The
L/L Research
Channeling Archives

Transcripts of the Meditation Sessions

Volume 10
November 13, 1988 to March 13, 1990

| Don Elkins | Jim McCarty | Carla L. Rueckert |

Copyright © 2009 L/L Research

All rights reserved. No part of this book may be reproduced or used in any form or by any means—graphic, electronic or mechanical, including photocopying or information storage and retrieval systems—without written permission from the copyright holder.

ISBN: 978-0-945007-84-5

Published by L/L Research
Box 5195
Louisville, Kentucky 40255-0195

E-mail: contact@llresearch.org
www.llresearch.org

About the cover photo: *This photograph of Jim McCarty and Carla L. Rueckert was taken during an L/L Research channeling session on August 4, 2009, in the living room of their Louisville, Kentucky home. Jim always holds hands with Carla when she channels, following the Ra group's advice on how she can avoid any possibility of astral travel.*

Dedication

These archive volumes are dedicated to Hal and Jo Price, who faithfully and lovingly hosted this group's weekly meditation meetings from 1962 to 1975,

to Walt Rogers, whose work with the research group Man, Consciousness and Understanding of Detroit offered the information needed to begin this ongoing channeling experiment,

and to the Confederation of Angels and Planets in the Service of the Infinite Creator, for sharing their love and wisdom with us so generously through the years.

Table of Contents

Introduction 6
Year 1988 8
    November 13, 1988 9
    December 18, 1988 15
Year 1989 19
    January 1, 1989 20
    January 15, 1989 26
    January 18, 1989 35
    January 25, 1989 38
    January 29, 1989 44
    January 31, 1989 53
    February 12, 1989 58
    February 19, 1989 66
    February 26, 1989 71
    March 8, 1989 77
    March 11, 1989 82
    March 12, 1989 85
    March 19, 1989 89
    March 25, 1989 96
    April 9, 1989 106
    April 12, 1989 114
    April 16, 1989 119
    April 23, 1989 127
    April 30, 1989 135
    May 7, 1989 143
    May 14, 1989 151
    May 28, 1989 159
    June 18, 1989 167
    June 21, 1989 176
    June 25, 1989 183
    July 2, 1989 189
    July 3, 1989 196
    July 9, 1989 203
    July 16, 1989 211
    July 23, 1989 219
    July 30, 1989 227
    August 6, 1989 233
    August 13, 1989 240
    September 10, 1989 246

September 17, 1989	253
September 24, 1989	260
October 1, 1989	266
October 8, 1989	274
October 15, 1989	282
October 22, 1989	287
October 29, 1989	295
November 5, 1989	303
November 12, 1989	310
November 26, 1989	315
December 3, 1989	323
December 10, 1989	328
December 17, 1989	332
December 31, 1989	338
Year 1990	**346**
January 7, 1990	347
January 21, 1990	352
February 4, 1990	356
February 11, 1990	362
February 25, 1990	368
March 4, 1990	372
March 11, 1990	377
March 12, 1990	384
March 13, 1990	390

Introduction

Welcome to this volume of the *L/L Research Channeling Archives*. This series of publications represents the collection of channeling sessions recorded by L/L Research during the period from the early seventies to the present day. The sessions are also available on the L/L Research website, www.llresearch.org.

Starting in the mid-1950s, Don Elkins, a professor of physics and engineering at Speed Scientific School, had begun researching the paranormal in general and UFOs in particular. Elkins was a pilot as well as a professor and he flew his small plane to meet with many of the UFO contactees of the period.

Hal Price had been a part of a UFO-contactee channeling circle in Detroit called "The Detroit Group." When Price was transferred from Detroit's Ford plant to its Louisville truck plant, mutual friends discovered that Price also was a UFO researcher and put the two men together. Hal introduced Elkins to material called *The Brown Notebook* which contained instructions on how to create a group and receive UFO contactee information. In January of 1962 they decided to put the instructions to use and began holding silent meditation meetings on Sunday nights just across the Ohio River in the southern Indiana home of Hal and his wife, Jo. This was the beginning of what was called the "Louisville Group."

I was an original member of that group, along with a dozen of Elkins' physics students. However, I did not learn to channel until 1974. Before that date, almost none of our weekly channeling sessions were recorded or transcribed. After I began improving as a channel, Elkins decided for the first time to record all the sessions and transcribe them.

During the first eighteen months or so of my studying channeling and producing material, we tended to reuse the tapes as soon as the transcriptions were finished. Since those were typewriter days, we had no record of the work that could be reopened and used again, as we do now with computers. And I used up the original and the carbon copy of my transcriptions putting together a manuscript, *Voices of the Gods*, which has not yet been published. It remains as almost the only record of Don Elkins' and my channeling of that period.

We learned from this experience to retain the original tapes of all of our sessions, and during the remainder of the seventies and through the eighties, our "Louisville Group" was prolific. The "Louisville Group" became "L/L Research" after Elkins and I published a book in 1976, *Secrets of the UFO*, using that publishing name. At first we met almost every night. In later years, we met gradually less often, and the number of sessions recorded by our group in a year accordingly went down. Eventually, the group began taking three months off from channeling during the summer. And after 2000, we began having channeling meditations only twice a month. The volume of sessions dropped to its present output of eighteen or so each year.

These sessions feature channeling from sources which call themselves members of the Confederation of Planets in the Service of the Infinite Creator. At first we enjoyed hearing from many different voices: Hatonn, Laitos, Oxal, L/Leema and Yadda being just a few of them. As I improved my tuning techniques, and became the sole senior channel in L/L Research, the number of contacts dwindled. When I began asking for "the highest and best contact which I can receive of Jesus the Christ's vibration of unconditional love in a conscious and stable manner," the entity offering its thoughts through our group was almost always Q'uo. This remains true as our group continues to channel on an ongoing basis.

The channelings are always about love and unity, enunciating "The Law of One" in one aspect or another. Seekers who are working with spiritual principles often find the material a good resource. We hope that you will as well. As time has gone on the questions have shifted somewhat, but in general the content of the channeling is metaphysical and focused on helping seekers find the love in the moment and the Creator in the love.

At first, I transcribed our channeling sessions. I got busier, as our little group became more widely known, and got hopelessly behind on transcribing. Two early transcribers who took that job off my hands were Kim

Howard and Judy Dunn, both of whom masterfully transcribed literally hundreds of sessions through the eighties and early nineties.

Then Ian Jaffray volunteered to create a web site for these transcriptions, and single-handedly unified the many different formats that the transcripts were in at that time and made them available online. This additional exposure prompted more volunteers to join the ranks of our transcribers, and now there are a dozen or so who help with this. Our thanks go out to all of these kind volunteers, early and late, who have made it possible for our webguy to make these archives available.

Around the turn of the millennium, I decided to commit to editing each session after it had been transcribed. So the later transcripts have fewer errata than the earlier ones, which are quite imperfect in places. One day, perhaps, those earlier sessions will be revisited and corrections will be made to the transcripts. It would be a large task, since there are well over 1500 channeling sessions as of this date, and counting. We apologize for the imperfections in those transcripts, and trust that you can ascertain the sense of them regardless of a mistake here and there.

Blessings, dear reader! Enjoy these "humble thoughts" from the Confederation of Planets. May they prove good companions to your spiritual seeking. ♣

For all of us at L/L Research,

Carla L. Rueckert

Louisville, Kentucky

July 16, 2009

Year 1988

November 13, 1988 to December 18, 1988

L/L Research

L/L Research is a subsidiary of Rock Creek Research & Development Laboratories, Inc.

P.O. Box 5195
Louisville, KY 40255-0195

www.llresearch.org

Rock Creek is a non-profit corporation dedicated to discovering and sharing information which may aid in the spiritual evolution of humankind.

ABOUT THE CONTENTS OF THIS TRANSCRIPT: This telepathic channeling has been taken from transcriptions of the weekly study and meditation meetings of the Rock Creek Research & Development Laboratories and L/L Research. It is offered in the hope that it may be useful to you. As the Confederation entities always make a point of saying, please use your discrimination and judgment in assessing this material. If something rings true to you, fine. If something does not resonate, please leave it behind, for neither we nor those of the Confederation would wish to be a stumbling block for any.

CAVEAT: This transcript is being published by L/L Research in a not yet final form. It has, however, been edited and any obvious errors have been corrected. When it is in a final form, this caveat will be removed.

© 2009 L/L Research

Sunday Meditation
November 13, 1988

Group question: Concerns the concept of the chosen, or the elect, mentioned in the Bible by Jesus, when he said that the elect would see the Kingdom of Heaven, mentioned by the Jehovah's witnesses when they talk about the 144 thousand, and in the new age, when the chosen people are mentioned as "those that are going to be lifted off the planet by the UFOs when they land." So, we're looking for comments upon the elect, the chosen. Is this a valid concept, or is this a distortion of something else?

(Carla channeling)

I am Ira, son of Mishdad. I come to you in the name of Jesus Christ, my Lord and Savior. We must identify ourselves to you who are servants of love and light, for we have been some time so identifying ourselves to this instrument. We have had no trouble passing this instrument's challenge, but this instrument was displeased that we were not members of the Confederation, but rather what you might call an ascended master. The significant incarnation for this humble one of Jerusalem was that of Ira, son of Mishdad, for it was in that lifetime that I followed Jehoshua, as he was called in his own dialect. You call this teacher Jesus. I was not worthy to touch his clothing, yet it was my joy to follow Jesus as my Lord and Savior.

Because there has been much, much distortion concerning the import and intent of the sayings attributed to your Jesus, we find that in certain sensitive channels we are able to create a subtle channel. The method of impression is quite different from that which this instrument is used to, and we feel the instrument coping, and suggest the instrument not cope, but rather simply realize that the pace of speaking may be as brisk as possible, for we have no need to regulate speech, as we are using a somewhat different form of concept communication.

In the spirit of love and in the spirit of Christ, let us pause to praise and thank the Father of All, and to worship at the feet of the one Father. Much is misunderstood that my teacher said, and I am most happy to share what in my own opinion was that given about what this instrument calls the elect. This is a grievous distortion of the true intent of Jesus' saying. Where to begin?

Along many dusty roads I walked, trying to catch a word or two of his private conversations, and when he spoke he spoke quietly, yet clearly and with much pride and authority, although he was always begrimed and dusty from the road. Somehow we all looked up to him without knowing why, even before we had heard what he had to say. I believe that the true importance of the idea of the elect is already clear to each who has become aware of the concept of service to others and service to self. The numbers of the elect are not exact, but symbolical in intention. It was the way of the rabbis to use numbers symbolically. The number twelve meant completion. Twelve times twelve meant a completion of completions. All eventually which have self-consciousness shall be of the elect, shall be of service to others or service to self, shall choose, shall be the seed planted in good soil. However, at the end of a given period of experience, some shall be ready for the next step, and some not.

I believe that Jesus' intent was to prepare humankind to meet the challenges of infinity and the larger life that lies beyond these Earthly vessels we call bodies. The concept of elitism or choosing one person above another would have been inherently distasteful to my teacher. Yet my teacher knew that one can offer information, but yet cannot expect that information to flower in every heart that receives it. It is certainly so in my own mind that my Savior felt himself to be the least and lowest of any man, indeed, the servant of all. This compassion would never be stinted by such an idea as a true elite in which some children of the Father were invited into the mansion and others not. This is not so, and this is not true. This was not the intention of my Lord and Savior, Jesus Christ. The road of my Savior was a road that asked all people to seek for something called the Kingdom of Heaven.

Each who hears my voice may choose himself to be the elect by choosing to live a certain kind of life, by choosing to attempt to be of service in the spiritual sense, by intention, in as much of the experience as possible. These are those things, this manifestation of love, this thinking about love, by which each of you creates the condition of the chosen. It is you who choose yourself. You have not my experience in walking in Galilee with the Master. You have not my personal experiences, and I realize that because you did not experience these things, they will never be real to you, as they are to me. Yet I say to you as honestly as I know how through this instrument, that there was no intention in the one known to you as Jesus, but to me as Rabbi, or Jehoshua, this entity precluded, excluded no one, but took all potentially within the heart, yet never, never would the Master presume, always was he patient, except with those who did not tell the truth.

I ask you now, you who have not walked with Jesus, to listen and pay attention to his true message, and to shut out of your ears and refuse to listen to the self-important bragging of those who depend upon anything but faith and call themselves chosen or elect. Yes, there shall indeed be the elect, and you shall indeed elect yourselves. That which is within your Holy Bible is a pitifully poor account in terms of volume of what the Rabbi had to say, of the impact that he had on people personally, of the transformation we all felt when we were in his presence, of the astounding miracles that he did. The Master was a free person. He relied completely on the moment, and he listened within. This voice through which we are speaking we call a human channel, for that which he spoke was not his, but that which he received from the Father, although he often made the joke and the pun upon his own accord, being a somewhat humorous person by nature.

And as we leave this instrument, we suggest that each may find it valuable to study the path that my Lord and Savior took, to think about the words of the Rabbi, to evaluate them, and to grasp the truth within this life story, for through lifetimes of unbroken desire to seek the Father in the way my Lord and Savior taught, I have been able to achieve that state which is between the third and fourth of your densities, as you would call them, that state in which I am in whatever position I wish, doing whatever service I wish.

It is rare that we are able to speak consciously to an instrument such as this. Normally we speak in visions and dreams. We are honored at this rare opportunity, for we are not wise; we are still awaiting the beginning of what you shall call social memory complex. We are still, those of us who have harvested ourselves, by the grace of God, doing the work with those who would wish to be the chosen and the elect by their own choice, by their own election.

We are happy to speak with this instrument at any time, whenever there is a call for this sort of information. We do find that in working with this instrument, we shall come under certain restrictions upon information—for that, you will have to forgive us—but we find, as this instrument is giving us validation—she is very far from full consciousness, but we are able to communicate with her well …

We must pause. We are losing contact with this instrument.

Carla: I lost it. I'm sorry. It was real faint, but it was real clear. Very interesting. Thank you, Ira, son of Mishdad. I've still got some pressure there.

(Carla channeling)

I am Ira, son of Mishdad. I greet you in the name of Jesus Christ. We are sorry for the breakup, and this communication will be breaking up, as this is very tiring to this instrument, we find. This instrument has an unusual access to its subconscious.

We wish to offer one more concept before we leave, if we are able to get it through this instrument quickly enough, and that is that there was a question about the name, the importance of the name. We find in this instrument's song, the hymn, "At the name of Jesus, every knee shall bow," "Blessed be the name of the Lord." We find many such phrases in this instrument's worship. The naming is that which is the nature. When a person chooses a different nature and becomes passionately bonded to that nature in such a way that it will change the life, and seals the change by a name, that is a name of power, because that is a person of power. When a person chooses a symbol for perfect compassion and divine love for what this instrument calls the highest and best of all things, the seeker must name the symbol.

If the seeker's faith is in itself, it will name itself. If the seeker's psychological makeup is such that it is aware of its many errors, and wishes to lean upon an idealized portion of itself, it may call upon the name of Jesus, for it is in that consciousness and in that consciousness only that you may be called elect, that you may choose to be chosen. You must become your journey, and your journey must become you, and the name of the consciousness that is your journey is Christ. You may choose your Christ, but it is in the name that the power lies, for the name is the nature, and the nature the name, and the I AM of consciousness is symbolized in its idealized form by my teacher, Jesus. I leave you in that blessed name.

We are thankful we were able to conclude this communication, for it would be very bad manners for us to leave you without blessing you, urging you to good works, to loving God in Christ, and loving each other as yourselves. So our teacher has taught us, those of us who have stayed behind to aid each of you to make the great choice. Your little life is not long, and you shall be called to account. If you have not chosen—and we speak to those who may only read those words which we speak—choose now. Choose that symbol for which you would die. Choose that faith that is the I AM for you. Choose your consciousness. Choose to be a certain way. Choose to be chosen. If my teacher is not yours, I leave you in peace, and bid you quickly, get hence, and right quickly, seek and find your true symbol, but let that symbol be the Christ to you, and may you seek to be the servant of all, for it truly is in serving that you shall grow, that you shall become strong and that you shall be healed of all bitterness, sadness and grief. We offer you the blessing of Jesus Christ. Go forth in peace, rejoicing in the power of the Spirit. Know that that Spirit is with you always. Amen. Amen. Amen. I am Ira, son of Mishdad. Amen.

Carla: Are you getting anything, Mickey? I'm not.

J: No.

Carla: Let's just meditate for a minute.

(Carla channeling)

I am Hatonn. I greet you in the love and in the light of the infinite Creator. It is indeed a privilege to speak through this instrument, and to this group, and we shall not long abide. We merely wished to acknowledge to the one known as C that we were with him, and to say just a few things that may be interesting at this time.

We realize that the world is an angry and present reality in many ways. We see the path of the frightened prey, and the stalking of the hunter. And by that, we mean simply that we feel that feeling that the difficulties of the illusion may generate, part of that feeling being the feeling of victim. Part of the same feeling, the guilty knowledge that one is the hunter as well as the hunted, that one cannot be one without being the other. We realize that no matter how excellent in behavior and thought one attempts to be, one must face—and, indeed, it is painful in your density—the completeness of the self, the fact that one is a full circle, an infinite universe of personalities, possibilities and choices. So with each of you, my friends, is a mixture of the good and the bad, as you would call it. This is the nature of your illusion.

Yet, if one is a disappointment to oneself, it is because one has not been good to oneself, but bad to oneself. Were we to ask you if the Creator forgives, "Yes," you would say, "I believe so." If you ask your brother if he forgives you, he shall think and say, "Yes, I believe so." Yet the one who has not forgiven the self is caught upon the tenterhook of harsh, self-inflicted guilt. Is this, my friends, a service to yourself, this guilt? Are you helping yourself to grow spiritually, by speaking harsh words to yourself about past errors?

My friends, as always, we encourage meditation and contemplation, and in this instance, encourage you to take into meditation the forgiveness of the self by the Creator, by those you have supposedly wronged and by yourself, for you are but the grade school child, adding the sums and getting an incorrect answer. Keep your eraser sharp and check those sums constantly, and when you find the error, use the eraser, but not the tongue in self-castigation for that self-same error, for you are here to encourage yourself to be the willing servant, to feel the freedom of the joy of service. You are here to help, and the first person you must help is yourself, that you may be free from self-inflicted woe, and so single-hearted and able to turn gladly to service to others in compassion, in peace, and always with a light touch.

We thank you for calling us to your meeting, and would at this time leave you. We would close through the other instrument, if the instrument would be willing. I leave this instrument at this time in love and light. I am Hatonn.

(Jim channeling)

I am Hatonn, and greet you again in love and light through this instrument. Before taking our leave of this group, we would wish to offer ourselves in the attempt to speak to any further queries which might remain upon the minds of those present. If there is a query, may we begin with that query now?

C: Hatonn, I'd like to thank you for being with me tonight. I have been thinking about starting to act as a vocal channel again, but I find that my reasonings to do so are not truly pure. I find that I had begun to have doubts lately, as I've begun to introduce new people to this group, I find that I doubt my ability to adequately convey knowledge which I have received, and am afraid that I will misinform them and not truly be of a service to them in their beginning of their seeking.

I also find that I have feelings that know I would once again like to channel, that the true reasoning behind it is a selfish one in that I feel that I am going at it from the viewpoint that my status with the new people would be elevated, and I know this is a selfishness on my part. So while I feel the urge to channel again, I have very serious doubts …

(Side one of tape ends.)

C: I know I still have the ability. I know that by speaking now, I am channeling in a way. Would you speak to me, please?

I am Hatonn, and am aware of your query, my brother. May we say that it is a great joy for us as well to blend our vibrations with yours this evening, and together seek upon the path of the seeker of truth.

Your desire to serve those who have recently joined this circle of seeking is commendable, for you have once again felt that call which originates from within your own heart to offer the self to others, that that which you have found helpful in your own journey might offer assistance to them as well. The means by which you pursue the offering of assistance is, of course, that which is of your choice, and we would offer our assistance to you in making this choice by commenting that the desire to serve without regard for return is at the heart of all successful service.

We would also suggest that you must, in order to be most effective in offering yourself, find the most appropriate means of so doing that which has its foundation uncluttered with personal desires within your own heart. The attempt to be of service as a vocal instrument is one which requires, as you know, a great deal of personal discipline and willingness to put the self in the position that may seem quite foolish. This is the area in which you find your current doubts arising, and we might remind you that all instruments feel some degree of this foolishness or liability to foolishness, for in order to serve as an instrument, one must move aside those reasoning portions of the mind, and allow the less frequently used subconscious mind to form a channel through which information might be moved, and which might become perceived and transmitted by the conscious mind.

This is a process which requires that one open the self to this inner conduit, or channel, in a fashion which does not leave one firm footing or grasp of the situation, or, shall we say, a control over it. Thus your doubting has a fundamentally sound reason for its existence, and thus we do not find personal doubting to be a significant obstacle for any who would serve as a vocal instrument.

As always, we would remind each instrument that the placing aside of the doubt each time that one begins is perhaps even a helpful and humbling experience that allows the channel to be opened in a manner which contains as little personality coloration, shall we say, as possible for the proper blend of vibrations to occur. However, the point to which we feel the greatest attention needs be given is that point that serves as the motivation for your taking up again the service of the vocal channel, and we cannot speak more specifically to this point, for we do not wish to take from you the opportunity to find your own way through this maze of desires, some of which seem upon the surface to conflict. We can only encourage you, my brother, that should you again wish to work as a vocal instrument, we are most happy to blend our vibrations with yours in this pursuit of service.

Is there another query, my brother?

C: This is the most comfortable I've been in a long [time] during meditation. I feel a definite kinship with you, and I'm very comfortable in your company. Thank you.

I am Hatonn, and we are most grateful to you as well, my brother. We rejoice in the opportunity of blending our vibrations with you and we thank you.

Is there another query at this time?

Carla: One short one, and it's just an asking for your opinion on a couple of things. You can either give it or just not, it depends on your concept of free will. First of all, was the purity of the channeling of the contact, Ira, satisfactorily pure in terms of my channeling? Or do I have work to do before I can channel that energy? I couldn't tell.

I am Hatonn, and am aware of your query, my sister, and now we see, my friends, that even the more experienced also have those needs to quell the doubt which arises from the effort which has been offered. And it is well that each instrument wishes to improve itself and to offer itself in the highest manner that it may stably do so. We commend each instrument for being careful and considerate enough in the vocal channeling efforts to constantly monitor those services which are offered to others.

The contact of which you speak, my sister, was one which was, as you are well aware, quite unexpected, and thus is something of a mystery to you. The contact utilized your abilities in a fashion which has been quite efficient in producing the manifested form of concept communication which the entity was desirous of transmitting this evening, due to the query which this group offered as the focus of the gathering.

Thus, we would commend your efforts both in the maintaining of the contact and its reception as well. We are happy that you have found that this contact is of some interest, for there are many of this kind of contact which want or lack the ability to find channels through which to speak. And this entity is quite happy that it has been able to make itself known to this group through your instrument.

Is there another query, my sister?

Carla: Yes. Thank you for that answer to that. It was certainly unexpected, and it was certainly—I mean, I wasn't just getting the concepts, I was getting whole impressions, and it was really hard to keep up. Actually, it was, you had to, instead of being real careful and choosing just the right word or something, it was like scrambling to keep up. It was, you know, I couldn't use the analogy of baseball, really. I imagine that that's the way inner planes channeling works, and I was just doing some of it, and that's probably why I was getting tired. I don't exactly know how to do that, that's why I asked if I needed more training. Perhaps at another time, when we have more energy, I can ask specifically, you know, what I might do to better fit myself for such channeling as that, if I deem it advisable for this research group.

But the other question was, would working with this channel detune me for work with the Confederation? If I could know that, I would like to know that.

I am Hatonn, and we find that your work with this new contact is work which would blend well with the work you have accomplished and may yet accomplish with those who have joined together within the Confederation of Planets in the Service of the Infinite Creator. The vibrational nature of a contact is the determining factor, not the status of belonging to the Confederation of Planets, thus the work with those of Ira is work well accomplished, my sister.

Is there another query?

Carla: You said, "Those of Ira." I though Ira was an individual. Was it a manner of speaking? Rather than, I mean [is] it your impression that this is indeed a multi-personed personality? Or are you referring to each life that Ira has lived, and that he's just manifesting one, but that he's all of them? I don't understand. I didn't mean to ask another question, but you just caught me off guard there.

I am Hatonn. We find that we have made an error in communicating through this instrument. We do not wish to give the impression that the contact with Ira was a contact with more than one individual entity.

Is there another query at this time?

Carla: Very well, thank you. Many, many thanks.

I am Hatonn, and we again give our great thanks to each present for allowing our blending of vibrations with yours this evening. We are very pleased that we have been able to exercise the instruments present, and have been able to join again this group which has for a great portion of your time been a home base for us. We shall take our leave of this group at this time, leaving each in the love and in the light of the one infinite Creator. We are those of Hatonn. Adonai, my friends. Adonai. ✾

L/L Research

L/L Research is a subsidiary of Rock Creek Research & Development Laboratories, Inc.

P.O. Box 5195
Louisville, KY 40255-0195

www.llresearch.org

Rock Creek is a non-profit corporation dedicated to discovering and sharing information which may aid in the spiritual evolution of humankind.

ABOUT THE CONTENTS OF THIS TRANSCRIPT: This telepathic channeling has been taken from transcriptions of the weekly study and meditation meetings of the Rock Creek Research & Development Laboratories and L/L Research. It is offered in the hope that it may be useful to you. As the Confederation entities always make a point of saying, please use your discrimination and judgment in assessing this material. If something rings true to you, fine. If something does not resonate, please leave it behind, for neither we nor those of the Confederation would wish to be a stumbling block for any.

CAVEAT: This transcript is being published by L/L Research in a not yet final form. It has, however, been edited and any obvious errors have been corrected. When it is in a final form, this caveat will be removed.

© 2009 L/L Research

Sunday Meditation
December 18, 1988

(Carla channeling)

I am L/Leema. I greet you in the love and in the light of the infinite One. May we express our feelings of blessedness at being called to your group this evening. It has been some time since we spoke with this group, and we are extremely pleased to join in your meditation and to be a part of the perfect circle of love, that which generates a kind of light most visible to us, enlightening done by so many entities and groups about your sphere at this time. It is indeed marvelous to observe the lightening of consciousness among many of your people during this season which you call Christmas. It is equally interesting to note that the extreme opposite is also true, that is that this season is that season which kills, which reopens remembrances of failures, of past grief, of recollective worry, of that which one wishes one could do over.

There is a great deal of difference between the light that you see when you gaze out the window, and the light that is both terrible and wonderful which moves in its own metaphysical rhythm within your yearly cycle, as this instrument would call it. That is, there are metaphysical reasons for both the elevated consciousness and the downcast consciousness during your short days and long nights. The metaphysical light may be associated with that new infant spiritual self that is being born day by day throughout an incarnation within the incarnate self.

Quite often this process is not recognized at any point during an incarnation, however, it moves inexorably, bringing entities who are not yet conscious, as well as entities who are already conscious of metaphysical dimensions to their lives, doing the job that [it] was intended to do, offering to the archetypal mind that vision of spiritual work which your story of infant Jesus recapitulates so well, for within each of you dwells the Christ. It dwells within you as a potential, as a part of an eternal birthright, for you were birthed first of all. Before any manifestation was, consciousness was. The creation is truly that which was offered to consciousness. There is a kind of rightness that entities upon your sphere feel in the domination of consciousness over the sphere upon which you enjoy existence.

However, this small spiritual infant which is potentially born, reborn and nurtured each day is not an entity which one may distinguish from one's ordinary everyday self. In fact, this season of the year is most important, specifically because it insists that each consciously seeking spiritual entity think at least briefly about the implications of a spiritual rebirth or the birth of the spiritual self, as opposed to that self which has come from dust and to it shall return, as the book which you call the Holy Bible states.

This infant soul is more your child and your responsibility than any child of your loins and womb, certainly far more important than any other single consideration which your mind may entertain in the course of the everyday existence, for this self is that vehicle which is, in a deeper reality, your Self, that continuing Self about which you know so little, and about which you desire to know so such more.

It is that Self within each to which we speak, hoping that some turn of phrase, some retelling of the story we tell over and over, will trip the mind, will trigger the emotion, will serve to inspire a seeking soul to seek more accurately, more carefully and more persistently. That you exist, and support that existence without being a burden upon others, may be perhaps seen as what this instrument would call the outer reality. This same kind of responsibility is one which we would suggest each consciously seeking entity entertain, that is that the nurturing and the self-sufficiency of the infant and growing and needful self be seen to as if each entity were the parent of its own spirit, of its own soul, for the soul needs the nurturing that will allow it to grow, just as you need your sunlight, or the hope of sunlight in the depth of winter. So the soul is bleak, unfocused and half-forgotten, for even those who attempt to be conscious of their spiritual selves, in many cases, for lack of some understandable, specific and practical way to practice the awareness of that soul self, and to practice that which will make it more healthy and more strong and more and more ennobled.

In some ways we might say that this is like this instrument's memory of the cliché concerning the carving of the statue of an elephant out of stone. When the artist is asked how he is able to seek and manifest the elephant within the stone, the answer is from the artist that he chips away everything that does not look like an elephant. This is only understandable by one with equal facility as an artist. In the same way, each entity sits within the illusion, which is your existence within the incarnational experience, like the block of rock which has within it the perfectly faceted gem, the perfectly carved statue, or whatever image one could most satisfactorily call up to enliven something as inert as a block of stone.

We have always offered one basic, practical, daily tool or resource to use in the discovery, rediscovery and nurturing on a continual basis of the soul-self. That tool is meditation. We do not encourage long periods of meditation nearly as much as we encourage a persistent dailiness of practice, for like any other thing, that which occupies the mind on a daily basis as an instinctive and reflexive recall is learned in a way [in which] that which is approached only when necessary or periodically cannot hope to match.

The meeting together to share love is also a kind of Christmas, and we would suggest to remember when each entity inevitably will feel downhearted during this period, that each day can be a small Christmas, if it is remembered that the Christ within is small, needs nurturing, needs attention, and needs most of all to be in the company of the infinite Creator. This is done by the turning of the attention. Meditation in and of itself tends to bring one to a realization, on a continuing basis, of the mystery and fascination of infinite intelligence, tends to bring one to a reckoning with love, and with one's relation with love itself, that which created all that there is.

Yet, if it is simply remembered that Christmas is far more important symbolically than literally, then you may keep Christmas within the heart, and then "bah-humbugs" are at an end forever, for the Christmas within you is the mass of Christ, is the thanksgiving for your relationship with the infinite mystery which for want of a better word we call love, the one original Thought, the Logos, which created all that there is. That relationship is direct. Thusly, what you wish for at Christmas is not presents, as in gifts, but the presence, or the communion with the infinite One.

Thus, as one goes into meditation, we very much suggest using readings, mantras or some inspirational thought which leads one towards the intention to tabernacle with that which is holy, with that which is the infinite mystery of the Creator.

We encourage each further, whenever the feelings are depressed, at whatever time of year, to recreate within the mind the Christmas experience of great darkness, short under-lit days of shadow and bleak cold, and a piercing and poignant joy of that infant spirit that against all odds, and without the acceptance of the darkness, moves into darkness as light that is not recognized. You yourselves are full of light which you do not recognize. It is not sunshine; it is not light in a physical sense. You are the carriers of precious treasure. You carry the infinity of the love and the light of the infinite Creator. Picture it. Symbolize it within yourselves as the Christ child, and give it room, encouragement and attention that it may grow each day.

As always, we encourage each to remain light of heart in the face of failure as perceived by the self. In the first place, we assure you, you do not know that which you do, and you shall not know until the veil has been lifted and you are no longer within the experience you now enjoy. In the second place, the recognition of an error perceived is all we encourage you to think of it as, emotionally neutral, much like a roundly worked puzzle, once the logically correct answer has been discovered, it is a matter of using the eraser and correcting that which is within your own mind so that it is in harmony with the divine laws, shall we say, as perceived by the self as a nurturer of the spirit.

We ask each, in sum, to take a very long view of Christmas, to release Christmas from any literal meaning—for those meanings have been very much distorted among your people—and to reclaim for yourself the glory, the splendor, the wonder, and the mystery of spiritual growth.

It has been a privilege to speak through this instrument and to this group. We would at this time release the floor, that the one known as Latwii might conclude this session. We are known to you as those of L/Leema, and leave you with jingle bells and Christmas carols and nervous relatives and all of the somewhat disheartening aspects of an illusion that in its way attempts in the midst of darkness to teach about light and love and beauty and mystery. Adonai. We leave you in the love and the light within you, all about you, everywhere of the one infinite Creator. Adonai. Adonai vasu borragus.

(Carla channeling)

I am Latwii. We have decided to use this instrument because there is some difficulty with the one known as Jim. We have a fairly simple task through this instrument, because we shall not be able to ask for questions. However, we would address a query from the one known as R. This was our intent as we moved to the one known as Jim, and we find it permissible to do so through this instrument, as there is no spoken question at this time to rattle the instrument's, shall we say, somewhat shaky intellect. Actually, we may say that those words were perhaps more hers than ours.

One who wishes to know how to move into the unveiling process may well view the courting process. The deeper portions of the mind are pure, more sensitive, and far more delicate in structure than those portions of the mind which are in heavy, everyday use. The deeper portions of the mind are those portions which react to impersonal and deeply felt rhythms and energies which flow into the energy web of the individual. The process of unveiling that deep mind is one which will spin many, many incarnations, and, in short, our opinion—and we stress that it is our opinion, and fallible—is that entrance into the deep mind should be as careful, loving and concerned as the suitor with damp palms who offers a corsage to his date for the dance.

It is truly a gentle thing when done well, and a slow process when done well, to lift the veil, not by intent, but by the process of disciplining one's waking personality. That is, one does not successfully assault the deep mind, rather, one prepares oneself to receive from the deep mind that which it is prepared to give, and then through the process of meditation, the process of the daydream, the vision, and the dreaming within sleep, it is in these ways that the deep mind yields its fruits to the conscious mind.

The way to stop the flow of information from the deep mind is to ignore information from the deep mind. That is not to say that one should be without discrimination and if one feels one has had a vision one must then do it. We do not encourage this sort of lack of discrimination at all. What we are saying is that it is well to seek gently, persistently, as the suitor would court the beloved, allowing the deep mind to reveal that which was previously unrevealed in a natural manner.

The difficulties which one discovers, if one attempts to move into the archetypical mind with a bulldozer, is that one will destroy the very scenery one has come to enjoy, without ever understanding its character, for there are many portions of the deep mind, and those which are won by force are those which shall be archetypes not particularly helpful to one upon the path of service to others.

Remember that all that there is lies within your consciousness, therefore you are as capable of receiving information perceived as negative from the deep mind as information biased towards love, kindliness and an over-arching ennoblement of self, of purpose and of life. Therefore, it is to the gentle person, to the persistent person, that the deep mind offers its beautiful, sweet-smelling bloom. Enjoy each new realization without holding onto it, and know that the veil is there for a purpose, and is not to be ripped away or to be torn asunder, but rather it is to be that through which necessary information will come to the one who daily waits and watches at the tabernacle of inner silence.

We are very happy to be with this instrument because this instrument enjoys telling bad jokes, however, we have no bad jokes to tell you, so we are going to leave this instrument at this time. It has been a pleasure to be with you. We are most happy to have been able to speak with you, and we would at this time leave each in the love and in the light of the infinite Creator. We are known to you as Latwii. Adonai. Adonai.

Year 1989

January 1, 1989 to December 31, 1989

L/L Research

L/L Research is a subsidiary of Rock Creek Research & Development Laboratories, Inc.

P.O. Box 5195
Louisville, KY 40255-0195

www.llresearch.org

Rock Creek is a non-profit corporation dedicated to discovering and sharing information which may aid in the spiritual evolution of humankind.

ABOUT THE CONTENTS OF THIS TRANSCRIPT: This telepathic channeling has been taken from transcriptions of the weekly study and meditation meetings of the Rock Creek Research & Development Laboratories and L/L Research. It is offered in the hope that it may be useful to you. As the Confederation entities always make a point of saying, please use your discrimination and judgment in assessing this material. If something rings true to you, fine. If something does not resonate, please leave it behind, for neither we nor those of the Confederation would wish to be a stumbling block for any.

CAVEAT: This transcript is being published by L/L Research in a not yet final form. It has, however, been edited and any obvious errors have been corrected. When it is in a final form, this caveat will be removed.

© 2009 L/L Research

Sunday Meditation
January 1, 1989

Group question: No matter what the sophisticated or old-fashioned method of consciousness expansion a person tries, what spiritual growth really seems to boil down to is a lot of trial and error and being able to deal with a lot of disappointment when we see ourselves fall short of our ideals. Would you speak to the idea that there really don't seem to be any shortcuts in spiritual growth, and to the part that disappointment and faith play in the path of the seeker of truth?

(Carla channeling)

I am Q'uo. Greetings in the love and in the light of the one infinite Creator, on whose behalf we have been called here to manifest those thoughts of love and light that may perhaps find a ready listening ear, so that we may be of some small service. For this to be possible is the height of our hope at this particular point in our development, and we cannot thank you enough for enabling us to speak through this instrument.

Upon this subject, the subject of the spiritual journey, [it] is one which we could begin speaking of in one way, find another way of gazing at the same experience, and in always relevant fashion we would be unable to exhaust the ways in which one may gaze at and imagine the true structure of the spiritual journey. That is, there is nothing particularly spiritual about the journey. It, like any other ordeal, is a matter of certain, shall we say, natural laws with the ever-balancing axis at ninety degrees, always, to those laws of the unpredictability of free will.

But this evening you have chosen to gaze at the spiritual journey in terms of time commitment, in terms of whether by taking thought one might accelerate the pace of spiritual growth. My children, if we of Q'uo did not believe that it were possible to accelerate the spiritual growth of careful and persistent students by means of inspirational messages, we would not be working with this instrument, for it is no part of our intention to waste our time. However, the truth is that it is extremely possible; that is, it is possible in almost any degree desired by the entity to accelerate the pace of spiritual growth. The difficulty from within the illusion is that a particularly difficult manifestation of accelerated spiritual growth is emotional pain, irritation with oneself for having failed, and other negative emotions.

The extremely simple reason for the seeming paradox is that in times of greatly accelerated growth, large-scale changes are being made in the road map of various portions of the program and metaprogram of the mind, and, especially when these changes have reached the initiatory or metaprogrammic phase, many, many feelings, actions and so forth will seem to have been those of an oversensitive, immature and imbalanced person.

This person will consider itself the least of all those who seek, for it is not manifesting cheerfulness, gaiety, merriment and freedom, but, rather, suffering under a burden.

However, when the memory has wound its golden bands about these times, and that which you call time has elapsed so that one may gaze back upon that golden-shrouded memory, one may see again and again the rapidity of growth side by side and inexorably tied to the most nauseating and humiliating of failures. It is for this reason that within the illusion it is most often felt that there are no short cuts, and that one must simply bumble along by trial and error.

In point of fact, when working with the deeper programming of the metaconsciousness, the movement of feeling within may be in such a powerful way that it may seem irresistible and perhaps counter to usual politeness. These expressions, however, are to be credited as part of the mind, not part of something called hysteria or emotions, but rather those times when the metaprogram has once and for all time changed a deep, deep program. There will be some sort of release from such a deep change that you do not understand it, and the fact that you may, perhaps, be disappointed in yourself must be accepted by you as a condition of your attempt to live a life based upon the faith that there is, indeed, a kindly Creator, a Creator made of love, which loved us first, and to Whom our response is faith.

Now, with those things said about the difficulties of progression and the lack of shortcuts being incorrect, let us say that a person does, indeed, use tools to move himself toward such a time of vision, a time of initiation, a time of change and metamorphosis. A person may use the techniques of deprivation known in many, many systems of expression toward the infinite Creator—the fasting, the changing of the daily routine to one of silence and devotion. All those daily acts of meditation and worship, whether it be for a moment or for a minute or for an hour, in their dailyness they keep you, the pilgrim soldier, upon the road. You are battling something you may well call disappointment. We would prefer to call it the uninformed intellectual mind. Your minds, my children, are very, very full of those opinions based only upon what this instrument would call conventional wisdom. Within your heart are stored the natural laws. It is well to know how to act lawfully within your society. It is well to act lawfully within that society.

It is also extremely well for you as a spiritual self to know who you are and who that individual that carries you around is. This is most important to you. If you do not know the large bipedal animal upon which you so depend, if you do not appreciate it, provide well for it, accept it, nurture it, and take care of it, then you as a consciousness will find it more and more difficult to spend intensity and time upon the spiritual search.

So, let yourself be the nurturer of yourself. When you are disappointed in yourself, let your nurturing self remember that you are only disappointed within the illusion. You have no idea, my children, of what a blessing your hopes, your intentions, and your ideals are. The light of those ideals is the light of your planet. Your zest for truth, your fidelity to the Creator, your living by faith and never by words; these things go beyond that self that carries you about. These things are what you really are: a being of faith. In times of disappointment, allow that being to nurture, protect, comfort and soothe you, for it is difficult to move quicker than the body is ready to go, than the mind is ready to move. It is a hard thing to change, and, indeed, it should be carefully resisted. Each change should be seen, considered and approved by your discriminating and entire self, a self always informed and centered by daily meditation.

To sum up, my children, each of you has spent many years accelerating the course of spiritual growth. Each of you has seen the most fruits come into manifestation in the midst of iniquity, error, mistake after mistake, and self-perceived sin. Each is able to see that compassion has grown during pain, beyond one's limits, and beyond the pale of that which would not disappoint one. Yes, you shall disappoint yourself again and again, and may we say, the more you disappoint yourself, the more you are trying to do, and the more we salute your brave spirit. Never, ever, allow the words that your mind can create to attack your faith and your hope that all that is painful will also be fruitful, and all that is difficult will also become that which is golden, that which brings the compassion to the heart, the understanding to the mind. For at the end of each and every failure, at the end of each and every limitation, once accepted and forgiven, can the self find the corresponding compassion for that same limitation in each and every other human being which it encounters in the same situation.

May you grow sweeter through adversity, and, most of all, may we say perhaps our greatest hint to you, as those who would like to continue speeding up the rate of acceleration or growth spiritually, learn to work as hard during those times perceived as positive as those times perceived as negative, and the negative events shall not need to occur.

In order to gain from the positive, one must do what would be impossible were not one familiar with negativity, that is, one must push against one's own standards of excellence, attempting at all times to give more and more praise to the Creator, more and more of one's conscious hours, attempting more and more, in moving into the sleep pattern, to program the self for the learning, and the setting of new metaprograms closer to the one great original Thought. Do these things faithfully. Work during the easy, the happy, the contented, and the peaceful times, and your lives shall become ever more peaceful and contented. The work must be done, my children. You have designed this into your incarnations. You yourselves will judge yourselves at the end. Yes, it shall be as the greater Self, but it shall be you, specifically and personally, that must riffle the pages of this incarnation.

Claim your disappointments now. Face them and learn from them and grow sweet with compassion. In this way, may the disappointment at seeming failure become, appropriately and in a balanced fashion, appreciation of and forgiveness of one's limitations, of the history and the tracks of one's change into an impersonal source of love. Then when, without the veil, you stand and gaze upon your life you shall see that you were aware, that there is no such thing as Earthly disappointment, but only the sounds, the experiences, the side products, the pain, and the difficulties of transformation. May you intend always the highest and best that you know, and may each limitation, disappointment and seeming failure become for you the opportunity of self-forgiveness, appreciation of yourself, and the nurturing of your growing spirit.

We would at this time close the session through the instrument known as Jim. We leave this instrument with thanks and love and light. I am known to you as Q'uo.

(Jim channeling)

I am Q'uo, and greet each again in love and light through this instrument. At this time it is our privilege to ask if we might respond to any queries which remain upon the minds of those gathered this evening.

T: Yes, I have a question. This maybe—I don't know, it almost seems like what we're doing here right now, channeling—but my question is, could you comment on spirit guides and how do you know when what you're seeming to be getting is real, other than it just feels right. That may be the answer. Anyway, would you comment, please?

I am Q'uo, and we are happy to speak to this subject, my brother. Indeed, we know of no way that the contact with those entities which you call the spirit guides can be proven in an unshakable way, for all that is of value, in our opinion, within your illusion, rests within the boundaries of mystery. And when one attempts to grasp firmly any concept or quality of value, such as purity, truth, beauty, goodness, mercy, forgiveness, one moves through the quality and discovers that there is nothing that can be known without doubt.

We are in agreement, my brother, that the most helpful means for giving assurance to the seeker that a communication has occurred betwixt it and those who watch over its evolutionary process may be determined through the feeling that is the response from the seeker when it has felt or become aware of a communication, whether that communication is understandable or not, for many times there are communications that are not perceived by the seeker that come from those entities that have the honor and the responsibility of serving as the guide or teacher in an unseen manner for the incarnate third density entity. Indeed, there are many, many experiences which each of you undergo each of your days which have been touched and guided by those unseen spirits that are ever-watchful [for] the opportunity to present the student with an illustration, an inspiration, a guiding hand, a warning whisper. There are many times that the coincidences of one's life pattern become more apparent and the seeker then will begin to wonder to itself if there might be a larger hand within the plan of the daily round of activities.

Again, from time to time when the moment is appropriate for the seeker's growth, there may be given to the seeker a confirmation of one kind or another that is given by those we are calling guides. The book or person or event that is placed within the seeker's notice at the appropriate moment is the most usual means by which such guidance occurs, for within the life pattern of each seeker, there are, shall we say, imbedded or programmed the opportunities that will open a new avenue of seeking, perhaps of serving, always of learning. And these avenues are oftentimes triggered, shall we say, by a combination of events which are both rooted within this illusion and without this illusion, as the preincarnative choices of the seeker meet the opportunities that have had the guiding hand propel them in just such a manner that the desired meeting then occurs, and from this point, the free will of the seeker to respond is paramount, and at this point, it is the seeker itself which proceeds upon this particular portion of the journey, having previously set the groundwork, shall we say, and prepared the self for the reception of certain impulses or ideas that will then become seeds that will produce a continuing interest in the seeker.

May we speak in any further fashion, my brother?

T: No, thank you, that's fine. Thank you very much.

I am Q'uo, and we thank you, my brother. Is there another query?

Carla: I had a couple. One was about the term, metaprogram. I haven't run into it before, and I was thinking about physics versus metaphysics. Unfortunately, the only reason it was called metaphysics was that the books were next to the physics books on the shelf, and *meta* is Greek for "next," and it was named that at Alexandria, so that doesn't make too much sense. But I think *meta* means sort of "beside," okay, so you're saying metaprogram, so it's a program beside that program which is in our conscious mind, so I was thinking, well, what would that be? And then I thought, well, it's the computer that makes up our computer, that puts the stuff in our computer in the first place. Like, if we changed the metaprogram, the program would change in a lot of different, subtle ways, because it would be changing our basic biases, and that would mean that the metaprogram was that personality of ours that does survive, and it's the personality of the spirit. Now, do you have any comments on any of these things? Am I in any way correct? Or what is a metaprogram, as opposed to a program, in the mind?

I am Q'uo, and if we have perceived your query correctly, we would equate the metaprogram with the preincarnative choices that have been chosen by each seeker, that there may be the opportunities for learning and then the reciprocal opportunities for serving according to that which has been learned in the life pattern. The programming of such opportunities consists, in general, in the imbedding, shall we say, of certain biases with the subconscious mind and in the conscious mind, when helpful, as well, that will allow opportunities of a certain nature to occur when these biases come in contact with a certain set of circumstances.

For example, if an entity has, for a number of its incarnations, concerned itself with the concept of abundance and its opposite, that being the seeming lack of abundance, then the degree of progress, shall we say, that has been achieved in the mental attitude that sees some degree of abundance or lack of abundance within all situations will be triggered when there is the coincidence of a situation where there is the need for enough of one quality or another, substance or another, to be present within the life pattern for the seeker to feel a certain degree of satisfaction or comfort or the feeling that it is cared for, provided for, and is secure.

Thus, as the seeker moves through various circumstances where it finds itself in need of more of a quality or commodity, then will its programming be triggered so that its attitude will be brought to bear upon the situation which is, in itself, relatively neutral, the coloration of an emotional nature coming primarily from the subconscious mind, according to the program of the seeker.

Thus, the metaprogram, or preincarnative choice, will allow the seeker to pursue the degree of balance that it has chosen previous to the incarnation, and to continue to refining, or in many cases, simply approaching, this degree of balance that will allow the seeker to achieve the goal which it has set for itself prior to the incarnation.

May we speak in any further fashion, my sister?

Carla: If you would, I have another completely different question. Thank you for the answer to that one. I'll enjoy reading it. The other question, I'm honestly a little bit baffled by, because I got a

Christmas card from a perfectly lovely lady, but she does something that has through the years irritated me more and more every time, and I guess I'm just getting old and judgmental. But she's a perfectly well-grown-up woman, and instead of saying, "A relationship I'd put a lot in on failed, but I was really lucky; I fell in love with somebody else that same year," she had to say that she had done a great deal of work with this wonderful person, but that they had talked together and decided that their work during this incarnation had come to an end, and so they blessed each other and went their separate ways.

And there's a lot of that sort of thing going around, where people try to take every single bit of guilt or wrongdoing off of people leaving each other. And they just don't accept the fact that there's been a failure of any kind. They figure, well, they just had all these different people that they had karmic ties with, that they had to clean up in one incarnation, and that's why they've been sluts or womanizers or whatever, and it just never did ring true to me, cause it seemed to me that what somebody was doing was just doing the same lesson over and over and over again, and it didn't seem to me to be like cleaning up karma at all; it seemed to me to be like making the same error or failing each and every time and not owning up to it. And I need to write people like this with compassion, because a lot of people that I speak with talk with this sort of vocabulary, and I'd really appreciate your showing me where I've gone off the track.

I am Q'uo, and am aware of your query, my sister. May we begin by reminding each present that no matter what the lesson that is attempted during any incarnation within your third-density illusion, each is attempted imperfectly, each is imperfectly perceived, and each is only approached in the ideal, to some degree or another. For within your illusion, it is not possible, as far as we are aware, that one may become absolutely certain, without any shadow of doubt, as to the true nature of any particular lesson, for the mystery of the Creator is great enough to encompass all that is known or thought, and to provide yet further layers of understanding to those who persevere past certainty within their own mind, past achieving what they feel is complete. For, within your illusion of limits there exists the infinite quality of each concept that each seeker has built the incarnation out of. There is the possibility for each seeker, then, to pursue any lesson or any service in an infinitely refined manner, and to continually learn more from every opportunity that it encounters, to learn more upon reflection, to learn more upon future application, to learn more within the silence of the self in meditation, to learn more within the face of each fellow seeker that one greets within the daily round of activities.

You have in your recent experience encountered this communication that has for you brought to your mind a particular quality of relationship and responsibility that stands first within your experience as that which deserves care, honor, work and commitment. These are qualities in your own experience which you have found to hold a certain charge, shall we say.

Before we continue, we find that we must pause in order that this instrument utilize the recording devices. We shall pause. We are those of Q'uo.

(Pause)

I am Q'uo, and am again with this instrument. We shall continue. We were attempting to illustrate the response which we gave to the previous query, that being that the preincarnative choices or programs will allow the seeker to experience a triggering mechanism upon the encountering of certain situations, which of themselves are a neutral nature, shall we say, the bias coming from the subconscious and conscious minds of the seeker. Thus, upon the reception of the communication concerning relationship, it was your experience that your dedication to getting one's utmost effort to the constructing and maintaining of the relationship then was triggered. For another with less dedication in this particular area, there may have been little, if any, emotional response to that particular communication.

Thus does each seeker pursue a path that wends its way through experiences according to the programmings that it has provided itself and according to the guidance that it receives in a loving and wise manner from those unseen spirits whose hands yet ever enfold the seeker within their protective and nurturing grasp. We would recommend that when you desire to communicate to others your experience or understanding of any quality or concept, whether it be of relationships, of commitment, of seeking, of desire, or of whatever nature, that you give fully and wholly of yourself with as much clarity as is possible and also with the qualification that that which you give is your opinion and your learning, for it is a dynamic process that one is engaged in as one pursues the path of the seeker of truth, and this dynamism is a fundamental necessity for one who would teach and instruct others, for if one teaches what one is learning, then one is engaged in a living and growing process, rather than the recapitulation of dead facts which have little bearing upon one's life experience.

It is helpful also to make the qualification to any who would seek to hear what you have to say in these areas that the opinion is that which you share, and that it may not be completely appropriate for another being, but that you have found it thus and such in your own life experience. Therefore, you may speak with as great a degree of commitment and passion as you feel, without fearing that you shall, in your passion and, perhaps, in your eloquence, overwhelm another and divert its free will in a manner which is not appropriate for its own incarnational pattern.

May we speak in any further way, my sister?

Carla: You did exactly grasp the thrust of my concern. I would just finish up by asking you if you would accept that work in consciousness, or indigo ray work, is basically metaprogramming? Is it a congruency of terms there?

I am Q'uo, and we would agree, in general, with the use of these terms, for the metaprogram is the program which has as its goal or its essence that which is somewhat hidden by its mechanics or its technique. Therefore, the factors which may be necessary in order for a program to be set in motion are more mechanical [in] nature than is the desired outcome from the setting into motion of the program. Therefore, the work in consciousness that is attempted is a work which one must diligently seek more as, shall we say, an aftereffect, having discovered that the outcome of a certain series of events was greater, shall we say, than was first noticed or presumed.

Therefore, it is often the case that the more diligent seeker will continue to look at what has been learned in any experience, so that the first fruits of that experience, then, are not the only fruits and, perhaps, not the central fruits that were possible in the experience. One who continues in this way to assess, to meditate upon that which has been learned, will find that not only are there layers of learning leading to the heart of the learning, but that there are correlations and extrapolations that may be found and applied in other portions of the life experience that were, perhaps, not seen to have a connection to the experience just completed and that which is being pondered. Therefore, the life experience of the more diligent seeker will become more unified in that each lesson, each experience will have a more universal application within the life pattern.

May we speak in any further fashion, my sister?

Carla: Not tonight, thank you. I feel the instrument's probably pretty tired. I really appreciate your answers. Thank you so much.

I am Q'uo, and we thank you, my sister. Is there another query at this time?

(Pause)

I am Q'uo, and it appears that we have, indeed, exhausted the queries for the evening, and we would like to thank each present for inviting us to share our opinions with each of you, for it is in this manner that we discover more of that which you seek and find valuable in your life patterns. And by observing and partaking in this process of sharing, we are also able to find that which is of value in our own life patterns. We cannot thank you enough for your generosity in continuing to open yourselves to our words and our thoughts. We would remind each, as always, that we offer that which is our opinion, that which has been found to be useful in our own life journeys. We do not wish any word to offer a stumbling block to any other seeker. Take those words which have value to you and leave those which do not.

At this time we would take our leave of this group, again thanking each for inviting our presence. We are known to you as those of Q'uo. We leave you in the love and in the light of the one infinite Creator. Adonai, my friends. Adonai. ☙

L/L Research

L/L Research is a subsidiary of Rock Creek Research & Development Laboratories, Inc.

P.O. Box 5195
Louisville, KY 40255-0195

www.llresearch.org

Rock Creek is a non-profit corporation dedicated to discovering and sharing information which may aid in the spiritual evolution of humankind.

ABOUT THE CONTENTS OF THIS TRANSCRIPT: This telepathic channeling has been taken from transcriptions of the weekly study and meditation meetings of the Rock Creek Research & Development Laboratories and L/L Research. It is offered in the hope that it may be useful to you. As the Confederation entities always make a point of saying, please use your discrimination and judgment in assessing this material. If something rings true to you, fine. If something does not resonate, please leave it behind, for neither we nor those of the Confederation would wish to be a stumbling block for any.

CAVEAT: This transcript is being published by L/L Research in a not yet final form. It has, however, been edited and any obvious errors have been corrected. When it is in a final form, this caveat will be removed.

© 2009 L/L Research

Sunday Meditation
January 15, 1989

Group question: Has to do with passion. How does one develop passion? How does one direct it most efficiently for the spiritual growth?

(Carla channeling)

I am Hatonn. I greet you in the love and in the light of our infinite Creator. It is a great privilege and blessing for us to be with you, to be called to your group in its search for information that may be useful upon the path towards truth.

We would like to pause, if we might for a moment, and move about the circle, simply enjoying each of you. If you will allow us this moment, we shall pause.

I am Hatonn, and am once again with this instrument. The beauty of each soul within the circle is unique and perfect, and to join with you is a cause for thanksgiving. Before we begin, we would like for you to know that we are, as you, pilgrims upon the path. We are not authorities to be unquestioned. We are those as yourselves, with opinions. Perhaps our opinions come from more experience than you, for we have been the way that you now trod, and are, perhaps, a few steps further along that infinite path towards the mystery of the Creator. But we would not be a stumbling block before you. If anything that we have to say to you disturbs or does not ring true in your own opinion, then it is not your truth, and you should and must discriminate carefully that which you take in, for you shall recognize, as if remembering, those truths that are your own, those truths that fit the situation, the biases, the person that you are this time. Do not attempt to force yourself into anyone else's mold, dogma, doctrine or way of thought, for such will only impede your natural progress toward the light and the love of the infinite Creator.

With this said, we shall turn to the question of this evening, that being passion—what it is, how to get it, where to find it, how to use it. It is a subject we are most pleased that this instrument take up, for it is a subject about which this instrument knows very little, for passion is one of this instrument's natural gifts. That which has not been learned is not understood. Therefore, we are pleased that this instrument shall one day read that which we say, that it, too, may learn.

This instrument has spoken already this evening about the climate, the environment of the everyday daily round of activity which those within your society call a normal routine of living. We find that its most blatant characteristics are distraction and somnolence. Either entities help themselves to refrain from thinking by constant activity, or they achieve the same objective by a near complete lack of activity and the companionship of the television, we find this instrument calls that series of speaking pictures which is aimed at those of your people who have not yet grown to adulthood.

In short, the density of technology within your society so far outstrips the density of concern for that which has no objective referent, that the mysterious ceases to raise the true imagination or engage the deep interest of most entities. Most entities are not aware that all of science and all of technology rest upon mysteries, mysteries that point towards a greater mystery: the Maker of those mysteries, the infinite Principle which created all that there is.

If you may go with me now into the mind, clearing it of those daily interests which so often clog the arteries of thought, you may begin to see another universe emerging. In this universe, all that is, is energy. Mass is an illusion created by gravity, which is also a mystery to your scientists. The electricity, the electronics, the electromagnetics, all work upon principles that are completely mysterious to scientists. Yet, they do work. They work according to natural law. And that these mysterious things work according to some natural law is interesting, is it not?

You each are consciousnesses, portions of the one infinite Creator, and about you is gathered the material which makes it possible to you to be incarnate at this time, this exciting time upon your planet. That is free will. Each of you is a mixture of the infinite Creator and free will. You begin the path of seeking with free will greatly to the fore, and the self, which is the Creator, almost entirely unknown, except for feelings that one thing is, perhaps, correct to do and another thing, perhaps, not. This is the beginning of the journey, and so the sensitive soul decides to seek a little harder than that for the truth of the mystery of the Creator, for in that mystery lies who each truly is, who each is in relationship to the Creator and what we may do in response to that Creator. And so we come to passion.

Let us make one thing very clear—as the characters in this instrument's head have been known to say many times (we refer to former presidents)—the first passion is not one for which you are responsible. The great and original passion is the passion of the Creator to know Itself. In that great passion, in that love, It created each of those portions of consciousness that sit as one being in this circle of seeking this evening. It created each of you before time and space began, for time and space are but a stage upon which consciousness may play out its many, many roles and learn those lessons which it has chosen to study, that the Creator may know Itself in the windows of each entity's eyes, in the mirroring of each relationship, in the transactions of all people.

Thus, the first passion is that you are loved. You are loved enough to have been created. You are loved enough to have been given free will. And you are loved and trusted enough to be set completely and utterly free, your mind carefully shielded and veiled from the deeper portions of its archetypal self, so that you cannot remember who you are, what your make-up is, what your relationship is to the Creator, or how you wish to respond. The call to a life in faith is a call to remembrance of the passion that created you. Therefore, the first element of passion is remembrance that infinite passion is the basis for all that you see, for all that you see was created because it was loved—and loved because it was created.

We draw you a picture of a seemingly needy Creator, a Creator needy for you, for your love, for your reactions, for your information, and in a biased way, this is indeed so. There is that portion of the Creator that lies beyond desire. Most of the creation, indeed, rests in love unexpressed and uncreated. You are portions of the active principle of the Creator, the Logos, or for want of a better word, love itself.

Now, each activity within an entity's life may take upon itself the tone of ordinary dailyness or the tone of communion. We suggest to you that when one has contemplated long upon the love the Creator has for oneself, then, perhaps, the second step to finding passion is a slow, gentle allowing of the self to awaken to that love, to listen to the bird that sings for your ear, and, yes, my children, it does sing for your ear, if you can but listen, for the breeze that blows so beautifully, for pearl-gray days that soften and gentle the harsh edges of winter moods, for sunshine and joy. In all these experiences, you may remember that this has been a gift of love, and that you are completely satisfying your Creator, no matter how quickly or how slowly you advance, simply by being and reacting in a natural and spontaneous way, or in any way whatsoever, to those things which occur.

There are those things which block this simple process from gaining in momentum. When one is distracted from the natural creation of the Father and when one has great difficulty seeing the Creator in each pair of eyes upon which one looks, one begins to move off of one's center, away from one's remembrance of love, and passion dies and numbness sets in, or anger or another negative emotion, but, indeed, we find that among your people the quality of numbness is marked. We ask you by a slow process of daily meditation to allow these layers of protection from that against which you do not need to be protected, to drop, simply to be let go. Then, with that done, call to remembrance that natural reaction which one may have to being loved so deeply that one becomes absolutely necessary for another's existence.

This is your situation. You are absolutely necessary to the Creator. You are timeless metaphysical entities, and you are beloved, with a passion and a love so far beyond any of your words that we must humbly beg for forgiveness for the paucity of our language. But, ah, my children, when you can remember, then you may dance the joyful dance of the heart and laugh the merry laugh of the child, and in that childlike way know for the first time the love that is the answer to love, the passion that is the answer to passion, the life of the spirit that is the answer of a clouded consciousness, to a wonderful light-filled mystery that calls to remembrance. You are beings of love, created in love, and you dance through life your own dance. You are aware that many are the steps that are awkward, clumsy and hurtful. Your jail cells, your prisons, your orphanages, your madhouses, are all full of people whom your society could not find ways to love but by secluding them.

Thus, you cannot look toward your society, your culture, for anything familiar to find your own passion for existence, for joy, for vitality, for the Creator and for love itself, yet it is there within you, coiled like a tiger's spring. Your heart is the heart of the Creator. It simply needs uncovering, remembering, finding and experiencing. Now, one way to accomplish this in an accelerated fashion, other than daily meditation, is the pushing of oneself beyond the limits, moving by simple exhaustion into a state where the utter joy and passion of life may be felt in a steady state, much as one would feel the sensation of orgasm at the climax of a sexual experience. This is the steady state of the universe at rest. This is the passion which you have for yourself, for your neighbor and for the Creator. This is how strong and how powerful your feelings truly are, and the fact that they have been so greatly shut down in your society is simply a matter of that which must be in order for you to have a free choice of whether to serve the Creator and others, and thus move towards growth of spirit, or serve the self, controlling others and bending them to your will, following the path of self-aggrandizement or service to self.

You have this choice to make. This is your basic choice in this density. Each time you choose to serve another instead of serving yourself, you become a more powerful being, a being more expressing of love. Yet, before you express love, let it be that you have first experienced the love of the infinite One. Let this experience be to you that subjective reality which does not have to be proven from the outside, which cannot lend itself to intellectual speculation, which is simply, utterly experiential. This is the basis of your own perception, of passion, of truth, of love.

What are those things that stop one most quickly from feeling? Primarily, my friends, it is fear that keeps one from feeling. There are many kinds of fear. There is fear connected with earning one's livelihood, fear connected with gain and loss in relationships, fear connected with learning more about a subject which one distrusts or suspects may be more of a subject than an entity wishes to take on. There are many, many fears, and it is well to identify them and allow them, once they are found, to fall away in a gradual way so that change is not too uncomfortable. For, my friends, when we ask you to experience the Creator, to tabernacle with the Father, we are asking you to change. In the process of meditating and focusing in inward silence upon what the Creator may have to offer to you this day, one learns may things. One becomes aware of a grasp of knowledge or a point of view that is broader and different than before, and you have begun to change.

Thus, the way to passion, the way to love, is not easy, for you must along the way empty out of yourself many armorings and defenses against those things which you fear which you do not have to fear, thus freeing the attention so that it may rest upon the fundamental mystery of consciousness. Focus upon that fundamental mystery until you begin to feel the desire to experience, to know more. Let that desire build ever more. If you are not satisfied with the level of your desire to seek as we said, you may simply dance or sing or move or run or swim or do anything which moves one past one's limits. Then sit and meditate again. Some of the veil will have been lifted because when one is quite exhausted the seat of consciousness rests far more in the subconscious portion of the mind. There it is that feelings are stored. There it is that passion lies waiting for its remembrance. The key is remembrance.

There is much more which we could say about this most fundamental topic, yet we sense that there are many questions in this group, and, thus, we would somewhat shorten this particular answer, that we may make room for other concerns and other questions. When you first feel the love of someone who loves you, the natural response is fondness in return, if one does not have fear. Your relationship with the Creator is self to self, but, my friends, you are very, very young creators, and your free will has remained willful. We urge you, through the process of daily meditation, to lay that will before the mystery, and ask, and simply wait. For that which you are to do shall come to you, early or late, and if you yearn for it more and more, it shall come to you more and more. As you desire, so shall you find. May you desire to experience the love of the infinite One. May you glory in the remembrance of that love. May you respond with equal passion to the Creator which wishes you in turn to create for others the manifestation of that love, not through your own limited resources, for you cannot love, even a day; the illusion is very heavy about you, and there is not the energy within you for such. By yourself you have enormous difficulties.

However, you are not alone. You are one with an infinite Source, an infinite Creator, which is at the same time intensely personal, intensely in love with you and waiting for your response. In your holy work, the relationship of the one known as Jesus the Christ to the people of Jesus which was, perhaps unfortunately, called the Church, was the relationship of bridegroom and bride. There is no more intense passion upon the physical level than that which draws a mated couple together. This same level of passion is felt for you by the infinite Creator. It is a matter of removing from yourself the armorings, those things which fill up the mind with triviality, and turn the attention within to the light within, and without to the beauty that speaks in the creation. May you feel the stars laugh. May you feel the joy of the seeds beneath the ground, resting, hoping, seeking that first warmth. May your hearts lie as fallow and your souls seek the light as the seed beneath the ground. You are beings of great passion, power, strength and majesty, yet also you are entities completely free to express in whatever manner you wish. It is a subject for thought, is it not?

We hope you will choose always to gaze at the light, to see the creation of love in the eyes of each whom you meet, to seek the love within and to remember how loved you are. We thank this instrument, and would leave this company at this time, that another entity, perhaps better suited to the questions and answers, might speak through the one known as Jim. We thank you once again for your seeking and the beauty that we perceive in each of you. We are known to you as those of Hatonn, of the Confederation of Planets in the Service of the Infinite Creator. We leave you in the love and the light of the infinite One. Adonai.

(Jim channeling)

I am Latwii, and greet each of you in the love and the light of the one infinite Creator. We are most happy to be able to join this group this evening. We thank each one of you for extending the invitation for us to do so. It is our honor to offer ourselves in the attempt to speak to those queries which may yet rest upon the minds of those gathered this evening. As did our brothers and sisters of Hatonn, would we also remind each of you that we are your brothers and sisters who have moved perhaps a few steps further upon the same path of seeking, and we do not wish any word that we speak to provide a stumbling block to you. Therefore, forget any which do not ring of truth and use those which do ring of your truth as you will. Is there a query with which we may begin?

Carla: Well, since B may be shy, she would like to know about the death process, what happens, where they go and all that.

I am Latwii, and am aware of the query, my sister. You may look upon the life which you experience much as the laboratory experiment, and the time in between the lives that you experience beyond the door which you call death as similar to the lecture which you would receive in one of your schools or colleges. When death's door has been passed through from your life into that which waits …

(Side one of tape ends.)

(Jim channeling)

I am Latwii, and am again with this instrument. We shall continue.

As the entity is joined by those which have served as its teachers, its friends and its guides, it is at this time, as you would call it, that the entity reviews the life experience which has just been completed, in order that the essence of the experience might be assessed and it might be determined those lessons which have been well learned and those which yet remain to be learned. For each entity, before entering the incarnation, sets before itself those programs of study which will allow it to know the Creator more fully and will allow the Creator to know Itself through the entity's experience. Each entity has a great variety of choice as to those lessons which it wishes to pursue. Within your particular illusion, each lesson revolves about the concept that you would call love or compassion, the unconditional acceptance of all that is as the Creator. As the life experience is reviewed, there are those portions of the experience that point toward new lessons that are called by the experience which has been completed. For as any course of study within your system of schooling, the life experience is that which may be enhanced and refined and utilized in ever more broadening, deepening and intensifying means.

As the review of the life experience is completed, the entity then is able to choose those areas of study, shall we say, that it shall pursue between the periods that you would call the life experience of the incarnation, in order that it might gain what you might call the theoretical basis of the next incarnation. This course of study has no limit of time, but is completed in the unique rhythmic manner which is the property or nature of each entity as it develops its own character structure, shall we say. This is a general type of experience which may be had between the incarnative experiences within your illusion.

At some point within the progression of incarnation, there comes the time that one may call the harvest or the graduation, for as all courses of study, there is a point at which the entity shall have learned those lessons of love which it has set about to learn, and shall then progress in the evolution of mind, body and spirit to those lessons which await beyond the beginning of the learning of the lessons of love. This harvest or graduation concerns itself with the entity's ability to welcome the love and light of the Creator within the entity's being in a manner which allows the entity to utilize this love and light in a dynamic fashion to further expand its understanding of that great mystery towards which it moves, the nature of the creation, and the nature of the Creator, and the nature of the self.

Thus, at the time of graduation, the entity moves toward the great light and welcomes the light unto the being, until the light grows too glaring. At this point the entity moves from the light and finds itself within what you might call a new vibration of frequency that shall be the area or density of light location which shall provide it with its succeeding lessons. Thus, the process of evolution is a progression by which the entity demonstrates its ability to extend or expand its point of view so that it is able to take in more of the creation, more of the light and more of the Creator, and is able to utilize this expanded understanding either in the positive manner of radiance or the service-to-others path, or is able to absorb the light in the negative or magnetic fashion which may be called the service-to-self path.

At this point, we feel that we have spoken, perhaps, enough without giving too much information that would tend to overload the understanding.

May we speak in any further way or to any further query?

Carla: Well, just, I think that she also wanted to know where this takes place. Does it take place within the time/space portion of our planet, our planet's atmosphere vibration?

I am Latwii, and am aware of your query, my sister. The location of this experience is a concept which is somewhat difficult to describe. It may be said in one sense that the location is the same as that which you now experience, but upon what you might call inner planes or levels of experience of this planetary sphere *(inaudible)*. The exception would be the time of the harvest or the graduation, when the entity would, perhaps, upon the graduation find that a different location would better suit the need that the entity has discovered within the self. At that point, the entity would then move in what you would call the etheric or form-maker body to that location that it deemed appropriate for further study.

Is there another query, my sister?

Carla: Only a very selfish one. Are you still studying our planet's color spectrum, and if so, what color are you?

I am Latwii, and we are, as always, most interested in the emanations of light from your planetary sphere and the populations upon it. At this particular time, we study almost exclusively within the area that you would connect with the heart chakra or energy center, that being the green-ray energy center.

Is there another query at this time?

Questioner: Yes. There are some religions on Earth that believe that this life, this reincarnation cycle that you're speaking of, is a struggle that you break free of itself, to break free of the constant reincarnations, in other words, that the life that you call our illusion is a negative thing, or at least something that's very difficult for a person to bear. Does this conform to the way that you understand it happening? Are we somehow breaking free, or are we simply, as you're saying, we're on a learning path?

I am Latwii, and am aware of your query, my brother. The process of learning which is accomplished by the utilization of lifetime after lifetime within this illusion of forgetting is one which, for many, is quite difficult, for as one enters into this illusion, one must forget that the unity of all creation exists for each entity, and, indeed, for the self. One must forget the exact programming of lessons that one has set for the self and operate within the illusion only by the smallest and simplest of impulses, that which has been called by many of your peoples, "the still small voice within." One must forget that there is, in truth, no danger or difficulty so great that one cannot find the necessary love to overcome all.

The forgetting is necessary in order that those lessons which are set for the self might be chosen out of free will within the incarnation, and by this choosing, become imbedded far more deeply within the mind/body/spirit complex that is the entity, be imbedded in such a fashion that the learning and expression of the lesson becomes a portion of the self far more efficiently than if the forgetting did not occur. It is as though the game, shall we say, needed to be relearned completely within the incarnative experience, and when this relearning has occurred, then the lessons have been learned, and there is no need to break free of anything, for the entity has freed itself as a part of a natural progression of incarnative experience, each building upon the previous learning from that which was not well learned, building as one does a structure, firmly upon the stone, and carefully placing each portion of the structure.

The difficulty that many feel within the incarnative experience that leads many to feel that there is the need to break free from this cycle of birth, death and rebirth is just that quality which allows the lessons to become more vividly experienced, more intensely expressed and more purely a part of the entity in order that it, through each lesson, might know itself and the Creator more fully.

May we speak in any further fashion, my brother?

Questioner: Yes. You speak of lessons, of learning, sort of reviewing this lesson and programming ourselves for this lesson in between lifetimes. Actually, I have a double question. Are we being guided by other entities from other densities? For example, we think during this period between lifetimes, through mentors from other dimensions? And if so, are we, during our incarnate lives, are we also being guided directly, in other words, do we have some form of guardian angel, as we would say here?

I am Latwii, and am aware of your query, my brother. Each portion of what you have spoken is in some degree correct. It is true for each within your illusion that the first guide or guardian is a portion of the self which has been called by many names, some of which are the "higher self," the "oversoul," or "that which overshadows the small self" within the incarnation. This is a portion of the self that is far more clearly a part of the creation and the Creator and which exists at [what] you would call a higher level of vibration, having, shall we say, the overview or the road map which describes the territory which shall be covered, but which does not guide to the point of overriding the free will of the entity, but with the cooperation of the entity within the incarnation plans before the incarnation the general nature of the journey which shall be experienced, and during the incarnation may, with the assistance of others, provide the entity within the incarnation the opportunities, the stimuli, shall we say, that will remind it of that which it has come to accomplish. Many times there is the meeting with just the right person at just the right time or the presentation of the appropriate book or program on your television or on any system of instruction which leads the entity in a manner which will allow it to travel as it has wished to travel and to learn that which it has wished to learn.

Each entity has, besides the higher self, a male guide, a female-oriented guide and that which may be called somewhat of an androgynous guide, that is, that which has blended the polarities and has found balance in the blend. There are, as well, various friends which have been drawn to the entity according to the nature of the seeking which the entity has expressed and experienced in incarnation after incarnation. Some of these friends are as the entity, however, they are at the time of the incarnation discarnate themselves, and serve as guides, shall we say, that may speak in concept, image and symbol within the sleep and dreaming state, or within the meditative state.

There are many entities which are drawn to assist each entity within the incarnation, so that all possible opportunities for learning may be taken advantage of without the imposing of any choice that would override the free will of the entity during the incarnation, for it is the exercise of this free will that is of paramount importance, as the entity chooses its steps within the incarnation.

May we speak in any further fashion, my brother?

Questioner: Just a little clarification. In the disincarnate state between lifetimes, between our lifetimes here, are we more aware of this whole experience you're talking about? For example, would I be able to communicate more directly with you, or would that even mean anything, in between lifetimes, without the problems of our physical presence?

I am Latwii, and am aware of your query, my brother. It is true that each entity between the incarnations sees far more clearly the nature of the self, the nature of the creation and the journey that the self makes through the creation. The entity between incarnations is able to see and assess all previous incarnational experiences, as one of your entities would look upon the courses of study within the school system that has been completed for the entity. The entity between incarnations is far more aware of the unity of all creation and the binding quality of love which holds the creation together. The entity between the incarnations is able to see the purpose of its existence, and is able to see the efficacy of the incarnational experience in that it offers the entity a far more accelerated means of evolution than should be offered the entity if it were not to enter into the incarnational experience, for as we mentioned previously, the lessons which are learned beyond the veil of forgetting, within your illusion, carry far more weight within the total beingness of the entity than the simple recognition of these basic truths outside of the veil of forgetting.

Is there a further query, my brother?

Questioner: Are you in between incarnations yourself?

I am Latwii, and we, at this time, are within the incarnational experience of that vibratory frequency which you would liken unto the wisdom or light-oriented density, that which follows the learning of the lessons of compassion and love. Thus, we move as you, within incarnated bodies, however these are somewhat more filled with light and somewhat less easy for you to detect than are your own.

May we speak in any further fashion, my brother?

Questioner: No, thank you very much.

I am Latwii, and we thank you, my brother. Is there another query at this time?

Questioner: I'd like to know *(inaudible)* to explore past lives *(inaudible)*.

I am Latwii. We find that there is little of the physical danger for most of your entities that would seek to explore previous incarnational experiences using the tool of hypnotic regression. The greatest danger, or, should we call it, difficulty, that we have noticed experienced by most entities is what we might call an over-interest or preoccupation with the concept of previous incarnational experiences and the attempt to discover what these experiences were and what exactly transpired in these experiences.

If the entity desiring such information has as its motivation for such exploration the desire to explore a thread or line of learning, a quality or concept which it is currently working with, and feels that there might be information helpful to this program of learning that is buried within previous incarnational experiences, then it is a deed well accomplished to explore in any direction possible for the entity. The simple curiosity that develops into a preoccupation with who one was of this or that nature in previous incarnations oftentimes distracts the seeker of truth from further seeking, so that there is what one might call the side road or the detour that must be experienced in order that this preoccupation be satisfied and the entity then take up again the great seeking of the central purpose of the incarnational experience.

Is there another query, my sister?

Questioner: I thank you very much. What I would like to know is, this life, we have obsessions about things *(inaudible)* interesting to find what these lives *(inaudible)* maybe to smooth these obsessions *(inaudible)*.

I am Latwii, and we believe that we grasp the thrust of your comment, and would agree that the desire to understand a current obsession, as you would call it, by exploring previous incarnations is a use of this tool called the regressive hypnosis that may, indeed, prove helpful to such an entity with such a desire.

Is there another query, my sister?

Questioner: *(Inaudible)*.

I am Latwii, and am aware of your query, my sister. The process by which one accomplishes that which you have called the astral travel is a process which requires the body that is associated with the heart-ray energy center to leave or exit the physical vehicle of your third-density illusion, and to move from that vehicle, connected only by what we find your philosophers have called the silver cord, and travel in a manner which may be likened unto the projection of thought, and find as the destination that location or quality which is likened unto the answer to a query, for the process of astral traveling which is well used by the seeker of truth is contained within the asking of the query and the seeking of the answer.

There is amongst your peoples a significant amount of this type of experience that is to be had within the sleep and dreaming state, and for some within the meditative state in a more conscious fashion as well. That the traveling in this fashion is to be found mostly within the unconscious realm is due to the need, shall we say, within your illusion to maintain the free will of each entity in order that those lessons learned might be the product of the exercise of free will choice. Were the ability to leave the physical vehicle more of a conscious process, the seeming barriers which limit the movement, not only of the astral body, but of thought and of the mental process of thinking and imagining, in order that this thinking be focused, the process of such thinking and imagining then would be seen to have far less of a barrier and the ability to focus upon the lessons at hand within the incarnation would be somewhat reduced.

Thus, for most entities, the ability to exit the physical vehicle and partake of the experiences that are provided elsewhere is a subconscious or unconscious process. It is a process which is utilized far more often and far more consciously between your incarnational periods.

May we speak in any further fashion, my sister?

Questioner: *(Inaudible)*.

Questioner: I'm interested in knowing a little bit more about [what] you're saying of vibratory planes, as you say, of existence. I've read in different materials that we have available—that fourth density is somewhat comparable to what we've seen in movies like Star Wars, and I hope you understand what I mean. And I don't know too much about the fifth vibratory plane, but what I am interested in knowing is, do you have what are similar to what we call emotions? Do you get angry? Do you have individual emotions, or are they collective emotions? Could you speak a little bit about that please?

I am Latwii, and I am aware of your query, my brother. We have one central emotion, as you would call it, or as close as we can come to approximating that which you call the emotion, for emotions are those mental qualities which carry a certain weight or charge for entities within your illusion, and it is these charges set upon the mental qualities that allow the learning of certain lessons, all of which evolve about the concept of compassion or love. That we also experience this emotion of love is the central quality of our being, for it is the lesson of the fourth-density entity to find within its being this quality of compassion for all experiences and entities that should come before its notice. When it is noticed that there is any other response to an entity or an experience other than that of love or compassion, then it is that the entity so experiencing that deviation shall learn from that deviation in a manner which will eventually bring it full circle in order that it shall then experience only love and compassion.

We have within our experience as a group, or as what we find some within this group would call a social memory complex, been fortunate in our own evolutionary experience to be able to develop this quality so that as we look upon any situation, any entity or any concept, we see first and foremost to the heart of the experience of the entity or of the concept, and see at the heart the one Creator knowing Itself through that experience, that entity, and that situation. Thus, we have little of the deviation that one would normally associate with what you call emotional responses. Rather, we feel the great upwelling of love for the creation that we see about us and for the creation which lies before and ahead of us upon our journey of seeking.

We experience our illusion as a group or as a race of beings, each blending with the other with a harmony that is difficult to describe, but which makes it impossible to hide our nature or to desire to hide our nature. Our communication is instantaneous by what you would call telepathic thought transference to those which are not a part of our social memory complex. Our communication with each other is an instantaneous knowing, so that which is known to any is known and available to all. Thus, we have at our disposal a great library, shall we say, of information that allows us ever more intricate, infinite and delicate means of observing and serving the one Creator which we see in all of the creation.

May we speak in any further fashion, my brother?

Questioner: Yes, that's very interesting. It sounds like that in your density that things are pretty easy, in other words, compared to the way that we live here, that your plan, your direction is sort of plotted out for you, that you just have struggle more and more, or study more and more. I don't know exactly how to describe it, but is sounds like that you do not experience what we would call unhappiness. Is that true?

I am Latwii, and we do not experience that which you call unhappiness, for we find that that quality has within it the properties of the illusion in which you now find yourselves moving, that is, the quality of failing, shall we say, to see the Creator in each experience. Rather than feeling that which you call unhappiness, we feel, as close as we can approximate, the incomplete service of the one Creator. We seek ever more refined and efficient means of being of such service. Within your illusion it is true that you have a far more challenging experience. You have, because of the need to forget that which you shall remember and that which you are, the inability to express this remembrance. You in your illusion are bound by the limits of the illusion, but experience also a greater potential for acceleration …

(Tape ends.) ❦

L/L Research

L/L Research is a subsidiary of Rock Creek Research & Development Laboratories, Inc.

P.O. Box 5195
Louisville, KY 40255-0195

www.llresearch.org

Rock Creek is a non-profit corporation dedicated to discovering and sharing information which may aid in the spiritual evolution of humankind.

ABOUT THE CONTENTS OF THIS TRANSCRIPT: This telepathic channeling has been taken from transcriptions of the weekly study and meditation meetings of the Rock Creek Research & Development Laboratories and L/L Research. It is offered in the hope that it may be useful to you. As the Confederation entities always make a point of saying, please use your discrimination and judgment in assessing this material. If something rings true to you, fine. If something does not resonate, please leave it behind, for neither we nor those of the Confederation would wish to be a stumbling block for any.

CAVEAT: This transcript is being published by L/L Research in a not yet final form. It has, however, been edited and any obvious errors have been corrected. When it is in a final form, this caveat will be removed.

© 2009 L/L Research

Intensive Meditation
January 18, 1989

(Carla channeling)

I am Laitos. I greet you in the love and in the light of the infinite Creator and thank you for the privilege of being called to your meditation this evening. We are most happy to be able to use this instrument to work with those of you who wish to learn the disciplines necessary for a considerably more careful use of the self for service than perhaps would be possible without some guidance. The guidance that we give is not only for the service of vocal channeling. Those tools which you bring to the preparation of the vocal channeling as service to others are also those tools which are needed to do any of the works done with a completely open heart. Healing, art, music, dance, architecture, all the expressions of aesthetic authenticity spring from an entity who knows who he is and what his ideal is.

Thus, it is not only those who work as vocal channels who may, perhaps, be able to gain some small benefit from considering these matters, but, indeed, any who truly wish to be of service to others. My friends, service to others begins with the self, for, indeed, all about you are faces of yourself. Those things which most distress you about others are those things which are the reflection of yourself, and in those things you may see a distorted version of that which is occurring within you. Thus, each relationship is like a mirror in time that moves with you along that river, showing to you your own face in a biased manner which may provide catalyst so that you may work upon the self.

It is obvious, but we will say it anyway, that in the normal run of things, an entity, no matter how sincerely seeking, may not have the luxury of a simple path, nor of a path which is without some conflict. It is not, in our opinion, and we stress that it is only our opinion, of moment whether or not there is conflict in a relationship, for honest disagreements may be harmonious. The only thing that is important is the priority which this disagreement takes within the relationship and within the structure of catalyst for the individual who is seeking to discipline and learn the workings of his own consciousness. Thus, to express emotion in an honest and spontaneous way is not behavior we would at any time discourage. We encourage, rather, the gazing at those spontaneous expressions with an eye to bringing a wider point of view to them.

All of the teaching which this instrument is so aware of concerning the clearing of lower energies has to do with the safety, physically and metaphysically, of one who is learning to enter into one's own guidance in a deeper and in a more coherent and controlled fashion. If the energy of the infinite One is not full in its surge through to the heart, then that heart energy will find doing work in consciousness a burden. We would hope that it may [be] seen to be practical, if one wishes to seek spiritually, that these moments that are burdensome may be as few as possible, for there is enough trauma in the process of becoming truly aware of who you are. One needs to have a steady stance and a firm grip upon an Earthly peace-filled existence before straining toward a destiny which involves both joy and responsibility; that is, there is no greater joy than knowing for the first time who you really are. On the other hand, once you know who you are, you are far more responsible for expressing and manifesting the fruits of that knowledge.

When the work has been done in consciousness with persistence, and we underline persistence and doggedness, a simple keeping on and keeping on, when all looks hopeless, as well as when all looks rosy, you shall, perhaps, come to the place where that which seems to be responsibility and duty has become the joy, the passion, the fun, the true service. This is a long process for each. Sometimes it is shortened. Sometimes when we speak to new instruments, we are speaking to those who have already moved through a good deal of this material. In these cases, development may seem to be quick. In actuality, it is simply that we have come in upon a different portion of that entity's incarnational learning. For the most part, when one is seeking to find out the truth about the self and the Creator and the about the relationship between the two, one is, for the most part, rather uncomfortable, confused, pondering, wondering and doubting.

We are sorry to tell you this. We would like to paint a rosy picture, for we would like very much for those of you upon the planet who are interested in working for the light to do so. Yet we must begin by explaining that there are costs to this work, and one of the costs is that it is hoped that it may be seen that if one is to express love and service to others, so it is that one must love the self in a final and holy way, for you are divine, each of you. Not in your Earthly form, but wrapped deeply within you lies the infant babe that is your pilgrim spirit. It sojourns here within that which you call a body, and you move about in this body, upon this plane of existence, upon this small sphere, this globe, this island in space and time. What is your wish for this experience? Would you wish to live without ideals or with them. Without faith or with faith? Without hope or with hope? Without consolation or with consolation? These are the choices you may make. It is your universe; your opinion rules your creation.

We ask you to consider one thing this evening, the concept of tuning. We are thankful that this instrument has taken the time to write out that which we need not repeat over and over within the material which she has given you to read. You are aware of the concept of tuning, the idea of the self being a receiver and transmitter for concepts and feelings. We work with instruments such as this one largely through concept; that is, we give concepts to this instrument, this instrument clothes them in words and gives them forth. The experience is exactly as if the instrument were speaking her own thoughts. This is very puzzling, however, when one is tuned to the very highest and the very best of spiritual frequencies that he or she may hold in a stable and safe manner, not straining the attention, not straining the qualities of self, but knowing the strong points of the self, moving onto them, standing on those strong parts of the self, moving ever deeper into the self to find those strong places, until at last you stand both in the physical world and in the metaphysical world as a true pilgrim citizen, one who may speak with authority, the authority of self-awareness and self-confidence.

To know yourself, to forgive yourself, and to love yourself is the first business at hand. This forgiveness needs to be complete. This is necessary for the tuning to the self, for if you are to love and serve another, you are to love and serve them as you would yourself; so it has been written in your holy works. If you do not love yourself sufficiently, how shall you love another? Therefore, your first work is the healing of the self and the setting of a goal, the goal of experiencing and knowing imperishable truth, of coming into realization of the natural laws of spiritual existence. Gradually, these things will become second nature to you, if you persevere.

For right now, we simply ask that whenever you catch yourself being negative about the self, that you remind yourself that you are an orphan on a very unusual planet, and that you must mother yourself and nurture yourself and care within your heart for yourself, until those sore and painful places are indeed nurtured and healed at last. Until there is forgiveness and redemption within the knowledge of the heart, not only of the mind, then may you tune upwards, seeking ever higher for a more beautiful, lovely and perfect ideal, a more clarified and fine version of love divine. What do you seek? How much do you want to know? Sharpen and hone your desire, for it has been written truly in the work you call your Holy Bible, "Seek and ye shall find; ask and it shall be given to you." Be very, very careful about that for which you would ask, for it is divine law that in one way or another you shall receive everything that you truly desire. Tune your desire, and so you shall learn to tune for channeling.

For this evening, we will content ourselves with merely greeting you. We would like to exercise you briefly by simply urging you to relax and allowing us to move first to the one known as Jim, and then to the one known as C, and then to one known as A so that we may say simply, "I am Laitos." We wish only to let you feel us, if, indeed, you are going to feel us, and to speak our voice so that you may see that when you hear in your mind, or see, or are aware of the phrase, "I am Laitos," it will seem to be your thought. We wish you to have this experience this evening, for we wish you to ponder the difficulties ensuing from doubt because you think that we are your own thoughts.

You will notice how long this instrument has been speaking. This instrument did not know her first sentence; she does not know her next. It is not this instrument—we are principles of being. We are, in our own way, real.

We hope we are helpful. We hope, indeed, that we do not disturb you by any experiences that you may have in experiencing our energy. If there are electrical experiences or the movement of limbs in an uncomfortable position, or the using of the neck in any way that is disliked, indeed, if anything is uncomfortable, we will be with each for a short time, simply making that first contact and working to adjust to a comfortable fit, shall we say. We have worked many times with the one known as C, and shall be most happy to work with him again. To the one known as A we say, "Fear not," but simply let that which seems to come, come, without disturbing the experience. Allow the experience in the same way you would allow a story to be so, until the story has been told. In this way you may distance yourself in a safe place, while experiencing the sensation of our contact.

Then we ask each to spend the intervening time before the next meeting considering the implications of the channeling seeming to be the self. It is one of the central problems of new channels. You must begin to acclimate yourself to the atmosphere of doubt which you will enjoy for some time. You will not know if it is you, or if there is truly another who is speaking through you. It is only through practice that you begin to be able to distinguish. There will, in conscious channeling, always be a portion of yourself in every channeling that you give. This is desired by us, and we feel that it is the strong point of conscious channeling, that is, that we have a very simple story to tell, a story of one great original Thought, a love which created all that there is, a love to which all shall one day return. This story is too simple for people to understand. They must make it more complex, so they may attempt to understand. It may be said that understanding is not something that may happen within your illusion, but it is part of the illusion that people wish very much to understand that which is not understandable.

(Pause)

I am Laitos. I am again with this instrument. We are sorry for this pause, but were having to contend with this instrument's variation in form of trance. This instrument almost—we believe the phrase is—went to sleep. We approve of the one known as Jim squeezing this instrument's hand; it is helpful, but we would not advise it for long. To continue. We would move now, so that each may feel that which he cannot, will not, and shall not understand. We are with you. We hope we are helpful. There is, indeed, no harm in us, and we would like to make our presence known to each. Thus, at this time, we will leave this instrument, simply to greet each by our own name. I am Laitos.

(The rest of the session was not transcribed.)

Intensive Meditation
January 25, 1989

Group question: What is the first step to open your channel and what does it mean to open your channel?

(Carla channeling)

I am Hatonn. I greet you in the love and in the light of the infinite Creator. It is a great pleasure to be called to your group. We especially thank this instrument for removing from our signal that of our counterpart. The amount of subtlety necessary to disarm the negative entity is much appreciated. We wish to say to the new instruments how very happy and blessed that we feel to be able to work with two people with such determination to seek the highest and best path that they may travel through the "valley of the shadow of death," for that is, indeed, that which life is. We realize that the topic to be discussed is channeling itself, what the first step is and what the nature of channeling might be. We shall answer the questions in turn, with great thanks for the strength in the circle and this great entity and unity of this great circle.

We are very pleased at the orderly way that these questions begin, for, indeed, there is a first step for which the instrument, perhaps, has not been giving a central enough place in its teaching in the past. The protection of the physical body is a very sensible and apropos caution to take before attempting any work whatsoever in consciousness, whether that work be that of the artist, the writer, the musician, the worker, the meditator, or the magician.

Anyone who attempts to do any of the improving of the self to meet one's ideals needs to be aware this is the path of polarization of service to others, and the more successful one is at it the more one will run into instances of the negative, or groups, or entities which are delighted to attempt to undo the work that has been done or, even better for them, to change the polarity of the student to be of service to self by deception. This is often done, in fact, and when they see the service-to-self aspect of many groups which have formed so vital camps to survive the catastrophes to come, indeed, that is not the action of those who wish to be shepherds of the flock which shall be frightened indeed at that time. The sensible precaution is the protection of the physical body, and we shall gratefully go over one great way to achieve an acceptable physical aura.

Now, we are presuming, we ask you to understand that there is within each a determination that drives to live a life in faith. Without faith in the positive and in love, there is in the end no protection. It is the decision without any objective evidence to live a life based on faith, abiding peace, joy, freedom and hospitality that such words as a channel, saint, mystic, seer, shaman, so forth, can in actuality mean.

Here is the direction for a specific protection of the self. We shall do it with you if you will safely follow along, for the energies which are energized, shall we say, by this protection are universal, having to do not with the body which you know and have but the length of energy which is your true body.

Picture, if you will, yourself sitting in a cross-legged Indian position or in a lotus position, if that picture does not bring you acute discomfort as it does this instrument. Rest the backs of your hands upon your knees in a comfortable place. Curl the thumb and forefinger together, a trustful but somewhat defensive posture, and picture at the base of the spine, in the groin, and just above where the generation of the species takes place, a red fire. See it within yourself. If it is not bright, allow it to brighten. If it still will not brighten, ask that it brighten. Then watch it spin. If it is not spinning, ask it to spin. And ask it to be clean and pure that the energy of the Creator might move upwards.

Visualize, then, at the middle of the abdomen, an orange fire. It must be brightened and then spun into crystal colors, and the prayer that all be clear and clean, that the energy may move forward and upward, may be made. Help may be asked for any way you may deem appropriate.

Then upwards toward the navel area, the pit of the stomach, where there is a yellow fire, do the same with this energy center. Whirling it, and seeing a green energy center at the heart level. Brighten it, and then spin it.

It is this energy that you need clear, and clean, and pure. It needs to be this way that you may receive those messages or even information to the self about the self which will truly be full of the love and light of the infinite Creator. If these lower energies take from the supply of that prana or living air which the heart chakra needs to brighten and to spin and to move the energy upwards, then the channeling work is compromised at best. Consequently, you continue with the green light center until it is clear, flashing and brilliant.

Now, it is to be hoped for that the blue center, that is, the communication center, in the throat may be brightened and spun.

And so the indigo center above and between the brows or the forehead.

It is, however, not necessary to do this work for these energy centers to be crystallized and clear. It is safe to do this work as long as there is energy into the heart chakra of sufficient magnitude for the weaker energy centers to take the energy from the supply of prana and still have enough energy to change the energy of self to the highest and best, most energetic and deepest self, that one may be a citizen of the universe.

Once all of the energy centers have been energized, it might be imagined that there is an eighth chakra, the crown chakra, which is white. This energy may be seen as either a glow or as the white that brightens and then spins. It is part of the self but also part of all of creation that is the Logos, and therefore may be seen, indeed, in both configurations within the same energy.

Take the white energy that you have brightened—we correct this instrument. We must pause.

(Pause)

I am Hatonn, and we greet you again in love and light. We are sorry but this instrument was drifting from the tuning of which we were talking about, and therefore we needed to pause. The condition of this contact is again satisfactory.

Vision, if you will, the white color moving down the left side of the body and picking up the red energy of the red survival chakra. Mix these two colors.

Add in that amount of the indigo ray and the blue ray chakra energy which you consider you have upon a stable basis achieved by your tuning. That is, if you do not feel that you are perfectly clear in blue and indigo ray, then ask for a limited amount of these colors.

Take a mixture of these four colors—red, indigo, blue, and white—and move them about the body until the body is in your visualization painted completely.

Take, then, that center we may call violet. It is always as it is and is not visualized. However, it is that as you are. Therefore, after the physical vehicle has been protected as well as you can, visualize it for the condition you are in as a channel.

Then visualize yourself covered again with the violet ray that is your own indication of character.

Over that, draw then the white light of the one infinite Creator, not that which is from yourself, that may brighten and spin, but that which is as a cloud or nimbus about the self.

Visualize that as a shield of light that covers every portion of the outer physical vehicle, allowing no thing which does not love the light within the sacred confines of the temple of the one infinite Creator which is your body. This protection is important for both.

There is further protection which we will emphasize before the one known as C. We are concerned that this entity moves even in the phase of discomfort into a fairly deep state of meditation. The toll of the type of labor which this instrument does to provide for those he loves has taken its toll in the sense of enabling spiritual growth by allowing work of such a nonintellectual kind that the mind is free to move into a relatively meditative state at nearly all times since there is not a large portion of the intellect involved in challenges.

We would suggest that this new channel that is new for this particular time might improve the background state for active awareness by a variety of experience within the confines of those hours that can be spared for leisure. This would aid the channel somewhat.

However, we are concerned with the protection of the channel under any circumstances, and would suggest to the one known as C that the entity, when it feels it may have gone too deeply into a meditative state, when it feels it might be uncomfortable, it needs simply to count upwards first to ten, and then if that is not up enough, to the full measure of years which the entity has lived upon this planet in this incarnation. When the last number of years the entity has lived [is reached] the entity will be fully awake and need only remain in a thoughtless, loosening, alert mode, for this is the appropriate environment for this type of channeling.

We speak only vaguely on the nature of channeling itself, for we feel we have taken too much time for information and perhaps have gotten the new channel a little concerned about how long it will be before they channel a long time.

One step at a time, my children. It is enough for now that we are able to work with you and move a small baby step. If we may do that each time, then we shall progress many, many miles, as the tortoise beats the hare in the story which this instrument is familiar with.

The nature of opening one's channel might be considered similar to beginning to understand a root system of consciousness which has geometry and form in a metaphysical sense, and which at the very bottom, just as the Earth has a molten core, of white air. So the center, the very, very deepest part of your consciousness, is what you might call a black hole. That small speck of water that is so heavy that it is gravity that somehow draws all things into it, only to have all things disappear.

That is your destiny, your omega, to be at one at last with infinite intelligence. Not to know God, shall we say, but to be. You are at this moment a portion of all that there is. You are a portion of the Creator. You are a unique portion of the Creator. However, you are skating upon the surface of your consciousness.

To open the channel is to open the door to approximately 98 percent of the content of your consciousness as a conscious channel, in the sense of being one who is conscious of a channeling process within self, has an opportunity to work within those times to deepen the understanding, to listen, to give self respect to those knowings. They are one's own truths and that which is one's given service.

One does not make up one's mind to do this or that, rather, one's feeling and one's heart as well as mind are led to the service that is of the Creator, for the Creator speaks within with a small voice easily drowned out by one's own small will. Thus, it is most important that the daily meditation be established and that, for the most part, at least adhered to.

It is not a disaster that one day is missed. We just ask that you do not allow that missed day cause the discouragement to lead to a second or third day. But allow each day to be itself new. Just as you yourself is made new with each dawn.

As you open your channel you shall find first those voices which speak only to you. That is your internal guidance. If you wish to receive internal guidance only we strongly suggest that the hands be crossed and the feet be crossed, that the electrical circuit of the body be closed so that one may carefully filter out any outside influence from the physical body.

This is not foolproof, however. If the guidance continues to be positive and helpful, then it is sufficient. It is, in the majority of cases, sufficient, may we say. There are some natures whose electrical properties as entities as such are that the circuitry of the physical body is changed in enough ways that this is not sufficient protection, this instrument being one of those people. This instrument has always wished to wear the crucifix about the neck, and the reason is simple. The instrument needs the protection and the reminder of the faith which creates within the instrument the love necessary to banish those influences which would speak of negativity.

When the channel is open anything is possible according to one's gifts, and the possibility of serving the Creator becomes almost certain. The life pattern may be such that beyond the simple vibratory nature of the self no dramatic work is expected. Simply the loving of those which are hard to love, the smile to stranger as a charity to those who need it. Others have more dramatic ways of being channels of love and life. All ways of service to others are equal.

The importance given to some methods over others of living a life are false. The various reputations which one encounters because of various entities' levels of schooling or other credentials are all false. When one is vibrating as a channel an infinite source comes through which sees the essence of all entities, that deep, mysterious Creator at the very bottom, at the very essence, at the very root of each organism which is conscious of itself and therefore has consciousness.

Within this state the nature of channeling is such it is well to choose, from the bounty of all that there is, one way of directing the channel. Some are healer, some are teachers, some are simply wise or loving. But it is well to focus one's energy in the direction which feels most helpful, good, pleasing and pleasant, for the path of service is part of a life which must first of all be joyful. Thus, the tuning of the self becomes important, the knowing of the self and so forth. And of these things we shall speak again but we feel we have worn out your ears.

And now we shall give you some respite by speaking far more briefly through each of you. We shall attempt only to greet you with a sentence or two. But if, then, you instruments feel a further thought to come up after we announce our presence and give greetings and the love and the light of the infinite One, then we would be happy to continue sending. It is simply that we do not wish to do more than a very small bit at each working, for this enables the new channels to do quite a bit of thinking about what is occurring in the process.

We would first ask the one known as A to relax, to allow the rational mind to rest, to empty itself, as if there were pockets in the mind, of the small change of daily life. Put all these things upon the dresser and return to your meditation with an empty, new mind. And then, if you think, "I am Hatonn," say it speedily and quickly and we shall offer another thought. The experience is indistinguishable while speaking your own thoughts, and we are aware it takes a certain amount of time to achieve a long enough contact to convince the self that it could not have, on its own, could not have created the precise message.

You will find in time that no matter whom we speak through our message is consistent and our points made in the same spiritual direction. You will be aware that you could not have created this pattern of thinking within the self because the self does not contain these particular patterns of thought in just this way. You would have said it differently or perhaps not thought of it. Then will come the time for each new channel when it puts aside the question of who we are. We do not wish to convince you before you are ready to accept the responsibility for knowing that there is an invisible world which is far more fundamental than the visible world. Certainly, there are many, many worlds but we are close to your own world, and speak to you from a relative near position, in metaphysical terms.

Please just let it all go, let the mind relax, and when we must speak, in you then immediately repeat the phrase in the parrot-like fashion, realizing that you are going completely on faith and will be doing so until that magical moment comes when the subjective evidence for our reality is clear to you personally. Each must earn that for himself.

We would now, with thanks to this instrument for the work upon the subject question, move to the one known as A. I am Hatonn.

(A channeling)

(Inaudible)

(Carla channeling)

I am Hatonn, and am delighted with the ability that the instrument had to put up upon the fairly subtle signal which we were able to give. We assure this instrument that it shall become clearer as we adjust to the instrument's particular vibratory complex. We also apologize that we cannot offer this instrument words in the French language, that we were aware that you were receiving our contact in French, and we wish to encourage the one known as A to go ahead with the visualization of these words even though the other entities within the room will understand little of what you say, for the purpose of learning the mother tongue is, indeed, perhaps best, and the one who attempts the concept communication in a second language makes the precise handicap that it meets when it attempts to cloth any concept in the second language's vocabulary. It is always easier to describe or relate a concept using the mother tongue. We thank the one known as A again, and hope this is of some help.

We would now go to the one known as C, with gratitude that this instrument picks up again that path which it has trodden so many times so faithfully. We are most humble before the persistence of this entity and wish to encourage the entity to realize the intensity of the desire for seeking for [that] which has sustained this pilgrim through the times when it knew not what to do or how to do it. It is a quality that is especially useful in spiritual work which is slow. This is why we so often encourage people not to be discouraged, for patience is most important in the spiritual search.

(Carla channeling)

I am Hatonn. I am again with this instrument, and again greet you in love and life. We will continue. We would ask the one known as C to realize the safety of his metaphysical position, to experience the feeling of safety about the person, for it is that realization or faith in one's protection which validates it and intensifies it, and we are very interested in aiding this instrument in feeling safer and stronger in the face of the disturbing swings in level of trance.

We ask the instrument to remain alert and simply to relax, as we have asked many a time, my brother. We would now translate. We would correct this instrument. We would now transfer to the one known as C. I am Hatonn.

(Inaudible).

(Carla channeling)

Hi. I greet each of you in love and life through this instrument. We are very pleased with the progress of the one known as C, who has demonstrated this evening, and assure you that we are pleased to be with you. It is a matter of persistence in gaining the whole form, shall we say, of this instrument. At this time we would offer ourselves to speak to any questions that may remain on your minds of those here this evening. Is there a query to which we may speak?

Questioner: I was wondering if there is an actual *(inaudible)* and if we add to *(inaudible)* experience to *(inaudible)*.

I am Hatonn. We find that the condition of the headache is one which has a connection to these undertakings for you at this time as a result of a mental tension which you may describe as a worry that you will not perform the vocal channeling in a satisfactory manner. This quality of worry or mental tension comes not only before we exercise one of your instruments but is most easily in the form of a headache as you have the opportunity after the channeling to assess not only your progress but your likelihood of advancing your [art], shall we say, in what we shall call your future.

This concern or worry is that which may be seen as quite normal in any new or experienced instrument in some form in that each wished to offer itself in the purest manner possible with a strong desire to serve others. The desire to serve others may be stepped down or distorted, shall we say, into a worry that the service will fall short of what is possible. Thus, we commend the desire and recommend that the lighter touch of the taking the self less seriously be employed as the remedy of this aching of the head.

Is there another query, my brother?

Questioner: *(Inaudible).*

I am Hatonn. Is there another query?

Questioner: Yes. It is awfully good to hear you *(inaudible)*.

I am Hatonn. And there are various ways of relieving the type of nervous energy which one may experience as a result of quieting the mind and the reaching through to a source of results that is find imbedded in the greater self, that in some cases may manifest its vitality as a kind of nervous energy. In taking part in the physical exercise which brings one to the physical exhaustion is as one means as simple as walking rapidly or jogging will remove this energy in a short period of time. The opportunity to do this not being present, one may also engage in conversation with those gathered about it and converse for a lengthier period of time. And if one is especially well trained, one may visualize the feeling of one's energy and seeing it being dispersed as a kind of shotgun blast, shall we say, as the mind sees the energy moving through it and moving in a rapid fashion into the area by directly placing it into the field of [inner] vision, and [allowing it to] continue to move as would the fire hose expel the water through it, so that the energy is moved rapidly through the being in a mental fashion.

Is there another query, my brother?

Questioner: *(Inaudible).*

I am Hatonn. Is there any further query at this time?

Questioner: What about counting downwards? You said counting upwards should make you more alert. What about doing the visualization about it all going away and feeling calm? What about counting down a number at this stage and visualizing it again, and then counting down a number, and so forth, until it feels right. Would that work for this instrument?

I am Hatonn. It is a possibility that the counting down would be of some assistance. The instrument needs to be aware of that it will to find two balancing points, between the over-excitation of the physical and the mental complexes and the relaxing of the physical and mental complexes upon the point of entering the deeper states of the trance. We suggest that the entity utilize any of the aforementioned meanings that feeling most nearly correct at this moment in its trance.

Is there another query?

Questioner: I'd like to follow up on that. Is there a downside to that? Is there a possibility to put yourself right back in the soup by being low in a trance real fast if you were counting down? If not, is there a possibility of that? Then it is not a suggestion I would want him to take.

I am Hatonn. There is this possibility. We suggest that the instrument take care in the utilization of the effect that he in order remain more liable condition.

Questioner: Is one number safe? Going down one number from your age?

I am Hatonn. This is enough.

Questioner: Thank you. I thought it might be. It was just an idea of mine. B used it all the time. I never knew why but it seemed to work.

(Transcription ends.) ❦

Sunday Meditation
January 29, 1989

Group question: Is there individuality in our lives, or are there forces that guide us that are beyond our perception—for example, astrology, predestination from previous incarnations—that goes into decision-making so that our lives seem to come out with relative order in relationship to the chaos? And how might all of this, in a general sense, relate to S's current condition in which she feels a great degree of stress and would like to have some inspirational word or message that might help her make sense out of this all?

(Carla channeling)

I am Latwii, and I greet you in the love and in the light of the one infinite Creator. It is a great blessing to us to feel your call and have this opportunity to serve you. Indeed, it is you who serve us, as our means of learning further at this time is service to those such as you who would at this time wish for thoughts which we have to offer. As always, we ask that no word be taken as authority and that each person discern that which is its own truth for itself, for all that we have to say may not be the truth of one or another of you. We are those brothers and sisters who travel the same path. We share opinions. Thus, we ask that you do not take us to be without error.

Our plate is nicely filled this evening, my friends. We have more things to begin with than we know what to do with and we are most excited about the possibility of communicating with you, for those things which you wish to know are, indeed, central to the continuing search for your own truth.

You wish to know who you are. What part of you is yourself, and what part influence only. The answer will be a paradox, yet it is what we have to tell you. You will find that the nature of spiritual seeking is such that paradoxes occur quite frequently. You are consciousness, and within consciousness lies the total experiential series of illusions which make up the experience of the creation within this creation's octave. However, these halls, shall we say, or temples of intelligence and information, inspiration and imagination are carefully guarded, and it is unlikely within the illusion you now enjoy that this portion of yourself would be available in any understandable fashion in its entirety. This is a real Self. It is also that which you call the Creator, for it is out of that which you call the Creator, out of that great singular consciousness which we find we must call love, since there is no stronger word for this feeling in your language, that is your being. Each [mote] of illusion is instinct with the Creator self.

This is not that which one hopes for when one asks a query concerning individuality, however, this is a portion and a most important portion of the individual self, and that is the Creator Self. It is this Self which must be reckoned, as this Self is the destiny of the self which at this particular time, as you would say, is indeed your individual self. You are both an individualized portion of consciousness and All That There Is. The important portion to focus upon within the experience of the illusion is first of all the self that you are within the illusion. The purpose of entering into this experience using this physical vehicle and moving through all the joys and sadnesses of an incarnational experience is to work toward decisions, biases within the mind and the heart. This individual self is the only self that may make those decisions within the illusion.

What we suggest that each entity does, basically, is to put the individual self back into perspective as a portion of the great unified Self, which is love. To say that another way, all are a portion of a consciousness that is beyond all intent or desire. Each of you through the action of free will moves towards desired ends. That from which you sprang, that one great original Thought of love, had, through the use of free will, made one choice, that being self-knowledge. Each individual portion of consciousness, thus, is offering to the Creator the experiences which it registers and the extremities of bias or intensities of feeling which its portions of consciousness can create and experience. The more intensity and color, shall we say, the more resonance and undertone one's internal experience expresses, the better, as far as the Creator is concerned. Thus, the Creator is interested alike in all things.

However, there is a bias that has been set in place within this density, which does, indeed, tend toward a suggestion that the Creator, being a Creator of love, has created in the path of love for others, a path which is more easily and joyfully taken than the path of service to self and control of others. Thus, each of you is, indeed, an individual, each of you is here for one basic purpose, that being to make a choice between one path and another, and then, that choice being made, to attempt throughout the remainder of the incarnation, with dogged and continuing persistence, to follow that choice and to make other choices which support and undergird the first choice of service to others.

Now, when one decides that one is to be of service to others, when one commits oneself to taking oneself seriously enough to enter into meditation, enter into the silence, and make that link between the small self and the Creator Self, one is bound to expect an experience which is more than usually full of new ideas, new feelings, and therefore discomfort. For as the changing process—that is, the process of change within an individual which is the inevitable fruit of the spiritual quest—is happening, discomfort and pain are also occurring. It is uncomfortable to change, and this is what each who makes the choice to act in a polarized manner does. The choice implies a long, long list of other choices involving being of service to another.

We may recommend for those who are at the beginning of this path that the first step in such a path is not to be of service to others, but rather to know and love the self and come into communion with the self so that one becomes to oneself the individual that others are to the self, but the self seldom is. It is often the self which criticizes the self the most harshly, the self which has an internal voice which pulls and tears at one's feeling of self-worth. These negative voices from within need to be reckoned with, need to gazed at and brought into balance. These voices are speaking to you of pain, and the pain must be investigated and all involved forgiven.

Most of the forgiveness that is needed at the beginning of the spiritual search is the forgiveness of the self, for one forgives others far more easily than one forgives the self. It is most centrally important to forgive and love and care for the self in a nurturing manner in order that one may love one's neighbor as oneself, as it is said in your holy work, the Bible. How can service to others be performed by those who do not love the self, for all other selves are in truth as the self? All are beloved and intimate, for all are brothers and sisters of one infinite Creator whose expression to all of us is much, much love. This Creator is most interested in each, tastes and relishes the experiences of each, and we, in return, those countless brothers and sisters of the creation, move evermore intently toward reentering that same awareness, which is the consciousness of love itself.

As the choice is made, things rapidly become chaotic. Indeed, the method of experience for any entity within your illusion is that of alternating order and disorder. This is due to the fact that the consciousness which is used by the surface mind is a type of, what this instrument would call, biocomputer; its one function is to answer queries "yes" or "no." It answers millions and millions of them each second, as the mind decides what it will apprehend with its senses and offer to the mind as information and what it will filter out as noise, rather than signal.

This biocomputer is programmed to accept certain information. When change is desired, the program of the computer itself must be written, or in many, many cases, concerning relationships especially, a program must be dumped and a new one written. This is the specific source of the discomfort of change. One is moving into the programming of one's biocomputer, and one is having to use more of one's internal character, shall we say, or will, in order to most beneficially reprogram the computer. Further, the act of meditation is a rapid accelerator to this process because it allows an opportunity for the higher self to work with what we may call a metaprogram, or greater program, which influences how one uses one's various programs within the information.

The act of meditation opens one to the experience of the Creator in a worshipful or personal manner, that is, one awaits and listens for a dear friend or a beloved one, one has the feeling of intimate expectancy. This is the beginning of the listening process, a desire as if [one is] before a lover or one who would read a beautiful poem that meant a great deal. This attitude is that which opens the heart and the mind in a way which gives much energy and power to whatever it is that is willed or desired by the entity. If the entity wishes to move ahead quickly and learn, then the entity will, indeed, be changing quite rapidly.

Those who are in relationship with such an entity are advised by us to join with the mate in this endeavor, since the changing otherwise causes one of the mates to gaze upon the other and say, "You have changed and I do not know you anymore." We find that the strongest and most comfortable or sturdy of the alliances that one may make in the spiritual search is that of the mate. The mated couple which has managed to clear away the many petty disagreements of everyday living and has agreed to work together may greatly intensify and accelerate the process of spiritual work in consciousness because one who is supported and loving, but truthful and honest, is a far better mirror than that one made of glass.

Many relationships between your peoples are those which offer the very distorted picture. Indeed, it is a great service to be a mate and offer an objective, loving and truthful picture of the other self. This is a worthy and service-to-others attempt. It may not sometimes please, but if it is truth to you, then allow it to be communicated, and in that communication shall you find unity, strength and more understanding, more awareness than was there before.

No two entities can walk the same path, and when mates attempt to walk a spiritual path together it must needs be seen that each is, indeed, an individual, and not an individual that can change easily, but an individual that is the result of biases gathered over incarnation after incarnation after incarnation. Gaze upon your babies and your youngsters and ask yourself, "Are these young souls possibly the product of their incarnational experience alone?" My friends, ask any parent, and it will explain to you that each entity is born an entity that knows upon its own rhythms from the beginning until the end.

Now we move to the question of influences. Yes, indeed, my friends, you are most influenced, and most of the influence is to distract you from the game at hand. For just as school is a game in which one attempts to pass the test at the end, so is life itself, and life after life after life part of the game in which an individual entity that is a consciousness or a soul, that is, in part, a part of the Creator, is intended to go through experience after experience after experience in each incarnation, testing the biases that have withstood the test of many, many, many experiences, so that by the gradual process of erosion of bad habits, shall we say, or habits that you decide are bad, and by the continual encouragement of that which seems to your deepest truth appropriate, you may change your choice more and more toward the polarization of love; love for yourself, love for the Creator, and love for all those whom you meet, all those who are alive and all things that are alive, or by being the product of man's hands are in that way alive.

We are sorry to say that experience of chaos continues, and the more it occurs, the faster the entity is changing and the more uncomfortable the entity will be. Any sort of chaos in the metaphysical sense, that is, in the sense of unpurposeable energy, is an illusion, for in an energy there is an inherent purpose or else it would not move. Within the illusion which you experience, the chaos is, almost always, a question of the point of view. It is well, in the sense of being, perhaps, the most accurate of gaining the largest amount of clarity, to move away mentally from the side of the sphere upon which you now enjoy an incarnation, until you can no longer see either the planet or its sun. From that standpoint, things look somewhat different. The frame of time and space has opened up, and there are many fewer things which are of importance. Some things, however, are timeless. These are the principles and natural rules of creation which it is well to observe.

These rules are very simple. Free will is uppermost in the so-called Laws of Creation. That is, each entity is an individual and has complete free will to make its choices. That is the whole point of this entire process of consciousness from alpha to omega. Thus, encourage yourself to be ever more conscious and ever more self-conscious, without becoming so self-involved that one forgets that once the self is in hand, once the self is peaceful and meditating and ready to serve, then the hand needs to be turned to the present moment.

Many people feel that they cannot be of service if they are not of dramatic service. This is not so. Each entity is of maximum service in the exact moment in which he asks the question, "How may I be of service?" by opening the eyes and gazing at what is in front of him. There lies the first service. Usually it is not a new service, but, rather, one which has elicited from the self a somewhat less than totally positive service-to-others feeling. There is your first challenge, your first choice. Gaze at that situation and ask yourself what you need to reprogram within your biocomputer in order to express and manifest the love and the light of the infinite Creator to that entity in some form of service.

The basic service of each of you is to be in a certain way, and this is that which we would especially point to our sister known as S. The entity needs to be concerned first with allowing the self to become cheerful, merry, lighthearted and gay. If the experience is that of hardship, this is not unusual. Many are the prisoners, those in pain, and those in many other kinds of distress. No entity which is lonely, downhearted or distressed is ever truly alone, for it is as though there were a communion between each which is suffering and all others which are suffering. There is a commonality to this experience of difficulty, and in the face of seemed or perceived negative experience, it is often a great challenge to present an honestly positive affirmative and cheerful view of life, a smile or a light in the eye. If this is a difficulty for any, we recommend stopping any question of being of service to others, and allowing that to remain upon the list of things to do someday.

For your first service is to be the individual that you are, for you are unique. You carry perfection within you, but you have molded it and distorted it in an unique way. Each of you is as a gem. Each, perhaps, feels very flawed, and expresses itself in a flawed manner, imperfect in many, many ways, yet each is also the Creator. When this is seen, the difficulties of achieving peace, cheerfulness, a positive attitude, are made much, much smaller, and with the aid of meditation, affirmations and prayer, and for those such as this instrument, the use of some gift such as singing, the state of mind which may be called centered may be achieved without purposeful or pompous effort in a relatively short number of years, considering how many lifetimes that you have been working upon how to love yourself, your Creator, and those whom you serve.

It is not surprising that the acceleration of this learning process would take a bit of time. It is well to do that which makes one's body, mind and spirit sing with joy. Failing such ideal circumstances, it is well simply to have hope, to be able to nurture and console the self and to wish to console and nurture others. Love, you see, is that which we come to speak about with you. It is too simple a thing to be drawn out by so many, many possible channels. That is why we always encourage those who wish to offer the vocal channeling as a service to others, for each entity is, indeed, an individual. Each entity brings to the channeling, which it corroborates with us on, its own unique experience, vocabulary and thinking processes.

We are aware that there had been a question earlier within the group concerning a trance channeling versus the conscious channeling and speaking only for the Confederation of Planets, we find that in most cases we do prefer that the instrument be in less than a complete state of trance. We enjoy the state this instrument is in, which is a, shall we say, medium amount of relaxation compared to sleep, but within the range which we find this instrument would call alpha.

We began with paradox, for as we say, we cannot speak of that which is spiritual without speaking in terms of paradoxes. We are a voice upon the wind. Are we this instrument's wiser, deeper self? In a way, that is true. Are we those of an independent identity? We are indeed.

We are sorry—if that is the correct expression—to leave entities in a state of some confusion. We would like to be clearer, but there is only so much clarity possible within a limited language system. We find that one of your poets said if he contained multitudes, then so be it. My friends, each of you does, yet all of these multitudinous parts of the creation are part of your character, and that which we call character is expressed within your particular illusion by that which is called desire or will.

Once you have identified your goal, spiritually, seek it with persistence. Will to know that which you do wish to seek, whether it is a clearer idea of the nature of yourself or your situation. Whatever portion of experience you are working upon, allow the desire to be very clear and understandable to your conscious mind and acceptable in every way before you will it to be so, for that which you will to be so will come to you one way or another.

Sometimes one wishes and receives that which one has not carefully thought out aforetimes, yet still one receives that which was requested. We ask you to be careful about that which you desire and to review that which you desire at intervals to see if you do wish to change the programming somewhat in your biocomputer. We encourage you to be intent …

(Side one of tape ends.)

(Carla channeling)

… you may take one thing away with you and leave all the rest, that would perhaps be our first priority.

We would like you to get to know yourselves, and in the process of getting to know yourselves you shall know the Creator, you shall experience communion with the Creator in the way that you yourself may comprehend. And from that point onward, you shall have a feeling of yourself, a sense of yourself, a comfort within yourself which may nurture you and strengthen you and empower you when all around you does seem to be negative and difficult. We would ask each to take it very easy. If there is intensity that is causing difficulty, back away from it. If there is a sluggishness that you feel has paralyzed you, back away from it.

Move to something that makes you merry, that causes you laughter, that moves the rubber band about the soul so that you may breathe, so that you are not constricted. Let yourself have fun; let the child express itself. Then move back with a full heart and single-minded devotion to your goals. Let them be those of service to others, and let your efforts be the best that you can produce. And let there be no emphasis placed upon the outcome of your efforts, for your efforts may fail or succeed, yet it is not important to your own choice-making procedure, as long as you may see that the best which you could [do] is done, the outcome does not matter, for when you are expressing from a centered, loving portion of being, you are, in fact, acting as a channel for a higher self, still yourself, yet more beautiful, more focused, certainly more enduring. You are able to shine a light through yourself, and you are then a great blessing.

We would end by a word about destiny. You asked us many questions, my friends, and it was hoped that we would be able to say more, but we find that this instrument is telling us we must speak briefly and leave, so that there is time for questions. We would say a few words about destiny and the stars.

Very briefly, the understanding that we have of what you call stars is that they are entities, radiant with the love and light of the one infinite Creator, that they send into the energy web of each a certain energy which affects that higher or finer body which may be called the form-maker body in a metaphysical sense, so that certain subconscious feelings and biases are part of the geography or topology of the mind just below the surface mind.

Therefore, on a given day, the influences of what the instrument would call heavenly bodies may be noted and charted as astrologers, we find, do. It is very much the same as gazing at a map of roads which cover your nation state and saying that because there is a map of these roads, the journey is predestined. One may take any road which one desires, but upon that road, one will find certain things. One will find whatever one sees to be a certain way based upon the self that one is. There is always the subject bias which moves from total consensus reality to the individual perception.

Each choice is, indeed, made with free will, however, and the higher self, which is you also, had quite a meeting before this incarnation, my friends. Each of you knew this was an important one for you. Each of you knew that you were very lucky, and shall we say, more than lucky, that you had earned the right to this incarnation, for there are many more souls who wish to incarnate at this time than there are opportunities. This planet is in a state where much may be learned quickly, if one has determination and persistence, for it is a painful, difficult ordeal to move through the valley of the shadow of death and to look at each experience without attempting to make anything of it.

The basic kind of experience one has within your illusion is that of loss, as we find this instrument heard the one known as Joseph Campbell say, "Life is loss." This meant a good deal to this instrument, and we use it with thanks. This is indeed so. It is the self within you which chooses to respond to the love inside which is felt within, to the love outside which is perceived by gazing at the creation without it.

It is that will and faith which has been developed within and without, not gazing at the affairs of the day, but by gazing within at consciousness and without at the world of what this instrument calls the natural world that one begins to develop a sense of the beauty and the goodness and the consolation and the light and the joy that is reality. For all that you experience in this third density, or in our density, is illusion. None of us sees plain. Yet, within may we experience more and more purely the love of the one great original Thought of love.

Thus, you have chosen to learn certain things, and those certain things will make up your incarnational pattern. If you do not like the pattern as it is at this time, make up the mind with determination to desire to learn the lesson which is being offered to you. Gaze at it. Find the love in it. Analyze it. Meditate upon it. Allow your intuition to develop. Yet, always, if it is too serious, if you are unhappy, if you are tense and troubled, back away and sing a song or play or laugh or move the body in rhythm or make something with whatever portion of yourself desires to create freely. The universe, as far as we know, exists at a steady level of joy. You know it when you experience that which you call the sexual orgasm. That is the steady state of reality. That is the intensity which created the physical vehicle in which you now express. That is the beginning of one way of understanding the Creator.

May you be blessed in your search, my friends, May you be comforted within and may you comfort and serve each other in love and in joy. We are those known to you as Latwii. I am a Latwii, however, and if I become confused, I may immediately ask any other entity which is within the complex calling itself Latwii to you this evening, and are able then to, perhaps, gain a deeper understanding of how we wish to be of service in the answer. Thus, I am Latwii and we are Latwii. We and I would wish at this time to transfer to the one known as Jim in order that we may close through this instrument. I transfer at this time.

(Jim channeling)

I am Latwii. We greet each again in love and light through this instrument. At this time it is our privilege to ask if there might be any queries remaining upon the minds of those gathered. Is there any query at this time?

Questioner: *(Inaudible)* ... around the greatest or a significantly large part of our energy through [our food] yet there is great evidence that a greater part of the energy comes from without. And I would like your response to that question as it affects the vitality of all people. How much of the energy that actually drives our body and our spirit comes from without *(inaudible)*?

I am Latwii, and am aware of your query, my brother. Your physical vehicle is similar to the furnace which must be stoked in order that it might provide the means by which it shall move through your daily round of activities. The physical vehicle, therefore, is the primary beneficiary of the food which you ingest. However, the physical vehicle is also enlivened, as is the mental and as is the spiritual vehicle, by those energies which are not of the food description, shall we say.

Each moment of your existence there is fed into your energy centers or the system of chakras, as many have called them, a kind of energy which is described in many ways by many of your peoples according to their study of their culture and their religious or spiritual histories. Some would call this energy the prana, the breath of the Creator. Others would call it love, others light. Others a combination of these qualities, a kind of intelligent energy which is the daily and moment by moment gift of the one Creator. This energy enters into the physical vehicle or the electrical energy fields, the aura of the physical vehicle, through the soles of the feet and thereupon through the base energy center located at the foundation or base of the spine, moving upwards through the various centers of energy which represent the qualities of one's character as a human being, thus allowing one to participate within the realm of the humankind to the degree that one has chosen previous to the incarnation and, increasingly, as the incarnation, progress as one has chosen in a conscious fashion to utilize.

The mental and spiritual complexes or bodies of each entity are motivated in large part by this intelligent energy, with the spiritual complex partaking also of a quality of energy that one may describe as unity, or, as we find some in this group would call it, intelligent infinity, which is the quality of beingness that the one Creator draws upon in order to create the creation and each portion of it. This quality of beingness, then, that enlivens the spiritual complex is the primary connection that the entity partakes in with all of the creation. It is that which ensures and sustains its very essence, the being that is never separate from the one Creator or from any portion of the creation.

The mental complex or body is somewhat nourished in what you might call a second-handed fashion, therefore, by its connection to the spiritual body and partakes of the quality or energy of beingness through that connection. The love and the light of the one Creator are the primary energy sources that are daily utilized in a conscious acting by each entity, as these energies move through the chakras or the energy centers, thereby, one, enlivening the need for survival and reproduction; moving upwards, two, the relationship with the self; moving further, three, the relationship with those of the family and friends known well to the entity; moving upwards further, four, the relationship of the self to all about one, whether known or unknown; moving further to five, the establishment of clear and freely given communication with all of those about one, sharing freely that which has been learned; moving further up the energy centers, six, to the quality of being that radiates without words; moving to the final center, seven, the reunion of the entity with the one Creator as the energies have been activated one upon the other by the conscious application of analysis, prayer and meditation upon the daily round of activities that have been made possible by the infusion of the intelligent energy, the love and the light of the one Creator, through the energy centers. All this in turn taking place because the physical vehicle has been energized by these energies as well as the food that powers its movement and its existence within your reality.

Is there another query, my brother?

Questioner: It appears when I hear how you speak of your entity that you are part of this group which are communicating psychically, which means … First of all, is this true, and secondly, can you also understand our thoughts psychically, and those are the two preliminary questions. The main question I want to know—is it possible for us to communicate between ourselves psychically? Is this a skill that we can learn?

I am Latwii, and am aware of your query, my brother. Our communication is quite simplified by the fact that the nature of our illusion, our reality, is one which is quite transparent. We are both unable and unwilling to hide any thought or any quality of our being from another within our complex, for it is our nature at this point within our evolution to share freely and openly all that we have learned of the one Creator, of our evolutionary journey and of our desire to be of service to others.

To move to the second query, we could telepathically perceive those thoughts within your mental complex if we desired to, however, it is our desire to respect the privacy of each entity that calls for our service. Therefore, we restrict our abilities, shall we say, to those queries which are verbalized, in order that we may not only speak to the point, but may respect the privacy which those of your peoples value greatly.

To move to the third portion of your query. The means of telepathic contact and communication may, indeed, be learned by those of your peoples who have great persistence, not only in attempting to learn this specific skill, but in attempting first to explore the self to the degree that is necessary in order to provide a, what you would call, clear channel transmitter and receiver, for many are the thoughts and tangles and thoughts waiting untangling that serve as a kind of static, shall we say, that interferes with this ability to communicate in a telepathic sense.

We find that the Logos or that great Being of the octave level of intelligence which is responsible for this portion of the creation has found it helpful for those within its care and guidance to depend within the third-density illusion upon the verbalized and symbolized communication, rather than the telepathic type of communication, for this enhances the use of catalyst, shall we say, or the opportunity to learn that is the purpose of your third-density illusion.

To state this in another way, were the ability to communicate in a telepathic manner widely utilized and ordinarily utilized within your illusion, there would be far less mystery as concerns the unity of all of the creation and far less motivation to penetrate this mystery. Therefore, the added challenge of verbalized and symbolized communication is seen as a means by which the evolutionary process might be enhanced for your peoples, causing as it does the increased desire to know more of the nature of the self and of the creation.

Is there another query, my brother?

Questioner: Just a verification. Does this mean, when we pray, if we're praying to the Lord for help or whatever, [should we verbalize it?]

I am Latwii, and am aware of your query, my brother. It is not necessary to verbalize such prayers or invocations, though it does not affect their quality, shall we say, for as one prays in a certain manner and to a certain entity or quality or concept, there is developed a certain, shall we say, pathway that moves quite accurately and swiftly to the source or focus of the prayer, and is as the ringing of the telephone within your culture, so that whether the prayer is mentally given or verbally spoken, the intent of the prayer and the content of the prayer are those qualities [which] are of importance and which will receive an answer of one kind or another.

Is there another query, my brother?

Questioner: No, thank you.

Questioner: I've increasingly become interested in a—been reading about a form of psychotherapy which has as its basis, I think, that the free flow of energy through the body is essential for human happiness and human function.

They contend that when the muscles of the body harden, as a way of reacting against negative situations, for example, that occur in your life, that are reacting the same way, certain muscle groups in the body become—"hardened," is the only way I can say it—against this particular negative thing, and they claim that this hardening impedes the flow of the energy in the body. And I guess I just want you to comment on this. Indeed, is this true, because I've always thought of the energy of the body as flowing through the nervous system more than anything, but if the muscles are restricting in an abnormal manner, does this restrict the flow of energy to the body?

I am Latwii, and am aware of your query, my brother. This, in a general sense, is, indeed, quite correct. However, it is more the outgrowth of a more fundamental blockage of another energy flow. This energy flow is that which is of the mental nature, for the lessons of your illusion, the catalysts of your illusion, move first to the mental complex, for the process of evolution within the creation is primarily a mental process whereby the consciousness that is developing its individual expression of the one Creator slowly but surely widens its point of viewing until it is able to see, accept, love and forgive all about it as it would the one Creator, for, indeed, it eventually sees all as the one Creator, including the self.

When there is a limitation of the viewpoint, and the mental configuration of an entity is unable to accept some portion of its experience, some portion of itself or another self which represents itself to it, then that energy which moves through the entity is constricted to some degree according to the limitation of the viewpoint which the entity has placed upon itself.

This continuing blockage of energy of the mental nature, when allowed to be prolonged without significant movement in understanding, then is given to the physical vehicle in some symbolized manner that will be noticed by the mind more quickly, it is hoped, than it was noticed in its original mental configuration.

Therefore, the hardening of certain muscle groups, as you have called them, as well as many ailments which move into various of the organs and structural portions of the physical vehicle are representations in a symbolic fashion of the original blockage of energy which first took place within the mind complex.

Therefore, the removal of the physical blockages of energy and their various expressions or manifestations is most effectively undertaken first upon the mental level and then allowed to move into the physical level as a result of working first upon the source or root of the blockage. The focus upon the physical blockage only, or before focusing upon the mental, tends to work primarily upon the symptoms, shall we say, or the outgrowth of the root cause.

Is there another query, my brother?

Questioner: No. Thank you very much.

I am Latwii, and we thank you, my brother. Is there another query?

Questioner: Yes, I have one. Actually, two, which in some way seem connected. The first is simple, and that's to ask you whether all of the entities who exist within your complex or your density, whether at one time did they all live on this Earth? And the second part of the question is, is there one religion on this Earth which is more valid or beneficial than any other?

I am Latwii. To speak to the first query. We are not native to your planetary influence, but we have had the honor of sending many of our peoples to your planetary influence in order that they might partake within your incarnational process for the purpose of lending their light to your planet and its evolution. Each such entity which undertakes this honor and this responsibility of service goes through the same process of forgetting that which has come before the current incarnation as does each of your planet's population. It is hoped that each entity which offers itself in this capacity of service will at some point within the incarnation begin to remember a portion of the reason why it has done what it has done, and will begin to offer that service which is its service peculiar to itself, to offer those about it in the attempt to lighten, shall we say, the vibrations of your planet. We offer ourselves in this capacity as a means both of serving those of planets such as your own and of moving our own evolutionary progress further along, for it is by service that we learn most effectively and it is a great honor and joy for us to do so.

I am Latwii, and we thank the one known as Carla for reminding us of the second portion of the query. We feel that each of the religions and philosophical stands which have been taken and followed in the history of the cultures of your planet each have a great deal to offer those which have the character necessary to follow each. This is to say that we do not find one particular …

(Tape ends.)

L/L Research

L/L Research is a subsidiary of Rock Creek Research & Development Laboratories, Inc.

P.O. Box 5195
Louisville, KY 40255-0195

www.llresearch.org

Rock Creek is a non-profit corporation dedicated to discovering and sharing information which may aid in the spiritual evolution of humankind.

ABOUT THE CONTENTS OF THIS TRANSCRIPT: This telepathic channeling has been taken from transcriptions of the weekly study and meditation meetings of the Rock Creek Research & Development Laboratories and L/L Research. It is offered in the hope that it may be useful to you. As the Confederation entities always make a point of saying, please use your discrimination and judgment in assessing this material. If something rings true to you, fine. If something does not resonate, please leave it behind, for neither we nor those of the Confederation would wish to be a stumbling block for any.

CAVEAT: This transcript is being published by L/L Research in a not yet final form. It has, however, been edited and any obvious errors have been corrected. When it is in a final form, this caveat will be removed.

© 2009 L/L Research

Intensive Meditation
January 31, 1989

(Jim channeling)

I am Hatonn, and I greet each of you in the love and in the light of the one infinite Creator. We are very grateful that we have been able to make a good contact with this instrument this evening, for it is unused in to making the initial contact and has some reservations about it and delivering the opening message, shall we say. Having partaken in the question and answer portion of the meditations for a great length of your time this instrument, as all instruments, has the ability to serve as a vocal instrument in a relatively stable and clear fashion, but also has the need for exercise that will improve its ability to serve as an instrument. We commend the diligence and perseverance of each that seeks to refine and nurture the desire to serve as an instrument.

As you each have discovered in a way that is personal to each of you, the service of the vocal instrument is one which has a great many ramifications that carry over into each portion of the life activity. As one serves as a vocal instrument the necessity becomes clear for opening the self to that which is unknown to the self, and for allowing a contact that is other than self to utilize the self and its personality, its history, its experiences, its ideals and its terminology, for the expression of information which may have value, not only to the self but also to others.

As seekers of truth pursue the journey of seeking this process of opening the self to that which is unknown, [it] not only draws into the instrument's mental framework those concepts which are, for the moment at least, unknown to the instrument, but tends to place upon the life experience that which is similar to the magnifying glass, as we give this instrument a picture in its mind of the glass that magnifies, held before the face so that all which comes before the notice is enlarged, is enhanced, and, perhaps, is intensified in some degree. This effect of throwing into larger and clearer and more intense relief the life pattern is both a blessing and a challenge, for the instrument that experiences this effect has the opportunity to utilize the daily round of activities as a kind of food, shall we say, which will allow it to focus upon the portions of the life experience which are in need of refinement, of analysis, of balance, of the attention that will provide the proper utilization of the catalyst. This is the opportunity, this is the blessing.

The challenge, of course, is that the continuing process of intensifying the catalyst in the daily round of activities requires that the instrument be ever attentive. That the relationship which it develops and pursues with any other self be a relationship which has as its foundation the desire to be of service in a clear and compassionate fashion. This, of course, is the basic lesson, shall we say, of your particular illusion. And it is ever more clearly and forcefully made apparent to the instrument that this process of building upon compassion each relationship that it finds and continues is the most important quality of a life experience.

Thus, as one pursues the art and service of serving as a vocal instrument, one will become more available, shall we say, to the effect of catalyst. One will find that this intensification of catalyst does not occur only when the instrument is ready or most ready. There are the moments of mental, physical and emotional and, perhaps, even spiritual fatigue that occur as a natural portion of each entity's cycle of being, the rhythm of the pulse of life as it moves through each entity. These moments are also filled with the more enhanced catalyst, so that the ability to respond in the desired manner may be reduced from time to time, and it is during those times of seeming regression or moving backwards from the ideal that the instrument will be tested, shall we say, by its own desire to match its life pattern with the ideals which it has set for itself.

We may look upon any instrument as [being] similar to the crystal. We see the diamond as it is usually cut and faceted by those of your peoples as being likened unto the instrument or any entity which seeks in a conscious manner to be of service to others. Each facet maybe seen to be a certain mental attitude, a certain symbolic representation of ideas, of thoughts, of the ideals of the strength and of the weaknesses that are to be found within the personality, within the character of any instrument.

The energy of the Creator, that which you may call the prana, the love, the light, the intelligent energy of the Creator, which moves through each entity, then may be seen to move through the crystallized being, that is, the seeker of truth, that is, the one who would serve as able co-instrument. As the facets of the personality become more harmoniously balanced due to conscious attention and work upon them, become balanced with each other in a regularized configuration, the intelligent energy of the Creator then moves through the crystal, so that it is reflected in a balanced manner, and the crystal, then, because of the sure and sturdy construction of its angles, is able to utilize the intelligent energy and to move it through the entirety of the crystal that it might be returned again to the source whence it came. The contact that we establish with each new and each experienced instrument travels this same path as does the intelligent energy of the Creator. It partakes of the same framework or pathway through the crystallized being where there is an area or portion of the self that is not well understood, or is not functioning as well as it is understood.

There is the lapse, the break, the opening, in that portion of the crystallized being that needs to draw a portion of the energy towards itself, as does the magnet draw the iron filings. For those portions of the entity which remain to be understood and which remain to be set into the motion of the daily round of activities serve as a kind of vacuum that draws to it any available energy that might be utilized in the—as we use the analogy—electrical sense, to organize the more random nature of that portion of the being. Thus, if the entity desiring to serve as a vocal instrument has neglected over-long a certain portion of its own evolutionary journey, a certain portion of understanding of the self, understanding of the self in relation to others, then there is the drawing into the area of whatever energy enters the being so that the expression which manifests or is sent from the entity has a certain imprint, a certain manifestation, a twist to it, that is characteristic of that area. Thus, the contact that is sent through this particular area will have in some degree a biasing, so that the energy which enters and then exits as concept, word or deed has a bias to it that will reflect the inner landscape of the personality, shall we say.

Thus, we find the conversation that was held prior to this session's beginning to be most helpful, in that it reminds each instrument that whatever areas within the self that yet await the refining and purification that is the task of the conscious seeker, will lend their certain bias to that which is the vocalized channeling. The concept here with which we deal is that each instrument will in some degree offer a portion of itself to the contact, to be blended with our concepts and vibrations in order that the collaboration between us and the instrument might produce information of use to others in their evolutionary journey. The portion that is of the instrument, then, needs must be made as stable, as clear, and as full of the vitality of the self as is possible. Thus, it is always recommended that as the vocal instrument chooses to pursue its art that it heed the advice given also to those who would serve as healers, and that is that it is well to first heal and balance the self as far as is possible at any particular time, in order that that portion of the self which is offered in the vocal channeling be the highest and best which the entity has to offer.

It is often possible for the instrument to momentarily clear the energy centers and the mind of the concerns and the distortions which might unduly influence any channeling process and to successfully serve as an instrument in the moment of this clearing, shall we say. However, it is not a process which can be depended upon to provide the instant remedy, shall we say, each time that the entity desires to serve as a vocal instrument. Therefore, we recommend the continued watchfulness and observation of the self by the self, so that the foundation of service may be built upon as strong and sure a base as possible.

We are aware that each instrument here has this information well in its mind and has through long experience put this information to work in the daily life. We mention it again at this time in order to amplify the words which were spoken prior to this meditation's beginning. For we have noted many times previously that there is great desire seen in almost all entities which serve as vocal instruments and this is quite commendable. However, the desire is often not matched by the careful practice of the knowing and healing of the self in each of the many ways and areas in which the self expresses in the daily life. Therefore, we beg your indulgence that you listen again to that which you have heard before.

At this time we would attempt to transfer this contact to the one known as C, so that this instrument may continue in reinvigorating its ability which has been proven over time to serve as a vocal instrument, and may, shall we say, begin to shake and scrape some of the rust from the instrument. We again would remind the one known as C that it is well that this instrument find a means of attaining that depth of concentration in the meditative state that is comfortable to it, that it visualize in some manner a method of bringing itself higher out or up from the levels which are too deep for it to function as an instrument. Whether this be the visualization of the numbers from 1 to 10, with each number allowing it to reach a higher level of alertness, the steps seen in front of the inner field of vision which allow the alertness to be increased as each step is ascended, or to simply utilize the words which are being transmitted through it, so that the words themselves may be willed by the instrument to bring it to the desired level of alertness as the words are spoken.

We wish the contact with the one known as C to be as comfortable to this instrument as possible and recommend that this instrument ask mentally for any adjustment of our contact that does not feel comfortable to it. We also recommend to the one known as C that it vocally speak any discomfort that it feels could be alleviated by the assistance of those gathered about it this evening. We would at this time transfer our contact to the one known as C in order that we might speak a few sentences through this instrument. I am Hatonn, and we now transfer this contact.

(C channeling)

I am Hatonn. We greet each once again in the love, light of the one infinite Creator. We would remind this instrument to allow the words to flow rather than try to analyze each. Irrational mind. This instrument is … We are having some difficulty at this time maintaining contact. We would … attempt … We would … I can't seem to hold it …

(Jim channeling)

Hi. I am Hatonn, and I greet each again in love and light through this instrument. We thank the one known as C for making a good effort to receive and speak those concepts we gave it and we commend it on its fidelity and its desire. We find that there is a certain degree of distraction within this instrument's mental complex this evening, and we recognize the difficulty with which the instrument deals and can only offer our support as it works with those distractions which are upon the mind.

We would recommend that this instrument engage in the daily meditation at a time which is convenient to it, so that it might be able to receive our conditioning vibration when it meditates, and might recognize our presence and be able to offer the challenge and then to allow the meditation to proceed in a silent manner from that point onward. This daily practice of recognizing our contact and taking time for the self to relax into meditation we see as a potential means of allowing the instrument to not only work upon the recognition of our contact, but also to work upon the quieting of the self, so that those distractions which move through the mind might be able to be studied in a more relaxed atmosphere rather than being only part of the conscious activity so that there is more than the conscious mind that is able to offer the viewpoint during the meditation periods.

At this time we would open this meeting to the queries which we will be happy to offer our opinion upon, if there be any queries at this time.

Carla: While I was experiencing your contact I was and still am to some extent receiving something else which I merely asked if it was here in the name of service to others and if contact was to be made. Can you say anything about what this other contact is?

I am Hatonn. We observe the presence of the quality or essence of what you may call a guide or a friend which has offered itself in the hope that it might aid the one known as C in achieving the proper level of meditation, in order that the contact with ourselves might be possible without the one known as C moving too deeply into the meditative and then too deeply into what's known as the trance state. This presence is one which is quite happy to respond to any mental request which the one known as C would offer to it. Therefore, we suggest that the one known as C offer any request that it feels is appropriate to this entity and that this presence might also be utilized in any meditative practice in order that the meditation might be conducted in the same fashion, that is, without entering too deep a state of trance, shall we say.

Is there another question?

Carla: The contact was exceedingly strong. Has this friend or guide been around before? Is this one that I knew in younger days?

I am Hatonn. We wish to give that which is appropriate at this time, without the infringement upon the free will, and may suggest that this contact of which we speak is one which has long been with the one known as C and has offered itself more in a more obvious fashion at this particular time, as the one known as C is undertaking again the exercise of its vocal instrument with the desire to be of service to others.

Is there another query?

Carla: I don't think so. It's kind of nice if it's who I think it is. It's old George around again. We'll have to get him to tone it down just a hair.

I'd like to ask a question. In an instance like this, Hatonn, is it a good teaching practice to encourage the student to attempt to vocalize the contact of the, you know, the inner planes entity which I also sensed was there, but which I had no authority over since it answered the challenge and since it was doing almost nothing as far as I could tell during the time I was challenging it. But then, on the other hand, C looked real dark, too, as if nothing was real active there, too. I have things to learn. I wonder if you could comment first of all on, would it be good practice when an inner planes guide is felt very strongly to encourage the student to go ahead in a safe confines of the challenging in the group and get a little bit closer with it or is that not such a good idea, and then any comments in addition about why I didn't see that C was, perhaps, a little uncomfortable. I usually see it in terms of light and I didn't see the light, I didn't see the energy moving.

I am Hatonn. We would recommend that the one known as C utilize the assistance of the guide as an enhancing factor in the attempt to reestablish a clear contact with ourselves and others of the Confederation that would attempt to make contact with this instrument. It would be well that this contact be well established in a way which the one known as C is familiar with from previous training before any attempt is made to contact a new source of information.

The ability to sense another's distress is one which is natural to you, my sister, but one which is also subject to refinement and improvement through the continued observation that you have made this evening. We would recommend that you continue to, as you would call it, patrol the perimeter and note anything that is of significance and to then check that with those which are gathered at a time after the meditation has concluded, or to check the observations in the question and answer portion of the session as you are now doing. In this way you shall receive the necessary feedback that will give you the hints and clues that are necessary to improve this ability to sense the nature of the circle, as it is being experienced by the group.

Is there another query, my sister?

Carla: Well, let me ask again, let me refine the question a little bit and see if I can … What was the metaphysical situation, forget the entity, I looked at C and I saw him as being basically, completely, excuse me, completely dark, that is to say, I didn't see any energy moving. Now, I was missing the fact that he was uncomfortable. I want to know if you can tell me what metaphysical area I should look at in order to become able to be more subtle in my seeing, if that makes any sense. Because I feel that my students depend on me to some extent for a backup, and I want to be there for them and I don't like it when I don't know something like that, like being uncomfortable, and I would like to learn.

I am Hatonn. We find that the degree of discomfort was not great and was not within the scope of your sight, shall we say. The viewing of the energy as it moves through another is best accomplished by holding that person in the mind, in the foreground of the vision and using, as we see you are aware, the inner senses to feel the degree and quality of energy present. We feel that your ability in this area is that which exceeds most entities' abilities, and we commend your desire to improve. However, at this time we feel that you have a good enough grasp of this process that it is simply a matter of continuing to exercise this ability that will increase its sensitivity to the degree that you will be able to notice the slighter discomforts. We can speak no further at this time.

Carla: Thank you, Hatonn.

I am Hatonn, and we thank you, my sister. Is there another query?

C: This entity … now that I become aware of … ah. I wish to reassure Carla that I wasn't in distress more, I was feeling more distracted than anything because it was something I was not used to experiencing while trying to channel, ah, and if this is who I think it is then this entity has really been a part of me for a long time. I simply have been unaware of it until tonight. I am curious now why the area of the bridge of my nose is so sensitive to contact?

I am Hatonn. The location of the indigo-ray energy center is found at this precise point within the physical vehicle. The activation of the indigo-ray energy center, though not critical for one who would serve as a vocal instrument, is that which is most helpful for those which are able to avail themselves of the activation of this center of energy, for through the indigo-ray energy center flows that quality of beingness that steadies and amplifies the carrier wave, shall we say, that attentiveness yet quietness within the mind upon which we infuse the concepts and words that are our contact. Thus, for one which has been able to activate this energy center, there is the ability to enter into a state of relaxation that is both profound and more stable than would be possible without the activation of this center. Thus, we would suggest that …

(Tape ends.)

L/L Research

Sunday Meditation
February 12, 1989

Group question: This concerns the spirit world and how much of the thoughts that we experience in our daily lives are influenced by the so-called world of spirits, guides, teachers, angelic presences, and so forth? And what is the real difference between whatever influence this supposed other or outer world has and that which we experience interiorly?

(Carla channeling)

I am Q'uo. I greet you in the love and in the light of the one infinite Creator and share with you the blessing of consciousness. We are most grateful to be able to share consciousness with you at this time, and we find the circle of seeking to be as a lighthouse upon a somewhat turbulent and darksome sea, yet, many, many lighthouses there are. The numbers are increasing, and we are most grateful, and most especially at this very instant of time, as you would call it, to you who seek to know the truth.

You have called us to your group this evening to speak of a subject difficult to speak of because the nature of the integrity of an entity is not understood within your people's vocabulary. Consequently, we shall be working somewhat athwart of the presumptions which are connotated by many words which can be mistaken within your language, and for this we apologize, but there is no substitute for the language of the entities to whom we speak. We must, indeed, use those words known and attempt to [blend] them as we may, with art.

The entity that each of you is is much other than you may, perhaps, perceive yourself. The actual portion that is imperishable of your consciousness, that which will take many bodies, that which will learn many things, is not a portion of the self that can be seen or measured or even differentiated from influences upon the subjective experience of the entity. However, the entity remains at the heart of the web of experience, choosing the biases it shall add permanently, or increase once the bias has been added. This is the imperishable self, that is, the infinity of the Creator surrounded by the distortion called free will. This is your consciousness. Your goal as a creative spirit is simply to advance from being a person of free will which wishes to seek the Creator to being a person which experiences a consciousness of the Creator's presence in the way best understood to the self.

In this context, each and every mundane and daily event is altered because of the contact with the presence of the infinite Father. The manifestations which come from this change in attitude are, perhaps, best described as polarizing strongly along the path of service to others.

Now, we speak first of the true character of each portion of infinite Consciousness, because we now will remove all the structure seemingly from the experience of that metaphysical and perfect creature that you, indeed, are. Each of you is at all times channeling in several different ways. Let us look at them as briefly as we can do this.

Firstly, there is the programming which one chooses as one observes during the younger years of the incarnation. The choosing is that of separating that which will be absorbed and attended to by the conscious mind and rejecting those signals which it is receiving from various points of … we fail to find a word in this instrument's mind for the various kinds of intentional spreading of various thoughts. However, the process of choosing what one will become aware of is very much affected both by the biases of those which are incarnate and are teachers of the young spirit—the parents, the family in general and the teachers or friends—but also the younger entity is much more aware of the priorities with which it came into incarnation, and is, therefore, even at so young an age, asking for aid in understanding the truth concerning such questions as what is death, and so forth.

Therefore, as the young entity develops its network of noise versus signal decisions which will for the remainder of the incarnation determine what the entity will see and hear and react to, there is much help given, so that even the very, very basic program which runs the computer of the mind has been much aided by spirits both incarnate and discarnate. This continues to be the pattern throughout the incarnation.

Each entity may, if it desires, form a cordial and mutually loving and helpful relationship with any of three guides or angelic presences, as this instrument might call them, which are, in fact, entities which partake to some extent of the self and to some extent of the imperishable greater Self which is the Creator. Some are more comfortable with a guide that is female, seeing that special nurturer as the gateway to the subconscious. Others are, perhaps, happier with the male guide or higher self, as, perhaps, that may have the connotation of good advice and so forth. Others prefer the third guide, which is androgynous in nature and understands each of the sexual polarities without being in a unbalanced or needing relationship, one or the other way. This kind of dispassionate guide is sometimes requested. Each of these are always with each. There is no shortage of available aid, and the ways of requesting it are, in many cases, subconscious. Bringing them into the conscious mind is always recommended if the growth is to be accelerated.

Once one has begun to accelerate the program of spiritual growth, there are many, many others which may become attracted to the entity. These are some of what you would call inner plane entities, that is, those who have completed their work in your illusion of third density, but have elected to remain behind to encourage and inspire those who wish to graduate into the density of love and compassion at the end of this particular lifetime. These are available by request, and are heard, by those who do not have the refined psychic ability, best in the dreaming process where, when one approaches the sleeping state one simply places oneself within a tuned and protected atmosphere, and protecting the physical vehicle with the crossed hands and the crossed legs, or legs together, invites the teachers of the appropriate vibration to express to you within the dreaming state that which you truly wish to work with, to grasp, and to begin to understand.

There are also those whom we may call the loyal opposition, those negative entities which are always drawn to one who is attempting to polarize [on the] service-to-others path. In brief, the ways of observing temptations being offered to one are simple. First, the temptation shall be power. That temptation has subtleties. There are different forms of power. It is helpful, perhaps, to look at the holy work this instrument calls the Bible in which the one known as Jesus the Christ was said to have been tempted by the devil in the wilderness. We do not verify the existence of the devil, but feel that there is a good parable to be told here. That is that the temptations were, first, the power to create food and have it to be eaten. This would indicate to the supposed devil that the one known as Jesus was, indeed, the Son of the one Creator. This was a temptation which the one known as Jesus refused. When one is in the position of impressing another, it is well in a metaphysical sense to understate the impressive fact, and, indeed, to be quite hesitant, shall we say, to manipulate others with such information.

Another temptation is that of kingdom and there are many, many kingdoms. Manipulation is [as] subtle in the kingdom of the home as your Machiavelli, as this instrument remembers the name, was in the history of Italy. In the parable we have been speaking of, the one known as Jesus was offered all the kingdoms of the Earth if he would worship someone else besides the one infinite Creator. This also was a temptation that the one known as Jesus avoided. Temptations of kingdom are indeed to be avoided, and when one perceives that one has power over another, one needs to speak with that other in such a way that the power is in some way limited and the other has some rightful voice, no matter what the relationship.

The third temptation which keeps an entity from the spiritual path of good suggestions is that of glory. In the parable, the one known as Jesus was offered the chance to leap from the top of the temple in Jerusalem so that angels would catch the one known as Jesus and set him safely upon the ground, thus glorifying the Father. The response that the one known as Jesus gave was, "Thou shalt not test the Lord, thy God." When things go poorly for an entity, it is then that this particular temptation encourages negative entities to speak to you in ways which seem to be persuasive, and we suggest to you that it is not helpful to rail, become upset with, become mad at or test the Creator. It is far, far more along the lines of service to others to have faith and abide in the faith that whatever is occurring to you is appropriate in order to teach a lesson which, though it may be challenging, will in the end be fruitful.

Now, we have covered the fact that you are virtually soaked through with the channeling of entities besides the consciousness that is yourself. Do not let this cause any to be concerned that the entity is any the less. This is not so. Help is simply there, because the lessons that all of us are attempting to learn have to do with service. And because we cannot serve an infinite intelligence which we cannot ever see, because we cannot manifest a mystery, we must turn to the Creator in awe, and to serve the Creator, we must serve you. Indeed, it aids us greatly to serve you, and we would not have you think that we are noble, for this is our path of learning and growing and refining our wisdom in compassionate service to the one infinite Creator.

In some, there is no time when an entity is not channeling. There is no time when an entity's thoughts can be said to be purely and specifically based upon the conscious thinking processes of the entity. Each entity has many, many influences upon the psyche, both discarnate and incarnate, which form the consciousness itself which takes up and attends to the structure, the fabric, the resonance as you perceive it.

Now, my friends, if you wish to alter your perceptions of reality to a more strongly affirmative and positive level, it is necessary to move into not only programs which move from the first program, that is, the attending program, one also must move into that metaprogram, that great program which lies behind the others and gives one the material for one's other perceptions and realizations.

If you wish to alter your perception of reality, it is well that thoughts be examined for associations and relationships that do not make logical sense. In the tracing of triggers for illogic lies much self-understanding, and, therefore, an increased ability to alter the basic program which chooses that which you will perceive. This work is best done, as always, in an atmosphere of meditation on a daily basis, and, perhaps, a period of reflection or meditation at the end of any given day, so that one may work with one's own subjective material in one's own way, be it serious, humorous or a mixture of the two. That, too, is a portion of programming which you may wish to change. We do recommend inserting as much humor into the biases of the personality as possible, for that light touch will hold you in good stead as you weave your way through the many, many ways of channeling the love and light of the one infinite Creator.

We wish you the luck of your endeavor, and perhaps more than anything, we know and hope that you realize once again that we are, as you, seekers upon a path. We have our opinions, but we do not have irrefutable knowledge; if we did, we would tell you so. Therefore, we simply ask that anything which may help or inspire be kept, and anything which does not seem to be your own truth be left behind.

At this time, we would transfer to the one known as Jim, that he may conclude this session. I am of those known to you as Q'uo.

(Jim channeling)

I am Q'uo, and greet each again in love and light through this instrument. At this time it is our privilege to ask if there might be any further queries to which we may reply?

Carla: Well, I notice that you didn't directly address the inside versus outside question, but, rather, said that you could think of them as inside or outside.

Do you want to leave it at that? Do you want to comment on that?

I am Q'uo. As each entity which has had its origin, as all have, with the one Creator, moves through the cycle experience that shall be its means of returning to the one Creator, the, shall we say, degree of difference that is apparent begins to shift, so that within the consciousness of those entities that move from your illusion to those of a higher vibration, this apparent difference begins to be noticed as less and less significant. We speak here of apparent difference, for there is the shared heart and very spark of life that always undergirds each expression of the one Creator.

As an entity begins to move in what you might call an harmonic resonance with the heartbeat of the creation, we shall call it, for want of a better term, the similarity and identity between the Creator, the creation, and the entity approaches oneness, so that the experience of the entity begins more and more to reflect to the entity the shared consciousness that may be likened unto the entity discovering that its sphere of consciousness, that with which it has become familiar and has called its own, is indeed larger than it has supposed, so that there are within the entity that likened unto veils removed to aid the sight in traveling to new boundaries that again will provide the entity with that experience that is necessary for it to understand, shall we say, in order that it might then use that understanding as a further stepping stone to move into those areas that again reveal unto it an experience that is unmistakably its own, and yet that which seemed other than the self before it had taken the step which led to this experience.

Thus, the entity, in retracing the journey to the Creator, does so in a fashion which may be likened unto the moving into experiences which become its own as it moves into them, and becomes the self as they are experienced. This is always the case for any entity, whether it has consciously experienced that which surrounds it as a portion of the self or not.

However, it is the perception of the entity with which we deal here most centrally, and as this perception is able to be widened in eyeshot, shall we say, so that entity becomes more able to penetrate outer illusion and see the truer nature of not only itself, but of the creation about it, the entity begins to discover that there is an harmonic resonance that permeates the entire creation, and as the entity moves into more profound or deeper realms of the self, the entity then becomes aware that there is far more to the self than it has previously supposed. An effect that has previously seemed to be of an exterior origin is seen to fall within the newly defined and experienced boundaries of the self. However, until the entity has completed this great cycle of being, the entity shall continually find that not only is there a greater and greater degree and breadth of selfness, there is also an increasing call from that which is yet to be experienced of the self which pulls the self onward in its journey of seeking the nature of its own self, of the creation, and of the journey of the self through the creation.

May we speak in any further fashion, my sister?

Carla: Well, it's in a tangential fashion, but I could really use your opinion, because it's sort of what I do for a non-living. I'm a Christian person, as you well know. We went around and around about that one earlier, but I am a mystical Christian, and I do not care whether Jesus Christ lived historically or died. The important thing for me happens to be the story and the way one can use it to approach the highest polarity in service to others that I have ever found of any way. Now, I realize, therefore, in terms of the actual function of Christ within the myth of Christianity, that Christ is acting as just what he said, the way or the bridge, in between our everyday, mundane selves and eternal Self. And what I've been doing, working with New Age people, is substituting words like "error" for "iniquity" and "sin" and stuff like that and "self-forgiveness" for "redemption" or "forgiveness" because of Jesus Christ. And I have found that to be somewhat difficult to get across to people, because they are so hard on themselves in the New Age; they haven't figured out any agency of forgiving themselves, and so they tend to carry around bunches of guilt and push guilt on other people, too. And I'm just wondering, how could I better communicate with the people that I would like to help?

I am Q'uo, and am aware of your query, my sister. We find that there are many entities which fall within the realm of qualities of which you speak. There are many which have other distortions or characteristics that make them unique, one from the other. As you meet each individual within your daily round of activities which requests from you assistance in one way or another, we find that it is most helpful to remember that each is, indeed, an unique individual which has needs that are as unique. Thus, to give a general means of seeking to assist such entities is to forget this primary fact of entities and the means by which they choose to experience and to express the life pattern.

Thus, we would recommend that the desire to be of service be that common thread that binds together all of your efforts to be of any service whatsoever, that you allow the moment to determine the wording, the phrasing, the concepts, and the feeling tone that is used to convey the information which then may be called through you, and in many cases, from you, that will be of assistance to such entities. Thus, you will add those portions of your own experience which are pertinent and which rise naturally to the mind and then to the lip.

You will also allow, we are hopeful, that information which may reside somewhat beyond your conscious grasp to blend itself with that which is within your grasp so that there might be the intermingling of sources, shall we say, that will produce in each instance the quality of concept communication that is most nearly appropriate for the situation and the entity which seeks from you assistance.

Again, we come to the question of the source of information, and we agree with you, my sister, that the ultimate source is not as important as is the quality of the information which proceeds from whatever source. The nature of the transfer of information is likened unto the speaking of the cells of the body to each other so that one portion which has been long removed from another might begin to reacquaint itself with that which is, indeed, a portion of itself and which is called to the self by the self.

Is there another query, my sister?

Carla: That was very thought provoking. There is one small query, and it's just because of the fact that I know that I have a real strong bias towards the belief that most of the people that I've worked with over the years, their biggest single problem, besides the fact that they were willing to live chaotic lives in terms of relationships, was that they carried around a lot of anger and guilt and stuff about themselves towards themselves, so they basically felt unworthy or had fairly low self esteem. And it seemed like this was the greatest real impediment to seeing the rest of the world compassionately. As a matter of fact, they tended to be better at seeing the rest of the world compassionately than themselves, but on a very subtle level it was keeping them from doing work in consciousness, and, actually, it happens to be my problem too, and I have a very strong bias towards working on that problem with my people, and I know that the help that I get is probably oriented according to that bias. Would [you] confirm if it is a good bias, or comment if you feel there is some thought I might take?

I am Q'uo, and we must pause briefly in order that this instrument complete its task with the recording devices. We shall return shortly.

(Pause)

I am Q'uo, and [am] again with this instrument. We would ask that the query be vibrated again, as this instrument was distracted by the recording devices.

Carla: Gladly. Q'uo, I just have a prejudice, a bias, that one of the important things to teach to people who come to me for lessons is to forgive themselves in some way. I can't use Jesus, but I need to get the feeling of self-forgiveness because a low self esteem seems to block work in consciousness better than just about anything except bad relationships, and I wondered if you would either validate my opinion and bias, or comment on it if you feel it needs some instruction.

I am Q'uo, and am aware of your query, my sister. The ability of any entity to move itself along the journey of evolution of mind, body and spirit is dependent in large degree upon some amount of dissatisfaction, of a kind of angst, if you will, otherwise the entity would remain as it is—happy with that which is and content to be that which it has discovered itself to be up to that point in its own experience. Thus, there is within each entity within your illusion a certain quality that may be seen to be as a kind of self doubt or self-inflicted perception of unworthiness which can be used by the entity as a motivating factor, shall we say, as it seeks to understand those qualities which comprise the self and seeks to match, shall we say, these qualities with those ideals which it has formed also in a mental fashion as the standards against which all shall be measured.

The task of bringing the self to the point where the components that comprise the self are seen as whole and perfect is a task which requires that the entity investigate the, shall we say, polar opposite qualities that also exist within the being that is known as the self, for as those qualities are explored that already exist within the perception of the entity, the entity will find that each quality calls into the realm of experience that which may be seen as its opposite so that when, for example, loving acceptance is experienced in sufficient quality, shall we say, there is a natural setting up of that which is not accepted as well. For as one defines that which one may accept and accept in a loving manner, that which does not reside within the definition in some degree partakes of that which is not accepted.

As the entity begins to explore that which is accepted and that which is not accepted and begins to conduct this exploration in a conscientious fashion in an ever-widening reach of the life experience, illuminating those dark corners of the consciousness, the entity will find that there is a closer and closer connection between the self and that which has previously not been accepted, so that as this process continues, the entity is slowly able to expand that realm of that which is acceptable and that which is loved.

Thus, as any entity looks upon those qualities of the self which are or are not accepted and continues this research with intensity and perseverance, the entity will begin to discover that each quality leads to other qualities, and all qualities eventually are seen to have a very close connection with the self. The ability to conduct this kind of exploration is the inner work which all religious teachings and philosophies have advised as that which is the necessary foundation work for the traveling upon the path of the seeker of truth, as it is called.

Thus, the dissatisfaction that any entity may feel for any portion of the self or any portion of the outer environment which is seen as a reflection of the self can become a motivating force that will eventually allow the entity to not only accept each quality in turn, but allow the entity to accept the polar opposite of each quality, will allow the entity to accept greater and greater portions of the self, and eventually allow the entity to accept an ever-widening field of vision that includes all about it.

Thus, the ability to forgive the self is an ability which is accomplished in slow stages, as if one were peeling the layers of the onion and discovering that each is the self.

Carla: Does that make it not a good thing to teach? Since it's going to be natural?

I am Q'uo, and am aware of your query, my sister. The definition of that which is natural is the definition of all that occurs. Thus, to attempt to aid another in the discovery of the path of self-forgiveness is a portion of that entity's journey which will have the appropriate impact upon the entity and affect it as it is ready and able to be affected.

There is, as you are aware, no mistake that occurs within the life of any seeker, and, indeed, as all are seekers, all that occurs is that which may be used as a teaching device for the perceptive eye and the listening ear.

May we speak to another query, my sister?

Carla: No, thank you.

I am Q'uo, and we thank you, my sister. Is there another query?

Questioner: I've [been] listening to this and having a lot of thoughts about the neurolinguistic programming model that I've been using with myself and with other people. It seems to accelerate this process of self-acceptance and forgiveness of self and others very effectively and beautifully. And I don't know exactly what question I have about it, accept to ask if you have knowledge of this learning and of how it can best be used and shared, if it might be a valuable thing to share with Carla in relation with her work with other people and her own family, and just in particular, suggestions that would be pertinent to me, as I learn and, one of the—I think that I've noticed a certain amount of caution in my approach to sharing this, because it seems to be a very powerful way, and I'm aware of just wanting to be in tune if I'm going to be using that, and in a way I think I think that I need to know more and more to be, I guess, skillful at using it, and yet, listening, I know that I can trust, in fact, do when I work with people, in my prayers and my meditations to be a channel, as I work, for the service of that person, and that what I consciously learn, what I've consciously learned to aid in this is always going to be assisted by a power and a knowing beyond that, an ability to help beyond whatever I've learned. I don't know if that's a question clear enough to be answered or not, or do I need to be more succinct about the question? I asked one earlier, but then I kept talking.

I am Q'uo, and we believe that we have discerned the query that was intended. We are not familiar with the technique of which you speak, though we may suggest that any technique which offers to an entity a model by which it might view the evolutionary process of its own being is a technique which will, indeed, speed this process, for the process of evolution is one which occurs even though an entity be not consciously aware that it occurs. There is a turning point, however, when an entity comes consciously to the recognition that it is, indeed, upon a journey, a journey which will reveal to the self greater portions of the self and of the creation of which it is a part and will allow the entity to make connections between portions of itself and this creation that will enhance its being and its ability to express that which is itself and that which moves in harmony with the self.

Thus, as an entity becomes more consciously aware of a process of evolution, whether this process be described in one language, one structure, one concept, or another, the process of attempting to put a model or a structure to this journey is the beginning of the intensification and the speeding up, shall we say, of the evolutionary journey. As an entity finds that it has success with speeding this process in any degree, it begins to define itself using a broader scope or vision, and allows to itself by this enlarged definition a greater ability to experience and express that which it now sees to be the self. This new experience and expression will allow further refinement of the model, whatever its structure may be.

Thus, there may be within a culture such as your own many, many different models that describe the nature of this process of evolution, the nature of the discovery of greater and greater degrees of the self, shall we say. Whatever the model used, there are entities that may profit from this use and move many steps further upon their journey by such use. As each model becomes refined in a more personal sense, the entity begins to gain what you might call a certain momentum in this journey of seeking. Always and ever, however, is there the ability of the entity, and, indeed, the necessity, for continuing to redefine and refine the perspective, the perception, the means by which the entity structures that which it believes, that which it follows and that idea of the self which it constructs as a kind of stepping stone that will carry it to the next level of understanding, shall we say.

Thus, we can offer no direct suggestions as to whom this may benefit or how the offering of such service to tendered, other than suggesting that your own intuitive abilities will first find whether there be an harmonic resonance, shall we say, at a deeper level of being that may wish to be expressed in a conscious fashion with another entity that may profit from learning a model which you have to share. Thus, we leave such decisions to your own discernment, wishing only to offer the general guidelines for such decision making.

May we speak in any further fashion, or to another query, my sister?

Questioner: There's still a slight question in my mind about my own slowness in spite of what has eventually become a lot that I've put into learning and developing my understanding of how to work with this model, and in a way that is individualized both in terms of how beliefs and understanding and in terms of any individual I'd be working with. I, nevertheless, have exhibited a slowness to be very, very active. I offer it out very quietly and almost tentatively, which in a way doesn't really result in a lot of interaction. And I've been sort of relying on the fact that there is an apparent wisdom in this timing, and yet I more and more have a sense that it is time to have more interaction and to be sharing this more, and I'm not quite sure either how to go about it or whether I'm stopping myself in some way, I need to simply encourage myself more?

So the question has to do with my own personal, the word that comes to mind is ambivalence, and how I might speed up the process of sorting out whatever I need to about, that would allow me to go ahead and share this more with other people and just be more clear about the fact, you know, just state that.

I am Q'uo, and in this regard we must speak carefully, that we do not infringe upon the free will of another, for the nature of the query which you have asked is one which is, indeed, personal and is that which benefits most by the introspection that discovers that which is within the being, and we would suggest that the feelings which you have described are those feelings which are most important in the discovery of what action shall be taken by you in your future. The feelings of value attached to the process described must be investigated and the ambivalence connected as is appropriate in those areas where there is doubt. Any art which offers itself to others as a service has value first to the entity which practices it upon the self. As the self experiences that which may be gained from the art, then does the self become convinced of the value, not only to the self, but in a more general [sense] to other selves as well.

Thus, the suggestion that we may make without infringement is that there may, perhaps, be the reevaluation of the effects upon the self of the practice of this particular means of programming the mind to experience new levels of being. Thus, the reevaluation is a process of offering to the self that which, perhaps, shall be offered to others with the self as the, shall we say, guinea pig that first experiences and then re-experiences and discovers those areas which may yet be held in doubt that they may be reaffirmed and reintroduced in the evolution of the self and be made more whole and functional, shall we say.

Is there another query, my sister?

Questioner: No, that's very helpful, thank you, and confirms my intuitions and extends them. Thank you.

I am Q'uo, and we thank you, my sister. We feel that this is the appropriate time in this particular session, due to weariness of several gathered, to bring this session to a close. We are most grateful to each present for inviting our presence this evening. It has been a great honor to blend our vibrations with yours, as we each travel the same journey, to walk hand in hand with those who also seek as do we is a joy which we cannot describe, but for which we are most grateful.

At this time we shall take our leave of this instrument and this group, leaving each, as always, in the love and in the light of the one infinite Creator. We are known to you as those of Q'uo. Adonai, my friends. Adonai. ☥

L/L Research

L/L Research is a subsidiary of Rock Creek Research & Development Laboratories, Inc.

P.O. Box 5195
Louisville, KY 40255-0195

www.llresearch.org

Rock Creek is a non-profit corporation dedicated to discovering and sharing information which may aid in the spiritual evolution of humankind.

ABOUT THE CONTENTS OF THIS TRANSCRIPT: This telepathic channeling has been taken from transcriptions of the weekly study and meditation meetings of the Rock Creek Research & Development Laboratories and L/L Research. It is offered in the hope that it may be useful to you. As the Confederation entities always make a point of saying, please use your discrimination and judgment in assessing this material. If something rings true to you, fine. If something does not resonate, please leave it behind, for neither we nor those of the Confederation would wish to be a stumbling block for any.

CAVEAT: This transcript is being published by L/L Research in a not yet final form. It has, however, been edited and any obvious errors have been corrected. When it is in a final form, this caveat will be removed.

© 2009 L/L Research

Sunday Meditation
February 19, 1989

Group question: How does one decide what particular action to take in any situation where neither the culture, the religion, or any other normal means of deciding right and wrong or good and bad do not any longer apply. When one is able to see both sides to a question, and there is no obvious right or wrong, how does one decide one's actions?

(Carla channeling)

I am Hatonn. I greet you in the love and in the light of the infinite Creator. We feel most privileged and blessed to join in your circle of seeking to share with you the beauty that lies within each whose spirit thirsts for the truth. We are most pleased to be called to your meeting this evening. It is for us our chief way of being of service at this time in the world of action, and, therefore, tied to service to you is our own growth and development as entities. Thus, we are grateful to serve and we assure you that we are more than compensated for some few thoughts we may share with you, none of which is given absolute authority by us. We consider our ideas opinion and would ask that each take what is seen to ring with a personal truth and leave that which does not without a second thought.

We do thank the one known as M for the question concerning ethics. It is perhaps, should we say, our speciality, and it is the kind of question which strikes at the fundamental nature of those spiritual entities which you call human beings.

You see, each of you is an imperishable portion of the Creator, an immeasurable spark of divine creativity. It is, shall we say, well hidden within a material physical vehicle, which is an analog for the rest of the outer illusion, a series of electromagnetic vortices, making it possible for that which is the imperishable you to experience and learn within an environment which is illusory and designed to challenge your perceptions, your judgment, and your maturity. Over and over again you shall receive lessons about that one great subject which you all came here to learn, that is, how to love.

How to love is that which you seek to know, because the very nature of the Creator, as closely as can be defined by your words, is, indeed, love. Love made manifest is the creation. That it is manifest is an illusion. You are within this illusion to gaze upon it, to learn and to offer the best learning, the best thinking, the most beautiful spirit that you may, back then to the Creator, as you move into the larger and more spacious light of the spirit, within a much, shall we say, more light and agreeable physical vehicle.

We agree that many things within an illusion which is designed to be perfectly imperfect would appear to be moot questions, that is, endlessly arguable. The nature of the illusion is specifically this in order that each of you may make choices which will advance your own spiritual seeking and maturity. The way to move into a more interesting classroom, shall we say, than the one in which you now exist is to learn to love enough so that you think about the concerns of those whom you love just a bit more than you think about your own concerns. That is, the work you face in this particular classroom is the work of wholehearted and sometimes sacrificial love. Inevitably, then, you are constantly moved into situations where it is difficult to love. Love comes from within the self. That which is described as love, that which moves in and out of the pattern of light for each in relationship, is that poor analog of love which is imperishable, which is that which is possible to that human animal with spirit which you are. That is, you will be unable to love at all times; you will run dry; you will fail. This is inevitable.

Eventually, each spirit decides to seek a love that is greater than the love it has been able to manifest, that it may know it and thus manifest it. This is the true end of all ethical thinking and spiritual seeking. This is the true end of humankind—to learn well enough how to love that death from this illusion rises to life in a far more lovely and more challenging grade of study. You are here to make choices, and you are here specifically to make one central choice—to honor and worship the Creator within you and you within the Creator by serving others, moving towards unity of self with all others, moving toward peace, concern and passionately held ideals, or controlling others for the good of the self, manipulating those about one and making choices which separate one from the loved ones, from the society.

The way of separation, the way of fear and terror and those things which are called negative, has its own ethics and we will not explore those. But the way of service to others is very straightforward about its ethics, and perhaps these ethics may help as you seek to learn the lessons of love in this very difficult and challenging illusion of yours.

Cast your minds back, if you will, to the words, "In the beginning." You have heard them many times, and many stories have you heard of the beginning of things. This is ours.

In the beginning there was the Creator. To the best of our knowledge, the first thing that occurred besides the Creator was that which is called free will. Thus, free will is that which is to be valued above all others things.

The second thing that was created by free will working upon the uncreated Creator was that which is called the name of Logos. We prefer to call it Love, to be careful in our delineation of our understanding of the nature of the Creator. The active principle of the Creator is creative Love, that which makes all that there is, that which takes all that there is back into Itself, that which is intensely curious about each thought and action and choice that you make, that each of you is the Creator, and through you the Creator learns about Itself. Thus, Love is the second priority in ethics.

The third thing that was created by the active principles of creation, love or Logos, was the photon, that so-called particle-wave of yours which light is created from. Its nature is mysterious to the scientists of your planet, yet this light may be considered to be the physical manifestation of what may be called compassionate wisdom. That is, the light of the Sun, for those who wish to be fundamentalists or literalists, is the nearest and most obvious manifestation of the Logos. Its consciousness has not moved from being one with the Creator, and its nature is that which may be seen to be the most understandable parable, shall we say, of the nature of the Creator: fiery, intense, compassionate and immensely generous and powerful and radiant.

Thus, in a situation in which there is no obvious answer, the first question one may ask the self is, "Where is the free will in this situation? Which choice would limit someone else's free will? Do I have the right, by family or matedness, to express thoughts that might infringe upon the free will of this entity?" This is of the highest ethical consideration at all times.

In a situation which that particular ethic does not address, one gazes at the situation to discover how one can best express the love and the light of the infinite Creator. Some things are reasonably moot or arguable, yet a patient waiting and asking and listening within the inner realm of silence and meditation will yield for you the bias of feeling of compassion and love that will enable you to address the situation.

In cases where even this is denied you as an ethical basis for making a choice, one must simply rely upon one's own inner compassionate wisdom or light. That is, one must allow creative possibilities to move about within the mind to the utmost capacity of the mind to be intuitive, loose and creative.

Each option, then, would be gazed at with an eye for compassion and wisdom. Some of your philosophers have suggested ways to evaluate wisely. Each way of evaluation has virtues and desperately dangerous faults. We would not advise any to be an "ist," that is, what this instruments calls those which are Marxists or Communists or Creationists. We do not feel we need to go on. We suggest strongly that one interested in true ethical considerations be aware that there are no two situations alike, and that ethics are, indeed, personal. We do suggest, when one is dealing in relationship, that no matter what the status of the relationship with regard to those expensive pieces of paper—which we find this instrument calls the wedding certificate—the ethics of the native contract rely upon agreements made. Changes may occur if talks between the two within the relationship reveal to both that it is time to change. Thus, one is not permanently tied to an agreement, but one is tied ethically to an agreement one has made until such time as one has expressed the need to change the agreement. This is an ethical guideline which is very helpful in determining those actions in relationship.

We have, perhaps, said that which we would most hope to cover, and being told by this instrument that it does not wish to channel over-long, we hope we have given you something to think about, and if you have further questions, we will be very happy to answer to them as soon as we transfer this contact. We would like to thank you once again through this instrument for the most delightful chance to share our opinions with you. We would now transfer in love and light to the one known as Jim. We are known to you as those of Hatonn.

(Jim channeling)

I am Hatonn, and greet each again in love and light through this instrument. At this time it is our privilege to ask if we might speak to any further queries which those gathered may find value in the asking. We remind each again that we offer that which is our opinion, but we offer it in joy and in gratitude. We do not wish to offer it as an infallible opinion of any kind. Is there a query at this time?

Questioner: Yes. Could you speak a little bit about the different densities? I would particularly like to know about your density, the fourth density, I believe, if that's correct. What differentiates you from us, and where are you bound?

I am Hatonn, and am aware of your query, my brother. The densities of this octave of creation are composed of light. This is that which is more or less dense within each succeeding density or dimension. The octave of creation itself may be seen as similar to the octave of notes in your Western scale of music, beginning with that which is analogous to "do," ending with that same note at an higher octave.

Thus, that which is the beginning in this octave, the first density, has a certain vibration of the photon of light that vibrates at a certain frequency and with certain angles of rotation that provide a discrete environment in which simple awareness may exist. That awareness is what you would see as that of earth, wind, fire and water.

After a certain portion of time, as you know it, has unrolled its scroll of beingness, there is the increased vibration of rotation and angle of rotation of the photon that allows a quantum leap, shall we say, that is significantly altered or expanded, and which provides for an enhanced experience of awareness—that which seeks the light and that which moves and that which is identified by your second density of plants and that which you call animals. These entities, then, have their experience, during which they attempt to gather about themselves an individualization of consciousness, and move from that which is the group, whether it be the herd, the flock, the school, etc.

When this has been accomplished in the cycle of beingness, there is again the great quantum leap in possibility and potential in consciousness, until that which is the third density of creation, that which you inhabit, which comes into being by the increased rotation of vibration of the photon of light and the angles of rotation that again allow the greater experience of consciousness as each portion of consciousness of the one Creator moves from that complete unity with the Creator into the individualization that allows the gathering of experience that will allow the Creator to know Itself in each of its portions, and which will allow each of

Its portions to know the Creator through this experience.

When consciousness within your third density has been individualized to the point that the choice can be made in either the positive or the negative sense—that is, to be of service to others, to give of that energy of the Creator to others, or to absorb that energy of the Creator in the negative or magnetic sense—when either of these two choices have been made as to how the further seeking of the Creator shall be experienced, then it is that another leap, shall we say, in consciousness is possible.

This is the movement of consciousness into that density of love and understanding which it is our honor and our privilege to inhabit. Within this [fourth] density of creation, the form of the body that has been chosen in the second-density experience of plants, of animal, to be invested, then is again used, as it was in the third density, but is used in what you might see of a somewhat different form, that is, what your peoples frequently call the astral body, that body which is lighter in your material gravity, shall we say, but is more densely packed with light. This body, then, is far more responsive to thought, and may move far more freely in time and in space than your bodies move.

Communication within our density of creation is most frequently in the form of what you would call telepathy, but in an expanded form of telepathy in which complete concepts or gestalts or pictures or information may be transmitted instantaneously. There is no ability or desire to hide any thought at this level of seeking the one Creator. We who have the honor of inhabiting this density of creation have found it helpful to join together with those of our kind, such as your planetary population might at some point in its future choose to join its seeking in service to the one Creator, each offering to the group or social memory complex that which it has learned in its journey of seeking, so that the entire complex of entities has at its disposal a great wealth of information, each experience of each entity becoming available, then, for use in decision making and in the attempt to continue the evolutionary process in service to the one Creator and each of Its manifestations.

When we have been successful in turning our beings entirely to the service of the one Creator, then that particle of consciousness that moves within each cell of our being as light shall again be offered the opportunity to leap forward to an expanded potential for awareness. This potential within the fifth density of light is that which offers the opportunity to gain that which you might [call] wisdom, so that the great compassion that is gained within our illusion of the fourth density might find a means of being focused in a manner which is most helpful, without interfering overmuch within the evolution of any other entity that we seek to serve.

Thus, the wisdom density, the fifth density of light, is that which seeks to create a form through which service might be offered in both a wise and a loving manner. When this lesson has been learned, there is again the opportunity to experience the leap in consciousness and the potential for greater perfection, as the point of view is widened to take in a greater portion of the Creator and the creation and to see it as the self.

The density numbering six is that density in which the unity of the Creator is again approached as love and wisdom are balanced, each with the other, and that which might be called a spiritual power is gained, the power to be of service without the infringement upon the free will of another. The sixth-density experience of light and of the creation is one in which those who have traveled both the positive, or radiant, and the negative, or absorbent, paths are again joined, so that seeking after this point within the sixth density continues apace without the great polarization in consciousness that begins within your third-density experience and continues through the fourth, the fifth and into the mid-sixth density.

When the lessons of unity have been completed, then it is that entities move into the seventh density, that gateway density of foreverness which allows the movement towards the complete reunification with the one Creator which is completed within the eighth density, as you would call it, thus completing the great cycle of experience, with all experiences gained by each entity offered to the Creator as means by which the Creator has been able to know Itself offered as that which shall become the seeds for the next great octave of experience.

The eighth density is the complete reunification with the one Creator, and is seen by your physicists and astronomers as that which is called the black hole, for within this level of being, all experience, all light, all matter, all of creation is indrawn into the one Creator, so that the fruits of the great journey may be gathered and become the foundation for the further experience and expression of the one Creator.

Is there another query, my brother?

Questioner: I'm trying to clarify as to your density, the fourth density particularly. From what I understand you do have the physical form, and you also have said that you continue to have polarization, perhaps even greater polarization that we have here. Does this mean that you have dissension? Does it mean that you have problems? What are the problems that you have in this density? And what are the things that make you happy? To me those are very basic. And what are the things that make you fulfilled in your existence between yourselves, not in dealing with us?

I am Hatonn, and am aware of your query, my brother. We must first preface our response by suggesting that the experience of each succeeding density beyond your own is difficult enough to describe in words that at some point it becomes impossible within the confining boundaries of words (to describe) that which is quite beyond description. However, we shall attempt to speak to your query.

We, indeed, inhabit physical vehicles which, as we mentioned previously, are those which were derived from the second-density creatures within your own illusion. The ape form is that form which was chosen by the Logos to invest with the potential for completing the evolutionary process through the octave of densities. This form is chosen in approximately 5 percent of the planetary influences within this galaxy of which we are aware. There are other forms chosen in other planetary influences. This form is maintained through the fourth-density illusion and into the fifth-density illusion, at which point the mastery over one's own being proceeds to the point that it is possible within the fifth-density illusion to create whatever form is most helpful at the moment, as the service that has been requested is offered.

That which enriches our being and brings the greatest joy to our hearts is our ability to offer service to other portions of the creation which seek or ask for that which is ours to offer. We have within our social memory complex of entities a great variety of experiences upon which we may draw to decide how best to offer our services. There is not dissension as you know it amongst our beings, in that we do not seek to gain advantage over others for our own gain, but there is frequently difference of opinion as to how best to offer our service to others, for in offering service, one must be most careful that the free will of those whom one wishes to serve is not abridged, which is to say, that we do not provide specific directions as to how an entity should move in its daily round of activity and how specific choices in the life pattern should be made. Rather, we seek to offer the principles of the evolutionary process which we have found helpful in our experience, that those whom we wish to serve may interpret in their own way and in their own life patterns.

May we speak in any further fashion, my brother?

Questioner: Do you have wars? You said that you have negative polarization entities that go into the fourth dimension, and positive. Once they get there, everybody's so happy to get there? Do you have wars in fourth dimension?

I am Hatonn, and am aware of your query, my brother. This is a topic which is quite difficult to enunciate with enough clarity that confusion may not be brought about. We again shall attempt to respond. In a situation such as that which pertains to your own planetary influence, your population of entities …

(Tape ends.) ❦

L/L Research

Sunday Meditation
February 26, 1989

Group question: "The soul is the essence of remembrance." What is the meaning behind that phrase?

(Carla channeling)

I am Latwii. I greet you in the love and the light of the one infinite Creator. May we say what a great blessing it is for us to be called to this circle of seeking. We thank and bless each for the privilege of sharing the beauty of your vibrations and your meditation. We join you in honoring and praising that infinite Mystery, whose face is love. We are most happy to be able to work through this instrument, for this instrument has the inner characteristics which make it possible for us to more easily express ourselves humorously, and we always appreciate the ability to express our opinions upon the most serious of subjects with a light touch, for there is great frustration in seeking the truth within an illusion as complete as your own. No word and no concept of which we now know can encompass the great mystery of the infinite Creator. In the face of such a complete unknowing, it is well to have a sense of humor, to feel free to be merry in one's search, for long faces are not good environments for the rapid growth of spirit. And as each within your often painful illusion must wear the long face from time to time, we hope to encourage in one's spiritual seeking that most blessed quality of joy.

One other introductory remark is a caveat. We are your brothers and sisters, not those who are infallible. We would not give you an erroneous opinion knowingly. However, we are still learning, and even our teachers express their own lack of final understanding. Consequently, be aware that this is a note passed from a group upon the road of spiritual seeking to another point of light upon that same road. See yourself, my children, as candles, lit, vibrant and moved by the wind of spiritual guidance. And in each meditation, seek to listen to that wind which contains that still, small voice, as your Holy Scripture puts it, within which lies all those things we cannot say, all those memories which are your birthright and which, when you hear them again, you shall recognize.

And this brings us to the question of this evening, that being a request to comment upon a statement received in meditation by one known as R, that "the soul is the essence of remembrance."

Let us move first to ground that of which we would speak in the earth of metaphysical structure as we see it. Each of you is a portion of the infinite One, which has been sent forth by the infinite One as Its free choice to learn about Itself. Through each experience that you have, through each bias that you gain from responding to the experiences that you have, you become, through many, many life experiences such as the one you enjoy at this time, more and more aware of yourself as an unique entity. Eventually, all that you have learned and found beautiful moves with you of your free choice back to the Source and the beginning, and the prodigal sons and daughters, as this instrument would call all upon the spiritual path, come home at last. It is a very long pilgrimage, extending through many dimensions and illusions, through many kinds of experience.

This particular experience which you enjoy at this time may be considered the dimension of choice, for if the face of the Creator is love, then a response of that created one to love is also love, yet it may be love of others or love of self. It may be the path of service to others or the path of service to self. In this illusion, where focuses of energy appear to be solid and thoughts that are stronger than those energies cannot be seen, the stage is set for a choice to be made in complete free will, for within the illusion the truth cannot be known in any objective fashion, but must be sought within through guidance and inspiration, through meditation, contemplation and discussion with others upon the path.

The choice is to radiate the love of the one infinite Creator or to so magnetize the self that one draws into the self-control, and becomes as the Creator, using each other spirit as power for the self. We are aware that each within this dwelling and this circle at this time has chosen the path of service to others, the path of radiant love. These foundation stones of the structure of your experience we thought were necessary before moving to a direct discussion of the statement concerning the soul as the essence of remembrance.

Let us define that which is called the "soul" as that portion of your being which is imperishable, that portion of your being which was before your world was formed, which was before earth and sky appeared and which shall be when all that you know now has become naught. This imperishable being which is earned as an unique consciousness, your soul, is at all times a gift to the Creator, from the active principle of creation, which is curious, which learns and which goes through a process called remembrance.

Let us gaze at the word "essence." That which is an essence is not that which meets the eye. It is not that which is usually particularly easy to determine from inter-group acquaintance with an individual among your peoples, for part of your illusion is the veil which has been dropped betwixt the conscious and unconscious mind, for by rendering your inborn capacity to communicate by concept and thought useless, you are forced to communicate with words and point, thus, constantly away from the essence of your self, which lies far too deep for words.

Let us now gaze at "memory." We find that this instrument's conscious approach to this question is much the same as if two Neoplatonists, a Stoic, a Sophist and a follower of Anaximander were wrestling within the instrument's mind. This is true, not only of this instrument, but of the great majority of those who attempt intellectually, logically and pragmatically to consider philosophical and spiritual questions.

Memory is thought to be a time-bound phenomenon, that is, an event occurs, one observes the event and registers it in memory. This, my children, is not the case, not at the beginning and not during the entire process of memory.

Each perception, moment by moment, which each seeker has is the product of many, many choices, made upon a subconscious level, according to programs, shall we say, in the biocomputer of the brain, which were often set so very, very far back into the young days of incarnation that the seeker simply does not know its own program of perception. You see, because of the nature of the illusion of time and the limitations of the biocomputer given each, it is improbable that an entity will use more than perhaps 5 percent of that which is perceived by raw senses and fed into the biocomputer as raw sense data. You do not know that which you are throwing away, that which you are overlooking, because you have already eschewed it. Thus, if there are difficulties in remembrances within this incarnational experiences, it is well to move back to the time that the programs were set in place.

Now, as you may deduce, the biased amount of information which you have received from the senses—that is, biased in accordance with conscious, and most often unconscious programming—then goes through a complex procedure of choices. The choices concern how or whether one will respond to that which has been perceived. Perceptions are hierarchical, in terms of survival being the first consideration of any entity, concerns of the self being second in importance, concerns of relationship being next, concerns with society being next, and all of these things coming before that which is the first purely spiritual concern, that of opening the heart, not to one or another thing, but in terms of strengthening, empowering and [crystallizing] one's authority as a channel for the love and the light of the one infinite Creator.

Thus, one's memories have no chance of being objective at any time. They are biased from the beginning, and as your memory becomes older and dimmer, it moves through one of two simple processes. Either it is gilded with a loving hand, to emphasize its beauty, its depth of meaning, its poignancy and its truth, or it is simply blocked and segregated as that which seems too self-destructive to allow within memory or to be healed at that particular moment in space and time.

At the end of an incarnational experience, you, as an imperishable being, have changed because of this illusion which you now enjoy. It is not that your intelligence has changed, for you do not carry that with you from incarnation to incarnation. It is not the personality, as you may think of the personality as the social butterfly or the teller of the jokes. It is that imperishable point of view which has been biased or polarized, either towards service to others or service to self and domination over others.

We are upon the servant's path. We do not deny that there is an opposite path. We simply do not teach it. Through many, many lifetimes, beginning with experiences as earth, air, wind, fire and all the elements, you have built your biases, your uniqueness, as a spark within the infinity of the Creator. You have experienced everything that you see in the world about you and from experience of rock or sea or cloud or blooming flower, you remember, not the entire experience, but its essence. And that essence is to you unique, for you are not anyone else. You are perfectly your own self. Each entity is correct for itself, for it is the sum of what it has learned. That you each wish to accelerate the process of learning is much to your credit, for there is much to do, and the world that cries out for more lightened consciousnesses will now have the essence of remembrance of the elemental density and the density of plant and animal as part of your imperishable self, as part of your gift to the infinite One.

Now you sit in the midst of the greatest decision you shall make within the entire octave of experience of what you would call men and angels: the choice to love or to be obeyed. Once you have made the decision, it then becomes your task, "if you wish to complete it," as "Mission Impossible" would say, to choose ever again to give, when you could receive, to console, when you yourself need consoling, to care and feel and love when others turn away in scorn and dislike. Each small choice is, in fact, a larger and larger choice, for as one positive choice builds upon another, so your spirit and soul grow in strength and power, and you begin to be, in feeling and in conscious thinking, that which you truly are—a metaphysical being, alive eternally in an infinite universe, peopled with nothing but yourself in the guise of many, many mirrors. Gaze into anyone's eyes—they show you yourself. Gaze at the trees, the skies, the stars—they, too, are yourself.

When you have graduated from this classroom, learning the first lessons of love, then shall you, in what some have called heaven, and others, paradise, enjoy a somewhat more comfortable atmosphere, yet you shall not be without your work, for you shall be learning. That is the essence of the soul, for the soul is the stuff of which the Creator is, that being love, combined with free will. And free will is ever-curious and ever-restless. And free will truths do not last forever. Only the mystery of that which is unknown is as truly imperishable as are each of you.

Thus, that which you are at this time, which may be called a soul, that is the imperishable part of you, is the kernel, the feeling and tone left behind by catalyst, the stain that remains from the spillage of experience. And these things you hold in an ever-shifting remembrance. Thus, the quality of your soul, to some great extent, depends upon the quality of your remembrance, that is, your ability to abide in faithfulness to the truth that lies within you, which you may know only through experiencing your own biases and seeking ever in daily meditation to dwell with the infinite One, and so open the door to your birthright, to your memory of all that you truly are and all that you truly feel.

We would direct your attention to that portion of the Christian faith whose liturgy is called the Holy Eucharist. Common to almost all Christian denominations is the inclusion within such a service of quotations from the holy work you call your Bible. The one known as Jesus the Christ took a simple, homely article, the bread, which was the bulk of a meager meal. This entity gave thanks for the plenty of his bread. He then broke it and offered it, saying, "Take and eat this in remembrance of me." And so, too, with that wine which was the usual libation in that less than cleanly age, "Drink this in remembrance of me." This entity did not wish to be remembered as an entity, but as a channel for that which flowed through the entity and transfigured it, the love and the light of the one infinite Creator.

Each of you needs a Eucharist, a way to focus upon a remembrance of those things which are beautiful and true, that your soul may be most faithful in remembering. Again and again we suggest the daily meditation with silence and the listening. And we offer in this case a simple rationale: "Do this in remembrance of me." And by me, we mean we ourselves no more than did the teacher known as Jesus, but rather we mean I AM, that is, Consciousness Itself, the one great original Thought which created all that there is. It is this we call to remembrance. It is this which centers our memory, it is this remembrance that ennobles the essence of memory.

To remember the small change of a lifetime is not altogether helpful, for there is not the focused power and a singular path for one's daily experiences. The effort needed to put into place a structure whereby one may give daily thanksgiving and remembrance to the one infinite Creator is a structure each must choose for himself, yet we say to you, that if you wish your imperishable self to rise as quickly as possible into the light of what you would call the Kingdom of Heaven, the greatest tool is daily remembrance of that great Thought, whose name in your language is love. Love has created you. Love sustains you. Love that is alive and caring and with you, guides you, aids you and protects you.

The words that you hear at this time are a very humble part of the system of discarnate spiritual aid that is available to those who seek it. There are many, many channels, many various ways of offering the information of the Creator [to] the children of the Creator, which are yourselves, and the eternity and full knowledge of yourself as Creator, which is ultimately your birthright. Yet, this birthright shall come to you not because you become more and more powerful and, therefore, are able to wrest it from the arms of the Almighty. This power descends upon one who has surrendered the free will of variousness to a far more impersonal kind of will, that deep will found within the self for good or service or love.

The desire to learn and the will to persevere may seem like those things which are taught to one in business school, that one may be a better salesman, yet we say to you that the faculties of desire and will create your experience. That which you desired to learn before this incarnation you set in place, not specifically, but in kind. You allowed yourself any number of attempts at each lesson. Thus, if you are seeing the same pattern over and over again, you know that there is a lesson of love in this pattern, and that the answer to this pattern lies along lines of the seeking of love within that pattern. Once this has been done and love has been found, the pattern is balanced, and one may go on to the next lesson one has offered oneself for the learning. Thus, you may see that your soul is, indeed, in your hands. You may learn, you may polarize, you may reclaim your birthright. You may advance as you wish—slowly, moderately or quickly. We would advise each never to run, but to take the careful steps, building slowly, nurturing the spiritual self, nurturing …

We must pause. I am Latwii.

(Side one of tape ends.)

(Carla channeling)

I am Latwii, and am again with this instrument. We find the recording devices somewhat humorous, but we understand the necessity of recording this deathless prose in some way.

To continue. We encourage each to nurture the infant soul within, for, indeed, each of you, in terms of the full spectrum of experience which you shall have within this octave of creation, are very young souls. You are doing your most important work at this time—not your hardest work, by any means, my children, for refining upon the choice is a challenge that takes, in your measurement of time, millions and millions of years. We hasten to encourage each by saying that we do not perceive time in our dimension as you perceive time in your own. We are most emphatically not bored, as one would be at the thought of spending millions of years in the same physical vehicle.

Soul is the essence of remembrance. What have you impressed in memory upon the essence of things that shall bias your soul this day? What do you wish for your soul? How and what shall you remember?

We very much thank each again for asking us to speak upon this interesting question. We would, of course, note that it is always so that there is a measure of meaning in any communication betwixt one's own private guidance and one's conscious self, which it would be an infringement upon free will to express. That is a portion that [is] unique to the self asking the question. The generalities we may offer, the twist or quirk that makes the information personal to one person is not ours to discuss. We hope that the one known as R grasps this and is able to, after assimilating this information, move forward in the freedom of its own choices, its own study and its own progress towards a more perfect, true and whole essence of remembrance, to a more entire identity with the Creator, the Soul of souls, the Self of selves and the Love of lovers.

We would at this time transfer this contact, with a merry heart and thanks to this instrument, to the one known as Jim. I am Latwii.

(Jim channeling)

I am Latwii, and greet each again in love and light through this instrument. At this time it is our privilege to ask if there might be any further queries which may be upon the minds of those gathered this evening? It is our great honor and joy to entertain any such queries at this time.

Carla: It would be logical to figure, if one person is its memory, that the Creator, in its active principle, anyway, is Its memory. Is that true?

I am Latwii, and am aware of your query, my sister. That which you call the active portion of the one Creator is, indeed, not only that which is Its memory, that which is the memory of each of Its portions, but is also far more this, for even the active portion of the Creator has that which is the potential and which has infinite ability to be. Thus, that portion of the Creator which has moved Itself into the creation and which experiences all that is experienced is enriched not only by all such experiences, but by the potential which awaits the free will choice of any portion of Its being. Thus, there is a great waiting beingness, shall we say, almost, if we may so surmise, an eagerness to be and to know.

Is there another query, my sister?

Carla: Would that suggest that the Creator has emotions? Besides love?

I am Latwii, and am aware of your query. The emotions are not properly present within the mind of the Creator, if we may use these terms, for terminology in this area is somewhat mythical, too [fancifully] constructed. However, there is a desire on the part of the Creator to know Itself in Its fullness, and as It knows Itself through Its creation, to love that which is created, that which is experienced. Thus, this desire to know and this great, overwhelming feeling of love may be seen as the equivalent of emotions, in your terms, on the part of the one Creator, as far as we can ascertain. We do not claim to have full knowledge of the great mystery which the one Creator embodies.

Is there another query, my sister?

Carla: Just a final one, logically following that. Would that desire spring from the free will which is a part of the active principle of the Creator? Just as it springs from the free will in us, that we're curious to know more?

I am Latwii. We do not wish to play with the word, shall we say, but it is more nearly correct, in our opinion, to say that the free will provides a means by which the desire of the Creator to know Itself may be fulfilled, for it is the desire of the Creator which comes before the means for its fulfillment. Thus, free will follows desire in this particular case.

Is there another query, my sister?

Carla: No, thank you.

I am Latwii, and we thank you, my sister. Is there another query at this time?

(Pause)

I am Latwii. At this time, therefore, we shall again offer our great gratitude to each of those gathered this evening for inviting our presence. It is a great joy for us to be able to share our opinions, our desire to know more of the truth and our joy with each. Again, we would remind each that we do not wish for any word that we have spoken to be seen as infallible. If any word does not ring of truth, please do not hesitate to forget it at once, keeping only those words that add to your own understanding in a way that is harmonious with it.

At this time we shall take our leave of this instrument and this group, leaving each, as always, in the love and in the light of the one infinite Creator. We are known to you as those of Latwii. Adonai, my friends. Adonai. ✣

Intensive Meditation
March 8, 1989

(Carla channeling)

I am Q'uo, and thank you for calling our group to your meeting this evening. It is a great pleasure to be with each of you and a privilege to share this meditation time with you. Our hearts are filled to overflowing with the joy of your presence and we love and bless each.

We are sorry for the delay experienced but this instrument was engaged in the successful challenging of a negative entity after which this entity was gone, but after which the channel challenged this entity until this entity was blue in the face. However, we thank the one known as Carla for this caution. It is caution of this type that we encourage each to use in the life and in action, for the tuning is sometimes one which may slip and the challenging that is not pure and wholehearted results sometimes in impressions upon which one may act which are not totally of the service-to-others path.

Now, each of you uses a kind of telepathy at all times. There is a strong connection which links the learning of the channeling and the living of the life, for one is a channel, in one sense, for specific discarnate entities which are carefully named and accepted by the instrument in those cases where the contact is stable. So it is in the daily life. The reason for the meditation is that it enables one to be a clearer channel. As this instrument would unfortunately put it, "a kinder, gentler," channel.

This is one of the great goals of the incarnation, for the gentle, peaceable and harmless life experience is that one which reflects inner peace, and this is the first step towards graduation from third density. This requires a type of channeling. We have never done anything but applaud this instrument's desire to teach the vocal channeling. But the reason for our wholehearted thanks was not only for the one-in-a-thousand which continues in this service, but that we realize that the process is one which one may use in the daily life.

If you are telepathic with the self within, you are in contact with the Creator. The essence of eternity is the realization that the present moment will last forever, and if one is not present at the present moment in the present tense as the new student of life, much of vital information and perception for the far-seeing thinker will be missed. This cannot be done by will or intelligence. This must be a subconscious bias. The work upon the subconscious is through the waking and the sleeping states.

In speaking of telepathy, we shall briefly speak of the dream state of telepathy, which is the satisfactory and deeper equivalent, physiologically speaking, of the meditative state—as more than one of this instrument's group has demonstrated at some point during a meditation by offering a snore.

We may take this moment to note that this instrument's original statements earlier this evening were those which do agree with our own, that the physiological part of the meditative process is not the significant part of the experience, unless, and we do repeat that there is significance if one desires to spend one's life in meditation or to go into retreat and think intensively of the Creator.

We feel with the instrument, the danger to the integrated personality of forcing the self to live with the intensity necessary to be with the Creator, it is, or could be, dangerous enough to the integrated self that the self moves apart and the mental balance is lost.

The request we make to avoid excessive periods of meditation is simply that we do not wish the accelerated process of change involved in meditation to disturb the seeker past its limits of endurance. If the entity experiences the difficulties in personality, other types of meditation, such as the working in the soup kitchen and, in short, any activity which brings forward a feeling of unity with the Creator but is active, is recommended until the self can once again tolerate the degree of change brought on by meditation.

It may be seen that we are aware that meditation is the key to service to others, to knowledge of self, and to knowledge of the Creator.

We must pause that this instrument may retune. I am Q'uo.

(Pause)

I am again with this instrument. I am Q'uo, and greet you in the love and in the light of the infinite One.

Let us move on in this discussion of the lived life. For you see, the reason for the meditation is not that it is an end in itself but that it is a tool through which one may focus one's will and one's faith. It is—if we may speak in Christian terms—a communion, a thanksgiving, and offering a Eucharist. It is the time that is, if you are seeking the Creator, the center of the day. It is time that you call to remembrance that Thought which created you. It is, within the illusion you experience, as much a family matter as concern for your relatives, and upon the level of seeking, replaces one's concern for any loved ones. Sharpen the desire, sharpen the faith, and this shall be done through it's use. Will and faith together; simple, dogged persistence; going on when you don't feel like it; getting up when you are tired; honoring the Creator to make that mysterious entity a part of your real, everyday life.

You shall experience change. The change is partially the dailyness of yourself, and so shall your true adventure begin as you learn what you truly desire as meditation changes your point of view and, again and again, truths leave, new truths come and the imperishable truths glow and glorify the one infinite Creator. May you be daily—may you see that you were following metaphysically a path which cannot fail. May you be aware of your process of change and so be tolerant of those who are not changing at your speed. Make the allowances reflect the Presence within.

We welcome each upon the path, we walk with you, and at your mental request, we are with you in silence to worship the one infinite Creator and to be with you in a deepening state of meditation.

I am Q'uo, and I know I speak for all of my brothers and sisters of the creation, some of whom are, perhaps, more akin to your vibration than we. Ask for that entity with whom you are acquainted, which to you is the clearest and most shining voice of your own truth, and allow that silent Presence to be with you by mentally requesting it. There are no words, there is no message, there is only you and the Creator part of you, and telepathically there is communication from self to self within. You are many levels, and, in the end, my friends, you are the Creator. Allow yourself to allow the energy of your life to pour out as a fountain in the infinite radiance of the one Creator. It is merely spending enough time each day that shall enlarge your viewpoint.

I would now transfer to the one known as Jim, if there are any queries. We are those of Q'uo.

(Jim channeling)

I am Q'uo, and greet each again through this instrument in love and in light. At this time we would ask if there might be further queries to which we may speak?

Questioner: Would you speak about the state which is between waking and sleeping that Carla spoke about earlier, that she called the hypnogogic state?

I am Q'uo. The conscious attention of the seeker begins, as the meditation is entered or as sleep is turned into wakefulness, to pass a point that is available from either direction. As the conscious mind relaxes and as the sleeping self awakes, there is the point of awareness which partakes, in some degree, of both the conscious and the unconscious mind and its abilities within each mode of being. At the state which you have called the hypnogogic state, the seeker is aware that it is aware, and yet what it is aware of and how it is experiencing this awareness is markedly different from the conscious awareness of the daily routine. The hypnogogic state may be seen to be that of pure listening, shall we say, being before action, in which there is the greater receptivity and the closer examination of that stimulus which is received.

Most usually, the source of the stimulus, however, is inward rather than being a product of the external environment. The perception or awareness is one which allows the seeker to partake more fully with that which is perceived that there is less distinction between the perception and the perceiver, yet enough that the seeker is, indeed, aware that it exists in what seems, in some cases, to be a dual reality. This experience is one which may allow the seeker to receive communication from deeper portions of the self and from other sources that may be external or more relatively unavailable to the conscious self. For the hypnogogic state may be seen to be somewhat similar to the carrier wave, shall we say, in your radio-electronic terms, as we believe they are used. This carrier wave allows for the placing upon of information, be it in images, in symbols, in feelings, in verbalizations that are inwardly heard. These communications may be the product of conscious querying over a fairly significant portion of the life experience; may be the focus of conscious concern that is intense in nature and, perhaps, shorter lived in drawing the attention. The communication has the purpose of providing an insight into the point of concern, whether it be conscious or unconscious. The use of this state over a prolonged period of time is quite helpful as a means of communication to the subconscious mind and of retrieving information which has been recorded there and which may lend an insight or direction to the use of catalyst in the conscious mind and in the daily round of activities.

We feel that we have at this time given a great deal of information which we hope has not been confusing in this area and would, at this time, ask if there might be another query?

Carla: I have one more that I think as a follow-up to this one is kind of important. You're saying, then, basically, that dreaming is a kind of telepathy or meditation—telepathy between the subconscious and conscious—a way to retrieve information from the deeper and wiser parts of ourselves that are working with the same catalyst that we are consciously working on. Is that correct? You can just validate that or not.

I am Q'uo, and this is primarily correct, my sister. The unconscious mind, however, works not so much upon the catalyst, as does the conscious mind, as it provides the conscious mind information in various areas which very likely are the areas of use of catalyst by the seeker. However, the unconscious mind may also provide information which lies somewhat outside of the realm of the patterns or lessons. The use of the catalyst is by the consciously seeking entity. For example, the unconscious mind may be used in the manner of which we previously spoke to engage in the problem solving, as we believe you call it, where information is requested that would allow a completion of thought and activity to occur or another step upon this journey to be taken.

Is there another query, my sister?

Carla: Just a conclusion. So, keeping a dream notebook, then, and working with your dreams is a good part of the meditative process if you use it right. Is that what you're saying?

I am Q'uo. Indeed, the working with the self within the dreaming state is one very helpful means by which an entity may come to know the self in a manner that provides a richness and variety of points of view.

Carla: But can it reach to God, the Creator?

I am Q'uo, and we would suggest that as the seeker of truth attempts to know the self by whatever means is chosen, the seeker is making itself aware of the face of God in one aspect or another as it is expressed in the incarnational pattern. Thus, to know the self in the deepest sense is to know all selves; is to know the creation; and is to know the one Creator.

Carla: Thank you, Q'uo.

I am Q'uo, and we thank you, my sister. Is there another query?

Questioner: I had a dream several days ago that I described to my child and my child explained it to me and it seemed the explanation was really sharp. My question is, does it mean that my child has talent, or does it mean that some people have talent to explain dreams, or talking about a dream, God would use a child to clarify—God would use instruments to clarify dreams, because it is difficult to be objective with our dreams?

So my question is really, do the talents some people maybe have about reading dreams and maybe how you go and work on it? I'm not sure I'm very clear.

I am Q'uo, and I believe that we grasp the thrust of your query, my sister.

There are, indeed, those which express a talent for the translation, shall we say, of the dream images. These entities may have previous experience within other life patterns working with the subconscious mind and the, we shall call it, language or archetypical nature of the subconscious mind of your peoples. For each race of entities—or in many cases, each nationality—shares similar experience in a general and most basic sense that is available to each entity within the population in a way that may be translated and understood by those familiar with the archetypical journey of each human entity which is expressed within the mythology, shall we say, of each culture.

There are many which study—as any field of inquiry may be studied—the nature of the subconscious mind, and, more specifically, the process of dreaming. Therefore, there is the progress that might be made through study that may enhance the natural inclination of those who find themselves drawn to working with the language of the subconscious mind as a means of being of service to those who also find value in this endeavor.

Is there another query, my sister?

Questioner: No, thank you very much.

I am Q'uo, and we thank you, my sister. Is there another query at this time?

Questioner: Is it possible—and, if possible, useful—to gain active control of the consciousness within dreams so that you might be an active participant in the dream, in making decisions within the dream?

I am Q'uo, and am aware of your query, my brother. Though this is, indeed, quite possible for the student which not only shows a talent for this particular field of study but which also perseveres for a great period of your time, the ability to move consciously within one's subconscious mind is properly an activity which is possible only for those most adeptly trained in this area. The training is by experience and desire, working with a portion of the being which one feels holds great resources and which one honors and respects in a way which is reflected in the daily round of activities [and also through] the insights gained within the dreaming state, utilized as living portions of the conscious awareness of the seeker.

Is there another query, my brother?

Questioner: I didn't understand the answer. There are more primitive cultures on Earth—or supposed more primitive cultures on Earth—who have within their culture a technique of going back into a dream and actively controlling their consciousness within the dream. As I understand, you say that this is extremely difficult for us to do, even though in the particular culture that I'm referring to, children can do it or learn to do it. Can you speak about that aspect?

I am Q'uo, and we shall attempt clarity at this time. The ability to consciously move within the dreaming state is, for most entities within your current culture, an activity reserved only for those much practiced at the use of the dreams, for there is less respect given to the use of dreams, in particular, in the use of the subconscious mind in general, within your culture than there is within other cultures, some of which you have described as being of a more technologically primitive nature. Yet, these cultures are much more aware through their own beliefs and teachings of the value of the unconscious mind and the dreams in particular. And, therefore, the ability to move within the dreaming state in a conscious manner is a more natural part of their culture than it is of yours, and because it is a foundation stone upon which their culture rests, is an avenue frequently traveled and the doors, therefore, are more open to such travel for such entities.

Is there another query, my brother?

Questioner: No, I understand now. Thank you.

I am Q'uo, and we thank you, my brother. Is there a final query at this time?

Carla: If no one else has a final one, I do. I suppose, really, that it would be an infringement of free will, but can you give any comment whatsoever on our decision which has been tentatively made, but not finally made, to stop the teaching of channeling itself from long distance and to offer instead the experience of the channeling without teaching others to channel unless they're close enough to be able to stick with it for a long period of time?

I am Q'uo, and as we find that this query still rests as a query within each mind, we do not wish to infringe upon either free will by biasing in one direction or the other. Therefore, we must beg your forgiveness for finding our inability to speak to this query.

Carla: That is perfectly acceptable and understandable. I kind of expected it. Thank you anyway, Q'uo. God bless.

I am Q'uo, and we thank you for your patience and your understanding, my sister.

At this time we shall, with great joy in our hearts, thank each for inviting our presence this evening and shall take our leave of this group, leaving each, as always, in the love and in the light of the one infinite Creator. Adonai, my friends. Adonai.

L/L Research

L/L Research is a subsidiary of Rock Creek Research & Development Laboratories, Inc.

P.O. Box 5195
Louisville, KY 40255-0195

www.llresearch.org

Rock Creek is a non-profit corporation dedicated to discovering and sharing information which may aid in the spiritual evolution of humankind.

ABOUT THE CONTENTS OF THIS TRANSCRIPT: This telepathic channeling has been taken from transcriptions of the weekly study and meditation meetings of the Rock Creek Research & Development Laboratories and L/L Research. It is offered in the hope that it may be useful to you. As the Confederation entities always make a point of saying, please use your discrimination and judgment in assessing this material. If something rings true to you, fine. If something does not resonate, please leave it behind, for neither we nor those of the Confederation would wish to be a stumbling block for any.

CAVEAT: This transcript is being published by L/L Research in a not yet final form. It has, however, been edited and any obvious errors have been corrected. When it is in a final form, this caveat will be removed.

© 2009 L/L Research

Saturday Meditation
March 11, 1989

Group question: Focusing around the phrase, "the willing suspension of disbelief" and the clearing of the lower energy centers, information concerning the red, orange and yellow.

(Carla channeling)

I am Q'uo. I greet you in the love and in the light of the one infinite Creator, of which we all partake. It is a great blessing and privilege to be called to your group, for it is our way of being of service, to share our opinions with you who call upon us with a certain vibration of seeking in service to others. It is also the way we ourselves learn and progress, so you are teachers to us as we are teachers to you. And we are companions together upon a very, very long journey.

The journey that we are all upon is much like a very, very long story, a story that takes place in an instant, simultaneously, and yet within your illusion and our illusions and those in between and those before and those beyond us, in rivers of time and space, so that there are pastures of experience along which you may feed and grow and learn. And when you are participating in your story, you are the hero and the heroine, the villain and all the bit parts. You are the audience, and you choose when to ring the curtains up and down. And in any story, in any fiction, in any narrative, the first requirement of the reader and the observer of that narrative is that that observer suspend willingly, out of free will, the faculty of discrimination or disbelief.

Note that it is suspended, while the action is taking place. It is not suggested that after the story is finished there be no afterthought, no process of discernment, no attempt to come to many various terms with all of those things which have happened within the story. "The willing suspension of disbelief" is a phrase taken from literary criticism, however, it is an equally important staple of the diet of heavenly food which nourishes and strengthens and enables the seeking soul to learn and grow.

It is all too tempting, within your illusion, to work with the negative energies of judgment. Turned in upon the self or out upon others, this faculty is equally damaging to the one who generates it. The entire lifetime experience, then, we are suggesting, is the period of the narrative of each entity's incarnational story, each entity's incarnational journey. Because it is an illusion that is nearly perfect and complete, it is most important to withhold judgment upon the self and others completely, in that one is never condemned but is seen as an entity which shall be, and indeed truly is, perfect, for the reality which you are experiencing at the same time that you experience space and time is the reality of the present moment, or to put [it] another way, the reality of eternity. The appropriate time for careful judgment is that moment called the day of judgment by that holy work which you call the Holy Bible, and that day shall arrive for each, and the judge shall be yourself. It is you that you must please. It is you that you must convince. It is you that are the critic. It is you that will write the outline of your next play, when you decide in the far more enlightened atmosphere outside of your particular illusion what biases you still wish to emphasize and what ones to de-emphasize.

Now, within any extended story cycle, which is, indeed, the life experience, there are many times of transformation and epiphany, many new beginnings, and it is at those times that we do, indeed, encourage each to take stock of the present moment, to remove that suspension of discrimination and disbelief and to examine, as deeply and as completely as possible, using rational and intuitive faculties alike, what it is that the lesson just experienced has been catalyst concerning, and then, as you gaze at the present moment and move into the river of time and space in the future, you may think carefully what you wish, what you desire, for what you feel passion, hunger and thirst. And when you have found the intensity within yourself, you know the direction you wish to go within the new situation, within the new story, within the new cycle of being that moves as the seasons do within the emotions to heart and the mind of each entity which [is] ensouled within a body within your sphere of existence at this time.

There is another phrase which may lend some illumination to the phrase, "the willing suspension of disbelief," and that is a phrase used by, shall we say, one of your more angst-ridden Christian apologists. That phrase is, "the leap of faith," for you see, the willing suspension of disbelief can only be done in the faith that it is safe to disbelieve—that is, to the intelligent, rational mind—like saying that it is safe to jump off the cliff without a moment's thought for how deep the cliff may be or what lies below. This is what faith is about. It is a choice made in a vacuum. The choice is very simply to abide and to have faith. What shall you have faith in? We would not call it anything more specific than love, for love is the closest word you have in your language to the terrible, awful, beautiful, creative and infinite love of the infinite One, the Father and Mother of all that there is.

It is not easy to leap into space within one's mind and heart, having nothing to hold onto but the faith itself which you have decided is your first choice. You have decided to trust the process whereby you shall learn what you came here to learn, and you take the step; you cooperate with change and you are in midair almost immediately. Not only has your disbelief been suspended, you yourself are suspended upon nothing but faith. This will occur time and time again to one who seeks.

This cycle of an experienced faith and a faith only hoped for is the necessary cycle of the seasons of the soul, for no soul can learn with unmitigated suffering, nor can any soul learn with unmitigated joy. The dynamic of the desert and the oasis is that which gives dynamic, interest and detail to each seeker's unique path. Let us say that each of you is on a very long journey. So does the one known as Jesus speak of the prodigal son. We find that in this connection, this story is helpful in illustrating the willing suspension of disbelief, or the leap of faith. In the first place, we would point out that that entity which did not go upon a journey, which made no mistakes, and had no good or sad adventures, was incapable of rejoicing, whereas that prodigal son, which had done so many things incorrectly, had squandered his inheritance, and was living with swine, was able to experience deep and intensely felt emotions of sadness, longing for home, hunger to be even a slave in his father's household.

And so, footsore and weary to the bone, hungry and thirsty for home, come we all along the road, along our story, along our journey. We know that our Father greets us with joy and gives us a feast and we know that joy. We can anticipate it. And all of these feelings are within a story, that story that is unable to be felt except upon an inner level.

So, too, you may choose to see your story in everyday, mundane, logical and pragmatic ways. Yet, you shall not learn as a soul by this technique. Far more shall you learn if you seek to suspend all disbelief in love, if you leap into love, whether it is a void or whether it is full and can hold you completely, you must make that choice always at each beginning, at each turn in the path.

In order to do this, it is very much necessary to meditate upon the daily basis, to put oneself in the Father's house at the Father's feasting table for just a few moments in the day, so that you know who you are and Whose you are. You are not your own. You do not belong to yourself. You are a story in the mind of the infinite Creator. May you leap into each leg of your journey with faith undiminished, ready to run the race in love, in joy and in hope of wisdom and compassion.

About the lower energy centers and their blockages we could speak for many, many hours, yet much has already been spoken about these blockages. We can only say that there is no body of philosophical or spiritual material upon your planet, of which we are aware, that has not within it some good insights into the voyager's search for the peaceful inner self. Thus, it is not a matter of pointing you in this direction or that, this religious system or that, but rather, perhaps, we may say in a very general sense that those things which keep energy from pouring at full volume into the heart energy center are those things which are not of love, but are distortions of love, seen in the faces and voices of those who have experienced pain. The essence of that which robs the heart of energy is separation. Thus, if you anger yourself, you must sit down and find that self within you which may forgive, find the grace within the self which redeems and makes one new. When the difficulty is perceived as being another, let it be clear that in some way you gaze upon the Creator and the self. From this you may learn if you are capable of remaining faithful and abiding in an inner peace which allows one the larger point of view.

Impulses towards kindness are sometimes not helpful in clearing lower energy centers, for there is a distinct difference between pleasing another and serving another. Before an interaction takes place, ask the self what spiritual principle is being called upon in this interchange and what role am I playing within the dynamics of love within this situation? For that which you wish to offer to others is that which may enable them to grow spiritually. Sometimes those things are not pleasing to those whom you would wish to serve, yet, if it be your light, given to you as your own truth, that to serve, this and this must be, then this and this must be the way that you act, in kindness, in compassion, and in unity, forgiving and being forgiven. To experience forgiveness, to allow it to be generated through one, is perhaps the shortest way to the clearing of the lower energies.

Perhaps the only other thing we would suggest in this regard, because of the shortness of the time period in which we have to work, is that each in its meditation move to that portion of the self which is the inner room deep within each heart and soul, and within that inner room offer the self up in complete and total surrender to the Creator which awaits within the self, but which will not come into conscious relationship with the self unless that relationship is thirsted for and hungered for as if it were the very food and drink that sustains life, and may we say, my children, in a metaphysical sense the presence of the one infinite Creator is, indeed, absolutely necessary for the soul's health. May you invite it. May you greet it, thank it, bless it and allow it to enable you to open the heart, to leap faithfully, joyfully and abidingly into the clear, unobstructed air of the grace and blessing of love itself. It is infinite, and it certainly seems void. And sometimes you will experience it as void and dark, and those are your desert times. Rejoice in them also and worry not if you feel blocked, because just as surely as you have entered the desert, so your steps shall bring you to the garden.

We are those of Q'uo, and we would transfer this contact to the one known as Jim. We are those of Q'uo.

(Carla channeling)

I am Q'uo, and am again with this instrument. We greet you again in love and in light, and offer the blessing of the infinite One. We find that the one known as Jim has explained to us that we must not linger. Therefore, we would bless each, thank each and remember to suggest once again that each seeker may best participate in his own story by treating all things as if they were heavenly food, including the self. They are to be blessed, and then to be broken and given to others that they may multiply. So does service multiply itself in love. Each entity who dwells in love creates that which it could not imagine by its mere persistence. May your light shine persistently. May your life in faith never need words, but only deep feeling and faith. We offer each the peace of the journey to the Source. We leave you in the love and in the light of the one infinite Creator. We are those known to you as Q'uo. Adonai, my children. Adonai. ✣

Sunday Meditation
March 12, 1989

Group question: Concerning how our (most importantly) mated relationships are perhaps a manifestation of our love for our self. And to carry this further, how all relationships that we might come in contact with, however brief or long, intense or shallow, might also be some kind of a manifestation of our love for our self.

(Carla channeling)

I am Q'uo. I greet you in the love and in the light of the one infinite Creator, and rejoice to be called again to work with your thoughts and offer some opinions that we may have. We are honored to join in your meditation, and we do thank you very much. We must be sure that you understand, as always, that we are not infallible, and that each truth that is your own truth is that which is recognized rather than learned. You already know the truth—it is at a level of your mind complex which does not use words. However, when the truth is clothed in words, the deep self remembers and recognizes that personal truth. Truth is, as far as we have learned, subjective, in that all of experience is subjective.

This leads to discussion of the thought offered by the one known as R that the mate is the gift of love of the self to the self.

Firstly, we would like to remove one aspect from this commentary quickly, and that is the always challenging difference betwixt the male and the female entity. Although it could equally be said, for instance, that each mate is an accurate reflection of the subconscious of the other, yet still, to the female energy is given the freer access and the greater energy and power of intuition and the half-knowledge of that which is veiled which is called intuition or inspiration. And to the male is given the reaching for that inspiriting.

To look at it in another way, one might see the quandary of a Creator which creates a companion for Itself, only to find the companion is not happy spending all of its time with the Creator, but rather feels alone without his own kind. We are not saying that this is the way creation in your density began. We are simply saying that the concept there embodied in the female being the artifact of man and man's desire not to be alone is far different than the original statement of the loved one as a reflection of the love of self for self. For in this debased picture, the two perfectly dovetailed species, male and female, are offered less than equal roles in a creation. Thus, we must pluck from the concept of the outer world of experience being created by the self's love for the self, we must broaden the horizons of this concept, as the author of this concept rationally had already begun to do, so that it includes all that there is.

Now we may gaze at the nature of the entity within third-density incarnation, and we say that this statement is a statement of an ideal nature of a certain kind. It is a spiritual ideal which is invoked. Indeed, the greater Self or the Creator is invoked in this concept, that is, the sense in which this statement is correct and literally accurate, is that the self, which is in the end the Creator, somewhat young and confused within third density, and certainly remaining confused by our fifth-density experience, somehow still contains that perfection which created all that there is. And in that sense, the Creator gazes at the Creator and knows that all has been created because of love.

All that is is a reflection of the Creator's love for Itself, and further, Its desire to know more about Itself, to communicate with Itself for the enlargement of Its personality and to learn that which seems to be subjectively true, beautiful and perfect, that which, unlike the physical vehicles of your density, is imperishable. In the sense of the God-self residing within the many layers of distortion and confusion that abound within third-density experience, the statement is accurate. However, we would quickly add that it is misleading to consider to oneself that one is capable of living in the God-self for any length of time and having this experience be a steady state. It is not that this is not possible; it has been done by those who ruthlessly remove themselves from anything but the sitting, the silence, the meditation, the breaking down completely of the self. When one resides, acts and reacts within the societal structure which is your best environment for learning, one cannot remain the God-self. Thus, as one gazes into the eyes of the loved one, one may upon one level try to remember that one gazes at the gift of love of God for Itself.

On another level, it is well to remember that you are gazing at yourself. You may well not love yourself. Therefore, you will not be pleased with the face of another, the conversation of another, or the actions or thoughts of another. The more disturbed or upset that face is able to create the catalyst for you to become, the more that self has to teach. We do not suggest that any learning difficult lessons attempt for any length of time to remain consciously the God-self, for it is a dangerous choice of personas, a risky choice of masks. The risks to one who walks incautiously upon the path of learning [are such that one] finds that one has been waylaid almost inevitably, for one's energy, unless taken from what you may call the world full time, is most usually not equal to the task of remembering who you really are.

Now, you are here to learn, rather than to dispense information and learning to others. The learning is primary; the fruits of that learning, secondary. Thusly, that which comes to a seeker from the faces of those around the seeker will reflect various facets of that seeker to itself, as a mirror may reflect accurately or in a most distorted fashion. Indeed, all of the mirrors are distortions, in some way, of love, yet the catalyst that this distortion of love may bring is far from a joyful experience.

We would like to take a few moments to talk about a very basic subject, that subject being meditation. It may well be said of those of the Confederation of Planets in the Service of the Infinite Creator that we sound one note very often, that note of meditation—daily, constant meditation. The reason for that is not one thing, but many, all concerning, however, the progress which each of you, the pilgrims that seek, may make.

As we allow these pauses, we are hoping and asking that you may begin to feel a presence, a presence called to this group from beyond us. We practice at this moment the presence of the one infinite Creator. Allow your heart to open to the greatest amount it may stably open. Do not ask it to become brighter or more crystalline than the power that is moving into it, but allow that to bloom. Allow the feeling of being in the presence of the Creator to bring to you praise, worship, adoration and thanksgiving. You sit with the Father and Mother of All, infinitely available to all, infinitely loving and infinitely unable to speak.

Each of you, then, by the changes made by meditation, may begin to perceive differently throughout a lifetime of sincere and openhearted effort in love, not duty. The viewpoint may change and widen and deepen and strengthen greatly in balance. As one meditates, one is intending to experience firsthand the Creator and the environment of the Creator, which is love, light and eternity, all of those in infinite quantity. With enough repetitive, impassioned silence and listening, one's reactions begin to change because one's consciousness has begun to change.

Meditation does other things as well. One great aid that it brings to the meditator is simply the strengthening of the bridge betwixt conscious and subconscious, intuitive and rational; all the parts of what a medical person would call the encephalos, working together and not at odds. We find often among your peoples that there are many voices within, each with a different viewpoint, each with a different program, if you would speak in terms of a computer, and all together having mutually opposing agendas. Meditation, taken daily, systematically and without the long, long meditations, but, rather, short meditations followed by the feeling of being strengthened, the mind begins to remake the basic metaprogram of the biocomputer mind in order that it may complete the process of integration so that one may become more and more a positive, unified entity, capable of a singleness of heart, a singleness of purpose, and a singleness of passion and love.

That which works—that is, that which functions within meditation—is not much affected by the meditative state achieved. The meditative state may, for most of your peoples, never be satisfactory in a subjective opinion, the self of the self. This is due to what this instrument would call your lifestyle; that which is full is ever a little fuller and details clog the arteries of inspiration. With meditation, intention, desire and passion are all, for the process is not a physiological one, not unless what you are attempting is the relaxation of the physical vehicle. Meditation is spending time with the infinite One and with Infinity Itself. It is a completely metaphysical act. Indeed, it does aid a person to be relaxed in order to meditate, but even the strong desire to meditate, pray, contemplate or worship has the desired effect; it opens a door behind which stands a Creator who will not knock, who will not ring the bell within the head, who waits patiently to be asked to come in, to join with the seeking soul and to offer it light, love, healing, peace and joy.

Yes, indeed, my friends, the Creator loves, and all of you are part of what it loves, for all of you are part of Itself. It desires to know each of you with a passion that is incomprehensible. All of the reactions which one has in love, about love, with love are shadows of the Love that created all that there is, the one great original Thought that is the Creator. We encourage you, therefore, not to see love in every face if you do not, but to take it into meditation without judgment, for you are as you are; each pilgrim, with its self-perceived strengths and weaknesses is unique. The Creator does not judge, but loves. Thus, we urge each never to force or push the spiritual seeking, but to allow it to occur naturally. When the seeker finds itself impatient for more knowledge, more truth, the seeker needs to realize that this is not a means to an end; this is the end desired. The Creator's hope is one thing more than self-knowledge. It is self-love.

We urge and encourage and exhort each to love each other and to see the face of Love in every face. We equally urge each never to judge the self or to become discouraged when this is not occurring, for that which is occurring is that which needs to occur at the very moment you experience that which is occurring. It is the raw material which, when refined, will become the gold of compassion, wisdom and humility.

We find that there are assorted concerns, and would transfer to the one known as Jim, that if any wish, they may query further of us. I am Q'uo, and I leave this instrument in love and in light.

(Jim channeling)

I am Q'uo, and greet each again in love and light through this instrument. At this time it is our privilege to ask if we might speak to any queries which yet remain upon the minds of those gathered this evening.

Carla: Well, if nobody else will kick it off, I'll ask a question you can't possibly answer, but I was curious. I sensed another presence here and patrolled the perimeter and found it, and was having a lot of trouble dealing with it for a few seconds. I was holding up an imaged cross. So, instead, I put this cross down and put my arms out and let the cross be big enough for me to be on it and challenged again in the name of Christ, and the entity vanished as quickly as I've ever seen one go. If you can make any comment on that, I'd be interested to know what was occurring with the challenging process?

I am Q'uo, and am aware of your query, my sister. The effect that was accomplished by exchanging the small visualized cross for that upon which you might place yourself was to magnify the intensity of your challenge to the point that the purity of your desire to serve in the positive aspect was overwhelming to the entity towards which the challenge was offered. Therefore, the entity found the need to take its leave of this group.

Is there another query, my sister?

Carla: No, thank you. That was a lot more than I'd hoped for.

I am Q'uo, and we thank you, my sister. Is there another query?

Questioner: What did that entity intend by its presence?

I am Q'uo, and am aware of your query, my brother. This entity of negative polarization was hopeful that it might be able to make some inroad into the channeling process, as is the habitual desire, shall we say, of those of the negative polarity, hoping that by their insertion of their philosophy into the positively oriented of a group such as this one, that they might in some degree partake of the power that is generated when entities of a positive nature gather together to seek more of that which they call the truth.

Therefore, this entity was hopeful of being able to, shall we say, bleed away part of that power, and, if successful in that first step, then be able to take a larger and larger role in the contact with this group, hoping that, perhaps, its information might become more predominant as a focus or concern for this particular group.

Is there another query, my brother?

Questioner: What density was that entity?

I am Q'uo. The density was that of four. Is there another query, my brother?

Questioner: Not from me at this time, but I would like to thank you for an extraordinarily illuminating answer, from my perspective, to the question that was originally posed.

I am Q'uo, and we thank you, my brother, for posing this query, for it has allowed us to speak upon a point which we felt was of some importance. It is by queries of this nature, and, indeed, by the seeking of each heart gathered this evening that we are able to have a beingness at all within your illusion, and to serve in the humble way in which we have the opportunity to serve.

Is there another query?

(Pause)

I am Q'uo. Again, may we thank each for inviting our presence to your group this evening. It is a great feeling of joy that overcomes us when we receive the invitation to join your circle of seeking, for with the invitation comes the opportunity of walking more fully with each of you and feeling your presence, your desire to know and your desire to serve, which when generated within the heavy chemical illusion that you inhabit is all the more precious for the great spiritual effort that has gone forth on the part of each of you to create these desires of a positive nature. We appreciate the illusion in which you dance and realize that it is not an easy task to continue your daily round of activities, which seem so burdensome so often, to then move the concerns from the daily round of activities to that which lies behind each activity, to that which lies within each self and each beating heart, to look for those clues of the Creator, to follow that trail of love, no matter how trying the journey. We salute each and share with you that which is our love for the Creator in each. We are those of Q'uo. At this time we shall take our leave of this group, leaving each, as always, in the love and light of the one infinite Creator. Adonai, my friends. Adonai. ❧

Sunday Meditation
March 19, 1989

Group question: Taking potluck questions tonight.

(Carla channeling)

We are Hatonn, and we greet you in the love and the light of the infinite Creator. May we say what a blessing it is, and an honor, to be allowed to share your meditation and to join your circle of seeking at this time. May we ask that each in the circle realize that there is only one being, one consciousness, amongst all seekers. Each is unique, but each a part of the same movement, the same process, each of you companions on the road from the Creator to the Creator. We ask that you settle down, perhaps, a bit deeper in order to serve as batteries for this instrument. We ask that this tuning procedure be enhanced if necessary by visualizing a small globe in the midst of the circle, and it moving until all are within that globe, all within the light, all protected and united in their seeking.

We have been called to your group this evening by the thoughts and desires of those who are here. We come gladly because it is our method of service to others to be with you at this time. We would perhaps recognize the motives of service to others that moves some among your peoples to go to those other peoples upon your sphere which are needy and teach the ways of using the environment to their environment. So, too, we wish to aid entities in another environment than that of the physical bread, the physical food, the physical existence. Each of you also is an awakening spirit, and each of you begins to awaken to the need, not only for food of the spirit, but for tools and resources, that one find the means of growing the wheat, of removing the chaff, of grinding and breaking that which is hard within you, that the newborn spirit, that the wheat, that the gold which you have made and found within yourself may glow and become a channel for the love and the light of the infinite Creator. This is what all of us seek to do, and this is the adventure at the beginning of which you now gaze with a fascination that this instrument would say would be shown by Dorothy in the Wizard of Oz. She knows she is not in Kansas anymore, but she does not know where she is.

We feel that it is a kindly universe, a most loving and loving and beloved Creator, and we find that our fates, as far as our teachers know, are most benign, and that our end is never; that we are imperishable beings, created to be the active portion of the one Creator, cells of an infinite Mind, which learns about Itself because of the interaction of all of us, all of you, all those of your sphere, all of your galaxy, all those of the billions of galaxies that you may see, all those in the infinity of the illusion of this octave of experience.

We of the Confederation of Planets in the Service of the Infinite Creator come to you with a very simple message. We come to you with what may be said to be a message so simple that it cannot be heard. We come to say that there is one great original Thought; that thought is Love. Not a love as you know it, but a full and complete love, a love both beautiful and terrible, the love of the Creator to know Itself. In that love, It created by using free will that which is called consciousness, self-consciousness, shall we say. Each of you is a mixture of the very stuff, shall we say, of the active principle of the Creator, that is, you have a God Self. However, to it was bonded free will, and in the immature, shall we say, seeker, that free will shows as willfulness, variousness and unpredictability in choice making. Indeed, many do not see that each day and, perhaps, each hour a decision that is to be made, that may seem very small, actually bears upon a spiritual principle. One could be working upon one's development as a polarized service-to-others entity. Many, many times, one misses the opportunity because one is far too much involved in that illusion which you call the everyday life.

We come to speak of a love that is so great that it does not run out. It is infinite in supply. We come to urge each to participate in that great original Thought of Love, for the more that one participates in the great original Thought, the more one's point of view regarding the mundane and everyday experiences of the life experience become infused with the light of the one infinite Creator and the compassion that is felt by the Creator for Itself, all parts of Itself, those who love the dark as well as those who love the light.

The greatest and most powerful pathway to an experience of the infinite Creator that is available in a way which will remain with the entity is persistent daily meditation, for in meditation one moves oneself through the door into the inner room in which stands waiting the Creator. The Creator is most willing to dwell and abide with each entity, but it is each entity's decision to open that door to the inner room of silence, meditation, contemplation and listening. If you may do one thing to accelerate the pace of spiritual growth, it is simply to choose a place and a time in each diurnal period where the meditation may take place in silence, and the listening within may be uninterrupted.

The process is most difficult to judge, we find, from those within the illusion, for within your society the mind complex is requested to be very active at all times and the body usually also. This makes it rather difficult for what this instrument would call the western or Occidental entity to participate in a passive meditation with much true quietness of mind. We ask you not to be discouraged on that account, for the work that you do in consciousness by meditating and listening is that work of the will, the will to discipline the personality, to change willfulness into that phrase from your holy work, "Not my will, but Thine," in other words, not the will of free will which is various, but the will of the Creator Self which is a will to love. To this, we ask you to surrender, as the finite surrenders before the infinite, as the past and the future surrender to the resonance of the present moment. Intersecting with the present moment at all present moments is eternity. One may think of it as, shall we say, perpendicular to all things. It is enmeshed with you. You dwell in heaven at this time.

Oh, my friends, we urge you to open the eyes and gaze about at the creation of the Father. We ask you to see the cooperation and the joy that there is in the green cathedral of nature. We ask you to seek the trees and the bushes that breathe out that which your species must breathe in, that breathe in that which your species must breathe out. The cooperation is great, yet completely without thought. Again and again within the world of nature, one may find not only beauty, but cooperation, harmony and a way of living in which each may exist and be wild and free and beautiful. That is still your heritage.

You see, you carry about with you a second-density creature. This creature is your body. You yourself have the consciousness of third density, but you must walk about upon this particular heavy physical density of illusion, and so, you carry about with you a certain kind of animal. This human animal is a delightful thing, and we ask each to honor it, to understand its needs, to harmonize and cooperate with that which some have called the temple of the soul. We would prefer the term physical vehicle, for you use it much as you would use a car; it gets you around, and through its senses you perceive much. But please reckon with this animal and know that it, including its ability to reason and to have instinct, is not informed in the same way that one which has chosen to become conscious of one's hope of accelerating spiritual growth is. You must realize that part of the willfulness that must be regularized so that the will may be turned to work in consciousness is that of the outer illusion, one's relationships, both in society and most especially with those with whom one is intimate, one's family.

It is well to do the very best one can to place one's creature in a good position for survival, so that one may go about the business of polarizing in consciousness. Do not allow the intellect or the instinct to rule the behavior, but turn again and again to the glory, the unity, the peace, and the joy of the presence of the one infinite and mysterious Creator, that Thought of love which created all that there is. Do not choose to be that which carries you around. Do not choose to be willful forever, but choose instead to will to surrender to that greater Self within. Ah, my friends, what a jewel rests within you, what light, what love! You are unique, each of you, unique as snowflakes. You have experienced much. You would not be here upon this planet within an incarnation at this time if you did not have a good chance of choosing to be of service to others to the extent that you polarize enough to graduate from this density to that density of love and understanding where the veil between the conscious and the conscious mind is lifted, and much is seen and understood that can never be understood within this illusion.

We do not mean to suggest for a moment that there is any hurry about this; it is one's choice completely. We do not mean to suggest for a moment that the fourth density is easier than the third. This is not so; it is simply different. The fourth density is a density in which one refines one's ability to love and one's knowledge of love, one's ability to be love and one's knowledge of being love. However, because there is a fourth density negative, there is a dynamic tension, and both those of positive and of negative persuasion may speak to your people. We ask you, therefore, to discern and discriminate carefully with each piece of information that you hear, including ours. We are fallible. What we have to say to you is, we believe, helpful. We hope it is. But if it is not, my friends, we ask you to let it go, for we would not be a stumbling block before you in any way.

We would not ask you to meditate for the long periods of time, for we find that the process of spiritual growth among your peoples causes a good deal of change. It is well that the change take place slowly enough that one's mate may deal with it as well as one's self. The process of change is sometimes painful, and we urge each to be extremely courageous and pick oneself up after each and every self-perceived failure to turn one's face again to the mysterious face of the Eternal One. We join you on this journey. We hope that you will meditate each day for a short period of time, not the long. We hope you will enjoy the changes that you perceive in yourself. We hope that you may again and again and again choose love and serving others over that love which takes, controls and manipulates.

See those activities and behaviors within yourself and start making other choices. These things you can do—not out of your own strength, but because you spend time with the Creator. May we say to you, the basic, single, most thorough-going advice we may give to you is to meditate on a daily basis, for one moment with the Creator can make one feel joyful, peaceful, centered and ready to meet that which comes later. Then when one is in a difficult situation, one may cast one's mind back to that centered place and in some way draw eternity into the most difficult of situations. It simply is a matter of spending time with the Creator. This mysterious Entity created you. It is infinite, It is intelligent, It is invisible. This much we know. The Creator is still a mystery to us as well. But the Creator intersects with your life at this time and at every time, for each moment is the present moment, and each moment is eternity. May you spend your time with the Creator so habitually that this becomes a resource that you may become a channel for the love and the light of the infinite One. And then, my friends, you shall shine like a lighthouse, like a beacon, for you shall be a channel for love, that which does not stop, that which is infinite. It is the lightening of the consciousness of the planet Earth that is our hope at this time.

With this thought, we would leave this instrument, and transfer to the one known as Jim. I am Hatonn.

(Jim channeling)

I am Hatonn, and greet each again in love and light through this instrument. At this time it is our privilege to ask if there might be further queries upon the minds of those gathered this evening to which we may speak? Again, we remind each that that which we offer is our opinion, offered freely and joyfully, yet with no desire that our words be seen as anything other than our opinions. Is there a query at this time?

Questioner: I have one. I believe that my higher self has created the illusion of my being here on Earth at this time. I believe in incarnations, since all time is one. Do I have all of my incarnations simultaneously working together now in and out of my being that is here in this room?

I am Hatonn, and am aware of your query, my sister. The simultaneous nature of time is a difficult concept to express in your words, for the nature of words themselves is that which works against, shall we say, the understanding of time at its heart. For within your illusion, time moves as does a river, with that which is past, that which is present, and that which is future moving sequentially in order that the mind complex may grasp in a specific or narrowed function certain lessons, shall we say, or concepts that shall require this focused attention in order to be realized within the depths of one's being. Therefore, time, as you experience it, is greatly distorted for a purpose, that you might learn intensively and with focus and purity. However, the larger view of time and of your own being includes a great deal more than this concept, than this illusion, and more than our humble words can begin to approach, though we shall attempt this process.

Your, as you have called it, higher self is what you now would call your fully potentiated self at a point in time that you would call your future. This higher self has what you might see as a road map laid out for you that has the beginning point, the ending point and many possible avenues of journeying between these points. The higher self has resources available to it upon which you may call through your desire to know more of the mystery of yourself, of this illusion, of the creation, of the Creator.

As you begin to request information of this nature, you are guided, shall we say, by your higher self to meet the various entities, activities and resources that are necessary to satisfy your desire and to allow you to continue upon your process of evolution. One of the resources which may be called upon in this process you may see as your various incarnational selves which exist within your being as probabilities or possibilities, infinite in number, and which contain, within their realms or boundaries of being, information gathered through experience within these incarnations which may prove useful in your current incarnation. It is more accurate to see the incarnational process in the simultaneous time framework as a kind of parallel existence which has no beginning or no end, if one explores carefully one's own connections, not only to one's present self or those that one might consider past or future, but also one's connections to each portion of the creation of which one is aware. For as you have become familiar with the concept of unity of self with all of the creation, this concept indeed begins to make itself more obviously apparent, or shall we say, apparently obvious, as one sees the connections between the self and each particle of the creation, and begins to see that there is that of value in each portion of the creation and is that which might teach or inform the self as the self moves through its currently perceived experiences.

All this is to say, my sister, that your supposition, though correct in its foundation, is somewhat oversimplified, as is our explanation in response to it with the words we have used, for the nature of one's being at the heart of one's being partakes of this unity which is unshakable and is the primary foundation stone upon which all of the creation is built.

Is there another query, my sister?

Questioner: I had an unusual experience that all of a sudden I had an insight, as if everybody that I was with in this particular room at a given time was me and I was them. I zoomed into them and they zoomed into me. Is everybody in this room tonight and everybody I come in contact with "other me"?

I am Hatonn, and am aware of your query, my sister. At the heart of each being, this is, indeed, true for each. Indeed, each entity which one meets in the daily round of activities is an other self, not just because each entity projects from its own conscious and unconscious mind a certain image of the self that serves as a kind of filter or eyeglass through which one sees one's universe, but even more profoundly, each entity is, indeed, the one Creator, and as the One exists in all, then all exists in the One, and, indeed, in each other. Therefore, the experiences that each entity accumulates in each incarnation are available as a resource to all, if each entity is able to move through the deeper levels of the mind complex to that place within the subconscious mind where this unity is more obvious and more profoundly in effect within each incarnation and each portion of each entity.

Is there another query, my sister?

Questioner: Not at this time.

I am Hatonn. Is there another query?

Carla: Well, I'll jump in while everybody else is thinking. I've always wondered about simultaneous time. If some past life version of you does something differently, like have another kid or die early and doesn't have kids or whatever, does the future all change? I mean, simultaneously?

I am Hatonn, and am aware of your query, my sister. This again, though correct in its basic premise, is somewhat oversimplified, for there is not just one past or one future; there are many, many of each, each with a different response, perhaps in degree or in quality, to those events which are occurring in a simultaneous fashion for the entity in one portion of its being that is seen within a certain framework of time. As we are sure that you begin now to see, the process is one which is dynamic in its interaction and the connection with not only deeper portions of one's own being, but with the entire creation about one as well.

Is there another query, my sister?

Carla: No, thank you.

I am Hatonn, and we thank you, my sister. Is there another query at this time?

Questioner: There's been a lot of study going on in life after death experiences of people that have come back, and from everything that I've understood, people go to a light, the source of God, as we believe it to be, as I understand it. There have been some that have not gone to this light. Is this not just in your own thought of what life is? And once you have passed through this period of time, are you not with God at that point, even if you have fear, even if you have a sense of evil or bad, do you not spend the time and still return to God? Instead of, for instance, hell? Is there even a hell?

I am Hatonn, and am aware of your query, my sister. Indeed, each entity, whether within the incarnation as you experience it or moving through the door of death, as you call it, to a different form of existence, each entity always is within the presence of the one Creator. That presence is perceived in a fashion which responds to the, shall we say, beliefs or structure of beliefs which the entity has formed within the current incarnational pattern. These beliefs may again, to use our former analogy, be seen as the spectacles, the eyeglasses upon the face through which the entity views its environment.

Thus, that which is experienced immediately following the process you call death partakes most fully of this distorting factor of belief that filters that which is, so that it is seen and experienced according to the beliefs of the entity having the experience. Thus, there is much of confusion for many, as each entity has formed a unique system of beliefs to some degree during the incarnation and must, at the time of the death process, first view that which is to come through this structure of beliefs. As the entity becomes more accustomed to its new environment, it begins to allow certain of the more distorting and obviously less useful beliefs to fall away as a natural function of the continuing process of transferring consciousness from one illusion to another less distorted illusion. Therefore, the entity begins to see …

(Side one of tape ends.)

(Jim channeling)

I am Hatonn, and am again with this instrument. Is there a further query at this time?

Questioner: As I, in this physical being, pass into death, and I take all of my biases and my prejudices and my learnings with me, and certain distortions fall away on the other side, whatever period of time I choose to stay on the other side, does a refined spirit come back through to the next incarnation in body?

I am Hatonn, and am aware of your query, my sister. As you begin to penetrate the realms of what we find called Etheria or the higher realms of the astral planes after moving through the death process, you become aware that there is a greater self towards which you move, until this "self" which has completed one incarnation, and the "self" which has not only lived each incarnation but has served as a repository of those lessons and experiences gathered in each, then becomes the [new] self, so that you are again unified with what may be called the essence of the self, or as most of your peoples call it, the soul.

This being, then, with the aid of others who have served as the guides and the teachers, and with the aid of the higher self, reviews the incarnation which has been completed in order that that which has been gained of learning and of service might be compared with that which was desired and planned before the incarnation. Where there has been less efficient learning, there is the renewed desire to pursue that which was left undone. Where there has been the completion of lessons, there is then the addition or refinement of these lessons so that the experience that is to come within the following incarnation might offer to the self an enhanced opportunity to know the self and to know the Creator, and also to allow the Creator to know Itself through the self within the new incarnation in a fashion which is also enhanced or refined, shall we say.

Thus, one may compare succeeding incarnations to the succeeding grades or classes within your schooling system, so that that which has been learned previously begins to form a foundation upon which the structure of the greater self might be built.

May we answer a further query, my sister?

Questioner: Is the greater self ever-changing, as God is? I mean, is there no—since there's infinity, is the greater self still going to expand and expand and expand for all eternity too?

I am Hatonn, and am aware of your query, my sister. As there is a limit, shall we say, to the dimensions or densities within one octave of being, there is a definite opportunity provided to each entity or portion of the one Creator to know the self, the creation, and the Creator. This progression of opportunities to know the Creator, at a certain [point] within the process many, many, as you would call them, millions of years in what you would call your future, moves to a point at which the unification of the small self with the great self with the higher self and with the Creator becomes so perfected, that, indeed, the self becomes the Creator and returns in a fashion that might be likened unto the workers bringing the harvest home, in order that the Creator, then, at this point might be able to utilize those fruits of the harvest, those experiences and lessons and services gathered as the seeds for a further octave of beingness that will begin as this one began, with the most basic elements of being: the earth, the wind, the fire, and the water blowing and burning incandescently in what would be seen as a chaotic fashion until again there is the beginning of the organization of consciousness and the moving forth into a new octave of experience that will allow further explorations for the Creator within the new creation, this process being infinite in nature, as far as we are aware.

Is there another query, my sister?

Questioner: Thank you, no.

I am Hatonn, and we would ask if there is a final query for this evening?

Questioner: I have one. If a person is, in their heart, interested in helping others, and the particular area they're trying to help in is dangerous, is putting their mind on the level of a criminal mind, is following in those directions to help our society from becoming victims, so to speak, of these people, what does a person need to do to protect themselves or to look at?

I am Hatonn, and am aware of your query, my sister. We find that this query is far more complex than its simple statement would presume, for within the query are various presumptions, some of which work against others. We would suggest that the greatest protection for any entity in any situation is to see the self and all other selves as the Creator and to have as the foundation stone of any interaction between selves a true and heartfelt love for the other selves. Whatever actions may then depend from this basic attitude of love, compassion and acceptance may then proceed within the boundaries, shall we say, of the greatest protection that is possible. For to those who move within the ways of love, there is no fear of any other self, for all is seen as the Creator.

Within your illusion this attitude of total and unconditional acceptance is not common. Indeed, within your illusion, most entities go through the daily round of activities in a fashion which is far removed from such an attitude of acceptance, and within this separation of self from other self, there is room enough for fear to grow to the point that one would feel the need to shield or armor the self in a more practical or physical fashion from others. These activities of shielding and armoring the self are those activities which provide the potential within the being practicing them for the swinging of the pendulum, shall we say, so that the attitude, through a series of testing and trials, becomes more amenable to the removing of the boundaries and the recognition of shared existence within your illusion.

In order to accomplish certain mundane or more worldly goals, it is often necessary to form the boundaries and the narrower ways of viewing a situation. This is well for the entity engaged in such activity, for each such activity will provide the entity a further step along its journey of seeking, yet shall not be the end of the journey. Each entity within your illusion, then, has as one of the primary goals the dissolving of boundaries so that there might be seen and experienced more and more of the unity of the self with all other selves, with the creation, and with the Creator. This is a significantly long journey, and oftentimes there is much of trial and trauma, in your terms, that must proceed before each step must be taken upon this journey. Yet, the steps are taken, and the journey is successfully accomplished in some degree by each entity within each incarnation.

At this time, we will make our gratitude known again to each for allowing our presence within your circle of seeking. We feel that we have exhausted various of the entities within this circle with, in some cases, an overabundance of information and, in others, a paucity of information. For this we apologize, but will attempt in succeeding gatherings to refine our ability to share our opinions and our joy at having been invited to your circle of seeking. We are those of Hatonn, and at this time we shall take our leave of this instrument and this circle, leaving each, as always, in the love and in the light of the one infinite Creator. Adonai, my friends. Adonai.

L/L Research is a subsidiary of Rock Creek Research & Development Laboratories, Inc.

P.O. Box 5195
Louisville, KY 40255-0195

www.llresearch.org

Rock Creek is a non-profit corporation dedicated to discovering and sharing information which may aid in the spiritual evolution of humankind.

ABOUT THE CONTENTS OF THIS TRANSCRIPT: This telepathic channeling has been taken from transcriptions of the weekly study and meditation meetings of the Rock Creek Research & Development Laboratories and L/L Research. It is offered in the hope that it may be useful to you. As the Confederation entities always make a point of saying, please use your discrimination and judgment in assessing this material. If something rings true to you, fine. If something does not resonate, please leave it behind, for neither we nor those of the Confederation would wish to be a stumbling block for any.

CAVEAT: This transcript is being published by L/L Research in a not yet final form. It has, however, been edited and any obvious errors have been corrected. When it is in a final form, this caveat will be removed.

© 2009 L/L Research

Sunday Meditation
March 25, 1989

Group question: How do we reconcile the concept of death with our earthly lives?

(Carla channeling)

I am Latwii. I greet you in the love and in the light of the one infinite Creator and am most pleased to be with you this evening and to have been called to your group by voices seeking truth, by ears open to hear, by hearts hoping to understand. We find each of you to be most beautiful in your vibrations, and we bless and thank each for the opportunity to share in these vibrations and in this meditation. We would ask that you attempt to stay awake, but we promise you that we shall not complain too much if there is the occasional snore. It is all right, for we shall simply speak that which we have to speak, knowing that that which is not of truth which is acceptable or recognized by you will be and must be ignored and put aside, for we would not be a stumbling block in the way of any. We have our opinions, but they are not infallible. Perhaps we have walked a few steps further, but our feet are still dusty with the walking of the same journey upon which you now plod, trudge, skip or dance, according to your mood.

When we speak with you about the nature of the death experience, we cannot speak completely in general. We would like, if we could, to back up from that death experience and speak of those things which the one known as M lightly considered a portion of his query, that is, the question of faith, that is "faith," rather than "belief in." We, of the Confederation of Planets in the Service of the Infinite Creator, do not greatly advocate "faith in" this or that, for that which may be formed into words shall one day ring false because of the change of time and thinking and the illusion.

Thus, the concept of faith must be divorced from all objective reference. One is best prepared for the death experience when one has learned to live a life in faith. Basically, this faith has no objective referent, in that the Creator is not an objective referent. This is no palpable, tangible, testable, visible Creator. Rather, the Creator is infinite intelligence, a concept which cannot fully be expressed using your language. The closest we may come to the active principle of that one great original Thought, which is the Creator in its active phase, is that inadequate word, Love. Consequently, that which one has faith in, if one must have faith in everything, is Love Itself, that which creates, that which destroys, that which is wonderful, that which is terrible, that which is all that there is.

Divine and creative love is a great mystery. To have faith in a mystery is to truly have faith, for faith is that which does not rest upon surety, but upon things unseen, unknown and unproven.

If you wish to live as a faithful person, faith works in the following way. A person of faith will, by centering oneself upon the first and great original Thought of Love, attempt to listen to those interchanges which come to one, and before responding, ask oneself, "How may I indicate compassion, support, wisdom and understanding, and most of all, love? How may I be of spiritual aid to this entity speaking with me?" This is the life and faith. It contains no dogma and no doctrine.

Many there are who have found the path of an orthodox faith to be the path that aids the seeker most ably along the journey of prodigal sons and daughters that we all walk. Others find that this walk is incomprehensible and therefore the walk must be created as a personal, shall we say, myth of self, Creator and the relation betwixt self and Creator. However, all these are things which one does with one's mind in order to exhort oneself to an ever-deeper intensity of desire to focus and center upon the presence of the mystery of Love, that is, the presence of the love and the light of the one infinite Creator. If one is able to die, knowing one is dying, and recalling one's faith in love, one's transition is the easiest possible.

Now we shall talk about those things within the physical incarnation which distort and confuse the question of death. Although it is completely known that each entity will and must die to this life before entering a larger one, yet still, we find among your peoples a profound fear of the loss of the animal which carries you about, that which [you] call the human being. We find this instrument noted it has also been called a featherless biped, but we merely add this for the humor. In any event, this animal, of whatever name, is not you. Are you in your toes? If you cut one off, would you disappear? If you cut off your leg, would you go away? What portion of yourself could you remove and no longer be yourself?

You are consciousness. And consciousness has natural laws. The greatest of these depends upon your choice, for you must follow the natural law towards quicker and more efficient polarization in consciousness, one way or the other, in order to have accomplished those changes in consciousness which you yourself, with aid, created the opportunity for before your incarnation.

We wish each to remember that this incarnation is most special, for at this particular, what you would call, time, those wishing to participate in the polarization of consciousness upon planet Earth are far more than the opportunities for animals which may house these consciousnesses. Therefore, souls to move into these human-being animals are chosen by seniority of vibration. This means that each of you is capable within this lifetime of achieving a harvestable attitude towards love. That is, each of you is capable of caring more for another, more for loving another, understanding another, comforting another, consoling another, forgiving another, than each cares for being understood or being loved or being consoled or being forgiven. This sacrificial nature of love, where one spends more of one's time concerned with aiding others than one does concerned with aiding oneself, is a tremendously helpful way to move in polarization ever closer to the point where, when you do enter the larger life after the death of the animal which has carried you about, you shall be able to use the requisite amount of light from the infinite Creator.

Now, we would not want you to feel that there is only one path. There is also the negative path, which we feel is very difficult, and is not that which we teach. It does, however, have a validity, although this validity is limited, and one cannot move the entire journey to the Creator, as far as we know, without having finally to reverse polarity to the positive, for that is the truth of the creation: love, unity and oneness. All of you and all of creation is one thing. You experience yourself as having boundaries. This is necessary for you; it is also necessary in terms of the experience within this illusion. Your very heavy physical vehicles, your animals, protect you from each other and from your own subconscious, for in this relationship you do the equivalent of taking the first real step in a mature and carefully considered way, a step which then must be pursued with persistence through many experiences, through several densities and through many, many refinements.

The death that you experience watching others grow old and leave their physical bodies is that death of the animal. It is unfortunate that death often contains a period just prior to the leaving of the physical vehicle where there is a great deal of pain. This occurs, as does everything else in life, to get one's attention, to allow one the opportunity or the reason to consider the great mysteries of the incarnation that has been experienced.

Now, those who are unaware of a life in faith, those who have spent a great deal of time working to manifest physical possessions and loving those physical possessions, shall find it difficult to become those who care more for others than for the self, although if one withholds the possessiveness which one may feel for one's possessions, and sees them rather as a gift from the Father, one may train oneself to think of oneself as a steward of the Creator's goods. Thus, if there are already many possessions, stop thinking of them as yours, and realize that you are the steward that is taking care of that which is the Creator's in every atom and every energy circle. These are those things which keep one from having the easy transitional experience.

There is one more thing which may cause a very difficult experience, and that is a very intense focusing upon some Earthly matter. The soldiers in the battle sometimes are not aware that they have been killed for some time, because it has happened so suddenly. Those with an obsession may be so focused upon the object of that obsession that they may become Earth-bound spirits, until the object of that obsession is gone, or until some entity helps the Earth-bound spirit to free itself from the blindness of the lower, what you would call, astral planes.

So, we suggest to each that during the lifetime one begin with the daily meditation to ground oneself in the Creator's love and light, to focus upon service to others, to love oneself and love each other, and to have no fear of death, for there is no break in consciousness; there is no snuffing out of the flame of consciousness; the animal which has carried you about simply becomes unviable. Among your peoples, this event is very moving and poignant, and, indeed, in our density too, we mourn our mates and our teachers. But we do not hold onto them, nor they to us. Each has the freedom to stay or to go, whereas within your illusion, sometimes entities do not know what freedom they do have.

Thus, one could experience many different things upon the occasion of the physical death. Some things are purely physiological and most uncomfortable. May we wish each a comfortable death? We certainly would not want to wish the contrary. However, once the physical body has been dropped, there are any number of experiences that may occur, depending upon the consciousness of the individual. In many cases, there is healing work to be done. In some cases, the healing work involves creating an atmosphere which equals the happiest time of the previous incarnation, and this primary healing technique is used until the entity is strong enough to face the rest of a difficult incarnation. At other times, the entity is conscious enough of the angelic guidance received during the incarnational experience that the entity moves without fear and with knowledge of the journey and with curiosity into whatever amount of light that entity can absorb comfortably and use.

Thus, eventually each is healed, each moves to a portion of the creation which has the light density which is comfortable for it, and from this vantage point, with its higher self, and, we always add, with that which we can only call grace, the entity judges its incarnation. The entity gazes back and leafs through the pages, or to use another metaphor, looks closely at the woven tapestry of emotion and thought and action which made up a life. Is your tapestry beautiful? Have you used rich colors and loving emotions? Is it stark with cold emotions or disturbing with anger? How are you making the tapestry of your life? It is you who will judge yourself. Please yourself today. Then judgment will not be so difficult.

Once the incarnation has been reviewed, and you have judged how well you have learned the lessons that you came to learn and what lessons remain to be learned, you may then plan your next incarnation. At this particular time in your density, many of you are hoping for, and some of you will achieve, harvest, thus going on to a more light-filled density, the density of love or understanding. If that is so, then the concerns of the higher self for that incarnation will be those of the new soul in a new situation which wishes, as always, to offer love. This is the beginning of the social memory complex that our colleagues known as Ra have spoken of through this channel.

We ask you to become aware of the present moment. All of eternity exists now. Time is an illusion, space is an illusion; your consciousness is not. Many, many confusions occur because you live in an illusion with the x-axis of time and the y-axis of space. There are other illusions, but they are illusions. The reality is closer to you than your breathing, but one is completely unable to find it. It is your consciousness. Work with it until you are happier with yourself today than yesterday, and at the same time, as always, we caution each never to be discouraged, for each day is a new day and a new start. Each day is the present moment. Each moment intersects with eternity, and in each moment there is the presence of the living and infinite Creator.

Why spend your time skating upon the pond of life? Break through that thin ice and dive into the deep, pure, warm waters of deeper consciousness. Visit the tabernacle of the Most High in meditation, for it is within you. You do not stand upon holy ground. You are an earthen vessel, but within you lies the holy ground of the infinite One. Honor this within yourself, emphasize this within yourself. Let this self open a conduit through you, that this self may flow through you in an infinity of energy you could never sustain. The more time that you spend doing this work in consciousness, the more you will die to yourself.

Perhaps the best advice we could give to those who are interested in the death of a body is to point them toward the true death that the choice between positive and negative paths demands. You have the power to choose. This is your time of choice. This is the heavy illusion in which you must make your choice. It was designed that you would have very few clues of a clearly overt nature as to the true nature of the mystery of the Creator. You make your choice in darkness, a shadowland where you can see nothing clearly. Wrong seems not-so-wrong and right seems questionable. There is nothing within the illusion that suggests ideals, ultimates or superlatives. Yet, we say to you that you yourself are absolutely unparalleled by any other spirit within the infinite creation. You are unique. You are very, very important to the Creator and much loved. When you know this, perhaps it is easier to open the heart to love in return. Perhaps it is easier to open your mouth to words of praise and thanks. Perhaps it becomes slowly easier to think of things from another person's point of view or from some larger point of view which alters provincial and petty thinking.

Now, each of you shall lose your physical vehicle. As you do so, our best advice to you is to have lived a loving life, to have encouraged within yourself a consciousness of love in the presence of the infinite Creator. It is a matter of allowing it to occur. It is a matter of asking for it, of desiring it. That which you desire, you shall receive. If you wish proof, we suggest that you join those technicians which are called scientists among your peoples who create many, many gadgets, using principles that are a mystery to them. They will not admit the mystery. Do you wish to live in a world of observations, repetitions and tests? Or do you wish to live a life of love and faith? Then take heart. Take courage and do it, persistently, one day at a time, and one day you shall die and you shall experience that which you have prepared yourself for.

May you all move into fourth density positive. May you all find so much love for the Creator and for yourself that you can love others even more than you love yourself and see in them the infinite One. Then shall your death be a change of clothing. A moment, no more, of transition, and you shall be where you need to be, reaching your hand out to those whom you wish to greet you. Fear death not, for it is benign. While you are here, do not question that you have a reason to be here. As long as you are alive, you are fulfilling that which you came to do. Natural death will occur when, shall we say, your hitch is up, for you have signed on to a very difficult assignment, a very difficult tour of duty.

May you find that in yourself which is of faith and love and wishes to give, and through meditation and desire, nurture it until the tapestry of your life becomes jewel tones upon jewel tones and patterns upon patterns and you become a poem to give to the infinite Creator, the fruit of a life in faith—peace, love and joy; also sorrow, suffering and death. See all these things as your brothers and sisters. They all equally teach; they are all equally blessed. Gaze with love upon all, and when you gaze upon death, you shall think of the Creator, Its light, Its love, and you shall be instantly in a wonderful, beautiful place.

This is the preparation we would suggest, the turning of the attention to love, the nurturing of the awareness of the Creator by meditation and by frequent, tiny thoughts during the day to bring one back to center. The physical death is momentary. You are spending this incarnation preparing for, shall we say, the final exam that shall occur thereafter. Do your homework, my children.

We would at this time thank this instrument for using us to channel, for this instrument is itself a terrible joke teller, and we are able to express more of our humorous personality through this instrument than in some groups. We hope you do not mind our lightheartedness, but it is our firm belief that without the light touch, the spiritual path can become far too serious and thereby lose its intensity and its joy. We hope for each to find joy as well as progress on this stony path, peopled by so many companions, my children.

I would now transfer to the one known as Jim, with thanks to each and encouragement. I am known to you as Latwii.

(Jim channeling)

I am Latwii, and greet each of you again in love and light through this instrument. At this time it is our privilege to ask if there might be further queries which remain upon the minds of those gathered this evening. We again remind each that we share that which is our opinion, and though we share it with great joy, we do not wish to offer that which would seem to be infallible to any. Please take those words that we speak and use them as you will, forgetting those that speak not to your heart. Is there a query at this time?

M: Yes. First of all, I want to thank you for your answer to my personal question. It was very touching for me. I did have a couple of questions, though. You spoke of death as being—that there's no break in consciousness. And you also spoke of the notion that time and space is an illusion. I have experienced a break in consciousness, I presume, for example, when I've been operated on, I've been put under into unconsciousness. Is this any way comparable to death? I go through a period of time where I do not even recognize the existence of time, or I have no idea where I am or I have no idea of my own self. Is that a kind of unconsciousness that is comparable to death?

(Side one of tape ends.)

(Jim channeling)

I am Latwii, and am again with this instrument. The experience of entering the subconscious mind via the drug-induced procedure that is utilized by those of your medical profession is one in which the door to the subconscious mind is momentarily opened, and the consciousness enters by a means that it is for the most part unaware of, and exists for the most part in a similar manner. Therefore, the experience, though it has some similarities to moving through that door which is called death, does not truly approximate this type of transition, for the experience of the process of death is one in which a remembering occurs that informs the conscious mind of more of its own beingness, that which has always been with it and has in its own way at the appropriate moments informed the conscious mind of certain pieces of information that would be helpful in a certain situation.

The experience of becoming so engrossed in the moment of your conscious existence, which is often called the daydream, or the—we find the colloquialism used of "spacing out" in the consciousness, is also, though similar in some respects, removed from true analogy to the experience of the process of death, in that the daydreaming provides a pathway, shall we say, into the upper reaches of the subconscious mind by invigorating the intuitive connection between the conscious and the subconscious mind, so that there might be the refreshment, shall we say, that the subconscious mind can provide the conscious mind when the conscious mind has been properly stilled in order that it might be informed or imprinted with another experience.

Is there another query, my brother?

M: Yes, thank you. Along the same line of questioning—in other words, you're saying, if I understand you correctly, that at death there is a kind of awakening to a lot of experiences that you may have even forgotten. I assume that that means that you're still aware of the life that you've just finished living, and yet what I find is that there seems to be very little communication between those who have died and those who are still living. Why is this?

I am Latwii, and am aware of your query, my brother. For the most part, the reason that there is so little of communication between those who have moved through the door of death and those who remain within the conscious incarnation is that there is little, if any, attempt made by those remaining incarnate to communicate with those who have moved into what you would call the discarnate or state of consciousness on the other side of the door of death. There is little belief amongst the majority of your peoples that such communication is either possible or advisable if it is possible, for that which is unknown amongst your peoples is feared to a large extent, and it is much more comfortable to most of your peoples to allow that which is unknown and that which is feared to remain untested and to not set foot within such mysterious fields, shall we say.

Another reason why there is little communication betwixt these two groups of your peoples is that, for the most part, those who have moved through the door of death have within their being a feeling of completion for the incarnation which has just ended and have a great feeling of the desire to explore that which is obviously awaiting them on their own journey of seeking, so that there is little desire to move back, shall we say, to that illusion which they have so recently left.

There are instances, however, where there is a final communication with those who have been the loved ones within the incarnation just completed. Oftentimes, this communication will take the form not of words or spoken concepts, but of a feeling of the essence of the entity being blended with the one with whom communication is attempted.

Thus, the one who now moves through the door of death and enters a larger existence will find a great deal to draw the attention onward in order that the evolutionary journey which is now more obvious to the entity than it was within the incarnation will become the sole focus of the attention in order that there might be further progress upon it.

Is there another query, my brother?

M: Just another one, and then I'll let somebody else ask questions. Just to clarify that. As I understand what you're re saying, most of us who are living sort of do not believe that we can actually communicate with our loved ones who are dead, but I also seem to understand that if we did, or if we attempted it in the right way, that it would be possible. First of all, is this true what I'm saying, and secondly, are there any peoples on Earth who are doing that? Or are interested in that and are doing it in a way that is visible?

I am Latwii, and am aware of your query, my brother. The ability to communicate with those who have moved beyond the boundaries of the present illusion is an ability which may, indeed, be learned by those who have the intense desire and the persistent practice that is required in the area of becoming, shall we say, a clear receiver and a clear sender of consciousness upon which information may be placed. This involves the careful examination of the life pattern, in order that the system of energy centers or chakras within the human physical vehicle might be utilized in a clear and lucid fashion that will allow the passage of the intelligent energy or love of the Creator through these centers without significant distortion.

This process is involved enough and demanding enough of the ruthless honesty, shall we say, of the seeker of truth that there are few who have mastered the ability to first communicate with the self in terms that are clear and unmistakable that will later allow communication upon nonverbal levels with other entities, be they incarnate or discarnate.

Therefore, we are unaware of a great number of peoples upon your planetary sphere who have mastered these disciplines of the personality to the extent that is required for such communication to occur. There are, however, various groups of entities within your planetary environment that are able to utilize their dreaming state in a manner which allows a more, shall we say, ephemeral type of communication to occur, that which occurs within the inner planes or the astral planes of this particular planetary influence, while one entity who is incarnate is involved in the sleeping process in which the dream is the meeting ground between the discarnate and the incarnate entity. There is the ability to communicate in this manner which has been developed by a number of peoples upon your planetary surface, primarily those that you would describe as living a somewhat more primitive existence, that which is closer to the natural rhythms of your planet and within the environment of your second-density plants and animals so that there is the familiarization with more, shall we call them, organic rhythms than is generally possible within your more industrialized and populated nation states.

Is there another query, my brother?

M: Not for the moment. Thank you very much.

I am Latwii, and we thank you, my brother. Is there another query?

K: Yes. My name is K, and I live in Missouri, and I am grateful for the opportunity to be here and listen to your message. My question is, recently I just completed a channeling class in St. Louis. I would like for you to comment upon my progress, if this can be made properly, and also about the extreme coldness that I have felt on the front of me in recent days.

I am Latwii, and am aware of your query, my brother. We find that we must in this particular case speak in terms which may be more general and less personally specific than you would desire, for a portion of your experience is significant enough to your own personal growth that it is well that your own free will be allowed to have full sway in this matter. However, we shall speak in a manner which we hope does not infringe upon your own free will.

We are aware that your desire to serve as a channel or a vocal instrument is one which at heart has the desire to be of service to others motivating it. We are most grateful that you would wish to offer yourself in this type of service, for there is much of service that may be offered in this manner. The practice of the vocal channel is one which requires a great degree of study, of practice and of persistence, for it is not an art that might be learned and perfected in a short period of time. Therefore, though we would commend your efforts in pursuing this means of service as you have done, we would suggest that it is but the beginning, the opening of a door, shall we say, that must be done in a careful and persistent manner. There is the possibility for any new instrument to move more quickly, shall we say, than is normally advisable for one seeking to be of service in this manner, for as one serves as a vocal instrument, one is placing oneself potentially closer to a source of light and of power than is normal for any seeker of truth.

This placement of the self in the close proximity to light and to the power that it generates is a step which has some risk, for there is the attraction to this light of beings that are less than desirous of being of service to you as you move toward that light and attempt to reflect or channel to others in a manner that might be of service to them. There are entities, shall we say, of the loyal opposition, those entities who are of the negative polarization who also would seek to control and master the power that is generated by the light that you would attempt to give to others through your vocal channeling. Their presence is a possibility which each new and, indeed, each experienced instrument must take the proper precautions in order to provide protection that will not allow their influence within your circle of seeking while you are practicing the art of the vocal instrument.

We find that you are familiar with the concepts of the challenging of the spirits by the name or concept of that which you hold most dear and that which is the central sun around which your desire orbits in order that you might be of service to others. The challenging of spirits is most centrally necessary at each opportunity that you take to serve as a vocal instrument. It is also quite necessary before each such session to prepare oneself in such a fashion as would be analogous to placing the dial of your radio squarely upon the station that you wish to receive. This we have found this group calls the tuning of the instrument. By this procedure, whether it be by the singing of the sacred music, the visualizing of light, the reading of those inspirational words of meaning to you and to your group, or by whatever means has significance to you, is necessary in order that your desire during the channeling process be only that to serve others and to serve to the fullest of your ability while serving as a vocal instrument.

When these precautions are properly taken, there is little chance that entities of a negatively oriented nature may influence one's efforts, for the light that one generates by these efforts of tuning the instrument and challenging spirits is that light which shows the truth to those about one and reflects it back to those who would seek to disrupt those efforts that you offer in service to others. When these precautions are left undone or poorly done, there is the possibility that the efforts may for that sitting be contaminated, shall we say, or influenced, and the contact mixed. The feeling of coldness is a sign, shall we say, that such entities have made their presence known.

We can recommend that when this feeling of coldness is felt, that one might retire to the meditative state and find within that state the greatest degree and purity of unconditional love that one can within one's being and send his love to whatever entity or entities are responsible for providing the feeling of coldness, in order that they be bathed in your love as much as is possible for you to generate, and then this love may also be seen as light which you form about you as a type of shield or armor against further incursion. This procedure may be repeated for as many times as is necessary to remove the influence that leaves its feeling of coldness as a sign of its presence.

Is there another query, my brother?

K: I thank you for answering my question in such detail. I feel that I do understand it.

I am Latwii. Is there another query, my brother?

K: I have been interested in UFOs. Can you comment properly, without infringement upon my free will, of any close contacts that I have had?

I am Latwii. It is with apologies that we must answer in the negative, for this area of inquiry is one which must remain totally within the boundaries of your own free will, for the mysterious nature of such occurrences has the purpose of drawing the attention not only to the experience itself, but to the larger life that the experience that the experience occurred within.

Is there another query, my brother?

K: I would relinquish any further time to anyone else that had any further questions.

M: I would like to ask a little bit further about the idea of creating a life of service. I think this is a very noble ambition, and as I understand it, it's also very useful for our evolution. However, there seems to be a paradox, and maybe you could help me understand this. I would like to develop this ability to serve and be of service more than I have it now, and yet to me that seems, in that very light, it seems kind of selfish to want to do that. I don't understand. In other words, is this process a process that one can learn? Or is it a process that should be a natural process that develops naturally as you evolve? Am I expressing myself okay?

I am Latwii, and we are, indeed, aware of your query, my brother. The desire to be of service to others in order to enhance one's own evolutionary journey does partake of a certain degree of what you would call selfishness. We find that all actions within your third density illusion begin from the center of the self and then move outwardly in a certain fashion that is unique to each entity, until the area of concern for the entity moves from being centered solely upon the self and its needs for survival and for learning, for growth and for all those experiences which offer themselves within your illusion, to that point at which time the concern begins to touch upon other selves and, indeed, becomes so focused upon the well-being of those about one, that one has, shall we say, tipped the scales so that there is a greater percentage or intensity of concern for others than there is for the self.

This process, as we stated previously, must begin with the self. It may then be a process of learning through the necessary interactions that are a portion of the daily round of activities, to be of service to others through the, shall we say, necessities of the moment, where, without thinking, one becomes involved with other selves, other entities that move about one and which make requests of one, either overtly or by their very presence. Therefore, there is the ability to learn first upon the subconscious level to interact with other selves to the degree that one begins to see this interaction and a serving of others as a natural portion of one's own being and activities.

As one becomes more aware in a conscious fashion through one's own seeking of the purpose of life and the possibilities of the life pattern, then this service by necessity, shall we call it, becomes expanded so that there is taken a certain degree of pleasure in the serving of others. The continued conscious seeking of the nature of the life pattern and its purpose will provide the seeker of truth with renewed opportunities for providing those services which are unique to each seeker to provide other selves. Then we find the seeker of truth discovering that there is even greater pleasure in serving others than there is in serving the self, while realizing that there is a certain, shall we say, base requirement of needs which the self must provide the self in order that the self might continue in its third-density experience.

There is a point which we see is at a slight distance beyond the 50 percent level of service, at which time the desire to be of service to others exceeds the desire to be of service to self, while the desire to be of service to self may, indeed, be yet significant. It is acceptable, shall we say, for the percentage of intentions to serve others to be fifty-one percent or greater for the student to be available for graduation or for harvest, as you may call it. It is necessary that the student have the persistent desire to be of service to others in excess of the 51 percentile in order that this student might be able to withstand the more intense light emanations that are the normal boundaries or givens, shall we say, of the fourth-density experience.

The experience of the fourth density, therefore, is enough more demanding in the way of providing further opportunities of growth that the student is required by its own ability to be able to offer itself in service to others to this degree, that being the 51 percent or greater. Such a student is able to begin at the lower levels of the fourth-density illusion and continue its learning at that point, having the fourth density, therefore, as its resources upon which to draw for further learning and further service.

Is there another query, my brother?

M: I think you've been very kind in your detail. I have one troublesome … This is the last question I'll ask tonight. Along those same lines, we've been talking about human beings who have a choice, but I'm interested in human beings, also, who do not have a choice, such as people who are born severely retarded in consciousness or people who are born insane or people who become insane or people who are aborted even before they have a chance to be born. Can you speak about this? How are they allowed to evolve? Or is there something so wrong with their choice that they just have to start all over again? Can you just answer that a little bit?

I am Latwii, and am aware of your query, my brother. We would remind you, my brother, that the current incarnation, though it may seem all of existence and all of possibility at this moment for you and for your peoples, it is, in truth, but a moment in the progression of any entity through the third density illusion. There is the choice available to each entity that enters the illusion concerning the manner of its experiencing of the illusion. There are some who, for specific reasons and previous experiences in other incarnations, have the need to experience the more intensified form of the incarnational pattern within your illusion. These you find in many situations, those which you have just spoken of yourself and many, many others as well, where it seems that the entity has little conscious choice within the incarnation as to how its incarnation shall proceed and what may be gleaned from such an incarnation.

We again remind each that experience of any incarnation within your third-density illusion has the purpose of balancing those experiences which have been gained in previous incarnations and also providing the beginning point, shall we say, for further balancing that shall occur within what you would call future incarnations.

Therefore, there is no incarnational experience that is lost. There are many, many experiences that are not understood while the experience is ongoing. However, upon the cessation of the incarnation, when the incarnation is reviewed before another is attempted, there is the greater range of viewpoint, shall we say, that allows the entity to see those forces in movement while it was incarnate that were a result of seeds it had itself planted, either previous to the incarnation or within the incarnation, so that whatever fruit was gathered might be utilized in the overall growth of what you would call the soul or the essence of the entity. There are many incarnations which fall far short of that which was hoped before the incarnation began; however, none are lost, for though the lesson learned may not have been the one that was anticipated, all incarnations and all experiences do, indeed, teach in the overall sense and scope of the soul.

Is there another query, my brother?

M: No, thank you. That was very nice.

I am Latwii, and we thank you, my brother. Is there a final query at this time?

Carla: Well, I have a question. There are two kinds of people that write to us at L/L that have trouble finding time to be of service to others or feel that they haven't been of service to others, and that is the person, man or woman, who has a business or works for a business that takes a lot of hours and gets one really tired so that one can't meditate very well and one can't spend a lot of time thinking or reading, or the caretaker, usually a woman, who is keeping house, taking care of children, chauffeuring around, going to the grocery, going quietly crazy, and really it's a very noisy environment, not a lot of time ever to sit down and just relax, especially with small children. And I tell them, you're being of service to others by your very consciousness. It's the best I can think of. Could you comment on that? And expand in any way on how those people are being of service and how they set that up?

I am Latwii, and am aware of your query, my sister. The inundation by the daily round of activities amongst your peoples is an experience which is quite common, for it seems that the details of the day are by far the most important concerns which the entity shall meet, and these concerns must have a proper resolution in order that one move the attention further to other concerns and other entities.

We would suggest that each entity be reminded that it is the desire that is found within the heart of the being that is of most importance in any incarnation.

The desire to imbue each relationship and each activity with as much love and service as one can find within one's being is that quality which shall provide the entity with the peace of mind, shall we say, in the ultimate sense.

We are aware that each entity looks at its own life pattern in a manner which is less than complimentary in this regard and sees the self as falling far short of those goals which one has set in the metaphysical sense. That one constantly falls short of that which is desired is unimportant in the overall growth of the soul. What is of importance in this growth is the desire to seek, the desire to serve, and the desire to continue even when one feels one has been nothing but a failure. We would remind …

(Tape ends.) ✣

L/L Research

L/L Research is a subsidiary of Rock Creek Research & Development Laboratories, Inc.

P.O. Box 5195
Louisville, KY 40255-0195

www.llresearch.org

Rock Creek is a non-profit corporation dedicated to discovering and sharing information which may aid in the spiritual evolution of humankind.

ABOUT THE CONTENTS OF THIS TRANSCRIPT: This telepathic channeling has been taken from transcriptions of the weekly study and meditation meetings of the Rock Creek Research & Development Laboratories and L/L Research. It is offered in the hope that it may be useful to you. As the Confederation entities always make a point of saying, please use your discrimination and judgment in assessing this material. If something rings true to you, fine. If something does not resonate, please leave it behind, for neither we nor those of the Confederation would wish to be a stumbling block for any.

CAVEAT: This transcript is being published by L/L Research in a not yet final form. It has, however, been edited and any obvious errors have been corrected. When it is in a final form, this caveat will be removed.

© 2009 L/L Research

Sunday Meditation
April 9, 1989

Group question: The question this evening has to do with the issues that exist between the Orion, or the so-called renegade UFO type of entities, and the Confederation entities, both of which seem to be [in] contact with the population of our planet. What are the issues between them and how does our planet fit into the scheme of things and to the scheme of issues between the Orion and the Confederation entities?

(Carla channeling)

I am Q'uo, and I greet you in the love and in the light of the one infinite Creator. In this service we come to you. We greet and bless each and thank you with our whole heart for allowing us to blend our vibrations with your own, and we thank you for calling us by the energy and intent of your seeking and the nature of your questions.

We of the Confederation of Planets in the Service of the Infinite Creator are those who wait for the call, for we are those upon the path of service to others, and where there is no call for service it is not within the bounds of our free will to offer it. Therefore, we rejoice at this opportunity to share our opinions with you through this instrument, although we do wish you to remember to discriminate carefully in all that you may hear, for all that you hear through this instrument are our opinions. We have moved through many more experiences than have you. We have been where you are and we have gone forward, yet we do not know precisely the end of the road ahead nor do we feel the end of our identity, and we know that these things will occur at somewhat, shall we say, the same time.

Thus, we are as you, pilgrims upon a very, very long and rewarding road, the road that seeks the mystery, the road that is the mystery of the one infinite Creator. You are all energy; that which you see as form and manifestation is, instead, an higher organization of energy fields. This will be helpful to remember as we speak with you about your question of the Confederation of Planets in the Service of the Infinite Creator and its possible differences from the so-called Orion or Orionis group.

There is an energy that radiates outward, blessing, shining, warming. The sun that you experience is a good example of such radiance. This is the radiance of unity, and in its promise lie the bloom of many kinds of qualities that may be considered positive and radiant—love, peace, unity, consolation, hope and joy. There is another sort of energy which may be worked upon to empower it, that is magnetic or attractive energy, in which the entity creates the self as the Creator and controls the creation about it as would a king his kingdom.

These two energies manifest in many, many different ways; they are two sides of the one coin of the infinite intelligence that created all of the densities of space and time through which in this creation we shall move. The trip may be longer for some than for others because the basic choice that this particular density asks the seeker to make is the choice of which energy to use in order to further understand the mystery of the one infinite Creator, the one original Thought or Logos that created all that there is. This choice may seem a simple one to make when gazed at theoretically, however, this particular illusion is designed to confuse and befuddle and trap, fool and mystify any and all attempts to make black and white out of the warp and woof of speckled gray that is this illusion.

Thus, this choice must be made with the only real evidence pointing in the direction of personal power as more effective than the radiant path of acting as the servant of all shining upon all freely, spontaneously and generously. Therefore, the person who has not thought deeply upon these matters moves through his life doing one good turn for a neighbor and then cutting another off in traffic, feeling murderous toward a fellow worker, and then noticing how beautiful is the sky at sunset upon the return home. The net result: dead zero; the changes in consciousness have moved back and forth in the gravity well of indifference.

Now let us describe these paths from this point of choice until the point at which they move together again in the density beyond our own, that is, the sixth. The positive polarity in fourth density is learning how to love completely, manifesting that love by creating a social entity of itself, that is, a single group memory. Thus, we call ourselves Q'uo to you, I myself who am speaking to you am an individual within that population which has chosen to serve at this time in this manner. However, I have access to the experiences, ideas and thoughts of all of those who work with me at this time.

This is the work of positive fourth density; it is work that is not as difficult as the work you do now within the heavier illusion, for we can remember that which you cannot. We remember the long, long line of choices that has brought us to the point at which we now find ourselves; this is in forth density. Therefore, although there are many disharmonies, the disharmonies are understood. It is more possible by far to communicate and disregard differences [in] culture, sex and race. Full concept communication, or telepathy, is most often used in this density, thus eliminating the need for comparison of symbols which because of different racial archetypical minds can never be translated from one culture to another.

There are those of us who in this fourth density turn back toward the third to offer themselves as teachers. There are those of the fifth or wisdom density that do the same, and we are one of those groups within the Confederation. There are very few sixth density entities which still attempt to communicate, for much happens within the sixth density, you see. The fourth density is a density of love or understanding. All the lessons that you are learning now have to do with how to love the unlovable, how to accept the unacceptable, how to remain radiant though all of the negative seeming experiences of the illusion, how to refrain from armoring the self.

These are very, very difficult problems to deal with within your heavy illusion. Therefore, there are those of us in the love density and in the wisdom density which turn back to aid as teacher. But, in the sixth density, wisdom and love must be combined and it is wisdom's final conclusion that we all are one. This creates within the negatively-oriented entity the terrible, tragic, unbelievable knowledge that it can go no further in its seeking for the one Creator unless it sees all others as the self. It can no longer manipulate others and fool itself that it is being otherwise all-compassionate. This is a great crisis for those upon the negative path, for those upon the negative path in fourth density create the social memory complex in a very rigid pecking order. Thoughts are shielded whenever possible and no one is truly trusted, for personal power remains that which is sought in order to use the Creator's light, and much, much learning is available to those willing to think only of the self at all times.

In our opinion, the positive path is much, much to be preferred. The other is, however, a viable though somewhat more difficult and certainly longer path. In fifth density the negative entity remains very much by itself, learning from its teachers and remaining completely solitary. It is in the sixth density that the negative entity must come face to face with this terrible difficulty, for the sixth density is the density of unity, and in this density those who have worked so hard to develop negative polarity must, as quickly as a magnet could switch from South to North, move to positive polarity of the equal strength. This is a supreme act of will and is the unification of the children of the Creator.

You may consider all of yourselves as those involved in the polarity betwixt the positive or radiant path and negative or magnetic path. Now, in the fourth density there are many who are on the negative path who move into this density during windows of opportunity which are allowed by the one infinite Creator under the premise that one with free will shall make a choice far more powerful than one with only partial information.

Therefore, you may hear, perhaps, even a majority of negatively directed information pass through your hearing apparatus. This is not an indication of the Creator's opinions; this is the stuff of an illusion made of energy. You are to make a choice in a seemingly negative atmosphere to be radiant and positive and loving, to offer the self as servant for all, to humble the self and surrender to that Self within, and in this you have help. You have us who have been called angels to you. There are those upon the inner planes that have refused to go on, although finished with third-density work, concerned that so many sit at this time upon the fence unwilling or unable to bring themselves to that final cornerstone decision, "Yes, my life will be service to others in the name of the infinite Creator, in the name of the mystery that I shall seek imperishably."

We hope that each that is in incarnation at this time will realize the opportunity of free choice within such a heavy chemical illusion. It shall make a far deeper etching upon the picture, shall we say, of the self. It shall delineate more biases of polarity done in incarnation than can ever happen outside of incarnation, when all is known and choices are obvious. Those upon the positive side, seeing that the negative entities attempt conquest at this time upon planet Earth, do in thought [join] battle [with] what one may fancifully call the forces of darkness.

However, that Armageddon, shall we say, has been raging for two hundred of your years already upon the spirit plane and seems to be that which has no probability either way, for the good [in] winning loses its polarity and must fall back to regroup, at which time the negative moves forward to take light. The battle is a delusion of fourth density, which fourth density entities learn for themselves the wisdom or folly of. However, you are more than pawns in this game. These entities are not more powerful than you, not in the metaphysical sense. That is, perhaps they might, in some negative manner, cause the entity to cease living, cause the discomfort or the pain, the embarrassment or the humiliation or the fright, but they too are bound by the basic laws of free will and prey largely upon those whose minds are not complex in their thinking processes.

You are the kings and the queens and the knights upon the board. You are the players in this game. The game, my friends, however, is too simple for most entities to grasp—to love, to smile, to have the light touch, to consider cautiously to reserve judgment, to encourage each other, to care for those whom you know who may need it. These are simple things, yet each act offered in humility increases your polarity in just as much power as does the more obvious power of the entity who gains power by his charisma and his skillful manipulation of entities about him.

All of those within the Confederation are not within one galaxy. All of those in the so-called Orion group are not within that galaxy, and all about you you will find some positive and some negative entities, some positive and negative planets. This is part of the plan of this particular creation laid into place and moving as smoothly as the working of a clock. Please understand that both space and time are illusions and that each of you is energy, a thought, or consciousness, if you will. Do not gaze at the phenomena of negative and positive. Gaze within the self in silence and pray that your energy may be always radiant and never that which sucks, like the vampire, the energy of those about you. When you need help, radiance is in accepting it, and in the one who gives, it in giving it. These is no circumstance whatsoever in which one cannot be of service by the cheery smile, the light touch, the gentle word, and the listening ear.

We are all pilgrims, and in talking with each other do we encourage each other to move onward and to seek the Father's house. Oh, prodigal daughters and sons, whatever your condition your Father awaits you and all of us with rejoicing, and we are all hungry for home. Yet, let us vow in whatever place we may be to pay attention, to see, and observe, and perceive that which our catalyst is attempting to give us in the way of lessons about love. Do not lose any opportunity to ask yourself in difficult circumstances, "Where is the loving thing to do; where is the love here?"

Yes, negativity and positivity exist, and it seems prudent to both positive and negative entities to form alliances in the positive sense so that we may share in one higher self which is a common memory of us all. In the negative sense, there are various reasons, shifting and restless, for combination. They all have to do with conquest. About those things which are political we wish to remain silent, simply reminding each that phenomena are manifestations of energy. The energy may be understood very simply. Gaze at any phenomenon and ask yourself, "Is it radiant and giving and loving and unifying or is it frightening and painful and difficult to bear?" Are you requested, or are you told and commanded? Judge for yourself the polarity of entities and situations, and know that armies will clash until entities tire of that game. The mystery of why the Creator chose to offer us these challenges and these ways of learning remains unknown to us. It is as well to accept, for now, that such is the case and to move always upon the positive path, thinking of others more than you do the self, giving more than you receive, understanding more than you are understood, being content to love. You are loved, loved most passionately and imperishably as the imperishable and unique soul that you are. The Creator is fascinated with you and wishes to know the tapestry of your feelings and thoughts and ideas and intentions. Offer to the Creator a passionate life, a life filled with caring and giving and loving and sharing. Let the colors be true and rich and let yourself have those periods which are the desert times, for those colors, too, must be in a truly beautiful painting or tapestry. Know, as you go through the dark times, of all the life that awaits to burst forth through the soil at the first drenching of blessed rain, and know that you shall as a soul receive that rain and walk once again in the lush oasis of joy.

We thank you for allowing us to come to you this evening. We are being told by the one known as Carla that we have, perhaps, talked long enough for this evening. We, therefore, at this time wish to transfer to the one known as Jim, that that entity may conclude this session. I am Q'uo.

(Jim channeling)

I am Q'uo, and greet each again in love and light through this instrument. At this time it is our privilege to ask if there might be further queries to which we may respond before leaving this group. Is there a query at this time?

Questioner: Where do the fourth, fifth and sixth dimensions exist?

I am Q'uo, and I am aware of your query, my brother. Each portion of the creation vibrates in complete harmony with the one infinite Creator which contains within Its being all the densities or dimensions which are the means by which each portion of the Creator shall know himself and shall know his Creator and, conversely, shall the Creator know Itself through each portion that It has created. Thus, each portion of the creation, your own planetary sphere, for example, has within its force field each density of light vibrating completely and fully. However, within your planetary sphere there is the activation of only the densities one through four at this time, with the fourth density that which is in the process of beginning its cycle of evolution as your third density illusion completes its cycle. Thus, the fifth and sixth and seventh densities of your planetary sphere remain, for the most part, in potentiation, serving only as vibrational frequencies to be utilized by those of like vibration from elsewhere, shall we say, at this time.

Is there another query, my brother?

Questioner: Those of like vibration who are for going to the mind of the One versus those of the like vibration who are moving towards material. How do their vibrations differ in feeling and aura and sound? How do we recognize those who are different vibrations here on this planet?

I am Q'uo, and, as we understand your query, those of your population, that is of the third density, would be for the most part unable to recognize the vibration of entities of densities beyond their own, whether the entities were of the positive or negative orientation, unless these entities chose to make certain portions of their being known to those of your population. However, there are many among your peoples that have awakened the abilities of the initiate and have become somewhat sensitized in a manner which would allow them to perceive with finer tuning, shall we say, some of the qualities of entities of advanced densities.

For the most part, the aura of the negatively-oriented entity will have in his field a predominance of the colors of the lower energy centers, those being the red, the orange, and the yellow. The positively-oriented entity, on the other hand, will exhibit the colorations of the higher energy centers, beginning with the heart and the green, the blue, and the indigo. The entities of the negative orientation will, when making their presence known to an entity of your third density, exhibit the feeling of coldness and will set in motion a subtle feeling of agitation or fear. The positive-oriented entity will seek to engender only those feelings of brotherhood, of inspiriting or inspiring those entities that they touch with any portion of their presence.

Is there another query, my brother?

Questioner: What about those who have gold auras, and those who have gray auras, and those who have triangular shaped auras? Are these walk-ins or inter-breds?

I am Q'uo, and I am aware of your query, my brother. To the first query, we may respond suggesting that the aura that is of gold or the aura that is white with the gold appearing within it as a living color are entities that are, shall we say, from elsewhere of a positive orientation who have chosen to return or to come for the first time to this planetary influence for the purpose of offering their service in whatever way might be possible for them. The entities that exhibit the more unusual configurations of the aura of which you have spoken, being the grayish aura and the triangulated aura, are entities that have become, shall we say, a portion of the play between the forces of what are called light and the forces that are called darkness upon your planetary sphere, and have become, shall we say, influenced in a way which we would rather leave to the free will thinking of those who are interested in such riddles, for there is a line beyond which we may not move in giving information without infringing upon the free will of those to whom we speak and, in some cases, the free will of those about which we speak. For this we apologize, my brother.

Is there another query?

Questioner: The auras that are triangular shaped and people who have triangular marks on their body, what does this signify and where are they from?

I am Q'uo, and I am aware of your query, my brother. As we were speaking previously, these entities are those who have had contact with entities of an origination other than your planetary sphere, who have, shall we say …

(Side one of tape ends.)

(Jim channeling)

I am Q'uo, and am again with this instrument. We shall ask if there is another query?

Questioner: How do we know if we are walk-ins, inter-breds, hybrids or we have been tagged? Must this information be protected from us or is there a way to discern?

I am Q'uo, and I am aware of your query, my brother. For a general response to this query that does not risk the infringement upon the free will of those who seek the mystery of their own being, we must suggest that one look within one's own being within the state of meditation or of prayer and for those who are accomplished at working with their dreams within the sleeping state there might be sought information in these areas that is not readily accessible to the conscious mind. The part which desires with great intensity to know the nature of its own being and the purpose of its being shall, with dogged persistence, continue to seek within the meditative or prayerful state this information which the subconscious mind contains in full and which it will release in symbolic form to the conscious mind in order that the conscious mind might be informed in the manner by which it has sought information.

This is the means by which one knocks upon the inner door that it might be opened and there might be an exchange of information and experience between the conscious and unconscious minds. The masks, shall we say, that each entity wears within an incarnation are placed as they are by the entity and its free will choices prior to each incarnational experience in order that certain potentials might be offered for learning certain lessons and offering services as a result of these experiences. Thus, each entity has the mystery that surrounds it that offers to it the constant opportunity to penetrate the veil of forgetting, as it is called, in order that a glimpse of that which lies beyond shall inspire the seeker to continue on this journey, finding a glimmer of light here, then there, then here and there, and, putting together these pieces of illumination, might begin to understand the nature of its own being and its connection to all of the creation about it.

Is there another query, my brother?

B: The people, the beings who come in from the Confederation, do they contact and take people for experimentation only with their permission? Or do they feel that they have a higher ethical imperative which overrides those of us of the lower dimensions?

I am Q'uo. It is the desire of each entity and group of entities that comprise the Confederation of Planets in the Service of the One Infinite Creator to offer those services to the population of your planetary sphere that are requested, as long as these services do not infringe upon the free will of those requesting the service. Thus, the interaction between those of the Confederation and your planetary population is one which is carefully guarded for the benefit of the population of your planet, for if there is interaction that is too, shall we say, open or blatant and which gives answers too easily, the student will not benefit from the interaction. Though it shall know the answers to the, shall we say, test of life, it shall not be able to move upon its own direction without the assistance of those who are more informed. This is not a situation which is desirable for the entities on your planetary sphere or those of the Confederation of Planets.

Thus, the positively-oriented contact will be one which is most subtle, in most cases. There are, of course, anomalistic situations in which these general guidelines may not apply, however, there is always the great desire to insure the exercise of free will by those of your population so that there is no infringement of this free will and no interaction that causes undue fear, if this can be avoided at all. Thus, most of the contacts that occur between the Confederation of Planets and those of your population are contacts which occur upon the, shall we say, inner planes or the astral level of experience which is accessible through the sleep and dreaming process or the meditative state. There are few contacts of a positively-oriented nature that occur in the face to face encounter, as we find you have called it.

Is there another query, my brother?

B: Yes. Those who are renegades, do they have a different ethical imperative that allows them to override the ethics and values of those of the third dimension? That is, do they work against our will without us having a say?

I am Q'uo, and am aware of your query, my brother. Those of the negatively oriented polarity have chosen the path that is magnetic or absorbent in nature, shall we say. That of light, of power, of energy or of fruitfulness of any nature which is about such an entity shall be controlled, shall we say, by that entity, in order that its own power might be enhanced. Thus, the entities of the negative orientation have chosen to travel a path in which the subjugation of the will of others is a natural part of that path, enabling those who gain power over others to exercise that power in a manner which does, indeed, infringe upon the free will of those who [are] brought under the control of the upper, shall we say, echelons or ranks of this polarization.

The interaction betwixt these entities and the population of your planet has as one of the cornerstones the engendering of the emotion of fear in order that the population of your planet might look with a feeling of fear and separation at the entities that comprise your population and at the concept of contact with extraterrestrial beings in general. The concept of fear then can be utilized to divide, shall we say, the desire of your peoples to travel the path of seeking the light, if that path can be shown to be strewn with difficulties and the unknown and fear-filled quality of beings that populate it. Thus, with the ignorance that is engendered by such fear and separation can the population of a peoples be controlled and utilized as what you might call the slaves that produce endlessly that which is desired by the master.

Is there a further query?

B: I have a final question. Those who seek the light, is there a way we can protect ourselves from those who seek the darkness?

I am Q'uo, and am aware of your query, my brother. We are most grateful that you have queried in this regard, for there is, indeed, the means by which any seeker of light might provide itself with a protection from such influence. Though it seems quite a foolish thing to do, the means is to enter, within one's own heart, within the state of meditation or prayer and to find as much heartfelt love as one can generate and offer it to those that would wish one less than well, and to bathe these entities in this love and in that light and to offer to them that unconditional love from the heart which is so sweet and delicate to those of the positive polarity but which has the opposite effect upon those of the negative polarity.

However, we must remind each that it is necessary that the intention for such a protection be not to resist or to cause the entities of negative polarity any discomfort at all, but to simply offer the heartfelt love to such entities and then to bathe the self in the armor of love and light and to offer this love as often as is necessary in order that the protection and wall of light be constructed about the entity in a pure and heartfelt manner. Thus, the positive and negative poles offer a natural boundary, shall we say, or resistance, each to the other, for a certain portion of time and experience before the unification of these polarities is accomplished within the sixth-density illusion, as we spoke previously.

Is there another query, my brother?

B: No, thank you.

I am Q'uo, and we thank you, my brother. Is there another query for the evening?

Carla: Just one small one. If someone has an implant, is there a way to remove it?

I am Q'uo, and am aware of your query, my sister. We shall offer this response as the final response for the evening. The implant that has been utilized so frequently in the contact betwixt the negatively-oriented entities and some of the peoples of your population is a device which is not readily responsive to the technology of your medical profession at this time …

Carla: Um-hmm. I was wondering about radionics, actually …

… for it is that which has properties that are, shall we say, multidimensional in nature. The ability to affect or remove these implants is present in those who seek to work in the metaphysical realm using the techniques of visualization and the, as we find you have called it, the laying on of hands in order that the healing touch of love and compassion might be directed according to the visualization which sees the implanted substance being dissolved by the intelligent energy which moves through the one serving as healer to the one seeking the healing.

This means of dissolving the implanted particle may be enhanced by the prayerful attitude of the one seeking the healing and any other entities of an harmonious vibrational character which would offer themselves in the healing circle at the time that the healing is attempted. Whether the circle is in the same location as the healer and one to be healed is unimportant. The important quality here is that the assistance is given at the time that the healing is attempted. There is the necessity of preparing the place of working for this healing in order that it is of a purified nature and offers only the most positively-oriented vibrations possible, so that the healing energies might be attracted and channeled with as little obstruction as possible from the lower vibrational nature of any place of working before it has been purified.

The purification of such a place of working might be accomplished in whatever manner has meaning to the one serving as healer and the one seeking the healing. Whether this be by visualization of light filling and cleansing the room, whether it be by the reading of sacred words, by the singing of sacred songs or chants, or by the physical cleansing that will symbolize the metaphysical cleansing that is desired is up to the discretion of those partaking in the healing service. Therefore, it is necessary to carefully prepare the place of the working and to prepare those that shall partake in this working in order that the energies provided might be enhanced as much as is possible.

Carla: May I ask a simple yes or no just to end? Would this by any chance be what Jesus meant when he said some demons can only come out by prayer?

I am Q'uo, and am aware of your query, my sister, and this is, indeed, the basis of the instructions which we have shared with you this evening. There is no greater healing power than that of true, heartfelt compassion given without condition and offered as a prayer to the one Creator which exists within one creation and which responds to the heartfelt plea for assistance.

Carla: Thank you. God bless.

I am Q'uo, and we thank you, my sister, and thank each within this circle of seeking this evening for inviting and allowing our presence. It has been a great joy and a great privilege to be able to blend our vibrations with yours and we cannot thank each enough for allowing this great experience of blending our vibrations with yours this evening. We at this time shall take our leave of this instrument and this group, leaving each, as always, in the love and in the light of the one infinite Creator. We are known to you as those of Q'uo. Adonai, my friends. Adonai. ☙

Intensive Meditation
April 12, 1989

Group question: The question this evening has to do with dreaming, the use that we can make of dreams in our lives and the various kinds of dreams that we might experience and how each might have something to offer us.

(Carla channeling)

I am Q'uo, and I greet you in the love and the light of the one infinite Creator in Whose service we answer your call for information this evening. We thank you for calling us to you and giving us the opportunity to share our thoughts with yours. It is most kind of you and most helpful to us, and we hope that we may in some humble way offer you a thought or two that you may use. However, we do warn you that we are not infallible, and, as always, we ask for you to use careful discrimination in absorbing any information, using your discernment and your own inner remembrance and recognition of what is true for you.

There are several types of dreams for all entities and for some there are more specialized types of dreams. We shall go over what this instrument would call the garden variety of dreams first, and that is the typically half-remembered, somewhat chaotic dream which has elements within it which are recognizable from the recent past. That which occurred within the recent past was not the appropriate solution for your mind or your emotions or your physical vehicle or your spirit and thusly a proportion of your mind is working out different ways of experiencing the situation which was not satisfactory to you or which held a meaning to you that was subconsciously recognized at the time. Thus, in the non-dramatic dream where the images are scattered and do not seem clear, it is important simply to recognize that you are more than casually troubled by something within the experiences which are being rehearsed within the dream experience in whatever distorted form. These are new items of distress and have not yet descended to the level of deep dreaming. These are the easiest dreams to work with, therefore, for although they may not seem as clear or as important, that small change which is dealt with in a daily manner, when balanced, becomes a very, very large amount over the long run.

It is important to remember the absolute necessity of the dreaming process. Therefore, even if you cannot remember the dreams at all, at least at first, never fear that you are lacking in the dream experience but assume that there is some other reason for the dreams to be removed from the ability to recall. In some cases, perhaps it is not well that the conscious mind deal with that which the subconscious mind finds conflicting and difficult. This will, however, cause the one who does not remember the dreams finally to experience a clearer dreaming process, perhaps in a more dramatic manner, say, than one who remembers dreams in a regular fashion and works with the images and their impact upon waking reality and what your own spirit has undergone in order to withstand or bear the catalyst that you re-experience in the dream.

The other, shall we say, garden variety type of dream is the so-called clear dreaming where one feels one is conscious within the dream. It is unusual for an entity to be able to cause the dream body to move and accept the living consciousness of the living self, therefore it is difficult, for instance, to cause the self in the dream to move limbs, eyes or mouth, however, it is perfectly possible to observe the self and these dreams are normally easier to remember. These dreams of clarity come to you after a certain amount of suffering.

It is not always relationships that cause one to suffer. One's progress through life may be a course which is causing suffering. One's lack of excellent equipment may be holding one back from what one feels to be one's true career. There are many, many things, beginning with those experiences within your younger times, that are linked in a chain throughout the years, where you as an entity have continually avoided balancing some certain disappointment, difficulty or challenge. These dreams often recur. Common themes are loss of control, lack of preparation for a test; basically those feeling times which indicate some sort of fear or negative emotion which the self is attempting to deal with while maintaining the integrity of the conscious mind. Dreaming is to be welcomed as it is an absolute spiritual necessity, an absolute physical necessity, [and] emotional and mental necessity. Therefore, not only the sleeping but the dreaming is to be valued for these two simple things alone.

Yet there are other types of dreams. There is the prophetic dream. This is caused by a sensitive instrument's picking up the simultaneous time in the future—which is actually simultaneous with right now—when something usually disastrous may happen. If it is a very clear dream, do not be surprised if it comes true. This is not a particularly common occurrence but is common enough to be mentioned. Also to be mentioned in this regard, with more interest, is that sort of clear dream which prophesizes in a parable or extended metaphor concerning choices to be made in the near future. These are dreams greatly to be valued and carefully to be studied.

There are two very esoteric types of dreams, which some have at some point within their lives, and some do not. It simply depends upon where that particular spirit is in its evolution. If one has come to this plane of existence from another in which memories are retained at some level, it is not surprising that some who call themselves wanderers would dream of adventures and heroics of one kind or another in the service of those who are desperate for help.

This is an experience which those who choose the path of service to others will inevitably go through. Thus, you are remembering that which has happened to you in another illusion and you need not expect it to make sense except as a fantasy; let it be a fantasy to you.

This is not an important type of dream, for you see you are now an Earth person. You have incarnated and are just as much under the planetary, natural law as any third-density Earth native. The real work of living a life in faith is living it within this illusion, at this time, with no evidence of glory or perfection outstanding. The challenge is to feel the glory and the majesty of creation, to feel the life that is lived now, to feel oneself opening as a flower to the Creator. These memories of aid do not truly help the émigré to Earth, for it is here that each spirit has chosen to make—once again—that great choice, of service to others or service to self. And we have all come with balanced karma, but we will not leave unless that karma remains balanced. Consequently, we urge each in this sort of dream experience to acknowledge that you, perhaps, had unusual adventures. But remember always that you are here to love and to accept love, to be wise and accept wisdom, to feel the time, to feel the space that is the appropriate time for each thing.

There is one more type of dream that some do have who are very intensely working upon the indigo-ray center, that is, who are doing work in consciousness. Such will remember being with a teacher but will not remember what is taught. This is, of course, as it should be, for those things which are of true help in taming the unruly spirit of mankind are far below the conscious level of control.

The aggressive impulse that has come to you through the type of body which each chose to inhabit, the variousness of free will, all of these things cause you to experience a normal, human experience. However, within the dream state, it is possible to receive instruction that may, over a period of time, aid in the instinctive reactions to challenging situations in order that your spirit may be calm and untroubled while the concern is put aside and the problem at hand approached as an enjoyable challenge. With this type of dream as well, it is very unlikely that you shall be able to remember that which you have been taught. On some occasions there will be one thought or one sentence which you are left with. It is well to write that down, for these are your teachers, these are those who are with you always, these are the Comforter which vibrates in that vibration which comforts you. So bless and welcome your teachers, they have much to tell you.

We have not touched upon the nightmare for the nightmare is not a different kind of dream. A nightmare can be that which was caused by the happenings of the day, that which was caused by repeated trauma in childhood. The classic, shall we say, nightmare is simply that type of dream which is very, very useful to examine, for what is feared, how it is feared and what the situation that is feared is actually like, this sort of working with the dream is most helpful.

Now, we are aware that it is felt sometimes that there is some help in offering difficult images in the dreaming process. However, we may suggest that you protect yourself by praying as you sleep, that is, as you enter the state of sleep. A simple prayer, the Lord's prayer or a simple childhood rhyme, thus surrounding yourself with the love and the light of the Creator which you remember instantaneously and Who instantaneously sheds grace abundant upon you.

The psychic greeting dream does exist but is so very specialized that it is extremely rare. Realize that your own lives have shown you abuse, terror, shame, humiliation and many extremes you would much prefer not having experienced. All of this is catalyst and is dealt with largely on the subconscious level. So your nightmares are actually attempts to heal and are to be valued as much as the happiest dream, for they represent a valiant and courageous subconscious mind which is quite determined to see you through that which has made you fear something or someone.

There is a waking dream which is identical to a sleeping dream in terms of the brain wave pattern of an entity. This is called the day-dreaming process and is closely linked to dreaming. It is recommended that this process be monitored, much as the dreaming process is monitored, that you may discover what it is that your mind is focused upon, what your true desires are. This is what you wish to know from within yourself.

So, as you approach your sleeping time, ask yourself inwardly to dream truthful dreams and to remember them well, and, if you can, write them down. We think you will find this most helpful. It is to be remembered in analyzing dreams that a principle this instrument has learned from psychology is true. That is: each character in your dream is an aspect of yourself. This is a very large key to the analysis of many dreams.

That which you do not realize, do not remember, and will never know, that which makes sleeping and dreaming utterly necessary, is that heavenly food and drink which each sleeping entity receives by the grace of the one infinite Creator. Much healing occurs in sleep, much forgiveness is engendered in sleep. Sleep is rest not only for the body; it is food, nourishment, absolutely necessary for the Spirit within. For you starve that Spirit, my children. You do not give that Spirit its wings in the daytime hours. You do not become excited passionately about what you are doing often enough. You have not enough zest. We encourage you to learn from your dreams, to grow from your dreams, and, taking one step at a time, to allow reality to become that which you, by analyzing your dreams, have found to be the peaceful, appropriate way of joy and dance for you.

At this time we would transfer to the one known as Jim in case any have questions at this time. I leave this instrument in love and light. I am known to you as Q'uo.

(Jim channeling)

I am Q'uo, and greet each again in love and light through this instrument. At this time it is our privilege to offer ourselves in the attempt to speak to those queries which may remain upon the minds. Is there a query at this time?

Questioner: One question. I have attached a significance before to people in dreams that are new to me. People that I don't know who appear in my dreams seem to be very significant. Would you please talk about that?

I am Q'uo, and am aware of your query, my brother. The significance, in general, for entities which appear in the dream are—we correct this instrument—is that the entity represents some aspect of the self. That this can be the case with a stranger underlines the quality of the self that has been seen, or as you might say, projected, upon the entity that is the stranger. In this instance, we would suggest that the unconscious mind is able to perceive a quality within the stranger that is obvious enough in importance to the conscious mind, being a significant aspect of the self, to bring to the attention of the self this quality. The quality may be felt rather than defined by the unconscious mind, therefore the strange entity, one unknown to the conscious self, is chosen in order that this feeling tone might be easily made apparent rather than finding this quality within a known entity and risking the coloration of the quality with what is already known in the familiar friend.

Is there another query, my brother?

Questioner: I feel like the question that I have has already been answered so I won't ask it again. I appreciate the answer, that makes sense.

I am Q'uo. We thank you for your query, my brother. Is there another query at this time?

Questioner: How, in a few sentences, could you tell someone that writing down dreams would help the spiritual life? I would like to interest some friends in doing it but I don't know how to tell or explain how it could be useful to them.

I am Q'uo, and we will do our best, my sister, to be brief with the description of the value of the dreaming process.

The conscious mind, the conscious entity, moves through its life observing itself and its interaction with others. This, many have called the Observer, that which talks to the self, critiques, motivates, reacts. Just so, the unconscious mind has such an observer quality that has a far broader point of view and a greater wealth of resources to offer in its commentary upon the conscious life. Thus, through the dreaming process is this commentary made available to the conscious self in order that both the conscious and unconscious portions of the mind—that male and that female quality—might be utilized in a fashion [that] when well done is of a balanced nature. Therefore, to rely only upon the conscious mind and its analysis of the life pattern is to utilize only half of the resources which are available to each entity within your illusion.

Is there another query, my sister?

Questioner: No, thank you very much … I had a question, it may not be interesting to everyone. I often have a dream where I see someone asking for help and I wonder if that is me asking for help?

I am Q'uo, and am aware of your query, my sister. The possibilities begin, of course, as we have said, with the self. One may see various aspects of the self painted into the dream landscape so that one may see each portion of the self as a piece in a larger puzzle or portrait. The utilization of other entities and situations may well make correlations between a portion of the self and the environment outside of the self and how the self relates to that environment. It is well in viewing any dream or portion of a dream to ask the self—we correct this instrument—to ask the self, if it is not obviously apparent, what each portion of the dream represents.

When there is uncertainty, it is well to begin a process of, shall we call it, "What if …?" What if that is so and so? What if that is myself as I relate to this person? What if that is this portion of myself from childhood? What if that is a portion of myself that had a certain experience recently? Ask any question which you can think of, for the conscious and unconscious mind will at this point feed likely possibilities to your conscious mind as you consider the dream and its meaning. Imagine as you consider each possibility that this is true for the time that you consider it. As this is done with each possibility, each "What if …?" examine the feeling within your heart so that when there is a recognition below the conscious level that you will be aware that the unconscious mind has resonated in harmony with that possibility. Thus, you may utilize both the conscious and unconscious mind in the analysis of the dream episode.

Is there another query, my sister?

Questioner: No, thank you.

I am Q'uo, and we thank you, my sister. Is there another query at this time?

Carla: If it wouldn't detune the instrument, I've often wondered why some people dream in black and white and some people dream in color. Please don't answer that if it would detune the instrument.

I am Q'uo, and am aware of your query, my sister, and appreciative of your concern as well. We shall do our best to speak to this query, though this instrument is somewhat dubious of our ability.

The dreaming in the color as is the life experience is a quality or ability which is not as widely utilized as one would imagine since it seems logical that the dreaming process would faithfully reflect the day-to-day experience and the record made by the eyes. However, for many, the process of dreaming contains enough filters, shall we say, that may be utilized for a variety of purposes that some dreams are remembered or rendered in more simple qualities, that of the black and white as you have called it. For some, this is the result of the distance one feels not only from the dreaming process, but more importantly and saliently, the distance one feels from the life experience. When there is little of the—we look for the correct words—*élan vitale* or gusto as you may call it, the zest that enlivens the daily round of activities so that there is little of the numbness, little of the lack of feeling, but great feeling and motivation from within the self to partake in the life experience, thus the filters that one has put in place, shall we say …

(Tape ends.)

Sunday Meditation
April 16, 1989

Group question: The question this evening, J, has to do with the basic sounds, shapes, colors, and mathematical equations that are found in nature. Is there a fundamental mathematical equation or relationship between any, or among all, of the basic shapes, the manifestations that we see in everyday life within the primal nature environment? Is there a correlation between the manifestation? Does it have a shape and a sound and a color and a mathematical equation that will tell us what it is if we only know one of those factors about it?

(Carla channeling)

I am Yom. I greet you in the love and the light of the infinite Creator. We are most pleased to be called to this group. We have never used this instrument. There is a good reason for not using this instrument. This instrument is very ill equipped to speak in scientific language. We shall, however, do the best we can with this instrument as your subject is one which, shall we say, we cover when it comes to the type of call that comes to Confederation entities. We tend, shall we say, to specialize so that each of us may learn a somewhat different lesson in service, given that we have a certain gift in our culture for one thing or another. For us, it happened to be that science led us to what you would call religion rather than religion leading us to science. Therefore, we are those of faith who learned through science rather than those of faith to whom science may seem to be an adversary. Thus, this is our subject and we are most grateful to have this call from you. We do apologize for this instrument's paucity of acceptable technical vocabulary, for there is much within your scientific jargon which we could use if this instrument were aware of the words. This instrument does not wish to go into trance, therefore, we shall have to give you the layman's version of our studied answer to your query which was, although awkwardly phrased, an important query we thought, and one which deserved, perhaps, to be restated in terms of its central question.

That is, is there an order to nature and does it somehow coincide with a metaphysical order? We feel that this was the question that was attempting to be asked, and it is a large subject. First of all, let us address the subject of order.

In the sense which most of your measuring devices could discover, there is only observed order and not true order. In terms of metaphysical order, the universe gives certain hints of the nature of this order. It does not occur to entities how fragile their physical vehicles are and how probable it would be, were there not absolute order, for there to be enough significant variation in the habitat of creatures such as yourselves that life would not be possible. One may gaze at the starry sky and notice that the light is neither imploding nor exploding. The stars remain fixed, although, we may note, there is always the oxymoron in spirituality. You gaze at the past as you gaze at the order of the universal sky. There would have to be infinite order, for the Creator is without order. Anything that is created is created first because the Creator had a Thought, a Thought of Love. It decided to create beings of Itself, so that they could exist in illusions, react as free conscious entities and send back to that Self that is the Creator within that information about the self to the Great Self.

Thus, the Creator created a principle, a Thought; it was Love. Love chose, out of all the ways to create, the particle called the photon. Light is your constant in a metaphysical way that is not at this time measurable by your scientists. The radiance of the sun which may physically be measured is notable in that it moves in a constant rate of speed. This velocity organizes and is the tune of love. It both is and moves. It is that which creates space and time.

As all is a unity, all things within the creation that is local are, indeed, fractions of that which you may call unit velocity or the speed of light, for the photon creates all that there is and creates it, not as your scientists believe by the creation of mass, but by the creation of vibratory energy patterns in a severely hierarchical and mathematical order.

The link between many unrelated observed simultaneous periodic happenings is a link that is tangential to that basic common denominator which you call the speed of light, it being the vibration of intelligent energy and that which your universe must be builded from. There are hierarchies of order. Much as in your classifications of plants and animals, there are the phyla, the genera, the species. So in anything which the Creator has wrought, there are hierarchies of energies. Thus, within the world which you call your natural world, there is a good deal of order.

Now, some of this order must seem somewhat random because it has to do with time rather than space. We have trouble expressing our thoughts through this instrument but will forge ahead as best as we can to try to explicate this hierarchy. It is as though there were one universe which contained one great principle, that principle being Love. In all forms, from animal to mineral, to the vegetable kingdom, to spirits of air and water, wind and fire, to gods and goddesses and planets, to all the mythical thoughts of all the cultures, there is, indeed, an order. Yet some of this order is, shall we say, the "y" axis, and your scientists move along the "x" axis. The intersection at the very middle is the constant. The universe is one and expresses itself as love.

Now, it is understandable that gazing closer and closer at an object with the tools at your disposal, your scientists would gradually find that nothing can be measured. You are part of an intelligent infinity. You are all one thing. Finitude is apparent but it is an illusion. Press that illusion and it shall fail. The average, as this instrument would say, man on the street does not know how to press the illusion except by the use of mind-altering substances. The thinker, the religionist, and the scientist have far more resources. And they shall discover chaos and order and chaos and order once they discover the hierarchical nature of consciousness, for all is perfect in its consciousness and life and all is the Creator, yet there are various manifestations of consciousness, from the least conscious rock to the self-awareness that each of you who seek now show as you choose to seek the truth. Can you measure yourself? Do you have order? Yes, my friends, you are creatures of geometrical order. Your mind can be understood. Its resources may be used, but may we say to you, that along the "y" axis of time, there is that which is called patience. All the emotions are those created by time. Emotions are to be given their due in understanding as best you can that which is the natural order of the self-conscious entity.

Therefore, each of you must think and feel. And you will find that your scientists will make their breakthroughs not only as those who use those numbers which have proven effective in creating useful things in the past, they will also be using themselves as instruments—their intuition, their deep knowledge, the discipline of their personality. To this approach will the illusion offer the most clarity of observation. We know not how to offer you a mechanical way to gaze with this wisdom at the world of nature. We cannot, because of the restrictions of infringement upon free will, discuss the qualities of such things as the use of the voice in speaking or singing, or instruments in making tunes or colors or shapes. We can say specifically that one may think of some of the shapes which one may see among your peoples as you might think of the brands of your cattle.

This instrument is challenging me again. Pardon me, we must pause.

(Pause)

(Carla channeling)

I am Yom. I am again with you. This instrument is very keen on the challenging, we must say. She hurls herself at us, and we would be most fearsome and want to leave, indeed, if we did not come able to say, "Christ is Lord." This child has Christ as Lord, thus, we may say that. We may therefore stay, but, my goodness, this little entity is very fierce.

Now, we were speaking of the metaphysical order of the human personality. It is to be, because of the needs of time, a slow and gentle penetration of the subconscious by the conscious mind. It is a very, very good idea to remember that that which is the most real thing within this illusion, that is, the human spirit, has both the "x" axis of space and the "y" axis of time. It is, therefore, an entity of love and it must be approached lovingly. The subconscious must be wooed, not only gently, carefully, discriminatingly, but also with gentleness, with returned passion, with respect, with praise, and with honor.

It may seem unnecessary in meditation to approach the silence as one would approach a lover, yet we ask you to sit and listen as you would listen to the one you adore, waiting with bated breath for that moment when you are aware that you and the Creator are lost in light together.

This experience is the teacher that is the basis of all of those inquiries that each field of study shall make that shall offer a more appropriate model of the illusion, for once one understands the reality, one may see, of course, the illusions are carefully, systematically and hierarchically engineered. We may suggest one application that a member that is present in this group would find especially interesting, and that is that there are connections between sounds, shall we say, and color, however, perhaps the most satisfactory blending of "x" and "y" axis is the use of the human voice in the chanting and praying simultaneously. For there is the notation, black and white upon the page of music, the words to speak clearly, and then the "y" axis of emotion, the breath of finitude, the time factor. You see time as a river. See time, rather, as a woman and woo her. Enjoy her and honor her, for that is one of those measurements which is beyond knowledge. Lost in infinity, the parentheses of birth and death in an incarnation is not measurable. There we have a random effect, yet it is not random, as many things are not random. They are choices made at some hierarchical level of creation by a Creator, which above all things in the vast illusion of the infinity that we call space and time …

We must pause. We are Yom.

(Pause)

(Carla channeling)

We are Yom. We are again with this instrument, but we find that we have a fatigued instrument and we are losing this instrument, therefore we would attempt to transfer to the one known as Jim, if this instrument would accept the contact.

We will now leave this instrument in love and light. We are known to your group as Yom.

(Pause)

(Jim channeling)

I am Yom, and greet each once again through this instrument. This is a new instrument for us, and we are grateful to be able to speak our thoughts through it, however, it may take some coordination, shall we say, upon our part and upon the part of the instrument as well, before we have a satisfactory contact. We are happy to work with this instrument and shall do so as we complete that thought which we have begun through the one known as Carla.

My friends, as you are trapped within the infinity of all that is by your experience within your illusion, you find yourselves pondering the relationships between yourself and that which is about you. And we have spoken this evening of those relationships having as their unifying factor that quality of the Creator which is called amongst your peoples the photon—light, my friends. You travel and are at your very heart moving within this light which has love as its product, love that is formed in such and such a may according to the vibrations of light that has formed all that is. You find yourselves attempting to penetrate the mysteries of your existence, which means that you attempt to penetrate the nature of love and the nature of light and the nature of free will which has created both of these qualities, the nature of the one infinite Creator, that Creator which has chosen to set in motion the creation as you know it, and the creation that lies beyond that which you know, that which rests in mystery.

As you explore on the equations of your relationships, on the qualities of your experience, you will find that the components of these equations can be reduced to your ability to accept more of yourself, of the creation, and of your experience as being whole and perfect within itself, lacking nothing. There is within each human heart the ability to express this acceptance in a direct ratio with the sincere desire to know what you call truth, for as you sincerely seek the truth of your experience and of yourself, you will find that all has the foundation of love and the qualities of light as it vibrates in a specifically defined field that gives you a framework or an environment in which to exercise your love. Thus, the creation has been made that you might play, as it were, study, romp as does the young kitten in the fields of experience that are made possible by the vibrational frequencies of the light which enfolds you and the love which empowers you.

At this time, we feel that we have spoken upon this point in relationship to the ability of these instruments to express, in general terms, an introductory exploration into the unifying factors of shape, of sound, of color, and of the conceptualizations that depend therefrom. Therefore, we shall at this time ask if we may speak to any further queries which those present may have for us, realizing, of course, that we have a difficulty with the vocabulary of these instruments.

Questioner: I have a question. You mentioned that sound has a relationship with color. Does sound or vibration also have a manifestation as form or shape?

I am Yom. The phenomenon of sound that is the vibration that is perceived by the ear has not only the color that is caused to spring to the clear mind, but may have a shape according to the, shall we say, receptive abilities of the one who hears the vibration. This is to say that there is an interrelationship and an interaction between the vibration which is heard and the mind of the one who hears the vibration. The color correlation is more nearly, shall we say, of an objective nature, and may be formed according to the desires of the entity experiencing the sound vibration. There is, however, also the possibility that if the source of the sound vibration desires, there may be a transmission of concept or form in what you may loosely call the holographic picture that may be perceived, then, by the receiver. There is in that case, then, a more definite image which is possible to construct according to the construction of the sound vibrations, these vibrations being multiple in nature in order to construct the image.

Is there another query, my brother?

Questioner: Yes. When a thought is created, does this thought become a vibration or is it already a vibration that, again, is manifested as a form?

I am Yom. You may see each thought that is created by the thinker as being similar to the message written upon the sand next to your body of water. The action of the waves will erase the drawing if it is not repeated often enough. The thought, which has but small duration, then, does not retain its integrity over a long span of time without the re-thinking or re-creation of the thought.

Is there another query, my brother?

Questioner: Yes. Within the electromagnetic spectrum, we are limited in our instruments to visual phenomenon, auditory phenomenon and tactile phenomenon. Are we also limited to shapes within these phenomenon and creation of forms? Are there some basic shapes that we are locked into in this field that we exist in? Are there basic—five or six basic shapes reoccurring in nature?

I am Yom, and within your third-density environment we find that this is, indeed, true, for the experience that you now enjoy has certain parameters that preclude further construction of shapes that would exist beyond those which you now know as the fundamental geometric shapes. We find that it is difficult to describe with the words of your illusion that which may lie beyond the illusion in terms of the shapes, those that would partake also in time. Therefore, we must apologize for our inability to describe beyond the limits of the words and the limit of this instrument's vocabulary.

Is there another query, my brother?

Questioner: Yes. Are the basic shapes squares, triangles, lines, pyramids …

(Side one of tape ends.)

(Jim channeling)

I am Yom, and am again with this instrument. As we perceive the query, we might suggest that the basic shapes which you have described are those which are, indeed, fundamental to your illusion, and we would suggest that the limitation that exists is one which is related, as we spoke previously, to the parameters of your illusion which make it possible.

Carla: I have a question. Do circular shapes and spirals have more to do with the "y" axis than the "x," more to do with time than space?

I am Yom. These shapes have a great deal, indeed, to do with that which you call time, for their construction suggests that which is eternal, that which has no beginning and no end and their utilization as a form of metaphysical geometry, if we may use these terms, is to suggest to the deeper mind the concept of eternity and the mystery which surrounds it in order that the seeker might utilize these shapes as a type of visualized mantra that will awaken certain portions of the unconscious mind that has contained within it the more fundamental perceptions regarding the self in its relationship to the current illusion and the movement beyond the current incarnation in order that the seeker might begin to relate itself to those qualities that it currently sees as beyond the self, but which, in truth, are contained in a larger perception of the self.

Is there another query?

Carla: So even the DNA double helix points directly to the mystery of the Creator in infinity, is that right?

I am Yom, and this is quite acceptable, my sister.

Carla: Thank you, Yom.

Questioner: I have another question. If … is the point of the "x" and the "y" axis our present incarnation? And if so, then we exist also in the … beyond the present incarnation at the same time and we create and generate forms and realities coexistent with the present incarnation. Is this true?

I am Yom. We find that your observation has a basic correctness to it, though we are unsure as to our ability to add significantly the ramifications which we feel are significant. The intersection of the, as you have called it, "x" and "y" axis, is a point within an incarnation, as well as being, perhaps, seen as the incarnation itself. In this description, then, you may see the point as not just the point, but as describing a progression or that which would begin to appear as the moving line as the incarnation itself progressed. However, this again lacks refinement, for the line does not move in a singular path, but has variation according to both the "x" and the "y" axis as well as varying according to certain, shall we call them, internal rhythms or predilections of each individual seeker.

Therefore, there is oftentimes a contact with or an awakening of latent portions of the personality or of the greater self which would add a certain influence that would also need to be registered upon the point that has become now a line, which again begins to move in other directions so that there is described that which begins to shape—we correct this instrument—begins to take a shape or a form, so that the point then becomes the line, then becomes three-dimensional, then begins to take the form of a picture so that you might see the incarnation as completing a kind of sculpture, so that after a certain point, the analogy of the "x" and the "y" axis becomes too simplistic in order to describe the entire range of this process, that is, the self moving through an incarnation that moves through a creation that is itself moving within and beyond itself.

Is there another query?

Questioner: I'd like to ask that a different way. We exist in the third density but we also exist in the fourth, in the fifth, in the sixth simultaneously, and probably more. And we are able to leave the present density and see different times and spaces and personalities of ourselves. Is that right?

I am Yom. Again, we do not wish to mislead by oversimplification, for there is a great deal of what you would call complexity and extrapolations and ramifications to this simple statement. For many, this is, indeed, true, that there are parallel existences that may, in certain instances, be tapped into, as you may call it, so that information might be received in one fashion or another, whether through dreaming, through the creative process, through the intuition or through information that simply appears within the mind complex.

There is, through this communication to the self from other portions of the self, the attempt to widen the point of view so that there is the possibility of enhancing the current incarnational experience in a manner which fulfills the goals for the incarnation that were set prior to its inception. However, there are some entities that have as their primary experience this incarnation and this incarnation alone, for their objectives have a far simpler construction and are in need of the more, shall we call them, nuts and bolts type of experiences that will allow for the beginning of the construction of the larger conception of the self that shall at a later incarnation, shall we say, be added upon.

We would ask for another two or three queries before we finish this session with this instrument.

Questioner: I have a question.

Questioner: Go ahead. I have one more, but I'd like to … I've been dominating, I'm sorry. Somebody was ask …

Questioner: I would like to ask a question. This is kind of not on the same subject but it's a … it's a kind of a burning question. Is it possible that—is it possible to make a wrong decision? I have to make some very important decisions with people that I associate myself with in the next few days and there are many possibilities, there are many ways to go, and no clear-cut answers as to which way to decide, and is it possible that we can decide upon a destiny line or is it already preordained that we have to go through certain experiences? And if so, can we make our own decision? I guess I just need to be more at ease about that.

I am Yom. This is a question that has merit and we appreciate the opportunity to speak to it. Within your illusion, and, indeed, within any illusion in which conscious entities exist there is only experience which may be had. It is not possible to make what you would call within your illusion a mistake, for the experience which has been set out for you by you with the aid of others under whose care you exist has been programmed, shall we say, into your subconscious mind in a fashion which will allow you to perceive within others and within various situations that which you need to perceive, in the way that you need to perceive it, in order that the opportunity be presented to you to pursue those lessons and those services which you have felt appropriate within this life experience. This is to say that there is a subconscious lens, as it were, through which all experience is perceived.

Thus, two entities may look upon the same situation and draw from it separate conclusions according to those lenses which have been placed previous to the incarnation and have been refined through free will during the incarnation. As you make choices, you will discover that you perceive that which is within your ability. Therefore, to perceive, it is necessary that you allow for the greatest expertise in perceiving to determine that which you feel is of importance to you, that which is your desire, that which you ask or expect from a situation.

When you have decided this through contemplation, through prayer, and through meditation and have done so with sincerity, you will discover that there is a certain ordering of priorities that becomes more apparent to your conscious mind as you pursue this ordering of priorities. You will provide yourself with those opportunities that you have determined to be appropriate previous to the incarnation and you will have provided yourself with these opportunities in the most efficacious manner that is possible. Though there are, indeed, no mistakes within your experience, or within any experience, there is the possibility of greater or lesser ease in presenting the self with that opportunity to learn. Therefore, we suggest that you take the necessary time to ask yourself what it is you desire so that those choices that await you might begin to become more clearly ordered according to their appropriateness at this particular time within your experience.

Is there a further query, my brother?

Questioner: No, thank you.

Questioner: I have a question. Earlier you said, if I understood it correctly, that basically we do not create with a single thought, thought only one time. If I understood that correctly, could you elaborate just a little bit on the process of reinforcement of creation by thought when that thought is reinforced through repetition?

I am Yom, and we shall use the analogy of the artist. The first thought that one may begin to create with is as the beginning idea with which the artist begins. If the idea has no merit, if the artist has not the time to pursue it, the idea, perhaps, will fade. If the artist feels, however, that there is merit, perhaps the first outline of a sketch will present itself in the mind. Perhaps this shall be carried further and shall be put upon the paper with the outline. If there is further inspiration for this beginning work of art or thought, perhaps there shall be the elaboration, the adding of color, the refining, perhaps, after the preliminary drawings have been made. There shall be the sculpting in clay; perhaps the final product shall be bronzed.

As an entity begins to think a thought, and finds that the thought holds the interest, that it has merit, the entity will begin to think further upon the thought within the mind, adding the ramifications, deciding that there is a small thing that might be done now to aid the vitalization of this thought. Perhaps continued thinking will produce continued action. Perhaps the entity shall then find that the thought begins to take upon itself a certain life of its own, and there is a communication developed between the entity and the thought, with the thought seeming to offer suggestions as to how it might become a thing within the experience of the thinker.

It is necessary in this process that there be some action of a concrete nature taken at some point within the thinking process, for though it is true that the mind is a powerful tool that has the ability to create, it is also true that, as with any form of what you might call the ritualized white magic, there must be grounding within the physical material illusion of that which is within the metaphysical realms at its inception. Therefore, as you continue the dialogue between yourself and the thought, you will find a natural process of creation being played through this dialogue. Then you will begin to discover that this is not an exotic process reserved for but a few, but a process which is constantly being utilized by each entity at all times.

There is, however, the possibility of utilizing this process within any sphere of one's experience and not just within the more mundane levels of the daily round of activities, as one easily visualizes the running of errands, the attending of the class, the doing of the work. These become as easy as the breathing, the walking, and the looking. The ability to utilize this process in a manner which is new to the seeker is what is generally called the creative ability and is one which needs only the refinement in order to be utilized within the life experience.

Is there a further query, my brother?

Questioner: I have a final question I'd like to ask. When the time and space axis creates a physical entity that we are in this creation, what happens when another consciousness enters in that with us, such as intervention by star people or so-called possessions? Do we have a dual consciousness and does one subjugate the other? How does that work?

I am Yom. Whether an entity has a shared experience with those of the, shall we call it, extraterrestrial nature or an experience with a terrestrial entity of the same family and neighborhood or geographical location, the consciousness that experiences the blending of energies, for however long it might last, is a consciousness that remains intact and that which has the ability or the power to continue exercising it's own free will, unless it shall for any reason, conscious or unconscious, choose to give that power to another, as those who study your psychology and sociology will attest.

There is, in the relationship of human beings, the continual trading of the power over the self between various entities for a great variety of reasons, each of which has a relationship to the central theme of the incarnation, the ability to give and receive love under a great variety of conditions, therefore, the relationship that has as its foundation the complete power to exercise free will vested within each entity, each entity having a variety of lessons and services that it desires to perform, and therefore when it joins with any other entities there is the interrelationship and interaction that affects both entities in a manner which is described by the preincarnative choices that, in themselves, form the lens of which we spoke previously, that which is the subconscious predilection to see certain events in certain ways.

At this time we would ask for the final query.

Carla: Well, thank you. I didn't think that I was going to get to ask one. I was really interested in something, uh … twice, well once, you gave … and then I went ahead and channeled it but then I stopped and challenged a fairly specific piece of information, and I know that you were a little irritated, but I really did need to know, and the second time you were starting to say something and I thought to myself, I'm going to challenge before I channel that and then I thought, oh gosh, you know, I'm really tired. Maybe I'd better not leave the responsibility of challenging to myself. I'll just stop and see if Jim can get it past the challenge and Yom passed the challenge to you.

Now, was the reason that I was able to get that information about sound and words that I didn't channel was just you'd given me the concept and I just refused to channel it without checking with you? I'd really like to know, is it because it's a validation of something the person interested already knows? Or is there some other rule in your area of information where you can give more specific information?

I am Yom. The point which you query about is a point which we did not feel was potentially that which could infringe upon the free will, for the description of the vibration of sound in this instance was a description which we find has been made available to this group through a previous contact and was therefore that which already existed in the memory of this group.

Carla: Hmmm, not mine. Ha. Thank you.

Therefore, we find no risk of infringing upon the free will when the free will has been made aware of information previously.

Carla: Very good, thank you.

I am Yom, and we thank you, my sister. We apologize for the necessity to bring this particular session to a close but we find that each instrument has had a somewhat wearying day and this makes concentration necessary for a clear contact somewhat difficult. Therefore, we shall express our great gratitude at being able to join this group and utilize these instruments this evening. It has been a great span of your time since we have had the honor of joining your group as other than observer. We thank each for extending this invitation and look forward to any future opportunity in which our service might be appreciated. We are those of Yom and leave each in the love and in the light of the one infinite Creator. Adonai, my friends. ✤

L/L Research

Sunday Meditation
April 23, 1989

Group question: The spectrum of queries for the evening revolves around the concept of is there a basic descriptive equation or simple set of factors that can tell you what a fern can be made from, what a musical phrase can be made from, what a human being is made from, sounds [are made from]; what is our relationship to each portion of the creation, and how can we know that we have a relationship to it? Is it worthwhile to attempt to find the reason why an acorn will produce an oak tree every time, and why any specific seed will grow a specific plant each time that it is grown? What's the basic equation to which each can be reduced? And how are we related to each thing that has being?

(Carla channeling)

I am Yom. We greet you in the love and in the light of the infinite Creator. We are most grateful to be speaking with you this evening. Although this channel, as we have mentioned before, is not one which has a large capacity to speak in scientific terms, yet may we say to you, my friends, without seeming to be anything but informative, that we welcome the use of instruments such as this one, even though the instrument has not the vocabulary which might, perhaps, make things clearer to a, shall we say, technologically oriented person, for this instrument is more sensitive to the tuning process and is resistant to detuning.

We must preface all remarks tonight by expressing that our intent is not to explicate the mechanical aspects of the creation which may be measured or predicted in one way or another. The gift or service which we hope we have to offer to those of your planet is an ever-increasing realization of each entity's own capacity by will and faith to grow in love and light, to more and more become one with the infinite Creator and more and more to be a channel for an infinite love and an infinite light that humankind does not have in its native design, nor was ever intended to have. So we shall be speaking with a philosophical or spiritual slant, and, therefore, we are satisfied to use this instrument, ignorant though she is.

We also thank this instrument for persisting in the challenging process. There were multiple challenges and a very persistent negative entity has now left the vicinity. We say this because we know that each of you is a channel, and each of you channels each and every day. We strongly suggest the use of the challenge or the simple question, "What spiritual principle does this action, does this person, does this relationship, does this interaction call to mind? How would I prefer to accelerate my spiritual growth or aid another in its spiritual growth at this point?" This we hope is something that is never far from your minds through the day, and whatever you may ask us, it is an eye to the practical as well as the theoretical that we make our answers, for we are not those that simply say that the Creator is love and love is the Creator. This is true, but this gives the student no steps to take from the miasma of the confusion of everyday life to the truths of eternity.

Thus, listen with the inner ear as well as the outer to what we have to say, and above all, as always, refrain from thinking of us as an information source that is always right. We consider ourselves fallible, and we hope you do too. Trust your own intuition, your own sense of recognition of the truth. If it does not ring true for you, it is the truth which does not work for you. Simply toss it aside and move on. You will meet it again one day, and it will be helpful, or you have gone past it already. Waste not time in worry about whether what we have to say is true or untrue, for you shall recognize truth as if remembering it.

The spiritual principle that governs the likeness of forms upon various levels of the hierarchical nature of your creation is "as above, so below." That is, you will find repeated again and again certain motifs which are those motifs which express the Creator's original creation of a certain kind of life form which was designed to carry a certain amount of consciousness, or what you would call, perhaps, Christ consciousness, that is, the God-self within. That which is elemental is that which is made up almost entirely of the love and the light of the infinite Creator. There is only minimal consciousness; therefore, there is no need for movement or thought. The ground upon which you stand, the rocks, water, chemicals, the wind, the fire are of a simple mind, completely lost in the Creator.

Thus, one who is a true magician that may cause changes in consciousness at will, one with faith, may, indeed, move the mountain or cause that to happen which seems a miracle. Such is the nature of the will at the level of humankind.

The nature of the air and the fire is that of radiance or movement. The nature of earth and rock is that which complements and is fecund to wind and fire. That which is called the water is to the elements the Eucharist or blessing or thanksgiving which does bless and balance in the sense that a mother balances a family, the Earth plane. It is the only element besides that of fire which contains movement. The movement of fire expresses the excellence of destruction, the other side of the coin of knowledge. The water is the nurturer, the mother aspect of the Creator and is a blessing to first density as well as second and third, it being of a crystalline nature, much as is the rock. It is, therefore, more able to be charged with consciousness. Wind and fire may be charged with consciousness, but only momentarily because of the movement therein.

When we see the various intricacies of development of life forms within the animal and the vegetable kingdoms, we see that there are many, many roads which the Creator tried in an effort to find life forms that would be satisfactory to this particular sphere which you call Earth. The design of it was careful, and there was an attempt at balance so that each species had a reason for being, a natural food which was available to it, and that group mind which is the level of consciousness at that level of being. That is, the being has movement and moves towards the light. This recapitulates the very beginning of the life force, which is the spiral.

The Creator's variety of life forms is difficult to grasp or believe. The generosity and creativity of the infinite One in creating ways for consciousness to express are most wonderful, and we know that each of you as you have gazed at the beautiful flowering trees and shrubs, the plush greens of new leaves and fresh lawn, the forests coming alive with birds and deer, that you are aware of the particular beauty of your planetary sphere at this time. Realize that this sphere was designed according to a metaphysical law that is far more important to understand than the mechanical laws of growth, and that is that the creation serves each other. Each species controls the population of another species and, in turn, itself is controlled so that all may have their fair share. The trees that grow upon your planet, those great beings, and all that is green, exhales the oxygen which is needed by second and third-density entities, who in turn offer back to those green things around, in symbiotic fashion, the carbon dioxide which is needed for their growth and blooming. It is a creation whose spiritual principle is unity. The term that your scientists have used to describe the basic unity of any environment is ecological balance, or the ecology of an environment.

We believe that is all we shall say about the repetitive shapes of those life forms which exist in each case, though one may find the predictive mathematical formula for prediction of that which is grown from that which is within the seed. That which cannot be predicted and cannot be measured by your present scientists is far more important, and that is the level of consciousness within the plant. For just as some people within your culture are born only to die young and have little energy, so it is with the smallest seed. It may make the creation that follows the pattern of the spiral energy of life within it, but it may be a weak, poor specimen and die quickly, its consciousness returning to the genetic pool from which that particular species springs. Other seeds or acorns or any sort of reproductive material may be full of a metaphysical vitality which includes that which you know of as will, the will to live and bloom and flourish.

Now, the relationship between you who are above and the plants and animals that are below is that you with your consciousness may affect that which is of second density, or even that which is of first, by your love of it, not because it is mechanically able to be predicted, but because it is life and is part of the one great original Thought which unifies all of us. The response to that thought whenever you see it, if you are centered, is to love, or, if there is not love in the artifacts of the moment, to do that which must be done for love's sake, your love of the infinite Creator. The equation need go no further than that. This alone is a perfectly acceptable reason for action. Thus, an interaction that you may have with animals, with plants, even with those things of first density, may invest them with more consciousness, more love, more beingness, until finally the consciousness that has permeated this life form which is so miraculous does not move back into the gene pool of that particular species, but has become individualized and has begun the walk towards the third density and full self-consciousness.

It would be predictable, you see, that nature would repeat itself, as the shapes of nature, that which may use fuel and live within this atmosphere, though they are only limited by the imagination of the Creator which is infinite, are, indeed, limited by the necessities of finding a way to fuel the physical vehicle during its life experience. Gaze through the microscope at anything, and you will find many, many, many interesting things. Gaze in the telescope, and you will find the same interesting things. The more sophisticated your knowledge, the more mystical you shall become as a scientific inquirer, for the more that you will be able to see the part that is played by the wills of those third-density entities which observe that which is occurring within the acorn, the seed, the animal behavior, and so forth.

The key to this is "as above, so below," a saying very old in your culture, but very, very true. You may think of the culture in which you live, the ecology in which you live, as the very tip, lower tip of an upside-down tree. And as you ascend this tree, it grows many, many ramifications and becomes larger and more complex. And finally at the end of a lifetime of seeking, you have moved up the tree of knowledge, and you move into the root system, rooted in what you would call the Kingdom of Heaven. And you find that this tree is eternal, and that life forms recapitulate themselves because of the Creator's sense either of aesthetics or humor.

Now, when you gaze upon the artifacts of humankind, you may not count and rely upon the naturalness of these artifacts. There are those artists which draw or speak of reality peculiar to their own self-consciousnesses which may not resonate with other's consciousnesses. However, for purposes of personal growth, may we suggest the extreme efficacy, when the mind is in turmoil, of turning from all that seems confused, moving into a natural atmosphere if possible, and raising the voice in song. For with your breath, your consciousness, your faith and your will, you may change that consciousness and remove yourself from that confusion. At the end of your time of singing, you have cleared out much emotion that, kept inside, is not liable to redound to your comfort and general health, shall we say.

Thus, we may say to you, yes, it is interesting and permissible for you to move into nature with all the measurements, observations and so forth at your command, but there is always the consciousness factor. There is a growing amount of consciousness as one comes closer to third density. And when one finds oneself in third density, we may tell you, if your will is strong enough, those who should die and will to live, live. Those who should live and will to die, will die. This is the degree of free choice which your consciousness permits you. Thus, we suggest that you heartily move towards a consciousness which thinks of the mystery of the love of the Creator; that your purpose in picking up each piece of paper, in doing your chores, in doing the most menial of jobs, your purpose is to express your love of the infinite One. It has nothing to do with pleasing others, relating to others or dealing with others.

The first step in consciousness is that decision which you make to remain within the purview of what this instrument would call Christ consciousness. For that which is metaphysical in third density becomes completely sovereign over that which is of the material of the physical body, and, indeed, in cases of those with unusual gifts, shall we say, the disposition of objects outside the physical body.

The reason that the singing is most important is that the intellect does not know what the subconscious knows. The intellect, therefore, will take upon itself the concern, the worry, the analysis, and so forth. In more than half of the cases, shall we say, of humankind's concern, once an analysis that is accurate has satisfied an entity, the faith and the will need to replace the concern, the worry, and the fear. And as you raise the voice in praise and thanksgiving, in joy, in laughter, in fun, so you occupy your mind and allow the strength of your faith and your emotions to move to the situation at hand and with their greater wisdom subtly rearrange things, so that as you finish singing, as you finish praising the one infinite Creator, or as you finish meditating in silence, that which seems to be thus and thus transforms itself because of your faith in a positive outcome.

We realize this seems to stray far afield from the land of microscopes, repeating patterns in nature, and so forth. But the Creator's order is such that were there no consciousness, all would move in an animalistic and balanced fashion which would support all. It is the distortions of humankind which have created the situation which rests upon your planet at this time. By your body you can only manifest the fruits of that which comes from within [of your] love for this planet and for each other and for the one infinite Creator.

That which is designed a certain way finds itself to be a natural form which has an equation, is interesting, but that that same form is completely a consciousness of service to all that is around it is a far more central truth, for that which you understand with the heart results in communication with the consciousness within, that natural shape about you. And it thrives upon your words of love and encouragement, just as you thrive upon the inspiration of the one infinite Creator. You are not the Creator, but your consciousness is one quantum leap ahead, and so it is as if you were turning back to help the little ones to grow as you speak to nature and express your appreciation, your heartfelt emotion, your caring and compassions and love of the beauty that is all about you.

You too, you see, grow according to natural genetic laws. The spiral of life within you without consciousness is as, shall we say, soulless or dead as any other flower that springs upon the planet, blooms in its brief hour, and passes into the compost heap. You must not take your bodies too seriously, but live by will and faith. It is good to care for the body, for it is spiritualized by your consciousness, and as you take care of it, so you shall be able to serve longer and more efficaciously. Thus, to take the best care you may understand of your physical vehicle is not selfishness, but merely a recognition that your physical vehicle is the temple of your consciousness, the God within.

But your essence, my friends, and the essence of all that is, is not that which can be measured in the acorn, although it is in the acorn, that which cannot be measured in the fertilized ovum. It is a matter of the strength of will and faith that that life form may be capable of. You have all seen the flowers and trees and shrubs that are strong to grow, and grow regardless, and those that seem hothouse flowers, unable to deal with the rigors of life in the sun and wind. So it is with entities, yet you, my friends, are self-conscious, and you know the value of desire. Desire carefully to seek the truth of the creation. Desire compassionately to love each other, and much more shall be learned than the gazing at the order which permeates this local illusion. It must be remembered that the order is complete and the illusion is complete; therefore, all order will eventually break down as the illusion is penetrated. This does not mean that there has not been order; it simply means that the illusion has been penetrated.

This illusion was not meant to be penetrated. It was meant for scientists and artists, workmen and musicians, and all humankind alike to labor under the shadow of unknowing, because it was designed for you not that you grow in such and such a way; that information is stored in each cell of your body. That which you seek upon this planet at this time is a consciousness that moves closer and closer to the one great original Thought of love. As you do this, you increase your vitality, your will, your ability to abide through difficult times, and your courage in being able to leave that behind which has not worked, and to grasp that new experience which holds the promise of transformation.

You, my friends, are entities of choice. The order of the second density is such that there is no choice. Each living being moves towards the sun, in some way is affected by each rhythm daily, monthly, seasonally, yearly, and so are your second-density bodies affected. Of course, it is well to understand that which affects the physical vehicle. And among your scientists there are many who are studying those physical vehicles which were used to create the physical vehicle which you now enjoy. One may learn much of the animal within by doing the research …

(Side one of tape ends.)

(Carla channeling)

… corrupted, shall we say, and changed, not transformed, but simply moved back into that which is the producer of future fertility for other second-density life forms.

It is when an entity becomes self-conscious that an entity enters into imperishable things. Scientists may use science to come to the conclusion that there is a great mystery which must be taken notice of. Those who work with artistic muses find an easier time of coming to grips with that fact, for they are working more with the subconscious than are those which measure and calibrate and reproduce and hypothesize. Nevertheless, any form of living whatsoever that you have chosen for yourself will contain those things which you need to learn at this time, and if you become uncomfortable or feel that you are no longer learning from a situation, then you have the freedom given you by the one infinite Creator, in spite of the inevitability of how you had to grow, based on the fertilized ovum of mother and father. You have freedom to make choices, to will to be, to will to do, to will to say. You may will to live by faith; you may will to abide.

You have become a co-creator with the Creator. Value the artifacts of humankind in this light and see what those with special ears or eyes or hearts may offer in enlarging your sympathy, and, if we may use the word, understanding of the deeper self which is never plumbed by the biological self, but is needed desperately by the self which, as a spiritual, imperishable entity, wishes to learn to live by faith.

We are aware that this has been in some ways a most unsatisfactory discussion, yet we felt it would be helpful to each to reemphasize the center of learning about all things that is the inner room. When you enter it within your heart, shut the door, and be alone with the Creator. Do not attempt to visualize this occurrence; let it occur to you as it will. But ask. Ask with much intensity of hope and desire that you may be with the one original Thought of love. For you love that Creator, and you wish to do all that you do out of love of that Creator. And in that consciousness, much shall begin to become apparent to you about the entire range of human knowledge, depending upon that upon which you work, that was never clear before. It is a matter of getting the self, the questioning, curious, restless, gypsy self, put to one side long enough to sit in silence with infinite love. That infinite love is not far away. It resides within your inner room, yet there is the door that you must open yourself. It will never be opened for you in the normal course of events. Remember to open that door, to step inside, and to make use of the deepest portion of yourself, that self which moves in a geometric and regular and, yes, a repetitive way, hierarchical, into the racial mind, the planetary mind, the archetypical mind, and the mind of the Creator.

It is possible that [the] mathematician that is a mystic shall be that person who is of most help to the beginning of those in fourth density. But may we say that at the end of third density, what we feel would be the most help is not physical, is not explanation of the order of nature, but rather an insistence upon a gaze at the spirituality of all that there is, the thought that each thing that one does is done for the love of the Creator. There need be no other reason, there need be no higher path. Anything that is done may be done for the love of the Creator. And as long as you are practicing that presence and the Creator is with you, all that you do, though it may be the most menial and undramatic thing possible, is blessed and appreciated, and you are loved.

Indeed, if you do nothing, you are still loved. You shall always be loved. The only difficulty in third density, truly, is learning to trust that love, to rest back in the love, and to have the courage to return that love, although its recipient is invisible and infinite. As you spend time with the Creator, as you converse with the Creator, you will find that there is no circumstance in which the Creator cannot be a conscious part. And you will find your scientific concerns falling into appropriate perspective.

We find this instrument is requesting that we transfer this contact, and so we shall move to the one known as Jim, with great thanks for this instrument's being willing to channel us this evening, in spite of some fatigue. We leave you in this instrument's mouth in love and light as we transfer to the one known as Jim. I am Yom.

(Jim channeling)

I am Yom, and greet each again in love and light through this instrument. At this time we feel that we have spoken sufficiently to begin that portion of your meditation which is the question and answer portion. If we may speak to further queries, we would be most happy to do so at this time.

M: I would just about like to thank you for being with us tonight, and query about something that you spoke about in the latter part of your message tonight, and that is, you said, "If you do nothing, it's just as …" The impression I had was, if you do nothing, it's about the same thing as if you do a lot of research and thinking and whatever. This brings to my mind the question of responsibility. My question is, what are our responsibilities as human beings to ourselves and to the other people around us? And also in a universal sense? Is a human being supposed to be doing something, or is it simply a question of what he feels like doing?

I am Yom. In truth, my brother, we would suggest that you, as any creature of the one Creator which contains the quality of free will, may do as you will, for each action shall, in some degree, teach. To learn of the self and to learn of the Creator and the relationship between these concepts within all of your creation is the purpose of your existence and of the existence of all of the creation. That you shall find standards by which you shall live, and shall take upon yourselves responsibilities, as you call them, as a result of what you learn from what you do and from what you seek is the natural outgrowth of experience which has had analysis and which has generated further thought and action.

Thus, as this process becomes more and more a conscious process, the seeker of truth shall find that there are more appropriate ways in which to conduct this process which take into account the welfare and needs of other entities about it, the welfare and needs of the environment in which it moves and has its being, and the welfare and needs of the inner self, shall we say, that portion of the self which seeks to be informed and to extend the boundaries of experience and identification. Thus, from the beginning command, shall we say, for lack of a better word, that command being, "Do as thou will," comes a progression of learning and a refinement of this process in a conscious manner.

Is there another query, my brother?

M: I guess that what I'm thinking about is just the point of it all. I mean, it sounds to me that, based on some of the knowledge I've gathered from other meetings such as this, that kind of education that we are supposed to attain out of each lifetime is—and correct me if I'm wrong—a kind of experiential education, as you just said, that in a sense, anything that you do is based on the need to learn a particular lesson, so in a sense, however we proceed is a kind of fulfillment of this education. So, in a real sense in terms of our evolution, is there any point in trying to attain another kind of education which is one that we create for ourselves, the kind of education we create which is through science or through metaphysical gatherings such as this tonight? In terms of our evolution through reincarnation, will this kind of created education, will it be helpful for us in our evolution?

I am Yom, and each such means of learning shall serve as a catalyst that one might accomplish what is at the heart of one's desire, whether the mind which creates the course of study is aware consciously of what is at the heart of the desire to learn. Thus, you may pursue any particular path of your so-called created education and because of the biases within your subconscious mind you will see and experience this created education in a manner which is congruent with your true desire. Thus, it shall be a vehicle for the accomplishment of that which you have set out to do.

Is there another query, my brother?

M: No, thank you. That's very reasonable. Just a query about you, the entity of Yom. This is the first time that I've had the pleasure of meeting with you. Could you tell me what density you are from and anything else about your background that you care to talk about?

I am Yom, and am seldom requested within this particular group, for our specialty lies in an area which is somewhat akin to those explorations of your more scientifically-oriented entities, though we do not call ourselves scientists in that strict sense. We are as many within the Confederation of Planets in the Service of the Infinite Creator, and that is a race of beings which have joined their conscious seeking so that it is unified in its direction and purpose. We seek at present within the density of light which is, according to the numbering system we are familiar with associated with this group, being five.

Is there another query, my brother?

M: No, thank you.

P: You said earlier that you had some hesitation about the quality of the answers that you were giving in that it was maybe not what was expected. But I'd like to say that I appreciate the direction of the answer that you gave and understand the direction of the answer that you gave. A question I have is, you spoke earlier of a time when—a time when a person has confusion, that they should sing, and the question I have, is singing in that manner the same as playing a musical instrument or expressing oneself creatively, or do you literally mean singing with your voice?

I am Yom. It was our intent to suggest the creative activity in general in order that the conscious confusion could, for the moment, be set aside so that the channel to the subconscious mind might be opened and allow the information which is being blocked by the confusion to be transmitted in some form to the conscious mind. The singing is one means by which this may [be] accomplished, as it effectively removes the necessity for further thought. The playing of a musical instrument would accomplish the same goal, for when the muscle memory, as we find you call it, is allowed to produce its patterns of creativity, then the conscious mind may for that period of time be emptied of the confusion, so that a new beginning might be had and the progress toward a solution to the problem at hand might be enhanced.

Is there another query, my brother?

P: Another thing I'd like to ask about that you spoke of, penetrating the illusion and that the illusion was not meant to be penetrated, but that it might be, and I'm unclear what you were speaking about there.

I am Yom. We speak of illusion, for the environment which each of us inhabits is more than it appears to be, and by being more than it appears to be, invites the seeking as to what that more might be and how it might be related to the self. Within your particular illusion, the nature of the illusion is quite dense, shall we say, in relation to those which follow it. The density of your illusion, the heaviness of it, has the purpose of providing an unbiased field of experience for free will to be exercised in a manner which is consciously directed for the purpose of eventually choosing to move in a certain fashion rather than another.

To be specific in this instance, your particular illusion asks that you choose to become aware of self to such a degree that you are, indeed, conscious beings, which then may choose the manner of your progression in evolution, either by choosing to be radiant and giving of that which you have found of value in your own searching or to be absorbent or magnetic and to take unto you that which you have found to be helpful, not only within your own experience, but to require that those about you serve you as well.

Thus, your illusion offers the opportunity to make this great choice and the ability to penetrate this illusion in any degree is in direct ratio to the desire and persistence with which the seeking for truth, as you would call it, is conducted by each seeker. Thus, there are moments of inspiration and illumination which are the natural outgrowth of any sincere seeker's experience, and during these moments of illumination a glimpse may be had into a wider point of view that has not so many veils hiding it from the inner eye of the seeker. However, even with many such glimpses of the truer nature of things, the seeker shall find that far more is unknown than is known.

Is there a further query, my brother?

P: Yes. Is the penetration of the illusion related to a term that we use called magic? Or is that not related? I should say, successful penetration of the illusion.

And we shall make this our final query for the evening, for it has been a lengthy session this evening. The term magic, as you have used it in relationship to the evolution of consciousness, may be seen as the conscious ability to gain access to the unconscious mind. The most often used definition within your culture which describes this term is the ability to create changes in consciousness at will.

We find that the conscious ability to utilize the subconscious mind is the foundation principle which allows the ability to create changes in consciousness at will. The persistent desire and practice on the part of the seeker of truth to persist and to analyze and meditate upon the results of the seeking is the quality which aids most in the development of this ability to create the changes in consciousness at will, for as the seeker explores the mysteries of creation, the seeker will discover that the journey does not move far from the self, but, indeed, focuses upon the nature of the self. And as the seeker begins to know more and more of its own self, it gains the ability to form that self in a fashion which is the result of conscious choice rather than the unconscious programming received in the early years of the life that was designed previous to the incarnation.

Thus, as the conscious seeker becomes aware of those programs within the deeper self that it itself has placed there, and begins to untangle the riddle of the self and its purpose, the seeker gains a mastery of the self that allows it not only to move the self as a result of conscious choice, but to move the self in an harmonious fashion with entities about it and with the environment about it as well. For there is an harmonic resonance that the seeker may become aware of that proceeds outward from each portion of the creation and which may be utilized in a fashion which is likened unto singing with harmony with another being, so that those songs which are sung then become the means by which the further evolution of the self may be accomplished.

We are aware that it is growing late, shall we say, and we shall take this opportunity to thank those who have gathered here this evening and who have invited our presence by their desires. We are most grateful for the opportunity to speak through these instruments that we might share that which is our joy and our passion. We ask that each evaluate according to what is within the heart, taking that which has resonance and leaving that which does not. We are known to you as those of Yom, and we leave each at this time in the love and the light of the one infinite Creator. Adonai, my friends.

L/L Research

L/L Research is a subsidiary of Rock Creek Research & Development Laboratories, Inc.

P.O. Box 5195
Louisville, KY 40255-0195

www.llresearch.org

Rock Creek is a non-profit corporation dedicated to discovering and sharing information which may aid in the spiritual evolution of humankind.

ABOUT THE CONTENTS OF THIS TRANSCRIPT: This telepathic channeling has been taken from transcriptions of the weekly study and meditation meetings of the Rock Creek Research & Development Laboratories and L/L Research. It is offered in the hope that it may be useful to you. As the Confederation entities always make a point of saying, please use your discrimination and judgment in assessing this material. If something rings true to you, fine. If something does not resonate, please leave it behind, for neither we nor those of the Confederation would wish to be a stumbling block for any.

CAVEAT: This transcript is being published by L/L Research in a not yet final form. It has, however, been edited and any obvious errors have been corrected. When it is in a final form, this caveat will be removed.

© 2009 L/L Research

Sunday Meditation
April 30, 1989

Group question: As our world becomes more interrelated and interdependent there seems to be a new generation that is experiencing a breakdown of traditional cultural and religious mythologies in the way that we are raised, so that there is a blending of some of these various traditions from person to person. Could you speak to this reforming of the various traditions and to a personal mythology or path to the Creator? And is there any difficulty that might come from the radical change in our upbringing so that there seems to be fewer reference points made between the way children are raised now and the way they used to be raised.

(Carla channeling)

I am Q'uo. I greet you in the love and in the light of the one infinite Creator. The Creator's blessing and ours be upon you, and our thanks and gratitude to you for the honor of being called to your group this evening to discuss the question of old and new mythologies, and, perhaps most importantly, the dealing with the young ones among you in the face of the teacher/parent's having found that the older and settled mythologies are not acceptable.

This is a large subject, and we shall do no more this evening than scratch the surface. However, we would like to give you some ideas, reminding you, [as] always, that we are prone to error, as any which is not whole and entirely within the Creator. As long as we have an identity of our own, there will be biases, and we ask always that you remember to discriminate carefully, and to keep those truths that seem helpful, to keep those inspirations that seem to be truth that you remember and recognize for the first time, and if something jars or is unhelpful, lay it aside and move ahead. That is part of what creating a personal myth consists in.

Now, let us lay some groundwork. First of all, the words mythology and religion should be far more interchangeable than they are. The difficulty is that in myth there is no judgment between one myth and another, whereas in religion those of one religion square off with hostility against those religions which in some way contradict it. Thus, we prefer to talk of all paths of spirituality as personal myths, including classical paths such as the path of mystical Christianity, the path of literal Christianity, the path of mystical Buddhism, the path of literal Buddhism, and so forth.

Realize that the essence of myth is to move the seeking entity by its own faith and its desire to know the truth over a kind of rainbow bridge, a magical covenantal span that links time and eternity, that which is known and that which is a mystery. Those who dwell in that which is known have a deadness inside them, though they live and their hearts beat. Those that dwell from time to time in eternity have a livingness that only crossing that span into eternity may offer. Certainly, there are those who naturally and unaffectedly spend each moment in the present moment. These are, for the most part, the young souls which parent/teachers are responsible for aiding in their growth and nurturing in the agony of constant change as growth occurs.

Therefore, we do not wish to engage in judgment betwixt settled world religions, except to describe how they create the rainbow bridge to eternity. Within the Oriental religions, the consciousness is considered to be spiritual, and that which is honored is the continuation of living eternity: father to child, to its child, to its child, and so forth. This mythological path is a path of ethic and wisdom. It is somewhat passive and unsuited to the Western, shall we say, mentality, as this instrument would put it.

That which you may call Buddhist is a group of paths covering exercise, breathing, work and worship. It is, perhaps, the most passive of the paths that are traditional, in that the goal is to cleanse the self of preferences so that one may see clearly and be unmoved by the illusion. This is a path of wisdom. The Muslim and the Jewish religions are those which have the God which acts for and against entities on a sometimes apparently capricious basis. This is a religion of ethic and one is taught to do certain things which shall span the rainbow bridge to eternity.

The many kinds of Christian religion are, to some extent, the more active of the world religions in that there is a strong ethic implied, an ethic of excellence, purity and good behavior, yet also an ethic which states quite clearly that by no means shall action bring one to paradise, to eternity, over the bridge. In this particular spiritual system it is acknowledged that there must be the bridge in place that by faith can be crossed. The Occidental part of the world finds this ethical and mythical system in its activity more suited culturally, and, indeed, though all the so-called world religions have much to offer, it is probable that the parable of the channeling of Jesus the Christ, being part and parcel of the culture in which each present dances, is perhaps the most accessible and the most useable.

Now, we speak of Christianity, Buddhism, Shintoism and so forth as if they were singular. This is not so. Each of these religious systems has one thing in common, and that is a call to mysticism, a call to a life in faith. That faith is what makes the bridge between time and eternity firm. Faith is fed by desire. Thus, the beginning of the creation of the personal myth is a burning, passionate, consuming desire to know the truth, the truth of who you are, of that which you are constructed, of your relationships to eternity and imperishability. Consciousness is malleable. It is plastic. And you are either at the helm of your consciousness or being dragged along by it, having lost the reins. Therefore, when deciding to create a personal mythology it is well first to grasp the reins of desire and discipline and passion, to hone and whet the edge of the need to know, the desire to understand. If you seek the Creator, your path will come to you.

Now, if one looks at any of the world religions—and we shall concentrate, since we are speaking to those of western culture, on Christianity—one may see that the images, the parables, the myth of the life of Jesus the Christ itself has very little objective referent to the time in which you now experience this illusion. It does not fire the imagination to think of the images and the stories which Christianity has to offer. The younger one is the more true this is, simply because the parental generation may well not have offered the child the experience of organized religion, and the child, therefore, may not have a clear image of that for which it hungers, for at any age a spirit will hunger and thirst for spiritual food.

Thus, in relation to the children we would suggest very strongly that if the parents do not engage in traditional church-going, it is well if there be an altar or holy place, small as it may be, within the dwelling or close to the dwelling that may be dry from the weather and accessible in all temperatures so that one may go there and meditate each day. When children see how seriously the parents desire to know the truth, when they see dailyness and discipline in seeking, they will, by osmosis and acting like the parents, imitate and grow to feel that place within themselves that hungers for heavenly food.

In short, what we are saying is, what you use to make the bridge should be a product of your desire. That which you can have imperishable faith in will come to you. Accept nothing that does not feel solid, and if it does feel solid no longer, leave it behind and move onward, for truth recedes infinitely in front of the pilgrim, remaining always a mystery and allowing one more and more, as one grows more and more mature and aged, to see the great depth, breadth and height of the spiritual path, the amount of glory and strength in service to others, the amount of joy and peace indwelling in love and light with those who also seek. To have companions along the way is most important.

There are other reasons for the rejection of ancient myths than that of their being irrelevant to that which is occurring at this time upon your planet. That is, few people, for instance, breed sheep; therefore the thought of the one known as Jesus as shepherd is difficult to manage, and the leaving of the ninety-nine for the one that is lost nothing more than a cosmic joke. Those of you in the West have experienced and are extending to all portions of the Earth the experience of heightened technology. Science has mistakenly assumed that it is separate from spirituality. This is a fatal flaw within science, and it shall be corrected, although within your particular life experience, it may not yet be evident science and spirituality are one.

Knowledge has nothing to do with faith. Dogma and doctrine are deadly enemies of faith. To live a life in faith is simply to say, "I have faith that I am a survivor, that I am held in the gentle arms of a kindly Creator, that that which is happening to me right now is what is supposed to be happening to me right now." Those who wish to polarize towards to service to others add upon that faith by attempting to listen carefully to others, that they may know how best to serve—not how to please, but serve.

The materialism within your culture and the work ethic within your culture both mitigate strongly against an appropriate attitude towards creating a personal myth, for though it is well to have good ethics and good moral behavior, the bridge to eternity is made almost entirely of the deep and intuitive portions of the mind, the feelings, the emotions, and the inspiration.

We ask each of you, honestly, what inspires each? We see confusion in your minds at this question, except for this instrument who has chosen its own personal mythology as mystical Christianity. Thus, we say to you, concentrate upon this creation. Begin to know who you are by processes which may be described easily—that of keeping the diary, that of keeping the dream diary, that of moving back in mind to painful experiences in the past and working with them until there is balance and forgiveness.

You see, without the bridge to eternity each entity is stuck fast in the mire of time and space. Things will go on and on, a road that never ends. This is an unreal picture of reality, but a true picture of the illusion in which you find yourself at this time. The key to forming a personal mythology, then, is to discover that which you may have faith in; that is, not belief, but simple faith. It often works best, for those who are new to the concept of being, to act as though one had faith in a kindly Creator and a redeeming Creator, and therefore to be able to forgive yourself and others simply by the strength of your faith. It is not faith in anything or anyone, perhaps, but merely a faith in the general kindliness of the one infinite Creator and of your own preference to serve others, to polarize towards the positive rather than to serve the self and control others, to move along a negative path.

How does one create a personal myth? It begins, as most things do, with the process of coming to know the self well, coming to feel the yearnings, the frustrations, the strong and the weak points of the self. Coming to find out what the self really desires, then honing that desire, sharpening that desire and becoming passionate in the desire to know the truth of the infinite One and your relationship to the infinite Creator.

When you have determined that which creates the bridge to eternity for you, we urge you to cross that bridge as often as possible. The ideal which was shown by many Christed entities is to live in such a way that the entire life experience becomes a channeling, a parable of the journey to infinity, of the ridding of oneself of the dross of perishability and the winning through of the understanding that your consciousness, more and more refined, polarized and uplifted, is, indeed, imperishable and is your true self. The more time one spends having crossed the rainbow bridge into eternity while in the physical body, the more one is able to offer in consolation, in forgiveness, in peace-making. For to one who has faith, there is no problem too great to solve, and that which is unsolvable is acceptable. Each day and night is its own entity, appreciated for itself, experienced for itself and action done for love out of faith. This is the life in faith.

Some entities require a very simple myth of a personal nature, and those within the so-called New Age movement demonstrate the simplistic nature of the path to infinity. It is, however, a path which is difficult to remain upon, for the nature of the illusion is to challenge and test the growing entity again and again. Those who feel that there is naught but love and light may be most distressed and confused by that which happens in the life experience which may be called traumatic or devastating. The impulse is to remove the faith and replace it with anger. Avoid such impulses, for the Creator is not simplistic. The Creator and you, together, have designed quite carefully the kind of lessons of love that you are to attempt to study within this life experience. To study them as a materialistic entity who lives and dies is, perhaps, all too often to remain asleep to the possibilities of challenge.

To face each trouble, difficulty and challenge with confident faith and quiet sureness in that bridge is to distance oneself from time and space, and, with that longer point of view, to gaze upon experience and choose the reaction which the hero would have. For this is the essence of myth. The hero, whether it be the Christ known as Jesus, the Christ known as Buddha, the Christ known as Lao Tsu, or the Christ known as Zoroaster, makes very little difference if one is mystical in one's faith and non-literal. The great difficulty with all settled religious systems is that they have become combative, materialistic and an artifact of the world and the culture in which you live.

Many are the priests in all faiths that attempt with every fiber of the being to retrieve the parables, the mythology, the story which initially sparked the spiritual movement. However, divisive elements, competitive elements within the nature of humankind create an ever onward going series of schism, splits, disagreements and steps backwards from unity into discord. Thus, many choose not to frequent the established spiritual system of myth for public worship. There is, however, an instinctive need for group worship. There is a need to come together as the children of the infinite Creator to worship, to offer praise and thanks and to ask for blessings.

Thus, there are meetings, such as these and many other of the so-called New Age type, which aid the seeker in the creation of his own story. The personal myth is that of the hero or the heroine who must go on a very difficult and challenging journey. During this journey, this entity will lose everything which it has, but by the aid of the infinite Creator, in one form or another, that which has been lost miraculously revivifies and becomes imperishable. This is the basic parable or story of the hero.

Let us look at the compelling myth of the Holy Grail. It has perhaps seized the imagination of mystics in a more direct way than any spiritual system, for it involves entities in a myth which is adventurous. The hero must go forth alone. It must pass impossible tests. It must bring back that which is unavailable, seemingly, and it must do it for the love of the infinite Creator. It is, of course, in the journey itself that the transformation of the hero occurs. When the hero returns, this entity, then, becomes the teacher, able to speak in parables and stories, anecdotes that may make sense to those about one.

What is your story? Have you conceived of yourself as a hero or a heroine? Have you learned to love the self and realized the consciousness of the self as blessed and holy …

(Side one of tape ends.)

(Carla channeling)

… and to become able to hollow the self of those things which are materialistic, greedy, grasping and worldly? The hero must lose a great deal of emotional and mental baggage, must unlearn the biases of pain and suffering found in childhood experiences and adult experiences as well, so that the life is self-forgiven, the self is seen as consciousness, which in essence is holy.

By sending oneself upon the metaphysical journey of the pilgrim, one sets out for the Holy Grail, the impossible dream. One has nothing but faith, whether the personal myth combines well with traditional spiritual systems or whether the personal myth has been created by the self, the entity needs to see itself as a true hero, one who wishes to serve, to sacrifice, and to learn. With the heart open, with the intellect disciplined, the traveler begins to learn to feel the natural feelings of consciousness.

The feeling we hope most to encourage you in is the emotion of worship or thanksgiving or praise. For the infinite Creator, the Imperishable One, is indeed Head of all, Source of all and Omega to all. You are all, indeed, a portion of the infinite Creator. And when your personal myth, your personal journey has been enough refined—and we are not at that state yet, at all—you shall one day gather that consciousness in its purity, having burned away all the dross of illusion, and move once again into the uncreated love of the one infinite Creator.

To sum, we encourage you to do two things. Firstly, to realize the central importance of living a life which points towards imperishability on a daily basis. In this way shall the pilgrim slowly discover its power, its strength, and its service. Secondly, we wish to encourage each parent to allow the children to see an active worship period on a daily basis in the home for those who do not attend the traditional places of worship. And for those who do attend the traditional places of worship, let there be the daily practice of that particular form of worship within the home environment. In either case, the young spirit shall, by identifying with the father and the mother, which seem like the Creator to the young spirit, will then have solidly, firmly in the subconsciousness of childhood for the entire life experience of the feeling of the presence of the one infinite Creator. This is a great, great gift to give your children. It demands discipline upon the part of parents, for it is difficult to do anything upon a daily basis. We are aware of your work ethic. We are aware of your busyness. We ask that you make the time to worship each day, standing upon the holy ground that is beneath your feet wherever you stand, for within yourself there is holiness.

Encourage yourself in your pilgrimage and love one another. And although you need not believe in Jesus Christ or Buddha Christ or whomever, we ask that you have a consciousness of faith and live a life of faith to create that which you were born to be—a living string in the plangent tonality of infinite love.

We are glad to be with you in your daily meditations or spiritual observances. You have only mentally to ask, and we will be there silently, attempting to aid in deepening the meditation or increasing the intensity of the spiritual experience.

We thank this instrument and would transfer at this time, in love and in light and in the joy and in thanks, to the one known as Jim. I am Q'uo.

(Jim channeling)

I am Q'uo, and greet each again in love and light through this instrument. At this time we are honored to offer ourselves in the attempt to speak to any further queries which may remain upon the minds of those present this evening. Is there a query at this time?

P: You spoke of ridding oneself of pain and suffering of experiences in childhood. Could you speak about this a little bit longer?

I am Q'uo. This topic, my brother, moves into that area of the examination of the life pattern which seeks to understand the roots of that life which has grown to the point at which the self now finds it expressing itself. The attempt to look at those formative experiences within the young years of the life experience is an attempt to see the means by which the preincarnative choices have been set in motion. It is during this portion of the life experience that the seeds of these choices are planted within the fertile soil of the young child, for at this time the child has a far more active subconscious mental capacity that is more malleable, shall we say, and which shall, as it is formed, continue to feed the parameters of the formation to the growing and soon-to-be dominant conscious mind of the entity.

Thus, it is well to explore how this process was carried out in order to gain a clearer understanding of those patterns and preferences which have become, to the observant student, repeated themes within the life pattern. This study may be undertaken in a number of ways, or should we say, there are many methods by which this study may be accomplished. To begin the searching of the conscious memory and analyzing those remembered experiences of significance is recommended, for the conscious mind does retain a great deal of information to the student which seeks the resources contained therein. Oftentimes this study, beginning with the conscious reflection, is well accomplished in the recording of a journal or diary that may be shared with others that are seeking the same goals for themselves, for though one may remember significant experiences, oftentimes it is the comment of another that will show the experience in another light or perspective and will add to the depth or richness of the reconstructed experience.

A natural outgrowth of the conscious reflection is to look within the subconscious mind for that which resides there in memory concerning these same experiences. The subconscious mind may be accessed by the hypnotic regression or by the recording and revealing of the dreams that have been received as a result of continued asking of the subconscious mind to give the conscious mind the information that the conscious mind seeks. The dream episodes at some point then will begin to reflect the formative experiences which are felt to be significant to the seeking entity.

There are many means by which information gained in such a manner may be analyzed, and it is well to review the dream landscape by the method which feels to the seeker to have the most to offer. There may be an interchange or blending of techniques from time to time. It is always helpful to engage in such review and analysis with others, for, again, the insights of the objective observer are oftentimes helpful to the seeker, which may not have the same perspective as another would have. To then utilize this information, however it has been gained, to gain a larger view of the life pattern and to begin to observe the roots, shall we say, of cause and effect, is the goal which the student will seek by such methods. There is the possibility, then, that by understanding the reasons for certain behaviors, that the student will begin to accept these behaviors and then the self in a greater degree, so that there might be more affecting of the conscious evolution in a freely chosen manner in the present moment, rather than having the behavior continually moved as is the marionette by forces that reach far back into the early years of the incarnation.

Is there another query, my brother?

P: No, thank you. That explained what I was wondering about.

I am Q'uo, and we thank you, my brother. Is there another query?

Carla: I have one about children, something I've been thinking about for a long time. I myself was raised with extreme responsibility for my age, and older than my age. I find myself, as an adult, able to deal with children in an authoritative way which escapes all my friends. My friends' children seem to be only under a very limited amount of control, and in some cases, such as my friend B, no control whatsoever. Yet, I may go into the same situation and establish my own relationship with the same young entities, clearly define the limits which I find acceptable, and am able to make a perfectly reasonable relationship with the children, whom I see as young souls who have just as much to say as I do. I am puzzled. I realize that each child is different and each child needs special things, but I wonder what the effect is of so many children these days having very elastic limits in every direction, so they truly do not know what would be the correct thing to do at any one time? Or am I simply uptight in wanting to control the situation for my comfort in asking children to behave?

I am Q'uo, and am aware of your query, my sister. The, shall we say, more modern theories in the raising of children have evolved, as do all theories and thought, from that which has gone before, and each portion of the process has that which is helpful and that which is not. Each attempts to build upon that which has gone before, and yet there is oftentimes a, shall we say, lag in the development of a truly superior means of achieving any goal. Much trial and error must take place before there is true progress.

The tenor or tone of the raising of children in years previous to those now experienced by your present culture was one that partook more of what we shall call wisdom, the clearly defined rules and limits that would be enforced with the harsh word and the rod. There was, as a general rule, less concern for the feelings, the rights, and the development of the young entity. This tenor or tone has, through the years and the modification of each generation, moved from that which we have called wisdom to that which we might call compassion, where there is, indeed, a great deal of concern for the feelings, the rights, and the experiences of each young entity. There is, perhaps, in our humble opinion, an overbalance in this case, of compassion, which has replaced the clearly defined limits of wisdom. Thus, the child is placed at the center of concern with, in many cases, little to guide the child as to the appropriateness of its choices when its choices infringe upon the rights of others.

It is helpful to be able to blend both the wisdom to set limits and the compassion for the child's development, so that the creative nature of each child finds a free range of expression within a certain field of experience, the field of experience being defined in the large part by the parents with the aid and assistance of the larger community of the educational system, the cultural mores, and the inspirational or religious direction. Thus, the child would find that it was free to a degree, with the freedom and range of freedom enlarging with the passing of years and the gaining of experience which would inform the decision-making process for the young entity that is now maturing into the entity which has discovered that its field or limits have also enlarged with its own experience and increasingly fall within its own free will choices.

It is difficult for any of those parents of your present culture to reconcile the discipline with which they were raised and the difficulties that many experienced with this discipline, and to reconcile these conclusions with the strong desire to give to the young entity a feeling of selfness which the parents have determined is important for the child to be able to express itself in those ways which are available to it. Thus, there is the ongoing process of refining the techniques by which the child is nurtured into adulthood.

Is there another query, my sister?

Carla: No, thank you. Thank you very much.

I am Q'uo, and we thank you, my sister. Is there another query?

Carla: One last one. I know that after we have come back with the Grail, as heroes or heroines, it is time to stand as a light on the hill, as the Christians say, so the city may see it. And I wondered what your opinion was on ways of doing that—being, doing, serving in soup kitchens, meditating? Is it equal for everyone to do whatever they do, or are there some services that are over others in preference?

I am Q'uo, and am aware of your query, my sister. Though, in the absolute and objective sense, there may be seen great inequality in one service over another, yet it must be remembered that each entity which incarnates within your third-density illusion has programmed those means by which that which is learned may be turned outward and shared with others by any of the means which you have mentioned, and by an infinite number of others as well, for within each life pattern there is presented the opportunity to learn those lessons which were considered appropriate for the incarnation, but also are offered those opportunities to share with others that which has been learned and that which has been taken within the being of the self, and which therefore colors all that proceeds from the self in a manner which has subtle or easily noticeable effects upon those about one or the environment in which one lives and works.

Thus, there is the pattern of experience laid out before each entity that includes both the learning and the teaching, and that which is appropriate for the entity is always provided for the entity so that there is little need to concern oneself overmuch with how to accomplish this or that goal. The most easily obtained means of achieving such goals is to notice that which is before one's sight, before one's experience, and to look upon each experience as that which holds the opportunity for both the learning and the serving.

Is there another query, my sister?

Carla: Just a follow-up on a personal note. I personally have had years of trouble—and it intensifies from time to time and it's pretty intense now—dealing with increasing amount of disability and feeling that I'm really useless because I can't fix dinner or iron or wash or sweep the floor or anything like that. About all I can do is care about people and communicate with them and do the channeling. And ironically, a lot of my friends feel that they're not doing anything, because all that they're doing is cooking and cleaning and so forth, and they're not doing anything dramatic. I wonder where the peace is for a feeling of being of service? A very nebulous question, but a real one.

I am Q'uo, and am aware of your query, my sister. In this regard may we say that peace within your illusion has a small place. There is a time that occasionally occurs for each entity in which it will feel the peace and the contentment of that which has been accomplished and will feel a quiet and joyful anticipation of that which is to come. Yet, for most a great deal of time is taken up within the incarnation agonizing over just those points which you have raised. This angst is that which might be seen as the motivator to seeking, for if one were always peaceful and satisfied with that which has occurred in the life pattern, there would be little to move one into further learning and further service.

Thus, the dissatisfaction that may tinge to a greater or lesser degree all that one accomplishes within the life pattern, and, indeed, the life pattern itself, may be seen as the, shall we say, grease which keeps the wheels turning. Thus, we recommend that even this dissatisfaction be valued for its motivational qualities. However, it is also helpful to keep the process lightly in mind, with a certain perspective that allows for acceptance of the self as one queries inwardly what the most appropriate means is to learn and to serve next. The light touch, that which retains the wider point of view, is a great ally to the seeker, and is the balance to the overdone angst, shall we say.

Is there a further query, my sister?

Carla: No, thank you, that is all, Q'uo.

I am Q'uo, and we thank you once again, my sister. Is there a final query at this time?

(Pause)

I am Q'uo. We are most grateful for being invited to join your circle of seeking this evening. We have been most heartened by the queries, which we feel have struck close to the heart for the purpose for the incarnation and the means by which the purpose shall be discovered and enacted by each seeker of truth. We have enjoyed sharing our opinions, and we do remind each that we have shared opinions. We do not wish our words to be taken too seriously, shall we say, if they do not sound a note of harmony within.

We shall look, as you would say, forward to those times in your future during which we shall again have the opportunity to blend our vibrations with yours and to walk more closely on that path which you now find yourselves on, that path which leads ever onward and ever homeward. We are those of Q'uo, and we leave each at this time in the love and in the light of the one infinite Creator. Adonai, my friends. Adonai. ♣

L/L Research

L/L Research is a subsidiary of Rock Creek Research & Development Laboratories, Inc.

P.O. Box 5195
Louisville, KY 40255-0195

www.llresearch.org

Rock Creek is a non-profit corporation dedicated to discovering and sharing information which may aid in the spiritual evolution of humankind.

ABOUT THE CONTENTS OF THIS TRANSCRIPT: This telepathic channeling has been taken from transcriptions of the weekly study and meditation meetings of the Rock Creek Research & Development Laboratories and L/L Research. It is offered in the hope that it may be useful to you. As the Confederation entities always make a point of saying, please use your discrimination and judgment in assessing this material. If something rings true to you, fine. If something does not resonate, please leave it behind, for neither we nor those of the Confederation would wish to be a stumbling block for any.

CAVEAT: This transcript is being published by L/L Research in a not yet final form. It has, however, been edited and any obvious errors have been corrected. When it is in a final form, this caveat will be removed.

© 2009 L/L Research

Sunday Meditation
May 7, 1989

Group question: About feelings. As we move through our daily round of activities, day after day, we come into situations in which we have various feelings that we either accept and let move through us, or, if the situation seems to be something we want to avoid for any possible reason, we might cut the feelings off, armor ourselves against them, and push them aside. When we actually begin feeling the feelings then, does this feeling of the feelings help us to move through the situation and to increase or enhance the general flow of energy through our energy centers or chakras and to make our experience more vivid or harmonious or real?

(Carla channeling)

I am Q'uo. I greet you in the love and in the light of the one infinite Creator, and wish to thank you and bless you for inviting us to share in the beauty of your meditation and the earnestness and sincerity of your seeking. We, too, are such as you, earnestly seeking, perhaps a step or two ahead, and so we have chosen, for this moment in what you might call time, to offer service, yet we cannot give you this service unless you request it, for when one works in positive polarity, as the Confederation of Planets in the Service of the Infinite Creator does, one must observe the cardinal importance of free will. So we are most honored by your call, for it is our manner of service, and it is a joy to be with you.

We must tell you that we are not infallible, but pilgrims on the way, such as yourselves. We can give you our understanding, such as it is, but it is limited. Therefore, because we know that that which we say is biased to some extent, we would appreciate it if each used careful discernment. If that which we say rings of truth and seems to be a dim memory, suddenly clearly remembered, then by all means keep that which we have given, for it has achieved its goal. If that which we say, on the other hand, disturbs or makes one indifferent, then we have not achieved our goal of expressing a truth which is relevant to your particular point of departure, shall we say, on the spiritual path. We would not be a stumbling block to any, therefore we do ask that you practice discernment.

We are most happy that you ask this question about feelings, for feelings are the distilled intelligence of many, many lifetimes and constitute the actual personality which is your imperishable self. The temptation of the illusion is to place the identity of the self within the mind. The mind is created to make choices, so that one may survive within an environment. The so-called frontal lobes, however, which are designed for work in consciousness, have not been overly used among your people. Indeed, less than 5 percent of all of the brain which you possess is put to use. That is, like any statistic, variable and therefore false, but it is a pretty fair average. The illusion is that you are a creature with the body and the mind, and as one achieves the height and weight and years of an adult and grown-up person, one learns to act in ways which are approved of by the society.

In your particular society, those known as women live longer than those manifesting as men because of the variation in the behavioral rewards given for various behaviors to boys versus that given to girls. For instance, if a girl might have a fight, she is considered to be less of a girl. If the same-aged male engages in the same fisticuffs, this entity is considered to be better than he was before, especially if he is able to win. Therefore, women are not trained to be competitive to the extent that men are trained. In other words, within your culture, women are encouraged in many subtle ways to act out their feelings. Crying is accepted. Feeling tense, nervous, afraid and many other emotions are accepted because of the mistaken notion that the particular subspecies called woman is an inferior race.

Indeed, what is occurring is that women are fulfilling that balance of the male and the female which is called the yin and the yang. The female is storing spiritual and emotional energy, the deeper portion of the mind.

Let us consider that the mind is a pond which has been filled with water and alcohol. Let us consider that the alcohol tends to rise to the top of the water and not to mix. Now, as one might skate across frozen alcohol, or as one would swim in the alcohol layer of life, one would be dealing with the material of the surface mind, the conscious mind, and very little of that which [is] from the deep mind would be allowed to come through the veil between subconscious and conscious. Women are given permission to move into the deep water. Men, for the most part, attempt from time to time to move deeply into life, but as they duck their heads, they do not, perhaps, go far enough, and one cannot breathe alcohol, if we may continue the metaphor. One must get to the water, for that which is at the very surface of the subconscious mind is perhaps not quite as confused and jumbled as that which the surface mind is sorting through in its process of making choice after choice after choice. However, it is dealing with topical, daily, ordinary material.

The imperishable personality, the true intelligence of each of you, the Christ-self within, that spark which makes all things one, is contained in deep feelings. This is true intelligence. It will never be seen as so within your culture. Indeed, there is no culture which has moved in any way towards mechanism and more crowded conditions in general of living that are able to encourage both sexes to find working with the deeper feelings natural. Therefore, men within the culture of, shall we say, Europe and America, as you call these various geographical locations, are a difficult testing ground in which one must dig through the alcohol and dive deep into the water to experience what one really thinks. Because feeling in a deep way is actually the thinking of many, many life experiences.

Now, we, having shown that feeling and emotion, especially the deep emotion, is very important to the growth of the spirit, would suggest tools with which one may approach learning how to feel feelings. May we say that in our opinion, the easiest way to feel is to begin with that which you feel most deeply. It may seem to be that which is furthest from you, however, the decision, the choice—and we emphasize this word, choice—to take a path of faith and live it, day in and day out, as this instrument would say, is central to opening the heart to feeling, to moving deeper into the water consciousness of the deep mind.

Therefore, we would suggest starting the day with a hymn of praise to the infinite One, as you know that higher power to be. Worship is so much easier for the Creator than it is to see the Creator in others, simply because the Creator is an abstraction which is mysterious, yet which has created all that there is. The wonder of this, the beauty of this, is enough to send someone without experience into ecstasies. There is beauty unbounded upon your sphere within the plant, animal and mineral lives. There is much beauty of character in your people. There have been many, many beautiful thoughts and songs and pictures and resonances of reality sounded by artists and philosophers, poets, essayists and writers. These entities have moved into their feelings, into the true intelligence of the deeper self.

It does not matter what you choose for your personal faith. Or to put it another way, in the words of Joseph Campbell, which this instrument recently saw, "It does not matter how you construct your personal myth, however, it must do certain things. It must be a myth in which all the mistakes and errors and misjudgments of the past can be washed away, forgiven and forgotten, just as you can forgive that which has been done to you."

Forgiveness is very difficult without a kind of bridge or shuttle between the conscious and the subconscious mind, for the upper levels of the subconscious very much wish to make the behavior more perfect in many cases, or perhaps one has given up, but yet sits upon the surface of life and tells sad stories. To start the day, opening to the Creator, is very helpful. If it is only thirty seconds as you lie in the bed upon waking and think to yourself, "Creator, I love You, I adore You, thank You for this day," you have begun speaking during this day to the one imperishable portion of yourself, that being the infinite Creator which is a part of each of you, which will enable you to take the material that the day's catalyst gives you and give you the resources to see difficulties as challenges and good things as wonderful gifts for which one gives thanks. When one has realized how much the Creator loves one, one begins to love back. It is easy to love the Creator. That love is unconditional.

And so, in whatever form your myth takes, you must jump into it in faith, with no proof, with no idea where the road may lead, with terror, shall we say, and one then lives this way each day, each week, each month, each year, through the life experience, doing all that one does for the love of the one infinite Creator, and therefore becoming a portion of that one great original Thought of love. As you give to others, as your love of the Creator begins to manifest in your life in the cheerful smile, in the recognition within the self that one is self-forgiven, one is redeemed, one is holy and sanctified if one wishes to be by simple prayer. One begins to become a light to others—and it is not because that entity is clever, for cleverness can be devastatingly terrible—it is because that entity feels love. Love created all that there it. That is the key.

Now, when one loves another entity, one is loving a distortion of the Creator, the distortion caused by free will acting through many incarnations upon the personality of the one that is loved. True love occurs between entities when one looks into the eyes of the entity and sees not only the familiar self, but the Creator. This is a deep, deep feeling, a deep recognition, but must depend upon that first great choice which must be taken in ignorance. Faith has nothing to do with belief. Belief is for those who need that structure in which right is always right and wrong is always wrong. Within your illusion, this is simply not so, and within the wider view which one's imperishable soul would take, many, many choices which the brain makes are quite irrelevant to the aiding of the spiritual growth of the self.

We emphasize worship, worship of that which is infinite and invisible, that which loves without stint, that which may be seen most clearly as a symbol as the sun—radiant, generous and ever outpouring. It blazes forth in ecstasy and fusion, in unity that is so powerful that it keeps each entity upon your sphere within the ability to live. Such generous love has your Creator for all of you, all of us, all of the infinity that is the creation, all of the illusions contained within that creation.

Before we leave this topic, we would address the subject of whether finding and feeling the feelings and realizing that one is feeling feelings is helping to one's physical body. We may say most certainly, "Yes." There is no question but that what has been called as a cliché, positive thinking, is correct thinking. It is appropriate to think hopefully, with love, and with trust. Those who feel too vulnerable to do that will armor themselves against a world in which they cannot trust. Yet until one can trust, the heart cannot open, the deep self cannot come forward. One must begin; one must make the choice to have faith, to have hope, to have trust, to have this cluster of words that can barely express something called love.

Now, it is true that when one trusts entities, sometimes the trust is broken. One learns from these episodes, too. But one does not, if one is seeking to emphasize spiritual growth, armor the self, blame the self or blame the other self, but simply sees that a process is taking place and that all is well, and love does abide, whether in the present or in memory.

Entities in any walk of life, whether it be long or hard work in the outdoors or long and hard hours at the desk, are not hampered from dwelling upon holy ground and loving the Creator, for all that one does may be done specifically for the love of the one infinite Creator. This hallows the entire life experience and creates many opportunities in which one may move into the deeper part of the mind in conversation with others who recognize an entity who can truly speak of substantial things.

And so a network of love, a web that grows, begins, and little by little, one begins to know more and more entities who love unconditionally that which they see of Christ, if we may use that word, or the Creator in you. Each within the circle wishes to learn to love and to love each other. Those who feel they are not doing enough for the most part are loving already, but they are blocked from their own ecstasy, from their own joy at love, because they see the illusion of work and toil, of shadow and arguments. They see the daily things upon the surface of life, but they never reach the life-giving water of heavenly food, which is the deeper self.

Therefore, to encourage one's feelings, we encourage reminding oneself how much one loves the Creator or how much one loves the weed by the road, the tree at the top of the hill, the house in the middle of the city, the river as it meanders downstream. Anything that is truly, truly loved by a seeker may be dwelled upon, and as one does any chore whatsoever in life, one may do it and ennoble it because one does it for the love of the one infinite Creator. In this way, feelings move. They are safe feelings, they are feelings that are silent, they are feelings to be tended, as was the Christ child, swaddled and rocked and fed and kept very silent, because others would harm a young entity that is opening to bloom.

Others do not understand why some wish this process to occur, and are content to swim along the surface, enjoying the gusto. Protect yourself from these entities by speaking not of that which you feel. But let yourself feel, and you will find that as you love the Creator, you will begin to realize your other loves. There are things which each love, there are people which each love deeply, irrevocably. To be in touch with those feelings and to be in touch with a feeling of self-forgiveness about all that occurred or occurs between these two entities or between you and that particular career or thing which is loved, is simply the outgrowth of the original love which is infinite, intelligent and what you would call divine. Love runs through you as a river, and as you make that choice to leap into a life in faith and not look back, you do a great service to yourself and to the consciousness of planet Earth, which is improving greatly at this, and we thank each of you that is a part of that.

The feelings are very effective in controlling the energy and the passage of energy through the chakras. One who is dwelling in love and doing that which one does for the love of the Creator moves fairly easily in this consciousness through the challenges of difficult relationships or problems, through wearying times, trying times, sad times and happy times, exhibiting always an awareness of that which is going on—we do not wish to speak like Pollyanna—but realizing also that beneath these daily occurrences of life and death within the illusion there lies an imperishable, infinite point of view that is made entirely of love. This realization quickens and crystallizes each of the chakras, as you yourself seek and feel the excellence of that which the Creator has made. So it is always helpful to one who feels very tired, very disappointed, very downhearted, or very depressed, to visualize each chakra and open the self to the love of the one infinite Creator and allow it to rise until the heart expands and sorrow has had its day and the heart now sings with the love of the Father.

You must realize that the Creator is Father/Mother, rather than Father; that is, the Creator creates, but also nurtures. There is comfort there for the seeker by simple mental request. There are those which are with you always. So as you wish to know what you truly feel, ask before you sleep; ask when you awake, after you have praised the one Creator; and keep asking. Do not make it an obsession, but make it that which you are most curious of and wish to learn, for it is those who seek who find. Respect and use your deep intelligence. Allow the experience of many lifetimes to inform you. Allow all of the intelligences of the universe which flow through you to speak to you. Go ever deeper. Jump ever further in faith. Trust ever more in a kindly but mysterious Intelligence that is love. Trust love. All within the illusion will fall and fail at one time or another; that is because free will is various. But that within you which is imperishable is safe, and that is where you must repair to lick your wounds, to soothe your soul, to ease your mind and to seek your deepest heart. Come to your safe place often and experience love from the one infinite Creator and love for the one Creator.

This instrument is telling us that we are speaking too long, but we would speak about one more facet of this equation, shall we say.

We wish to emphasize that the reason that some mythical systems not only exist, but last for many, many centuries is that they are myths which do things which are needed to move someone from [finitude] to infinity. The leap of faith needs to be taken holding someone's or something's hand. There must be the feeling of safety while being the fool. No one within the illusion can talk oneself into the belief that one can do everything perfectly and unravel the secrets of the universe by the self. You go into uncharted waters, and you will change by seeking in this manner. You must determine that in which you have faith, and if you need to make up a figure, so be it. If you need to visualize a quality, visualize it as a figure of some kind that demonstrates that quality. But allow the means of moving from time to eternity to be personal to you, to be an object of worship and love, for it is the bridge of faith that moves you into the present moment which has all the resonance of eternity. We cannot express to you what hero you may have, what great teacher you may follow, or what you may make up, feel and follow as your own path, but make it personal and own it faithfully and live in faith, abiding in faith and hope, no matter what the outer illusion indicates. This is the basic choice toward positive polarity, to live in faith. For in faith, one does love others, one sees the Creator in others and, finally, one makes that move from loving the Creator in someone to loving someone with all the foibles, the character defects, and the aggravations.

The first challenge the seeker has is the self. The first work must be done to forgive and love the self. That is why a personal symbol of redemption is necessary. Each workable myth creates a means of that redemption. Thus, those who move through that particular program of belief system experience the emotion of faith. We encourage you to experience the emotion of faith, no matter how slender your faith. Do not make it pretentious or show it upon the outside. Let it be personal and real and authentic, and if it takes years in the growing, so be that. You have years. Take them. It is most important to you.

Again, we thank you for this most insightful question and affirm the deep, deep importance of one's true intelligence, one's deep feelings. We would at this time thank this instrument and move to the one known as Jim. I am Q'uo.

(Jim channeling)

I am Q'uo, and greet each again in love and light through this instrument.

(Side one of tape ends.)

(Jim channeling)

I am Q'uo, and am again with this instrument. Is there a query at this time?

Carla: What are the important elements of a personal myth? Besides redemption?

I am Q'uo, and am aware of your query, my sister. This is, indeed, a large field of investigation which this query begins to uncover. We shall attempt to speak in a fashion which covers only briefly that which is of great depth and breadth.

The nature of any mythology is that which offers the model, the blueprint, which provides the seeker a means by which it might move itself in a general fashion, made more specific by application, with the goal of enlightening the self with the love and the light of the one Creator in a relatively pure fashion.

The first element of any workable mythology is the hero which may be identified as any entity who places itself upon the path of the pilgrim who seeks the answers to the great mysteries of the life pattern, the nature of the life, the nature of the self, the purpose of both and their relationship of each to the other, the nature of the Creator, the existence of such, the relationship of self to the Creator and all those created entities about one.

Then there is the journey of the hero that symbolizes the life pattern through which the hero moves, encountering difficulties and dangers, as it would seem, as these are the means by which the desire of the hero is strengthened, then tested, then strengthened again, and tested once again as those riddles of the life pattern begin to [be] answered in a small degree, and by the answering reveal yet more mystery which remains unsolved and which draws the hero onward upon this journey.

As the hero continues upon the journey, the hero learns that there are those forces, both seen and unseen, which may be called upon for assistance when there is a particularly difficult problem that is set before the hero and which yields no easy solution and yet which must be solved in some degree if further progress is to be had. These forces take many forms, depending upon the culture in which the hero is placed, for each culture produces those who have gone before the hero and who themselves have been heroes in their own lives. And yet these entities, once mortal, also called upon that which was greater than they and received an answer, assistance, which empowered, inspired and motivated the hero to continue. These forces then become a source which is seen at first to be exterior to the hero and his or her personality.

However, after a relationship is developed between these powers which are greater than the self and the self, there is seen by the perceptive hero or seeker a connection betwixt these forces and the self which seeks their assistance, so that the seeds of realization of this connection are planted within the being of the hero and provide one of the many opportunities for transformation which take place as the hero moves through various phases and cycles of the journey for that which is in many cultures called the Holy Grail.

As this realization of that which is greater being within the self grows in the heart and in the mind of the hero, the hero finds new abilities within the self, and yet with these new abilities, finds new challenges, that the answers to the great riddles which the hero seeks may be driven ever more deeply into the conscious mind and into the very being of the hero.

Thus, as the hero continues the journey, the process is of that which is identification, the identification of the small self with an enlarging view of the self, so that the hero might begin to place the viewpoint in a manner within the self which experiences a wider and wider definition of the self to include that which is experienced.

The matter of redemption plays a vital role in this process, for as the hero begins to identify the self with a growing viewpoint of the self to include more of that which it views or has viewed as exterior to the self, there is the necessity for allowing the smaller viewpoint to fall away, which is another way of saying that as the hero continues upon this journey, it finds that that which has impeded its progress is its own definition of itself in various modes or manners of expression that have taken root within the perception of the self by the self within the incarnation.

Thus, as these limiting definitions are discarded, there is the need to forgive or to redeem the self which has held these limiting points of view, limiting only as the hero has felt the necessity to move beyond them. For each new point of view or definition of the self will serve the hero for a certain portion of its experience, until it is ready to move beyond this point of view as well. At that time, that point of view will become a hindrance to further progress until a larger point of view is found and the smaller point of view is discarded. This is a simplistic means of describing the process of redemption or redefining of the self.

This process is much aided when the hero entity has other forces or sources of inspiration that are seen as greater than the self to call upon for the sustenance that they provide. However, as the hero continues upon this journey, it begins to identify itself with these forces to such an extent that at some point this journey is seen to be completely interior. The hero is beginning here to see that the self is all—and all is the self—and all are one.

This is a long process, and yet, as the various stages or cycles of this process are traveled, the hero begins to identify the self with a larger and larger point of view until the realization of unity with all is accomplished, at which point the illusion has provided the means by which the hero has been able to transcend the illusion, for however brief a time. And as the hero has been able to transcend the illusion, it then begins to reflect the nature of the illusion more and more faithfully within the life pattern.

Is there another query, my sister?

Carla: No, I'll think about that. And if I ask another question, I promise I'll ask it as the question at the beginning. Thank you very much.

I am Q'uo. We thank you, my sister.

H: I'd like to tell you what I'm thinking about. A friend of mine is sixteen and has been going through a very severe mental breakdown, and I'd like to support her as much as possible. And if you can give me any clues as to how to go about that. She seems to have lost her concentration and her ability to connect, comprehend, and I'm not clear whether she'll ever get that back. And I really … I know I can love her and I can be with her, and that's important, but I feel a little bit at sea as to how I can help her.

I am Q'uo, and am aware of your query, my sister. The desire to be of service to another is the place where we would suggest the beginning be made. The opening of the heart to another with the desire to share that which may be of healing assistance is the key which may be able to unlock the door, shall we say, that will open a new point of view to the one seeking the healing. The opening of the heart is the first step which allows that word or gesture or concept to move through to the one seeking the healing in a manner which is most appropriate to that person at that moment. We do not find that there are strict rules or techniques beyond the honest sharing of that which is available to the self by opening the heart in this manner. As you are aware from previous experience, there are, shall we say, surprises to the self which occur when one honestly opens the self to another and moves with those intuitive feelings that rise naturally to the conscious mind from the subconscious mind when the desire to serve another provides the bridge betwixt these two portions of the mental complex.

Thus, perhaps our greatest aid in this instance would be also to suggest the trusting of one's own self and the intuitive recognition that comes to the self as one desires to serve another. It is also quite helpful to provide an environment which supports and makes comfortable the one seeking assistance. This is done more by the relationship which is developed between the one seeking assistance and the one desiring to give it than the physical placement of either entity. To provide the loving words, understanding, sympathy and embrace is to make safe the relationship and trust which are most necessary for any assistance to be received.

Thus, the true caring that you bring to the effort to assist is that which shall allow and enable the intuitive connection to be established within your own being and between the one seeking your assistance and yourself, so that that information which moves through your own intuitive process will move as freely as possible and will be received as clearly as possible.

Is there another query, my sister?

H: I think that's quite clear to me. Thank you.

I am Q'uo, and we thank you, my sister. Is there another query?

H: I would like to create my life with some way of [aiding] … I don't know, a connection, a spiritual connection, such as what is going on now, in my own … when I'm away from here. And, I'm not a channeler and I don't have a church that I feel comfortable in at this point, and I'm wondering if you have a suggestion for me?

I am Q'uo, and am aware of your query, my sister. Without infringing upon your own decision-making abilities, we can suggest that there is for each entity such as yourself a, shall we say, library of information that is available within your culture that offers inspiration that is found to be more or less useful to those who seek a daily inspiration as a means of centering the self and moving from that center in service to others.

For each such entity, we may recommend that a portion of the day be reserved solely for the inner seeking and reflection which may provide the seeker a drink, shall we say, of the everlasting waters which truly nourish. The time for meditation may be at one's own discretion and be joined with the reading or listening to inspirational information which has been chosen for its special feeling of connection with the seeker. By setting aside a certain portion of each day in a regular manner, one consciously speaks to the subconscious self which has the ability to respond by offering guidance so that a dialog begins to be constructed in which the seeker consciously asks for assistance and also gives thanksgiving for that which has blessed the life pattern.

Thus, the affirmation of the blessedness of the opportunity of each day is given, not only as an affirmation of the day and of opportunity, but as an affirmation of the resiliency and determination and nobility of the self as it seeks to understand the incarnation and its purpose and to share in some manner that understanding as a service to others.

Is there a further query, my sister?

H: No, thank you. That was nice.

I am Q'uo, and again we thank you, my sister. Is there another query at this time?

(Pause)

I am Q'uo, and we have apparently exhausted the queries at the same time as we have exhausted this instrument, and we are most grateful for each query and for this circle's invitation to us to be a part of its seeking for this evening. We are most grateful for this opportunity, and are hopeful that our words have provided a small insight into those matters which are of great concern to each, as each moves upon that great journey which the hero undertakes in the heart of each entity. We are those of Q'uo, and we shall leave this group at this time in the love and in the light of the one infinite Creator. Adonai, my friends. Adonai. ☥

L/L Research

L/L Research is a subsidiary of Rock Creek Research & Development Laboratories, Inc.

P.O. Box 5195
Louisville, KY 40255-0195

www.llresearch.org

Rock Creek is a non-profit corporation dedicated to discovering and sharing information which may aid in the spiritual evolution of humankind.

ABOUT THE CONTENTS OF THIS TRANSCRIPT: This telepathic channeling has been taken from transcriptions of the weekly study and meditation meetings of the Rock Creek Research & Development Laboratories and L/L Research. It is offered in the hope that it may be useful to you. As the Confederation entities always make a point of saying, please use your discrimination and judgment in assessing this material. If something rings true to you, fine. If something does not resonate, please leave it behind, for neither we nor those of the Confederation would wish to be a stumbling block for any.

CAVEAT: This transcript is being published by L/L Research in a not yet final form. It has, however, been edited and any obvious errors have been corrected. When it is in a final form, this caveat will be removed.

© 2009 L/L Research

Sunday Meditation
May 14, 1989

Group question: Has to do with how we might recognize adversity in its early stages, so that we might do whatever is necessary in order to diminish the more traumatic effects, shall we say, or to avoid it completely.

(Carla channeling)

I am Q'uo. I greet you in the love and in the light of the one infinite Creator, and am so very happy and blessed to share this meditation with you and to be a part of your circle of seeking. As always, when we answer your questions with our opinion, we do ask you to be discerning upon your own behalf, for your personal truth shall be as if remembered, not learned but recognized, not for the first time: those things are for you. Other things which have no meaning to you or present a stumbling block are not for you, and we ask you to leave them without a second thought, for we would not wish to be a stumbling block. Anyone has the right to the path of his choice, and those things that we say are of a very decided polarity, that being of service to others. Also, we understand that although our distortions have been refined from your harsh illusion, yet still, subtle confusion persists and the mystery of the universe draws us ever onward.

We must do a bit of background speaking before we can speak upon the subject of adversity and how to recognize it in its early stages. First of all, we would like to specify that it is our opinion that each of you is in part perfect and of the Creator, that in truth all of you and all of we are one together with all else in creation. There is nothing dead; all is alive and all is a unity. The illusions are formed by a series of electromagnetic fields. That is all. We know that the illusion can be very, very trying, tormenting and painful. You, yourself, have designed this to be so, and we will tell you why.

At this time in your planet's history, it is approaching a time when conditions for third density will become most difficult, and it will not make a great deal of sense to attempt having third density life forms upon this planet. Consequently, we speak to those who are, shall we say, advanced students, old souls. In order for each of you to have been born at this time, you had to be able, through the use of faith and will, to achieve service to others of a 51 percent grade or higher; that is, you are capable of serving others more that you serve yourself. One might describe it as giving the other person the larger half of the sandwich instinctively. That is a simplistic way of describing the attitude of service to others. It is not that one is hurting the self—one takes a little less and gives a little more. This is the path of the suffering servant, but it is also the path of unending joy.

Therefore, before you came into this incarnation, you planned for yourself temptations, trials and troubles aplenty. You may have piled your plate very high, or, as this instrument has put it about herself, you have done the equivalent of taking a twenty-one hour semester. It is not advisable, but there are certain souls which are advanced enough that we permit even an ambitious lifetime, for if the ambition turns into fruit, it shall be great fruit. And those who suffer are those who bear fruit, therefore, each of you has chosen difficulties on purpose, not for your abstraction, disgust, apprehension, fear or worry, but for catalyst, that you may learn the lessons of love that it his been given you to learn to make the choice of service to others.

Now, we must do a bit further background work in establishing the actuality of this adversity. Within the illusion, adversity is most real, and, for the most part, normal. It impinges on one, and one reacts to it. In actuality, it is part of a plan set up by your deeper self and the Creator, and it has a sense about it which, when one has lived long enough, yields to inspection. There is always the pattern of the incarnational experience. Over and over again has come the same experience, the same disappointment, or the same betrayal, the same anger or the same love, the same difficulty or the same needs. And after a time one may begin to see an incarnational pattern. Perhaps one is learning patience; perhaps one is learning to love without expectation of return.

That is within this instrument's mind because this instrument believes it is her personal reason for choosing to incarnate at this time as opposed to the work of channeling that she is doing. To love without expectation of return is a most important lesson to learn. To reach out and console, to bring into unity—these are the traits of a strong character whose control is not over others but for the sake of others. And to be in control for the good or for the bad, you must begin and end within yourself.

The first item on the agenda of one who wishes to recognize adversity in its early stages is to know, in a systematic and organized fashion, oneself. This is done by examining the reactions one has had and the behavior one has advertently or inadvertently done during the day. It is best done in contemplation or analysis in the last portion of the day, perhaps when one is drifting off to sleep. And if there has been difficulty and pain to you, your first duty and honor is the healing of yourself. You must be your mother in the sense that the Creator is your mother. You must nurture and cradle yourself and allow the hurt to fall from you. Allow forgiveness to pour into you, for there is no end to forgiveness if it comes through the entity and not from the entity.

Do not expect, as a human entity—that is, one who participates in the senses which perceive third density—to be able to do this quickly or easily. We urge you simply to intend the best and highest that you can in this regard. This is in order that you may be self-forgiven and that you have forgiven that which has pained one. In other words, instead of attempting the difficult and sometimes impossible matter of being understood for oneself, one must first become oneself to the point that one does not react, even to adversity, but acts doing what one wishes to do in that particular situation. Perhaps one does not like what one is doing, but it is well when one's behavior consists of positive choices.

That, perhaps, is the heart of what we have to say to you, but there is more upon other portions of this same subject. The communication with the mate and with the family is most important. The young souls, the children, are those who are open and honest and will indicate and act out in some way when they need to speak and be heard. The adult or grown-up, so-called, person is, on the other hand, inclined to choose not to communicate fully due to ambivalence about subjects or honest confusion and pain. In order to nip adversity in the bud, this adversity—which may not come from illness, pestilence, plague or famine, but from the minds and the hearts and the tongues of each other—one must search deeply within to be sure one is speaking in an honest fashion. There is an authenticity about speaking in a fully open and honest fashion which is unmistakable.

If those about you are unable to deal with the fact that you as a seeker have become an actor in the play who writes his own lines, not one who mouths the lines given by mother or grandmother or mate, one simply does not be concerned that others are not understanding, that others do not seem to be loving. For the satisfaction of being a true, independent, metaphysical spirit is in the loving. However, communication is, indeed, a prize worth pursuing on a daily basis with the mate. However, it is not necessary to achieve the ability to see adversity coming and the ability to become an actor rather than a reactor in the situation.

Much can be said about the quality of faith in this regard. Every entity will have the time of temptation in the desert, the time of confusion, loss and heartsickness. One does not know how long these seasons last or when the oasis shall appear, and in each mated relationship it is only after much work together that entities move in their moods together. Most often entities move according to their own rhythms and have not unified with the other entity enough to experience the same emotional life. Therefore, one of the mated pair may be stolid while the other is excitable. One may be calm, while the other speaks quickly and enthusiastically.

Communication is most difficult. To practice it, simply practice telling the truth to yourself, the whole truth as you see it. When one says it out loud, one hears it about oneself for the first time, and one may, perhaps, learn that one has not got the right of it yet. So, in communication with others you open yourself up to the mirror of your mate, your friend or whomever you are speaking to. And this mirror, if the mirror be objective and kind, is the most incredibly helpful mirror that you may have. If it is objective and critical, it may be painful, but it is still helpful. If it is critical and inaccurate, it is to be ignored. It is most important that you filter that which goes into the self to avoid the constant drain upon self-worth to those who honestly wish to give sacrificially within this illusion in order to polarize sufficiently to graduate into larger life.

We ask that you remember the Christ, who suffered unto death willingly, if not enthusiastically, because it was the will of the Father. We take this example because it is most important to each of you. Each of you is upon a journey, upon a quest. What you are to do is directly in front of your eyes. It may be the scrubbing of a pot, it may be a great adventure, it may be professional work or waxing the car, but if it be done for the love of the Creator, then shall it be blessed and nothing shall be unholy within your spirit, your heart and your mind. For as you do all that you do, you do it for the love of the Creator, and adversity then seems much further off, much more distant, and you are strengthened by your faith and by your will to be yourself.

That God-self within you waits to come forth as you tame your will; therefore, will to know the Father's will until finally your will is one with the Father. Ask always, "Not my will but Thine," for in this harsh chemical illusion you cannot see every desert experience ahead of time. Through the grace of the one infinite Creator, you may be led to instinctive actions. Trust those instincts if they are helpful, if they bind wounds, if they create better situations. Trust those instincts that you know not quite how you found. Ask before sleep the solution to that which puzzles you. Ask at all times and strengthen your will to know, your will to seek the truth.

We are afraid that each of you has chosen a sacrificial life to a certain extent for the express purpose of working towards a greater polarization in your native density. That is, we are saying that each of you is a wanderer, each of you comes from elsewhere in order to aid this particular planet at this particular time. You need not remember that you are a wanderer, indeed, it is not important at all, for you are now naturalized citizens of Earth, dressed in a physical body and soon to die—soon enough, that is; we do not wish to alarm you. When you are now free of the physical body, then you shall examine all those adversities that you met and see if you acted within adversity as well as good times with integrity and authenticity, being yourself and being as kind and compassionate and self-assertive as possible, feeling your worth and feeling others as well.

We remind the seeker of the phrase, "In quietness and confidence is our strength." This is in the mind of this instrument and is from your holy works. You are imperishable spirit. You have chosen to come into a harsh kind of boot camp, shall we say. It does not last long, but it is intense, and within the situations of your life, which keep repeating over and over, you have many attempts to learn the same lesson. Therefore, the solution to an early end to adversity is to feel the friction mentally and emotionally of resistance, a sliding friction of ideas or feelings which comes from resisting that which has created the adversity, whether it be someone or something someone has said.

In other words, in this instance and in every instance you are the instigator of your own pain, others are merely catalyst for you. You must stand upon your own two feet metaphysically and see that, yes, you are responsible, yes, you do not know why, perhaps, you are in a situation, but, yes, you have the faith that it is no mistake whatsoever, but what should be happening, and, yes, you have the will to endure, to love, and to serve.

Be yourself, for you are part of I AM, you are part of consciousness, you are part of All That There Is. Do not be discouraging to yourself, but give yourself every encouragement as would a mother, and do all that you do for the love of the Creator. If you are imperishable, you must ask yourself the question, when adversity begins and you feel that friction: "Shall I move with my catalyst and eat it as fast as I can and learn from it, or shall I surrender to it and be taken like a ship in high wind with no rudder out to sea?" Needless to say, you wish to maintain control of the rudder, control of the sail, control of the direction of your tack or sail.

You do this by being yourself and being radiant and positive where there is difficulty. Find that which is hopeful while recognizing the difficulty. For every feeling, there is the antithesis. For every incarnational pattern there are early warning signs which have mostly to do with that certain feeling that you are resisting change, that you are resisting catalyst, that you are not allowing the self to flow for fear that the self shall disappear. You each are perfect jewels. You can never disappear. You may ask yourself, "Will this be important in ten millennia?" If the answer is no, then you need not be concerned with it overmuch. If you see that within the answer there is a spiritual principle, apply that spiritual principle if you can, and nurture and forgive yourself and give yourself the strength to try again in complete forgiveness if, at this moment, you are not able to stop the catalyst from becoming your illusion, your reality. It takes patience, persistence and courage to follow the path of faith.

We speak to those who seek to have faith. Yet those who seek to have faith do have faith dimly remembered, do have passionate love for the Creator, and they seek to reach that within themselves. Make that connection, feel the true worth of the self, stand upon one's own two feet, metaphysically speaking, and that which is catalyst will then come to you as catalyst. And once one has discovered the basic lesson of the incarnation, one may quickly move, when the sliding resistance begins, into a positive attitude of asking for the change, asking for the experience, asking to change, opening that biocomputer of the mind to new programming, new selfhood, new ways of perception and new ways of storing memory.

Much of your brain is not at this time used. Start suggesting to yourself that a spiritual portion of your mind, so often symbolized by the third eye of the forehead but containing the whole of the skull, be recognized. Above all, we ask that you allow adversity, handled well or handled poorly, to mellow into sweetness within the character. Kindness and charity and hope and faith—all of these things are different ways of saying love, and that is the essence of your being, that is the essence of your Creator, that is the essence of creation itself.

As for adversity … ah, you have designed it to come upon you. You shall one day be interested, rather than fearful, of what the day may bring, for the entity which rules himself needs little but the infinite Creator and the ability and opportunity to love others.

When there are practicalities involved, we suggest that one use one's biocomputer as logically and carefully as possible. However, over against this caution, we assure you that you cannot truly make a mistake, for whatever road upon which you turn, you shall meet your catalyst again and again until you recognize it, love it, forgive it and move beyond. You are queens and kings, rulers of yourselves, all of you royal. Remember who you are, remember your birthright and remember that you live in a spiritual democracy where each entity is precisely, mathematically equal. The differences within the illusion come from your use of will through faith.

With this thought we shall leave this instrument and transfer this contact, with thanks to the one known as Carla, to the one known as Jim. I am Q'uo, and we would, as we leave this instrument, thank it once again for removing a somewhat negative entity from the circle at the time we began. We were grateful that that was removed. We would now transfer in love and light. We are those of Q'uo.

(Jim channeling)

I am Q'uo, and greet each again in love and light. We are privileged at this time to offer ourselves in the attempt to speak to any further queries which may have found their way into the minds of those present. Is there a query at this time?

Carla: I have one from K. I would like to know anything that you can tell me about the basic worthwhileness and use of crystals, whether they are just fashionable right now or whether they have use, and if they have use, what are the uses?

I am Q'uo, and am aware of the query, my sister. The crystal is a living entity, full of the intelligent infinity of the one Creator, and may be utilized as any other portion of the Creator's creation, that is, it may be used well or poorly as a tool for understanding and serving, or as merely an adornment.

The use of the crystal is a field of inquiry which is quite large, as once would expect. However, it might be summarized by suggesting that the crystal, through its facets in construction and the inner properties of geometry and geography, intensifying both the instreamings of intelligent energy from the creation and the vibrational harmonics of the entity that seeks to utilize the crystal in any consciously directed fashion. The crystal then may be utilized to aid the deepening of one's meditative state by desiring that this outcome be produced and by placing the self within a structure of a crystalline nature, such as the framework of a teepee, for example, which would funnel the intelligent energy of the Creator in a fashion that could deepen the meditative state of an entity which has placed itself in the middle of such a structure.

The smaller and more commonly used crystal gems may be utilized by one who seeks to be of service as that which you call the healer, for when the crystal has been chosen according to those qualities which are known to be a part of each gemstone, the appropriately selected crystal may be charged or enhanced by the desire of the one serving as healer in order that the interruption of the energy pattern of the one to be healed might be achieved. This interruption of the energy pattern would allow for another configuration, loosely known to your peoples as health, to be chosen according to the newer mental understanding of the one to be healed, realizing that it has learned what was necessary from the previous configuration of mind that produced the diseases, shall we say, within the mind/body/spirit complex.

Thus, the crystal may be seen as similar to a magnification device and an intensification device that may aid the healer in its attempt to offer its services …

(Side one of tape ends.)

(Jim channeling)

I am Q'uo, and am again with this instrument. Is there another query?

Carla: Yes. I would like to follow up on that with just a couple of small ones. I know there are objects which are also able to contain a lot of negative energy and people have magnetized them that way. Is the best way to demagnetize them … is it sufficient to use salt and water, holy water, or is it necessary to grind them up or otherwise destroy the form of such objects which feel negative?

I am Q'uo, and I am aware of you query, my sister. The use of the salt and blessed water is sufficient for the removal of negative thought forms or vibratory complexes from the artifacts of your illusion when utilized with the desire that is manifested to do so. That is to say, that it is helpful to devise a personally meaningful ritual, if one has not chosen an established ritual of cleansing and consecration of a place or a thing. Thus, we recommend the choosing of such a ritual to accompany the use of the salt and the blessed water.

Carla: Thank you. The other follow-up was having to do with water, especially salt water. Water just makes my arthritic body feel a lot better, especially warm water, and going to South Carolina and getting into the sea water, it seems like I really get better every time I go. Is there some kind of crystal quality to water, especially maybe salt water with minerals in it, that acts as do crystals to heal?

I am Q'uo, and I am aware of your query, my sister. The salt water of your seas and oceans has an especially beneficial healing effect upon the general weariness and fatigue of the physical vehicle. Water in general, and, more specifically, that water which contains salt, is a kind of demagnetizer, shall we say, if one can see the weariness and fatigue of the bones, muscles and joints of the physical vehicle as being that which has accumulated within the vehicle and which may be attracted outward from the vehicle by the immersion of the vehicle in the solution of salt and water.

Carla: Does it help to visualize this occurring cell by cell?

I am Q'uo, and this would be effective for an entity which consciously sought healing from the salted water and was able to visualize with some degree of effectiveness.

Is there another query, my sister?

Carla: No, thank you, Q'uo.

I am Q'uo, and we thank you once again. Is there a query again at this time?

J: I find myself that I am experiencing a lot of dramatic emotions around me, and within my reasoning I feel that it is unwise for me to participate in the emotions, and I find that my life is more pleasurable by simply thinking about things, becoming aware of myself and my surroundings, but yet I find it unnecessary to participate in the dramatic emotions that surround me. I'm just wondering—I find that I do that, so I'm wondering why I do that.

I am Q'uo, and if we understand your query correctly, we may not speak as to the motivation for your actions which is unknown to you, for that which is your heart's desire, if unknown to you, is that which you must seek by your own efforts. We would suggest that each entity in the life pattern takes those actions and thinks those thoughts and speaks those words that one feels are appropriate to the situation at hand. And yet if this entity will look at the motivations for each word, thought or deed, one may discover that it is not a simple matter to put the finger squarely upon the single reason for any thought, word or deed. For each of you, my friends, is a complex being with various lessons, abilities, desires, blockages and challenges to face, all revolving about the concept of love and compassion.

As one begins to move beyond the surface or appearance of one's motivations, one begins to see an interrelationship developing so that there are a number of influences proceeding from the subconscious mind into the conscious behavioral patterns affecting each and every portion of the existence and the being. Thus, there is much which can be learned by turning the curious eye inward and continuing to study that which is seen in order to glean the many fruits which await therein.

Is there another query, my brother?

J: Yes, let's do a little bit of clarifying on that. What I was trying to get, what I was trying to understand was that what I'm feeling about the way I react to these emotions surrounding me, I feel that it is healthy for me though I am not supported by the emotions, in other words, others may feel that it is unhealthy for me and that in the end I will lose the battle by choosing not to participate in the emotional pond, I guess. And I'm just wondering if it is healthy for me. I feel that it is healthy for me now, but I guess I'm wanting to know the future—if it's still beneficial at the same time or if I'm on the wrong path, I guess. I realize I have to decide my own path and react to the surroundings, but I guess that's a frustration for me now because I feel that I am alone in my decision to not become involved in the emotions.

I am Q'uo, and we shall attempt to speak to this query. Whether an action is helpful in the overall sense of one's soul development or is not helpful is a conclusion which is most difficult to reach within your third-density illusion, for much is veiled from the conscious mind, so that what seems helpful in one sense may be just the opposite in another sense when seen from a larger perspective, and vice versa is also true. That is to say, that which seems unhelpful in the short run of things, as you would say, may in the overall sense be quite beneficial.

One may look at one's tendencies or the possibilities which exist as one interacts with those about one. One may choose a certain action and attempt to carry it out in a conscious fashion, feeling that this is the most helpful action that might be chosen. This is a part of the overall learning of any entity, and will eventually bring the entity to that point which is appropriate in its own process of learning, and that is that its true feelings will be discovered, whether they were known in any degree before the action was decided upon or not.

That which is most helpful to an entity in utilizing the catalyst of the daily round of activities is the spontaneous and unrehearsed thought, word or deed which is carried out to its logical or appropriate conclusion, then reflected upon in a conscious fashion and utilized within the meditative state, so that any biases that are not deemed consonant with the highest ideals of the seeker might be noted and marked for future reference, so that the lesson which is embodied might be clarified and a certain set of actions might be associated with that lesson.

Thus, the entity begins to look upon the world with a new point of view that has been enhanced by spontaneous action that has been carefully analyzed, meditated upon, and placed within the proper perspective in the overall growth of the soul as seen from the viewpoint of the conscious seeking self.

Is there another query, my brother?

J: No, thank you.

I am Q'uo, and we thank you. Is there a further query at this time?

A: Yes. I would like to learn to deal with passion that relates to the human being—a passion which is destructive, which doesn't lead any place, which hurts. How to dominate it and how to make it less destructive? Maybe there is no way, maybe there is a way. What would you advise someone particularly in love with someone since a long time and doesn't know how to deal with it anymore and knows it doesn't lead any place. What would you advise this person to deal with so this person doesn't get hurt so much, that this person has no room to serve, or it diminishes the action of this person to really serve the others because there is this healing process going on, or this big hurt and wound going on?

I am Q'uo, and we feel much within your query which is unspoken and which speaks loudly as to the desire to be of service and the confusion as to how best to achieve true service in this regard. We may not give specific suggestions in this type of query, for that which is closest to the heart of the seeker is that which must respond only to the seeker's free will choice and not to words that we may give as teacher. For when the test is true there is the opportunity to express the learning which one has achieved at a time that may seem most traumatic, and it is at this time that the choice rests squarely upon the shoulders of the seeker which may be confused as to the direction of movement, the shape of the movement, and the final outcome. All of this is the nature of mystery which is at the heart of each incarnation.

But we might suggest that when the seeker of truth finds itself confronted with such a choice that is felt to be of great importance within the life pattern, that there is no time during which it is more important to remain close to the heart within and to move in the manner which the heart declares.

How to find this feeling of the heart; this is the dilemma of the seeker. Each will recognize the choices before one in such a situation. Much thought will be given to each. Prayers may be offered. Each possibility may be embraced within meditation. All of the attention of the seeker is placed upon each possible choice. Play out each within your heart of hearts one at a time, perhaps on separate days, when you feel a great desire to know and have the opportunity to meditate in peace and in silence. Observe your heart and your feelings as each choice is played out, and most especially the after-effects.

When you have played each choice to its logical conclusion and visualized the ramifications attendant to each possibility, then it is that your heart will speak; that this is or is not a possibility. As you eliminate possibilities, you will at some point discover the direction of the heart, for the heart seeks not only the welfare of the single self, but of those with whom the self has joined in the like pattern so that there is a harmony that the heart sees and reflects when the conscious mind asks sincerely.

Thus, we can recommend no specific answers to your situation, for it is such challenge that you have placed before yourself and which is of such importance that each step which you take to be most helpful in the overall growth of the world must be that which is freely chosen by your own desires.

May we speak in any further fashion to another query, my sister?

A: Thank you, that's fine.

Carla: So, what you are saying is follow your deepest desires no matter what. Follow your heart.

I am Q'uo. That is correct, my sister.

Is there another query?

J: I guess I have one that goes back to my original—my first question. If … the strong emotions, what part do they play in this density as far as the benefits in order to graduate to a higher level or whatever. What are the benefits of the emotions?

I am Q'uo, and am aware of your query, my brother. The benefit of such emotional biases is personal to each seeker. The stronger the emotional bias, the more intensity there is noted within the learning opportunity. That is to say, the greater the emotion, the greater the bias, and the more obvious the lesson which is being presented to the seeker, for there is but one response to any catalyst within your illusion that reflects a balanced point of view. That response, as you know well, is love or compassion. When any other emotion is noted within the mind/body/spirit complex of the self, then the seeker may assume there is catalyst there to be processed in order that a balancing may occur.

Is there another query, my brother?

J: Would you say that these emotions are the emotions other than compassion, love, which I feel *(inaudible)* there are purely instinctual, instinctive, anyway. I think they are more of logic, that you should have compassion, because that is giving for others. Do you feel that the other's emotions are purely self-centered and egotistical and have no benefit to the serving of others?

I am Q'uo, and am aware of your query, my brother. The benefit, as we spoke previously, is to each seeker in that the emotions alert the seeker to that which remains to be balanced. As balancing occurs, the ability to serve others is enhanced.

Is there another query, my brother?

J: I'm not quite understanding what you're saying.

Carla: Well, I'd like to clarify that, too. To me there is a distinction between surface emotions, which are almost always destructive, and deep emotions which are intelligent emotions.

J: I feel that anger and hatred and things like that are very destructive, but I can see that they would help the individual if they helped them, but only if they could be intelligent enough to become aware of what happened and how they can learn from the situation. But if the person's not intelligent enough, I guess, or doesn't want to be aware of the situation, is wont to display the dramatic emotions, I feel that that may be self-centered, but I'm not sure if it is, because it may have some effects, I guess. I don't know. I guess that's what I want to know.

I am Q'uo and am aware of your query, my brother. The ability of the seeker to consciously recognize catalyst is primary to any learning in a conscious sense. Most entities within your illusion have only the barest conscious glimpse of the value of the emotions which mark their biases and growth potential, shall we say. Such entities must experience the same catalyst, whether it is intensely felt anger or blandly experienced boredom, over and over again before the catalyst makes its mark within the conscious mind strongly enough to draw the attention there to discover the possibility of balancing that exists within every bias. Whether the emotion is small and superficial or deep and [perceived as dangerous], the lesson that is possible within any situation remains as a function of the intensity of the bias.

There may, indeed, be emotions within your illusion, as you are well aware, that are quite mentally or physically destructive. All of these ramifications of interaction are significant portions of the learning process. The more important the lesson or the transformation of point of view, the greater will be the price or the sacrifice that the entity shall need to make in order to purchase that which may, indeed, be a pearl of great price. Thus, great anger can teach as great a measure of compassion. However, each learning does, indeed, have its price.

Is there a further query?

J: No, thank you.

I am Q'uo, and we thank you, my brother. Is there a final query at this time?

Carla: Thank you, Q'uo.

I am Q'uo, and we, indeed, express our gratitude to each present this evening. It is a great honor to join this group, to blend our vibrations with yours. We cannot thank each enough for this opportunity. Again we remind each that if any word we have spoken does not ring true to the heart, that it should be forgotten immediately. We do not wish to place any stumbling block before the seeker of truth.

At this time we shall take our leave of this group, leaving each, as always, in the love and in the light of the one infinite Creator. We are known to you as those of Q'uo. Adonai, my friends. Adonai. ✤

L/L Research

www.llresearch.org

Sunday Meditation
May 28, 1989

Group question: Has to do with what we might call a spiritual kind of coincidence in our lives, which ranges from how the various events of the day that aid our learning and understanding occur, whether it might be we meet the right person, the right book or the right travel agent, or whether it might be that the entity that incarnates through us as a child comes into our lives. It is said by many that there are spiritual entities of various densities and degrees of understanding located within various of the realms of the astral level and of the devachanic levels of our Earth plane that are attracted to us by our current vibrations or understanding or seeking for information. How are all of these entities and ideas, peoples and events brought together in our lives in what seems later to be an appropriate configuration so that just the right learning occurs and just the right service at the right time?

(Carla channeling)

I am Q'uo. I greet you all in the love and the light of the infinite Creator. May we thank this instrument for removing from the group's atmosphere the negative entity which could have confused this contact. We appreciate this instrument's care in challenging spirits.

It is a beauty and blessing to us to be called to your group this evening. Joy washes over us as we enjoy your combined vibrations and the light of seeking which together you build, which comes through the ethers as a call which we may answer. For we are of those who desire to be of service through contact with those of your people who serve as vocal channels.

That which we have to say is opinion, and we ask you carefully to beware of authoritarianism in us or anyone, for all is opinion—nothing is known. This is not important in a final sense, for there is much to learn before the spiritual gravity within us calls us away from identity and back to the uncreated oneness of the Creator. Consequently, that which we have to say to you, if it is inspirational, please feel free to use it. If it provides for you a stumbling block, remove it without a second thought. We thank you for your discrimination and encourage it.

The question this evening concerns spiritual coincidence. It is a subject that may be approached from many ways, and we have debated how to approach it. We have decided that perhaps the best way is to express the grand principle of free will among all your peoples, all of humankind and third density upon your sphere. There is free choice at all times. There is that which is called faith or destiny, in that each of you with the help of the higher self decided what lessons you are to attempt within this life experience. However, there are many, many plans made because entities do not follow the dictates of their deepest free will, of their happiness and bliss, as the one this instrument is fond of—as Joseph Campbell would say.

Thus, let there be no talk of destiny disrupting free will, for free will is paramount. Each of you has the choice at all times of which voice to which you may listen, which instinct feels correct, which hesitation is born of fear and which of wisdom. The comforting thing about spiritual coincidence is that it continues as long as one is upon the spiritual path. As humankind misses by misunderstanding spiritual coincidences, patiently, carefully, the higher self organizes a probable series of actions which will teach the same lesson. It tends to have more force each time it is repeated so that the seeker may recognize the problem more easily.

To some, it may seem as if the Creator is progressively against them [to] these or those who have not awakened to the catalyst being that which is borne as fertilizer to the ground of faith and love and service to others, that fruit may appear from the suffering endured and learning the lesson. Why is there suffering, my friends? It is very simple. Suffering is a natural concomitant of change, and when something new is realized and put into action within the self and the self's thinking and behavior, change occurs. The energy of programs which have become useless may now turn to new programs, and so the student progresses upon the path of seeking the infinite mystery of the one Creator.

At any point, an entity may say, "This I cannot handle at this time," and may walk away from the catalyst. There is no loss of free will, nor is there merely one conclusion that may be drawn from the same catalyst. Each entity will experience a common catalyst in an unique way.

Therefore, we ask that you be aware that spiritual coincidence is not coincidence, but planning. Before your birth—and we may parenthetically add here that each of you upon this sphere at this time is capable of graduation into fourth density—has had the opportunity to make many, many choices, to see catalyst in a way that can be of service to self and others or in a way that is self-destructive and destructive to others. These coincidences are so that the one who is working along the spiritual path may be cheered and strengthened in faith. It takes nothing away from the free will of the entity to have a situation presented in which this lesson may be demonstrated as learned, this particular lesson that you interpret in this particular way. But if you walk away from this opportunity, this catalyst, you shall again encounter a similar catalyst, in different circumstances, in a different spiritual set of coincidences, so that you may further recognize that lesson you came to express and manifest.

We ask you to think of yourself in a symbolic manner as the Christ upon the cross. Each suffers; each dies. Each spends the life, no matter how happy, in some degree of psychic, spiritual, emotional, mental or physical pain. This is the road of service to others. This is the sacrificial road which each of you has chosen as service-to-others entities. Each of you loves each other. Each of you would step in front of the other to stop the bullet. This is service-to-others polarity, and this entire vibratory nexus which you call third density is that in which you make the foundation choice which each of you has already made to be of service to others and to live a life in faith. Your basic contribution is living the life in faith; not in being happy or melancholy or useful or productive, but in being a certain kind of entity, an entity that is able to shine through the windows of the eyes and the smile upon the lips with the light of the one infinite Creator.

While you are doing this, you are carrying the cross to which you are nailed. This is, shall we say, the valley of the shadow of death. To put it in completely another context, this is your boot camp. This is a difficult time for each seeking spirit, for you must begin to learn your true value as a child of the one Creator. You must begin to choose your service and to make that service so much a part of your life that it becomes your freedom and the inability to serve becomes enslavement.

Therefore we ask you, even though it is difficult, not to fear the pain of change or the sometimes bewildering energy that may accompany it. For change you will, if you meditate each day, and if you attempt to choose always to serve the one infinite Creator.

It was part of the question that there were many upon your inner planes which were at all times available and might aid the entity. This is indeed so. None is alone ever. Each is beloved not only by the Creator but by those who have chosen to be companions within the life experience of this spirit. Thus, the second thing which we would encourage in each is a program of daily, humble, simple, listening, silent meditation. There are voices deep within you of the Creator, of what this instrument would call the Spirit, and many others, the higher self, of guides, of the inner planes, of the deeper recesses of the self, which in a subjective sense is equal to the description of the outer spirits above, that can give information to you which you are unable to reach or have access to while in the normal waking state.

Thus, to put oneself in a state of listening is most important in opening the intuition and strengthening that rainbow bridge betwixt time and eternity, betwixt the past, present and future and now, the eternal moment. For all of you, you see, experience an illusion called time, and an illusion called space, that the great tapestry of your life may be woven by you, warp and woof, color upon color and pattern upon pattern, as a gift to the infinite Creator. In silence, these deeper voices may speak to you, and you find what you truly and most deeply wish to do.

We do not suggest that because you feel that you have heard this or that, you obey it. We encourage always the discrimination. But we encourage each to listen to the clear dream, to the sudden realization, to the result of meditation. For, my friends, your consciousness uses for its subtle spiritual work that portion of the brain which is called the frontal lobes. It is faith that creates the rainbow bridge betwixt the waking, thinking and creative self and the spiritual wilderness of most entity's frontal lobes.

Each of you which is doing work in consciousness needs to be aware that there is a simple physiological movement of the consciousness which is the cause of so many of the teachers of meditation advising the gaze upon the third eye within the forehead. It is not the gland itself that is so important; it is the physical matter of the frontal lobes which, when given attention by the deep mind, may open by faith that one may cross into eternity and look at situations from the standpoint of now, a now which is ten thousand years later, a now which may give the planetary view, a now which gives the eternal view.

It is said that all roads lead to Rome; we find this within this instrument's head. We assure you, you cannot make too many detours to move through the densities. It merely is up to you as to how fast you wish to progress. The faster that you progress, the more uncomfortable that you will be. If you truly wish to progress quickly, it is best to do it with another entity at least, for the energies released are strong. The revolution around meditation and balancing of the day's experiences or analysis of the day's experiences is most important. The taking of the life seriously is helpful, and the viewpoint of laughter, merriment and seeing the life as [a] cartoon is equally helpful. Both viewpoints are needed to form an accurate picture of that which occurs within the catalyst of your life experience. All that is tragic has the edge of humor. All that is happy and humorous has an inner side of tragedy. Polarity is a portion of third density.

We encourage you not to be concerned as to how fast you move along the path to spiritual enlightenment, for, in truth you are not seeking a specific gradation of light, but are seeking merely to progress. There is, indeed, a resistance point betwixt densities, a point of light which becomes suddenly of a different nature, so that those which truly cannot move into fourth density at the end of the life experience will be placed upon a planet which is having third-density experience. Those who are able to cross the threshold to the fourth density upon their physical death may move into a larger life, a life of glowing colors and harmonious entities, a life where all the lies and deceptions and the schemes and attitudes are known and loved and forgiven, and therefore are no longer needed as armor and are dropped; a density of understanding of each other, of being able to see which mate is truly associated with you and is truly to be with you, and in this instance we would refer to the query of the one known as P.

The choice of a mate is most important, for one who seeks may seek much more stably, much more objectively, and much more creatively if that spirit is, shall we say, in harness with another entity which likewise is dedicated to carrying the cross of humanity and suffering to learn the lessons of love. We are not specifically Christian, anymore than we are specifically Buddhist or Taoist or Shintoist. We are those who speak of love and light, and we wish each to realize that those who speak of a life experience as the proverbial bowl of cherries, as this instrument would call it, have in one way got it right, because this is an illusion, my friends, a complete and total illusion.

That through which you are going at this time will not leave a mark upon you—that is, your spirit—

unless you allow it to. This and that shall happen with difficulty to your mind, your emotions, and your body; all which is born, shall die. You are perishable, yet you are also imperishable, and the spiritual coincidences of this illusion give to you information, subjective personal information, not of use to others, not of general importance, not of proof, shall we say, but that which is subjectively interesting to you.

In daily meditation you sink into your intuitive mind, into your subconscious, and you build that rainbow bridge of faith. Above all things, we urge you to live a life in faith and love, faith that what is happening should be happening, love for all that moves and breathes, love for the elements themselves, love for the Creator, and above all, love of each other. Listen increasingly, as your intuition becomes more able to communicate with you consciously. Keep the dream notebook, keep the notebook of that which comes to you when awake, and see what your concerns are, what the pattern of your difficulties may be. Your so-called brain is a biocomputer which is of limited use. It is very useful as an employee of your spirit, and we urge you to place that ability to think and discern upon those things which have already happened which need analysis, though we urge you to keep the intellect in abeyance while experiencing intuitional information.

My friends, there is not a lack of free will, but each of you has a destiny. Each of you has come here hoping to fulfill some job, shall we say, some change in attitude, some feeling, some bias that before you were born you decided needed strengthening. Therefore, that which is happening to you is happening to you because you chose to be strengthened in a certain way. Let your intuition speak to you concerning the catalyst of the day and especially the spiritual coincidences that occur. For much information, in fact, all that there is, resides within your own consciousness which in itself is a portion of the one infinite Creator in its active state. Trust in your birthright, and do not be fooled by this little life that you live at this time. You cannot make a mistake within this illusion if you but shoulder your troubles and carry on, having faith that you have arranged for yourself in a perfectly simple and understandable manner that which confronts you. No matter how confused or difficult it may seem, there is a heart to it and in that heart is a lesson of love.

Do not berate the self as you fail in your own eyes, but simply start again, look again, meditate again, and persevere in the desire to know. For if you desire to know the truth, the truth will repeatedly come to you, some truths useful for a small period of time, some truths useful for all of eternity. When one truth changes to another, do not be afraid, for the basic truth is love, and its basic expression within your density, faith. You were born as part of the Creator and part of free will. You have within you love and variousness. As you move through the variety of experiences that your free will chooses, allow that Creator-spirit within to recognize the spiritual lessons which you are to learn. Allow that rainbow bridge to form, allow, shall we say, in a mechanical way, the use of the frontal lobes in which are stored all of creation.

At this time, we would transfer this contact to the one known as Jim, thanking this instrument for its effort upon our behalf, and especially for the ridding from the group of an entity with which we would have difficulty in keeping a clear contact. I am Q'uo. I leave in love and light and transfer at this time.

(Jim channeling)

I am Q'uo, and greet each again in love and light through this instrument. At this time it is our privilege to offer ourselves in the attempt to speak to those queries which may yet remain upon the minds of those present. Is there a query at this time to which we may speak?

J: Yes, I have a question. Earlier, Q'uo, in the channeling you spoke of if a person decides to go rapidly in your spiritual seeking and take the hard path, I believe you said, it is best to have a kindred spirit making the journey with you. I think I understand why, but could you elaborate just a little bit in case there's some things about that I'm not thinking of?

I am Q'uo, and am aware of your query, my brother. As one progresses upon the journey of evolution of mind, body and spirit, one will discover that the catalyst which aids in this progress is most usually configured in a manner which will present the challenge in order that abilities of the entity may be stretched, shall we say, to the limits and the possibility of enlarging these abilities then offered. If one chooses to progress in a more rapid or conscious fashion, this in the mundane world of your daily experience may well mean that the difficulties will be enhanced.

Thus, it is well upon such a journey to travel with a companion of similar desire that wishes above all else with you to make this journey of seeking, of learning and of service, for those who are of a like mind will far more surely find those clues within the catalyst that point the direction for the next step, and those who travel together will experience their catalyst and processing of same in an unique fashion, with one utilizing the intensity of experience at a time, perhaps, when the other has less intensity, so that there might be assistance given from one to another. The support of one seeker for another is crucial in those times during which the night of the soul is experienced and despair descends upon the perception of the one who is experiencing the battle of learning and of service. For there is much to untangle within each incarnational experience and when one seeks to speed this process, one is asking to suffer in the mundane world in order that the limits of ability might be enhanced and enlarged.

Thus, there is much of comfort and of solace and of support that each may provide the other as the goal of learning and of serving is achieved.

Is there a further query, my brother?

J: No, thank you very much.

I am Q'uo, and thank you, my brother. Is there another query?

Carla: Could you speak on the reprogramming of the mind?

I am Q'uo, and we shall speak but briefly …

(Side one of tape ends.)

(Jim channeling)

I am Q'uo, and am again with this instrument. We shall continue. The term "reprogramming" has some misdirection within it to which we would first speak. It is possible to assume by this term that one would change the program that has been set in motion in some fashion due to conscious desire and specific efforts. We would rather focus upon the completion of programming rather than that which would change programming which has been chosen previous to the incarnation's beginning. For the preincarnative choices that have allowed certain biases and tendencies to manifest within the incarnational pattern have the purpose of allowing a greater point of view or perspective to be achieved as the preincarnative biases are experienced, analyzed, meditated upon, and consciously worked with in a manner which draws unto them their appropriate complements, in many cases these being the opposite of the original bias.

Thus, one may experience a good deal of frustration and anger pointed toward the self within an incarnational pattern as a result of various what an entity may call mistakes and ineffective application in order that a greater love and compassion might eventually replace the anger and frustration which were the first distortions or biases with which the entity began. Thus, the continued experience of this anger pointed toward the self may eventually attract the attention of the entity to the degree that the entity begins to consider why such anger exists and what use may be made of it, all the while building the potential for eventual acceptance and compassion for the self and then for others about the self.

Thus, it is our recommendation that each entity seek to understand and to identify those biases or programmings which are prominent within the life pattern and to trace these behaviors of thought, of word, and of action to their deepest source within the being and to then note the effect that these programmings have brought about within the point of view or attitude of the entity. It is well to enter into the daily round of activities without pretense or predisposition to, shall we say, clamp down upon the self certain behaviors due to their being felt to be of an unhelpful nature, but rather to allow the natural response in each situation to find its expression within the self and to work with that response at a later time when the emotional coloration has left the mind and to work in the contemplative or prayerful or meditative state with these spontaneous responses in order that they might be enhanced to the point that their logical conclusion is seen and felt within the being.

At this point it is then possible that the appropriate complement that is meant to be drawn to the entity through these spontaneous experiences will make itself known as well within the field of vision of the inner eye. When this has occurred with equal intensity, then, at the deepest level of awareness possible for the seeker, it may be seen that the life pattern has the purpose in this instance of allowing this range of experience to be had in the life pattern in order that certain opportunities and lessons and services might be made available.

Thus, it is our recommendation that the conscious working with catalyst, that which may be called the reprogramming, be done as a function of the natural experience that forms the life pattern and be done in a conscious fashion with the desire to penetrate to the heart of the experience so that the surface appearance is soon left behind and the deeper significance is discovered, buried layer upon layer within the symbolic formation of this programming within the entity's life pattern.

Is there another query, my sister?

Carla: It says in the Bible, "By their fruits you shall know them," and that's sort of a biblical equivalent of the work ethic which Americans have. It sounds to me that you're saying that worldly ambition and the work ethic work, or can work, against living a life in faith or living a life by spiritual principles. Is that correct?

I am Q'uo, and am aware of your query, my sister. If one's focus of attention remains solely upon the surface of experience, that which you call the worldly ambition, then, indeed, it is so that such can retard the progress of one upon the path of evolution. For it is truly said that it is an illusion in which you now dwell. "It is far more than it appears," is another way of stating this point of view. Thus, there are various levels of realization that one may obtain from any particular experience. One may remain upon the surface of experience and realize only that which is mundane and worldly in your normal round of activities. One may chose at some point within the life experience to seek further the meaning of the experience.

At this point the entity will begin to see beyond the appearance of the illusion and the daily round of activities so that a pattern of purpose begins to form itself within the conscious seeking entity. Thus, the journey inward has begun and may continue for as long and as far as the entity wishes to pursue it.

May we speak further, my sister?

Carla: But you can do a job and make a living, as long as you don't take it home with you. It wouldn't matter then, right? You could still progress spiritually?

I am Q'uo. One may, indeed, complete the job, as you have called it, and provide a living for the self and the family and yet be able to take great strides of evolution. For all that comes before the conscious seeker of truth in the daily round may be utilized in a higher and higher sense, shall we say, once the mundane level of experience has been accomplished.

Is there another query, my sister?

Carla: Is the opposite true? Can one who does not do any physical service find a way to progress spiritually?

I am Q'uo, and am aware of your query, my sister. Within your illusion it is quite possible to progress in a spiritual sense without physically doing any particular thing, for the entity which is consciously aware of the process of evolution may utilize any experience, thought or desire in order to advance the ability to feel love and compassion for the self and for all other selves. Thus, it is only necessary that the desire to learn and to serve be present within the entity for these goals to be realized within your illusion.

Is there a further query, my sister?

Carla: No, Q'uo, thank you very much.

I am Q'uo, and we thank you, my sister. Is there another query at this time?

J: I have another question. I don't want to be a hog, but this has been bothering me the whole time we've been sitting here. It goes back to when Carla was channeling at the very beginning. Before she was channeling, just before we said the Lord's prayer, I was running a real negative trip in my head about a common friend and our experiences, and it was really just bothering me, because here we were about to start praying together and I was running all this real heavy negative stuff. And then Carla came and channeled and said and was thanked by Q'uo for challenging a negative entity. My question is, was this negative entity in any way involved with the intensity of my thoughts, my negative feelings? If this doesn't infringe upon free will, could you comment upon it, please?

I am Q'uo and am aware of your query, my brother. The entity of which we spoke through the instrument known as Carla was an entity which was attracted to the desire to be of service that was present within this circle of seeking. This desire is seen upon the metaphysical planes as a light This light is seen in its intensity to possess a power to transform. The negatively-oriented entity desired to influence this light in as great a fashion as possible in order that the light might be brought within its domain, for this is the nature of the negatively-oriented entity, to gather from whatever source possible as much light power as possible in order that its own power might be enhanced at the expense, shall we say, of others.

The thoughts of those within the circle of seeking, inasmuch as they would deviate from the harmony normally present within such a positively-oriented group, may be utilized by such an entity to provide a chink, shall we say, in the armor of protective light that this group or any such group provides by its desire to seek information in order to be of service to others.

Thus, the thoughts that were present within your mind complex were available as a resource for this entity which would have been happy to utilize them by enhancing their intensity and removing your positive contribution to the circle of seeking. This was in potential and was not yet a possibility for the entity, however, the entity was aware of such possibility.

Is there a further query, my brother?

J: In other words, from what you just said, this entity hadn't really focused on me, but was just aware, because this is not the first time this particular thought had been entertained by me. But you're saying that it really wasn't a focus at this time of this entity on my particular thoughts that made them so intense?

I am Q'uo, and am aware of your query, my brother. Without infringement, we may suggest that the notice of the thoughts of which you speak was as far as the entity was able to proceed, though the normal process for such an entity is, indeed, to intensify such choices freely made that deviate from the harmony possible for an entity. There is no ability of negatively-oriented entities to plant, shall we say, such a thought within the mind of another without the other first creating that thought of its own free will.

Is there another query, my brother?

J: No, thank you very much.

I am Q'uo, and we thank you once again, my brother. Is there another query at this time?

Questioner: Would you address the difference between judgment and discernment?

I am Q'uo, and am aware of your query, my sister. The hallmark difference from our point of view between the judging and the discerning is that in the act of judging an action, a thought, or an entity, one in some degree removes that thought, action or entity from the loving compassion that one would feel in a normal sense without the judgment. In the act of discerning, one looks at a thought, a word, an action, or an entity and attempts to describe what is occurring without removing this thought, word, action or entity from the heart, shall we say, and attempts to relate to that thought, word, action or entity in a fashion that is consonant with the feeling of compassion and love that each portion of the Creator has as a natural birthright.

May we speak in any further degree, my sister?

Questioner: No, thank you.

I am Q'uo, and we thank you, my sister. Is there a final query at this time?

Carla: I guess I'd like to ask the one that was brought up about the sevens. There were a lot of seven densities and seven sub-densities and so forth. Have you any comment to make on that particular arrangement?

I am Q'uo, and am aware of your query, my sister. Each density of light provides a certain vibrational possibility for learning and for service. Within your third density, as is true with each density before and after the third density, there is the primary division of the density into seven levels of vibration, each building upon the previous level in the possibility of obtaining experience, of learning through experience, and of serving through utilizing that which has been learned. There is within each sub-density a further division of seven that proceeds yet into further division of seven, until one may assume that the division is infinite.

Thus, possibility for learning and serving through the gradation of experience is also infinite. The divisions of each density and sub-density are not arbitrary or created by any particularized entity or group of entities, but are rather a function of the nature of the creation itself which has certain vibrational characteristics that naturally fall into those areas which in your numbering systems correspond to that which equals seven.

Thus, within your illusion, there are many mystery schools, shall we say, which find meaning in this division of sevens, so that in a mathematical sense there is the possibility of creating the model or the analog which approaches the deeper levels of understanding of the very nature of creation. Thus, one finds that the pursuit of the understanding, shall we say, of the mysteries of life, as you would call it, may be described in a general fashion by the application of the qualities that are associated with the seven levels of vibration of light which form the creation or the universe as you know it.

Thus, each entity within this circle of seeking and within the third density in general has reproduced within its energy systems, or those areas which you have called the chakras, the seven levels of vibration, each energy center or chakra containing also a division of seven levels of apprehending the basic nature or tone of experience that is possible within each energy center, with each succeeding center providing a finer or more refined application of the basic energy which enters through the root chakra and proceeds through the system of chakras or energy centers in the form of light, so that the entity is able, or potentially able, to apply its own level of understanding to its daily round of activities and discern those experiences which have significance in the journey of evolution.

Thus, the system of sevens provides each seeker of truth the ability to penetrate beyond the surface appearance of any thought or experience so that there might be gained from each a variety of levels of experience or symbolism that will enhance the evolutionary process.

At this time …

Carla: Could I ask just one more question? To follow up? It's just this. Excuse me—I didn't mean to interrupt you, but I was so curious. Would it be correct to say, then, that the peculiar plangency and heartfeltness of music, especially sacred music, is due to the fact that music is the physical analog of that spiritual truth, since it moves in octaves—seven notes and then the next note is the same as the first, only an octave higher?

I am Q'uo, and this is correct, my sister, for the vibration that is felt within an entity as a response to the musical notation being reflected through voice or instrument is a vibration which sets up the possibility of viewing the present experience of the entity from that level of vibration created by the music. Thus, certain music, as you call it, will excite certain centers of energy, and through that excitation the entity will feel various levels and qualities of inspiration. Thus, the perception of the entity will blend in an harmonious fashion with the music and provide the entity an experience that would not be possible without the presence of the music.

Carla: Thank you, Q'uo. I'm done now, and I just want to thank you for being with us tonight and invite you to join us afterwards for our merriment and laughter. Be with us, and we thank you so much, all of us. Adonai.

I am Q'uo, and we are most grateful, my sister, to each present for allowing our presence this evening, for without your invitation we would have no beingness within your circle of seeking. We are most grateful for the opportunity to speak those words which we offer freely and which are the fruits of our own seeking. We remind each that we offer that which is but our opinion, and we do not wish any word to provide a stumbling block to any seeker. Please accept those words which have meaning to you and use them as you will. If any word does not ring true, please forget it at once.

We at, this time, would leave this instrument and this circle, as always, in the love and in the light of the one infinite Creator. We are known to you as those of Q'uo. Adonai, my friends. Adonai. ♣

Sunday Meditation
June 18, 1989

Group question: Most people feel that the spiritual journey should become easier, happier and healthier the further and longer that you travel. This doesn't seem to be so. In many cases there seem to be more difficulties or challenges, shall we say, that are put in the path of the sincere and persistent seeker. Why is it that the path does not necessarily become easier or happier or healthier the longer that you travel?

(Carla channeling)

I am Q'uo. I greet you in the love and in the light of the one infinite Creator. We of Q'uo thank you for the desire which has come to make you one circle of seeking, one desire for truth, one unity of spirit. The question that you have asked this instrument to channel upon is one which this instrument will find interesting because this instrument has immediately previous to this read a similar message to a similar question. It is a good chance for those who have been channeling to see that there are nuances and subtleties to questions within a group that are personalized by the group so that although the end result is hopefully an inspiration which may be universal, it is carefully shaped to the questions between the lines of the question.

Within your culture, you have a condition of emotion, spirit and body which is called burnout by this instrument. The cause of this is that you have not given over those portions of yourself which are not good fruit and, therefore, that within you which is not good fruit tries to take over the good vine, as your holy book would put it. Now, we are starting from a spiritual standpoint, because we feel that to this group meditation, inspiration, integrity and singleness of heart are already in place. This is [the] spiritual atmosphere in which we urge each to come. Each of you comes already in this mode, centered by meditation and contemplation and a burning desire to serve the Creator and all of your brothers and sisters. Therefore, we shall move into the subject from the secular standpoint.

When you face a challenging task, it is often exciting, and if you are given the opportunity to finish the task before beginning another, there is much satisfaction. If you begin another large task while in the midst of finishing the first, the stress and anxiety of time allotment occurs, not because there is not enough time, but because you are depending upon yourself. This is a secular world, a secular culture, an unchurched culture. The offering of unity and unconditional love that the master known to you as Jesus offered has been so subverted and contaminated with doctrine and dogma that it seems that there is no longer the possibility of what one may call Christian worship.

Yet I say unto you, my children, this is an untruth. You may, in opening yourself to the less personal side of yourself, find the strength, find the time, and find the grace to know the will of the Creator and to do it. This cannot happen to you secularly or in a human fashion, for you are, in your waking consciousness, very, very little aware of the fact that all of you are channels. Therefore, you attempt to channel your own deepest love and service to others. And at some point, you reach your own limits and can go no further, and this seems to you to be a great failure.

We ask you first of all never to judge the self. That judgment will come, and you yourself shall be the God-self which evaluates this lifetime experience for you. As you well know, you are your own hardest critic, your own most difficult audience. To please yourself with what you do is the greatest challenge. Paradoxically, in order to maximize one's service, there is much of oneself that needs to be burned away, as the chaff from the wheat, so that the wheat may be gathered as it springs green upon the hillside, and then golden, and then ripens unobstructed by the weeds of daily concern.

So our focus, perhaps, to you this evening would be to suggest that a time be set aside, and, if possible, a special place where one may go to listen within one's heart, having opened the door behind which stands the consciousness of Christhood, the consciousness of Love. This consciousness is infinite, and one who trusts it and has faith in it is able to tap into that overflowing, beautiful and ineffable stream of the Creator's love. You tap into it, it flows through you, and you are not weary or disappointed or saddened, for you have done your best, you have done your work, you have prepared yourself, you have challenged each spirit and found that spirit to be true to your own beliefs.

Then there is no burnout, there is no tiring, there is simply to do more and more because of the joy in the doing of it. We may say that this is equally true of healing. Those who attempt to heal by the power of their own inner being, by anomalistic electromagnetic fields, or by any other means will soon find themselves beleaguered and truly unwilling to act anymore as a healer, for there is great heartbreak in working as a healer. Sometimes the healing involves the end of this particular physical body. Sometimes the answer to your prayer is a simple no. Always, you are asked to sacrifice the personal self in some way.

Now let us look at the process. You have given over yourself to the ideal of service to the Creator by serving as the Creator. You have opened that inner door, that closet within, and metaphorically knelt there in listening reverence. You have spent time worshipping in your own way. You have not begrudged those things which fall away from you, because they do so naturally to someone who is meditating daily.

At this point we feel each of you is at this time. Now what lies ahead of you is what one of your poets would call "the road less traveled." For we are not here to evangelize. We are not here to ask you to believe in dogma or doctrine. We are here because we are those of the consciousness of love, and we come to you as called for this particular kind of information which we give you in love, asking you always to remember that all that we say is opinion and not gospel. If anything that we say disturbs or disquiets you, we urge you to put that aside immediately, for you will recognize your own personal truth. It will be as if you remembered it.

After the first several years of an intensely lived spiritual life, some good habits and some bad habits are in place. The good habits tend to be that of dailyness and regularity and intensity in worship. More time is spent thinking about the one infinite Creator and Its loving nature; less time is spent considering the treasures of this particular illusion. Yet, there are always teachers which will urge you onward, and the primary teacher which always urges you onward is yourself, for you came into this incarnation blazing with zeal to do the Creator's will in whatever way it has been laid out for you to do. By faith alone can you silence each day, "What is there for me to do?" and find a feeling in answer. We advise that you sit in meditation until you reach the point at which you are illumined, may we say, and lost in the Creator, so that each cell of the body and mind and spirit-if spirits may be said to have cells-is comforted, strengthened, sustained and blessed.

Gaze about you in your mind's eye at the beauty of the surroundings that you have just traversed. It is a fragile beauty, blooming one day and dying the next. And yet each perfect bloom in its moment of glory is ineffably beautiful to the Creator and to those with the eyes to see. We ask you to see that nature itself, the second density upon which you so depend, works hard to renew itself, to heal itself of the wounds that mankind has inflicted upon it. We would ask you in your daily meditation to pray for the peace and the integrity of your planet, for as each of you does so, the consciousness of this planet is lightened and more and more entities are ready for graduation into the next density.

Now, you have already experienced that things become harder as one goes along throughout an incarnational experience. It may seem simplistic to you, but we ask you to think of your school system: first grade, second grade, third grade, and so on. Such is the classroom in which you are now in terms of the way we measure dimensionality. You lie at the very cusp of third and fourth density, finishing the old and beginning to feel the new vibrations. Those who are negatively inclined will be more negative. Those who are positively inclined will be polarizing more and more towards service to others, for there is no one upon this planet at this time who does not have a chance for graduation. Each of you has earned this incarnation, this precious experience, by seniority of vibration, by being able, by learning the lessons of this incarnation to make that step from thinking more about the self than others to thinking more about others than the self. If one were to be given calculus in the first grade and reading in the tenth, it would be rather chaotic, would it not?

Therefore, we begin slowly. The creation, first density of rock, sea, fire and air; the second generation or dimension of plants and animals, all of these are connected intimately with love. This is why many of you experience such a deep peace when surrounded by wilderness of nature, for it sways with the rhythm of creation and has an open heart for all beings around it. It even offers to each of you the oxygen that you breathe, just as you offer it the carbon dioxide which it needs.

So you learn the beginning of things first. You learn to turn towards the light in second density, and by the end of second density you have become an individual, whether you be an animal, a plant, or a rock formation. If it is invested with enough devotion and love from third-density entities such as yourself, it too will become ensouled within a physical body which is able to be self-conscious.

The third density, in which you now enjoy experience, is a density in which one thing is raised high before everyone's eye. And that is the choice: faith or doubt; light or darkness; hope or despair. Each time that you pass through the fire and find that you have learned something very difficult, you wipe your brow, metaphysically speaking, and say, "Ohh, I hope that is all I need to learn right now." My friends, your higher selves are ambitious for you. They are not content with a little of this and a little of that. They ask you for your life, and in return give you the sense of life eternal, which is the imperishable truth about each of you, for each of you is a consciousness which was before the world began. Each of you is a spark of God-self with a matching and appropriate amount of free will, set loose to make your own choices, to decide whether you shall serve others and serve the Creator, or serve yourself and so serve the Creator.

There are two reasons why things become more difficult as one goes along. Perhaps the most characteristic reason is that of the unlearned or incompletely learned lesson of love. Each lesson which comes to you, each challenge and difficulty and demand, holds a lesson of love for you. If you do not successfully work out this particular lesson through the aids of meditation, contemplation, inspiration and analysis, you may not learn the lesson in front of you. You may decide instead that perhaps you have a more glorious ministry, a more exciting gift to give to the world. You are impatient. Yet there is no room for impatience in timelessness, and, my friends, all of your spiritual growth takes place in the timeless present moment. Until you have removed yourself from today, yesterday and tomorrow, you have not contacted infinity, and it is infinity for which you yearn, for that is your birthright.

Any lesson, then, which was not successfully observed, analyzed, intuited and acted upon will in another way, but with the same dynamics of feeling, repeat itself in a more intense fashion so that you may hear more and more clearly the internal urgency of making the choice between the positive path and the negative path. One of the most terrible misconceptions of any group of seekers is elitism, the fallacy that because one is seeking, teaching, channeling or learning, one is better, elect and special compared to those who gaze upon your television sets and consume your alcoholic beverages.

Your higher self is very patient. It does not mind how long it takes for you to learn a particular lesson. It is gazing at you from the prospect of several million years. It is helping you as its gift; your gift to yourself from what you would call the future. Learn to trust in that gift. Learn to trust your own advice. Tackle the job. Talk it through and work it out the first time. There then need be no two-by-four applied to the forehead with a more stringent second lesson or an even more stringent and difficult third lesson.

Gaze at the pattern of your incarnation. What do you suppose the lessons were that you came to learn? What has your life been patterned like? All lives are a patchwork quilt when seen up close, bewildering to the eye. Yet when one backs off, one sees a pattern, a beautiful, carefully sewn pattern. All the pieces are stitched together, making the truth of love complete. And quilting is placed beneath the coverlet that you may be soft in your zeal, gentle in your speaking of the truth, never intrusive but always ready to witness to that which is in your heart when someone asks.

Therefore, the first and greatest cause of the feeling that things are getting harder as one goes along is that one is resisting a change. For in order to be of service to other people in a truly compassionate manner, one must stop making assumptions about what, in a human term, one would think this or that person needs, this or that person desires, this or that person should hear. You may drop the seed now and again. You may suggest a thought, but toss it as if it were a lighthearted shuttlecock in a badminton game. Let it flow gently and freely over the net of another's resistance. And if it is caught and hit-very well; you may move on. If it is not caught-very well; you may move on. It is not your responsibility to change anyone's life but your own. It is no one's responsibility that you have difficulties or joy. Each of you is a completely independent, metaphysical, equal being, equal in stature to any being in the creation, for that of which you are made is the Creator, and that of which all things are made is of the Creator.

We suggest to you, therefore, that whatever your strong point is-intuition, analysis, meditation, prayer or contemplation-that you focus upon this in a daily and earnest manner, seeking to know how you may offer love, asking that the opportunity be given to you to share that love with others. If one does this, the lessons will still become harder, but they will at least have the interesting factor of being different. It is when one resists the pattern that one must repeat the lesson again and again.

There is another reason that the road becomes stonier and rockier as one moves along. What you are seeking to do is to take a bipedal animal with self-consciousness and so far integrate that bodily self into the consciousness that every cell of the being may listen to the secret, small voice within the closed door of the closet of your heart. You shall not ever be satisfied with yourself. This is one of those facts of the illusion which may seem to be sad, yet there is no sadness here, for you are wanting to lose those odd little parts of yourself that do not serve in any way, and wanting to fill the places that you have made with the choices of service to others.

The third reason that the lessons become more difficult is simply that there is a great subtlety to the art and the craft of service to others. Very many of your people confuse this with pleasing others, and if they please others, they feel they have served. We suggest that this may not, indeed, be the case, and that each request for service be gazed at, not from the standpoint of pleasing the self or the other self, but from the standpoint of where the love is in the situation so that you may fasten on to that lodestar of love and light and act accordingly to those principles which stream therefrom.

How we admire you. We remember third density. It is the shortest of the densities, the density of choice. You are here to choose to serve the Creator by serving others or by serving the self and manipulating others. As you serve others, you may be asked to do outrageous things, to go beyond your limitations, to do what cannot be done yet which shall be done because it must. And in those situations we strongly advise that you release your personal personality and move to an impersonal portion of your deep self, that God-self of unmitigated and straightforward compassion. To determine what is pleasing as opposed to what is serving another entity is sometimes difficult, especially on the spur of the moment. Therefore, we ask you to steep yourselves as you would immolate a tea bag in the teacup in the love and the light of the infinite One, that what needs be done for you to polarize, for you to choose, may be done with what this instrument would call singleness and gladness of heart.

Much of the illusion is based upon the feeling that you are not all right, that you are imperfect, that you are flawed. In a human sense this is true. Each of you has free will and that free will causes you to act variously at various times. Some of those times are successful, some of those times are disgusting and failures. We do not ask that you succeed, nor does your higher self ask that you literally and in a worldly sense succeed in service to others …

(Side one of tape ends.)

(Carla channeling)

… you spirit, this polarization as the steps between the polarity you experience and the polarity you wish becomes smaller or shorter but much more intense, for you are burning away a great deal of what people may call personality. This is not to say that you should not be merry, full of laughter and joy, comforting and exhorting each other always in love. Each of you was put here for each of you. You have the freedom to be one with everyone or to single out the self as more important than everyone.

Now, there is a trick, which we may shamelessly call that, for aiding the floundering spirit, and that is this. The Creator, if asked, will give you what you desire. Indeed, this is so much true that in a way we fear to say the truth, for that which you wish you will surely get. And many of you wish sometimes for very self-destructive things because you are unhappy with yourself. Let no illusion trouble you, but remain in your heart, in your spirit, on your path, for all paths lead to the one infinite Creator.

Now, as you gain experience and service to others, you may find your work with other people in service changing, because you are changing. Change, of course, is painful, yet it is what you are desiring, each and every one of you. If you do not wish to feel pain, refrain from the meditation, refrain from helping others, be secure and safe within your own four walls and live your life. Perhaps in the next incarnation you shall take up the quest once again. You have all the time in the world, and we mean that literally. There is no hurry; there is no judgment; there is simply a large portion of the Creator which has separated itself by the action of free will that it may know itself, that it may know itself better and better.

This is not the first creation, nor shall it be the last. Each of you is old, older than you can imagine, wiser than you can imagine. But these attributes are very deep within the subconscious mind. When you desire to seek the true service as opposed to pleasing entities, it is well to spend time in silence, allowing all the situation, the feelings, the expectations of others and so forth, to wash through you, and then to tune yourself to the highest and best that you possibly know and can carry on a stable basis.

We speak simple truths. There isn't anything new about what we say. It is just that we have, shall we say, no ax to grind, no churches to build. All we care is to serve one person, one soul at a time, and we are most, most happily content, for each of you, my friends, is worthwhile, imperishable, perfect and beautiful. Now, the process that you go through in becoming a less personal servant and a more impersonal servant through which things come involves more and more sacrifice, adjustment, understanding and laughter. If you are not laughing and feeling merry at some times as you meditate, then it is time for you to learn to laugh, for you to release the spontaneity which is your birthright.

You see, each of you has complete free will. You do not have to follow the path of the Creator. You may stay in one place, or you may move in a negative fashion, controlling others and manipulating them to serve yourself. The choices are yours, and as you make one successful choice the strength is then given to you to try again and again and again. You will many times feel that you have failed. But remember, you cannot judge yourself, not until this illusion is gone from you and you can see the truth face to face. The very desire and zeal to be faithful and loving to one another is a light for the nations, a lightening of the planetary consciousness and the hope of your planet [at] this particular time.

Let us reckon with free will before we close in this instrument. You have an equal measure of free will and of God-self. This is your makeup. When you are small in stature and have not learned you are very self-involved. You are hungry, and you cry; you are wet, and you cry; you wish to be comforted, and you cry. Communication is very easy. The free will of the mother and father who nurture is not given many options, for it is in the nature of the relationship of parent and child that nurturing will in some way be done or at least attempted. But now all of you have passed that stage of living a free-will life and have found that the only true free will is the will to serve.

Thus, willfulness becomes willingness, and difficulty becomes a smoothly running river of love and light that cascades you know not where. You do not know whose lives you touch, but by faith your life itself may touch many and give them the light that they need to make their choices.

We urge each neither to proselytize nor to refrain from witnessing to that truth which is yours personally when asked. This is simple, solid, metaphysical information which has been written down many times in your holy works. But it is always new, as each day is new and as each day you are new. And so we turn to that which breaks the back of willfulness, and that is forgiveness. In willfulness you want to do this and you want to do that, and you will do this and you won't do that. And the God-self sits in a corner with Its hands folded in the closet of your heart, waiting for you to open the door. One day you open the door, but you see nothing. You go in and you seat yourself and you prepare yourself and you find nothing. Perseverance brings awareness, a subtle awareness of the God-self, the Christ-consciousness within.

It is inevitable that each grade, shall we say, is going to be more difficult than the last, more challenging, more interesting, for that which is before you now is based upon that which you have learned so far in this incarnational experience. Perhaps the key to being able to distinguish that which you wish to do is the letting go of the decision and the allowing of inner wisdom to inform you in your free will what seems the best service to perform. Then one can turn the will with a glad and merry heart to the task at hand, wasting no time in doubt, but only tuning yourself always to the highest and best that you can be, moving again and again to the center of your being, and, no matter how harsh the failure seems to you subjectively at any one time, to refrain from the judgment of the self.

Learning has always been a painful task. It is exciting, and when one looks back upon it, it is wondrous and adventurous. One feels as a voyager would, going to conquer new lands, going to embrace the world with love and light. Just about the time that you feel this way, the next lesson shall begin. This is what you planned for yourself for the utmost polarization for service to others.

(Pause)

We paused briefly, simply to enjoy the beauty of this circle of seeking, and we thank and bless each of you for calling us this evening to your meditation to share in your vibrations at this time. It is most blessed to us to be able to share our thoughts with you, our most hoped-for event, and we thank you, for as we speak with you, and as we share in the anguish and joy that each brings this evening, we re-experience the third-density illusion, the heaviest of all illusions, and we see and are inspired by the bravery, the courage, and the determination of those who wish to do the Father's will, regardless of what it costs.

We would at this time transfer this contact to the one known as Jim, thanking this instrument and each instrument in the group and all in the group, indeed, for acting as batteries for this instrument. We leave in love and light. We are Q'uo.

(Jim channeling)

I am Q'uo, and greet each again in love and light through this instrument. Before we take our leave of this group for this evening, we would offer ourselves in the attempt to speak to any queries which those present may have remaining upon the mind. Is there a query at this time?

Questioner: You spoke just now of how we act as a battery for the primary channel. Could you say more about that process?

I am Q'uo, and am aware of your query, my brother. As each has entered this circle of seeking this evening, there is the desire that is paramount in each heart and mind to partake in the seeking for some portion of truth, some portion of light that might be utilized to inspire the service to others within the self, to inspire the greater understanding within the self of how service is rendered and how one might evolve in the sense of mind, body and spirit.

Thus, the desire that each brings into this circle of seeking which has been enhanced by a lifetime of service may be seen as a kind of food or energizing force that, when taken cumulatively with each other entity's desire, provides a sustained level of energy for the one serving as instrument to draw upon. The desire, then, of the entire group might be seen to be likened unto the antenna of one of your radio devices which is able to receive a signal from a distant source in direct relationship or ratio to the amount of power or energy that is available to that antenna. Thus, each of you provides a portion of that energy, and for this service we are most grateful, my brother.

Is there another query?

Questioner: I had a question about the concept of a dark force, an evil force, and the light force. I've heard it said that the evil force is an illusion, and the only evil is between your ears, that it doesn't really exist, and we are in this illusion, learning, leaning towards the light. And my question is that, in that leaning, should one even acknowledge that there's darkness, that it is illusion?

I am Q'uo, and am aware of your query, my brother. We would first begin by reminding each that the creation itself is a finely wrought and intricately designed illusion which gives each portion of the Creator a means whereby it might come to know the Creator through experience, and the Creator might come to know each portion of Itself though that same experience. Within the illusion of the creation, there is that which is of the positive or radiant and that which is of the negative or magnetic. There are many terms that are used to describe the duality of forces which together form the dynamic tension which holds the creation in place as a manifested thought that might be utilized for growth and for service.

Within the illusion of this creation there is that which is not illusory, that from which the creation has been made, the one Creator, that which is beyond thought, beyond mind, beyond consciousness. There is that truth, then, of unity from which is created that which you know as the creation. There is That Which Is-unity-and That Which Is Not-and that is separation. From these two paths, then, come the two viable paths that might be traveled to the one Creator. That path which attempts to see the unity of all creation, to recognize it in each face that comes before your own, this is the path of service to others, the path of radiance, of giving and of positivity. Far more travel this path than travel that path of negativity, that path which enhances the concept of seeming separation and takes it to its logical conclusion, the path of service to self that attempts to gain for the self the power of the light and use it in subjugation of those about one in order that the power of each might redound to the one exercising control.

Within your illusion of the third density these two paths have been seen as good and as evil. This is a distortion, as you may be aware of the true nature of these paths. The more difficult of the path is that of the negative polarity, that which is called within your cultures, evil, for the attempt to bend the wills of others to one's own desire meets the difficulty of the dissipation of the power thusly gained as the ability to blend one's seeking with another is blocked by the separation that has been enhanced and pursued.

This path finds its conclusion within that density numbering six, where it is of necessity required that each entity wishing to proceed further in the path of unification with the Creator see all about one as the Creator. This is not difficult for those of positive polarity, for the path of positive polarity attempts as the fundamental quality of that path to see all as the Creator. It is difficult enough for those of negative polarity that the negative polarity must be abandoned at that point, and an immediate shift in polarity, shall we say, is then accomplished, for the power is the same, from the same source, and might then be reversed, shall we say, with some difficulty, in order that the seeking then proceeds with the eyes looking upon a new world and a new creation and a new sense of self.

Therefore, that which has been called evil or negative might be seen as that journey which turns upon its head all that is positive and in reverse fashion finds its pleasures in that which is dark and that which is hidden, in that which provides the opportunity for advancing the self at the expense of others. However, the end point and the final goal of each path is the one Creator, for there is no other goal, there is no other source, there is no other journey. There are, however, two means of apprehending this journey and of accomplishing its end.

Is there a further query, my brother?

Questioner: No, thank you.

I am Q'uo, and we thank you, my brother. Is there another query at this time?

Questioner: Another question. I was curious about what you said was the energy, as I understand it, showering down on the planet at this time. You said something about the negativity increasing or the energies that people are working with, if they happen to be of the resistant path, they're going to be increasing. I guess that is true on the positive path, also? And it will continue until the fourth density comes into completion?

I am Q'uo, and am aware of your query, my brother. We find that you have in essence provided the answer to your query, in that it is, indeed, our observation that as your planetary sphere moves into a new sector of time and space that the increased love and light of that sector is felt as it streams through the web of energy vortices of your planet by each entity upon your planet, much as would the print on the written page be enlarged by the magnifying glass. Therefore, the directions which have been chosen, either to the positive radiant or the negative and magnetic, be enhanced in their direction and vector.

Therefore, it is a situation in which there is more energy as a resource to call upon and therefore becomes a natural portion of the everyday environment, shall we say, so that each individual within your planetary cultures has available the stepped-up level of vibrational energy that is affecting the daily round of activities and the perceptions of the individual, so that there is an intensification of experience.

Is there a further query, my brother?

Questioner: No, thank you.

I am Q'uo, and we thank you once again, my brother. Is there a further query at this time?

Questioner: May I ask a question of a personal nature?

I am Q'uo, and we will be happy to entertain any query that is presented to us, however, we are bound by the desire that we not infringe upon an entity's free will by giving responses that would affect that entity's future or the personal interpretation of experience that is, of necessity, best left to the entity. With these caveats, we are happy to respond, my brother.

Questioner: I understand. I experience from time to time jolts of energy coming through my body which cause my head to jerk or tremble, even when I am not intending to channel healing energy, although it is quite prevalent at those times. And I am desirous of knowing what exactly that phenomenon is. What am I experiencing?

I am Q'uo, and am aware of your query, my brother. We find that we may speak in a general fashion, leaving the specific application to your own discrimination. For one who has offered the self in the capacity of serving as healer to those who are broken or incomplete in some fashion, according to their own perceptions, there is over a period of time and the experience of serving as a healer, a buildup of a certain kind of energy that is of an healing nature. There is within some entities the need to discharge a portion of this buildup of energy which has, in what might be seen as a consciously unbidden manner, moved into the energy pattern of the healer as a kind of natural reflex, shall we say, the path of energy having been traversed many, many times previously. Thus, the buildup has the need of discharge in order that there not be a, shall we say, back-burning of the circuits within the electrical body.

Is there a further query, my brother?

Questioner: No, thank you.

Carla: I'd like to follow up on that. Is that like … Never mind. I know the answer. Forget it. Thank you.

I am Q'uo, and we thank each. Is there a final query at this time?

Questioner: Tell us about our fondness for and our attraction to felines, particularly of the Siamese societies like these.

I am Q'uo, and am aware of your query, my brother. We look upon the second density which you have called within your culture the cat, the member of the feline family, and see an entity that has from ages past within your third-density illusion served as that which might be seen as the guard, that which watches carefully the path that is traveled by the seeker of truth. There have been many cultures within your planet's history that have revered the cat for this particular quality of serving as one which watches, as one which guards, and gives a certain nurturing care to the seeker of truth which travels the path of the positive polarity. Thus, there is the general attraction to this particular creature by those who feel a sensitivity towards the inward seeking.

There is in many individual cases a further attraction to the cat, having been established within previous incarnations in a culture which did, indeed, revere the feline creatures. We look especially to that culture of ancient Egypt which found great use for the form and the function of the cat, serving as guard to many of the rooms of the initiation chambers and rooms used for the learning and service to others. Thus, the cat is old within the archetypical mind of all of your peoples, and is especially placed upon a cherished point of focus for many individuals upon your planet who have had previous experience with these nurturing creatures.

At this time we would like to thank each within this circle of seeking for inviting our presence amongst you in order that we might share some of our thoughts upon some of those topics which are of greatest interest to you on your journeys of seeking. It is a great honor for us to be asked to such a circle, and we cannot thank each enough for this privilege. Again we would remind each that we offer that which is but our opinion, that which we have learned upon our own journeys. We do not wish any word that we have spoken to be a stumbling block for any present. Please disregard any words which have not rung of truth to you, and use those which have in that way which serves you most. We would leave each at this time in the love and in the light of the one infinite Creator. We are known to you as those of Q'uo. Adonai, my friends. Adonai. ✢

Special Meditation
June 21, 1989

Group question: It is said that our main goal or lesson is to learn to love, to serve, to give of the self to others. Is there a point beyond which one should not give, because it damages the self too much? For instance, giving one's free will to a dominating person or giving health to unreasonable demands of non-supporting family members or destroyed self esteem to the constant criticism by a mate.

(Carla channeling)

I am Latwii. I greet you in the love and in the light of the one infinite Creator. We are most blessed to be able to share our thoughts with you and to be called to this circle of seeking. We are aware that the question you have asked is multifaceted. And we shall do our best to look at the question from various perspectives so that rather than deciding for anyone what there is to do, we may simply lay forth the choices as we see them to be within your illusion.

The question has to do with the mistreatment of one entity by another, the second entity being unaware that he is mistreating the God-self within, that person which is hurt and the person himself. Therefore, though an entity may suffer from the vagaries of a domineering mate, one is not part of the difficulty that constrains the mate which is confused and striking out.

The situation in many, many cases, when mates begin to seek, is that one will seek truly, the other upon the surface; one with the heart and the other the intellect. Therefore, the one moving from the heart center will be changing and growing and the pace of growth accelerates as the journey moves along—not that you are aware of the milestones that fly by you. But if you are persistent in doing what you feel you should do, then you are the light of the world.

Perhaps we should say before we say anything else that it is time once and for all to banish any idea of inequality of any souls whatsoever. You cannot find a degraded, drunken person sleeping in his own vomit, for that person has consciousness and holds Christ within. No more can you misjudge those near and dear to you. Their behavior may be appalling, but you are still dealing with the Christ in each person.

Consensus reality within your illusion and your particular culture at this time suggests and, indeed, encourages the option of separation when one person has been traumatized by another. This is actually a perfectly good solution. There is only one problem. If the termination of the relationship occurs before a full understanding of the dynamics of that relationship have been reached, then that situation will come up again and in a more intensified way, so that you may learn the lesson you have set for yourself to learn. Therefore, in all but the most drastic cases, it is well to work with that which challenges the seeker at the present moment rather than seeking to change the circumstances so that the entity may feel more at peace.

You are all divine individuals. This is the key to your thinking about yourself. You view yourself in failure after failure, in disappointment after disappointment; but you do not see that free will within you has distorted that Creator-self into ways that were inappropriate, and it is from those failures that you have learned much, and it is from further failure that you will learn more. Consequently, though it seems paradoxical, if you suffer from being misunderstood or from not understanding the motives of one who seems to be abusing you, that is perfectly satisfactory. It is only necessary to continue to keep the heart chakra open and to refrain from judgment on any level.

Now, with that said, we would address the question of free will. The questioner posed a situation in which one mate has completely taken over the life, the thinking and the mentality of the spouse, and the spouse has become a kind of slave. The law of free will moves against this organization of illusion with the utmost compassion and force. The ways of natural law always tend toward the balancing of such situation. However, this balancing may take many, many years. Therefore, we may say very simply, it is extremely unwise to let anyone do one's thinking for one. It is unwise to allow another entity to belittle you and believe it. All insults should be shed as if there were a raincoat around your heart, so that they may be considered and analyzed with no hard feelings by yourself, and if the criticisms have merit, then you may use them. For the most part those who criticize others are those who are truly criticizing themselves.

When an entity has lost its free will to the point that it seems paralyzed and unable to move further, then that entity must needs go within and tabernacle with the Creator and listen very closely to the silence. Within that silence there is a love and imperishable beauty, a compassionate wisdom and an ever-comforting pair of arms that will rock you gently through the cradle of this incarnation until the chrysalis that you are becomes, in fourth density, the butterfly. The butterfly now is within you, waiting to occur. Honor yourself and let no man or woman take away from you your own knowledge of your own nature and birthright, for you are all made of love.

We encourage people to love each other. This is a blanket statement that has nothing wrong with it. However, we find that within your culture people confuse pleasing people with serving people. To please someone is a never-ending struggle, because no entity can be pleased all the time. Each entity will have its cycles of inward mood, regardless of outer circumstance. It is not your responsibility to take care of the mood level of those about you, but rather to maintain your own centered joy and peace.

In extreme cases such as you have queried about, there are options concerning communication or a simple action for the good of the entire family unit. But we cannot decide for any person where that point is. We can only say that if one perceives that one is at the point where one cannot go on in partnership, it is not a negative thing, lovingly to separate. It is also quite likely that if it is done with no rancor that the couple may be together once again on an entirely different footing—the footing of equals.

The great problem in most of your male/female relationships is the problem of inequality. This is a false and illusory concept, that is, that one entity may be worth more or [be] more important than another. We live in a completely, as you would call it, democratic creation. All souls are equal, for all souls are of the same Creator-self, mixed with free will.

The query then revolves in the end about free will itself and choices that one wishes to make, and there are no clear and hard and fast reasons and ways of thinking that can move one to right action. Sometimes the right action is to remove oneself and one's children from the situation. Sometimes the right action is to move along within the strong and persistent will of the self, doing in a difficult situation what needs to be done, and feeling that this is indeed the peace that you have found within yourself.

That is the important thing: to discover joy and peace within yourself. If it is being robbed from you, you must cut that cord that tugs your good times away from you. This does not necessarily mean that you physically no longer see the mate, the friend, or any entity that may hurt you, but that when you do see that entity, you are corresponding with that entity in the language of the Creator-self and not the language of free will. Realize that your own free will is completely predominant. You may decide to accept a very sacrificial environment because you have decided to learn a very difficult lesson about love, that generally being that one loves the ideal, but one sees the shallowness and foolishness. It is difficult to love shallowness and foolishness, yet this is the incarnation in which you must make the choice to love and be of service to others.

Therefore, if there is the strength within to continue loving despite the challenges of a troublesome mate, a good spiritual line of accelerated growth will spiral forth and you shall shine brighter and brighter. It is a myth that certain circumstances create more spirituality than others. Spirituality is that which is recognized within one's self.

Therefore, you have yourself, hampered only by your free will, which in the beginning is willful and moves you in various directions, and, indeed, in the case of one mate trying to dominate another, it is normal that the dominating mate not be aware of Christ consciousness in the other, and the one dominated being aware of the total democracy of spirits, and therefore being unwilling to be less than perfectly gracious, considering that each entity is the Creator.

Various entities may evaluate this data in different ways. The important thing to remember, we feel, is that you are responsible for your own thoughts, your own ideals and hopes and aspirations, your own prayers, your own consolations and your own peace, for Christ is within you; not far away, but a friend when there is no other. Open the door to your heart, reach out your hand and that consciousness that is you and the Creator is there.

So, in solving a riddle that cannot be solved, such as the riddle of how to deal with someone who is despitefully using you, it is well to take into meditation this dilemma, not urging one or the other way, but asking, seeking, hoping for an answer that may be more unitive, more loving and more effective in making loving gentle relationships occur.

There is that among your people which is called ambition. Perhaps the most destructive of ambitions is the ambition to save the physical world. There are many who fall from a very high state of consciousness because they are not content with working with one person at a time, but rather wish to manipulate the entire planet for its entire good. We do not have this bias. We simply ask you to evaluate carefully whether you have learned the lesson that this difficulty has given. When you have learned that lesson, you will feel a peace and a release from the situation.

Trust that meditative process. Trust that asking and seeking, and when you hear the answer, find the grace and the will to act upon it with a singleness of heart. For you wish to give glory to the infinite Creator, and no matter who you love, that you love is the glory of humankind. It does not matter if that love be twisted by another; it does not matter if that love be unknown or thrown away or despoiled. It matters only that you radiate the beauty, the peace, and the joy of a life centered in faith.

Turning to those about you for help will inevitably confuse. Yet, each person may have something interesting to say. It is always well to listen, for after all, all have opinions, just as we do. But in our way of thinking, we would simply suggest that in this very difficult illusion the main focus be upon centering oneself in love and acting out of love rather than reacting out of negative emotion. If in your evaluation of yourself you find that this is completely impossible, it is then time to attempt communication to work such difficulties out.

If these difficulties cannot be worked out, possibly being apart will effect some healing, so that when you come together again there is more of a realization upon both parts of the true nature of mated relationships. Mated relationships are a true adventure and ordeal. They are the sacrificing of two entities to become one. In addition to each entity, there is an "us," and that us does many, many things: raising children, running a house, living a life together, walking across the carpets and stones of daily life.

Thus, you cannot, within the illusion, see what is to be done with someone who is holding you down irrationally, who is mistreating you, who is abusing you, and who is taking away your self-respect. These are things that in the end you have allowed to happen, and it is, if you wish to change the situation, yours to change. Each is capable of looking at options, gazing at them clearly and choosing.

We ask only that you remember at all times that you are choosing as Christ would choose, that your mind is the mind of Christ, and if your willfulness moves your mind instead of your mind your will, you have put the cart before the horse, and you will go nowhere. Therefore, sit in silence and patience day after day, week after week, and allow the process of acceleration of growth spiritually to occur in a natural manner. When you receive an impression as to what would be well to be done, act upon it in a loving and compassionate manner, for truly you are dealing, no matter how else it may seem, with yourself, with the Creator.

Therefore, bring a sense of honor for the one who causes you pain. Rather than causing him pain, you may witness unto him of the light and the love of the infinite Creator by refusing to be beaten down, by moving from love imperishable into action, by reacting not at all to the negative things that move about one, but, rather, to put oneself in a protective shell and move through the life as one who is not quite of the life or the illusion.

It is a matter of the point of view. One cannot help or decide for another entity what path that entity may take, what thoughts that entity may think. You are the only guinea pig you have the right to work upon. Therefore, we ask that you gird your loins in situations of this kind, put on the armor of light and move out freely against any and all wickedness, knowing that love does overcome all things, and that all things besides love are distortions of love, no matter how depraved.

The situation the question describes is not a pleasant one. It seems full of anguish, sadness and even horror. It is absolutely unacceptable metaphysically for one person to enslave another, either by criticism, by keeping the entity within the house, by any kind of mental or physical force whatsoever, so that if this is happening to you, then you are aware that you are in a situation which is unacceptable. At that point we would suggest that you consider deeply and take into prayer and meditation the possibility of being the one who makes the compassionate change, not closing doors, but opening them, finding a situation that will be better than the one that exists at this time.

In conclusion, we would like to say that there are many angelic spirits upon your Earth who live with entities most difficult to bear and who are untouched by any pain or grief or frustration or anger, simply because they do not identify what the person says with who that person is. We would not want to lead you astray, and so we wish to state at this time that we are not suggesting that any leave a mate because of difficulties. We are simply suggesting that a thought process available to the analytical part of the mind may come in useful as the life experience moves into a pattern.

Once you see that you have found the basic lesson of love which you are to learn, then it may become clear to you why you have been associated with this difficult spouse in the mated relationship. This difficult spouse is breaking natural law by interfering with your free will. It is indeed difficult not to reciprocate. We urge you not to. We urge you to continue at all times to look upon each person as the Creator, but we do not urge masochism upon anyone, and if, after meditation, there is peace about the leaving of such an entity, then so be it. We find the idea of the so-called sin of divorce or separation to be misunderstood among your peoples. Mates are very rare. Many marry upon your sphere of existence, but few form strong teams. When one has a mate which is willing to work with one, one is blessed and should be humble before that and offer thanksgiving each and every day.

If one has the challenging relationship that tests one day after day, exhausts one, tires one, confuses one, then we suggest time alone, a walk, a meditation each day, a retreat to a beautiful place for the weekend, times when you—the entity who you really are—may sit down and contemplate the entire picture of your incarnational pattern that you may see a lesson of love you are to learn. Once you have seen that, the "slings and arrows," as this instrument would quote, "of outrageous fortune," though still hitting you, cannot penetrate, because you understand whence these negative feelings arise. This is not an easy task. This is not a task in which it is at all easy to be successful, for those who are in constant negativity tend simply to become too tired to do other than react to any situation at hand. We urge each never to become too lazy, too tired, too hopeless, too despairing to center in on who you really are and to move ahead that day as a child of the one infinite Creator.

We are aware that we have given little instruction, but merely pointed out some options and some thoughts about them. Because matedness among third-density entities is so completely misunderstood as being a kind of business partnership, it is no wonder that many relationships are emotionally bankrupt. We do not encourage cruel or unfortunate behavior upon your part in retaliation for what has happened. We do encourage prayer on behalf of the one which is disturbing you. But most of all we ask you to step back and look up at night at the infinity of the heavens and find within yourself that place which contains all those heavens. The tabernacle of creation lies within your heart. This you may seek again and again, and if you have courage and persistence, you will still seek again and again, but you will be moving more quickly.

Many entities at this time have chosen to come into relationship with entities which challenge them. This is because it is easier to push against a force to polarize than to polarize from internal pressure. That is to say, it is easier when there is a bad example to be a good example than when all there is about you is good examples.

One more thing that we would mention is the involvement of children in such difficulties of relationship between mates. The disharmony that is tolerable to a grown being is often painfully intolerable to a younger soul who is more sensitive. Find the nurturer within yourself, that you may nurture those young ones who are in pain.

Before you lie two realities. One is small. It contains things like garages, houses, relationships, jobs, chores and time. It is the surface of your life. But behold, underlying that surface is an incredibly beautiful, perfectly manifested God-self within. Seek that light that is brighter than light. Seek that love which ravishes and makes one whole. Seek to be with the Father. This is the most important thing which any entity may do to improve the level of vibration of your planet. The good deeds are helpful, but no more so than good intentions. That is the metaphysical rule: thoughts are things. So look at the infinite creation. It is a blessing, a beauty, and a transcendent joy and gauge yourself in the life of life around you. Be your own person with your own resources. Hold your head high in the face of challenge, resting in the mercy seat of the compassion of your heart, for if you have the will to tame your willfulness to the service of the infinite Creator, there is no kind thing which is beyond your ability to do.

May we say at the end that that which seems broken may be whole and that which seems to be lost may be found, for the Creator did not cause one to have a certain path throughout the incarnation, but rather placed certain lessons for us to learn. It is to those lessons we encourage you to look. It is the pattern of your incarnation we encourage you to analyze, but most of all, we encourage you to spend time tabernacling with the Creator and knowing that the place whereon you stand is holy ground.

As always, we of the Confederation of Planets in the Service of the Infinite Creator are with you at your mental request to aid you in your meditations, to urge you on and exhort you in cheer and joy and laughter. There is much to be let go of in a life which focuses on the spiritual. Much personal that must become impersonal that one may become a better channel. Sometimes relationships are created for apparently no reason whatsoever, but when one examines the dynamics of the relationship, one discovers the lesson that one needs to learn the most. In some cases, that is, "I am worthy." You are perfect, unique and ultimately worthy.

We would leave this instrument in love and light and transfer at this time to the one known as Jim. I am Latwii.

(Jim channeling)

I am Latwii, and greet each again in love and light through this instrument. At this time it is our privilege to offer ourselves in the attempt to speak to those queries which may yet remain upon the minds. Is there a query to which we may speak?

S: I just have one. I have a need to feel you. Will you touch me?

I am Latwii, and it is our great joy and honor, my sister, to pause briefly and to make our presence known to you. We shall pause.

(Pause)

I am Latwii, and am again with this instrument. We have enjoyed the blending of our vibrations with yours. Is there a query at this time?

(Side one of tape ends.)

Carla: I just have one, and I just want a validation. When I patrolled the perimeter before I started challenging, I found low level negative vibrations surrounding our entire group, and I wondered if it was because it was important to L/L Research. I banished them all, but it took awhile. They couldn't stand up to the Christ challenge, but I was just wondering why the unusual gathering at this time? And the validation I would expect is, because it is S and S is very much a part of us and we hope to stand as close to the light as possible. Comment?

I am Latwii, and we do indeed affirm the presence of these entities of which you have spoken. The reason is much as you have surmised, that being that the gathering of this particular group of entities is that which has a spiritual significance, shall we say. There is a great deal of desire to be of service amongst those presently gathered. There is, therefore, the notice upon the metaphysical of this light. This light attracts the attention much as does your electrical light attract the attention of the night creatures which fly about in your air. Thus, there are many of the negative orientation that are interested in this light, but for the most part have little other than curiosity to bring them to this light, for it is that which is of the moment at this time.

Is there a further query at this time, my sister?

Carla: I just have one, and you can skip it if you don't want to tackle it, because it's personal and long, but I have been struggling to accept my disability for a long time, and I really don't seem to have succeeded. And it's hard for me to feel useful or worthy. I find myself feeling the opposite of it a great deal because of the things that I can't do, and I wonder how best I could nurture myself so that I could stop dumping on myself. I can work so little in a day now that it drives me crazy.

I am Latwii, and am aware of your query, my sister. We would wish to relieve such suffering if there were not great rewards from the overcoming of such suffering that might be achieved by your own efforts which we also acknowledge are being made with a whole heart at this time. The fact that you have not succeeded to your own satisfaction in discovering the value within yourself of your existence and of the part that you play of this incarnation and of the planet at this time is that which would again remind you does exist. However, the finding of that treasure of great value within is a part of a journey which must be seen as a whole, for when you began this incarnation, there was much that you set before yourself to accomplish, and we would affirm that, indeed, much, much has been done in this regard.

However, the greater task—that being larger, shall we say, than the service which you might offer others—for your own beingness has been to discover that the self which is within that focus of energy that serves others has a great value and integrity of its own. That you look to that which remains to be accomplished, and that which cannot, due to limitations, be accomplished, is a portion of the means you have used to advance your own seeking, for that angst which seeks to complete that which is begun is a great motivating force.

However, as it has been a strength, it can also become that which is the weakest link, shall we say, in the chain of your own beingness, and we would advise your careful contemplation and prayerful consideration of the over-emphasis upon that quality of your being, that driving force to complete that which remains to be done, and look at those times when you do feel the need to do one thing or another.

Look then at that which has been accomplished and give praise for that moment to the one Creator for the opportunity and the privilege of accomplishing that which you have indeed accomplished. Look also at the Creator which gives those gifts of opportunities to serve in the manner which you have served and give praise for the ability to look with a longer view upon your own life pattern that you might see the wholeness and the completeness of this pattern.

Therefore, we have given you, my sister, we are afraid to admit, something of the old adage that it is well to count one's blessing. Such a simple reminder, however, when taken to heart, might be of great assistance in this regard.

Is there a further query, my sister?

Carla: No, thank you.

I am Latwii. Is there a final query for this session?

S: I just have a thought, going back to the three of us meditating and the low level of service-to-self entities, and I, too, felt those, and I went through some unusual things I usually don't have to hear. A thought came to me that perhaps that if we all lived in one location, a group of us, and why we haven't done it sooner, but why we think and hold on to the faith that we will in the future is perhaps the imbalance we would put on a larger location because of the concentration of one path, service to others, and that as long as each one of us have other drains on our energy that to—such as I with my children and Carla with her singing, Jim with other expenditures—that when we choose or when it is time for all of us to be together that the concentration of our energy in that one path is going to draw the other side and that we will need to be fully ready to support the battle that might develop or the strain of the two sides pulling? Does that make any sense or would you like to respond to that?

I am Latwii, and we believe that we have the grasp of your query, my sister. Please ask further if we are incorrect. The fact that when entities of a strong polarization towards service to others are gathered together and join in a seeking, whether it be for a short or a long duration of your time, that there is an attraction also of the, shall we say, loyal opposition of negatively-polarized entities, is a situation which is true for all positively-oriented entities. It is not a situation which, in our opinion, needs the, shall we say, alteration of plans of any kind, for it is simply the natural response to a given situation.

We would suggest that for each present and others which are also members of this particular grouping of entities, that should there come the feeling within the heart of being that there is now a need or an opportunity for blending the energies in a closer configuration in order that a service might be offered that would not be possible should this blending not be so close, that this possibility at that time be explored, but that there not be the over-concern given to such before this feeling has arisen within each entity or within those entities that would feel the need to alter their conditions of existence in order to bring about the joining of energies.

What we are hoping to convey through this response is that there is not the need for concern either that there is a great distance or time, in your measurement, separating entities or that there would a greater responsibility placed upon the group or any individuals within it should there be a joining of entities and energies at some point within your future. There is within each entity, and indeed within this group in its larger definition, a thread of, shall we say, logical existence or a preplanned design that has its outlines well in place, and there is always the opportunity for realizing a fuller description of that design for any entity that would wish to meditate carefully and sincerely upon that design, shall we say.

We wish to affirm to each that all is indeed well with the pattern as it has been and is now being lived. There is the fullness within each moment, even though that fullness may yet escape the conscious detection of any particular entity within the group at those times when the illusion is heavy upon the mind and strikes sharply to the heart. All is indeed well, my sister, and there is great opportunity that awaits each.

Is there a further query at this time?

S: No, thank you.

I am Latwii, and we are most grateful to have been asked to join this group and are especially grateful that we have been able to sit in silent and spoken meditation with the one known as S. We are never absent from this entity's presence, however, we do rejoice at the opportunity of speaking in a more ordinary, shall we say, way to this particular entity.

At this time we shall take our leave of this group, leaving each, as always, in the love and in the light of the one infinite Creator. We are known to you as those of Latwii. Adonai, my friends. Adonai. ✣

L/L Research

Sunday Meditation
June 25, 1989

Group question: Concerns self-esteem or self-worth. There are a lot of people in the world who, on conscious reflection of their life patterns, do not feel that they have produced enough worthwhile information, inspiration or products or service—enough things—to feel that they deserve to be on the planet, alive and living. Now do we, in the spiritual sense, look at ourselves and come away with a justified feeling of self-worth? In other words, how can you feel that you have a reason and a purpose and a value in your life? How do we measure such things spiritually?

(Carla channeling)

I greet you in the love and the light of the one infinite Creator. I am known to you as Oxal. It is a privilege to be called to this group, as we have not been for some time. This question, however lies more, shall we say, within our area than most of your queries, and we thank you that you give us this opportunity to offer our service, humble though it may be. We share the information that we have, knowing that we do not know the whole story, and hoping and encouraging each to realize also that we do not know the whole story. Therefore, we ask you to take that which is of value to you and leave the rest behind, for we would not mislead you or cause you to stumble on the spiritual path.

This instrument asks the question to which she knows the answer so well that we are very surprised we must channel to this instrument. However, we find that in this instrument the pathways which lead to tolerance of self are blocked. Therefore, we will speak in general about this blockage and about how one may estimate spiritually one's progress towards self-esteem.

Consider the *cul de sac*, the dead end alley. This is what the entity which judges itself chooses. One runs into the end of oneself. The human self can never judge the human self, for that is an illusion judging an illusion, and neither your consciousness nor your behavior are in any continuum most normally but that of space/time. Self-worth is a time/space activity and a tremendous inner discipline, and we would suggest none feel cocky or confident in any way, for each of you is at the beginning of a long refining process, as if you were crude oil and the distillation was to begin and continue until the finest of oil was made.

In this density you do the big muscle movement, shall we say, of the dance of creation: you choose your partner. Shall you choose a Creator that is loving and giving, and shall you be loving and giving? Or shall you seek a Creator that is self-serving and hungry for praise, and you yourself be self-serving and hungry for praise? This is your dimension; this is your choice. This is where you make the choice. You are in the right place. Each of you has made the choice, yet still each wonders about the spiritual excellence of the self. And each judges the self as the person would never judge another. The self is always hardest upon the self, for it is privy to its stream of consciousness and very aware of what this instrument would call the clay feet.

Thus, we would suggest that none upon your planet may feel self-esteem of any height, for each is barely beginning the refinement process. At the same time, you must realize that within each is the perfect Creator-self. Each of you has taken upon himself that Creator-self, has realized that the Creator does lie within, that the answers do lie within, that the great question of "Who?" only has its answers in silence. And so each of you spends time seeking the truth, hoping for advancement and probably judging yourself harshly for mistakes which you have made over things you have not done, but could have.

It would be simple to tell each simply to release the low self-esteem, to let it go, to loosen its bonds from the personality and see it drift away, but it would not be apt, because those who are saddled with the lower opinion of themselves cannot let anything go. There is a tightness and a tension to the self-destructive attitude that is as heavy cord, binding the thought form to the self. Attempts to change the thought or to let it go mean nothing, for one is virtually tied to the concern and worry. This is to say that one cannot, in one's human self, remove oneself from one's self-esteem being low and instead produce a new self with good esteem, good self-worth and a sense of normalcy. The capacity of the entity which you are at this time is finite. Consequently, each seeker must realize that it cannot, of itself, esteem itself, but can only esteem itself within the Creator that is the true self.

Now, this Creator exists before it behaves, before it thinks, before it acts. The creation is made up of the Creator's thought, the great original Thought of Love that is within each. Now each has the free will. In an immature entity it is willful and you are moved by the will as one may be moved by the tides or the wind. In others, willfulness has given way to willingness, willingness to work, to share, to love, to be a part of the good of creation. This is the basic struggle of third density, the taming of the free will, the discovery of true free will, which can be found only when one has decided completely and dedicated oneself utterly to one of the two paths and is following that path in a daily way.

Now, we have explained to you why everyone should feel low self-esteem and why all should feel quite high in self-esteem. We've also indicated that the progress or maturity which one attains upon the spiritual path within this density has to do with the use of will.

To will to do all things for the love of the Creator is not a very specific will. But when it is translated into practical ethics and workaday situations, one finds the Creator looking very odd sometimes—in the face of a strange woman or a peculiar man, someone who is attempting to get your attention, but who is irritating you. Or perhaps today the Christ appears in another way. Always there is that which may engage the self in selfless giving. Always there is the opportunity to be one who gives.

Now, when one who is willing to give is not able to give all because of bodily distress, as we find this instrument's case to be, or because of any other reason for limitation, we do not find that the being of the self has changed at all, but rather that the attitude becomes self-destructive because the entity judges a self which no longer exists. And in some degree, this progress of less and less activity as one becomes older, of less and less ability to have energy to help with projects and so forth, is universal and not to be mourned, but to be investigated as any other situation. There are many useful things about a situation in which there is much time for contemplation and thought. There is the opportunity at all times to do whatever one is doing for the love of the one infinite Creator. In that adoration, in that worship, lies the light of the consciousness of your planet.

This is your basic work and this is your basic worth. When you can bring into manifestation that which vibrates in service to others, the universe is happy with you, and those who receive the bounty that you give are happy with you. But if there is no production, if there is only the being and that beingness remains joy-filled and filled with thoughts of the one infinite Creator, thoughts of love, thoughts of unity, thoughts of peace, the entity continues, then, to function fully as one whose work it is, whose mission it is, whose job it is, whose choice it is to serve others, to help lighten the planetary consciousness at this time with so many brothers and sisters which have also come from afar.

We find among your people that low self-esteem runs rampant. There is a shocking effect of the speeding up of things occurring which is characteristic of a change into fourth density. There is the polarity of the evil, shall we say, or negative and good or positive, each showing more polarity. Of course, it is those of service-to-self polarity which normally are considered newsworthy, but there are many, many more who are polarizing positively than negatively at this time. Why does each have low self-esteem? Few escape the difficulties.

We gaze upon humanity and realize how deep the illusion is with you. You see yourselves as a rather pinkish-colored, two-footed creatures, with eyes so and mouth so, and hair this, and clothes that. And that is what you think of as you. We will tell you how we see your density. We see energy fields. Some energy fields are radiant and beautiful. Some come together as yours and make a light that we cannot describe, for it is truly said when two or three are gathered together, there is much universal power.

We think, perhaps, that there is no way to escape low self-esteem, given the willfulness of the natural entity. Even the most disciplined entity will from time to time be unable to deal with the spiritual path because of exhaustion or confusion or anger or fear. And then we say to that person, remember you are not alone. You have support. You may call us angels, you may call us UFO contactees. We do not care what you call those of the inner planes who wish to help. It is enough for you to know that you are never, never without comfort if you ask for it. And if you ask for it, you shall find it—a comfort that you cannot give yourself because you are limited, but a comfort that can be given to you because the nature of the Creator is love and compassion.

If you are able in this incarnation to serve others more than half the time that you are doing something, you have succeeded, and we are not speaking of ritualized ways of aiding people, such as the job and so forth, nor are we speaking as if one could not be of service to others in solitude. But it is the person whose will has been brought so into alignment with the desire of the infinite One that those things which one has to face each day are faced, realized for the lessons that they are, and assimilated. There is seldom going to be a perfect day, shall we say, for a human entity, because each entity has biases because of willfulness in past lives. One cannot explain these biases. One is merely aware that one has somehow fallen short. Indeed, that is part of the human condition. Indeed, each has fallen short. This is an excellent lesson for each student of truth. All fall short. All fail. No entity may find the kingdom of the Father by itself or with any ease. There must be dependence upon love, a realization, a brave willingness to realize that the Creator is real, that the Creator loves and forgives and has forgiven all that is mis-done, that the Creator has no low self-esteem, but rather, work for you to do.

Thus it is that one who would remove the self-esteem look to service to others, move into those places where something needs to be done and help with a glad and merry heart, a song upon the lips and a smile upon the face. Each day it is possible for that to be the day in one's own mind. If one meditates and centers oneself during the day, it is often possible to find a rather blissful rhythm to a period of daylight and a period of darkness.

We hope we have not confused by looking at the problem of low self-esteem from several points of view, but we simply wish to point out that it is not a simple question, and spiritually one cannot measure oneself; one can only attempt to improve the use of the will that it may desire the desire of the Creator. For the Creator has things for each entity to offer today in love and in light, as a flower its bloom, as a tree its leaves, as a house its shelter. Each of you moves through each day purposefully, you know not why. The purpose will be unknown to you until the moment it is revealed. It is the centered and canny watcher and observer that spots the opportunity for love, that finds the place to give a smile of hello or a welcome handshake, a cheery word or a pat on the back. It takes a will to serve others to bear the questions in between the lines of the questions entities ask you, that you may minister unto them according to the knowledge that is within you. All of these things are what should occupy the mind.

The judgment of the self we need not say is inappropriate to this illusion from within this illusion, for those within the illusion cannot even see that they are energy fields with consciousness. Each thinks each is solid and pink and two-legged. We ask you, how much more distorted a picture of the self could one receive? Yet, that is how you perceive and are perceived. Consequently, never judge the self, but each day groom the will to desire to seek the love and the light of the one infinite Creator, and then, if there is aught to do for the Creator that lies before you, do it with a glad and merry heart and singleness of vision for only one reason—for love. And that is your salvation.

We speak to you thusly not to keep you from being humble. We simply wish to allow you to see things as we see them. And, indeed, there is a glory to third density from those who have chosen to discipline their will to that will which is called divine will. May that be your goal in each day. And may you each cease thinking about the self. To the extent that low self-esteem even enters the mind, the mind needs to be concerned with how others are doing, what may be needed and so forth.

It has been a pleasure to speak through this instrument. We are at this time going to close through this instrument, that we may speak through the one known as Jim. We leave this instrument in love and in light. I am Oxal.

(Jim channeling)

I am Oxal, and I greet each once again in love and in light. It has been some time since we have had the opportunity to utilize this instrument and it will take some amount of adjustment in order to make our contact both comfortable and clear. We thank this instrument for offering itself in the capacity of speaking our thoughts, and we would at this time ask if we might speak to any queries which are upon the minds of those present.

Carla: Well, just the one thing that wasn't touched on—it was my question. I felt real bad because the instrument, Jim, has to give up so much of his life in order to help me have a life. I'd just be in bed without him, I think, and it doesn't seem right that one person should have to spend so such time with another person's upkeep. Do you have any comments on that?

I am Oxal, and would speak to that query by reminding you, my sister, that there are those who wish to accomplish somewhat more during a lifetime than do others, and more than, shall we say, the entity may have attempted with previous incarnational patterns according to the needs both of the entity and of the entities that it wishes to serve within an incarnation. The fact that there is what you may call a norm for relationships within your culture that proceeds from the ordinary activity and range of motion upon the mundane level is not particularly good reason to assume that a pattern that deviates from that normal pattern is either better or lesser than that pattern, to be thought less of or to be embraced, for in the ultimate estimation of the entire range of possibilities available to third-density entities, the situation in which you find yourself falls only somewhat more toward limitation and intensity of experience in a certain manner than does the great majority of life patterns upon your planet.

Thus, the individual point of view is that which is of paramount importance in any situation, for each incarnational pattern will contain the challenges and the resources to meet those challenges, and each incarnational pattern will have the potential to increase the intensity of the experience if that is the desire of each entity involved. That each moves through your illusion as a function of the exercise of free will is of primary importance, for some there are that prefer one type of lesson over another, some there are who prefer greater intensity to lesser intensity. Yet each chooses freely to engage in that which it is felt will be of the most assistance in both the learning of those lessons which are placed before the entity and in the providing of services to others as a function of giving of that which has been learned. Thus, there are various ways of operating within your illusion, of moving the self along the evolutionary path, and each is quite capable of allowing the seeker to explore those realms which it desires.

We recommend that each look at the situation that comprises the life pattern, and if there are areas which do not please the discerning eye, then we would recommend that these areas be investigated even more closely with an eye that sees with a somewhat different focus, looking for that which has not previously been found, the opportunities which lie waiting, waiting for the careful gaze of the patient seeker.

Opportunities abound, my sister. Where there is limitation and discomfort, yet do opportunities abound if one is able to look upon the life pattern with the discerning eye which does not allow itself to be confused by comparison to that which is more normal or ordinary within the daily round of activities for many of your peoples.

Before asking for a further query, we shall pause in order that this instrument might tend to its recording devices. We shall pause at this time. I am Oxal.

(Side one of tape ends.)

(Jim channeling)

I am Oxal, and am again with this instrument. Is there another query at this time?

Carla: In *The Ra Material*, some people are spoken of as coming from outside the solar system, coming from Deneb. Do they have a different set of archetypes? Do they have an archetypical mind that is different from the archetypical mind of this particular star system?

I am Oxal, and we consider your query, my sister. Those whose origin is of the Deneb system, as those whose origin is from any system outside of your own, will of necessity bring with them the archetypical resonances of their own system, which is enough different from your own that there is of necessity a blending of certain facets or features within the deep mind, so that there might be the continuation of the spiritual journey that calls upon these deep resonances in an harmonious fashion. Thus, all those who have joined your third-density experience from those solar systems outside of your own add to the richness of your own archetypical system, which may be seen as a kind of a blueprint or structure of evolution that provides resources for the enhancing of the use of catalyst within your illusion.

There may be some confusion for those who pursue the study of the archetypical mind in a specific and quite conscious sense when attempting to grasp qualities that may seem alien. However, when most of your entities engage themselves in the study of this portion of the deep mind, there is that quality of awe and wonder that easily accepts that which seems foreign within the realm of the personal experience in order that it might enrich that experience, for when the deep mind is explored in a conscious fashion, there is always the feeling that this is not only holy ground, but ground which the self in its smaller sense is walking for the first sense. Therefore, the additions of exterior, shall we say, archetypical influences offers less of a difficulty than it offers greater richness.

Is there a further query, my sister?

Carla: Well, the reason that I asked that question was because I had been praying for peace in China—not military peace, that has happened—but a democratic peace that didn't happen. And I'd like to continue praying for it, but I was thinking perhaps I was sort of holding up hope that somehow it would work out, that China would make it, and so I was sort of using that archetype as we know it from the Tarot that we studied with *The Ra Material*. But I wondered if there was a useful difference that I could add to my visualization that would make it more powerful to that other archetypical system of imagery, so that my prayers would be mate to them, to their aid.

I am Oxal, and your query is a thoughtful one. However, we feel that at your current level of development, shall we say, it is the sending of the love and the light in the general form, the simple vibrations and intentions for harmony and peace within the heart, that may with hopefulness be sent, and it then be realized that as all healing vibrations, these shall be used and be translated, shall we say, in a most general sense by those to whom they are sent.

The ambiance, shall we say, of the inner planes as they are related to this particular culture is enhanced so that there is a greater feeling of goodness, shall we say, of nurturing, of support that may be drawn upon by those which have distortions or biases in this direction. Thus inspired, these receiving such vibrations will then allow the resonance of these vibrations to influence the life pattern to some degree. All of this, of course, operates upon the most basic and general of levels of spiritual existence, thus enhancing the mundane life pattern which grows from that foundation.

Is there another query, my sister?

Carla: No, thank you, Oxal.

I am Oxal, and thank you, my sister Is there another query at this time?

(Pause)

I am Oxal, and would take this opportunity to express our great gratitude at having the rare opportunity to address this particular group. It has been a great portion of your time since we were able to speak through this group. We are most appreciative. We hope that our words have been of some small assistance, and we hope that you will disregard those which have not. We await your further calls with joy and the desire to answer such calls with that which we have found helpful upon our own journeys of seeking. At this time we shall leave this group. We are known to you as those of Oxal. Adonai, my friends. ✣

Sunday Meditation
July 2, 1989

Group question: Has to do with the concept of the kundalini energy. In many of the teachings of the East it is suggested that the student of evolution not attempt to energize or raise the kundalini energy on his own, but rather should attempt to do this only in the presence of a guru or an enlightened master, and when this is done with the guru, that it is much more effortlessness and much safer. And what we are wondering this evening, if it is possible in any other fashion for the conscious seeker to be able work upon the kundalini and to move it along its upward path?

(Carla channeling)

I am Q'uo. I greet you in the love and in the light of the one infinite Creator. We thank you gratefully for your gracious invitation to join our vibrations with yours at this circle of seeking and bless all who seek for truth. Our love is shared with each of you as we enjoy this privilege and hear through this instrument's ears the sounds of your quiet evening, the soft, soaking rain of summer and the seeking thoughts of those who wish to serve others to serve the Creator and to know the truth.

The query that you ask shall take us some untangling of vocabulary to answer because in the older established religions of your planet those words which at first were innocent and neutral in their meaning have become laden with emotional bias towards the positive or towards the negative depending [on] the entity which hears the word. So we shall try to work around the vocabulary that so greatly differs between what we may call in general the Western tradition of faith in the Christ and the Eastern tradition of faith in Buddha.

Now, the entities which enjoy Buddhism and Hinduism are those which have experienced many lives in a culture which has been set up to furnish certain spiritual lessons about love, just as your own situation is. However, those who move through those lessons are those of other temperaments, of other needs, of other feelings that they have had in gazing at the past incarnation. As a result, they will move back into that system of polarizing towards service to others and realization in the way [most suited] to them, life after life after life.

Now, in the Western systems—and we will allow the danger of over-generalization to occur for the sake of time—the Creator is sometimes barely noticed because of the devotion many put upon the guru of this particular religion, that being the one known as the teacher, Jesus. It was his intent to create a guru that would live and speak within each as the spirit within and that would give guidance, that would have a higher self, so that the situation between those who work with the kundalini in the Eastern way are those who are working with the multiplicity of divinities, but one teacher, whereas those in your

Western religion claim a three-in-one Creator and many, many saints, yet one entity stands out as the guru.

The Creator does not call the ordering of the growth of the human spirit. Each is co-creator and has completely free will. As a general suggestion, we suggest that in whatever culture one is, one take a long and mystical view of the religion of that culture, using that myth as the guru for protection, for inspiration, and for information. That which you desire to know lies latent within yourself. It is the process of recognition of that which is already known, the process of remembering that occurs during the raising of what you have called the kundalini.

Now, the outpourings of what one may call prana are everywhere and move from every point in every direction so that the universe is full of creative life and light. It moves this energy into the body complex with sometimes quite physiological feelings, sometimes none, and one who is doing work in consciousness may then lean back into the arms of the guru's meditation. In the case of Jesus the Christ, this leaning back is called faith. Yet, let us say in this regard that those of the Eastern tradition have a different kind of faith, so that the culture might be accommodated. They believe that which they see. The challenge of those who do not choose the guru that is living is to have faith that the guru, which is Christ, has its consciousness within you and will yield to the persistent knocking and opening of the door to that inner room within you, to that rag and bone shop of the heart, as the poet would say. The guru indwells each.

Because you are of the Western culture, those to whom we speak this evening, we would recommend moving along those lines, if the Christ myth is able to express each spiritual feeling and emotion, adoration and worship that you wish. The process of raising the kundalini is as simple as that of removing blockages or dams from a swollen river. An infinity of prana enters the physical vehicle which houses your consciousness.

If you are blocking energy by holding it at any chakra before the heart chakra, the kundalini will have a very quiet time resting within. The blockages of relationship that are not peaceful or a situation that is not helpful in the workplace, things of these natures, may well block and stop the universal energy which is the one infinite Creator from providing sufficient energy to the heart chakra. This is why over and over again we encourage that entities meditate and that they do so from time to time in groups, for in the group comes the universality of worship, adoration and love.

To have companions along the road of spiritual seeking is extraordinarily helpful, and to have the guru is, as we have intimated, nearly necessary in order to advance beyond a certain point. We say nearly necessary simply because anything is possible. However, the same physiological, mental and emotional changes occur within each, whether in the Eastern, or negating, tradition or the Western, or radiating, condition. Each has the guru in place. Now, this teacher is important, for not only does this teacher give information, but more than that and mainly, the time that is spent in communion with this teacher gives to that deeper mind which is the feelings, the emotions, and the biases the nourishment that it needs in order to see one's own blockages and difficulties, to see that one has created them, to see that they may be healed and forgiven.

The greatest danger we find in those upon your sphere is that of the attempt to open the higher energy centers without dealing first with whatever material the seeker has brought into his life as he lives it in the present. Many times the early childhood or the failed marriage, the groom left at the altar or the death of a parent, may completely confuse and befuddle the seeker and the seeker must rest. In this situation it is not well to go forward, for in confusion can come biases that are false and you wish to find out what you are, not what you are not.

Therefore, as one who is, as you call it, in the Western tradition of mystical seeking, we greatly encourage the spending of time with the teacher, that is, in silent meditation visualizing, if you will, the mind of Christ or Christ consciousness, allowing yourself to be bathed in it, allowing it to do with you what it will. This is very useful in bringing up energy to the heart chakra and in many cases such as the communications you hear this evening, the indigo chakra and blue chakra are also much involved in the service to which you come by spiritual coincidence.

It is necessary to have a teacher for one simple reason. The energies which each seeks destroy as easily as heal. The light does not blink at negative or positive, but is available to both. One who seeks erratically or without guidance, one who does not practice dailyness in offerings and worship, is either simply unawakened or, when the meditation does occur, may be open to receiving information or subconscious biases which are service to self. The teacher and the pupil is the relationship to be treasured above all. Yet, we feel that in the Western world the myth of Christ functions perhaps more appropriately at this time than the myth of Buddha because the responsibility for opening the door to the teacher then becomes completely subjective. You cannot get out of your car and open the door and walk into the room with your guru and sit and meditate and gaze upon the guru's face. The face of the mind of Christ you will never know. Therefore you are a faith-filled people when you are working at the parables of Jesus the Christ's life and the parable within the parable, each parable which he told, that is.

It is our feeling that it is more indicative of the joy of creation to move the kundalini in the Western manner for those who are of Western feelings and belief, simply because the physiological body needs, in most cases, a lifetime of preparation in order to move culturally into the subconscious rhythms and archetypes of a different belief system.

We hope that you are not at all surprised that you are not alone. Since the creation is within you, you are far, far from alone, for you have infinity within you. Thus, we urge each to the dailyness of meditation and taking oneself seriously enough in the intention of the meditation to move thoughts out of the mind that come into the mind, to continue refocusing and recentering for a short time, rather than sitting with the eyes closed and planning the dinner menu, as this instrument has been known to do. This is your moment of nourishment. This is the bread of heaven. Your energy rises as you put out the fires, shall we say, in red, orange and yellow chakras.

Now, how can this be done with the guru and with no speech in the Eastern tradition? It is done in this way because the Eastern tradition is passive and negative. It seeks a nothingness. It is not sacrificial, but, rather, joyful, and it demands of its priests—as this instrument would call them—that they be realized enough entities to perform some small portion of what Christ consciousness may perform. In that culture the teacher simply entrains the consciousness of the chela, or student, to its own impersonal vibration in adoration of the One.

In this Western culture of yours, such would be considered brainwashing. Instead, in this culture entities are encouraged to use the mind, the intellect, as well as the heart to discover a life in faith. This is unfortunate, in that it emphasizes that which is not important, that is, the specifics of the life in history of Jesus the Christ. In order for this entity, Jesus, to be a guru or teacher or rabbi, the entity had to dismantle several thousand years of brutal solipsistic thinking concerning the Creator. Against a backdrop of many gods, those who preceeded the one known as Jesus tried to cling to one, but they were not successful. Thus, the path was not single and progress was difficult.

Within the Western tradition there have, of course, been just as many difficulties, and so it is with the Sufis and Elijah and with Muslim and Allah. One cannot say this or that way of worshipping is perfect. One can only firstly assume that it is probably that the greatest grist will be ground from the mill of the religion of one's culture that one has been steeped in all of one's incarnational experience. We urge that careful attention be paid first to settling within oneself one's feeling about one's being and sexuality.

We realize that the one known as Jim was speaking of this previously, but what the Eastern guru does with the chela is put metaphysical training wheels upon the chela that are false, that is, they are of the guru, and as long as the meditations with the guru continue, then the meditations are satisfactory. But the guru is an entity, one who cannot move past the hump of humanness, that none can within third density. Therefore, these entities are weaker in wisdom and compassion often than the teacher known to you as Jesus. They all, each prophet, each savior, each figure, has something to add to an overall perspective, for it is agreed, if nothing else, that there is one Creator. Upon this point, most of the world's religions would settle.

Therefore, [if] you wish to ask the guru's help, that is, in meditation, ask within if there is a difficulty with the sexuality, with the feeling of being worthwhile, with anything which might threaten the stability and comfort of the body. This should be worked with consciously and rooted out, that that energy center may be clear and energy flow through it. We are not saying that each must have the sex life;

we are saying that each must feel good about having a sex life, whether one is or is not in a relationship at the time. One must feel not only tolerant but good when one thinks of one's passion and sexuality, for the passion that you feel at orgasm is your first experience of the steady state of the Creator. It is brief and fleeting, but it is an indication given as a gift and also as a perfectly practical means of evolving the species [offered by] the one infinite Creator.

When we move from red to orange, we gaze at the murkiness of relationships, and we say to you that if you are at odds with any, do your best at this point to seek forgiveness and to forgive self. If there are those whose forgiveness you cannot ask, know that you are forgiven, for others forgive you easier than you forgive yourself. The clearing of the orange ray and the yellow ray has a good deal to do with how one's conduct is, whether it is spontaneous, heartfelt and honest, or whether it is studied, positional and angular.

We are speaking of the Western tradition of living upon the very surface of the pond, shall we say, of life. People skate across the ice and enjoy the beautiful things that your planet has to offer without living in a state of praise and thanksgiving, without looking at each moment and asking, "Can I help? Can I love? Can I share?" The mind of Jesus is a most helpful interior guru. To move ahead without such an one to guide and govern these times is to ask not only for a lack of inspiration, but even a decline or regression in one's spiritual growth. The human entity does not have the simple, persistent strength to be daily throughout a lifetime without opening the door within to the teacher that bids you take up the cross, take up your condition, take up your humanity and follow in the footsteps of one who healed, who loved, who brought light, who brought union, who brought joy.

Within your culture you are tolerant of your Earthly priests, and this is healthier, we feel. You know that they all have clay feet—so do gurus. That is the difficulty, the one salient problem with the system of teacher and pupil both being incarnate. However, whether you learn from an Earthly teacher or whether you have your hand in the Christ's or visualize in some other way the identification of that consciousness and yourself, you will be less strong than if you can make a simple habit of moving in consciousness to the center of one's being, the open and compassionate heart.

When the red, orange and yellow energy centers are all functioning, spinning brightly and moving the energy well, the conditions are good for the seeker to undertake work in consciousness. It is not good to undertake work in consciousness of a higher kind before one has gazed at one's life and, to the extent it is possible, made amends, squared away debts and, in general, until the person no longer has the love of the wealth of the planet, but the love of the Creator as the motivating force. This change in attitude often comes in an instant, but that instant is preceded by a good deal of work. And when realization has come, then you shall find your next lesson and you shall find that the idea of becoming perfected and realized by yourself is quite impossible and not of this density. The teacher is there to guard, to protect, and to deepen the meditative state by meditating with an entity. You may ask any of us to do the same thing. We are happy to.

Each entity has his own understanding of teachers, gurus, guides, angels or the Holy Spirit. Do not let the differences in vocabulary cause you to think there are differences in the emotional and mental experiences of those who seek to live a life in faith. We believe it is well that the kundalini move easily and flowingly into the heart chakra and right up through into that measure of the vibratory rate of the self, the violet ray.

The problem one faces in achieving realization of the self within Western incarnation is distraction. You are the most bombarded society upon the planet. The music, the television, the loudspeakers in the stores, the traffic noises, the constant movement about that is characteristic of your society …

(Side one of tape ends.)

(Carla channeling)

… is that which puts out the light; which keeps the kundalini asleep. Now, we do not condemn any of your gadgets. We realize that—as is in this instrument's mind at this moment—there are interesting and informative and enjoyable programs of entertainment within the media. Information is passed about which one cares. And it is not necessary to move to a cave and block out all sensory input in order to work with the kundalini. For this kundalini is nothing more nor less than the way the body physiologically organizes the infinite instreamings of prana and those effects which various stars and galaxies have upon the entity, keeping it moving, keeping it alive, letting it flow through one. This is a goal much to be desired, for though the life has become simple and—as the one known as T would certainly say at this point—impersonal, it is also free, for the first time in the life experience.

Each of you is dragged about by the free will of each. That is the willfulness which masks the Creator-self within. There is that in you of the mischievous child, that which wishes to play hooky. Consequently, we urge two things upon you, first that you attempt a very intentional time of just spending time with the Christ consciousness each day, silent and listening, and we ask that you love each other, for in loving each other, you shall work very actively upon the kundalini. Love expressed is infinitely valuable. Know that it comes through you, not from you. Don't expect this to be a human task. It is a superhuman ordeal, but you have that within you which is superhuman, that is, above the state of third density. You have within you the Creator-self. It is simply that you begin your life experience somewhat deaf to the inner voice and the outer voices are so riveting to the young soul in the childhood years, that it is the rare child who begins to seek spiritually in any way except in imitation of the parents.

And in that regard, we may say [to] those with children who wish to help their children become more aware and to raise their own kundalini power that the most effective way to move children into relationship with the one infinite Creator is by example. It can be a totally unspoken example. There is simply one place where the mother, the father, go to sit and worship and adore and intercede and give thanksgiving and share hopes and talk and then listen. Silent prayer or meditation is the greatest key to spiritual growth.

We find that we have again taken up too much of your time. This instrument is telling us that she asked us to speak shortly, but, my children, we have spoken shortly; there is so much more upon the subject that we could say. This was the shortest we could make it. We wish you to know we were trying to coincide with your wishes.

At this time we would like to thank this instrument for allowing us to use it, would remind each that we are not an infallible source of information, but merely those in the group which has gone through the density which you now enjoy and has learned some further lessons. We are not perfect. We are far from it, my friends; we could be wrong. It is well for you to listen and discern that which is for you and toss the rest away, for you will be attracted to and recognize your truth.

And as that truth changes as you change, we advise you to let that flow also, as change is the hallmark of the raising of the kundalini. You may be often uncomfortable in, what this instrument would call, the fast lane of spiritual progress, for change equals discomfort. It is your choice. We encourage you to work on your polarity, to use your teacher, whether it be incarnate or discarnate and to allow some discomfort into the life, that one may burn away that which is not needed and temper the personality that remains to be flexible, gentle and very, very strong in love of neighbor and of Creator.

We shall leave this instrument now in love and light and transfer to the entity known as Jim. I am Q'uo.

(Jim channeling)

I am Q'uo, and greet each again in love and light through this instrument. It is our privilege at this time to offer ourselves in the attempt to speak to any further queries. Is there a query at this time?

T: Yes, I have a question. When attempting to go within and listen to the still, small voice within, there are times when it seems that I'm very sure that I am not bringing something out of my own everyday conscious mind. There are other times when I'm not, and there are times when I'm sure that it's just me, my everyday self saying this. How can one tell? Your thoughts on how one can tell you're truly listening to the Creator within, your own higher self?

I am Q'uo, and am aware of your query, my brother. We find that though you asked the query, you have determined to a large extent the answer, for you have discovered that there are times during which you feel that the information and guidance that you receive when you ask for the voice of that small and still voice, that the response is indeed that voice, and other times it is more of the conscious waking self's response. We may affirm that each entity has not only access to this voice, but has the means to determine the depth from which information comes.

For as you look upon your own mind, much likened to a tree that stands with roots traveling deep into the earth, that your own mind is like this tree; that you have a simple and sure connection to the voice which speaks from the center of your heart in simplicity and in clarity; that you listen to this speaking, and that the feeling that you have in response to the speaking is that which shall inform you as to the nature of that speaking and of the voice which speaks it.

Know that each guidance from within has come from a deeper portion of your own self and has been filtered through more or less of your conscious awareness according to what you might call the inner weather or conditions of that particular day or time, or as with the weather of your planetary sphere, there is a weather that is active within your own mind in both the conscious and subconscious realms that is responsive to various mental, emotional and experiential conditions within your life pattern. Therefore, there will be times when the inner communication is far more clear than at other times when the weather conditions, shall we say, might have a distorting influence due to the coinciding of certain rhythms or cycles within your own nature.

Thus, if there is ever doubt as to the nature of the voice that speaks from within, we would recommend that first you ask yourself the nature of this voice, that if doubt remains, that you at another time seek again that guidance. Do this until you are certain that you have received the clearest and most substantial information that you can receive. Thus, you take advantage of the varying inner conditions of your own being and affirm that which is given, or determine that you must seek again.

Is there a further query, my brother?

T: No, thank you very much. That was excellent.

I am Q'uo, and we thank you, my brother. Is there another query?

Questioner: I have one, too. At the beginning of this meditation, when I was holding myself in a state of openness, I felt an enormous power that I had felt before when I was very young in a dreaming state. Was this of the kundalini?

I am Q'uo, and am aware of your query, my brother. When we speak to matters that are of an intensely personal nature, we must take great care that we do not move beyond the boundary that signifies an infringement upon an entity's free will, for many mysteries there are in each seeker's life pattern that must remain mysteries until that seeker has of his or her own accord and effort discovered a significant enough portion of the riddle to be given hints and clues as to the further unraveling of such a riddle. The experience of which you speak falls within this type of information and mystery. We may speak in a general sense only in this regard in order that we do not infringe upon your own free will.

The power of which you speak does indeed have close relationship to the energy which we have been calling kundalini this particular evening. The nature of this relationship is one which is likened unto the guiding sign, shall we say—we search for the correct word within your language—the inner clue that reveals a possibility to the self from a deeper portion of the self by having a certain center of energy or chakra energized to the point that the feeling of overwhelming power elicits from your conscious self the desire to penetrate the mystery, to follow the thread left upon the ground and which leads into the forest. Thus, this experience is much like a letter from home, shall we say, and we find that this is the extent of the information which is permissible at this time to give upon this topic.

Is there another query, my brother?

Questioner: Thank you for that answer.

I am Q'uo, and we thank you, my brother. Is there another query at this time?

Carla: I've got a couple. I'm not sure if you can answer one. This is about the fifth meditation in a row that I have had to chase off fairly low level negative entities. This time it was all around the circle, not just around one side. Why are they hanging around? Can you answer that? They don't usually.

I am Q'uo, and am aware of your query, my sister. You may liken the gathering of this nature to the gathering of entities around the campfire at night in the woods. The entities around the campfire warm themselves by the heat of the fire, light themselves enough to see each other's face and communicate that which is of meaning at that moment. Many other eyes there are that see this fire and look upon it as that which offers something of interest, something of potential gain. These eyes from outside the circle may or may not be those eyes which wish the circle well, however, their presence is assured when the fire is lit, for elsewhere there is but darkness. That you have not been aware of the entities of which you speak previously before the last few of your meditative seekings is a function of your own ability to perceive that which is present and may be expected to continue in its growing acuity.

Is there a further query, my sister?

Carla: Yeah. This is the one that's general. I think I'm like everybody, in that with the best will in the world, I have three or four people in my life that simply will not forgive me for something they think I've done or not done or something. The people like the one known as N—you can get all that information out of my mind or Jim's—people that I have not been able to please and have attempted everything in my power to make things right with and have simply fallen flat on my face. And I wonder sometimes, is it acceptable to forgive the self until the other self forgives you?

I am Q'uo, and am aware of your query, my sister. You and each seeker would be quite surprised, we believe, if you knew the number of entities that may have yet to forgive some thought, word or deed that was your offering to them. It is well to forgive these entities and to forgive yourself for those offerings which missed their mark or have been misunderstood. Indeed, it is all that any individual can, for within your illusion, misperception and miscommunication are the rule, for you exist in an illusion, which means that you exist in a frame of reference that is other than it appears to the surface glance, and, indeed, is other than it appears even to the serious seeker that attempts to move beyond the surface appearance.

Thus, it is not important in the ultimate sense that one is fully forgiven by each entity that one touches in the life pattern. But it is quite important that one forgives not only each entity that touches one's life pattern, but that one forgives the self for those efforts which have fallen short of the desire to be of service. One is responsible for the self. One cannot learn for another. One can learn only for the self, and then share with others that which has been learned and forgive all for any misunderstanding or injury that has been done.

Is there another query, my sister?

Carla: Yes, just a quickie. And again, this may infringe on free will, and it's perfectly okay if you don't answer it, but I'd just like to check my perceptions, because we're working in an invisible metaphysical field here and there isn't anything but subjective proof, but if you could confirm this. I heard Oxal at the very beginning, but he was not wanting to give a message. He was wanting to be present and to give his blessing. Is that correct? Can you confirm?

I am Q'uo, and am aware of your query, my sister. We can indeed confirm that which you have correctly surmised. Those of Oxal offer their blessings to those that are of a nature to appreciate and welcome this blessing.

Carla: Well, then, would I be correct in assuming that Oxal was here to greet our new guest?

I am Q'uo, and this, too, is correct, my sister.

Carla: Okay, that works out. Thank you so much, Q'uo.

I am Q'uo. Again we thank you, my sister. Is there a further query at this time?

(Pause)

I am Q'uo, and we are most happy to have been able to speak to those areas of concern for each of those gathered this evening. It has been a great honor, and we humbly thank each for inviting our presence. Again, we remind each that we do not wish to provide a stumbling block for any seeker. If we have spoken any word which does not ring true, we ask that you forget that word and use those which do ring of truth to you as you will. We would at this time take our leave of this instrument and this group, leaving each, as always, in the love and in the light of the one infinite Creator. We are known to you as those of Q'uo. Adonai, my friends. Adonai. ❧

Special Meditation
July 3, 1989

Group question: Has to do with two concepts, the first of which being the necessity for remaining open-minded and willing to process new information and to change as we travel on our journey back into unity with the Creator, and the second concept has to do with the individuality that we construct that is our personality, the core of ourselves, which makes choices, makes decision, and is open. We would like to have some information concerning the relationship between the somewhat fixed and stable nature of the personality that makes these choices and the ability to remain open and flexible so that one can change and become a new being and eventually become more unified with the Creator.

(Carla channeling)

I am Q'uo. I greet each of you in the love and in the light of the one infinite Creator and thank each for requesting our service which we may humbly perform, for in our life experiences at this time, our service to those upon your sphere who wish to hear the words of light and truth is our way of progressing and refining our understanding love, compassion and wisdom. Therefore, you are being of great service to us, as well as to yourselves, by pondering those questions that have substantive meaning without regard to time or space.

The question that you ask this day seems to contain a paradox. This means that the questioner is on the right track, for the spiritual quest has as its signal virtue continual paradox. In this case, the paradox is "How does one be oneself while one is becoming oneself? How does one be, yet be open to change?"

Firstly, we would like to express that beyond any control of your own, you are. You have no choice but to be what you are, for you are an imperishable metaphysical entity, a form of light. The beauty of your vibrations is unique to each. The balance of service is unique to each, yet each is beautiful and cherished by us. And we thank all who seek the truth and turn their face towards the mystery of infinity and the Creator's love.

Each of you existed as a definite consciousness before the world you dwell upon was created and each will continue infinitely to be a consciousness for many millions of years into your future, as you would call it. Indeed, the infinity of our consciousness stretches before us too, although our teachers express to us that they are aware of those entities which have gained enough spiritual gravity or solidity or crystalline nature, shall we say, where compassion is enough perfected that the entity moves into the consciousness of the one Creator. That consciousness, then, is lost, but informs the one Creator and is part of the active principle of the one Creator.

By far the greater part of the Creator is not active but resides in a state of love, which force created all that there is, and which force each of you seeks to bind into your lives more and more naturally, more and more authentically, more and more deliberately. The thrust of this thought is that you cannot help being. It is within you, unquestionable, from our viewpoint, as to what vibratory complex each of you is. We realize this is not available to you in this illusion, but we assure you that you are imperishable ones and that there is no mistake that one may make that could eliminate the beingness, the consciousness of the self.

Now, let us turn our minds to the phenomenon of learning. Any learning experience is a kind of ordeal. The spiritual learning experience is one of a great deal of catalyst and change, for the spiritual seeker who attempts to accelerate the rate of his spiritual growth will discover more and more how uncomfortable change can be. So it may be that, in the darker moods, one wonders whether one is spiritual enough, whether one has stayed upon the road to the kingdom that awaits. One questions oneself.

We ask each to pull back the focus of attention, the point of view, as though you were a camera moving farther and farther away. First you see your entire block, then the entire planet, and then you are so far away that you can only see the Sun. This is a point of view worth attempting. The discomforts of the spiritual journey are all linked to the desire to change. It is a blessing to one who serves others when that entity understands that that which he is to do is prepared for him and sits in front of his face.

Thus, no one needs to use an enormous amount of discrimination in order to do the work necessary to make changes necessary in consciousness. The trap of those with spiritual pride is that they would rate dramatic services to others above the less dramatic services and those who render them.

This will never advance the cause of lightening the consciousness of Earth. Rather, it is a series of paradoxes which we suggest you consider—that is, the middle way, the *via media*—for walking in balance with the life about one in service to others. Non-dramatic services to others—those who tend the child, those who sweep the hearth, those who work in jobs that do not seem to have satisfaction in them—are just as capable as the most experienced seeker of bringing into manifestation within their creation the love of the infinite One.

Now, the paradox between judgment and tolerance or open-mindedness is solved only by faith; that is, the faith that we are, that each is, that oneself is an I AM. All you are responsible for, in that regard, is learning who you are. Many there are who get so caught up in spiritual growth that they do not ever establish for themselves the roots of their faith. Consequently, they move from one spiritual practice to another, never getting the satisfaction and consolation of spiritual guidance and service to others in community.

Thus, we would say it is well to know the self well, to know what the physical vehicle that moves each about needs, and to provide it carefully, to treat that instrument kindly, for it carries you about. Then one may turn one's face to the changing, assured of who one is, for in changing, you are not changing in kind but in refinement of quality.

Therefore, the open mind, the attempt of new things, will, of course, bring changes within the conscious mind and the programming of the subconscious mind as well, and this, as always, will be experienced as times of discomfort, frustration, sorrow, anger or some other negative stress. From within the illusion that is the picture that the eyes carry to the brain. This is not an accurate picture, for in retrospect one may always discover that where there was catalyst for change and the difficulty of changing in order to be of more service to others, there has also been the balance of learning that intensifies during traumatic events.

Thus, each seeking entity must do the work of discrimination and judgment for himself. Let no one express truth to you in a way which is infallible, but rather allow that which is infallible, the Creator-self within, to have constant daily opportunities to center and tabernacle with the one infinite Creator.

You would be very startled, my children, if you knew what your true spiritual temperature is. None of you knows himself to the extent that we do, simply because we may read you. We may see your vibrations and your balances in their uniqueness, in their crystalline purity. Within the illusion you do not see a crystal forming in consciousness, but rather you see lumps of bone and muscle and sinew, hair and various features, things very much touchable, and it is almost impossible to experience, without experiencing through the senses of the physical body with relationship to the physical world, the pain of change. In actuality, when the pain is occurring, frequently this is the time of the greatest step forward for an entity. The challenge of the catalyst has focused the attention and, therefore, the seeker is more ready to welcome change in terms of increasing one's polarity in service to others.

Now, we realize that none of you knows precisely how to know the self. May we suggest that especially in the mated relationship, the mate which is upon the spiritual quest with the other mate functions as teacher and mirror so that that which one hears comes into the biocomputer of the mind, is filtered through subconscious biases and thus becomes a rather distorted reflection of yourself. When conversation takes place, the two seeking entities are seeking to aid each other, to comfort each other, to console each other and to learn together. Thus, they become honest; they become malleable to speaking clearly on any subject.

Within your culture many subjects are considered inadvisable to dwell upon. The spiritual is a matter of life, and, in this illusion, death, for that which you do within this illusion, the choices that you make here, will in turn affect your being at the harvest, and the more polarized towards the light you have become, the more loving, the more compassionate, the more accepting, the more peaceful, the more joyful, the more light you may accept in joy and use. And in that term, light, we do not mean simply the photon, but rather the energy that is the Creator's. The photon is the manifestation of that great original Thought of Love.

So, we would suggest that each examine the portions of experience which have caused each to feel an emotion, for emotion is a very deep and purified kind of thinking. As one gazes into one's prejudices and biases, one has the opportunity to attempt to balance them, to acknowledge the paradox, the opposite, and to see that they are two sides of one thing, that all is one, that there is no separation. The practical difficulty which we find this instrument feels is so, is that there is a great deal of material which refers to philosophical and spiritual principles. Much of that material has been mixed with specific material concerning what this instrument would call eschatological concerns.

We do not deny in any way that there is the possibility of planetary disaster upon your sphere. However, we do suggest that the true nature of the New Age is that which comes after the death in this illusion and the walking of the path of light until one has found the light that one can accept the best and enjoy most fully. We ourselves are on that same path and we ourselves have a great deal of refining yet to do, for to understand how to blend complete compassion and wisdom is the study of much, much experience. Where you are now is in a decisive blink of an eye. The little life that you experience, great and whole and wonderful as it is, is very short, and at the end is the death. And those who dwell upon the last days and the New Age are receiving much information from the feeling portion of the subconscious having to do with the fear of death. Although it is inevitable and therefore seemingly uninteresting, it becomes a vital concern for entities as they approach the limit of the life experience and prepare to go on.

Now, one may polarize and continue changing in any circumstance or condition. We suggest that you see the balance and walk the middle road, using your discrimination after you have heard the ideas that are presented to you, not judging ahead or during the experience, but allowing each learning experience its own shape and space and color, allowing it to sink into that portion of the mind which is far more accurate, that portion of the mind which lies below the level of conscious thought. In meditation daily this is done, and it is well done to be daily in meditation.

But who you are is how you behave, and service to others is not pleasing others. These are thoughts to be pondered. Many attempt to polarize towards light by helping and pleasing people. The question that needs to be asked by each is this: "Has this person asked for my help? And am I able to respond?" If you can find no spiritual principle, yet you can help another by refraining from judgment and offering sympathy. If your advice is asked and you not know what to say, that is acceptable. You do not have to please the entity by making a guess at what the trouble might be. The goal, you see, is to be in a state of consciousness within which is preserved the feeling of unity with the one Creator, the experience of tabernacling in meditation, the experience of opening the inner door by meditation. Many times learnings will come to a seeker through dreams, daydreams or visions. These should never be ignored, but should be valued as deep indicators of who you are.

A paradox, too, is the result of a life lived in faith and service, for as one serves, one is served a dozen-fold, a hundred-fold, a thousand-fold. As one gives, one receives in plenty. Thus, the paradox is that compassionate feelings and actions in service to other entities by loving, by supporting, by sharing or by a brief smile to a stranger, these things commend you as a servant of the one infinite Creator, yet what you receive back from the creation is a thousand-fold that which [you] have expressed.

Thus, we suggest that each begin to become aware of the very core of the being that is joyful and merry and full of passion. You see, my children, when we say that we greet you in love and in light, we are only using words which are inadequate, because there is no word in your language for the extreme amount of infinite passion the one infinite Creator has for each of its parts of consciousness that are active and teaching the Creator about Itself.

Seek that inner fire. Seek to deepen the ability to worship the Creator, to give adoration, praise and thanksgiving to the Creator for all things, including those challenges which have been set up that you may learn what you intended to when you came here. You shall never be rid of your selfhood. It is only possible to be unaware of it. The practice of honesty with the self is the cornerstone of this basically analytical process.

In the case of the questioner and in many other cases the amount of learning that has been programmed into this incarnation is the maximum amount that the higher self felt that each was capable of in this density. Many entities, therefore, experience great difficulty and have designed that in place in the life experience for the purposes of learning to serve without expectation of return. This instrument has a great deal of trouble remembering that it is a service to receive, and we would remind each that those who receive are as blessed as those who give. The blessedness lies in the compassion between the two people. That which is done grudgingly is not going to polarize your consciousness towards the positive, so if it is impossible to serve cheerfully, it is well to move into solitude and meditation until one has the balance back, until one's faith is firm, until one no longer feels despair.

You have a choice to make, my children, in this incarnation, since is the last probable incarnation for each within this density. You have the opportunity and the ability to move into the next [density] …

(Side one of tape ends.)

(Carla channeling)

… yet you have some work to do in this incarnation in order that you may be harvestable as a service-to-others entity. Thus, the illusions of illness, limitation, financial ruin and any other life disturbing patterns may well not be disasters at all, but, rather, marvelous challenges that enable you to polarize thousands of times more quickly than we ever could within our density, which is the fifth, or any other density besides your own. The third density is the intensive density. It is the density of making the choice to serve the Creator by serving the self or to serve the Creator by serving others.

Now, you came, each of you, into the life experience with the biases which we encourage you to discover for yourself. You may then evaluate these biases for their polarity in service to others and in mutual love. Remember the great passion that is the Logos. You have been created with that steady state which you experience during orgasm in the sexual sense. This is the intensity of the Creator's love for each, and to be oneself in fact and not in conjecture, one needs to open oneself carefully and gaze with interest and an acuity of observation upon each and every situation, looking for the opportunity to serve and to share love.

As you understand your biases better, so may you work upon increasing the biases you feel worthwhile and decreasing the biases you feel not worthwhile. You may change your own consciousness, but again we say, your becoming is illusory, for in the ultimate sense there is no time, there is no space—there is the present moment which is infinite. Very few entities are able to dwell in the present moment, but, rather, they are chastising themselves or congratulating themselves on that which is passed or worrying about that which is to come. It is well to remember that each moment intersects eternity. We ask each to release the fear of living in this illusion, to release the fear of leaving the illusion, and to become content with whatever conditions prevail, accepting any condition as agreeable, even though it may seem to be a serious challenge or difficulty.

You are not alone, as you work towards becoming more of what you are. Basically, you are uncovering who you are as you refine yourself, for the original self that is your consciousness is the consciousness of the Creator, that great, intense, passionate love which calls into being the photon and from that point all manifestations of your illusion.

There is much to be said for sheer persistence and the refusal to rebuke the self, for the more unsparing you are of the self in the attempt to realize the Creator-self within in manifestation within the illusion, the more difficulties you will experience. Allow the fact that this is an illusion to sink deeply into the mind. Think of all that there is. It is made, we are aware that your scientists have said, of atomic and subatomic particles and combinations thereof. However, there has never been a sighting of an actual mass, merely the track of the energy has been found by your scientists. They see at first-hand the depth of the illusion.

May you too realize that you are a mind and body and spirit composed of complex energy patterns, that you are sensitive to the environment in which you dwell and the universe in which you find yourself. We believe that we have said what we wished to about this topic, although we are most happy to answer further questions. The art of becoming is not an art that is won easily. It is a craft, and you are the artist. It is a play, and you the actor. Know yourself as well as you can, and then listen open-mindedly to all information and put it to the test within and within you will come the answer, for you will recognize your own truth. Each entity has a slightly different path to the Creator. What is functional for one entity may be useless to another, with the exception of the practice of silent meditation and listening.

We wish you the joy of knowing, even in pain and difficulty and distress, that work in consciousness that you have planned for yourself is being accomplished fruitfully, beneficially and steadily, so that each persistent and faithful pilgrim along the way shall, by conscious decision and intention, live more and more the life of the instant which is eternal, bringing infinity into the illusory experience, bringing the vast point of view into the mind which is saddled with many words and numbers.

We wish you to be extremely nurturing of yourselves as you perceive failure within the illusion. You have no idea of how you are doing within the illusion. You will not know how you have done until you have left the heavy chemical illusion that you experience and are once again able to look at the life experience as part of what this instrument would call the Akashic Record, turning the pages of the life, gazing at the tapestry one has woven of love and sorrow and service and selfishness. May each weave the most beautiful tapestry he can. May each look to the life experience as to a poem, an attempt to write each line with grace and beauty. In this you are supported and are never alone, for the higher self, under any guise which you wish to call this energy, is with you as comforter and nurturer, and when despair does overtake the soul, we ask that you suspend all judgment, all discrimination of the self, and move into an awareness that one is being held in the infinite arms of the infinite Creator, that one is, in truth, nurtured.

We thank this instrument and would at this time transfer to the one known as Jim, leaving this instrument in love and light. We are known to you as those of Q'uo.

(Jim channeling)

I am Q'uo, and greet each again in love and light through this instrument. At this time it is our privilege to offer ourselves in the attempt to speak to any further queries. Is there a query at this time?

Questioner: I have one. To continue the question of the paradox just a little bit further. In the direction now of spiritual practice, when one meditates there seems to be a fine line between making an effort and letting go. Can you speak to the question of what the most effective way of meditating is, whether it involves the use of imagination or simply not thinking?

I am Q'uo, and am aware of the query, my brother. We cannot say that there is one means of meditating that is, in general, better than another, for each individual will approach the meditative state and the balance point of which you speak in an unique fashion. The ability to prepare the self inwardly, whether it be by the imagery or the mental ritual that is constructed for personal use or by any other means is the active phase, shall we say, of this preparation. The entity which wishes to set the table, shall we say, must needs prepare the self in whatever manner has meaning to that self. This is determined by the experience of the entity. There are a variety of ways in which an entity may go about this, and each may discover that the final choice is not so final when refinements are discovered.

We do not mean to, shall we say, dodge the query, but mean to express the nature of the flexibility that the seeker has at its disposal for preparing to open the inner eye to a field of vision and experience which is not available to the entity without such preparation within the meditative state. Thus, we recommend experimentation, choice, dedication, perseverance and, as the theme of this meditation has been, the ability to remain open to new ideas and possibilities. Thus, the seeker shall find that the experience is one which will offer itself—that is, the seeker—the continuing possibility for growth. There is much within each seeker which remains hidden and which through the perseverance and dedication to regularity will be revealed as the seeker [is] ready.

Thus, we find the most important point to emphasize in this regard is the dedication or the regularity in the practice of the meditation and the motivation for such meditation, that motivation being most helpful when the heart of the desire is to seek union with the Creator. When such dedication and regularity are a firm portion of the foundation of the seeker in its daily round of activities, there will be made available to the seeker those opportunities for refining the process which are appropriate at a certain time determined by an inner rhythm that is a great portion of the mystery which forms not only the larger portion of the Creator but the heart of the seeker as well.

Is there another query, my brother?

Questioner: No, thank you.

I am Q'uo, and we thank you. Is there another query at this time?

Carla: So, basically, what you're saying is we're like a block of stone and the friction of experience and catalyst chips away everything that's not an elephant, to use the old adage. Basically, is that what you're saying?

I am Q'uo, and am aware of your query, my sister. This is indeed a large portion of the concept which we wish to convey, however, this analogy is one which describes primarily the subconscious nature of experience for any entity within your illusion, for whether the entity seeks in a conscious fashion or not, there is yet the catalyst of each day which does indeed chip ever so slowly away at that which is not desired according to the overall plan of the incarnation.

However, at some point, each seeker will discover the beginning working of this process of evolution and will seek to accelerate this process in order that it might, in a conscious fashion, take part in the creation of the statue, shall we say, that is the self, the truer self, the ideal self, within certain boundaries or limitations, those limitations being set by your third-density illusion. Thus, the seeker seeks to become co-creator of that which it is and that which it experiences and seeks to place the chisel in just the right location and seeks to strike it with just the right force.

Is there a further query, my sister?

Carla: Yes, I just have one more. I have been working with a feeling of low self-esteem forever, since I started being disabled, and I wonder if you have any comments concerning work in the area of reprogramming early childhood misconceptions which one has mistakenly brought into the present as biases. How does one most easily go about the reprogramming process? I have as yet been relatively unsuccessful.

I am Q'uo, and am aware of your query, my sister. We find that you have at your disposal techniques which are effective in this regard, those being the working with the subconscious mind through dream states and through the keeping of what you have called the daily journal and the analyzing of the fruits of each endeavor in order to bring into a synthesized whole the overall picture of the incarnational pattern. It is well to have one with whom this type of activity might be shared so that there might be the comment and criticism that expands the viewpoint and enriches the conclusions.

Thus, we find again that the beginning of such activities and the perseverance on a regular basis is most helpful in this regard.

Is there another query, my sister?

Carla: No, Q'uo, thank you very much and thank you for coming.

I am Q'uo, and again we thank you, my sister. Is there a further query at this time?

Questioner: No, thank you.

I am Q'uo, and we are most grateful, once again, to each for inviting our presence. We cannot thank you enough for this honor. We look, as you would say, forward to each gathering in which we may participate as your brothers and sisters seeking the source of the same mystery which each here finds the center of the life pattern. We shall leave this group at this time in the love and in the light of the one infinite Creator. Adonai, my friends. Adonai. ✼

L/L Research

Sunday Meditation
July 9, 1989

Group question: Concerns abortion and the ramifications to both the entity that is aborted, what type of difficulties or opportunities are presented by being aborted, and to the entities that are conducting the abortion, what sort of difficulties or opportunities are presented to the mother and the father that decide upon an abortion?

(Carla channeling)

I am Q'uo. I greet you in the love and in the light of the one infinite Creator. We were sometime in passing this instrument's challenge, and we find her spirit to be very fierce. We are glad that we are the good guys. That is what we told her, finally, and it made her smile.

It is a great privilege to share your meditation this evening and to offer our opinions on a subject that you have a need to know the truth of. We will give you what truth we know. It is not infallible, and we may be mistaken, for we are pilgrims along the same road as are you, and though we have gone many steps beyond you, yet as we gaze ahead, we see only more to learn. Consequently, know that we give you the best information that we have, but we ask you not to regard this information as an authority, but rather look and listen and discriminate, for you will recognize your own truth. It will be as if you remember that which we say. When that occurs, when that resonance is felt, allow that thought to be a part of the good in your life, and we shall be most happy to have been of this humble service.

The question of abortion is much like all of the environmental questions of your ecosphere, that is, it is a question that would not be asked in any other density. In second density, propagation is natural and behavior instinctual. Seldom is an animal left to die because the mother is a rogue. When it happens, it happens. There are no abortionists for animals. If they have too many children, they simply die.

In the density to which you aspire at this time, the density of love and understanding and compassion, it would not occur to entities that were unsuited, to create new life, because each could see each other's radiance and particular aura and configuration of spirit. When there is no need for behavior or communication, then things become far more simple.

It is within third density that the illusion is so thick that each of you is unable to link himself to all else in the universe. Consequently, such things as the acid rain, the various pollutants of farming and those of war, all of these things exist because you are in third density, and in third density the illusion is that there is the dark and the light and it is for you to make a choice. Many things are misdone by entities seeking their path. Many may feel that they have erred in some way, but there is no more of an ethical nature to aborting an unborn entity than there is in polluting the air, polluting the water, and above all, polluting the minds of those within your culture. In your culture, passion is veiled; true passion, true love, for creation, for the Creator and for each other are not things that are intensely felt, appreciated, given thanks for among the majority of your people.

The same abuse is given to the body of the animal which carries each entity about. Instead of cooperating with this animal and using the human skills of reasoning and communication to make wise decisions about mated relationships, there are games within games, shadows within shadows and communication is quite unclear among your peoples, as you well know. Therefore the basic moral turpitude which has been suggested to be the lot of those who abort children is unreal. It is part of the illusion.

Now let us get to the meat of the question, that which interests us as well as you, and that is what dynamic moves an entity into birth, into incarnation, and in what way is this process guided and governed?

We wish each of you to know that you decided upon who your parents would be. Not only that, but as your higher self between incarnations, you drew the basic geographical map of the journey that you would take and the lessons that you would learn within this lifetime. This is why we encourage each never to be disappointed because you have seemingly failed. Because the only thing that is important is that you persist in attempting to communicate love and light. Causing it to be manifest is the gift of grace, not the hallmark of humanity.

Let us say that we deplore and find very sad the sleep that has overtaken most of the people that are, as this instrument would say, civilized. The basic numbness and indifference of the good entities within your density is quiet and low in profile. Your culture is oriented to examining in detail the negative emotions involved in murders, crashes and other disasters. Consequently, one becomes quite numbed to experience, and one does not feel deeply.

Furthermore, because of the—we search for a word—dinosaur nature of the established church, it does not meet the needs of entities who wish to have good moral guidance at this particular time in the face of a world which has no morals except those of capitalism, that is, the conservation of capital by all.

Different of your nation states do this in different ways, but that is the somewhat grimy nature of your density. It is built upon something that does not exist, that is true money, and therefore all of the society which depends upon this for personal verification is annihilated. Entities for the most part have no moral guidance which reaches the heart, which engages the mind and which stirs the passion. All of the religions that are established are moribund, soon to die, and those that will be coming are now in the making. You live in the darkness before the dawn. And you see much that is soiled and spoiled and sad. And you ask yourself, "How could this be a good world and a good Creator?" when all of the suffering goes on.

Let us examine the process of choosing an incarnation. Each of you has had enough experience as an entity of third density that you have the capacity within this lifetime of becoming harvestable. That is the only reason that you are now here: to aid in the harvest and to be part of the harvest. This includes wanderers and natives alike.

We cannot give you passion and wisdom and integrity. We cannot urge careful morals or ethics in any mass way, because it is simply not a message which anyone wishes to hear. Those who attend your organized religions for the most part are sleeping through the opportunity for group worship. The children then, because the parents are not fed the bread of heaven, also starve at the same table, and we would urge each parent to have a daily worship and to feel very strongly and passionately about it, for this is the way your children learn what life is like within this illusion. You are their teacher, each parent, and you hopefully will desire to give passion and love and a sense of peace that you feel within your heart to those children that are yours to teach and rear and tend.

Between the incarnations, after you have finished healing that which was unbalanced in the incarnation previous, each of you has gone through the process of deciding what the lessons are that need to be learned in this lifetime. Often there will be a former relationship which was unbalanced and a particular person will be in the life pattern against all reason for the simple advantage of the opportunity to be able to balance previous distortions of love and free will. The parents are chosen not for their niceness or for their wealth by most entities who are seeking to learn and to serve. Many put themselves in very difficult positions where they will have to do a maximum of thinking, analyzing, going within, and depending upon the self. Many of you have undertaken ambitious case loads, shall we say, this semester, who are taking perhaps more classes than you should. All we can say to each of you is, please have faith, for your higher self knew better than you know now that which was needed for your spiritual growth.

When one picks one's parents, one looks for the opportunity to learn the lessons of love that one has decided are still to be learned. In this instrument, for example, this instrument chose parents to whom she would be the parent and experienced a difficult childhood for such a young mother. This was, however, not because the instrument wished to hurt herself, but because the instrument wished to learn more carefully and fully to love without any expectation of return. Each of you can look back through the incarnation and see a pattern. The pattern is for you to transcend—not overcome, but balance.

Growth comes from within the self. Everything that is outside of the self, including the most intimate of relationships, is part of the illusion, is working within the illusion, is communicating within the illusion and will remain within the illusion. What must be done by the person who seeks to grow is to find what the entity in the relationship wants from you to determine that which can and cannot be done and to attempt as openly and as clearly as possible to communicate that of which you are capable and those things which you would wish of a relationship. May we note that this clear communication is very seldom seen among your people. We would suggest more of it for each of you, for each of you that has chosen a mate has chosen a mate as carefully as you have chosen the parents, and if you cannot learn the lesson that this mate offers and you move on to another, then you shall learn the lesson, but it will be more difficult so that it will get your attention completely and you will be moved to passion, to love, and to selfhood. What you are attempting to do is become a whole metaphysical being.

When a woman decides to have an abortion, what she is doing is taking away one opportunity for that particular entity to enter incarnation. It is sometimes a way in which painful relationships are balanced, for it is certainly abuse to be aborted, yet that same entity may well have needed this balancing so that that which you call karma would be balanced. Each entity within each fetus comes into the body at a different time. The more consciously entities live, the more that they will feel the call of the soul that awaits them and the more they will put personality into their thinking about the child to come. In this case, the bonding of mother and child is as flowing and instinctual as any other mammal's carrying of her young. It is the human's unfortunate aspect to be melancholy even when blooming to new birth.

Thus you choose; not for comfort in a lifetime, not for convenience, but for growth. It was each of your decision to experience that which you have experienced and that which you are experiencing now. If for some reason this situation becomes intolerable and you escape it, you will meet it again with a more fearsome face and a larger growl. The wolf at the door will come back again and again until you have turned into a lamb and have walked innocently and in a balanced fashion through the tattered remnants of what was a ruined relationship or a lack of love.

You see, my friends, it is possible to live one's own life, not in relation to another's life, but in essence and in depth the living of the life is a responsibility that must be seen to be completely one's own. Only in this way can each entity experience itself as a living imperishable metaphysical being. You do realize, we are sure, that no souls are lost in the abortion. It is merely that there is a carelessness and lack of appreciation for the sanctity and beauty of life itself in one thoughtless enough to engender such a child and then remove it. Many are those who skate upon the pond of life, as we have said before, and never ever find the magical kingdom beneath that thin crust in water consciousness.

Even though we say there is no moral or ethical problem about abortion, we do recommend that an entity who is pregnant go through a careful process of listening within to the intuitions and feelings of the heart. This deeper mind, this intuitive mind, is a medium through which may be transmitted answers to such thorny questions as, "Do I keep this baby?" It is at that level that the unborn child that has agreed to stay with you communicates with you, at all times, before birth and after birth, the surface communication being important, but the very deep communication always being there. So you do no one harm by aborting the body of an unborn one, but yourself, in that you did not value a relationship which, had you faith, you would perhaps have felt was acceptable under whatever circumstances there needed to be to allow a soul which had chosen you to be given the opportunity to experience you.

Now, there are guards put against childbirth for some. This is due to their having come to this plane for other reasons. These entities will not have children, but will not have the decision of abortion either. If an entity which has come here only for a spiritual path conceives, the child is simply spontaneously aborted, as the body's consciousness already knows that the mission of this particular entity does not include the luxury of loving a child, but rather the entity must face the fact that that work to which he gives his love and labor is his child.

I feel that there is some disappointment because we have neither said that it was good or bad to abort a child, except of course, in terms of the consciousness of the self. If there is anything that you can take away from this particular evening, it is that you are part of all that there is, and the more consciously that you relate to everything and everyone, the more honest, straightforward, open and clear you are, regardless of catalyst, the more you may become an interest for the Creator's light to shine in a very dim world. You cannot do this of your human self, therefore we ask you to go into meditation at least once a day for however long you can, placing yourself in the presence of eternity and the Eternal One Who is Creator of All.

As you go through your day, retain the resonance of eternity in each present moment if you can, and you shall do precisely that which you and Father have set out for you to do. It seems to be a muddled and imperfect world. It is, in fact, a nearly perfect illusion, and when you leave the chemical body you have used during this incarnation and are again a being of light, you will gaze back and thank that body that suffered on your behalf and died for giving you the opportunity to feel so intensely, that you discovered a passion that was stronger than death. That passion is the love of the one infinite Creator. When you feel the orgasm of your sexual union, you then understand the Creator's love for you. It is that intense as a steady state, and for that reason you can see why we find the word love to pale and not be adequate to convey what the Creator's love truly is. You can only imitate that love by returning it.

We would now transfer this channel, with thanks to this instrument, so that questions may be asked. I am known to you as Q'uo, and I leave this instrument in love and light.

(Jim channeling)

I am Q'uo and greet each again in love and light through this instrument. At this time it is our privilege to attempt to speak to those queries which may yet remain upon the minds of those present. We would ask if there might be a query with which we may begin?

C: If the lesson is repeated *(inaudible)* in the case where the *(inaudible)* will be passed along to the child *(inaudible)* that when the child is born *(inaudible)* that the child is *(inaudible)* is more difficult *(inaudible)*.

I am Q'uo, and am aware of your query, my brother. I many cases, this would be the situation which would pertain, however, in other cases, it is possible that the entity which decided upon the abortion and carried it out to its completion might have what you would call a change of heart and welcome the next opportunity that presented itself within the life pattern to conceive, bear and raise the young entity. The attitude of the parental entity is the attitude that is paramount in importance in this situation. For the entity which resists the lesson which it has placed before itself and resists with great fervor is the entity which will find that lesson somewhat difficult according to the degree of resistance. Therefore, the passing of the opportunity by abortion is a portion of the, shall we say, equation which determines the intensity of the lesson when it does appear again in the life pattern, and we may add that in most cases, the lesson shall appear again within the current life pattern, and if it remains incompletely processed in one life pattern, then it shall be available for future incarnations.

Is there a further query, my brother?

C: One further question. Abortion before the current *(inaudible)*. How, in a situation such as that, that the *(inaudible)*.

I am Q'uo, and am aware of your query, my brother. Each entity within a mated relationship brings, shall we say, the baggage, the lessons which await the learning, the lessons which have been processed to some degree, and the lessons which have been ignored or refused, shall we say. As the couple proceeds in the mated relationship, each shall find that there is the necessity of focusing upon certain lessons that are individual in nature and are shared in nature. Each shall find that it becomes a portion of the other's incarnational pattern, and must in some way process that other self's experience in order to find the harmonious or agreed-upon balance in the relationship in each area awaiting the learning. Thus, if an entity has …

(Side one of tape ends.)

(Jim channeling)

I am Q'uo, and am again with this instrument. To continue. If one entity in a mated relationship has chosen previous to the relationship to engage in any action which resists a certain lesson, that entity shall find at some point within the life pattern that the opportunity for learning that lesson shall again present itself in a form which is easier to distinguish, that is to say, which may cause somewhat more difficulty if the entity still presents the resistance to the lesson. If this is the case, then the entity's mate shall find that there is a further ramification to the relationship that shall also affect it in a manner which is consonant with the overall design or purpose of the mated relationship.

Therefore, each entity brings into the relationship those areas which each shall find the necessity of focusing upon. It would seem at first glance that there could be the possibility of unfairness or an injustice in such a situation, for those areas left undone by either entity would then present both entities with the increased need to focus the attention and to process the catalyst in these areas. We would suggest that in truth there is no injustice or unfairness, for when the mated relationship is entered into, this is a function of preincarnative choices that have set forth the possibility of a relationship which would offer certain opportunities or challenges to each entity within the relationship. The fact that there are certain areas within each entity's life pattern that may have been less well learned or processed is simply a portion of the overall nature of the relationship and those opportunities that the relationship has presented to each entity.

Is there a further query, my brother?

C: *(Inaudible).*

I am Q'uo, and am aware of your query, my brother. This occurs with some frequency within your illusion, my brother.

Is there another query?

C: When you talked about mated relationships that in the case where the relationship failed and the parties split, that one of the lessons that were to be learned would come back in an even stronger version. Is there the case where the lesson learned is that it is right for the mated relationship to end?

I am Q'uo, and am aware of your query, my brother. In this situation, we find that there are those instances in which the lessons which have been set forth by each entity have been learned to the fullest extent that each is able to achieve without some deterioration of the overall purpose of the relationship. In most cases, a relationship which is entered into is that situation which is most appropriate and beneficial for the lessons which remain for each entity. Oftentimes, however, there is a, shall we say, a souring of the catalyst which each feels due to the inability to balance certain distortions within the individual life pattern. In such a situation, the separation of the entities is much like the marathon runner discovering that at the midway point through the race it must stop and catch its breath, so to speak.

In each instance, whether it be the race or the relationship, it is advisable for each entity to consider well the obstacles that caused the need to catch the breath, in order that these might be worked upon as catalysts, so that there is a balancing of distortions that would then allow the beginning again of the race, whether with the same mate or with another is not of the greatest importance as is the beginning again of the race in order that the lessons which have been set forth might be worked upon as much as is possible, for the lessons have been chosen with great care and offer the greatest opportunity for each entity's personal growth and service to others.

Is there a further query, my brother?

C: No, thank you.

I am Q'uo, and we thank you, my brother. Is there another query at this time?

J: For the entity that was aborted, does that entity prior to conception, does this entity have the choice or is it a part of the process of the choice for abortion, and if so, of what benefit is abortion to this entity?

I am Q'uo, and am aware of your query, my brother. In many cases, the entity that wishes to enter the incarnation and which is the focus of the abortion, as you call it, does partake in the making of this decision, but not usually at the level of the decision to abort this particular entity, but rather has made a choice with the parental entities that it shall offer this opportunity and shall take part in the decision to limit the opportunity in order that that which can be learned from the overall process might be offered to those who serve as the potential parental entities. This is in some few cases. However, in the great majority of cases, the entity which has its opportunity to enter the incarnation stopped momentarily by the decision to abort will find that there are other opportunities which are then made available to it, for the experience within the metaphysical realms is more obviously multifaceted than is your own, although your own experience is indeed multifaceted as well, although you are aware that as one choice is made, those other potential choices that could have been made as well are then set aside and do not manifest within your reality. However, within the metaphysical realms, the entity which has had the opportunity ended in one area will find that there are other potential entities with which it has made preliminary agreements, each of course, needing certain conditions or prerequisites to be in place before the entry into the incarnation is complete. Therefore the decision of the parental entities to have the abortion rather than the child is a decision which then offers the aborted entity the opportunity to seek the entry into incarnation with other parental entities.

Is there a further query, my brother?

J: At the moment of conception, is the fetus at that point a spirit/mind/body complex, or is it simply physical, at that point lacking spirit and mind?

I am Q'uo, and am aware of your query, my brother. There is no general response that is accurate in each instance, for though the entity which is conceived is indeed a live being, at the conception, it is not always the case that the entity contains the mind/body/spirit complex. The very nature of the physical vehicle brings with it a consciousness which is intelligent, however, the entity which will eventually incarnate or desires to incarnate may not enter this physical vehicle which has consciousness until a point later in the gestation period, according to the needs and desires of that entity to experience more of the metaphysical realm prior to the birth or the need and desire to experience that which life within the womb may offer it. It is rarely the case that the entity defers entry into the physical vehicle until after it has been birthed into your illusion. However, this is possible and does occur in rare instances. Therefore, we can suggest that the point of entry into the physical vehicle created by the parental entities is quite various.

Is there a further query, my brother?

J: No, thank you.

I am Q'uo, and we thank you, my brother. Is there another query at this time?

Carla: I'd like to go back and look at what you answered C earlier about when people get together they take on each other's catalyst and work it as if it were their own. Just before Don Elkins died, I had a complete mental breakdown, and I have had several suicidal attacks since then, and it has occurred to me that what I am doing is getting well from the mental illness that Don had, as well as the one that I had. But I don't know if that is in any metaphysical way correct. Could you comment?

I am Q'uo, and we shall attempt to speak to this query in two different modes. Firstly, the statement that the mated couple may take on themselves each the other's catalyst is not exactly correct, for we wished to state in that response that the catalyst of either entity may be enhanced by previous experience which would include the resistance to catalyst. The effect this has upon each partner is to intensify the catalyst which each partner already possesses, for catalyst is of the subconscious mind, that is to say, is personal in nature, so that one entity cannot truly take upon itself another entity's catalyst unless that other entity's catalyst is already identical to its own. This is usually the case when an entity has a difficulty that it ascribes to another. It has, in truth, not taken the other's catalyst, but has used its own in another manner or in a more intense manner.

To speak to the specificity of your query, we would suggest that the relationship which existed between the one known as Don and yourself was a relationship anomalistic enough in its nature that it would be quite difficult and indeed quite inadvisable to apply what might be learned from it to another relationship. For that bond which existed between the two of you was unique in that it had been tempered by many, many previous experiences. Thus, we may agree in general with your supposition that you have been completing much of that which was begun during the life of the one known as Don, however we would not extrapolate from that experience and suggest that this is common amongst entities within the third-density illusion.

Is there a further query, my sister?

Carla: I have one on another subject. Thank you for that. That's very interesting and informative. I observed two coincidences tonight. One was that while I was cleansing and doing my prayers, I did something I hadn't done for a long time. I invoked the archangels, whom I've always loved. And when I sat down here and took a look around the watchtower—is the way I call it—took a look around the mental atmosphere in here, I saw the usual white, green far away of entities that are not good that would like to come in, and I got rid of them in an instant. But there was over arching all of this circle a beautiful golden dome, except that it did not have any end to it, it just went up and up and up. And it is very beautiful and I just wonder if that had anything to do with the archangels?

I am Q'uo and am aware of your query, my sister. We might suggest that you have perceived that which has always been so as a function of your own desire and invocation within your own being that this circle of seeking receive the added blessings of those who always watch from some distance, as you would say, such proceedings.

Is there a further query, my sister?

Carla: No, thank you, Q'uo.

I am Q'uo, and we thank you, my sister. Is there another query at this time?

T: This question doesn't follow the line of thinking we're pursuing this evening—yes, I guess it does in a way. When you have a relationship, specifically with a child/parent relationship, spouse type relationship, if you have a relationship where seemingly at a conscious functional level, one person in the relationship does not seem to be willing to face up to or even acknowledge that there is a problem or lesson to be learned or problems to be worked out in this relationship between the parents, can this carry over for the half of this relationship that is trying, say it's the child that is trying to work out the parent and they're not acknowledged, does this carry any karmic problems into later lives for this child where this child, where what he is is trying to work out the problems because the other entities would not agree to work out their problems, at least on a conscious level?

I am Q'uo, and am aware of your query, my brother. The lesson, whatever its nature, may be ignored in any degree by either entity, in which case this lesson shall be again chosen and faced and worked with to the point that it has offered complete harmony and balance, whether in this incarnation or another. For the entity that has given its fullest effort and has received little effort in return in the processing of the catalyst, the intention to process the catalyst fully will serve that entity well in that it shall find alternate opportunities, shall we say, to specifically apply that desire to learn and utilize that particular lesson or set of lessons. This is to say that the entity shall not find its opportunity ended or diminished because of the unwillingness of the other entity to engage in the processing of the catalyst, but shall instead find that there are other means by which this particular lesson might be learned, and the desire to learn this lesson will then, shall we say, ease the processing of the catalyst, whether that catalyst might be discovered within the current incarnation, which is most likely, or in a further incarnation where it shall be joined again with yet other catalyst.

Is there a further query, my brother?

T: So, just to take it a little further. One of the other entities recognizes that this is just a seemingly impossible situation, where the other will not do anything, and if he was trying to learn something to work this out, he'd probably be better off just dropping it than to try to get the other the other entity to work with him. Is that correct?

I am Q'uo and am aware of your query, my brother. We would suggest that it would be most appropriate not to cease the attempt, but to leave the door, as you would say, open so that if there is a change of heart or attitude upon the part of the other entity, that the processing of the catalyst might begin again. However, we would suggest that the entity continue in its desire to learn this particular lesson and make itself available, perhaps upon a more passive level if it feels that it is presenting a stumbling block to the entity which refuses to share the catalyst.

Is there a further query, my brother?

T: No, thank you.

I am Q'uo, and we thank you, my brother. Is there a final query at this time?

(Pause)

I am Q'uo, and we would take this opportunity to thank each for offering us the blessing of joining your circle of seeking this evening. We cannot thank each of you enough for this blessing, for we learn as you do within these sharing and blendings of vibrations. We learn of your great desire to know more of that which you call the truth, and we learn of your courage in persevering under circumstances which are obviously quite difficult to comprehend and to harmonize within the life pattern. And we learn that the desire to know the Creator grows strongly and brightly within each heart, as it does within our own. We thank you for sharing with us that which is of utmost importance to you, and we look, as you would say, forward to those opportunities when we again have the opportunity to blend our vibrations with yours.

At this time we shall take our leave of this instrument and this circle of seeking, leaving each, as always, in the love and in the light of the one infinite Creator. We are known to you as those of Q'uo. Adonai. Adonai. ✶

L/L Research

Sunday Meditation
July 16, 1989

Group question: The question this evening deals with the common situation which everybody at some point in their lives find—that there is difficulty that is almost unsolvable; that we have to find our way out of frustration, repeating patterns of behavior that continually bring us into situations in which we are tested. Is this test something that we have devised for ourselves? Are we being tested by some source outside of ourselves? How can we learn from our experience and find some peace or grace or means of dealing with the difficult situations that seem to add up to a cross that each of us bears in our life? Is there any alternative to bearing the cross? Or are we destined to suffer? Or is there some meaning in the suffering that we can take inspiration from, and continue on the same path with a better means of feeling about it, dealing with it?

(Carla channeling)

I am Q'uo, I greet you with great joy in the love and the light of the one infinite Creator. Our hearts are brim-full in thanks for your calling us to your meeting here this evening, for sharing with us your love for each other, your love of the Creator, and your earnest and sincere seeking for the truth and the mystery of creation.

Truth recedes, we have found, as the path is traveled, therefore we cannot give you final truths, for we are not a final source. We are ourselves pilgrims on the same road whose stones stub your feet and whose nettles may catch and scratch.

You have asked this evening about suffering: whether it is necessary, why it repeats itself, and what its uses may be. Let us lay a little ground work first. Each of you was created before your planet emerged from its timeless and chaotic state. This is, as we understand it, due to the fact that each of you was an unit of consciousness in the creation before this one, so that when the Creator began this creation, He sent out those agents of His active love housed in physical vehicles in many different illusions so that they might add to the complete knowledge of the Creator of Himself, for the Creator wishes, as anyone, to know Itself and It cannot know Itself without experiencing Itself as each of your Christ-selves within offer, as a gift to the Creator, all that you feel and suffer and think and manifest.

You are active agents of the Creator, part of your being truly a Creator-self. The majority of the people do not have an awareness of this fact. This is not necessary, this awareness, in order to make the harvest that is to come, a harvest of souls that have learned to be of service to others to the extent that they spend more than half their time in terms of service to someone else besides themselves. It is not necessary to understand, intellectually, any particular point, if the entity is a natural worker and has a feeling for the evolutionary process of humankind.

Now, as we gaze over the octave which all of us are now engaged in experiencing, we see the analogy of the classroom to fit fairly well, and we have used this many times, but, my friends, it is also a certain kind of school. It is a school for the evolution of *homo sapiens* into a new man, one who is consciously aware of the God-self within, and one who acknowledges it, treasures it, and attempts to experience and manifest its presence.

Each density in the octave of creation we now experience is a very long affair in terms of your time, millions of years passing in one density, as the problems to be learned have no resistance. There is no polarity in this type of learning of elements, animals and the vegetable world, for there is no self-consciousness.

In densities after your own, again you shall be spending what you conceive of as "time," for each density is an illusion, working to refine something that has been chosen the hard way. The density of choice, the density of sorrow, the density of the cross, the density of the hard way, is third density.

As we gaze within our memory at other third density planets, we may honestly say that some have done less well than you in producing a harvestable crop of entities who are ready to move on to more light-filled lessons. We feel very hopeful about many making positive choices and polarizing in power and strength in the spirit of love and light in service to the infinite One.

Each entity who dwells upon the planet at this time has the capacity to graduate into the fourth density, that density in which the veil between the conscious and the subconscious mind is lifted, and once again you may for yourself, without any egotism, see the Christ within, see the harmony—and those harmonies that can be so easily made harmonious, for no one is hidden from anyone.

The social memory complex is being formed and thoughts about being "One" are available, as in a data bank, to all others within that planetary population of entities which has decided to seek as one being.

The death of the illusion which you experience is tremendous. We do not minimize your task. Indeed, as we remember what you suffer, without understanding, as we remember how we suffered also, we can only, in humility, bow to your bravery and your steadfastness, for it is courage and persistence and will that lead one to an understanding that transforms suffering into a life of transcendent joy.

This instrument has a great deal of this knowledge locked within its subconscious, as do each of you, and is, perhaps, somewhat more transparent to it than to some, but to no one is it clear why the illusion is set up to be so difficult, so wearing, so difficult, so confusing, so irrational and in many ways so continually, endlessly negative—when all that you wish for yourself, or for those you love, is peace, harmony, joy and laughter.

These are very, very good things. These are, however, manifestations of a state of mind which can only be achieved when those things which trouble one, in the incarnational pattern, have been finally perceived in their spiritual sense, the challenge read correctly and the lessons well completed.

The reason that many times an experience will happen again and again and again is that the situation is one which demands change. And more specifically, change which can only be made by one who is confident within the self and who has no fear for the future. You may think of making difficult choices of service to self versus the martyrdom—which sometimes seems to be the essence of service to others—is difficult to sort out within the illusion—the kernel, the heart, the core, of the lesson about love one is attempting to learn. Therefore, the reason for the repetition is that you are obeying the dictates of your own deeper will, which lies deep within inside you, in the unconscious part of you, and it takes both a clear and logical mind and contemplative, meditative, intuitive consciousness to achieve a fair understanding of the love inherent in this difficult situation.

You have called yourself to this lifetime and have had the privilege of being incarnate at this very exciting time because you deserve to be here. Each of you is capable of moving into the fourth density at the end of this incarnation. It is no wonder, then, that you are receiving the final and the hardest lessons.

Now, let us take the lesson of the one who is under another's thumb, the one who is the slave. How can the slave feel spiritually free, how can the one who is habitually beaten down be dignified, whole and triumphant? The answer lies in change of perception about self. The answer lies in beginning to stop the resistance one naturally has towards change, since that is painful in this process, and urge oneself to become that better self which one has not yet been able to be.

If the slave frees itself, mentally, and chooses to do all for the love of the infinite Creator, the owner, no matter how mistaken in his feelings of possession, has no longer any true power to disturb the one who prays to change in freedom.

Now, what is the essence of freedom? Each of you certainly feels that it is "somewhere else" and certainly not in the present moment, or in the present life experience. And yet we say to you that full freedom is available to you within this experience, just as the Kingdom of Heaven is available to any who will do the work to transform themselves into a lighter being. Therefore, we ask you to have faith in your own self when you face repetitive problems. You have simply put yourselves into a situation which is a challenge to love the unlovable; to accept the unacceptable; to return the good for the negative; to be blithely oblivious of the negative, and see the good in all; to retain the hopefulness of close and deep association with nature, both second-density trees, grasses and blooms, and third-density entities.

Once you have been able to come to the heart of the repetitive pattern you may break it by forgiveness of that which may be forgiven, and by the remembering of the self by the self of the nature of the self. Each of you has, within you, the creation and the Creator. You are entities to be honored—you are all one, and you are all the Creator's children.

Now, when you began this octave of experience, each of you had made certain progress in a previous creation. You had made progress to a certain point, and to that point the Creator now knows about Itself. But the Creator is generous and curious and in perpetual motion. And so, when all of us come together at the end of what could be done in one octave of creation, then from the heart of the infinite One will set again a new creation, incorporating all of those things which the Creator had learned about Itself—making pathways for the evolution of the Christ-self within clearer and plainer with each octave of experience.

So, you see, you bring to this incarnation a pattern, what would be to you an infinite amount of experience, which has caused certain biases. Now, it is these biases, prejudices, and foolishly held opinions of the self that create an atmosphere of pain, of one entity to another. To one who has safely anchored within the gate of the Creator, the noisy clamor of the critical and foolish world comes as against a picture window all about one, splatters and falls like rain, leaving you untouched, for you are no longer finding it necessary to have that suffering.

But, as you finish one lesson, your ambitious higher self will prepare you for another. Thus, your incarnational pattern, if you do not learn the first lesson, will be an endless repetition of that pattern. If you wish to accelerate the process of growth, then you will take the harder and less traveled road. And when you have solved one riddle of love, another challenge shall be put before you.

It is the tendency of entities at this particular time, so close to harvest, to have made for themselves extremely ambitious processes of learning, wishing to learn to give love without expectation of return; wishing to see the Christ in the self without doubt, without pride, and with humility, and you learn to bend the will to that Christ-self so that the willfulness that is free will ceases being various, ceases enslaving one, and, instead, becomes guided by the will of the infinite One.

Paradoxically, when one has completely given the life over to the service of the infinite One, when one does all that one does, from the meanest chore to the most magnificent, one will be polarizing rapidly. Entities which you see about you are illusory. You also are illusory, but the one thing which is not illusory is your consciousness. Most of your people are not taking full advantage of this intensive experience upon your sphere at this time, but rather have diverted themselves into non-polarizing paths of existence. There is no harm in this, but neither is there any gain. Each of you has eternity to move through this creation and back to the one infinite source of all that is.

We find that each find it a bit difficult to believe that the basic self is what this instrument would call the Christ-self, for you experience the vagaries of your free will willfully. You do this and that, willfully. You have this sensitivity and that doubt, and this guilt and that lack, or limitation, and you do not see yourselves as the completely equal, quite perfect metaphysical beings that you are. It is not pride, nor is it arrogance to claim the Christ within oneself, for by doing this one is then able to gaze upon the difficult and challenging situation. If one is being misunderstood, one may attempt clear communication, but without attachment to an outcome.

Each of you is far more independent and strong than you may be aware of. This does not mean that there will be an end to suffering. It is possible to move to third density without suffering to the extent your peoples have. Your own planet has had many, many conflicts, which have added many negative biases to the thought patterns of the inhabitants of that fragile sphere. So, perhaps our best advice to you would be, if you wish to make an end to the repeated lessons: meditate, pray, ask to dream, and focus upon the love that must be, for you know by faith that that must be, in the situation that is repeating and repeating and causing you pain—the pain is the pain of change. If you may flow with the change and become that which is needed to balance the challenge, then you will have finished with that lesson and it shall not be repeated, except perhaps to make sure that you have understood the lesson.

Most frequently the challenges within third density are those of relationships. Entities who love each other do not know the depth of each other, yet they begin to discover patterns that are sometimes destructive to the relationship, in that there is a separation by this action within the relationship. Therefore, any action which is a separating action—we do not mean this literally, but figuratively—is to be regarded as an intellect solution, for you are at this time choosing to lead a whole and complete and unique life in service to others, polarizing constantly towards service to others. You are committing yourselves to a series of painful changes as the unnecessary portions of personality—especially that which this instrument would call low self-esteem—are simply vacuumed away by the realization that one does not have to take in that which is given, but can instead create a unity and end to discord simply as an act of will. Communication is very helpful, but there are few among your people who are capable of clear communication. This is due to the fact that the illusion is indeed so very, very convincing and there really does seem to be a bias within all that one may see of humankind towards the negative.

There will be a negative harvest from this planet, but it will be small. Most of you who graduate shall have graduated because you have polarized in service to others.

The question of martyrdom is interesting to us, for in fact one of the lessons of love is martyrdom. It is the most foolish choice, and therefore the most blessed of all choices, but if it is martyrdom for no good reason, then, though it may help you, it shall not aid the creation as much as if the concentration of the seeker is moving always towards questions of substance and changes of substance. For you wish to hollow yourselves out as an earthen vessel is described in your holy work, that sacred things may be held therein. Your earthly vessel has but a little time and it shall perish. Therefore, we encourage each to realize the incredible amount of aid each is to each, for when there is a relationship difficulty, it is often not the entities themselves who first grasp the lesson, but a third party, one who observes, one who makes the opinion known when asked, one who sees from the farther perspective as one who is uninvolved in this particular catalyst.

Each of you may do that, as a mirror for the other. Mated relationship is both the best place for this to happen and the place where it most seldom does happen, because of the way your lifestyle, shall we say, has been arranged by you. You seem to be a planet of scurrying, hurrying, worrying elves, with pickaxes over their shoulders, constantly whistling as they work, constantly trying to find the gold of life, the silver, and the precious stones. Look upon the ground before you—the simplest pebble sings of heaven. It is all an illusion. You can pay attention to anything you wish, and when you see that you are being attacked and the bias is unfair, you may perhaps choose to defend yourself. Or you may, perhaps, choose to create a new situation, to move with confidence against the challenge of criticism and say quietly and confidently, "All is well, let us move forward from here. We cannot resolve this today. Let us pray on it, and resolve it tomorrow."

Some there are who are skilled at communication, and when two such entities come together, the work that is done is very intense. But even in this case, there will be the repetition and the lesson may be somewhat more refined. The choices which one makes for harmony, union, love and an increase in joy, and, above all, the choice of the light over the dark thing to say or do, the more you become ready and able to see through the illusion, if only dimly, [and] choose not to suffer, but to be confident of the self to be humble before all and before the Creator, and yet to know at the heart of oneself is the Creator.

This is your birthright, this is your nature, this is your destiny. What you are building now is the cornerstone of that structure of personality, that disciplined character, which shall be reformed and refined and refined again, until compassion and wisdom have blended as one, and all that is possible to be learned by each unique entity within the creation has been learned. Needless to say, the process is infinite.

It is also, we feel, a great blessing. For we find it a blessing to be conscious, to be able to make our choices. We are building, shall we say, the skyscraper that is based upon the firm foundation you now are laying, the foundation of accepting the unacceptable, of loving the unlovable, of changing the insult into the light touch. You have the control to make these choices at will. Each of you has this within, but how difficult, my friends, it is to call upon it. As always, we move to the suggestion of persistent daily meditation, the listening within, the learning of who you really are, the centering of oneself within the creation, so that no thing is strange and no one a stranger. Nothing threatens, but only challenges.

Try to make your decisions for love with all the passion within your heart, with all the caring in your spirit, for the depth of your commitment to the positive path of service to others in the service of the one infinite Creator will be the measure of the amount of light that you may use and enjoy when this incarnation is at an end. We realize each of you wishes to be able to use the love and the light of the fourth density. We assure you the challenges and the problems do not stop simply because the choice has been made. It is a long, long process of refinement of the knowledge that one has gained, of the biases that one has earned.

So, when you see the repetitive event, analyze with the mind, ask the intuition, in dream, to speak to you upon the subject, begin to discover the nature of the change that will bring into the situation a balance of love. And when you have decided what that action is, quietly and confidently and doggedly do that, in the face of the repeated catalyst. Without the reaction of bias towards difficulty towards you, actions towards you meant to harm or inadvertently meant to harm, cannot touch you, cannot come close to you. You are forging the foundation of your very being as a metaphysical entity. In this particular density, by the choice you make in this density and by the excellence with which you make it, so you create the atmosphere for that which must be refined and refined and refined until that which is left of the personality is that which is of the Christ-self and the rest has been burned away, that one may be truly be the earthen vessel that holds great treasure. That treasure is your Christ-self.

Before we leave this instrument, we wish wholeheartedly not to be [discouraging]. You may think that you have made many mistakes. You may think that you have failed many times. This is not important, this is not what should be upon your minds. Rather, immerse yourself in the present moment, for each moment your life begins now, and each moment, the old life is ended. There is the constant opportunity of renewal, growth, inspiration and positive change. To learn to flow gracefully with the tides of experience is indeed the work of the pilgrim sailor who seeks the land of milk and honey. It is there, my friends, it is there. And all that is broken shall be healed.

You may yourself accelerate this process, with your trust, your love, your refusal to allow the weary world to influence your consciousness. We join in mediation not only at this time but at any time you wish to have a meditation partner. It is our honor to add our vibrations to yours. We do not speak at such times, but only share in the holy silence of sacred ground. Please be aware, as always, that these are our opinions and are not to be taken as absolute truth, for we know no absolute except that All is One. Each of you seems to be separate, yet you all are one. You all are part of the Creator.

We would leave this instrument at this time with many thanks to the this group for its excellent focus and energy for this contact, for this instrument has been much aided thereby. We are those of Q'uo, and would now transfer the contact to the one known as Jim, in love and in light.

(Jim channeling)

I am Q'uo, and I greet each again in love and light. We are honored to offer ourselves at this time in the attempt to speak to any remaining queries which those present may have. Is there a query at this time?

Questioner: Are there ways to learn clearer communication for people who have trouble communicating?

I am Q'uo, and am aware of your query, my sister. The easiest answer that we have for that query is simply to practice the communication. To be more to the point, it is well if one become familiar with what one feels in any particular situation so that one may have the deepest truth from which to offer the communication. It is also quite necessary that there be a certain level of trust developed between those who would seek clear communication, for the clarity of communication may reveal, in the same clear light, some indications or messages that may make one uncomfortable, and it is well that each in the relationship trust that there is no harm, shall we say, intended, that each is searching in virgin or new territory within the self and may be as perplexed as the other at what is found there.

It is well to enter into communication with the desire and the intention to speak that which is felt and that which is true for the self with the attitude that it is not the final answer and that it might become a stepping stone toward that which is desired, if the clear communication has uncovered that which, though not desired, is truly the case at that moment. Thus, the trust is the foundation stone between the two who seek clear communication. And upon that foundation stone of trust may be added the speaking of that which is truly felt as a portion of the communication that shall continue to reveal a balance and a harmony that can be found when the communication has been clear enough for long enough that the, shall we say, whole picture begins to be seen beyond the boundaries of what is felt and thought by the self, by each self.

Is there another query, my sister?

Questioner: Well, just the observation that from what you said it seems that in third density we have absolutely necessary suffering because of the fact that change is painful, and I was wondering what consolation, what boon/goal, what healing lies in place *(inaudible)* so that one is not so bruised, so that one has an ability to heal?

I am Q'uo, and am aware of your query, my sister. The boon, as you have called it, is the positioning for creation of the self [by the self] through experience and may take the form of the concept which you know of as faith, for though the trail may be long and difficult, there must be the faith within the seeker that there is a reason for traveling the trail. The seeker may turn to those sources of inspiration that are found in your literature which record the voices of those seekers of your past who have traveled this same trail and left records that illustrate the reality of their faith and of faith that might be found by others of their kind on similar journeys. One may look to such sources for a kind of inspiration that speaks to a deeper portion of the self that is beyond the confinement of your narrow, walled illusion and which vibrates in recognition of the truth when it is heard by these voices who have traveled the same journey.

Thus, the inspiration of others may speak to that spark of the self that we have called the Christ Consciousness and in which the still, silent moments of reflection and contemplation and meditation and prayerful attention cause a feeling of purpose and goodness and direction to well up from within and bolster, shall we say, the faith that has been nurtured by much experience through each seeker.

Is there another query, my sister?

Questioner: No, Q'uo, but I'd like to share with you a short hymn that I've been singing since I was a little girl, and I think it's really what you are saying. It's called "Temper My Spirit, Oh Lord."

Temper my spirit, oh Lord Keep it long in the fire Make it one with the flame Let us share but one *(inaudible)* desire.

(Inaudible)

Temper my spirit, oh Lord.

I am Q'uo, and we listen with joy at the resonance in our own hearts to those words of your hymn. We thank you, my sister. Is there another query at this time?

Questioner: How can a person know the difference between life situations which are a part of a general learning experience and negative life situations [which] come along that may be defined as a psychic greeting which appear to be an outward attack on a person, possibly as a result of their seeking and possibly as a result of changes they have brought about themselves as a result of seeking? That's my question.

I am Q'uo, and aware of your query, my brother. We would suggest that there is, in fact and in function, no significant difference betwixt the situations which you describe, for each offers the opportunity to learn, one at a level we would describe as ordinary, or common, the other at a more intensified or magnified level of—we search for the correct word within this instrument's mind—level of intensity is the closest which we may find. Each offers the same opportunity. The attention may be more focused by that experience which you have described, the psychic greeting, for the experience is more intensified, but though it has the component of those of the, shall we say, loyal opposition, the initial choice was your own, and you are thereby experiencing that which is yours in a more lucid or vivid fashion.

Is there a further query, my brother?

Questioner: So, just to get an understanding better, what you are saying is that we deal with each situation the same way without trying to make a differentiation of what it might be? Or do we have different ways of dealing with it depending which way we perceive it to be?

I am Q'uo, and am aware of your query, my brother. We mean to suggest that there can be no psychic greeting component without your free will choice in an area which lies within your course of study, shall we say. There may be no obstacles placed in your path by those who are of the loyal opposition, as we have described it, but those entities may magnify those experiences which you utilize, though we must at this time suggest that this phenomenon is far more unusual than most entities would imagine, for most of the entities within your illusion find themselves moving between the choice of service to others and service to self, and have not moved far enough in either direction to attract the attention of those who would choose to manipulate that movement.

We also suggest that it is not a point to be overly concerned about, for your life pattern will be as it will be, and will include those lessons that you have chosen, and there is no need to concern yourself about the factor or entity outside of the self, but there is great need to look carefully at that which is within the experience of self at the moment of experience in order that the heart of the self may be expressed as clearly and as cleanly and as spontaneously as is possible, whatever experience one encounters.

There will be those elements that are of an exterior nature, whether they be third density entities or those from higher densities. The important ingredient is the perception and attitude of the self as it takes part in and responds to those experiences that belong to it.

Is there a further query, my brother?

Questioner: No. I appreciate [the answer as it has been given.]

I am Q'uo, and we thank you, my brother, for your queries. Is there another query at this time?

(Pause)

I am Q'uo, and we wish to thank those gathered this evening for offering to us the desire to know more of the nature of your own experience and its relationship to the plan of evolution which each of us finds ourselves moving within. It is a great and mysterious journey that each of us undertakes when we seek to unlock the keys to the fundamental questions of the nature of our lives of the creation about us and of our source and destination in this great experience of life. We bless each which moves upon this journey, and we thank each for allowing us to join you for a step or two along your way. We take inspiration from your efforts and we hope that we may give you inspiration with our information that might be helpful upon your journeys. We cannot thank you enough for your very being and for your gracious desire to share with us. We are those of Q'uo, and we take this opportunity to leave this instrument and this group at this time, leaving each, as always, in the love the light of the one infinite Creator. Adonai, my friends. Adonai.

(Carla channeling)

[I am Yadda.] I speak only briefly. But wish to say to each here, there is one thing which acts as a brake, a stopping mechanism on the learning, and that is fear. When one is afraid, one cannot see whole and unity. Many of your concerns are only fears, and fear is an inappropriate emotion, for you have nothing to fear. Where can you go except the creation? Who can you be, except yourself? You can never be crushed.

It is simply that you, for a time, might decide to be afraid. What are you afraid of? Speak your mind and never worry about the reputation, the opinion of others, or even your opinion of yourself. But do the walk you came to do, and lose the fear which stops your evolution. Replace it consciously. Give it a good hour without fear. With hope and faith, these are the keys, not fear. Not the one who is unworried but simply the attitude of being a positive and loving positive and let people deal with you as they will. You are responsible for yourself. You may be as happy as you chose. You lose the fear, please.

We thank this instrument. She not challenge us to death this time. We have learned that we must follow her wishes or we cannot speak. So we thankfully [leave] in the love and the light of the One Who is All. I am Yadda. ✣

L/L Research

Sunday Meditation
July 23, 1989

Group question: The question this evening has to do with catalyst and the use of catalyst in the seeming synchronicities or coincidences in our lives where there is a change in direction or attitude or content of the life pattern. How do we utilize catalyst in this way? Do we draw it to us by our previous work? How do we prepare ourselves for it, and when it shows up, how can we best take advantage of it so that we actually do move ourselves along the evolutionary path?

(Carla channeling)

I am Q'uo. I greet each of you this evening in the love and the light of the one infinite Creator, the one original Thought of love. We thank you for the generosity of your spirit in asking for information upon subjects which seem abstracted from the daily pattern of mundane activity. Yet by calls such as yours, we recognize those who have committed themselves towards accelerating paths of their spiritual evolution, and we salute and greet each as colleagues upon the path of seeking the knowledge of the truth.

The question which you ask this evening is many-faceted. There is no error which an entity may make during which an opportunity for growth and learning is forever past. Each seeker has an infinite amount of time to learn the lessons of this density, to grasp the illusory nature of all that is born, blooms, withers and dies. Each of you hungers for a food which is spiritual, for part of you is an imperishable being of light and that portion of you is your reality. That consciousness is not only your consciousness, but within it, largely in the deeper portions of the mind, lies the entire creation.

The process by which each of you has chosen in an incarnational pattern for this incarnational experience, is one's own judgment of oneself. We realize that much has been said in spiritual literature about judgment, however, it is impossible within the illusion to judge in any way the effectiveness of what is being done. You cannot know what your score is. You cannot count up wisdoms or number strategies of meditation until you reach enlightenment. You merely put one foot before the other before a very long and dusty road. It is the road less traveled, as this instrument would say, and it does make all the difference. You have decided to seek in a theoretical and abstract way the nature of the composition of your consciousness. We find that this concern moves to the heart of the reason for third density being as intense an illusion as it is. It also explains the necessity of continuous spiritual coincidence, which some may call synchronicity.

When one first comes into the realization of one's own self-consciousness as being something more than the brain of an animal which carries you around, each responds by moving towards knowledge, seeking to know the answers to questions. Where one begins seeking is largely a matter of free will, for in few cases do the very young remember anything of the undistorted images of light which express a spiritual entity. So, each of you has planned before this incarnation, with the aid of the higher self, those things which are needed to be learned within the incarnation.

Now, each of you also came primarily to serve, and by focusing daily upon the Creator, you have served and served well. And each moment that you spend consciously aware of your relationship with the Creator is a moment in which the consciousness of the planet upon which you abide [is served]. You have no clear idea of the kind of light source that you can truly be and that each of you is from time to time.

Now, there is destiny, let us say, but there is not predestination, that is, in no way is an entity's life fixed. It is malleable as a soft piece of new clay. The entity begins the incarnation forgetful entirely of all its good reasons for choosing this parent, that sibling, this situation, that relationship. Rather than wasting the time of pondering these things, we might suggest that it is an act of faith to trust that whatever is happening at the moment is what should be happening at the moment, and the only important thing is that you approach the moment with the resonance of eternity within your consciousness so that the mundane and grimy world cannot touch the light being that you are, nor can it touch your ability to act as a channel for love and light to those who suffer in one way or another.

You and your higher self, before the incarnation, have chosen what in most cases is a difficult incarnational pattern. The reason for this is that each entity to whom we speak has the capacity to graduate to the fourth density, to accept more love and more light, and to live in a denser light within this illusion, each of you. Nevertheless, each of you came first to serve, and then only secondarily to work upon the personal consciousness. This is a situation such as your Red Cross might answer in case of peril on a large scale.

We visit you by thought because there is a great call for information of this type. As when people attempt to move into the established forms of doctrine and dogma of religion, they simply cannot any longer accept symbols that have become meaningless to them. Thus, you may find yourself creating a personal philosophy, religion or myth. The words are interchangeable. For it is important that those who walk the spiritual supermarket look carefully at each choice on the shelf, each path to the Creator, and then choose one and follow it persistently and deeply. Those who never begin to move toward the center of things, those who continue walking around the rim—we correct this instrument—the rim of the wheel of life, cannot polarize in either direction, and therefore will not be able to express the joy and the passion and delight in the light that is necessary for movement, comfortable movement into fourth density.

Let us speak now of spiritual coincidence. As we have said, there is destiny but not predestination. You are co-creator of your life. The portion of you that is co-creator is the portion of you that began the incarnation as complete, chaotic, unruly willfulness. The portion of you which remains ever the same is the Creator-self within. Now, because of this sameness, this complete congruency betwixt all individuals in their most basic makeup, the universe may be seen to collapse into a field of unified consciousness. This is the very long and slow movement back to the source which each prodigal son and daughter decides to take.

Spiritual coincidence is often used in order to offer proof of a subjective nature that one has hit upon something that it is important about which to think, or has somehow blossomed and begun to manifest in a new and different way, and signs are there for you alone, to reassure you that your job is being well done. Likewise in sadness, in grief and in frustration, there is always comfort available, for each is nurtured by the one infinite Creator and no entity need be or feel alone at any time.

Spiritual coincidence is also used in another way. It is used when one is attempting to learn a somewhat complex lesson and the higher self finds its conceptualized lesson to be distorted by the illusion in one way or another. This means that, for awhile, the work in consciousness which the seeker is doing is either delusive and even vain. At that point, often a spiritual coincidence will occur to express in some radical way the need simply to pay attention, to remember who one is and who one's Father and Creator is.

So, some spiritual coincidences are set up to encourage and console the weary-footed seeker. Other spiritual coincidences occur so that one may take another and different look at the same challenge of love. There are many, many things to learn about loving. Few there are who may love unconditionally within your density. There is always the temptation for the bargaining, the rights of each, and so forth. When two entities who are mated seek together, you may find the spiritual coincidences mounting rapidly because each mate teaches the other. Each offers a fairly undistorted mirror to the other self, enabling that self to see itself in an objective way; thereby, intuitive or rational decisions can be made and change occur.

Thus, when there is a seeming synchronicity that has entered your life pattern, allow yourself to be completely fascinated by it and to follow the trail that it leads you to. The forest of ignorance and unknowing and indifference blocks the sun from many. Thus, we urge each not to become calmer and calmer, but rather to become spiritual warriors. Those who take advantage of the challenges of this very precious, small portion of time which is your incarnational experience, you will find that there is a good deal of change involved in deciphering spiritual coincidence.

You will also find at the time it occurs it may seem to be a disaster, for when one decides to manifest in another way, when one decides to discipline or change one's personality, one must, in this instrument's terms, dump programs that have been working and set in place within the bio-computer of your mind for time long enough for the habit to be very difficult to break.

When you recognize synchronicity, there is the key, the clue, the harbinger which says, "Pay attention, find the love in this, this is your challenge, this is your pattern." Move and flow with it without resistance. We are aware that there is nothing harder for any entity to do than to have blind trust and faith that all will be well. When difficulties seem to be large, perhaps even insurmountable, when the juice of gladness and joy seems to have left and the life seems empty of true purpose, this also is an excellent time to meditate upon and to analyze one's emotional and physical environment, for a truly exhausted soul will often need to sit by the road for a time and refresh itself.

Thus, we encourage each to be completely non-judgmental of the self or others, to appreciate the validity of subjectively interesting spiritual coincidences, and to realize that the seeker enters an ordeal. The seek—we correct this instrument—the seeking of the Holy Grail might perhaps be the best way to express the journey that each is on. Each yearns for the food of eternal existence and in the day-to-day cares of the world, love can become sour, trust can become embittered, walls can be built that can't be broken down.

In order to avoid slowly building oneself into a fixed position which you [as] an entity do not like, it is well to make every attempt to flow through the changes and not hold on to any truth, but rather have faith that that which is true at this time is indeed valid, but that at sometime in the future you may find another learning which gives you a deeper understanding of the particular lesson that you are attempting to learn.

It is much more exciting for entities to learn efficiently, but we find that your people do not learn efficiently and we find that most third-density entities do not learn efficiently. The inefficiency of the illusion as far as its offering to the seeker any outer proof of the existence of eternity is simply not there. So each must gaze upon the catalyst before him and say quite seriously, "What has this to do with me? What would be the way to serve, the way to unburden, the way to console, the way to bring light?"

Therefore, we very much encourage each to recognize the great importance of subjectively interesting spiritual coincidence or synchronicity, and to gaze keenly at the situations either by intuition or by analysis or both, seeking out what pattern is being repeated in this particular situation. For each of you, my children, has an incarnational pattern with one or two basic lessons which you wished to learn.

Now, mind you, your anxiety is not because of your own learning, for each of you wishes far more to aid others than each may take seriously the self. We would suggest that each continue to attempt to serve others, but that each take oneself more seriously. We do not mean that you should lose your sense of humor. That is certainly necessary within an illusion such as yours, which is quite comedic, we find. But in order to avoid becoming a pawn in someone else's game you must grasp the dimensions of the understanding that is being asked of you, and then to the best of your ability attempt to learn and to manifest that new understanding, to undergo the pain of transformation and change, and to use the energy of that pain for a building of a new and higher truth for yourself.

There are few who examine the life minutely, moment by moment each day. Most entities are content to be intro—we correct this instrument—introspective from time to time only. It is well to never focus upon oneself to the extent that one is oblivious of other's needs, but it is also most important for each of you, my children, that you respect yourself, that you move within your consciousness as on holy ground, for all of creation, all of love, dwells within the infinity of your deep mind.

If you wish to work with spiritual coincidence more intensively, the writing down of the dreams when one awakens is an helpful adjunct to silent prayer and meditation. In the silent meditation, one simply is with the Creator, and slowly, the self of each self in that atmosphere becomes and is the Creator. This is the depth and the resonance of the present moment which infinitely intersects with eternity. And the more consciousness that each has of the eternal moment, denying time and space any final reality, there is a great opportunity for that entity to find knowledge that is being sought. Then there is the responsibility and the duty to put into action those things which are learned.

May we say in reassurance, that it matters not how many times you may misread the will of the Father for you, for in each situation—synchronistically, if you will—events will fall in such a way that you are presented once again with the area of learning to love that you have been working upon for some time. It is well to know one's incarnational goals, not only in service to others, but in terms of honoring the self as a portion of the creation enough to place that self in a meditative state where there is light abundant and food plentiful for the soul and the spirit.

Daily meditation, as always, is something which we feel is at the heart of one's acceleration of spiritual growth, but never think that you are being moved about by destiny. This is not so. The free choice is always your own. If you do not wish a lesson, if you are too weary, you may simply sit by the side of the road and let others go by for awhile. And when you are refreshed, you simply begin again where you stopped. There is no hurry, there is no worry, there is no concern, there is no attachment. There is only the challenge of the chase for the Grail and the infinite satisfaction of spending time with the one infinite Creator. Indeed, each time the mind turns to the Creator with a word of praise or thanksgiving, the service rendered thereby is incalculable. Each time that each may smile at the stranger, or comfort, or help one who needs it, each is expressing a kind of consciousness that one is attempting to learn, that is, unconditional love.

So it is as if, say for instance, you wished to drive to the town of Chicago, you may go by one way or by another. You may sail about the world or drive the distance in a very short period of time. Eventually, however, you shall arrive at that destination which is yours. So nothing is wasted and nothing is lost in processing catalyst in a biased fashion. You are, of course, attempting to hone out of the stuff of which you are made, that is, free will and the Creator-self within, a self in which the will has become disciplined.

And one thing that spiritual coincidence does for those who heed it is encourage them upon their quest. When one is in a deep feeling of despair, one is still a hologram of the one infinite Creator. There is no way one is not going to get to Chicago, if we may continue the metaphor. It is just that there are many, many roads, some shorter, some longer, some easier, some more difficult. The measure of an entity's spiritual mettle is basically the entity's ability to express faith that all is as it should be and that there is love in the moment. This takes a complete, blind trust and faith because the illusion has been designed for you to see a fairly large portion of negativity within the relationships one has, the friendships one has, and the wars and rumors of wars of those upon your planet who would wish …

(Side one of tape ends.)

(Carla channeling)

… The instrument has just informed me that she would wish that I transfer this contact at this time, for we seem to have spoken in enough of a volume of your time that were we to be longer, we would lose you, as this instrument would say, as each drifted sweetly off to sleep. Therefore, we would close this meditation through the instrument known as Jim. I am known to you as Q'uo.

(Jim channeling)

I am Q'uo, and greet each again in the love and light through this instrument. At this time it is our privilege to ask if we might speak to any queries which yet remain upon the minds of those present. Is there a query at this time?

Questioner: To continue the analogy that was presented in tonight's session about a trip to Chicago, I wonder if there would be the possibility of an accelerated path to Chicago, maybe to use an analogy like time travel. In other words, how does an entity accelerate along the path to reach the ultimate goal?

I am Q'uo, and am aware of your query, my brother. We may suggest that there is that which you call the accelerated path, that path being the one which is consciously chosen and followed. This is in contrast to the path which many of your peoples follow, that which is, as yet, less a conscious choice than a preincarnative and subconscious choice, that uses catalyst far less efficiently than does the path that has been carefully considered and has been consciously made the focus point of the life pattern by the seeker.

We are aware that you query as to the possibility of further accelerating the consciously chosen path. In this regard, we may respond by suggesting that as one carefully considers the daily round of activities and the seeming coincidences that present themselves in such activities, that one then follow the product of the intuition and the analysis as soon as one is aware that there is a direction which feels appropriate to the heart of the being. There is much within your illusion and your life patterns that is of mystery. As you are able to sort that which is of most value from that which is of less value, you will find yet that there are still choices to be made, and contemplation, meditation, and the prayerful attitude to be undertaken in the evaluation of the most efficient choice.

If one is able to move in harmony with these feelings and contemplative products of meditation and a prayerful attitude, one will be moving as quickly as it is well for one to move, for there is within each entity a rhythm, shall we say, of awareness that presents itself as a kind of pattern that offers the surest and most stable growth possible. If one attempts to move more quickly than one may successfully assimilate lessons and learning and service to the heart of one's being, there is danger of overloading, shall we say, the spiritual and mental emotional circuitry of the mind/body/spirit complex. It is well, therefore, to move with some stability as well as with [the] eagerness of the seeker which sees, if only faintly, the goal which is in reach.

Is there a further query, my brother?

Questioner: Not at this time, thank you.

I am Q'uo. We thank you my brother. Is there another query?

Questioner: Yes. I'd like to ask about … I'm a little confused about how the mirror image works in the mated relationship. I—it seems like maybe one person is really patient and the other person is impatient, for example, and I'm sure that's part of the Creator's way of showing us that each of us contains both the patience and the impatience. But what if you, say, if you consider you're the patient person and you're seeing the impatience in the other person, does that indicate that you need, or that you feel that you should become more patient than you already are … um … I'm kind of confused how this works, how to best utilize this system here.

I am Q'uo, and am aware of your query, my sister. We shall do our best to respond in the manner which is most helpful.

The mirroring effect that those within the mated relationship experience is an intensification of the mirroring effect that is experienced by each entity at all times when in contact with others. It may be noted within the mind, when there is an interaction between entities, when a thought, word or deed that has been shared remains within the thoughts that you think and remains with a certain charge, shall we say, when there is a response by yourself to any thought, word or deed of another that causes you to move from the center of your being, and causes you concern of any kind, you may notice the mirroring effect as it is generated from your own subconscious mind.

This is to say that you have before the incarnation chosen certain lessons upon which you shall apply yourself. You have therefore biased your perceptions in a manner which will allow you to see what we may call a neutral experience, or neutral catalyst, in such and such a fashion that is in accordance with your preincarnative choices. Thus, a number of entities may witness the same exchange of experience and respond by feeling a variety of responses. This is due to the unique nature of each entity's preincarnative programming and subconscious bias.

Thus, whatever experience you share with another that leaves its mark upon your memory is one which you would do well to consider within your own meditations, to look within your own self to see what significance this experience has. Then one may, in a meditative state, look at that experience within the life pattern to note the repetition of this experience or similar experiences, and begin by this analysis to discern the deeper pattern that comprises the lesson that you are attempting at this time to learn, and which has been signaled by the experience shared with another that registered a strong emotional response in your own being.

Thus, each life pattern is unique and the response to various stimuli or catalyst is also unique and may be observed for the impact that it has on the self.

Is there a further query, my sister?

Questioner: No, thank you, that was very helpful.

I am Q'uo, and we thank you, my sister. Is there another query?

Carla: Well, I'd sort of like to go back and look at the situation such as R's, which is very common, where a person is not doing something that he feels expresses himself, but rather puts on a mask and expresses a persona—a part of the self, but not the whole self. And again and again an entity has attempted to move into a different direction, yet each time, as R said this evening, there is some compelling reason to return to a kind of irreverent humor which is considered by the entity to be perhaps less than completely helpful in service to others. What is going on when this kind of yellow-ray difficulty occurs with the society, with work, and so forth?

I am Q'uo, and I am aware of your query, my sister. One may look at each life pattern as having various vehicles for expression. The relationship with the mate is one of primary importance. The relationship with those with whom one labors in the daily round of activities is another. Each relationship or situation of an enduring nature that one encounters in the life pattern may be seen as the vehicle through which the preincarnative choices find a field of play, shall we say. It is within such relationships that those opportunities to express the lessons and services preincarnatively chosen appear. It is less important to the supposed effect upon another entity that one may assume has been made than it is to observe the effect of the experience upon the self.

It is well, therefore, to look not so much at the vehicle by which or through which one is expressing the self, as it is to look at the feeling or tone within the self that is, shall we say, the motivating force for the expression in such and such a manner. We would recommend, therefore, that there be less emphasis given to the form or framework within which lessons are attempted and more emphasis be given to the motivation for those structures that are built and operated within for the purpose of attempting those lessons.

Is there a further query, my sister?

Carla: No, just an observation. You sounded … very good and I really appreciated it. Thank you.

I am Q'uo, and we thank you, my sister. Is there another query at this time?

Carla: I guess I do have one more. I was conjecturing it to myself earlier today. We were talking about time being different in different dimensions and being experienced differently in different dimensions and I thought, well, gee, you know, we experience time differently in a subjective sense in this illusion even. I mean, even with a clock ticking all the time and saying what time it is, if you don't look at the clock, if you're doing something you really dislike doing, a minute can last about three hours, and if you're doing something you love doing, three hours can last about a minute. So time is very malleable and obviously an illusion, a subjective illusion, even while the clock ticks on in the illusion, you can see through it even though you're within the illusion. It's one of the easiest things to see through, and I was wondering if in the higher densities, the reason that there is so much time in human terms, you know, millions of years to work on lessons, that perhaps, subjectively, that time is not experienced as a long, long time but rather, is experienced as a time of concentration in which all sense of time is lost while one attempts to learn a very refined lesson.

I am Q'uo, and am aware of your query, my sister. We shall attempt to describe this function of time by suggesting that the fluidity or quick passage of time is a function of the lack of resistance to experience. To state this in the positive sense, the ability to move in harmony with one's experience allows the dissolving of the barriers of time for that entity as it is able to move in harmony.

Is there another query, my sister?

Carla: Oh no, thank you, Q'uo.

I am Q'uo, and again thank you, my sister. Is there another query at this time?

Questioner: I sense that the energy of the instrument is getting low at this point, so perhaps maybe just a brief answer can be given about the use of magnetism, on what we know as Atlantis.

I am Q'uo, and am aware of your query, my brother, and we appreciate your concern for the energy of the instrument, for it is quite low at this time.

The entities within the Atlantean culture were in many respects quite successful in utilizing various means of tapping into what might be called the intelligent infinity or infinite intelligence of the creation, thereby bringing through a kind of intelligent energy which was utilized in many ways to technologically advance the culture. The use of the magnetic field of force as well as use of the energy contained within the atom and use of the crystal for penetrating intelligent infinity was made by a careful application of trial and error testing as is the way of the rational and, as you call it, scientific mind.

The utilization of these forms and forces was, for the most part, an exercise in the mundane application of energy for the use of but a few within the culture and at the expense of the majority of entities within that culture. There were those who felt that the mental discipline of the personality would yield far greater results for both the individual and the culture, and these entities, before the down-sinking of Atlantis, chose therefore to remove themselves from this culture to distant locations upon your planetary surface in order to continue the metaphysical studies that they felt would provide greater opportunity for learning and for service than would the utilization of the technological means of gaining and of applying the intelligent energy through the use of magnetic fields of force, through the use of crystals, and through the release of nuclear energy.

Is there a further query, my brother?

Questioner: No, thank you.

I am Q'uo, and again thank you, my brother. Is there a final query at this time?

Carla: All right, I have a question. The negative entities that seem to be coming among us at this time in spacecraft seem bent on manipulating our people for some reason. Could you comment on that at all?

I am Q'uo, and am aware of your query, my friend. Our comment upon this phenomenon in order to avoid the infringement upon free will must be of a general nature, for there is much activity within the various cultures of your planet at this time that is, shall we say, of the planetary again, and must remain mysterious in order for the free will of the general population of your planet to be maintained. When there is sharing and opportunity of sharing that which is helpful in the positive sense of service to others, as is the growing experience of your planet at this time, there must also be the balancing opportunity for the population of your planet to choose the path.

Therefore, the experiences of which you speak are a portion of this opportunity. The choice, however, remains always, with each individual to look upon the creation about it, either as that which is an extension of the self and that which is helped by the services of each entity, or as that which is to be controlled and plundered for the benefit only of the self or of the group to which the self belongs. Each experience and each entity shall therefore find a free range of choice available. The experiences that you refer to are much in the minds of those who work within the metaphysical studies at this time, for there is also at this time much of light and service to others that is moving as a conscious experience for a greater number of the people of this planet.

At this time, we shall thank each present for inviting our presence in your circle of seeking this evening. It has been a great honor to share that which is ours to share with you. We wish to remind each that we are but your brothers and sisters who have perhaps moved a bit farther along the same path that you travel than have you, but we do not wish any word we have spoken to serve as a stumbling block to you upon that path. Therefore, if we have spoken any words which do not ring true, please forget them at once and use only those concepts for which you feel affinity. We are known to you as those of Q'uo and we leave each at this time in the love and in the light of the one infinite Creator. Adonai, my friends. Adonai. ☙

L/L Research

L/L Research is a subsidiary of Rock Creek Research & Development Laboratories, Inc.

P.O. Box 5195
Louisville, KY 40255-0195

www.llresearch.org

Rock Creek is a non-profit corporation dedicated to discovering and sharing information which may aid in the spiritual evolution of humankind.

ABOUT THE CONTENTS OF THIS TRANSCRIPT: This telepathic channeling has been taken from transcriptions of the weekly study and meditation meetings of the Rock Creek Research & Development Laboratories and L/L Research. It is offered in the hope that it may be useful to you. As the Confederation entities always make a point of saying, please use your discrimination and judgment in assessing this material. If something rings true to you, fine. If something does not resonate, please leave it behind, for neither we nor those of the Confederation would wish to be a stumbling block for any.

CAVEAT: This transcript is being published by L/L Research in a not yet final form. It has, however, been edited and any obvious errors have been corrected. When it is in a final form, this caveat will be removed.

© 2009 L/L Research

Sunday Meditation
July 30, 1989

Group question: The question this evening has to do with the ability that many seekers have when concentrating carefully and working diligently to stay centered within themselves so that they are aware of their feelings, their actions, and the meaning of both. But what do you do when you partake in the daily round of activities and you don't have that steady concentration? How do you maintain a contact with the center of yourself so that you're able to take advantage of the opportunities for growth that present themselves? How do you keep from getting off the track and getting lost in the television, the mundane activities, the conversation, the emotions of the moment?

(Carla channeling)

I am Q'uo. I greet you in the love and the light of the one infinite Creator, and thank you for calling us to share with you what humble information we may have. About the subject of living the life of the monastery in the seeming non-monastery of the mundane world, we are most happy to take up this subject, for it is central to the process of polarizing in consciousness towards service to others and an awareness of the Creator's love for you and your adoration of the Creator who has made all things well.

As always, we ask that you remember that we are not infallible, that we still have much to learn, and that as long as we have identity, we will be making errors from time to time. The only lack of error lies in non-polarized love, and that love is a love so intense that it [vitiates] the necessity for a conscious personality. It is, therefore, stored within the Creator as the active principle of the Creator when eventually we each return to our source.

It is written in your holy works that the teacher known to you as Jesus stated that birds of the air had their nest, but that the son of man had nowhere to put his head. This was the simple truth. This entity did not operate from a home base of any kind, but rather was peripatetic and walked to different places to learn and to teach and to inspire and to fulfill that purpose for which he accepted incarnation in third density.

This entity's life, like all entities who are sons of man and daughters of man, was the experience of the endless journey. Those who choose to sequester themselves—we correct this instrument—from the mundane world by moving into monkhood or the nunnery or some specific way of organized religion supporting those who are contemplatives, these entities remove themselves, they think, from the catalyst that they would experience as ordinary citizens who are not specifically religious or of the cloth, as this instrument would say. This is a snare and a delusion.

Humankind is equally confused and unbalanced in various ways throughout all populations, whether they be monasteries, colleges, towns or countryside. The holiness, the steeping in sanctity that is available in this life of monastery living becomes the daily round, the normal routine, the working. Mundane personalities clash between brothers and between sisters. Authority finds itself in confrontation just as much within so-called religious orders as in any other job. This is not to say that we would discourage people from becoming ministers, monks or nuns. It is merely to say that the same temptations, distractions and waywardness will await those who move into a specifically religious lifestyle to the extent that each as an entity needs catalyst. The catalyst will be there. The thought of the protection of the monastery may well be comforting, but in years of experience of living in such a community, any thoughtful religious person living therein would say that there is mundane activity that must be done always, that there is no escape from the surface of life.

Now, we would like to offer you some thoughts on the subject. There are a variety of ways to gauge centeredness to your own satisfaction. We would first indicate that a way that is considered mundane of experiencing the Creator is the making love with the intention of experiencing the Creator, for within the Creator's love, the one original Thought is a manifestation in third density in red ray which you call the orgasm, and at those moments you are experiencing the love of the infinite Creator in an undistorted fashion. This is the steady state of the Creator. This is the nature of the Creator—joy, bliss, ecstasy and peace, all in the name of love.

As you gaze at each of your energy centers, though, those controlling your relationships with yourself, others and the society, you may find many, many ways to see the holiness and sanctity of apparently mundane things. Because you skate upon the very thin pond ice of life is no reason that you cannot make the hole in the ice and dive deeply into each moment. It is simply a matter of beginning to recognize that which is holy, that which is blessed, that which is beautiful, that which is true in the common, everyday round of activities. Any work, as this entity is aware [a brother once] has written[1], is completely spiritual if it is done for the love of the one infinite Creator.

We say this first because we wish you to know that it is not a hopeless task that you gaze upon, but rather an endless journey which is more and more rewarding. Going through spirals of learning, painful change, peaceful plateaus, and new learnings, pain and new peaceful repose—this is the surface of your life. Do not consider for a moment that your conscious mind is all that is responding to the perceived catalyst.

While the conscious mind is busy with the numbers, the letters, the chores, the subconscious mind is seeking the Creator in those who wish to move toward polarity in service to others. The foundation of this double consciousness, where one is capable of completing all mundane tasks necessary while remaining aware of the one infinite Creator, has its foundation in meditation, that is, the silent meditation of listening without any expectation, just listening.

Each entity will feel the presence of the one infinite Creator in a different way. Some feel it in the heart, some feel it more cerebrally, some feel it with a deep emotion tone that cannot be described. But once this direct experience of being with the Creator has been recognized, acknowledged and praised—and this is available to any who are able to make love—the journey is well begun and it simply requires a steady, persistent effort to observe the thoughts which move through your mind complex, to discard those which do not seem proper, or if unable to discharge them, to experience them, knowing it is a part of the catalyst of your particular lesson and feeling neither anger nor disappointment at the Creator or at yourself for becoming stuck in the mire of every day and loosing the contact of the heart with the Creator within.

It is very important that each who attempts to accelerate the pace of the spiritual evolution realize that this will be done through a series of failures as well as successes, each failure being as important or more important than the successes because of the situation in which one decides one must change. This changing to come more into line with full consciousness of the Creator in all that is is a long,

---

[1] Carla: The quote is from Kahlil Gibran's *The Prophet*: "Work is love made visible. And if you cannot work with love but only with distaste, it is better that you should leave your work and sit at the gate of the temple and take alms of those who work with joy." The flavor of the whole essay is that "to love life through labor is to be familiar with life's innermost secret."

progressive lesson, shall we say, a seemingly endless journey.

There are other techniques for training the mind to awareness that each present moment has the resonance of eternity. One way is simply to remind oneself of that fact as often as one thinks of it and to pause for a moment in praise, thanksgiving and adoration of the Creator which allows free will to its various parts, that they may learn freely, choose freely, and evolve each at its own rate.

Any of the senses can be used to remind one of the infinite Creator. The artifacts of humankind, especially the media, are excellent for the weary soul, however, this mass information exchange tends to entrain the mind, to manipulate the attitudes, and more than anything else, to emphasize the surface life which each entity finds, as it spirals through desert periods of its learning, to be completely inadequate to form a satisfactory life.

There is a good reason for this. We realize that in speaking of evolution, we speak of those things about which your culture is uneasy. However, we believe that it is true that you as entities have come to the near end of physical evolution in third density, which is surely reasonable considering how little of third density is left for each.

The future evolution of humankind will be what entities of your culture would call philosophical or religious. These are misnomers because that which is spiritual and that which is scientific are, in the end, congruent. And time spent pondering the various gadgets and contrivances which your people are so excellent at creating, you create the distraction, the unnecessary that seems to be needed, and underscore the surface of life for yourself.

Now, how shall you pull yourself up by your own bootstraps, as this instrument would say, to become true disciples of the one infinite Creator, to become those who truly wish to manifest the incredibly intense and infinite love that created all that is? To continue the point of view of gazing at the energy centers of the entity, we may say that once the full energy or prana or love/light of the one infinite Creator is able to reach the heart chakra, at that point the desk, shall we say, is cleared for work in consciousness. While one is mired in the surface details, one simply does not have the same consciousness. Therefore, we do not suggest in any way that any change the style of living, the way of laboring, the way of earning that which purchases food and clothing and shelter. We urge each to explore the resonances, the undertones and light motifs of everything from relationships to clear communication to any experience of any kind. In all experiences, you are on holy ground and the simple remembrance of this fact enables the seeking soul to polarize more and more in that consciousness of sanctity.

There is great polarization on your planet at this time, for harvest is near and some entities are as negative as others are positive and so many are neither negative or positive but simply unaware of a choice having to be made. To those we would say, drop a seed here and there, but have no attachment to that seed's growing in a way you would wish, for each entity will make its own choice for service to self or service to others. Each entity has an infinite time to do so. There is no tragedy that is truly tragedy, no loss that is truly a loss, and, conversely, no happiness that is complete on the surface of your life. But with a sense of humor and a merry will, not seriously but lightheartedly, as though it were a play, we urge each to systematically cleanse the self of separation and fear whenever it rears its head.

Fear is usually the cause of separation—fear that one may be hurt, fear that one may be passed over and so forth. Then there are fears that one may perhaps not be able to meet one's obligations. There are fears of the future and of the past. There is fear of illness, of so many things, my children, and this fear keeps you handcuffed to the surface of life. We urge each of you to dive as deeply as you can each day in meditation, and when an action is undertaken, especially in reference to other entities, whether it be the making love, the clear communication, the companionship, or the comforting, make a conscious intention of this love and pleasure, for the praise, the thanksgiving and the worship of the one infinite Creator, whose nature is so loving that it is to your third-density experience unbelievably explosive.

It is very helpful to have another entity or a group of entities with which one is seeking. This is the main use of the idea of community that is behind the monasteries, however, any group may be a support group, each to the other, if each, when the other is in difficulty and confusion, can remember that that is all right, that is acceptable, that is a portion, a natural part of the endless spiritual journey.

The spiritually polarized entity finds things dropping away, finds the life becoming simpler in an inexplicable way, and as the entity polarizes more and more in the manifestation and fruit of service to others, there is a growing and ultimately irresistible aid in that the more one polarizes towards service to others in a natural rather than forced way, the more one begins to view what is known to you as virtue with affection and fondness rather than a weary eye for legality and guilt. You do not live to yourself. You live to others and others live for you.

Realize deep within yourself that that which seems mundane and everyday, the workplace, each environment, is in actuality the Creator speaking with the Creator in one way or another. It is much easier to see the love, the joy, the bliss and the bloom of second-density creation than it is to see the same of each self-conscious, self-aware entity which has gained the right, the obligation, in its own time to make a choice betwixt service to self and service to others.

Therefore, each entity has its own, what this instrument would call, psychology of being. For some, the simple repeating of a spiritual phrase whenever one is not specifically thinking of something else will aid tremendously. For others, the cutting off of negative thinking and the application of trust and abiding faith and lack of fear does its slow but inexorable work of clearing the consciousness that it may see, not simply what the five senses of your physical body perceives, but what your entire entity perceives. The subconscious portion of the self is well aware of the Creator in all that is, of the worshipfulness inherent in being a child of the Creator. This is very slow work. The journey is long and, [to] those who attempt to discipline the personality, to live within the Kingdom of Heaven while functioning upon Earth, is somewhat intense.

We would not urge one single way for anyone to do this work, for work in consciousness is unique to each consciousness, which is also unique. The basic premise of our suggestion is that time spent thinking of the Creator in meditation and thanking and praising the Creator throughout each day in whatever way this is desired is the way to dive deeper and deeper into the present moment where there is no fear, there is no guilt from the past or worry of the future. If you may live in the moment, you are living, as this instrument would call, the Kingdom of Heaven. Those who are truly service to others oriented are most often in the thick of things doing that which has been given them to do within the mundane world creating service to others each in its own unique way. Each of you has an unique way to be of service.

Service is largely non-dramatic and impossible to detect by one who is not aware of the process going on within you. A simple smile, a soft answer to a hard question, a way of smoothing things over in the workplace—all these efforts, all these sharings of the self and the goodness of the self [redound] to the consciousness of the planet and lighten it for you to bear fruit and bloom each time you become fully aware that you are gazing at the Creator in all that you see, and that your response need contain no fear. Each of you lives within a perishable vehicle and there is much fear connected with the body complex's desire not to end the incarnational experience. We would, on the other hand, suggest that …

We shall pause. I am Q'uo.

(Pause)

We would suggest to each that this surface illusion begin to be consciously penetrated by the heart and the consciousness. It is well to spend much time …

(Side one of tape ends.)

(Carla channeling)

… planet, in its own way remarkable and unique and all the senses are teased and delighted with the lovely smells of the various second-density things which grow within your Earth and create such beauty for the eyes. But you are third density and hoping to become fourth density. This means that your basic philosophy is that of one who runs the straight race, as the entity known as Paul has written in the holy work known as the Bible.

Never force the self to be "spiritual." Never force yourself to be good, polite or helpful but rather when you have discovered a blockage within yourself and have communicated clearly that you have a problem, move deep into your consciousness and examine that difficulty, finding the love and the lesson in that situation. There is no way of which we know for an entity to make an errorless life experience. Even the entity known to you as Jesus, who is mistakenly worshipped by many who do not realize that this entity was a perfect channel for the one infinite Creator, [had] this confusion. Perfect bliss is available only to those who remove themselves in solitude so that no mirrors are held up to the self and one may go one's eccentric and idiosyncratic way seeking God as it will, seeking love and expressing love as it can.

You will find that each of you has gifts and talents which can be used to emphasize the progress of spiritual evolution within yourself. We know that you wish to evolve. The simple remembrance of that wish within you creates a call and a desire which will give to you subjective experiences that build one upon the other over long periods of time, so that without judging the self, one may honestly say, "Yes, twenty years ago I did not think so much about the Creator and my imperishable relationship with that infinite and imperishable Creator." Each of you has the answer within. This is why we began with such a direct and simple example of meeting the Creator in the act of love. There is no need for fanciness of thought or great stretches of the imagination but only unreserved compassion in order to polarize more and more towards being a consciously loving and serving entity.

This instrument has informed us that we have exceeded the required time limit. We are sorry to be so verbose but this particular subject is one upon which we could speak for many hours. We ourselves are still polarizing towards service to others. This is not a short journey. This is an uncomfortable journey that is real. That which you see with your five senses is a complete illusion. That which you hear from entities who are unaware that the Creator lives within them may convince you that there are some entities who are hopeless. All contain the Creator within and this is your great guide, this is why the meditation of silence is central and why it should be as frequent as possible, preferably daily and at the same time. It is especially helpful at the beginning of the day to think upon the Creator in one way or another by reading of spiritual books, by singing of spiritual songs or by the simple going within and opening the inner door to that presence which already lies within you whole and perfect, the Creator within.

We wish each the quality of faithfulness, foolishness and persistence; faithfulness in the face of adversity, foolishness in the face of those who do not believe ideals are worth holding to, and above all, an easygoing and joyful, light touch, so that you move lightly through the illusion, always gazing at the Creator.

Again we say to you, use your environment. There is no environment that is not full of the love and the light of the infinite Creator. There is no environment which is not ripe for you to be of service to others at the time at which it is asked of you. Many are the times one must wait, for one cannot be of service if one attempts to be of service in a way that is not pleasing to the one served. But if the willingness and the unconditional love of the open heart is maintained through clearing up all lower energy blockages, each entity has a more and more available opportunity to dive into the soul of reality and to experience and bring back to this world which you now enjoy the resonances of eternity.

We would at this time transfer this contact to the one known as Jim. I leave this instrument in love and light. I am Q'uo.

(Jim channeling)

I am Q'uo, and greet each again in love and light through this instrument. We realize that we have spoken overly long this evening, but we wish to offer the opportunity for further queries to be asked if there are any as yet remaining upon the minds of those present. Is there a query at this time?

Questioner: I don't have any questions, but I would like to say that that was a rather amazing channel, and it answered an awful lot of questions and it clarified directions for me and I thank you very much for the information and for the time and the love in which it was given.

I am Q'uo, and we are most grateful to you as well, my brother, for offering the query. Is there a query at this time from any present?

(Pause)

I am Q'uo, and we are most grateful to have been able to join this group this evening and to share those words and thoughts which are the product of our own seeking, for we seek as do each of you, my brothers and sisters. We seek on that endless trail which many before us have trod and many which come after us shall also trod. We thank all seekers that offer their supplications to the one Creator, that there might be those to respond to such calls for service and in such response be as blessed [as] are we this evening in answering your call.

At this time, we shall take our leave of this group, leaving each, as always, in the love and in the light from the one infinite Creator. We are known to you as those of Q'uo. Adonai, my friends. Adonai.

Sunday Meditation
August 6, 1989

Group question: The question this evening is: misconceptions and unclear communications seem to be a continuous difficulty in mated relationships. Could you recommend any practices or development of attitudes that couples could share in order to clear their communications and still be able to communicate from the heart?

(Carla channeling)

I am Laitos. I greet you in the love and the light of the infinite Creator and express our delight and gratitude to be called to this group at this time, for this question is a portion of information that we, in our particular social memory complex, have specialized in. That is, the relation of self with other self within the life experience. We thank you for allowing us to be of service to you by sharing our opinions, but we wish you to understand, as always, that our opinions are not infallible, nor are we a source that can be approached as one would a holy work. We are your neighbors and we have come to help at a difficult period. Therefore, take that which you find resonating within you away with you and allow it to work within your life. But if it does not resonate when first heard, simply drop it from your consciousness, for each person's truth is different and each person's time to come to certain truths is different and you are a unique entity with the right and the duty of choosing each and every step that you take.

As we gaze upon your mated relationship in your culture we find that there is a great need for understanding of the true nature of relationships that is lacking among your people. To become mated is to become one—one flesh, one line, and one spirit. If one is not able to commit one's respect and admiration, either physically, mentally, emotionally or spiritually, then the relationship is hampered from the beginning by the lack of the other's good opinion.

The true nature of the married relationship—or the mated relationship as we prefer to call it, marriage having confusing connotations—is that each may help the other upon the spiritual path that they are making through the seeming time span of their short lives. That is what each of you does. You walk one step at a time down a road whose end you can not and will not ever see. And to have a comrade at your side to share the dust of the road with, to share the enjoyment of nourishment and water when the oasis is found, simply to go through the same experiences and catalysts together, is a very, very great service from each to each, for each has much to teach and much to learn.

Thus, in an ideal sense, we may say that in a natural way of being, insofar as the body complex is concerned, it is the self-conscious choice of some entities not to be mated monogamously but to be mated whenever there is an opportunity. Thus, it is not the animal through which you express your being that is to blame if unwise sexual choices are made. It is the mind that needs to be gazed at.

Now, when two entities contemplate the ordeal that marriage is they must ask themselves if this is the person they wish to be yoked with until one of you dies. Is this the person you wish to serve until one of you dies? Is this a person whose conversation will not pall? There are many questions one may ask oneself. The fundamental question is, "Do you love?" and if the answer in regard to that relationship is, "Yes, I have love for this entity," then on some level of friendship, or more than friendship, is a natural and desirable outgrowth of such attractions of mind. However, entities within your culture believe, and no one has told them differently whom they can respect and believe, that it is well to marry for love and that one lives the "happily ever after" of the picture books. This is not so.

A marriage is the beginning of two paths converging together into one single, enhanced path for both. That is—we shall use the information from this instrument's connection with the one known as Jim, knowing that it is given us freely to do so. The struggle that entities who do not have instinctive understanding of each other is to communicate and it is such a challenge that people seldom are able to continue to communicate upon a subject that is difficult beyond a certain point. If entities were able to reason with each other, there would not be the discord. However, when one enters into marriage one enters into that which, by its very nature, has a strong potential of becoming an adversary relationship.

No two entities are alike. Their paths may cross here and there in the mundane sense, but no two paths are at all alike. Consequently, when one attempts to express oneself, to give information about the self to one of another sex, it is as if one is talking through a muffling device. And this is also true for women who attempt to communicate with men. It is as if all the words were somehow distorted. And this is, indeed, due to the fact that men and women do not think the same way. Women have a greater access to their deeper mind, which is the emotions, among other things.

So, you may see that the basic flaw that causes so many entities not to communicate and to have disastrous experiences with someone whom one loves, is in communication. Now, let us examine that to a certain extent. Communication speaks upon all levels of the consciousness of the entity. The giving of the self to the other's support is that which is most difficult for entities who are perhaps not entirely in agreement with their spouses. However, it is well to remember that each of the spouses is also an unique spiritual entity. Consequently, even if you are being treated as an adversary by your spouse, it is well for you to recall that you have made vows and pledged a promise to cherish an entity until this entity requests being released from the cherishing of you.

The nature of the animal which moves you about is relatively peaceful. That is, if you did not have a brain beyond that found in animal life of other species, your actions would not therefore become wicked, or what you would call wicked if you criticized your own behavior. It would simply revert to a more instinctual way of living. Each entity is free in its own right and no one can be possessed or possess anyone else.

These are all misunderstandings about marriage and mating that lead to many arguments, distressing differences, and ultimate separation Thus, it is wise to provide oneself with a partner with whom one may speak clearly. Then you merely have a fairly hard job rather than an impossible one. You and the other self make a pact to live a very poetic and beautiful life together, a life described within your scripture and your writings as most benign and helpful. However, it is not well for an entity to take for granted that because there was attraction at one time nothing will ever change. Changing is constant, especially for spiritually, consciously working individuals.

Thus, first of all, learn your own body. Learn it that you may balance it, and use it by your own will and not by its own will. This discipline of the red-ray energy is not suggested because of moral or ethical reasons. It is due to our love of free will. As the two who are yoked together to pull the consciousness of light and love into the Earth plane they may realize they have created between them the beginnings of a third entity. Each will have to change a good deal and give up much in order that one's own path and one's mate's path may remain close enough to communicate about. So, communication is always the key. The entity who loses the temper and raises the voice is going to accomplish nothing except a healthy release of frustration, which may well keep such an entity from ulcers or cancers. In that regard we applaud such honesty; in all others we see no use for it.

The animal, however, does have a strong fight-or-flight mechanism, and because of the derivation of your body forms you may well be aware that you are not particularly aggressive in the fact of your animalhood. For if you gaze at your animal predecessors you may see them cooperating in tribes and families. It seems that you have known and can trust this sort of pattern. The body, however, is controlled by the mind. Even those things which you call autonomous in the nervous system may be controlled by mind. Consequently, it is well within the limits of possibility that two entities who are aware of the ordeal that marriage will be and who wish to tackle it together would be [choosing] the best of all personal reasons for the mated relationship.

When one mates due to the physical attractiveness of the other, one mates with a shell, the inside of which may be rotten, sickly or undernourished. We ask out of respect to each of you as imperishable light beings that you respect and uplift yourselves to the highest and best mated relationship that you can imagine, this simply being the specialized case that those who are workers for the light will have their light dimmed or put out by a spouse that does not like or approve of the seeking that goes on in meetings like this one.

We do not encourage you to blame your body for the difficulties that you have with another. We encourage you to realize that the difficulties that you may have with another stem from your perception that there is a separation between you. Good mates, when finding this distance coming from the other, drop all things, run to the side of the one who has fallen into error in thinking, and correct the opinion as well as possible before returning to work. After just so long a while the entity will learn not to distrust, not to be afraid. Meanwhile, there is the comfort to give, even when one does not feel it is deserved.

Marriage is an ordeal. In this instrument's mind these words are Joseph Campbell's. They are also the simple truth. Life is an ordeal. All things are ordeals of one kind or another and the mated relationship is the greatest of all challenges in catalyst because it is the most intense experience of one entity living with another, with the opportunity to choose either to be on each other's side and to be one in thinking or to be over against each other in different opinions that are hard-held so that you are unable to compromise and that separation betwixt the two of you who were so in love once wanes and dies.

Therefore, we suggest that the greatest tool in working with relationship is silent meditation, sitting together in silence. Also are exercises appropriate by which each recognizes the other as the Creator. It is a matter of turning the will to the welfare of another entity above and in preference to the will of your own self. If there is no judgment of error, but merely a disagreement, then we always would suggest that all be talked out, resolution come and unity restored in the diurnal cycle in which it was disturbed. Do not allow difficult and unhappy feelings about the mate to extend past the time limit of one daytime period, for once one begins to refrain from saying those things that bother it, from then on it becomes more and more and more difficult to communicate until finally it is almost impossible within the perceptions of those who are attempting the communication. There is anger and fear and guilt instead of love and joy and peace.

This is completely the free will choice of mated entities. They need to know their animal selves. They need to know that the animal self they came from was indeed mated, that it is the mind of man and womankind that creates multiple sexual relationships. The reasons for this are quite simple and based upon survival. They stem from an instinct as deep as that which you would call Neanderthal. And that is that one's tribe is one's family, one's group is a coherent and cohesive group and will work all things out.

When you come together in the marriage it is well to remember what is ahead because what is ahead are startling discoveries about yourself and about the entity whom you love, about how life in general happens to people upon your planet. And you may choose not to learn from this but rather to become bitter and sour and be one who whines and says, "It's not fair." But the true mate, the mate that is desirable, is one who already knows that nothing is fair within this illusion, but that a trust level may be achieved between two persons which makes it virtually impossible under normal circumstances for that entity to feel separated in any significant way from its mate. You have no animal's excuse for moving from relationship to relationship. You only have the cultural preference that has been fed to you time and time and time again by those within what you call the media and within the pages of many books. It is a kind of fantasy life of your population which all too often is acted out rather than balanced within the heart as it should be.

Now, we would not for the world judge anyone who has wished to make love without benefit of marriage or who wishes to make love after marriage with another. We are not condemning from that point of view. We condemn simply the breaking of a promise before the promise is discussed. However, such events put a tremendous strain upon the relationship, and it is difficult in that situation for entities not to become adversaries even if they were in harmony before.

It is a simple choice, you see, of taking the time and the effort to understand the other person's point of view. It will be radically different than your own, for men and women do not think alike, although they often come to the same conclusions. They have, shall we say, a different interior mathematical framework.

Another tool one may use to become more and more one with one's mate and to avoid the adversary relationship is to allow the child within to have its freedom, to offer it swims and picnics and joyful companionship of all kinds. Never, ever, let the joys of childhood depart from you but rather find the child within your mate and let both children out to play. It keeps you as an integrated being, healthy and cheerful. This is very helpful.

The morning meditation and any other observances which one wishes to offer on a daily basis, this is very helpful too. And, perhaps, for one who has a certain measure of will, just an intellectual analysis of the situation which explains to one that one is becoming an adversary is often enough to rein in that person who does not wish to be an adversary to one's mate. There is nothing inevitable about matings becoming boring, adversarial or unhappy. The reason that they so often do so is that people are not aware that marriage is an ideal, not a reality. Mating, monogamy and so forth, are in the self-conscious individual a choice just like any other. A choice, in this case, that is truly service to others. It is a choice each makes day by day, from the simple standpoint of sharing sexuality. That by itself is transparent. There is nothing in the exchange of sexual energy to create the fear or the distress on anyone's part. Nevertheless, we note well that within your culture such things are considered transgressions, and we would, as always, encourage each to live according to not only one's highest moral and ethical principles, but also as much as possible within the dry bones of legality.

The adversary relationship is difficult to spot until it has become full-blown. Therefore, our last suggestion to you is that each mate become to the other more of a presence, more of a warmth, more the one with the self, so that there is the intimate feeling between two that does not need to be spoken. This inner peace of high trust level, one with the other, can pull both through the crises of the incarnational experience, as they will almost never have the same breaking point in any given situation. Always one will be able to help the other.

When you spot within yourself the beginnings of disagreement, ask for a meeting. When it is convenient have that meeting and express your preferences clearly. Then your mate may express its preferences clearly. This is the beginning of what may be seen as a negotiation within a company, which marriage basically is, an incorporation of two entities into one unit. Thus, the communication is very, very difficult, at first especially. However, one who perseveres will find that the companionship, while not replacing the ordeal, does enhance the ordeal, give it soul, spirit and heart and a vector towards the light.

So we ask you to love each other, my friends, and to serve them not as you would serve yourself but as they would have you serve them. We ask each who is ready to offer the bitter answer or a sarcastic question to stop and ask the self, "Am I uniting with my mate by this statement or am I separating from my mate with this statement?" If the realization may come, then the behavior should well improve as one becomes conscious that the actual reasons for seeming incompatibility and fighting within the mated relationship is within the person itself and not in the spouse. Then one has to move into a far more responsible position within oneself, realizing that as a student of the universe each is alone with the Creator and various other principles of light and love that aid in guiding one. Ask those entities to aid in your relationship also.

And realize that all relationships within the density that you now enjoy, with very few exceptions, go through difficult times. Not just once but cyclical. Do not be afraid of these times, but rather gaze at what unites the two rather than what separates you, one from the other. Do this for the love of your mate, for your love of self, and, above all, for your over-arching desire to be part of the good that comes to the Creator's heart.

May you lighten the consciousness on planet Earth. May each of you learn the way to inner peace. May each of you find soft answers to hard questions. Brothers and sisters, love one another. If you cannot do so right away, do not be discouraged. Nobody else can either. You have lots of time, but you must be persistent in your will and your desire to know and to manifest the truth within you, the glory and the splendor and rightness of the Creator-self within you. And that can only be crystallized and activated when the opening has been made for that energy to be moved with the help of those of us from other densities.

At this point we would like to thank this instrument. It has been a long time since we spoke through this instrument and we are most happy to have spoken with her. And we are also very thankful that the entity known as Carla who challenged [rigorously], due to the fact that the first entity that the one known as Carla challenged is already known to this group as a fifth-density negative entity capable of moving along the same basic vibratory rate as its counterpart in the physically positive sense. The challenge was successfully made and this very strong negative entity caused to move from these environs, and we thank this instrument that it does take care to preserve the purity of what we may ever so incoherently say to you.

I leave this instrument with thanks and love and in light. I am Latwii.

(Side one of tape ends.)

(Jim channeling)

I am Latwii, and I greet each in the love and in the light of the infinite Creator. It is our privilege to offer ourselves at this time, and we attempt to speak to any queries which those present may have upon the mind. We are very happy to speak in this capacity and would remind each again that we are not infallible beings but are those who wish to share as freely as possible that which we have found helpful on our own journey of seeking. Is there a question to which we may speak at this time?

Questioner: Yes. *(Inaudible).*

I am Latwii, and I am aware of your query, my brother. We find that the gathering together of three entities for the purpose of accomplishing spiritual work is a most beneficial circumstance when seen in a balanced sense. That is to say, there is the increased possibility of providing a framework through which and upon which work of a spiritual nature may be accomplished, for there is within the grouping of three a source of energy that is greater than the addition of each individual energy and is so in a manner which exceeds even the pairing that provides a oneness, of which we have previously spoken, that is also greater than the individuals composing it.

Three is a very stable number and form. If one observes the strength of the triangle, there is a bracing effect that is apparent in the triangular shape which provides a strength that is not matched by any other geometrical form that does not also take the triangle into account and into the construction. Thus it is as well within the mental and spiritual complexes for entities within a grouping of three.

We would, however, also suggest that due to the history of relationships within your culture, and, indeed, within most cultures of your planet, that there is a great inner and emotional resistance, in many cases, to the addition of the third member of the group, for there is quite often the competition, shall we say, that provides the catalyst within the grouping so that there is often either the spoken or unspoken voting that ends in the two-against-one verdict.

The communication that is so difficult within the mated pair becomes also more difficult within the grouping of three, for when there is the addition of another perception to a situation, there is the additional need for clearing the communication and making the effort to keep the communication clearly spoken. The chances for misperception and miscommunication are as enhanced as are the opportunities for increasing the growth of each individual within the group and of providing greater service to the group. Therefore, that which has been suggested for the clearing and maintaining of communication for the mated pair is also recommended for the grouping of three.

Is there another query?

Carla: If he doesn't mind, I'd like to follow up on that because it's—I'm very interested in that, because we have a third person coming and because we had a three person unit before. Before the three person unit worked because the two men were not jealous of each other because I had an agreement to be sexually faithful and a good friend, and that is all that entity desired, with one of the two. With the other of the two I had a celibate, worldly, yet primary relationship. And this was understood. I find myself all too aware at this point that it is possible that triangles can, and often do, become difficult because of the angle of the sexual desire for both other entities by the odd man out, shall we say. Could you speak to that?

I am Latwii, and am aware of your query. Our response to this query must, of course, be in a general sense, for each situation is quite different from any other. There must be in such a relationship, indeed, within any relationship of three, an agreement that is clearly understood and which is valued by each entity within the threesome. This agreement is that which defines the boundaries of that which is acceptable and that which is not acceptable. It is well for each entity within the grouping of three to consider well what each desires from the relationship, from the grouping, and speak clearly these desires to those within the group so that all may be clearly understood and utilized as the means by which decisions shall be made. It is often the case that there are secret desires that are not spoken, perhaps not even fully recognized by the one holding the secret desire.

Therefore, it is well for each entity before entering into such a relationship to explore carefully that which is within the heart, shall we say, and within the mind, exploring each possibility so that the self might be known to the self and then shared clearly and truly with the other selves within the group in order that the foundation for the relationship might be built upon firm ground.

There will be difficulties from time to time within the relationship due to misperceptions. These can be dealt with with clear communication if all has been clearly revealed before entering into the relationship. When there are hidden desires there is the increased possibility that there shall be the increased difficulty at a later time within the relationship that will need resolution.

Is there a further query?

Carla: There's something I've wondered about for some time and haven't been able to figure out why it is true. It is true that spiritually I'm far more compatible with my husband than I am with most of the people at the church where I go. Yet, my husband is completely unchurched, and I myself find extreme consolation in the Eucharist and in the church beauty in general, singing the sacred music and so forth. I had chances to marry Christian people who would seemingly share my path more exactly. Yet, it was given to me not to make those choices. There was just no possibility of my making that choice. It had to be with this entity who is so different from me but who somehow seems more spiritually kindred to me than meets the eye. I imagine there are a lot of things like this, a lot of relationships like this. And I wonder what is the key, when two people are so different? What brings them together? What keeps them together? Why is a spiritual path obviously not shared literally like, "If you're not a Christian you cannot share my path," but rather in a far more broad a sense of religiosity, that is, "We all need to find some way to come to God." If you can make a question of that.

I am Latwii, and am aware of your query, my sister, and we shall attempt to respond. The desire that is at the heart of each life experience is in truth for each entity the desire to know the Creator, to know the self, to know the purpose for the life. Many have called this the seeking for the Holy Grail. This desire is at the heart of all creation for it is the desire of the Creator, which is all creation, to know Itself. There are as many means of fulfilling this desire as there are portions of the creation.

There are many entities, such as those gathered here this evening, who have put form to this desire in a manner which has meaning to the entity. The form will undoubtedly vary from one entity to another because of the uniqueness that is the hallmark of this creation. Though the forms may vary there are certain attributes, shall we say, that are fundamentally of necessity in order for entities to take pleasure, shall we say, in sharing the parallel journeys that are moving each entity closer toward the desire to know the Creator. The ability to accept that which is other than and different than and even to find a fascination in that which is different from the self, is of paramount importance. The ability to open the mind and the perceptions to alternate expressions of selfhood and of the desire to know the Creator is most important; far more important, shall we say, than sharing each step of the journey in a congruent fashion, for there is the enrichment that comes from contrast and comparison that does a great deal to enhance the journey of each because of the other's differences.

There is also the necessity for the breadth of viewpoint to be arranged in such a fashion that a sense of proportion, or that which you call a sense of humor, is possible to experience within the life pattern. The ability to accept that which is other than the self and other than the self's journey and to view it with sympathy, as one views the self, provides the opportunity for the humor to infuse the relationship and the seeking within the relationship with a vitality which enhances the journey. That entities who are quite different in their expression of the desire to know the Creator might find traveling upon a journey an harmonious thing to do is due as well to …

And the instrument at this point has lost its track. We apologize, for the instrument was listening to another voice. We shall begin again.

… that entities who travel upon this journey may find the differences between to be an enlivening and harmonious experience is due to the ability of the wider point of …

(There was difficulty with the recording equipment and a loss of contact with Latwii. A reestablishment of the contact brought no more information.) ❧

L/L Research

L/L Research is a subsidiary of Rock Creek Research & Development Laboratories, Inc.

P.O. Box 5195
Louisville, KY 40255-0195

www.llresearch.org

Rock Creek is a non-profit corporation dedicated to discovering and sharing information which may aid in the spiritual evolution of humankind.

ABOUT THE CONTENTS OF THIS TRANSCRIPT: This telepathic channeling has been taken from transcriptions of the weekly study and meditation meetings of the Rock Creek Research & Development Laboratories and L/L Research. It is offered in the hope that it may be useful to you. As the Confederation entities always make a point of saying, please use your discrimination and judgment in assessing this material. If something rings true to you, fine. If something does not resonate, please leave it behind, for neither we nor those of the Confederation would wish to be a stumbling block for any.

CAVEAT: This transcript is being published by L/L Research in a not yet final form. It has, however, been edited and any obvious errors have been corrected. When it is in a final form, this caveat will be removed.

© 2009 L/L Research

Sunday Meditation
August 13, 1989

Group question: The question this evening has to do with service and the direction of our service. How we can discover the direction and pursue it and accomplish service in the most harmonious and effective way possible?

(Carla channeling)

I am Q'uo. I greet each of you in the love and the light of the one infinite Creator. We thank you for your call to us this evening. It is a great blessing to be with you and to share in your vibrations of meditation, service and love. To speak our humble words to you is our service, and we wish particularly to emphasize that it is a service that is not infallible, that all that we say should come under the discrimination of the individual, for each of you already knows all that there is. It is at a level beneath the conscious mind. However, when a truth is given that is new to the conscious mind but is a personal truth, there will be a resonance, a remembering, that this indeed is true—a subjective surety that makes all the difference. We ask that you keep only those thoughts that have this impact and allow the rest to be blown away like chaff in the wind for we would not be a stumbling block to any.

You have asked us to talk about service to others. The instrument has urged us to be terse. We must admit that it will be difficult to be terse, but we will attempt to be less wordy than we sometimes are.

Let us begin gazing at the nature of the one infinite Creator. It is not polarized. It is not good nor is it bad. It is not positive nor is it negative. It is. And the beingness of that which is the Creator is something called in your language love. Yet this love is the strength and intensity of orgasm. Thus, even in the red-ray experiences that seem so basic and unspiritual sometimes, you may find a Eucharist for the spirit in that experience wherein you know firsthand and are immediately with the infinite Creator. That is the energy that powers creation, that energy which is expressed by the red ray in the reproduction of children. This makes each of you very powerful people—powerful to yourself, for that which you decide to be the directions and movements of your incarnational experience you are completely free to follow. You are free to achieve that which you will. You are free to evaluate life experiences and make choices. Free will is utmost in importance within the system of service to others in love of the Creator.

Therefore, the first act of service to others is continually, daily, to spend time working with the discipline of the personality. The discipline of that willfulness that sometimes wishes to serve and sometimes wishes not to serve. The discipline of that lack of focus that causes one to feel needless negative emotion. The loss of that point of view of love that you are cultivating that causes you to behave towards your brothers and sisters as if they were not one with you and one with the infinite One.

Thus, we encourage each who wishes to be of service to others to move carefully and thoughtfully through each experience which has caught upon the mind as a burr upon the clothing. It is sticking there; it does not belong there; it is potentially painful. It is time, once this is realized, to balance this catalyst so that an understanding of sorts may be achieved and a balance found. This does not mean that you may cure yourself all at once of some defect of character that you subjectively apprehend. Indeed, due to the efficiency of the illusion many times you do not know when you are of service when you are not. Therefore, the primary service, especially that of wanderers who carry the vibrations of their home density, is to be free of care, free of worry, free of judgment, and free of negativity so that the spirit may soar, the heart be content, and the knowledge of what one wishes to do has an open door, unblocked by doubt.

The greatest tool in this first phase, and one which we recommend you never be without on a daily basis, is that of the silent listening meditation. There are other ways of doing spiritual work and they are excellent, but this first way of honoring the self and opening the deeper self which carries the Father within is central to the service of your life experience. Thus, meditate and listen. No matter what other prayers, songs or disciplines that you use for spiritual growth, always quiet the inner mind. It does not have to be a long meditation. It is only necessary that you begin to realize that you are standing upon holy ground and that the Creator lies within you.

In this way you may learn not to brutalize yourself with bad opinion. Not to rail against the conditions of life but rather to flow with them. To become, in short, a person whose life is spent in eternity while within the illusion of time and space. For each present moment has a very deep resonance back to the beginning of all that is and on towards the ending and the return to the Source. Open gently the doors to deeper knowledge. Never force it. Try not to allow yourself to become discouraged. Do not judge the self if the self misses a meditation, but simply move back into meditation the next day.

Results are perceived subjectively, differently by each unique personality. Therefore, we cannot say to you will feel blissful, peaceful and full of love as you meditate. For some, much is being worked through during the meditation on an unconscious level and it will be perhaps uncomfortable in some way. This is, we hope, acceptable to you because the meditative process is simply burning out those poisons which are close to the top of the unconscious mind at the subliminal level. It brings whatever is there that is negative out so you can see it. Recognize it for part of yourself. Take it to your breast and love that part of yourself as you would a child. You need to believe that you are whole. That is the first step towards service to others.

Now, in the illusion no one is whole. No one can perceive another as whole. When one becomes aware of the various facets of any personality one becomes aware of defects of character that are subjectively perceived by the observer. That these are defects may not necessarily be so, but for you and your universe, for your state of mind and your service, your opinion is all that there is. So gaze carefully, objectively and with a long view at the opinions that you hold. Encourage the ones that seem to create more positivity. Discourage the ones that are self-destructive, or in any way not of service to others but the self.

Now, each begins needing service to self almost entirely. Each of you recapitulates the childhood of the human race in infanthood for it simply cries out its demands and a kindly nature provides for all but a few.

Now, with this background in mind we would like to look at the concept of service to others. We have said this before and we feel it is an important point—namely that service to others does not equal the pleasing of others. Service to others is acting in such a way that you are full of hope in attempting to share with your colleague thoughts of inspiration, love, compassion, peace and understanding. It is not always that which someone wants to hear, wants to see have happen, that will be of service to that entity. And it is your discrimination only that will allow you the grace to know just what your service will be.

It is certain that you have a service and that it is front of you at this moment. That is true for all. The creation is one of order and each of you chose a life path which intended to learn certain personal lesson being of service in certain ways. Perhaps the most obvious of these ways is the one least appreciated, that being the rearing, teaching and nurturing of young souls. This has been extremely underrated and given over to those who are not parents but teachers to which the child was born. This is a most, most important service for you are cultivating and planting in the fertile soil of a mind that is hanging on your every word, the world which that young one will see to love or despise, to feel good about or to feel dyspeptic about. It is the parents in this non-dramatic and extremely difficult service who have the opportunity both to explain the idea and how important that is and to explain those gray areas, as this instrument would call them, which cover the human world of civilized nation states where every transaction is recorded upon the paper within the computer and so forth until the human race drowns in its own intellectual knowledge.

Each goes to work most every day and each receives a pay. When one is doing spiritual work one goes to work each day but one does not reap what one sows. It is reaped by those to whom you give. And those to whom you give will sow to you and you shall reap what they offer to you. And that which you offer to them will almost surely be reflected in what they offer to you. Therefore, simply being of a certain consciousness, being in love with life, being in love with eternity, being aware of the long view in truly wishing to serve others—these things are very, very important, but you should not judge yourself. And if there comes a time when you know something will please but not serve another, then it is that you must speak, gently and compassionately, explaining your point of view and allowing that person to learn from your point of view a more spiritualized way of gazing at the difficulty that lies in front of you.

Now there are many, many different kinds of service to others. We realize that in the New Age, as it is called among your people, nearly everyone wishes to take up some dramatic service. Some service that will make a large difference, some service that will be noticeable. My friends, this seldom occurs. Yet it is still true that that which is within your purview at the moment is that to which you may be of service and it is not by accident that you are in the milieu that you are. Your service is there. Your learning is there. When it not there any longer your life will move inexorably to the next step.

Now, those who meditate each day and work in consciousness shall spend a great deal of time being uncomfortable because they are changing. Change is almost always painful. When one has to stop thinking a certain way because it is incorrect and correct that thinking it is as if one were to take out an entire program of a computer. Dumping that program that you have decided is not service to others releases a tremendous amount of energy which is often experienced as great discomfort. Know that discomfort and bless it, for by it you grow. By it you polarize. By it you make choices for the positive. You yourself, however, are a servant. All who are of service to others need to cultivate, along with the knowledge of themselves as whole and perfect, the realization of the human self as being quite imperfect, quite locked within an illusion and very much in need of more information, more tools, and more resources to work with your path to the infinite One. No two paths are just alike and therefore we would suggest to those who wish to be of service to others the gathering together into groups and exchanging of ideas so that the group energy may develop service that to one person would not be possible.

It is not always the wise word or the compassionate smile that is of service to others. There are times to listen and say nothing. There are times to be confrontive and surgical, and blunt and honest because the entity you wish to serve has got to know your point of view. Do not do this unless it is asked of you. But when it is asked of you in a compassionate way, express yourself in clear communication, in brilliant blue ray. For, you see, your deeper mind is telepathic and often you may feel that you know things that you know not how you know. But the conscious mind is anything but telepathic. Indeed, it is almost guaranteed not to be telepathic without training, for the distractions, the noise, the activity, and the shallowness of the illusion that you enjoy do not encourage depth of being. This is what you are seeking as one who seeks to serve others—is more and more depth and resonance of being.

When you work upon yourself you begin to recognize the situations, to realize the opportunities whereby you may perhaps offer a spiritual thought or principle that may be of inspiration or help to a brother or sister. Many, many of these small conversations, these moments of listening and so forth, may seem like nothing at all, not a service but merely passing the time. This is virtually impossible. You are either wishing to be of service or not wishing to be of service; it is seldom that one is indifferent. However, many of your people are oriented very close to indifference because they have utilized the illusion to distract them completely from thinking or feeling those deeper things within which lie the mystery of creation and Creator.

To protect yourself as a servant simply surround yourself with white light and move into the world with the eyes of eternity. With the long point of view and whatever your skill is—and you will find that skill—do it first for the love of the infinite One and secondly because of the realization that that entity that you wish to serve is the infinite One.

Many entities among your people and those to whom we speak at this time feel much loneliness within your third-density illusion because it is difficult to deal with the vibrations that are harsh and confrontive and cause one to make choices without enough knowledge. That is the key. You are never given enough knowledge to make an intellectual decision. You must do the meditating, the listening so that you may be intuitively inspired to know when the time has come for you to concentrate every iota of your being in love and compassion for another. There is no service that is small. All service is gauged by the intensity of the intention to serve. That is what you will be looking for when it you review your incarnation.

Consequently, we ask each who wishes to be a servant to find that passionate surety that service to the Creator is perfect freedom. If one experiences one's need to be of service to others as a kind of job or chore it will never be done with a light heart and a merry tongue. Know you must take the light touch and the patient attitude and allow situations to develop until you see and are asked for a chance to be of service. Anything that may help you [help] another upon its path, any comfort for the discouraged, any consolation for the bereaved, any company for the lonely, any balm for the sick person, any visit to one who has not been visited. All of these things, even if you visit a stranger, are pure acts of love and service to others in the name of the one infinite Creator.

Consequently, to some may be given the gift of communication, such as this channel has. To another the gift of healing. To another the ability to teach/communicate very clearly. There are in infinite ways—we correct this instrument—there are an infinite number of ways to be of service, therefore your flexibility and acuity of observation of the present moment is as helpful as your sense of humor. The sense of humor is very important in your spiritual growth. One who becomes sober and solemn with the weight of spiritual service is not ready yet for this level of service and perhaps needs to find a more obvious service such as volunteering in prisons, in hospitals, in hospices, and so forth.

It is for you to gauge each opportunity and to see if your heart moves you towards that opportunity. Again the dependence upon meditation is simply that you wish to communicate with the deeper self within to find the point of view of eternity and to carry it with you in your consciousness through this life stream until the physical vehicle has done its job and you are once again free of the heavy chemical body that you now enjoy.

More and more people are beginning to feel the aspect of service to others which is involved in the idea of living in a fairly close-knit community where each may help each. This is the beginning of your fourth-density social memory complex. These stirrings, longings and needs within you to be in a communal situation, to be in the world, to be part of an effort to serve, these things are precisely what should be happening to each as third density draws to its close upon your planet and fourth density begins. Therefore, never undervalue like-minded entities, for those of like mind who both have faith—a deep abiding faith in things unknown and unseen—may be the most powerful light, the most powerful healing force that one is capable of offering within this illusion.

We suggest firstly that the meditative place be picked carefully; a place that is not used except for the meditation, if that be possible. At any rate, to meditate in the same place and at the same time of day is very helpful for the body is a creature of habit. When one goes out into the world, braced and refreshed by the breath of eternity, one has two choices. One may gaze at the smog, shall we say, spiritually speaking, of your sphere and the peoples upon it. Or, one may gaze at the possibilities. When one has the long view the level of possibilities is greatly enhanced. The service-to-others entity which meditates faithfully will find itself to be more and more intuitive, more and more creative in somehow knowing without knowing how one knows the thing that feels correct to do in order to be a service-to-others entity.

Now, each of you becomes different over and over again and you cannot expect that you will only have one service, for life situations change, paths of service change. This is the density of choice but as long as each choice is to be of service to others you will polarize and continue to polarize and by the intensity of your passion to help you will lighten the consciousness of planet Earth in a way that cannot be described except to say that it is the saving of your planet. Many, many more entities among your peoples are attempting to lighten and gentle the untamed will of humanity. Encourage these movements in entities about you. As for yourself, keep in touch with the true self. Do not be discouraged when you cannot find it. It is only misplaced. It has not been lost. Just simply continue persistently and faithfully. Although every instinct tells you [you] are making no progress, those instinct—we correct this instrument—those instincts are incorrect because each honestly made attempt to be of service lightens the planetary consciousness and polarizes you more and more. Each of you has the opportunity to graduate to fourth density, else you would not be here at this time. There are not enough bodies to hold all those who are within third density at this time so those who are experiencing an incarnation at this time are experiencing it because their vibratory level was such that they were capable—with work and prayer …

(Side one of tape ends.)

(Carla channeling)

You may attempt to be wise but you may fail. This is not important. It is the intensity of the attempt and the desire to help that polarizes an individual towards the positive pole. This is your goal—to become more and more positive, more and more filled with light, less and less trammeled by the trappings of materialistic society.

The instrument is informing us that we need to stop so that questions may be asked and we are sorry for there is more to say on this subject as we said at the outset. However, this instrument is somewhat adamant about the length of our discussions and it has been reached. Consequently, we thank this instrument for once again making itself available to us and in love and light we would transfer this contact to the one known as Jim. I am Q'uo.

(Jim channeling)

I am Q'uo, and greet each again in love and light through this instrument. It is our privilege at this time to offer ourselves in an attempt to speak to any queries which may yet remain in the minds of those present. Is there a query at this time?

Carla: Well, I have a question. I don't know if you can answer or not. The meditations we've been having lately have all been visited by entities who call themselves Confederation members but do not pass the challenge. It seems to be intensifying or it seems to happen much more often than it used to. As a matter of fact, it seems to happen just about every time. I wonder if you could speak to the general spiritual principles behind that and what one may do to continue to ensure discrimination.

I am Q'uo, and am aware of your query, my sister. The intensification of the desire on the part of those in this circle of seeking to be of service and to offer the self as an instrument for our words and the words of other entities in the Confederation of Planets in Service to the One Creator is likened unto a glowing light which attracts the attention of those entities which recognize the power of such a light and who perhaps may be of the orientation that seeks to be of service to the self and to take what power may be found where e'er it may be found and use it for the self. As this process occurs you will note the increasing presence of such entities and it will be necessary for you to exercise the challenging of the spirits of which you are quite familiar by this time.

You may in one sense regard this phenomenon as a kind of *(inaudible)* the work which you do, however, it does require *(inaudible)* vigilance in order that the contacts which you allow to speak might be of the most beneficial and positive nature possible. We commend your vigilance and can only suggest that it be continued, for as each entity moves further along the path of evolution there is presented to each entity an increasing array of what you may see as challenges which have the hoped for effect of increasing one's desire, one's discrimination, and one's ability in the final analysis to be of service in the manner which has been chosen. Thus, that which has served you well as you have pursued the service of the vocal channel—that is, the discrimination and challenging of spirits and the tuning required *(inaudible)* meditation's beginning—are those qualities which shall continue to serve you well. It is the faithful servant that gives of the self continually and which seeks to remain faithful that is most appreciated by those of us who treasure such contacts with your peoples as we are, through them, able to give shape and meaning to those concepts which are sought from us and which we hope shall be of service as we *(inaudible)*.

Is there another query?

Carla: No, thank you, Q'uo.

I am Q'uo, and we thank you, my sister. Is there another query at this time?

Questioner: *(Inaudible).*

I am Q'uo, and am aware of your query. We are well aware from our own experience that even with the purest of intention there may be, as you have discussed, the situation which arises that is les than that which was desired and indeed may seem deleterious to those to whom service was offered. This is the way of illusion, my brother. For each of us moves in one kind of illusion or another in which there is much which is other than it seems. The riddles and puzzles of creation within and without are those qualities which draw each of us onward to seek the final solution in unity with all.

However, upon that journey each shall—even with very pure intentions—find that the effort falls short. This is the way of all learning for there is the attempt to offer the self within an illusion in which the self and other self are seen less distinctly and clearly than truly do they exist. Thus, with such hindrances, shall we say, it is to be expected that there will be the efforts which fall short. However, to be able to reflect upon one's experience and to see each portion as a puzzle piece and to refine the fitting of each piece in succeeding efforts to serve is the means by which wisdom is gained.

However, within your illusion the intention, the desire, the motivation, the passion to serve is that which is of most importance, for it is the nurturing of this passion that opens the center of the heart that one may give in an universal and unconditional sense and by so giving express most purely the compassion and unconditional love which are the foundation for all of creation.

The refining of this great outpouring of caring is a work which will, shall we say, follow the nurturing of this passion in succeeding densities of experience. First the foundation must be discovered in the individual entity so that the beginning of conscious seeking and serving is placed upon firm ground. Let those errors in judgment fall as they may and nurture always that passion, that intention, that motivation. The refining shall find a time, a season within your being that is more appropriate for its expression. However, we are aware that as conscious beings each seeker and servant shall undertake a small portion of that refining as it continues one's journey in service and seeking. The motivating force that allows that journey to continue is passion, a great desire to be of service even if that desire shall fall short of the ideal.

Is there a further query, my brother?

Questioner: *(Inaudible).*

I am Q'uo, and we thank you, my brother. Is there another query at this time?

Carla: No, thank you.

I am Q'uo, and it has been a great privilege and pleasure to be asked to join your circle of seeking this evening *(inaudible)* thank each of you for this great honor. We remind each that we give that which is our experience and our learning and opinion and do not wish any word we have spoken to become a stumbling block upon your journey. If any has not the ring of truth to you please forget those words *(inaudible)*. We will be with each in what you call your future. Upon the request we are most happy to join each in silent meditation in order that meditation might be deepened. We do not speak in any vocal sense at those times but simply blend our vibrations with yours in order that we might tabernacle with you *(inaudible)* one infinite Creator.

At this time we shall take our leave of this instrument and this group, leaving each, as always, in the love and the light of the one infinite Creator. We are known to you as those of Q'uo. Adonai, my friends. ✢

Sunday Meditation
September 10, 1989

Group question: The question this evening has to do with the fact that when one observes the study of astronomy in the various cultures around the world, the roots of all the studies in the various cultures seem to show that each culture, whether independently or through some sort of cooperation or a trade of information, arrived at four cardinal points: North, South, East, and West, and what is normally seen as a mandala with the cross in the middle. Many also have a perpendicular point or line rising from that mandala, going into the infinite ethers, supposedly supporting the universe and also symbolizing a world or universal view, the structure or source from which we all come. And our question concerns, "How did each culture or why did each culture arrive at the same four cardinal points and have so many other similarities regarding the cosmological view of the universe through the study of astronomy?"

(Carla channeling)

I am Yaum. I greet you in the love and in the light of the one infinite Creator. It is a great privilege to be able to share the beauty of your silent meditation. We may see each seeking heart, each thirsting soul, and we realize that many upon your planet are asleep, but that there are those who have awakened, and are seeking deeper answers. Indeed, it is our belief that change will come about for your people when they start discovering which questions to ask of themselves and others before acting. There is much [within the world of nature] to which the Creator has given qualities which resemble those of the human being. The term this instrument uses is anthropomorphism, "the attributing of human characteristics to those who are not human."

We are taking this instrument to a deeper level, if you will pardon our pause We shall return soon. I am Yaum.

(Pause)

I am Yaum. We shall continue. There is the simple logic of identification behind those things which man does but cannot control. The fact that man cannot control his fate is central to an understanding of third density. A man can only choose his destiny. There is far further to go after that initial choice. But it is in the body that you experience now, or one very like it, with the veil dropped completely between you and the subconscious, that will do the work that you do in this lifetime to give glory to the one Creator, to find resources within the self and to be a radiance, a part of the good of other's lives.

It is inconceivable to most people, even at the present, for there to be that in the heavens which does not influence densities. One of the reasons that many different cultures have obtained the same basic information is that many sought the same information at a time when that information was ripe as the fruit on the vine and ready to be plucked for good or for ill.

Given that man is an entity with eyes that face forward, it inevitably follows that he has a front, two sides and a back. This is linear thinking, not three-dimensional thinking, and it bears no resemblance to the simple truth that each of you is standing on the side of a ball, and the directions are up to the heavens, and down to the Earth.

Yet, this is so. Consequently, people may move about, people may change all that they can of their life paths, but in the end the human entity is limited by its own configuration and in this configuration there are four directions: before one, behind one, to the left of one, and to the right of one, relative to nothing but the self. It is simple logic that entities would see this strength rather than the strength of all bonding together in a global mass. Therefore, each of the religions, as you have said, and many philosophies, talk about direction.

Another great reason, of course, that there is something called north, south, east and west was the discovery, many of your centuries ago, of the lodestone, which always points to magnetic north. Being able to use this and simple instruments to study the configurations of stars which do not appreciably change within one's lifetime, was to be able to be far more free to travel, to learn and to experience than ever before.

In the illusion, you are not the center of the universe. Within your own creation and within the personal myth generated by your thinking, your faith, and your will, you will discover that which works for you but you will find it difficult to free yourself of preconceived anthropomorphic notions about those who are unlike you, yet those who are your brothers and sisters.

The foursomes you are all familiar with are powerful constructions, whether they be positive or negative. The four horsemen of the apocalypse, for instance, is a very archetypal image, and it takes the four groups. If there were entities with persistence of a lifetime nature who wished to observe and contemplate, that person might well discover a theory that is most helpful.

As we have said, in our opinion the cosmology of the Earth plane is too simple to understand. You are here to learn the lessons of love and to love each other, but you will be limited by your physical self and you will think in terms not of up and down and around, but of "in front of you" and "in back of you," "to the right of you" and "to the left." This is a biologically based way of thinking, it relates to the body of the person thinking, and this personal realization of the Holy Ground is the result.

The New Age will begin—for those who still await the New Age—when they wake up within their next incarnation. Some there are who have not the need for spiritual discipline, being naturally spiritually disciplined. But most have the need for signs and wonders, of harbingers and telltale signs of all kinds that say that we are all connected, that when the one thinks about something, one will receive the answer.

Another reason for the north, south, east and west concept is the growing interest in the Middle Ages, in attempting to predict the activities of the stars, the activities which the moon causes upon the Earth, and so forth. Being scientists, it would be difficult for them to understand that the thought of Love, that powerful original Thought, is that which has brought this person to self-realization, and to self-responsibility.

We would offer you a suggestion, based upon these four, in that it is a good protection and can be done quickly. This instrument knows the exercises of the Middle Pillar, and so it is very easy to speak through her to this point. The phrase "Before me, Raphael, behind me, Gabriel, on my right hand Michael, and on my left hand Auriel." It is onomatopoetic in the literal sense but *(inaudible)* the mystical coincidences which occur to form lifetime situations almost always take one by surprise. You yourself are a lodestone, and Polaris for you is likely to be that shuttle of the spirit which enables one to tabernacle with the spirit.

The so-called L-shaped shift or ninety degree phase shift is an abstract concept difficult to imagine, yet out of each clime comes a certain set of deep feelings among those who have settled there. There are just as many deep feelings in those who are seated here, or any who may hear our words. It is not, in our opinion, a cruel or meaningless thing to drop the veil of forgetting over all that has been past, and over all that one consciously hoped for before the birth. Each lifetime is a fresh start, a blank tablet, and so each of you does work in consciousness, learning how to praise the one infinite Creator, but always there is the feeling, "The Christ before me, the Christ behind me, the Christ to the right of me, and the Christ to the left of me."

This is the way the master known as Jesus saw all entities whatsoever. The entity's compassion was complete and pure and very self-sacrificing. But here you are, in the twentieth century, still wearing heavy chemical clothing, before you put on your outer clothing, the chemistry of bone and blood muscle and fat. Perhaps it is time now to think seriously about working to accelerate the speed of your growth. You may do many things. You may keep a diary of your dreams, you may keep a journal of thoughts that come to you, but at any rate you are communicating with the Creator on that piece of paper.

It is not for anyone upon your sphere. It is also the third reason or strand of the rope which makes up the logic of the way things are done. It is also true that we can only respond to the call. We do not have the free will simply to plunge into your midst. We must be bidden by the question itself.

The one key concept that has never been understood is the ninety degree phase shift, because it is a logical oxymoron. But we say to you, my friends, that this is the way it is as far as we know.

Which direction is holy for you? Which direction is sanctified? May we suggest that you are in the culture which does not pay much attention to directions, which does not cover a good deal of geological or geographical detail. It is our feeling that the natural anthropomorphism of man is to a great extent responsible for the extremely heightened interest in astronomy and astrology. We would not suggest that any take up these tasks, or others of a spiritual nature, without careful consideration, because you will be in a sacrificial position. And unless you feel good about what you are doing, the love in the situation is lost. We would hope that you could find as many labors of love to do as possible. Love of each other is love of the Christ consciousness.

So, to sum up in a very mundane and prosaic way, you have two arms, which point out on each side; you look straight ahead, and your dorsal side can't see anything. The one who looks straight ahead and sees you clearly is Raphael, and he is rich in blessings. The subconscious is represented by that which is below; is it not said the first shall be last and the last first?

As this instrument would say, the world is full of many things. You begin to experience some of the inner work of consciousness by asking these questions. The question is the important thing, as we have stressed already, for if you are pondering these mysteries your mind is fixed upon the Creator and should you die at that time you would not have one regret, for your mind would be in service to others and bringing oneself to a higher realization of the self.

You will find some differences. Some of the races upon your planet, due to the fact that their archetypical system varies somewhat from the Eastern traditional, Western tradition *(inaudible)*. Yet, this entity, too, may be aided and helped. It remains for each of you to meditate persistently, daily, not necessarily for very long, but with extreme intention, so that we may separate ourselves from the anthropomorphism of our ancestors.

The only anthropomorphic symbol that the one known as Jesus used was that of the family. He spoke to the Creator as "my Father." He spoke that he was the son of man, and spoke, "Do not be afraid, for these things shall come upon me." It was an act of ultimate compassion, the giving up of oneself in hopes of saving the creation. But even this event was held close to the summer equinox. The older religions felt the influence of the stars more greatly. Firstly, because there were no lights to hide the sky. The pinkish glow of the city at night is not conducive to good gazing. Also, it is absolutely true that each star system and planet has a certain personality, those, of course, that are inhabited. The others dwell simply in the love and the light of the infinite Creator.

Many things are happening for you now. It is painful to change. We understand this, and you may have as much time as you wish in this type of environment of third density to learn the lessons of love. But if you do not wish to linger in the land of MacDonald's Golden Arches, then it is perhaps appropriate for a daily meditative pattern to emerge.

When you count your value upon how much you aid another you have put a great strain on that other person. He has to need you so that you have a reason to live. We do not suggest this kind of rationale. We simply suggest that those who are in incarnation at this time have a chance of creating enough polarity in consciousness to achieve fourth density, or in the case of wanderers, to move back to the home atmosphere. This information is not particularly interesting to those who do not believe in reincarnation and/or the Creator. Let them, with all of their measuring instruments, explain love. Explain the power of the unrestrained mind. Explain the most unusual things that have occurred throughout history. It simply will not wash.

Perhaps we have given you more information than you actually wished, since the simple truth of the before, behind, the left, and right is entangled, literally, with the fact that one has a face, a back, a right and a left. When the circle is put around that finity, the circle which has no end becomes that which holds finity, or finitude within the bounds of creation.

Do you wish to graduate, my friends? You cannot do it by good works, although you can be fed in such a way. You cannot do it by constant meditation and contemplation. You can do it only by being exactly who you are; this is, the undistorted Christ within. Some portions of the aspects of humankind are difficult. Those who have aggression towards women, those who steal, those who murder, etc. In other cultures, however, woman is looked to as the source of wisdom. So you see, there is nothing totally archetypical about this man/woman relationship. We believe that each entity carves out for itself the life it would like to have, once it has found a loving mate. But always recognize that north, in the sense of subjectivity, is straight up in the air; south is the direction at your feet; and there is no right or left, but merely a circle which the hands would describe if the feet turned around at the apex of the cross.

There is also some dogma which is quite unimportant within the Jewish community concerning these things, but because they are muddled enough we do not wish to recommend to you any reading upon the subject, but, rather, living that subject.

We are those of Latwii. It has been a great—we correct this instrument. We are those of Yaum. Those of Latwii are here, that is why this instrument took so long between the two contacts. She could banish neither of them, so she simply had to ask which one wished to speak. I am Yaum, connected with the one known as Latwii, and at this time we would like to transfer to the one known as Jim.

(Jim channeling)

I am Latwii, and I greet each in the love and in the light of the one infinite Creator. We have been waiting patiently for our turn to be able to speak to this group, and it is our privilege to offer ourselves in your question and answer portion with the hope that we might be of some small service.

We have listened with some degree of humor with our interest as the topic of the directions was discussed by our brothers and sisters of Yaum. Our humor has its source in that the most simple of concepts have been made so complex and difficult by that crowning achievement of your peoples, the rational mind. We do not wish to denigrate the achievements of your rational mind or of your desire to use it in the evolution of your kind, but find some humor in the over-complexity that often colors this great desire for advancement through the thinking.

Without further ado or comment upon our part, we would now offer ourselves in the attempt to speak to those queries which might arise within the minds of those present. Is there a query with which we may begin?

Questioner: Yes, I have a question *(inaudible)*. You ask if you wish to move ahead spiritually *(inaudible)* you don't have to. You mentioned several things you have to do *(inaudible)* just have to be yourself *(inaudible)*. I am presuming that you mean that you just have to make contact with the Creator within and basically structure your life according to that advice and that way of thinking that the Creator would give you. I have been attempting to do this and, as usual, I ran into the problem of what is my thought and what is the thought of the Creator *(inaudible)* being given to my mortal mind to act upon. Do you have any suggestions as to how a person can delineate between his everyday mortal thoughts and those which the Creator inspires in him?

I am Latwii, and am aware of your query, my brother. To clarify the statement, we would recommend that each entity realize that there is within each the program which has been placed in motion previous to the incarnation's beginning that contains all that is necessary for the entity and its progress towards the union with the one Creator and the service of each of its portions within the daily rounds of activities.

It is the task of each seeker, therefore, to allow the program to manifest itself, shall we say, within the conscious mind and within the daily round of activities. This program has been carefully considered by each entity with the aid of its guides and higher self previous to the incarnation and has been constructed because it contains those areas which are considered of most importance when viewing the entire beingness or soul identity, shall we say.

Each has traveled many paths and lived many incarnations and learned a great deal about the Creation …

(Side one of tape ends.)

(Jim channeling)

I am Latwii, and am again with this instrument. To continue. That which has been learned, therefore, becomes the foundation and the resources which may be called upon in the learning of that which remains to be learned. Each incarnation, then, is an exploration in mystery. The seeker will do well to refrain from placing its thoughts and its actions in too narrow a restriction, whether this restriction be philosophically, religiously or moralistically based, for that which waits to find full bloom within each seeker is that expression of the self, which has been carefully programmed, shall we say.

But, it is not necessary to burden the self overly much with the rules, the restrictions, the commandments, though it is well to have ideals and to attempt to bring an understanding of the ideals into the daily round of activities.

Thus, our suggestion to each is to allow the spontaneous responses to stimuli to occur. Then, to take these spontaneous responses into the meditative or contemplative state of consciousness in order that they might be examined for that which has the kernel of truth and that which contains the distortion of that truth. And then to find an acceptance within the being for each of these portions of the self, so that that which has been expressed becomes a food, or fuel, if you will, that continues to propel the seeker into the mystery of that which waits and that which shall further inform and inspire the seeking. When this is done, then there is a clearer channel through which the higher self or the Creator, if you will, might superimpose the inspirational direction, concept or thought.

Is there a further query my brother?

Questioner: No. Thank you.

I am Latwii, and we thank you, my brother, and is there another query?

Carla: I have a question. I don't know how close you can come to answering it, but it just seems like lately, I have to send people away, and away, and away, before I get a good contact. Luckily I challenge, fairly sincerely, and am fairly effective at removing them, but it takes time and I just wanted any kind of comment you could give me on what they're doing it for, and what we can do about it, because it is a threat to the channeling.

I am Latwii, and am aware of your query, my sister. Where there is food, there are frequently those creatures we call the "ants." There is attraction to that which is light. There is attraction to the power that is generated by a group such as this group which sits in a circle for the sole purpose of seeking some portion of the truth. The power that is generated by such a circle of seekers attracts the attention of those of many orientations. Some of those who are thusly attracted are not desirable in such a circle and must be asked, in all graciousness and firmness, to leave. It is the nature of the work which we do, my sister.

Is there another query?

Carla: Why is it increasing?

I am Latwii. We can only … *(inaudible)* that there may be a greater desire within the circle that is small and yet sincere, thus generating a great attraction.

Is there another query?

Carla: No, thank you.

I am Latwii, and we thank you once again, my sister. Is there another query at this time?

Questioner: I have a question about using intuitive ideas and concepts that come into one's mind and become manifest and tend to pull a person in a direction. Myself, I have become able to be aware of intuitions, and lately, maybe within the last two years, I have begun to follow up on some of them, and in some cases they take me places, physically. For instance, I am going to go to an archeological place, Indian place, called *(inaudible)* in about two weeks, and my point of being there is to be there for the Equinox sunrise; beyond that I don't know why I'm going there, but I'm going. My question, specifically, is, I don't feel like this will benefit anyone else, for me to be there, and my wonder is, why do I … should I be there … why should I follow that intuition, if it doesn't benefit anyone?

I am Latwii, and am aware of your query, my brother. If the seeker's desire to feed others with the radiance which has illuminated its own journey, must it not first be fed itself? That portion of the self which might be called the shadow, or the subconscious mind, is much more closely connected with the programming, shall we say, which has been chosen for your current incarnation, and as the teacher makes suggestions to the student as to possible means of solving the problem at hand, so does the subconscious mind offer to the conscious mind suggestions as to how the journey of evolution might be illuminated in some finer degree by this or that action, thought or possibility. Thus, that which feeds the seeker becomes a fuel for those with whom the seeker shall exchange information and illumination.

The journey for many is one which is roundabout, shall we say. There is much movement to and fro, in order that the overall picture might be more clearly painted and understood by the conscious mind.

Is there another question, my brother?"

Questioner: Along the same lines—and this would have to do, maybe, with the question that T asked awhile ago; I didn't feel like I got an answer for it, within the answer for his question—I can either blindly follow an intuition, when it first makes itself apparent to me, and not question it, or I can—I don't know what the right word is—I can come up with some rationalization that I should not follow the intuition, and I would like to know what your feelings are about that.

I am Latwii, and am aware of your query, my brother. This bears directly upon our comment at the beginning of our speaking through this instrument, which, in effect, suggests that the interplay betwixt the conscious and subconscious minds of each seeker is often that which is overly complex. If there were absolute honesty spoken betwixt the self that is conscious and the self that is beneath the conscious level of awareness, there would be a simplified communication that would be clear and succinct. However, because each of you dwell in a third-density illusion that contains a veil betwixt your conscious and subconscious minds, there is the need upon the part of the conscious mind to question, to question all experiences, to question, oftentimes, to the point of absurdity. When this occurs, it is well for the seeker to retire to the meditative state and to allow that jumble of thought to resolve itself by what we might call a kind of "sedimentation" so that that which is extraneous falls from conscious awareness, leaving only that which has importance or significance in the current efforts of seeking.

Thus, our suggestion to you, my brother, is that you look at that which is your desire, and focus carefully upon that desire, purifying it of that which is extraneous through your own meditative efforts; then ask clearly and forcefully of your subconscious mind that it might illuminate your desire in some way; then to attend to any symbols, imagery, or inspiration that you become aware of and act upon them accordingly.

It is well said that when the seeker knocks upon the door, the door shall be opened; when you ask, you shall receive the answer. We recommend simplification of desire and the simplification of questioning and the simplification of action. This, of course, requires a great deal of honesty, which is achieved by continuing to persevere in the seeking and continuing to meditate regularly upon the heart of your desire and to act faithfully according to that which is found in the meditative state to be the direction of thought and action.

Is there another query, my brother?

Questioner: I appreciate the answer very much. It's a helpful answer. I have one more question. I would like to know about a ninety degree phase shift that was mentioned earlier. I feel like I have heard of it before, but I don't know what context you're speaking of. Could we talk about it a little more?

I am Latwii, and am aware of your query, my brother. This shift that has been called the ninety degree phase shift is a movement in consciousness from that which is physical to that which is metaphysical; from that which is mundane to that which is sacred; from that which is seen to that which is unseen.

Each concept, each action, each manifestation, each thought within your third-density illusion has the mundane nature of your illusion contained within it, for within your third-density illusion that which is of central importance is most usually hidden and mysterious, awaiting the discovery of the persevering seeker. Thus, to shift one's consciousness or the phase of one's consciousness in a manner which is helpful to the heart of the evolutionary process for the seeker, is to move from what is apparent within your illusion to what is, shall we say, undergirding, sustaining and is the foundation of the illusion.

By this statement, we mean to suggest that one must penetrate the appearance of experience and of your illusion in general, in order to find that which is of the essence, that which is at the heart of all experience. This requires a changing of attitude, shall we say. Moving from the surface to the heart, moving inwardly in the beingness, in order to find that which sustains the beingness and to find the avenue, shall we say, the traveling of which will lead to the desire of the heart when it is discovered.

Is there another query, my brother?

Questioner: No. Thank you very much.

I am Latwii, and I again thank you, my brother. Is there another query at this time?

Carla: This is a specific question. I don't know if you can answer it or not. I doubt it. E *(inaudible)* has sent a list of good foods, most of which I don't recognize, to be fixed, and my groom and I never could get to fix them because I can't fix anything, and because he works all day, so it's never been done. Would it be logical to try to follow the one known as E as faithfully as possible, or is it just a waste of time? I don't think you can answer this, but I thought it was worth asking.

I am Latwii, and, indeed, a query well worth the asking, and, indeed, we cannot answer. For this we apologize.

Is there another query at this time?

(Pause)

Carla: No, I'd just like to thank you, Q'uo, for whatever happened between me and my mom, when Daddy died. She was pulling and pulling on me and now she seems to be quite fine and I really appreciate the answer to the prayers that I offered up. Thank you very much.

I am Latwii, and we are grateful that we have been able to speak through this instrument this evening, and to be able to share our humble thoughts with this group. We are always eager to address this group, for it is known for the breadth of the query and the ability to laugh with us at those foibles of all seekers of the truth. We share with you the laughter of each seeker which sees the broader point of view, in what you call the 20/20 nature of hindsight.

(Laughter)

We again thank each for allowing us this opportunity, and we shall be with you in your future as you continue in the seeking of the One. At this time, we shall take our leave of this group, leaving each, as always, in the love and in the light of the one infinite Creator. We are known to you as those of Latwii, and for those of Yaum and those of Q'uo, we bid each adieu. ✣

L/L Research

Sunday Meditation
September 17, 1989

Group question: The question this evening has to do with stress, and the predominance of stress in more and more people's lives and more and more intensely as our modern round of activities every day seems to include so many things to do, people to see, and hurdles to jump that a lot of people really don't have too much time to sit and meditate, or to even contemplate the more spiritual aspect of their lives. So, what our question this evening is is: How can we, in this type of society that moves so quickly and seems to leave so little time for the contemplative and prayerful and meditative of our lives, how do we manage to cope? How do we deal with our stress?

(Carla channeling)

I am Q'uo, and I greet you in the love and the light of the one infinite Creator. It is a pleasure, a privilege, and a blessing for us to share this meditation with you. We cannot thank you enough for calling for our humble opinions at this time.

The subject which you approach is a symptom rather than it's a basic cause; that is, stress is not free-floating but rather has its roots in the undisciplined personality. Therefore, we shall speak about personality and its discipline as a kind of base of information before we discuss the question of stress, the great difficulty of your culture with its speedy changes and cultural dangers.

It is, indeed, no wonder that entities feel stress, for the very planet upon which you place your feet is at this time under tremendous stress, for it must be birthed into fourth density and therefore the question of stress and how to deal with it is most important, because those of you who seek to be of service to others are primarily seeking first to be of service to the planetary consciousness, to lighten it and to lighten the burden of the Earth as it is birthed into fourth density. It is at this time having a somewhat difficult delivery simply because there is much misplaced strong opinion upon things which cannot have objective reference, and, therefore, cannot be proven or shared from person to person. Without communication possible, one is left with one's biases and the stress, basically, that you feel is that of non-communication or unclear communication.

The disciplining of the personality has two basic parts. The first part is that intentional effort made upon a daily basis to spend whatever moment one does have remembering, thanking, praising and praying to the one infinite Creator with a feeling of awe, wonderment and mystery, realizing that you are part of that mystery, that the Creator lies within you as well as within all those whom you meet, and all the beautiful plants and animals, and even elements. The human entity is a very vast illusion which makes it appear that each is separate and alone. This in itself is stressful, for to be completely alone is to rely upon the self even when the self would, perhaps, be aided by rest, contemplation or those quiet pleasures of leisure which are denied to so many who labor daily and long in order to provide for those whom they love.

The turning to the Creator within is a massive basic discipline. We have times without number stressed the importance of daily meditation, and we do so now again, noting that meditation can be as swift as the striking of the clock if you have trained your mind at the chiming of the clock to turn to the one infinite Creator in praise and thanksgiving for the good that is in your life. This takes only a moment, but during that moment you rest in eternity and it is a true rest. You cannot move too quickly for the spirit of love to find you and to comfort you. It is in the mental turning within, the mental face, that silent listening, even if only for a moment or two, will center one upon holy ground that can aid each no matter how busy with the daily round that is so stressful.

It is also true of your culture that the pace of leisure has become hectic and rushed also so that the more contemplative leisure activities often have given way to the socialization, the parties, the competition, and those things which, instead of relaxing the entity, add to the level of stress.

So, we would suggest those two things. First, momentary centering whenever possible. You may do it your own way. It does not have to be the striking of a clock. All entities have clocks that strike. It may be a whistle that you may hear that lets people out of a factory. It may be simply that you may remind yourself by looking at the time passing when you glance at your watch or your clock that you are on the Creator's time as well as the time of this illusion. And this realization of itself becomes your tabernacle and it will rest you. But you must turn within and allow the peace and the quietness and the strength of that which is real—that is, the love and the light of the one infinite Creator—to come deeply home to your heart so that you do not feel any longer alone.

The aloneness is part of the illusion that causes the stress, and that is why we constantly say to each of you, "Love one another," for those who console, those who pardon, those who listen and comfort, those who give because of the love of giving, may feel the same stress as others, but, as they cast that stressful effort in service to others, so washes back the love and the light that is the reflection of your service.

Now we shall speak about stress. In the first place, this illusion was designed to be uncomfortable, stressful, mysterious and confusing. We feel that the illusion is fairly good at providing these qualities. This level of confusion is necessary because each of you are in the process of making a choice of service to others or service to self.

Now, when we speak of service to self we are not speaking of the work in consciousness which must be done if one is able to be of service to others. We are speaking of the service to self that causes entities to manipulate each other, to attempt to change each other, and so forth. Avoid, at all costs, the attempts to improve, change and modify any situation in which you have not been asked, for silence is often the greatest comfort to another rather than reams and reams of good, but irrelevant, advice.

Thus, your service to others who are stressed involves the waiting patiently for the request for information. And when that information is requested, it is well for you to center deeply, to move into the deepest consciousness of which you are capable and with intuition and guidance from within you may then speak those words which are affirmative, not negative, which are stress relievers, because they show to the one you are aiding a longer view, the wider perspective. The lack of perspective, the getting too close to the illusion so that one begins not to see the illusion but its apparent reality, is the greater error which those upon the path of service to others may make, for it pulls one away from one's central deep beingness.

Now, we are speaking to those who are working consciously to accelerate their spiritual evolution. This message is not for those who are merely toying with the idea of meditating or are not serious in their seeking but rather [are] simply open-minded and interested. That which we have to say moves deeply into the part of the being that is all feeling, which has been so much ignored and so much repressed and denied that it is no wonder that there is a great deal of stress.

We understand why much of the illusion is ignored. In this instrument's case, for instance, if the instrument were willing to be fully conscious at all times of the physical catalyst having to do with the arthritis which it experiences it would stop this entity from its service to others and would turn the focus towards service to self. Therefore, some stresses are not negative, but positive. If an entity knows why it must be under stress, that in itself relaxes the stress. For instance, this entity knows that it will accept as much difficulty as the day will bring while continuing to attempt to be of service. There is stress involved in this, but it is the stress of one who seeks to serve, and in each case, whether the stress is because of illness or difficulty, because of difficult relationships or because of the simple organic beingness which has become burnt out, as this instrument would say, the stress needs to be approached in a positive and affirmative way.

Let us take a moment to use this instrument's mind and ears and senses to point out at this time the soft cry of animals which are without the building, the gentle creaks and groans of your habitation as it settles into the cool of the day, shrinking and becoming somewhat different, although that difference cannot be seen by the human eye. We are aware that as you sit in circle each of you finds joy in the seriousness of seeking of each other; each is able to build a trust because that goal is shared.

Therefore, when one feels most full of stress it is the time not so much to ask for help but to be of help, not so much to ask for comfort but to be of comfort to others. For, in dealing with others in a positive and affirmative way, one receives a hundred-fold that love which one has sent forth. Not that one loves in order to receive the bounty of love! This, indeed, is service to self and will not result in comfort. It is the genuine desire to serve and love, understand and console each other that brings peace to each and joy and affirmation to the one which you are serving and to yourself as you see the onus lightening, the yoke becoming easy, the stress level lowering.

The concept of money, rather than barter, or simply each being able to take what one needs and to give back what one does not, is so far from the pattern in your culture that it is remarkable. Rather than seeing spouses, children, co-workers, friends, acquaintances and strangers as the Creator, one who has not spent a moment upon holy ground lately is liable to view many or all of these entities antagonistically and confrontively. For, each feels that each has the right idea and therefore wishes to be of service by promulgating that right idea. This is a most stressful act. It is much, much kinder in a situation where one in whom you are in relationship with has difficulties, to sympathize and to await the giving of advice until it is asked. Simple sympathy and consolation and the expression of sure forgiveness of both self and other self is that which will lighten the load that each carries.

Now, each carries a load. There are no exceptions to this rule, for you are in an intense density. Many of you have come back to this density to be sure you understand the lessons of love. That is, that love is always given with no expectation of return. For wanderers, who are here to aid in the lightening of the planet upon which you dwell, this is very important.

Realize, each of you, that stress must not get in the way of the light touch, the merry joke, the smile, the grin, the laughter, the good times. That is your true nature. You are all children of the Creator, and the Creator is love and joy, merriment and peace. Therefore, it is a matter of shifting the point of view from gazing at stressful situations and realizing that they are stressful to gazing at the same situation and asking the self confidently, serenely and surely, "What may I do to be part of the good that is occurring upon the planet at this time? What service may I perform?" Many times you find that the only service you have been asked to perform is that service of preparing the personality with the discipline of the free will so that one is not at the beck and call of one's emotions, that is, the surface emotions of the uninformed and mystery-clad being, but, rather, moves from the deeper source that is the heart and the spirit.

The noise level of your society is stressful. We note that particularly because of the fondness that your culture has for the gadgets: the television, the video games, the armchair watching of others competing like gladiators. The noise beats against the serene and quiet mind and creates a cluttered mental landscape in which one finds it difficult to think clearly because one's attention is scattered, one eye upon the television, one eye upon one's empty stomach, another eye upon the consumer world relationship in the past or in the future.

It is well to discipline the personality to avoid this sort of free-floating thinking, worrying and being concerned. The answer to stress is action. For, in action one lets go of the stress because one is doing what one can, and when that is done there is a feeling, perhaps, of sadness that one subjectively feels that one has not been effective. But, metaphysically speaking, the intention to be of service, the effort to be of service, the sharing of the self is most precious and most relieving of stress, both for the giver and for the one to whom it is given.

We ask each of you to give each other the gift of love and peace and laughter and joy. What you cannot do for yourself you can do for others. Allow others to minister unto you as you minister unto them.

There are many, many activities which bombard each of you. The days, far from being relaxed and long, with each entity spending time in the second-density creation of the Father, taking heart, taking consolation from the beauty—indeed, many do not see second-density beauty of tree and flower and butterfly, for the mind is single pointed towards the next chore, the next activity, as if chores and activities were all-important and the heart and soul of yourself were only something that may be tended to in your off-hours. It is difficult discipline to move from that off-center perception of the way things are to the realization that the beginning of a life lived peacefully is the disciplining of the personality so that one sees not confrontive people, not angry people, not disturbed entities, not catastrophes but, rather, love at work.

Love gives entities the chance, again and again, to choose. Yours is the density of the first choice upon which many, many beyonds of your time will refine. Here you are intensely seeking that choice. That which will most get in the way, that which will most discourage one, is one's own feeling of failure at dealing appropriately with situations. We encourage each to analyze and balance emotions positive and negative so that you are, as much of the time as you can be, aware that you stand not only in time and space but in eternity, not only upon the good earth but upon holy and sacred ground, for the kingdom of the Creator is within each of you. All of your answers are within each of you. You, yourself, will be your teacher.

We may say things to you but unless they come to you as that which is remembered for the first time, that which seems perfectly obvious once it is spoken, it may not be your truth for this moment, and in that case we urge each to forget and pay no attention to those ideas which are unhelpful. We would not be a stumbling block to you and add stress to your stress by giving a long list of things which one must do to relieve stress. It is basically a pulling back of the point of view. The longer the point of view, the clearer the challenges of loving other people without expectation of return become. That is, the simple heart of living a less stressful life, becoming confident of your role within this illusion, this dance which you dance, for a fleeting moment, a parenthesis in eternity. To realize that you are eternal, imperishable and one with the Creator, to affirm that, to give praise for that, to give thanks for your blessings—these are things which take seconds but which may turn the mood completely.

Now, we have observed that among your peoples it is considered an acceptable hobby, shall we say, to worry, to be concerned, to question the self and to feel insecure. It would be a miracle if this were not so, for you have outstripped your spiritual seeking with the creation of many powerful gadgets. So, you are as if those in grade school, handling the materials that you shall receive many grades hence, and you must always remind yourself that you must turn your mind back from high-flying ideals and concerns to the moment, which is eternity, that present moment which resonates forever. When you are there you will hear the cries for help and you will be able to respond, not out of duty or out of feeling that you should respond, but because you see a soul in anguish and you wish to give comfort. That first soul in anguish is yourself. Therefore, we encourage each to work steadily on the disciplining of the personality so that when negative thought patterns occur they are recognized, discarded and replaced with an attitude of affirmation, love, praise and thanksgiving.

How can one who works from dawn to dusk and then has many responsibilities thereafter follow our suggestions? A radical departure would be to arise a half hour or an hour earlier and to spend that time in meditation and prayer. This is a drastic move which has helped many who were stressed almost beyond the limits of sanity. A great tool and resource for the reducing of stress goes with the larger point of view, and that is the sense of humor. Any illusion has its synergies and their …

(Side one of tape ends.)

(Carla channeling)

I am Q'uo. We shall continue. And if you gaze at the universe, not with a jaundiced eye, but with the eye of a merry child, one may see the comedy amidst the tragedy that is life as you experience it. The light touch, the sense of humor, is extremely helpful in lightening stress. To laugh is to be within the Kingdom of Heaven. To be in close love and harmony with another is to experience the bliss of that heavenly kingdom. These are things which are from time to time available to each of you. When these blessings surround you, recognize them. And when non-dramatic blessings occur, cultivate the habit of thanksgiving and praise.

You may give thanksgiving for simple things: for a crust of bread, for a roof to keep out sun and rain, heat and cold in their extremes, for clothing to make one comfortable, for the sound of bird cry and the rustle of bush and tree, the gentle pit-patter of rain upon your roof. So many things, my friends, so many things which are blessings which are easily overlooked.

When your mind is occupied with noticing the beauty, the goodness, that which is to be praised, that which requires thanksgiving, one is much too busy to be in stress. One has become of a different mind. And this affirmative mind is not that mind of a "Pollyanna," but simply a mind that is willing to appreciate light in the darkness.

You live in darkness, but your hope is your light. As you hope to become more and more of service to others, let the hope shine as a beacon before you, drawing you ever onward, reminding you to step back from situations and to find the humor, the pathos, the sympathy, those positive emotions which one may fruitfully share with another.

An excellent stress reliever in the physiological sense, and that is in terms of removing the chemical imbalances in the brain due to stress, is simple exercise. And we would suggest for each that some program of exercise be followed in order that the physiological components of stress, those chemicals within the brain cells which cause these feelings, are able to be learned away by physical effort. It does not take a terribly long time—this instrument would call the time of exercising, perhaps, one half an hour as being completely adequate to remove the chemical basis of stress from the mind. Now, this only removes that which has already been a catalyst for the individual as stress and has not been used as catalyst, and, therefore, has moved into the body and mind complex and manifests as stress.

You may see yourself as a kind of transmitter, as each of you are instruments, each of you are channeling from within yourself the portion of yourself with which you are in touch. The secret, my friends, is to move ever deeper within the self in gentleness and respect and care that you do not do violence to yourself, but that gradually you are able to move into that consciousness in which stress is unnecessary.

We may say in a practical manner that it is much to be desired that entities choose those means of earning their daily bread, those relationships which are close, which add to one's peace and bliss and love. The taking of the job which is not desired is a self-destructive action unless one is so convinced that one needs to do just that in order to support one's dependents that it is worth the sacrifice. In that case the stress level should reduce itself dramatically in that the entity is aware that it is playing a role on the stage of this illusion for which it has not been well cast but it cannot find other parts to play at this moment and so it is doing the best it can with what lies before it.

And that, my friends, is the heart of removing stress from the life: to do that which is in front of you, without worry, without concern, but giving thanks each time one looks out the window and sees the beauty of the creation of the Father, giving thanks for smiles received and given, giving thanks for any beauty perceived. It is a matter of attitude.

We cannot say that you shall not be worn out by laboring at relationships or employments of the self that are not appropriate. And when these things occur, we suggest a very deep internal gaze to find why this challenge has been given you. For, you see, there are no mistakes. What is happening to you is that which is designed by yourself before this incarnation to occur. What you did not design, what you could not design, was the action of your free will in dealing with the experiences of life. Thus, as always, one turns to faith and the will. Faith that what is happening to you, no matter how stressful, is not that which has defeated you but that which has challenged you to deepen and broaden your perspective, to learn the hard lesson that the master known as Jesus the Christ personified by carrying his own cross. This entity said, "If you wish to follow me, pick up your cross." The entity who said this was not feeling stress. It felt stress only before it had made its final decision.

Thus, we suggest that you work towards that fundamental choice: to do the will of the Creator, your greater self, which you and your greater self have arranged for you. This day and every day a life in faith is a life that glows from within. We cannot protect you, and we do not wish to protect you from the catalyst of your environment. It is intended to be challenging. It is intended to force you to make choices. Knowing what those choices are all about should aid each, and, as always, at any moment that you have leisure, move in consciousness to praise and thanksgiving for your consciousness, for those whom you love, for all the good that is within your life and for all that awaits you in that larger life of your imperishable soul.

You must refrain from seeing the self as victim, and, instead, see the self as student, student of life itself. This illusion was designed for you to study the laws of love and to become one who is radiant and has chosen to give love regardless of what it gets in return. This is your environment. The actions that you take within it are totally of your own free will, but if you have the faith and the will to know deep within yourself that these things that occur that are difficult are truly challenges to the spirit, then it is easier to do the work in consciousness that needs to be done. It is easier to recover a feeling of thanksgiving, a feeling of praise. It becomes easier to realize how incredibly blessed each is that each is experiencing and has consciousness.

Your being is most praiseworthy and worthy of thanksgiving. Because you have been, and are, and will be, you are an exciting portion of a most exciting creation. You carry that creation about within you. Find that part of yourself through constant realization that you stand upon holy ground and are not alone but one with the Creator and those servants of the Creator such as we and many others in your inner planes.

We are being told by this instrument that once again we have spoken too long and we do apologize. The instrument is capable of moving very deeply into concentration and is not aware of the time and we are afraid that anything to do with time/space remembering is difficult for us to gauge, as our reality is substantially different from your own. That is, our illusion is more transparent than your own, and, therefore, has less to do with the illusions of space and time.

We admire you, we wish very much to serve you and aid you. You are working harder than you will ever work again. But this is the important choice. This incarnation that you have now is an opportunity to choose once and for all to be a being of love, radiant, giving, sharing and loving. Make that choice and continue to polarize and the stress that you feel will bleed itself away as you find more and more things for which to give thanks, for which to give praise, for which to offer prayers. Do not see yourself entrapped in the illusion. It is an illusion. Look within to the great, vast reaches of the space within you, the space that is exemplified by the night sky. You carry infinity with you. Move into the present moment in thanksgiving and praise and rejoice.

We thank you for listening to us, though we are overlong, and would at this time wish to thank this instrument for being available to us, you for calling us, and would like to transfer this contact to the one known as Jim. I am Q'uo.

(Jim channeling)

I am Q'uo, and greet each again in love and light through this instrument. At this time, if we have not overstayed our welcome, we would offer ourselves in the attempt to speak to any further queries which those present may have for us. Is there a query at this time?

Questioner: *(Inaudible).*

I am Q'uo, and am aware of your query, my sister. It is indeed true that for each seeker that attempts to live a conscious life that this entity must begin with what is, whether that be within the self, within other selves or within the environment in which one lives the daily round of activity. This process of accepting that which is, whether it be easy or difficult, is a process of, in one sense, becoming able to appreciate each facet of the Creator that is revealed to you and to build upon this appreciation so that it becomes more natural to give praise and thanksgiving for all one's experiences. For, within the attitude of praise and thanksgiving, one smoothes the journey, shall we say.

This ability to accept that which is unacceptable is not easily won within your illusion, for there is much that is not as you would have it be. You, each of you, you seek for those qualities of unconditional love, of clearly illuminated wisdom and for the power to be of service to others. It is well to look at those qualities that are unacceptable, wherever they are found, and to see them as some aspect of the self, whether they are obviously of the self, or of other selves, or of your environment.

To look upon that which is unacceptable and upon that which is acceptable as portions of the self, or aspects of some portion of the self, begins to put the focus where it must needs be placed. For the perception which one has in viewing the world, the self and other selves, is a perception which has been constructed internally and, in most cases, on a subconscious level, having origins in preincarnative choices so that certain opportunities would be presented to the self according to the way in which the self would see or experience the incarnation.

Thus, when one begins to appreciate one's experience as being that which is completely internal, one then has the metaphysical feet, shall we say, upon firm ground and may begin to see not only that which is not yet acceptable but begin to see beyond the surface of that which is not acceptable so that there is not so much the reaction, or, shall we say, the knee-jerk reaction against that which is unacceptable, but there is the investigation of those qualities so that one may begin to understand their origins, their nature, their ramifications and their purpose within the being.

As this investigation is continued, it will be noted by the conscientious seeker that there is a certain freeing of the perceptions and the self that occurs when the truer nature of these distortions becomes known. It is well said that if one knows the truth the truth shall set one free. The careful investigation of those qualities which are unacceptable will eventually take one beyond the mere inability to accept certain qualities and will take one to those levels of the self which may be expressing in certain ways in order to attract the attention and allow a movement in the perception, in the consciousness, in a certain way that is indicated by the study of those portions of the self which are seen to be as unacceptable.

This new direction is that movement which has been planned, shall we say, preincarnatively and which offers to the entity the opportunity for releasing certain abilities, services and opportunities to grow that would not be possible without the biases and distortions that were first seen as unacceptable. That they are eventually seen is the hope that was born at the time of the incarnation so that these signposts, shall we say, would eventually lead the seeker in a manner which will yield the enhancement, the widening, the enrichment of not only the perceptions but of the small self which moves toward a union with the greater Self.

Is there a further query, my sister?

Questioner: No, and I thank you.

I am Q'uo, and we thank you. Is there another query?

(Pause)

I am Q'uo, and we are most grateful to have been invited to join your circle of seeking this evening, and again we apologize for speaking in a manner which is overly lengthy for most of your entities to appreciate. We so enjoy the opportunity to address those areas of your concern that we give too little thought, we fear, to your comfort, and we shall endeavor to be more brief in your future as you measure time.

At this time we shall again thank each for this joyful opportunity of sharing that which we have found to be helpful in our own journey of seeking and shall take our leave of this group, leaving each, as always, in the love and in the light of the one infinite Creator. We are known to you as those of Q'uo. Adonai, my friends. Adonai.

Sunday Meditation
September 24, 1989

Group question: The question this evening is a long one. Practices, such as long fasting for purposes of purification, whirling dervish dancing past exhaustion to achieve unitive insights, marathon running to the point of ecstasy, and any practice which takes us beyond our normal limits and which is done with the intention of expanding our normal awareness seems to be significantly effective in doing just that. They also seem to be small, intensive symbols of how an entire incarnation is offered as an opportunity for growth, as will and faith are continually taking us beyond our limits, and eventually result in the metaphysical realization of our soul's goals. Could you comment on the degree of accuracy of this observation, and expand upon it, please?

(Carla channeling)

I am Oxal, and I greet you in the love and in the light of our infinite Creator. This instrument is surprised to find us answering the call of service to your group this evening, yet the particular field of questioning we felt perhaps might be something we might aid you in consideration of. And so we gratefully thank each within this circle of love, service and seeking for allowing us the privilege of moving with your vibrations and thoughts, sharing in your meditation, and working with the poor tools of words to achieve concepts that instruct and inspire. This instrument has always thought of us as a very stern channel, and perhaps we are more quiet and careful with our words than other channels. We are also more difficult to receive, as our contact is more narrowband than most. However, we are grateful to be here, and we shall address the subject of the effects of moving beyond one's limitations, or what one perceives to be one's limitations.

In the first place, there are no limitations. That is part of the illusion. Each limitation is a special part of a general illusion. Everything is possible, but there is so much seemingly perceived evidence to the contrary that it is a rare entity that may have the faith to gaze steadily through the illusion of meat and bone and tree and farm and city, to move into a different way of looking at the self, a different perception or state of mind. Each of the disciplines which were described, the going beyond oneself in physical exhaustion, the altering of the mind through chemicals, points towards the same instinct, and that is to press through the illusion, open the doors of perception, and see things as they truly are.

In the purest sense, this is complete folly, for in your density it is not given to know exactly how things are. It is given you, rather, to know of an illusion which allows you to make many choices, and in this context we may speak of pushing beyond the physical limits in a different sort of way. When one wishes to become good at an activity within your illusion, one spends time and practice upon the skill involved. When a skill after which you are chasing is the skill of looking through the illusion, that becomes a challenging project. Your five senses are geared by your physical vehicle to receive impressions in an accurate and prioritized manner of all that is occurring about one within the illusion at any given time. There is much goodness in this illusion, and in observing the illusion, and making the emotional, spiritual commitment in blind faith that one can only make in an illusion as dense as your own. Nothing is clear in your illusion, nothing can ever be permanently clear. It is possible to place the mind within a different state of consciousness, because consciousness has little to do with the illusion. That is precisely what the Sufi who dances, the shaman who twirls, the runner who goes beyond his limits, or the entity which takes mind-altering drugs intends to do. It intends to move to a point of view which is less illusory and more full of that which all humankind seeks—truth.

There is much talk about the Creator, and love, and service to others, but before an entity can move sincerely and wholeheartedly into service to others, love of a mysterious and unseen Creator, it must somehow discipline the self so that the self realizes there is more to the self than the everyday experience. There is hardly any other reason to attempt spiritual evolution on an accelerated basis. One has to achieve what this instrument would call the mountaintop experiences as clues, harbingers and messengers of the more light filled illusion of one less distorted from the original Thought of love, that is, the one Creator.

Thus, pushing oneself, in and of itself, is not necessarily helpful. If one is pushing the self because one has worldly ambitions, it is, in fact, a deepening of the dreaming process of the illusion, and not until the entity becomes completely exhausted from that ambition can the entity begin to perceive that that in which he was interested is not all that there was.

Mystery abounds in your illusion, however those who are most respected within your culture do not deal with the mystery, but with the illusion which they can manipulate as they cannot manipulate the noumenal, the unseen, and the mysterious. Therefore, it takes a different kind of scientist, shall we say, that is, one who wishes to know, and that is the scientist who is a true scientist, who simply wishes to understand—if we may use that term—the nature of its illusory environment, and the steps, tools and resources that are necessary stably to move the self in greater and greater rhythmic harmony with the one great original Thought of love.

This is the search for truth. In many it expresses itself as the search for beauty, the search for justice, the search for the ideal proportion, for many are the personality distortions among your people. But among those who are thinking the most clearly, the opinion is, and it is one in which we concur, that the self is the subject for examination, with an eye to finding the mysterious part of the self, that part that is bound up inextricably in the great mystery of creation.

We find no actual harm in the shamanic twirling, in the taking of mind-altering substances, in the working past physical exhaustion, but we find little good there. These are side effects of something which is more important within the illusion, that is, discipline. The shaman which twirls is disciplined, concentrated, centered and focused, single-hearted. The one who runs beyond his limitations runs because he desires that altered state of consciousness. The [one] who takes the chemical substance to alter the consciousness does so because of a realization that there is an illusion to be penetrated. However, entities need to grow organically, step by step, inch by inch, little by little. To overstep the self is to cause confusion and pain.

Thusly, although we fully accept the value of the insights gained in going beyond the self, we urge each to consider using the consciousness itself, the analytical consciousness, the intuition, and all the tools and resources that you have gained in your spiritual study, to move into meditation in a natural and organic fashion, and to await patiently the altering of the consciousness that this will inevitably bring. It is not usual for this practice to bring enlightenment in a moment.

We find meditation more acceptable than the guru/chela relationship which this instrument is aware of, for though the teacher to the student, the student becoming a teacher and teaching the student, is acceptable, again the guru, which one adores rather than adoring the Creator, is perhaps missing the fact that the guru, the student, and the Creator are one, and all of them are love.

To achieve this consciousness in a steady state is to work day by day to keep the mind upon the present and eternal moment, to keep the senses alert and the sense of humor sharpened and honed to see the wit of the world as it passes by completely disheveled and most humorous. It is good to laugh at the self, for to laugh at the self is to heal the self. Move into meditation each day, and use the faith and the will that one would use in pushing past one's physical limits to quiet the mind, to hone and sharpen the attention, the listening of the meditation, and to remember throughout each day to move back into that consciousness achieved in meditation as it were a room to which you had access by grace.

This room is within you. It is the closet of the spirit, the sanctum sanctorum of the inner temple. There is perfect truth, there within lies perfect consciousness, undistorted, but it is buried very, very deeply. We still seek the truth, and we are those of the wisdom density, which is, shall we say, two grades above your own. Yet we are enthusiastic about the simple process of meditation, until one knows the truth of who one is, and one sees day by day the distortions and misunderstandings that have crept in because of a lack of trust, a lack of faith, or a lack of will. The key, permanently to changing one's perception of the illusion, is persistent, daily listening in silence, that which you call the silent meditation. Each of you, indeed, all who meditate, need constantly to be attempting, in this context, to push the self toward a pure, deeper communion with the one Creator, in that holy ground within. Yes, it is true that the fast run race and the sudden, startling, beautiful observation coming from an altered mind are charming things, but they are not organic, they are not of the spirit, but are tricks done to the physical vehicle in order partially to free consciousness from its vehicle.

Now, each of you needs, not simply the silent meditation, but the experience of true worship and adoration. It is for this reason that so many move toward the guru/student relationship. We would suggest that a support group of those who are of like mind, but who are considered colleagues, is a more natural and honest way of attempting to pierce the illusion, of attempting to see the truth, of attempting to move past the dragon and find the treasure that lies so deeply within you, each of you.

Thus, we encourage you to encourage each other, in love, by loving each other, by honesty with each other, by serving each other, by communicating with each other. The consciousnesses within each, then, are together attempting to move into a more centered and focused place within the mind where the illusion is not subject, and where the unity of all things may begin to be felt in an organic fashion so that it is not intellectual knowledge, it is not remembered knowledge, it is experienced knowledge, and not experienced because of something outside the self, but experienced because each seeks to know the truth, seeks to serve each other, and seeks to worship and love the one infinite Creator. Worship may be done in many, many ways. We do encourage each to cultivate the ability to worship, to bow down and give thanks, praise and glory. We do not feel that there is any semantic difficulty, for all stories about the Creator are effective to some and not to others. It is a matter of finding the path that is truly most excellent for you.

When in communion with others of like mind, the experience of each becomes a resource of all. This is the beginning of a social memory complex. Each may then be teacher to each by reflecting that person's image back faithfully, honestly and clearly, without prejudice of any kind. This is what is to be hoped for in companionship. That friend which is true and wishes to serve will tell the exact truth as it knows it, will encourage, exhort and caution when those feelings spontaneously come over one, will in fact be a living mirror for those within the community. This is an excellent and organic and, as far as we are concerned, most normal and healthful way of achieving an acceleration in spiritual growth, especially for those who are wanderers, and wishing to remove all karma before the physical death of this life.

To be able to live in love is not given to many. For most, the struggle towards the love that lies beyond our definition is a long one, and there is no proof that there is such a Creator, that there is such a love. Indeed, within the illusion, the finger points towards a creator of chaos, dishevelment, constant worsening of conditions, and an eventual suicidal end to the human race. You may gaze at the illusion, or you may seek in silence for the truth. If there has been no experience of worship in the life experience so far, perhaps it is not so bad an idea to use a chemical, or the shamanic dancing, or the Sufi dancing beyond exhaustion, so that one may at least feel an objective referent to the feeling that all are one, and all is love. But it is not well to depend upon any exterior influence, for the mind, the spirit, are not of you, which is true, and by mind we do not mean that bio-computer which is the brain, but rather the consciousness which uses that computer. Do not let the computer use you. Stay with the heart, stay with the emotions. Herein lies your deepest mind, your canniest intelligence. One must be cautious to ensure that one is not simply acting whimsically. One must take thoughts of change into meditation, and feel deeply the guidance that comes with each step which you have prepared for yourself within this incarnation. Move past yourselves by all means, for you are unlimited and imperishable beings. You are infinite and you are eternal. Seek to feel that consciousness. Seek to feel that worship, and that unity.

We wish you a brightly whetted ax of desire, and a tree of experience to cut down that is not so cross-grained as to make the incarnational experience difficult. There are those who choose the difficult incarnational experiences. There are reasons for these choices having to do with personal growth, for those who are dealing with some handicap are also pushing through into another state of consciousness, that is, one which is less aware of one's disability. Each of you are citizens of the universe. Gaze at the stars, and know that mystery lies within you. Seek for it, hope for it, pray for it, and wait for it.

We would at this time transfer to the one known as Jim, that this entity may answer any queries and then close the meditation. We leave this instrument in love and light.

(Jim channeling)

I am Oxal, and greet each again in love and light through this instrument. It is our privilege at this time to offer ourselves in the attempt to speak to those queries which yet remain upon the mind. May we ask if there is a query with which we may begin?

Carla: I feel as though the three of us in this room, and also Don, and some few others that we have met, are really like a family although we were born to many different mothers and fathers. Could you comment?

I am Oxal, and we may comment to a degree. Those of like mind form a kind of family. That the minds desire to serve and that the minds find a harmony within the self that might be shared with others, and that the entities with such minds have the will to offer themselves in a free and open manner are characteristics which create an environment in which the concept of family as you know it within your culture may take root and, indeed, may flourish. That entities discover these qualities within themselves and within other selves with whom they shall or do share experience, and have origins within this incarnation from many places, is explained in some instances by the reverberations, shall we say, of this quality of family that sound from another home, shall we say.

There are many upon your planet at this time that have removed themselves from other densities and planetary influences for the purposes of offering services that are needed as this planetary entity, which you call Earth, makes its entrance into the density of understanding[2]. Therefore, there are many who have found service in joining in incarnation with their own kind, shall we say. Upon your planet at this time there are many of these that you call wanderers that work individually, letting the life's experience shine to those in the immediate vicinity. There are others that join together with those that you may see as family in order that their services might be enhanced. You are aware of many entities with whom you feel this quality of family, and are aware that the overriding purpose of each entity's incarnation is the offering of service to this planetary sphere.

(Side one of tape ends.)

I am Oxal, and am with this instrument. Is there another query at this time?

Carla: I would like a validation. I understand that you can give validation if the person already knows something, and I do feel this is what happened, but it would be comforting to have it validated. Did my father say good-bye to me on the beach and in the water and when I was singing right after he passed into larger life?

---

[2] Carla: In some of the older material, I can remember this being used, most specifically by George Hunt Williamson's channeling of Brother Philip where Philip referred to fourth density as the density of love and understanding. I have tended more recently (post Ra Material) to use the "understanding" part for fifth density, however, and reserve the fourth for "love." I don't think that literal understanding is fourth—we have to love first, then go for the counterbalance of moving the mind in again.

I am Oxal. We have some difficulty with this instrument at this time. We shall allow this instrument to pause.

(Pause)

I am Oxal. The experience of which you speak upon the beach as you were feeling the movement of energy through your being was in part not just the reaching to you by the entity that was your father within this incarnation, but was also a reaching by you to this entity as a deeper portion of your mind complex was aware of his movement from the physical vehicle into the etheric body. Therefore there was, as you may call it, a natural attraction which was set up as this entity was able to penetrate the immediate experience of the passing from the vehicle and was able to take stock of its situation and offer a blessing to you as you were able to perceive that touching of the spirit, which is not a normal or easily perceived experience.

Is there another query, my sister?

Carla: No thank you.

I am Oxal, and we thank you, my sister. Is there another query at this time?

K: I have a question regarding the concept and process of worship *(inaudible)* particular view of the Creator, and particularly *(inaudible)* I feel as though I'm *(inaudible)* on the idea of worship *(inaudible)* not much idea at all of what the Creator is, and I realize that's to be expected because the Creator is mystery, but there's also the idea of the Creator being all that there is, and all that there is is the Creator, and I have difficulty figuring out how to offer worship at this time. I feel as though I need a certain focus for it *(inaudible)*. Can you offer any suggestions *(inaudible)*?

I am Oxal. The simple desire to find a means to worship is a good place to begin, for the giving of thanks, in gratitude, to that principle which is known as many names, concepts and ideas is a natural function of each portion of this same Creator, for each of the individualized portions of the Creator, however veiled their consciousness might be as regards their true identity, is to sing, shall we say, or to resonate in harmony with what might be called the primal sound of the universe as it is being created, destroyed and recreated moment by moment.

Therefore, for each portion, or entity, of this unity there is a note or means by which the entity may realign or tune the being to the greater, shall we say, symphony. We cannot direct the means by which this tuning, this worship, or this resonating of self with great Self is to be accomplished, for a part of this worship, as we find it is called by your peoples, is to discover for the self that which expresses the truest feelings within the being for that concept one seeks to give praise and thanksgiving to.

We can recommend that one experiment with any means which seems promising, and continue the experimentation until there is the satisfactory completion of this ritual. It can be as simple as giving thanks with each breath, if one lives a contemplative life in a finely focused manner, or as elaborate as the worship services that we find many of your peoples attend on this particular day, and we can even be *(inaudible)* in the *(inaudible)* and detail that is achieved. We find, however, that the elaborateness is far less important than the desire. When there is the appropriate desire present, the means to express this desire are far more liable to be discovered than if the desire is absent, and the entity finds itself walking in another's shoes, shall we say, and simply *(inaudible)* motion and posture.

Thus, we would suggest that you might begin with your desire, and give that desire whatever voice, large or small, that seems appropriate to you at that time. Let any beginning be sufficient, and let your desire be persistent.

Is there another query, my sister?

K: *(Mostly inaudible. About that inherent in the idea of worship the idea of separation between the created and the Creator, and trouble with shift to the idea of unity of created and Creator.)*

I am Oxal, and we would comment by suggesting that the illusion in which you move has, as a fundamental portion of its fabric, the seeming separation of each entity from each other entity, and from all other portions of the creation, so that it seems that there are many, many sources and factors that feed into one's perception of the creation and of the self. This fundamental nature of your illusion, therefore, colors and affects the forms of worship that are achieved by your people. There is within each culture and each religion a recognition, however *(inaudible)* or infrequently or frequently referred to, of the unity which is the true nature of all that is.

Therefore, each religion attempts to speak to this point in some means as a foundation stone of the worship and practice of the tenets of the faith. However, as the practice of each religion has proceeded throughout your ages there has been in the instance the continuing entry of the mundane and, shall we say, man-made affairs of the world into each religion and practice of worship. The means by which the fullness of the concept of unity might be expressed by any entity in the circumstance of your organized religion is one which requires that an individual's journey inward be accomplished in order to remove some of the distortions that have allowed a concept of the separation of that which is worshipped from those who worship to occur.

Therefore, we would suggest that the meditation of a prolonged nature be accomplished for the purpose of, shall we say, wiping clean the slate of perception, in order that that which is more appropriate to the individual heart be discovered in a manner much like peeling back the layers of the onion skin so that the heart's desire and its means of expression naturally work to give form to that which is felt.

Is there a further query, my sister?

K: No, thank you.

I am Oxal, and we thank you, my sister. Is there another query at this time?

Carla: No, thank you.

I am Oxal, and it has been a rare privilege for us to be able to speak in words to this group this evening. We thank you for your invitation and for your patience, for we are not an easy contact to receive and we are somewhat difficult as well to give voice to for this particular instrument. We shall be with you in your seeking and in your meditation. We shall leave this group at this time. We are those of Oxal. We leave each in the love and in the light of the one infinite Creator. Adonai. Adonai, my friends.

Sunday Meditation
October 1, 1989

Group question: The question this evening concerns worship. We would like to have some information along the lines of the purpose of worship in a person's growth, the elements that go into worship, concerning perhaps something along the lines of awe, of thanksgiving, of praise. We are wanting to know something about the means by which one can accomplish worship. Can it be done as simply as meditating and attempting to make a contact with the soul self, the higher self, the Creator, in a feeling of unity? Some people experience worship most profoundly when in the very strict and ritualized setting of the church. That would include singing of sacred music, the taking of Communion, the singing of song, and the listening to an inspirational message. Other people have begun to form their own "churches," shall we say, and find worship in meditation, in dance, in other types of ritual. So, we would like to have information concerning worship.

(Carla channeling)

I am Q'uo, and I greet you in the love and in the light of the one infinite Creator in Whose name we come among you as brothers and sisters seeking the light and the love of the infinite One. We were with this instrument prior to the meeting, reading over the instrument's shoulder, as it were, as the instrument studies the progress of those whom she is teaching. Consequently, we were swift to answer. However, this question strikes at the heart of that which is to be learned upon the Earth plane within third density at this time.

You ask about worship. We find that worship is a daunting word in your society. Worship denotes that which takes place within an acceptable church or temple. Worship is that which is finite. Worship is that which is ritualized, and so forth. In this way, many of those who are unable to deal with the proliferation of doctrine and dogma in settled religions find that they have lost the ability to worship, for they have lost their innocence, shall we say, and no longer believe that the Creator is separate and far apart from Its creation. Each seeker becomes aware subjectively that the Creator is imminent and at all times with each seeking entity. It is the entity's decision to open the door to Love.

This is a large enough subject that we ponder the most clear way of proceeding. We shall begin with the concepts which are foreign to the culture of which you all are a part. Within those who follow the path of the guru and the chela, the concentration of worship is seen as a continuation of student, teacher and the Creator, all being one. This, however, gives the devotee of the one infinite Creator a living entity to adore, with feet that may be kissed and with hands that may receive garlands of flowers. In this way, the adoration of an entity which is seen is accomplished, and that entity is seen as a representative, or as one with, the infinite One.

There are many distortions within this way of worship involving, of course, the unfinished business of humankind which the most enlightened teacher still has to experience. Thus, the adoration is often less than pure as the entity is less than a pure representative of love. So, we shall turn to the options available to those wondering whether to worship within a structure made by others, a structure made by the self, or simply in silent communion.

This instrument is a good example of the entity which is a natural mystic. The entity also experiences sensitively through each sense. We find that neither the word sensuous nor sensual has connotations in your language which are spiritual. Yet, the heightening of all the senses is an aid to the keenness and whetting of the appetite for worship of the one infinite Creator. This instrument has simply chosen to ignore those doctrines which it cannot and will never understand. Therefore, the instrument keeps its mind upon a pure emotion, ways of feeling that are private between the self and that greater Self, which is all that there is. Because of this instrument's persistence in this practice and because of its ability to move through the service discarding that which it does not wish to take in, it has been able to use a system of stimulation of the senses which is intended to evoke strong emotional release.

Prayers and worship are many, many things. They may be praise. They may be thanksgiving. They may be intercession. They may simply be a statement of adoration. Or, indeed, it may be the silent communion tabernacling with the One Who is All, knowing that self is indeed upon holy ground, standing at both the beginning and the ending of the great cycle of creation while it experiences the illusion of the passing of time.

The purpose of the emotions evoked through worship is to so purify and clarify within a seeker the emotions of unconditional love that the entity becomes aware of the Source of unconditional love. When it is realized that the Creator is truly within, and the whole creation also, then it may be seen that it is an internal matter: the small human self through purified emotion opening the gateway to a deeper and deeper awareness of the Christ-self, the Creator-self, that is the core, the reality, the beginning and the ending of each.

One cannot cause oneself to feel emotion. One may behave in such a way as to indicate emotion, but there is the inner knowledge of the depth of that particular emotion. And what the seeker wishes to do is to intensify, by steps which are natural and unforced, one's emotions of adoration and worship of that great Self which is at the core of all that there is. Many simply go through the motions, hoping that worship will strike from the sky as lightning. However, it is to the persistent, steadfast, daily plodder, the one who walks with slow, firm steps, who accepts the dust and difficulty of the spiritual path of service to others, who is best able to begin the discipline of the personality that leads one to be able to release the personality and the limitations of human understanding, if we may use that term.

The understanding which each gathers is extremely helpful within this illusion and is intended for instruction that one may learn how better to love. However, all things within the illusion are distorted, not only the general things but the specific things in each entity's life experience. Each sensibility receives and perceives information in an unique way according to the eccentricities or idiosyncrasies of that entity's personality. There is a great problem with those who have come to an understanding that the Creator is within. Does one wish to worship the self? One would think, surely not—the self with the clay feet and the foolish mind and the sometimes unsteady heart. Worship is not possible from any entity. Worship is an emotion that flows through the entity.

Now, the beginning of worship is a clear realization that the true self of you is the Creator, that you are love, and that within you is the capability of manifesting or channeling the love and the light of the infinite One though each of you are within a finite illusion and, therefore, are unable of yourselves to generate infinite emotion. Within your culture the attitude toward the teacher is not that of adoration and worship. Within your cultural nexus this would seem to be blasphemy. The next great step, then, in preparing oneself for worship, is to yield up the humanness of the self, gladly, willingly and eagerly, to release oneself from the limitations of making sense, of being rational, of analyzing, thinking, concentrating, pondering and so forth. An emotion is experienced; it is not *an* experience. It is that which occurs *to* one.

And why would this occur? Let us gaze at the nature and the face of the Creator. Oh, how many books have been written about the Father/Mother/Creator of all that there is. How many words have been written, how many paths have been taken, to attempt to gain from the self wisdom, knowledge and information that may make one holy, sanctified and blessed. This type of belief that understanding and information will move one forward, to the exclusion of purified emotions, is termed among people "gnosticism," and is indeed, though not heretical, an ambiguous and unsuccessful road upon which to travel in search of the one infinite Creator.

Now, you see many, many wish to be of service to others. Many feel the need to express love to others. But first there must be two realizations. The first realization is that the Creator loves you with a passion most intense, for you are a portion of the Creator experiencing Itself—love experiencing love. True worship is a response to the unconditional love that lies at the center of the universe and of your being. Within you is infinity and within that infinity, an infinite intelligence. And this principle is one of love and so all that there is is love.

Yet, you would wish, and we would recommend, that you strive to attain the emotion of worship, for within the process of moving toward worship one first dies to the self. That is, one releases oneself from one's humanity, one surrenders the self to the greater Self that lies within in complete trust that that which is love may be answered with the most profound and purified love in return.

The one known as Jesus was a teacher particularly adapted to offering these teachings. Yet, they were misunderstood, misquoted and, to some extent, lost, for this entity always declared that it was not he who spoke but the Father within, an indication of his own surrender to the infinite One Which lies at the heart of each and everything in creation.

Some entities feel emotions of any kind with far more ease than others. Thus, we ask each entity to move toward worship, allowing itself whatever latitude it needs to work with the distortions of the self, to bypass that which is not held in faith. Worship is not an artifact of belief. Worship is a purified emotion from the self to the Self to the self to the Self to the self. One self may be capitalized; that is the Self within. The other self is your outer shell which is as a shadow dancing upon the wall of reality.

Your physical shells are illusory. Your creation as you perceive it with your senses is illusory. And, indeed, the reason that many mystics are able to continue worshipping within the established church is that they have been able to separate themselves from the judgment of Self versus self and are able to see teachers, such as the one known as Jesus, not as objects of worship and adoration, but as worthy entities leaving a legacy of wisdom and compassion. Because of the times in which this entity offered its ministry, all of the senses were valued, and, thus, each sense was stimulated to align the mind to obedient and complete surrender to that greater Self within. The music, the incense, the taste of body and blood of heaven, the smells and feelings of those buildings which are considered holy and which have been upheld in prayer, occupy the surface consciousness to great extent, thereby making it far more easy for the entity to move deeply into the self and open that inner door which none other shall ever open, to find love waiting, love so profound, so undeniable, so joyful that one cannot help but love, worship and adore in return.

The Creator is, to use your word, holy and sanctified. Each of you is likewise holy and sanctified. But there is, shall we say, the surface illusion to be penetrated. As always, for this we recommend daily meditation and the daily contemplation at day's end of those things which have moved each so that one is familiar with one's human self and may find it easier and more safe to put aside, knowing that the surface self shall be resumed at a time when these purified emotions have surged through the spiritual shuttle which moves each into the infinite and eternal reality of the circle of creation.

People do not wish to worship themselves. Yet, as they go to the churches they cannot find a Creator to worship for they cannot accept many things about the experience of the so-called spiritual fellowship. Those entering in the spiritual fellowship are of all stages of development of self-awareness and, therefore, there is great pressure on many within your organized religions to manipulate, to impress upon others the idea one has of oneself, to do things a way which seems correct as opposed to a way which seems not. And that intensive effort which would be given to pure experience within a service is frittered away in, shall we say, church politics and busywork.

If the seeker seeks within the organized religions, let the seeker's seeking be daily and not dependent upon that which one does for service. For without worship, love and adoration of the one infinite Creator filling one's soul with inspiration, the services to others will not be of the highest and best that you may obtain in this stable manner. They will be distortions of that expression, distortions which are designed by the surface self and which therefore limit the infinity of the outpouring of the love that is the principle and nature of the Creator and of creation.

To be in worship and adoration is to walk the path of angels. To move from that path to the daily round of activities is a sorry shock for most. Yet, we would suggest that it is the daily grounding of the self in surrender to the great Self within that may bring that eternity, that infinity of love into manifestation through the very being and nature of the entity. There is much sacrifice in this path, but as the teacher known as Jesus said, "I do not come to bring peace, but a sword." That sword shall refine and refine the choice that each makes to be of service to the infinite Creator. The peace that is found in the service of that infinite Creator is a peace found only in complete surrender.

This is the sticking point for many who do not wish to surrender what seems to them their free will in order to worship that which cannot be seen, that which is intangible and has no objective referent. It seems equally improbable that one would worship another or that one would worship the interior of one's being. In daily meditation, in listening, and in opening that inner door to that principle of love which meekly stands waiting to enter, is to begin the process of spiritual evolution that results in what this instrument would call "praying without ceasing." When one is conscious always of the greater Self within, the life becomes effortless and flows naturally as the spring of love wells up infinitely through the entity to the surface entity and then into manifestation to others.

Emotions are not understood well or given appropriate importance within your illusion, for each prides itself upon its rationality, its practicality, and its common sense. These functions are those given to your bio-computer of your brain and these functions are extremely helpful in making choices, analyzing situations, and moving towards the spiritual by asking questions of this type. However, there will not be enough energy for anyone to sustain a manifestation of service to others unless that entity is feeding itself with the heavenly food of recognition, surrender and worship, and finally, dedication to be true to the enormous love between the greater Self and the expressing self within the illusion.

Each of you sees yourself as a being progressing through the years, growing older, and facing the leaving of the physical vehicle. What will you bring with you? What is your permanent personality? It is the biases that you have gained by dwelling in love, praise, prayer and thanksgiving, in seeking harmony, in seeking peace, in remembering the humility of one laboring under an impenetrable illusion. Know this about yourselves. You are not at all whom you see in the mirror. You are not at all that which expresses in casual carelessness from day-to-day. You are not that which is thoughtless. This is all of the surface. What you shall take with you upon the spiritual level at the time of physical death to the vehicle are those biases which have been created by purified emotion; that is, adoration, worship and unconditional love.

We suggest to those who wish to form …

(Side one of tape ends.)

(Carla channeling)

I am Q'uo. I am again with this instrument and shall continue briefly. For those who wish to enter ever more deeply into the covenant of Love meeting love, we can only suggest that with lighthearted merriment one observe the humor and, shall we say, the oftentimes ridiculous nature of the illusion while maintaining an awareness that at one's heart one is not foolish, one is not limited, one is of the Creator, one is love. Each day it is necessary to observe the self and begin to cleanse from the self those portions of personality which would keep one straying from the path of surrender to the infinite One. The fact that the infinite One is within means that this is work in consciousness to be done by the self with the Self.

The group meditations are most helpful in this regard and, indeed, it is true of worship in general that the greater the mass of worshipping, faithful souls, the greater the power of love that is experienced, not only by those who worship but, in the planetary sense, of the lightening of consciousness of planet Earth. It is for this reason that we never condemn any sort of religious practice which has as its goal, worship. We are not particularly interested in the specific means of attaining the emotion of worship and adoration. We are interested, and each entity needs be interested, in finding a path by song, by prayer, by whatever ritual required that opens the shell of the passing self, that self, that shell of personality that shall die and be no more, so that it may be broken apart as the egg broken into the dish. It is not the eggshell which those sitting in this circle are interested in; it is that which is within the mystery of that egg, that life, that miracle of birth.

If you are at this time only beginning to work upon the releasing of the surface self to the deeper and infinitely wiser will of the greater Self within, we may say, treat yourself as if you were a precious child, tiny, helpless, an infant which needs to be fed heavenly food. Find a way to feed that appetite through the singing, through the praying, through whatever has meaning for you, and do it persistently and for the love of the infinite One.

Worship, ecstasy, love—these are interchangeable words as regards the nature of the creation and the Creator. Your worship is only an answer to the Creator's worship of love, for Love worships love in all ways. The illusion is most complex. That which is to be worshipped, the reality behind the illusion, has no concept, no shape, no face. It is a great mystery. It is also a mystery to us. We do not believe we will plumb the depths of this mystery until we are once again without any surface consciousness of personality, so that we have become completely that which is in the core of our being.

This task is wonderful, but also dusty, hot and long. There are difficulties which assail one when one attempts to polarize persistently. There are the stresses of change as the human personality is gradually taken more lightly and less seriously. Above all, we would encourage each to be persistent, to wait, to allow, to expect, to hope that one may feel the presence of that great Self within, that one may feel that one is always standing upon holy ground.

Do not be discouraged. This is not the work of a lifetime. The work of your lifetime is specific lessons which you laid out for yourself and specific services which you wished to perform for the love of the one infinite Creator. Service to others without love has no real beingness metaphysically, and the so-called burnout of many of those who enter the helping professions is due to the limited awareness of the surface self and the lack of depth in seeking the heart of self so that those aids which one may give to others come through the self, not from the self, exhilarating and clarifying the self, not exhausting the self.

Emotions, when purified, are true thoughts. That which you consider thinking is simply that which has been given you in this illusion in order to make choices, and you make them well, my friends. But know this, that love is a steady state. As you tune into that steady state of the Creator's love, you are so loved. You must needs yearn and hold out the hands of prayer, praise and thanksgiving to the One Who loves you infinitely. And, in time, your return may become infinite and you may, indeed, live the life of praying without ceasing, of seeing holy ground under each footfall, of seeing the face of love in each and every entity regardless of its condition of life.

We have been informed by this instrument that we have once again spoken too long and we do apologize. The question asked tonight was, we feel, one of central importance, much misunderstood among your people who equate worship with action, worship with stewardship, with the giving of money and time and talent. These things cannot be done without the eating of spiritual food, and that spiritual food is the knowledge that you and the Father are one, and it is not you who speak, but the Father who speaks through you. In this purified emotional state of worship shall your soul grow in service to others and in love for the one infinite Creator which, when translated into a life experience, means an immense and glorious tapestry of love in relationship within the mystery-clad Self and with all those things both made by humankind and created by the one infinite Creator that move one to emotion: the thanksgiving for beauty, the poignant joy of birth.

We would now at this time resume this contact through the one known as Jim. We are most grateful to have been able to speak through this entity and we do thank it and leave this instrument in love and light. I am Q'uo.

(Jim channeling)

I am Q'uo, and greet each again in love and light through this instrument. We, at this time, would offer ourselves in the attempt to speak to whatever queries may be upon the minds of those gathered this evening. We wish to remind each that we do not wish to be as infallible sources of information but, rather, those of your brothers and sisters who have moved to a position from which we may see that which you see in a somewhat clearer light and who wish to share that vision with you if it is of value to you. Is there a query at this time with which we may begin?

Questioner: I have two students, one of which I have never actually taught, far away geographically who are working by themselves upon their channeling. What advice would you give in general to those who are beginning the attempt to be of service by vocal channeling?

I am Q'uo, and am aware of your query, my sister. We can suggest what you would call the basic information here concerning the necessities for certain parameters that must needs be observed in order to proceed along a path which has the capacity of sharing greatly with others. Yet, because of the great opportunity, there is also the great necessity for taking care that the path be traveled as surely and as carefully as possible.

There is the need for the experienced instrument within the group, for the process of serving as a vocal instrument is one which may be learned with relative speed, as you measure time, but must be refined with the dedication and practice that comes from the student and the presence of the experienced vocal instrument that can discern those instances where there is the need for special attention that might easily escape the novice or the beginner.

There is, of course, the need for the numbering of the group to be that of three or greater in order that there be a natural kind of support and protection provided by the desires of each being melded into a wall, shall we say, of light that serves to unify the seeking being, shall we say, that calls for contact of those, such as are we, that might give information and inspiration through that contact. There is always the need within any new circle of instruments to be able to rely upon the inspiration of an experienced instrument for those times when the difficulties or doubts do arise. Therefore, once again, it is well that such a group contain the experienced instrument.

We would also recommend to any such group that the desire to serve as a vocal instrument be periodically examined and intensified so as to continually place the tuning of each entity within the group at the highest point that is able to be sustained upon a steady level. It is necessary, therefore, to continue to work upon the self in what you might see as a therapeutic manner in order that those energies which may block or distort such contact might be kept within the balance point of awareness, shall we say. It is well to continue to work at least as hard upon the self as it is to work upon the process of learning to become a vocal instrument. This is being sure that the foundation for such work is placed upon the firmest of ground with great attention to its stability in order that any service which might be produced through the vocal channeling might have some hope of longevity and providing a continuing means both of learning and of serving.

We feel these points are a good beginning for the new instrument, and, indeed, are points which any instrument, no matter what the degree of experience, does well to continually consider as a portion of the process of serving as a vocal instrument.

Is there a further query, my sister?

Questioner: *(No further query.)*

I am Q'uo, and we thank you, my sister. Is there another query?

Questioner: Yes. I have asked this question before, but in light of the wonderful information that we have heard tonight—which, for me, is one of the best I've ever heard—I feel like I need to ask the question again to see if there is anything that can be added to it, or just to refresh me. When communing with the inner self when attempting to receive guidance to structure your life, or at least to *(inaudible)* your actions, I suppose, according to what you get from the inside *(inaudible)* sometimes I run into a very hard problem of differentiating between that which comes from the inner self and that which just comes from the mortal self that exists in the illusion. Could you comment further or reiterate?

I am Q'uo, and am aware of your query, my brother. As one moves into the meditative state, it is well to prepare for this experience by first contemplating for a short period the reason that one moves into meditation, to prepare for that meditation by structuring the conscious mind in a fashion which serves as the personal tuning, shall we say. One may ask of the self what it is that one seeks, why it is that one seeks, how it is that one seeks. This will begin to place the attention in, shall we say, the proper attitude so that as the meditation is begun the attention will have a certain vector or direction that is not only inward but charged in a specific way. And by this charge, then, the consciousness that has been focused begins to move in a more meaningful fashion through the tree of mind down the branches to the trunk and therefrom to the deepest roots that are accessible to the entity at that time.

How deeply the entity is able to move down the tree of mind determines the degree of, shall we say, distortion or lack thereof, so that whatever information is gained does contain helpful insights, more and more helpful as the entity moves more deeply into or down into the roots of the mind complex. As the entity moves more deeply, the distortion factor is reduced so that those insights that are sought and which are supplied have less of a factor of distortion or of the coloration that is of necessity placed upon information from deeper portions of the self when this information must need travel through the more conscious portions of the mind or that which you might call the personality.

Therefore, it is our suggestion that each insight that is gained be looked at within the meditative state and within the contemplative state after the meditation as that which is helpful and as that which must also be subject to discernment in order that whatever distortion might be present as a natural communicative function of the mind complex might be determined so that the information becomes as purely distilled as is possible.

We suggest that this is not as difficult a process as our lengthy description of it would suggest. There is the recognition of information that strikes to the heart of one's concerns that comes from the conscious mind as it considers that which has been placed before it. Therefore, we suggest that each piece of information be given careful consideration and be valued as that which has its origin within the deepest and purest parts of the self that touch unto the higher self.

Is there a further query, my brother?

Questioner: *(The questioner understands the basic description of the method of entering meditation and describes his daily meditative practice, but wants further suggestions as to what to do when seeking guidance in the middle of activity when there is no time to meditate. Also, how can one judge the validity of guidance received quickly in such situations when there is no time for considered reflection?)*

I am Q'uo, and am aware of your query, my brother. In such an instance, one may see the attempt to untangle the confusion by asking for assistance as the sudden and sharp stopping of the conscious mind and by the query itself, seeing the query move as an arrow or a bolt of lightning into the deepest portion of the self so that a response might as quickly be received as what is frequently called among your peoples as the "hunch," the intuition, the inspiration that is of at moment. This is an effective means of communicating with a deeper portion of the self. The degree of effectiveness is determined in large part by the degree of sincerity of the conscious question. By asking sincerely and desiring sincerely, the subconscious mind gives that which is of the instantaneous nature of insight—a word, a phrase, a concept, a feeling—in some form. It is well to pay attention to that which responds to the sincere query, that which is of the heart, for it is that portion of the self answering which contains that which is sought and communicates this in but an instant.

Is there a further query, my brother?

Questioner: *(No further questions on this topic.)*

I am Q'uo, and we thank you once again, my brother. Is there another query at this time?

(Pause)

I am Q'uo, and as we have apparently exhausted the queries for this evening, we would take this opportunity to thank those present once again for inviting our presence. We take increasing pleasure in being able to join this group, for we find the desire to explore the self in all its variety with honesty and clarity to be most refreshing, and we rejoice in the opportunity to be a part of your seeking for these gatherings. We again remind each that we would offer only those words and concepts which may have value to you and would ask that you discard those that do not. We would leave this group at this time in the love and in the light of the one infinite Creator. We are known to you as those of Q'uo. Adonai, my friends. Adonai. ☥

L/L Research

L/L Research is a subsidiary of Rock Creek Research & Development Laboratories, Inc.

P.O. Box 5195
Louisville, KY 40255-0195

www.llresearch.org

Rock Creek is a non-profit corporation dedicated to discovering and sharing information which may aid in the spiritual evolution of humankind.

ABOUT THE CONTENTS OF THIS TRANSCRIPT: This telepathic channeling has been taken from transcriptions of the weekly study and meditation meetings of the Rock Creek Research & Development Laboratories and L/L Research. It is offered in the hope that it may be useful to you. As the Confederation entities always make a point of saying, please use your discrimination and judgment in assessing this material. If something rings true to you, fine. If something does not resonate, please leave it behind, for neither we nor those of the Confederation would wish to be a stumbling block for any.

CAVEAT: This transcript is being published by L/L Research in a not yet final form. It has, however, been edited and any obvious errors have been corrected. When it is in a final form, this caveat will be removed.

© 2009 L/L Research

Sunday Meditation
October 8, 1989

Group question: We have a two-pronged question this evening, the first portion being, is there any additional way in which entities of the Confederation of Planets in the Service of the Infinite Creator, such as we contact in our group, can expand their contact with us and their teaching to us? For example, the inner-planes masters frequently take entities to other densities, or to other areas within the inner planes where [there are] experiences that are especially helpful to them. And then, once we have gathered information from whatever source, whether it be from the inner planes, from a guide, from a book, from a channeling, from a friend, or from whomever, how can we further put that information to work in our lives and produce more of the spiritual fruit, and the evolution of mind, body and spirit and the service to others that we have come here to accomplish?

(Carla channeling)

I am Q'uo. We are very pleased to be speaking through this instrument. We wished this instrument to reach a deeper state of meditation after the instrument was satisfied it had challenged us properly. We feel the instrument is now ready to proceed. We wish you a most happy and blessed evening together. It is our privilege to be called to this circle of seeking. We come in the love and in the light of the one infinite Creator. Our gratitude for your allowing us to share our opinions with you is great. It is you who help us, as any teacher may understand, for we learn, slowly but surely, truly how to understand and have compassion, truly how to temper that compassion with wisdom, by gazing at those who are going through what we may call the fire of decision. Yours is a stressful time, as you would say. It is so for a purpose.

We would now move to the question that has been asked. We of Q'uo are those of what may be called outer plane principles. That is, we have had the experience of working as a social memory complex, and we have chosen as one to move back to a density in which our humble opinions may be of value. That which we may offer is limited by the steel boundaries of free will. We may offer to you principles that are spiritual; we may attempt to contrive resources and tools for you to learn. But that which we do is as you surmised earlier, governed by a counsel which has found no single happening of that which was intended coming from a service-to-others physical appearance. It is always an infringement upon free will.

Consequently, we speak with you as those who love and those who wish to serve, and you serve us as you listen and consider. Please consider always that our opinions are finite. We do not have the knowledge of the one infinite Creator. We are merely a little further along on a path which is as dusty to us as it is to you, and as joyful.

Let us speak about the inner-planes masters, so called. These are entities which have personally evolved to be harvestable to fourth density who have instead chosen to remain discarnate and to turn back and aid those of third density. These entities are creatures of your illusion which have moved to larger life and are able to see, shall we say, the tree of consciousness down to its roots and up to its loftiest branches. They are out of the illusion, but they have not had the experience of the higher densities by working with a social memory complex. It is, shall we say, a choice. There are service-to-others and service-to-self entities within your inner planes. There are very wise ones within your inner planes. They have done very, very difficult work, and they are to be commended. However, they have halted their own learning process, turning back to aid, and knowing only that which has been realized within the incarnation that makes the entity at the time of the physical death able to move into fourth-density light.

We have chosen, shall we say, a path with a broader vision. It may be said, perhaps, that we have chosen to love the Creator more than we love those to whom we speak, whereas the inner-planes masters love their students more than they love themselves, for they are unable to progress while still within the inner planes of third density. They are, however, able to give very, very good advice and to speak to specific matters that on our part would be an infringement of free will.

No, we cannot come among you. That which we know of the service-to-others path is enough to allow us to have concluded that the most effective way to aid humankind in this third-density illusion is to speak to spiritual principles with a long view, a point of view that is far away from yours in time and space, if you wish to use those terms. We look at thousands of years, while inner masters speak to the daily needs of their students.

Each path of seeking among your peoples is acceptable. Those upon the inner planes have done the equivalent of crucifixion. They have not risen; they have not moved on. They have loved their brothers, and have so great a compassion that they stay within discarnate third density, and attempt to be of service to their brothers and sisters. We have chosen to learn to be, knowing that eventually we would be able to be of service by our being, and at this point in our development we have also conceived of the project of speaking with groups such as yours, and this has passed the Council, obviously, or this instrument who challenges so fiercely would not be speaking.

It is acceptable to seek the Creator either through the inner-planes masters, or through those such as ourselves who attempt to offer a cosmology and some tools and resources for entering into that which is infinite and unknown. This instrument would call it the noumenal. It is our feeling that as we seek the Creator and learn more and more within the social memory complex experience, we learn to become able to serve in such a way that we learn; and so our service is our learning, and all that we offer comes back to us a hundred and a thousand-fold.

The apparent difficulty, from the standpoint of an inner-planes entity, is that any kind of physical apparatus, even light bodies, must be maintained. The consciousness must be housed. We are uncomfortable, we have our catalyst, we are attempting to refine our understanding of the ways of wisdom. Learning is always less than comfortable. The inner-planes masters have the realization which they have achieved, and they are very comfortable, for they are only consciousness, and because they once stood upon the same planet as you, they may, through a materialization medium, come to you and speak specifically to you.

There are those who need the daily touch, the intimacy, the ability to converse, of the inner-planes master or guide. A large percentage of your planet's entities choose this method of seeking. Let us say that the teacher known as Jesus the Christ offered a clearer view, that is, a longer view, of the purpose of the choice-making density, by living a parable, which may be seen to be that which explains that the one who is the greatest is the one who has chosen to be a servant, that the one who is most centered and conscious is the one who moves to the least comfortable position so that others may have the comfort.

You all wish to be service-to-others entities, and, as of this evening, you have chosen to work upon the way itself; not upon the answers, but upon the questions. It is our honest belief, from this point of view, that the questions are far more important than the answers that this instrument prizes. The point of the path of seeking is evolution, and a movement towards unity, not through experiencing the self as the Creator, but in experiencing the Creator through the self. That is, we see in each of you the Creator. We see the patterns of distortions that you have woven about the tapestry of your life so far. We can see the incarnational pattern, the learning of love that you are doing, and the integrity and sincerity and intensity of your intention to seek the truth. This is what makes the call that reaches the tuned ear.

Those who seek from inner-planes masters are often of, shall we say, an entirely different planetary origin, and find the need of inner-planes masters or guides because they are unwilling or unable to work within third density, within the prison of the flesh, within the additional prison of the brain, towards realization within the illusion, towards a penetration of the illusion from within the midst of that illusion. This is interesting to us.

We encourage people to take a long view. It is our honest belief that it is better to continue learning to be, and then, as a side product, being able to serve, than to turn one's back on one's own evolution, and sacrifice and martyr oneself within the inner planes in service to beloved students. This is only our opinion. There are very many service-to-others oriented, positively polarized and excellent inner-planes beings, some of which you are aware. We find within this group a very burning desire to move on, to progress in evolution, knowing that service to others will be the natural byproduct of the sacrifice of comfort, the sacrifice of freedom, in the sense of having to have a physical vehicle and a place to be.

You see, my friends, consciousness is not as you feel that it is. It is not the thinking; it is not the doing. The closest we may come to the essence of consciousness is purified emotion. There lies your wisdom. That which inhabits your brain, that which is given you within this illusion, is by and large that given for the making of choices, this being the density of choice. Much as a computer answers a question "yes" or "no," time and again, to come up with any number of informations, so too does the mind choose what it will perceive, and then arrange that perception according to the distortions of its own biases and understandings.

We suggest that whatever a person has found its path to lead it to at this time, that it is well to follow the heart, the preference, the bias, not to move from one way of seeking, such as inner-planes masters, such as speaking with those of us of the Confederation. It is a free choice, and good information comes from both, if the channel be pure.

Now we would tackle the question of how you may be aided more by our beingness. We are parables; we are exemplars. We do not teach, we are the catalyst for teaching. We are the voice of the infinite One, and we speak with vast perspective, compared to your own. Yet we are called to very specific vibrations, such as this group's. Inner-planes masters are called to individuals. They may be channeled to others, but they are in essence entities which belong to one person alone, or one person which belongs to one entity alone, depending upon the polarization of the contact.

Humankind has for all of written history, this instrument would say, tried to become wise. It has written billions and billions of words in many, many languages. It has thought many thoughts, and proposed many proposals concerning the way things really are. Mankind has struggled to learn, to evolve, to believe in something that is real. There is a difficulty with that. Nothing is real. All that you experience, including your own personality, is illusion, shadow and distortion.

It is our belief that because of our longer point of view we are able to serve you in a way that is different than the inner-planes master, and it is our belief that you are in a position to serve yourself in a way that is different from inner-planes guidance, and that is by the conscious use of spiritual principles in living the very uncomfortable life of one who is attempting, while in, shall we say, marine boot camp, to work twice as hard as the other entities who are grabbing the gusto, the bowling balls, and the beer. Those of you who hear my words and seek to help others are those who have chosen the dusty path, the path of sacrifice, the path of discomfort, of woes and troubles and problems. You have chosen to expose yourself to all that is in whatever form you may experience it, be vulnerable to it, be open to it, and attempt to learn from it, by the conscious use of spiritual principles.

Now, spiritual principles end always in two things: paradox and mystery. Consequently, it is the entity who seeks with a literal mind who seeks the inner-planes masters. It is more often the mystic, the poet, or, shall we say, the wanderer type, who is interested in the abstract principles which theoretically govern a living world of reality. Within your own life, then, you may devalue certain aspects of the brain's limitations of choice, and realize that beyond the veil of the inner being, if one is careful, and like a lover searches for the self, the heart of the self, and the heart of passion, that one may find, little by little, the self, amidst all the variousness of free will, and may begin by will and intent, consciously to change the polarity, to evolve spiritually, not because there is a guide who may speak to you each day, and tell you what to do, but because you are upon a quest. You are in search of an unfathomable mystery. That mystery is love. You have only one tool at the beginning of that great search, that dusty, infinite walk, and that is your intent, your desire, your seeking. The one known as Jesus the Christ said, "Seek and ye shall find, knock and it shall be opened unto you." This is inestimably true on many, many levels. Be very careful of that for which you desire, as it will come to you. Be sure of your desires; have the purity to know and examine the self.

Thus, we are suggesting to you that what we can do as beings is teach you that it is perhaps, although seemingly a choice of selfishness, [better] to move on and learn more, and not to stay behind in the inner planes and help students. It is better to go on, seeking, asking, being an entity with personality, which means that one has not yet approached the heart of the Creator. It is possible with inner guides masters to experience egolessness, personlessness and nonbeing. It is possible to have great realizations beneath the threshold of the conscious mind, and to allow one's being to be moved by whatever intuition those realizations produce.

Eventually, each inner-planes master will decide to move on, for the will to evolve is so much a part of the nature of the active principle of the Creator that it cannot be forever denied. The inner-planes ones must take up their staffs at some point, must take upon themselves manifestation and learn more, refine that choice, that understanding, that realization, more and more, until that which is called free will is found to be the desire to serve, that is the free will. When the free will and the desire to serve the one infinite Creator [are one]—this instrument would say the "not my will but Thine" syndrome— then the entity is most prepared to take full advantage of the experience which this dance upon planet Earth at this time offers.

You do not need to be other directed. We give you these words hoping for inspiration and information, but without hope that any will have any particular reaction to our words. We give them to you as opinion. We expect that you will take what is useful to you and forget the rest. This is excellent; this is the way it should be, for those who are conscious teach themselves by the catalyst of gazing into the face of the Creator, in each other, in us, and in the self.

Take the long view, my friends. Find the lightness of heart that this gives you, the balance of opinion, and the thoughtfulness, and eventually, the faith that it offers. [For when there is no reason to anything within the illusion, then it is that that which is mysterious outside of the illusion has the only possibility of being real.] Gaze at that pontificated reality, and realize that that reality, that mystery, is love, an energy indescribable. The infinite intelligence of the one Creator is love, unpotentiated, unpolarized, unaware. It merely loves. The active principle of free will is chosen again and again by the Creator, Who chooses to make a creation and form active principles of Itself that It may learn of Its own nature. We already know the answer: the nature of the Creator is love; the nature of you is love; the nature of your circumstances is love. Whatever they may be, all is as it should be; all offers the catalyst that is required at the present time.

If one may have faith in this, and seek the one infinite Creator which is within the mystery, which is the mystery, and which is the core of the being of the self, then one may find one's way to a way of living that is beautiful, and makes of marine boot camp a very tidy place, a place of happy laughter and merriment, a place of lightheartedness and peace. For as you learn more and more about service to others, taking the punches, having the troubles, learning from them, and not from an inner guide who tells you what to think, so you become more and more aware of the humbleness of your own nature, and of your desire for servanthood. Servanthood is not as you may think of it. Servanthood is servanthood to the Creator. One may see the face of servanthood in the face of a mother or father, who serves the Creator and nurtures the beings that house those consciousnesses that are unique, just as each of you is unique.

(Side one of tape ends.)

(Carla channeling)

I am Q'uo. We continue with this instrument. Each of you has a special gift to give. That gift is the gift of the pattern of the self. Consider the snowflake, no two alike. So it is with spirits, as they grow in compassion and wisdom and service to others. Each one has a somewhat different energy nexus, a somewhat different emphasis or area of expertise. Each speaks uniquely to the Creator of itself; each has experiences no other in the infinite creation has had, and has experienced them in the idiosyncratic way of one truly conscious of the self within.

You see, my friends, you are a jailer as well as a prisoner. In most entities the jailer is the stronger of the two entities. And so the entity moves through the life depending on outside help. You do not need to depend on any outside help, my friends. You do not need us, you do not need any teacher. You merely need persistence, determination, and a kind of respect for the self that must be the foundation of seeking. The core of you is the infinite love of the one Creator. You are the Creator within. This is not evident; it is not intended to be. You must seek this beingness within. We can be with you in your meditations; we can strengthen your meditations. We cannot strengthen your persistence, your determination or your seeking. We cannot purify your intent, or widen your point of view. You must leave that to the consciousness that is within you, the purified and ever more purified emotion that comes forward as bliss, ecstasy, passion, intensity and, paradoxically, peace. All these things are within you.

This is where that which is called faith becomes evidently different from that which is called belief, for inner-planes masters are those who have believed certain things, who have certain pathways to follow to graduate from third density. They are legitimate. There is a blindness to them, since the higher densities have been bypassed by the entity's immediate realization of the one infinite Creator. This may seem to be a great advantage, but it is as if you were only visiting and must go home. The only way to move back to the source, the only way to become unpotentiated love once again, the only way to find and be the Grail, is to walk this dusty path, learning of the self, of the beingness, of compassion and wisdom and balance, in that order, so that one may at last, having experienced much, turn and offer to the Creator the one gift that is most excellent and holy: the self, with all the richness of its learning.

May you see yourself as beautiful, my friends. May you attempt to live beautiful lives. May your laughter be hearty and real. May you delight in each other. May you seek together, may you be persistent and daily. At any time you wish for us to strengthen your meditation, we are welcome to be with you. We will not guide you. We respect you. You will guide yourself. All that you need to know lies within you. When you hear it, and say, "Yes, now I understand," there is a part of you that would wish to say, "Yes, now I remember." For that which is personal truth comes to one as a long forgotten memory that has somehow found its way to the surface. We welcome you to the dusty path. We feel it is an authentic option, a way to learn, a way back to the Source, and we are most grateful for your seeking.

This instrument informs us that we have been much overlong, as we are wont to do, and we apologize, but the question was an interesting one, and we must admit to being fond of interesting questions. We would at this time transfer this contact to the one known as Jim, that he may conclude tonight's working. I leave this instrument in love and light. I am known to you as Q'uo.

(Jim channeling)

I am Q'uo, and greet each again in love and light through this instrument. It is our privilege at this time to offer ourselves in the attempt to speak to those queries which may yet remain upon the minds of those present. Again, may we remind you that we speak those opinions which we have found useful in our own journey. We do not wish our words to be accepted without discrimination upon your parts. Is there a query with which we may begin?

T: Yes, I have a question, or something I'd like to say. I'd like you to comment on it. I try to get an answer from myself or from within—you said earlier, there usually comes a point where you just feel it's right, when you know that this is right, and coming to accept this as a valid answer, or a safe answer, or however you want to say it—so therefore I trust it when it just feels right, and I believe I understood you to say earlier that this was the criteria that we should use when judging an answer or getting an answer. Could you comment on that, please?

I am Q'uo, and am aware of your query, my brother. The image that we give this instrument is that of the garden. This is an interior garden. There awaits in this garden many flowers, shall we say, that have been sown by the seeds of your desire, your interest, and the direction of your seeking. As you seek those answers from within, it is as though you continue to water this garden, and as you seek the specific direction of that inner voice you are accomplishing the same thing as though you were to pluck the flower from that garden.

Thus, by your own desire and your persistence you have tended this garden, and it provides you with those answers which are helpful in your daily round of activities as you call upon the inner garden for the beauty and the fragrance of the flowers whose seeds you have sown. In short, my brother, we affirm the query which you have presented to us.

Is there a further query, my brother?

T: No, thank you, that's a very nice way of saying it. Thank you.

I am Q'uo, and we thank you, my brother. Is there another query?

S: Yes, Q'uo. We are sometimes accustomed to distinguish *(inaudible)* energy between that portion which is manifest and that portion called the Godhead which is not manifest. I understand that we belong to the divinity, each in a unique way. This belonging is experienced by us in manifestation. What I would like to understand, explore, is the respect in which the manifestation of divinity is motivated within the Godhead Itself and to understand the sense in which factors such as emergence of will and desire come into play from within the Godhead.

I am Q'uo, and am aware of your query, my brother. This is a large and most interesting field which you have chosen for your query, and for the sake of clarity we shall attempt to be brief rather than to explore in depth this field. Within that entity or quality which you have called the Godhead there exists a desire. That desire is to know the nature of that which you have called the Godhead, to know the nature of that great Self, to know the Source that is unmanifested from which that which is manifested springs, to know the possibilities of that which is manifest, to know if there is any boundary to that which is possible within manifestation, to explore as an adventurer that vast plenum of manifestation.

This desire is that same desire which moves in each particle and portion of the manifested creation and, indeed, moves in a freely chosen and intelligent manner in each entity such as yourself and all within the third-density illusion in which the mind, the body, and the spirit first are joined in this great journey of seeking. Thus, that sense of yearning to know is that quality which one may call the will. Thus, that which has no form or manifestation of any kind has provided the spark of desire, of will, that enlivens and enables that which is manifest, that there might be this great exploration of the nature of all that is, and that each portion of all that is might partake in this journey of seeking.

May we speak further, my brother?

S: There is one point I would like to look at more closely, and this has to do with the way our seeking fits into the experience of the Godhead. From where I stand now there seems to be an ambiguity between an understanding I have that the one infinite Creator has begotten me, and the sense in which I feel a kind of self-origination out of a desire within the Godhead. As I find my way back slowly and through the densities to the Godhead, it is important to find my way back to the specific place of my origin. Is that why one is so scrupulous to attending to one's biases?

I am Q'uo, and am aware of your query, my brother. We shall take your phrase, "the place of your origin" not to be a specific location, for, indeed, you are from all places, but to be that frame of mind or attitude of unity from which each portion of the one Creator springs, and, indeed, this is true, my brother, for each entity has begun in total unity as an unpolarized and undifferentiated particle of that one great original Thought of love which has set all creation in motion. Each entity, therefore, finds its uniqueness in the means by which it is able to refine and define this unity from a perspective born of experience that becomes of necessity unique, for as each portion of the creation that becomes intelligent and self-conscious does so, its experience is at variance to some degree from the experience of any other portion of the creation, for the hallmark of an infinite Creator, my brother, is variety. By the free will choices that are possible to each portion of the creation, there is seen an infinity of possibility for each portion of the creation.

Thus does each entity such as yourself move in a rhythm that partakes of the great heartbeat of the universe, moving outward and outward, gathering experience, turning that experience into the power to serve, to love, to glorify the one Creator, and to continue on the journey, moving then back again to that place of unity from which all this began, having now gained the experience of moving through the cycles of creation. Thus, you are in microcosm the one Creator that has come to know Itself as you are now, and shall come to know Itself as all that is.

Is there a further query, my brother?

S: No, thank you very much.

I am Q'uo, and again we thank you, my brother. Is there another query?

Carla: I have one. In analyzing what I can remember of what I channeled, I was struck mostly by, well, in the past there has been a lot of emphasis on two things: faith and will, will and faith. Now thinking about the guru trip, the trip of inner-planes masters, incarnate or discarnate, and thinking that perhaps although there is much faith, the will is given over to a teacher that is perceived as apart from the self, and that teacher interacts with the student, and the student becomes able to deal with fourth density light, but it has not honed its faith. In other words, it thinks it knows something.

Whereas, the person who walks the road of spiritual principles and, shall we say, the hard school of knocks of life, instead of the ivory tower of talking with an inner-planes master, who has chosen to live the truth rather than study the truth, and because of that the only thing that moves one through experience is faith, and sooner or later it must be grasped by any one hopeful enough to continue to exist.

So, that is why you recommend working things out within your experience without undue attention to any opinion but your own, and that is because faith does not depend on facts or proofs or anything that is known, but faith just is faith that all is well and all is one with the infinite Creator. Could you comment on that? I thought it was kind of an important thought.

I am Q'uo, and am aware of your query, my sister. We shall attempt to speak to this point. It is difficult to generalize with accuracy in the manner which you have described, for with any teacher or student there is the likelihood that there will be anomalistic experience, that which deviates from the norm.

There are many teachers of the origin of inner planes that work with specific beliefs as you have noted. There are many students who work either with a teacher or alone who also work diligently upon the nature of beliefs and the power of the mind to affect not only one's behavior but one's ability to move along the spiritual path, shall we say. Whether one works with belief and concentrates little upon faith, or whether one works greatly with faith in that which is unseen and little upon belief, there is within your illusion a quality built in, shall we say, in which all efforts shall both fall short of the mark and shall produce some fruit.

The quality that we find most helpful to any student in whatever way the journey has been fashioned by that student, is the tandem, shall we say, use of will and faith. The desire to know, to grow, and to serve must be strong, and there must be the faith that such is possible, and we find that whether one has focused upon belief in certain principles, rituals or concepts, or has focused upon the direct application of faith, it is yet this quality of faith powered by the will, the desire, that is functioning either consciously or subconsciously, for each student has chosen—and in this sense we speak of those who are consciously seeking—to move the self upon the path of seeking to know in a way which implies and requires the exercise of faith in something, whether that something be a set of beliefs, a guru or teacher that personifies certain qualities, or whether it is indeed the faith itself, the faith that all entities share an origin, a journey, and a destination, and the surety that all is indeed well throughout the process of evolution.

May we speak in any further fashion, my sister?

Carla: Well that's very eloquent, it's just that I feel rather strongly that the organized religions, if you should take them literally, or take any body of teaching literally, or any spirit guide, following its directions literally impacts the will, and that's why I was saying that faith seems to have ascendancy over belief in being a good tool, because faith isn't faith in anything, it's just faith. If there's no further comment from you, than that was just—I thought that thinking for yourself and seeking your path did more to improve the strength of the will than the path of accepting that which a teacher has to say without question.

I am Q'uo, and am aware of your query, my sister, and we would further comment by suggesting that it is indeed the most frequently noted experience that the organized, as you have called them, religions do seem after a period of time to solidify the tenets of the faith or of the belief so that there is a more narrow path that is permissible to walk upon.

However, given this limitation of the hardening of the viewpoint and the narrowing of the viewpoint, there is ever available within each system of beliefs a path which is straight and true for those followers whose faith has remained unblemished and whose ability to awaken compassion within the beingness has ripened, shall we say, and has found a means of manifesting within the daily life.

We would agree that the hardening of the beliefs provides a difficulty for those entities who do not take upon themselves the responsibility of making those discriminations and interpretations and applications of the belief which will allow the awakening of compassion.

May we speak in any further sense, my sister?

Carla: No, I thought that was very enlightening. Thanks a lot.

I am Q'uo, and we again thank you, my sister. Is there another query at this time?

R: There is one other small, humble question. I get many sounds, and I wish your comment on these sounds. *(Inaudible)* before.

I am Q'uo, and we must apologize, my sister, for being shy of information in this regard, for we find that if we were to speak in this way we would be infringing upon a process of inner growth which is in our opinion most beneficially aided by your own efforts. There is a line across which we do not desire to move, and that is the infringement upon an entity's free will when there is the process of inspiration occurring that is of an inner nature which must be discovered by the student without the teacher, shall we say, giving hints for the homework.

Is there another query, my sister?

R: That was *(inaudible)*. Thank you.

I am Q'uo, and we thank you, my sister. Is there another query?

Carla: I guess we're through, Q'uo. Thank you so much.

I am Q'uo, and we thank each for allowing our presence this evening. It was a great honor to be able to blend our vibrations with yours and to walk with you upon your journey of seeking, which is indeed the same journey upon which we move as well. We take a delight in being able to give voice to our concepts and hope that we have been able to share some portion of our journey with you that might be of service to you. Again, we request that you apply your own discrimination rigorously upon those words which we have been privileged to share with you this evening.

At this time we shall take our leave of this instrument and this group, leaving each, as always, in the love and in the light of the one infinite Creator. We are known to you as those of Q'uo. Adonai, my friends. Adonai. ❧

L/L Research

Sunday Meditation
October 15, 1989

Group question: Pot luck.

(Carla channeling)

I am Q'uo, and I greet you in the love and in the light of the one infinite Creator, in whose service we come to answer your call this evening. May we say what a joy and blessing it is to us to enter your circle, and to aid in whatever way we may with the spiritual evolution of each, for, indeed, you do us a similar service by allowing us to serve you, for those who serve learn always more than those who receive. The teacher learns more than the student. Therefore, we are most grateful to you for continuing to be able to refine our understanding of compassion and wisdom. We find that we have been given a blank slate, a *tabula rasa*, this evening. It is good that the instrument is somewhat fatigued, for the sort of monologue which we would have through this instrument would perhaps be, shall we say, objected to if the instrument were less tired, for we shall touch on more than one subject.

We believe that we shall start with the general gaze at the nature of third density. If you could consider an ice that was not cold, but merely a skin over water, that is what your conscious mind is to the ocean of consciousness beneath the limen of consciousness. Those who yet have not asked what their purpose in life, or what their purpose in eternity might be, skate upon that thin covering, thinking that it is life. Indeed, it is a grand illusion, an illusion within an illusion many times. Why are you here? What do you wish for yourself? What is the truth? We have very simple answers, my friends, too simple for your questions, for the truth is so simple that it is difficult to accept. The truth is that there is one great original Thought which created the creation in order that It may know Itself better, and by the use of free will moved love—that is, the one great original Thought—into manifestation as light, and through the use of this substance, shall we say, or radiation, created all that you see outside of your physical eyes, all of it an illusion, and all of it designed to cause entities to make choices. Not simple and easy choices, like what to have for dinner, but the grand, major choice of this density, to serve others, in serving the one Creator, or to serve the self, realizing that the Creator is within.

We are not a service-to-self contact. We only teach service-to-others information. But we feel that we are speaking to a group who would wish only positive information, so we are satisfied that we are universal enough in our scope, but we did wish to mention that there are, indeed, two sides to the story of this particular sphere at this particular time, as each side, the positive and the negative, attempts to polarize itself to the point of being able to form a social memory complex and to make use of the denser and fuller light of fourth density.

This is the work in which each of you is engaged in one way or another. The choices are yours, and ofttimes distinctions are subtle, and difficult to judge accurately. This is acceptable, for within this density the whole idea is that you must work upon faith, that which is blind, as faith moves in many ways in the context of many wills, and no two entities follow the same path as they seek to form a polarity of service to others. But we encourage each at this time to realize that all those things which are outer within this illusion are in themselves illusions, that is, they are fields of energy, rather than the materialized objects which your physical eyes behold.

The nature of everything is consciousness. Thus, to move the focus of attention most well towards the one infinite Creator, it is well first to move the attention from the world of phenomena to the world of paradox and mystery, these two characteristics being the hallmarks of spiritual truth. Although the paradoxes are in later densities blended and unified, the essence of spirituality is an awareness of the absolute polarity of this density, and the dear necessity, the grateful necessity, of choosing and continuing to choose one path to the Creator.

For it is those who choose, those who risk, those who leap blindly in faith, those who will and hope, who move themselves in a most accelerated manner along the path of spiritual evolution. It is not those who seek this phenomenon and then that. This is what we may call the spiritual seeking, and each of the paths examined, it is well to examine. But in the end we ask that you consider very carefully the creation of your own system of faith. We do not ask that you believe in one or another story about the Creator. We ask only that you see yourself as a pilgrim on a very long road, that you see yourself in transit and know that the price that you pay for accelerating along spiritual evolutionary paths is discomfort and pain, because of the nature of the brain as opposed to the nature of consciousness.

The nature of the brain is such that when changes occur the programming of the biocomputer brain must be altered. This is a painful process. The old programs are, somewhat painfully perhaps, removed, and the energy created by that removal is used to form a new personal understanding or truth, and this crystallization of the self, the understanding of the self, its relation to the creation and the Creator, it moves, but it is difficult.

So we warn each seeker that the path is not a comfortable, joy-filled picnic at all times. There are the oasis times, there are the desert times. In terms of the dynamic of human personality it is necessary that these two basic states of consciousness follow each other seriatim, for there are truths to learn from mountaintop experiences, and there are the same sacred truths to learn when deep in the valley of mundane ordinariness.

Now, those who work upon themselves may find it easy to undervalue those who skate along the skin of life. Remember always that the universe is an utter metaphysical democracy, as all entities are portions of the one infinite Creator in its active principle, that is, the Creator is made up partially of its active principle, which is each entity with consciousness, each planetary entity, each sun entity.

We would focus upon the crystallization of one's will and one's faith. The desires which are within each must be fulfilled before the entity is free to depart this illusion for another, more light-filled illusion to learn further lessons, all further lessons being the refinement of the choice made in this density. Thus, we ask that you be very careful of that which you desire, for you shall get it, and that before you may move on to the next density.

Therefore, a prerequisite to graduation from this density is to have done all those things which you wished to do, and have purified the desire to the point where that which you desire is to know the will of the Creator within. It is very difficult to know that will until one has worked with the self for some time. The process of daily meditation in a listening sense rather than creative visualizations, we feel, is central, for in listening to the silence within, passages are opened from the conscious to the subconscious mind, and voices may come upwards from the roots of the tree of mind and break through the threshold of consciousness and enhance and sustain the life experience.

Now, how should one go about this task and this joy? One may begin in many ways. But once one has settled upon a daily spiritual time, a daily spiritual routine, a daily spiritual practice of the presence of the one infinite Creator, then we suggest that you stop looking up and down the aisles of the supermarket of spiritual values, thoughts and phenomena, and to move into that leap of faith, acting upon that which moves you the most greatly of any inspiration, thoughts and ideals with which you may have come into contact. Then it is persistence and persistence alone that brings the results that you wish, meditation upon meditation upon meditation, not done any fancy way necessarily, done on the run, done when the clock strikes, done when the noon whistle sounds. Centering and calling for the presence of the one Creator, even momentarily, is a steadying and stabilizing experience, a part of the crystallization of a personality.

Now, we are aware that there is interest in crystals in this group this evening. The crystals are a large subject, and we do not wish to instruct you in them, as there are others far more able to speak, within the inner planes of your planet, than we. But let us say this, that without the entity becoming crystallized, the crystals are only rocks. The crystalline nature is that which may hold a metaphysical reality. Now, within the illusion you are not real, you are a personality shell. In order to become real to the self, in order to become conscious of one's own self-consciousness, one must become conscious of the discipline of the personality, of the choices one is making, of the thoughts one is thinking, for the time is coming, more and more, when thoughts, especially negative things, move into manifestation with ease, there being much fourth-density energy already upon your planet.

The creation is a subjective thing. We have found nothing but illusion, and yet still we seek the one infinite Creator as we refine our path, as we become more rested, more trusting, more joyful, more relaxed and more intent upon a single-minded goal of practicing the presence of the infinite One. We find, as we have said, that we continue to find ourselves in the divine discomfort of learning, in the difficult and sometimes painful cleansing of the self of those idiosyncrasies which are not necessary and perhaps are seen [as] stumbling blocks to a continued, persistent and successful seeking to accelerate the rate of one's spiritual growth.

That one may so accelerate this growth is so, else we would not be here. However, my friends, we cannot tell you that the work is all joy, all love, all ease and all merriment. When one is dealing with mystery, when one comes up against paradox after paradox, one can be fascinated, but never comfortable, in the ways of those heedless ones who feel that they are but hairless apes which are born and then are no more.

Each of you is a portion of the infinite Creator. Each of you is precisely equal—the murderer, the rapist, the saint, and the fool. For each of you has the entire constellation of possibilities within, and it has been with each a matter of choice after choice after choice as to how to live the life, how to serve the Creator, how to practice the presence of the Creator, and how to serve others, perhaps the most difficult question of all.

We study this still. We have found that it is foolish of us to attempt to serve others before they request it. We heard you speaking of the individual that is voiced, "Yod-he-vau-heh," or "Yahweh," or "Jehovah." This entity, which was a group entity and a guardian of this planet, a member of the Confederation, was extremely helpful in finalizing our code of ethics as regards this planet, for the plan to create improved, healthy human physical vehicles for souls turned from a plan which was focused upon entities being more able to move more quickly in spiritual growth and in service to others into a disaster where those who were somewhat superior mentally or physically simply became bellicose and worldly, moving away further and further from service to [others].

The quarantine upon your planet was therefore placed after this experience, and we may assure you that the positive entity, whose name was described Yod-he-vau-heh, moves still in this density attempting insofar as it may to correct the damage it has done.

However, it is human nature that in an apparently separate universe—that is, each entity being separate from each—many would feel that the best way to serve others is to become strong in oneself, and this is easily turned by the entity who is not careful into an absorbing self-interest which removes the entity from the mainstream of human suffering and joy.

It is well to be painfully and vulnerably in touch with the dynamics of this illusion, for the choice-making is easier in the face of the facts. The decision to jump into the thin air of faith is made possible only because of an ultimate grasp of the fact that we understand nothing. All ends in mystery, regardless of where you pick up the string of phenomena. The string always leads at last into the mobius ring of eternity. Truth recedes before the seeker like a carrot upon a stick.

If one is not careful one can create one's own spiritual burnout. We suggest that the meditations be limited to perhaps no more than an hour per day, perhaps no more than a half hour at any one sitting. This is due to the fact that meditation is a very powerful tool, and the rate of change needs to be slow enough that the personality of your consciousness may have time to absorb knowledge and inspiration that it receives and make its choices in a timely and deliberate manner. It is not well to rush or to hurry the spiritual life, for the soul has its leisure, and in the fullness of time are things accomplished. It cannot be known within the illusion which day is the day of jubilee for one entity, and that is not important. To seek the happiness, the contentment, this is not important. To seek the presence of the infinite One, this is a great aid, and we suggest that we do this most gently, most lovingly, opening to the subconscious as a suitor with bouquet and candy, knowing the spirit to be sweet and precious, the nature of love.

When you are aware that there is that jewel within, that crystallized entity within, it then becomes the goal to find that center of self, to find who one is, what one wishes, and how one wishes to go about the process of one's desires. Meditation is always most helpful, as is paying attention to the dreaming, which is a large part of the life of the deeper mind, and can constitute, in one who keeps a record of such things, an auxiliary report, auxiliary, that is, to your experience as perceived on a conscious level, for within the dreams those dynamics which may not be seen upon the surface, those feelings which may not be acknowledged or even known, move across the threshold of consciousness, and in some symbolic way express and manifest themselves. Thus, it is well to work with this material, as indeed perhaps one fourth to one third of one's time is spent in this method of relaxation of the body complex and restoration of the spiritual complex.

We feel that we have spoken to those things that are most upon the minds of those present, in a general way, and although we could move on and speak of many things, we are aware that each within the group is fatigued, and so we would at this time thank each for its attention to us. We wish each to know that we are your brothers and sisters. We are on the same path. We have moved further along this path and we study the lessons of wisdom. We are those of fifth density, yet still we have, in order to experience that which aids us in accelerating our spiritual growth, a physical vehicle of a kind, which requires nourishment, companionship and the fulfillment of its nature. What is your true nature? Seek this, seek to know it well, for it is the one who knows who he is in no uncertain terms that may move into the world of discarnate entities, and be an equal among equals.

It is most unfortunate that many of your peoples feel that they must be overcome by a greater power. The great power lies within each. It is simply a matter of choosing to seek the highest and best of that power. This is not done in a day; this is sometimes not done in a lifetime, but for all the difficulties of the spiritual path, shall we say, of hard knocks, there is the joy of companionship, the joy of learning, the joy of experiencing immediately the love and the light of the one infinite Creator. These are the oasis times, these are the sweet honey times that sustain one through the next dry and bleak period within the life experience. Back and forth each entity goes, for there is much to be learned from both frames of mind, especially if an entity can begin to focus upon difficult situations as challenges, a kind of game in which one attempts to find the love hidden in the situation at hand. When one once sees and is able to grasp the principle involved in the lesson being learned, either by analysis or intuition, one may then simply will to complete that lesson.

So you see, all phenomena are corollary to the great work of consciousness itself, the disciplining of the human personality, the encouragement of the greater self within, the encouragement of its being able to speak in many different ways through the subconsciousness to the conscious mind, always this produces the longer view, the more compassionate and wise point of view, for always one begins to see the pettiness of one's concerns and the overwhelming importance of love.

This instrument requests …

(Side one of tape ends.)

(Carla channeling)

We shall continue, leaving this instrument. We discover that this instrument has tried very hard to get below forty-five minutes, but we have outfoxed her once again. We are most apologetic, we really have not the sense of time that we would need to be able to limit our sessions as to time. We are simply able to limit them by the strength of the group energy, and this normally is that which this instrument would call long-winded. We hope we have not bored you. We hope you realize that all truths are personal. That which is your personal truth you shall recognize. There shall be no struggle, you shall simply say, "Yes, I knew that, I remember that," and that is your truth, for however long it is your truth. Some truths are larger than others, some are fleeting, none are permanent except unity.

We would now leave this instrument, asking each to continue the daily, faithful, moderate meditation, the centering whenever possible, momentarily within the presence of the one infinite Creator, that the intersection of eternity and present moment may work its magic through you that you may bring eternity into the lives of those about you.

We would at this time transfer this contact to the one known as Jim, that this entity may conclude the session this evening. We thank this instrument and the one known as Jim also, both of whom are somewhat fatigued. We are most grateful for the willingness to be open to us, and we thank each for the service it offers us and for the call itself which is a great blessing to us. We are those known to you as Q'uo. We shall at this time transfer to the one known as Jim.

(Jim channeling)

I am Q'uo, and greet each again in love and light through this instrument. We would at this time offer ourselves in the attempt to speak to any further queries that those present may have for us, though we are well aware that there is a significant amount of fatigue within the circle. We would wish that we might be able to speak to any query which may remain upon your mind, however. Is there a query at this time?

Carla: I have none.

I am Q'uo. Very well then, we are most pleased to have been able to join this group this evening. We would remind each that we are but pilgrims upon the journey of evolution as are you, and wish that our words be carefully discriminated, that only those which are of value to you be kept in use. Please discard any that do not ring true. We would at this time take our leave of this group, leaving each, as always, in the love and in the light of the one infinite Creator. We are known to you as those of Q'uo. Adonai, my friends. Adonai. ✣

L/L Research

Sunday Meditation
October 22, 1989

Group question: How can people who are interested in pursuing in a life's work and being of service to others and developing their gifts discover what exactly the gifts are that they have, and then, if, say, they have more than one gift, how can people determine what the best way of service is, how to use the gifts or gift that they have in developing themselves, and then in being of service to others?

(Gifts, Part I)

(Carla channeling)

I am Q'uo. Greetings in the love and in the light of the one infinite Creator. It is a great privilege to share in this circle of meditation and seeking and to see the earnest hearts of those who wish to express their unity of all that there is in the very life that they lead.

We are aware that the illusion is a heavy one, and that missteps are inevitable and frequent. We urge each always to turn again in hope, to try once more, to be undiscouraged by circumstances, but simply to abide in this feeling that fills this dwelling place at this time, the unconditional love of the one infinite Creator.

The third density is not a density in which wisdom plays a great part. It is the folly of men to believe that there is wisdom in third density, and thus one may see the ideal of justice, an ethical, philosophical ideal which does not take into account either the nature of the illusion, the purpose of the illusion, or those entities which have come to self-consciousness within third-density illusion. In any real sense, there is little observable justice, for the plan which each has created before the lifetime often deliberately includes difficult, unfair and painful circumstance, and the more spiritually ambitious an entity is, the more difficult the lessons that that entity came to manifest will be.

We speak this evening to those whose worldly ambitions are a cipher, a nothing. This has been decided. This leaves the mind free, regardless of whether work is done in the mundane world or not, to ponder and contemplate those philosophical and spiritual questions that you may have. This is a great head start that you have over people who are torn between the world and the cosmos, between this life and infinity. Those who have awakened, such as you, to their true desire to be of service to the one infinite Creator by loving each other, are so often in the difficult position of having to adjudge their own service in the absence of any support whatsoever.

This is especially true of the mated relationship, and the raising of children. There is no greater or more sacrificial service than the raising of young souls, attempting to offer to those souls that information which is grist not only for making one's way in the mundane world, but for becoming aware of eternity, becoming aware that so-called human beings have a context into which they fit. They are not the be-all and the end-all of evolution. Evolution moves steadily on, and the progress, after third density, is all spiritual. Within this density you still need more of the personality in order to deal with the heavy chemical vibrations. More and more you will see yourselves as a spiritual discovery, finding and refining that truth which is within you until you become aware of your nature. Becoming aware of one's own nature may or may not sound simple. It is not simple in our estimation, unless one has the gift of faith as this instrument does and simply bypasses the intellect, moving instinctively toward intuition and what the instrument calls purified emotion.

For the most part, entities wish to do something which is of true service to the Creator, and it seems logical and right to entities who have observed great spiritual figures of the past and present to wish to be great spiritual figures and to be of service in that way also. One can even seek dramatic, publicized service to others, and within the limitations of mixed contact, since there is ego involved in such hope, such channels are able to do much good to bring many souls to an awareness of the mystery that underlies all that there is.

We always say to each that we do not wish to become a stumbling block, and we wish you to take only that which makes sense to you from what we say. And no matter how inspiring, if confusing, we ask that you release and forget the information, for it is not your personal truth at this time, and there is no need for you to change and struggle and strive. The spiritual path is one of allowing things to occur, for you have planned well.

Each of you would be unable to incarnate at this time upon this particular sphere, were it not possible for each and every entity to graduate either service to self or service to others, third density; that is, each has the opportunity of learning to use a denser and much enhanced cohesion of light. In this atmosphere, as the instrument has often said, thoughts become things. And as you are entering at this time into fourth-density space/time, thoughts are becoming things, over and over again. The negative emotions involved with lifestyles that are not helpful to the entity through anger, through feelings of rejection and so forth, cause much illness, much unhappiness.

It is difficult for the person who comes to this information as a neophyte to imagine that he or she could be of equal service to those who heal or teach or channel, for the latter three are somewhat dramatic. The entity, if positively oriented, is relatively without ego, as you call the need to impress or to control. We would like to extend this idea to form a true picture of spiritual service in third density.

Perhaps the greatest spiritual service you can do is to center and meditate and think upon the Creator, lovingly, gratefully, emotionally, in a purified and inner way, not letting your prayers float to the four corners of the room in which you are so that entities may hear you, but rather stepping into that inner room and listening in silence, waiting for the presence of the infinite One.

The difficulty for those within your culture is that people identify service to others with certain specific skills, which we would call dramatic skills, such as the vocal channeling and the healing. It is our opinion that each and every entity who has incarnated at this time upon the Earth has a beautiful, loving and right service to perform, planned beforehand, planned in such a way that one may be continuously rocked and buffeted by the winds of change that accompany realization.

This is true whether or not the service is the greatest service of all, that of knowing who you are, and of vibrating in that knowledge consciously, or of non-dramatic service. This is what confuses your people. It is your people's idea that some services are greater than other services. This is true only insofar as some desires to serve are purer than other desires to serve. It does not matter what is in front of your face. What is in front of your face is your service. If you can allow yourself to flow intuitively in the river of consciousness, you yourself will let yourself know, "Yes, I wish to do this," "No, I do not wish to do that."

Therefore, we suggest that in order to find out one's gifts, one do several things. Firstly, if one is of some substantial age and has had many experiences, it becomes extremely easier to gaze back over the incarnation and see the pattern of lessons to be learned. One kind of lesson will occur again and again and again, until you have mastered and balanced your ability to serve under those conditions. Basically, each entity goes through a lifetime process of accepting the unacceptable, of forgiving the unforgivable, of loving the unlovable, of consoling the inconsolable, of pardoning one in error, even when that error has cost you greatly.

It does not seem to be a service to be a parent, or a breadwinner, or any of the other myriad non-dramatic ways of living possible. What sets the spiritual seeker apart from one who simply lives in the mundane world without questions as to eternity, is that realization of the present moment as eternity, that ideal which says "I can have time spent with the infinite One, I can feel Its love and Its light. These experiences are meaningful to me." This creates an atmosphere within of trust, so that one may gradually, gradually relax, and allow the rhythm of life, as you have planned it, to overtake you.

It is not well to pray and affirm in the attempt to control the life, because that which is upon the surface of your minds is as the tip of the iceberg, and those things which are deepest within take some time to express themselves through dreams, visions or instant realizations after ten years of work. Some entities move quickly, others more slowly and more surely. All that we suggest to each is that each remain within the integrity of the self, feeling the selfhood of the self, feeling the discrimination and the thought processes of the self, so that as one listens to all of life, whether it be the weather report, a symphony or a channeling such as this one, one is listening with an ear to pray for the lost, to rejoice with the joyful, to give thanks for those who have had blessing, and to console those who are wretched.

Any form of loving one another is that action which expresses what this instrument would call the Christ consciousness, that which is deeply buried within you, that with which you are to some extent acquainted, but perhaps more to the point, of being able to love without stint, to give without thinking, to spend all one's energy, time, talent and what you call money, with the spiritual life central and in the mind.

It is possible to be of tremendous service while washing your dishes, for as one washes the dishes it is a waking meditation. The gestures are automatic, and it is possible in the meantime to be in a state of light meditation and listening, or in a state of contemplation, or in a state of intercessory prayer, where you are concerned for the health and the well-being of those you love. Thoughts are becoming things; your prayers are heard more than ever.

We find that it is unfortunate that entities who are upon the spiritual path that does not include orthodox religion, tend to wish that they may be of this or that service rather than allowing service to come to them. It will come; it has been planned. It may not seem dramatic or large or important, but the dish washed for the love of the one infinite Creator is a dish washed in a bath of love as well as soap and water, and that love radiates and lightens the consciousness of the planet. This is your greatest service, each of you, and you do it within the unmanifest being with no one to know, no drama, and no announcement of having done so.

You are working upon your evolution, and from third density forward all evolution is spiritual. Thusly, we would back up and look at how one may abide in faith, and have the patience, the persistence, and the faith to wait and do what there comes before the face to do. That, and that alone, for that instant, is all that is needed. It is never known to you when you have truly succeeded and when you have failed, nor is it important, for if you do anything for the love of the one infinite Creator, that radiant thought, however poorly the actions manifest, is a purely positive, loving and caring thought, and will add to the consciousness and the lightness of your sphere.

Entities within your culture are much bemused by gadgetry, much in love with foreign places, ambitious and restless and yearning, and thinking that what they hunger for is better money, a better position, more power, or more clout in some way. This is not the objective of living this particular incarnation in this particular density. You are attempting to drop that of yourself which does not seem to be loving, not in overcoming or repressing it, but by balancing it and understanding it within the self.

This is a difficult thing to do, painful for those with any sensitivity, for as you know, all of creation lies within you. You are all that is. Circumstances may have made it possible for you to move through the incarnation comfortably, or uncomfortable but honestly, or comfortably and dishonestly, or uncomfortable and dishonestly. Yet, within each and every situation, no matter how unpromising, lies that which may be a certain knowledge, a certain determined hope in that which is unseen, that the situation before one's eyes is exactly what it should be, and, painful or wonderful, is giving you what you need to take in and work with as catalyst at this time.

Each upon this planet at this time had a hand in creating the life pattern. Once one has discovered the lesson that one has set oneself, it becomes easier to see tiny moment after tiny moment, and small detail after small detail take on an aura of the spiritual as one seeks within such situations to find a way to manifest love where there is no love, light where there is no light, and union where there was discord.

We may say, because each is aware, that each is a wanderer who has come to this planet at this time to be of service to those who are attempting to graduate, who are not able to accept the consolations of any organized religion. We do not claim to be a religion, a church, a dogma, or a doctrine. We are those who have had experiences with the Creator, who have grown closer and closer to the Creator, and who expect to have quite a way to go before we are able to dissolve once again in the ocean of unmanifest love. The cycle is as beautiful as the beating of a giant heart, and the fact that anything that one does could not be one's service is to us improbable. Subjectively, one may feel that one has erred, made mistakes, been thoughtless, and so forth. It is well in those times to continue positive thinking, and move quickly towards a state of forgiveness of the self and of the one with whom there was conflict.

Perhaps the second greatest service upon your planet at this time, or at any time in third density, is the responsibility of parenting young souls who know and seek the truth with childish lilting voices and squeals of laughter. This particular service is looked down upon by most as being the lot of the one who is too lazy to work. We find the concept ludicrous in that children and a home are a great deal of work. There is no boss, there is no judge, there is only the parent attempting to be of service to the young one. And we may say that it is our opinion that the most helpful thing spiritually in the service of raising children, for the children, is either to bring them to any organized religious group for interaction with people of their own age and teachers, or, and this is undoubtedly preferable to many, to create a worship service within the home that is done daily and without comment. Emphasis is not put upon such spiritual discipline; it is picked up by young children as that stress or emphasis which protests too much. Happy are the parents who are settled in peace together and who may sit in meditation or whatever form of spiritual practice is desired, each and every day for a short time. This moves into the child's subconscious as that which is, and in our opinion this is the truth of that which is—that is, that the Creator is within everything.

It is impossible not to serve if one is loving the Creator while doing the service. At this time your planet is very polarized. Very positive entities gaze upon the havoc created by very negative ones, and negative entities gaze back at those who are polarizing towards the positive and see what this instrument would call "suckers." We urge each, therefore, to allow those things to happen which happen, and to ponder them and ruminate on them, and even analyze them—if one is of an analytical turn of mind—at the end of each day, that one may remain clear, confident and calm, centered in the love and the light of the one infinite Creator. We know of no other way to explain to you the difference between your view of service and our view of service than to say that to us there is no lifetime lived that is not potentially a life of service if things within it are done with a love of the one infinite Creator and in the love of the one infinite Creator.

This is not easy medicine for entities to swallow. Wanderers especially are quite certain they have a mission. Indeed, the mission may be an humble one. There are no missions that are not humble. Some seem to be more than humble services because they are dramatic, such as this instrument as she speaks without knowing what word will come next. This is interesting to people, a tightrope act, and therefore dramatic. Will the instrument lose the contact? Will the acrobat fall off the slim, round, slippery wire upon which he is walking between the present moment and eternity?

You are here to bring light to a dark world. It is as simple as that. The purpose for which wanderers incarnated is all one—to love, and to love, and to love, and to love. You will be hurt, broken, humiliated and defeated in the course of a life in faith. It runs directly counter to the culture in which you live to do things for an ideal reason, to focus upon the Creator which is unseen rather than all of the phenomena, all of the gadgetry, all of the amusements that are so delightful upon the surface of life in your density. Be aware that even in those situations you may choose to be of service by moving constantly in an awareness of the love and the light of the one infinite Creator. But also, and most of all, be aware, we ask each, that non-dramatic service is as vital as dramatic service, just as the mouth of an entity speaks many things, but would not be able to function without each and every other organ of the physical vehicle, which must be kept in some sort of balance in order that one may manifest any gifts whatsoever.

We may say that there is one thing that we would not advise in attempting to be of service and find one's niche, and that is to attempt to control the process. The conscious mind has very little in it compared to the unconscious mind, in which lies the roots of mind and the Creator Itself, covered over and over by distortion, but there, perfect and whole nevertheless: each one's true nature.

Now, we would suggest to this group, as it is doing somewhat advanced work, that it simply practice the presence as it moves about the daily activities, not berating the self every time one realizes one has not thought about the Creator for hours, but simply turning again and again to its simple ideal, the desire for the love of the infinite Creator, to love each other.

Almost any situation which seems difficult involves a lack or a loss of love. Hearts that are not opened to the love and the light of the infinite Creator can be mean and petty, hurtful and vicious, all in the name of service. Better it is that you do nothing but sit in one place and send love, than be active and confused, and somewhat negative as well as positive by desiring to control what happens to one.

For in the desire to help someone, there needs to be the realization that one must come to a halt within, and admit that one does not know all that there is to know about service to this entity, that one will need inspiration and intuition, so that one may call upon these deep resources of the self, which many call the higher self, the Holy Spirit, guardian angel, or inner planes master. All of these sorts of entities exist, the difference between them is only that of outer plane third density and inner plane third density. Those within the outer plane may come from other planes, those within the inner plane must have at one time been incarnate upon this particular sphere.

Thus, be aware, we ask you, [of] the service that you provide by your very consciousness, by your love of the sunlight and the dappled shades of autumn trees, by your love of the immensity of the universe and its noumenal mystery, by seeing life itself as sanctified, a blessing which oftentimes seems a most uncomfortable and inconvenient blessing.

Now, how shall you reach that point of faith where you refuse to accept that you are not of service and simply continue to be of service? As this instrument has said many times upon its own, due to its own experience with its intelligence, the intellect has almost no help to give a spiritual seeker, for those truths which will be helpful to one will be recognized from within as personal truths.

Thus, we urge each when listening to us, or any other spiritually oriented being speak, to discriminate carefully, not in terms of intellectual right and wrong and so forth, but in terms of the intuitional feeling of recognition or non-recognition of truth. Each has a different path.

This thing that is common to all paths in third density is that you are learning how to love and be loved. This is the foundation of a social memory complex which shall be your next lesson, that is, to see all that there is in each mind—and in each mind is the mind of the murderer, the rapist, the robber, the revolutionary, the despot—and yet accept the self and all others for the nature which has been given them in order that they might make choices with free will.

It is very important that there be negativity and difficult experiences that one may learn the humility of one who allows, observes and then acts, rather than reacts. To take the life into one's own hands is not to take control of what one wishes by affirmations and prayers unceasing. It is rather to realize that the plan has already been made, the pattern has been set. It is the best pattern you and your higher self could create for you, and all that you need do this time is allow yourself to be upon the path upon which you are, keeping your eyes open, watching your feelings, finding ways to manifest love, the smile upon the street, the kind word to a stranger.

This instrument is asking us to allow this to end, however we wish to make one more point before we leave. The instrument itself was concerned with its many gifts and its lack of desire to use the gifts of creativity in an intellectual or physical manner, such as the music, the dancing, the criticism, and the creative writing. In fact, all of these gifts are being used in the life pattern. It is simply that the gifts are being used to support that one thing with which the channel has been concerned and involved within its entire life experience, that being the living in a poem, the making of a beautiful tapestry of a life as a gift to the one infinite Creator.

We would at this time transfer this contact, thanking the one known as Carla and the one known as Jim. We shall close the session through the one known as Jim. I leave this instrument in love and light. I am Q'uo.

(Jim channeling)

I am Q'uo, and greet each again in love and light through this instrument. We would offer ourselves at this time in the attempt to speak to further queries if there are any remaining on the minds of those present. Is there a query at this time?

Carla: Well, if nobody else has a query I'll ask one that's real marginal, you probably can't help me, but … in talking about spiritual principles with someone who is traumatized by traditional Christianity, one needs a very different vocabulary than one who is a Christian such as myself would use, and I wondered if there were any way to express what to me is a reality, that is that one does not exist metaphysically until one knows who one is, and can stand firm on that, to the point of death if necessary, in vocabulary that will be neutral, and helpful to one traumatized by religious dogma and doctrine.

I am Q'uo, and am aware of your query, my sister. We find that as it is important that one grasp and master these concepts of the knowing of the self to the heart of the being and the expressing of that knowing as a form of tuning and as a form of challenging of spirits, that it is also necessary that when one speak of these activities that one do so in a manner which is of one's own nature, shall we say. If it is a stumbling block to speak in this manner, then perhaps the words may be written upon the page, after having been brought forth from the heart without censor, and then upon the page to be arranged in a manner that would be acceptable to the [one] which was not able to receive the words in their original form.

There are many ways of describing the, what we would call, basic principles of exercising as an instrument. There are as many ways as there are entities who have accomplished this task. Therefore, we are confident that one which has mastered this task can also redescribe or interpret that experience in a means which is acceptable to another, after having expressed that process as fully and as concisely as possible in the vocabulary and concepts which are natural to the entity, then accomplishing the translation, shall we say.

Is there a further query, my sister?

Carla: No, thank you.

I am Q'uo, and we thank you, my sister. Is there another query at this time?

K: I have a question. I've been in circumstances a number of times where those who are either not serious seekers, or those who are seekers within what appears to me to be a very narrow path, ask questions about my particular path, and I have often been at a loss as to how to answer them without either infringing on their free will, or seeming to place judgments on their views of life as being right or wrong. There seem to be such differences in viewpoints, and it's difficult for me to know how to answer the questions. Sometimes I feel that they shouldn't be answered at all, but again I'm at a loss to know how to do that without giving offense. Do you have any comments or suggestions on this situation?

(Pause)

I am Q'uo, and am aware of your query. We apologize. The instrument was tickled.

(Pause)

I am Q'uo, and am again with this instrument, who has now added the necessary recording device. When you are in the presence of those who ask of your path, and you wish to answer in a manner that is both accurate and compassionate, it is our suggestion that you first ask yourself how it is you wish to serve this entity or these entities, that you find that desire to speak both clearly and yet with an understanding of the position that is experienced by the questioner.

When you feel a desire to serve, then do not worry about the words that might be used to express that desire. Speak freely, as you serve as a channel from your conscious and subconscious minds concerning that journey upon which you find yourself. If one worries overmuch about the specifics of the question and its response, one may find the mind in a kind of tangle. However, if this worry can be circumvented by focusing upon a desire to serve freely and without judgment, then a clearer path is made to the subconscious portions of the mind which contain the clear and compassionate expression that will suffice as the reply to the query. Thus, one serves as an instrument in these situations that one might share that which has been helpful to the self.

Is there another query, my sister?

K: That was very helpful, thank you. I do have another question also, and that is, can you offer some suggestions on how to differentiate between serving and pleasing?

I am Q'uo, and am aware of your query, my sister. We find in our experience that there is a significant difference in these concepts. The desire to serve another is based upon a concern for the other self, and how best to aid that other self in its thinking or in its actions or in its being. The desire to please another self, however, has its focus upon your own self, and receiving a reward from the other self for actions which have been constructed with the hope of receiving that reward, whether it be the smile, the confirmation, the attention, or in a negative sense, the removal of criticism.

Thus, look to that which is desired from the action to determine whether it is an action that has the other self or the self as its central focus.

Is there another query, my sister?

K: Yes, along the same lines, if the desire is truly to serve the other self, there are still many circumstances in which I find it difficult to determine which course of action would truly be of service, and I find that I do not have the appropriate resources to determine that. That's the sort of situation that I'm really interested in. How do I decide what course of action to take with a person when there are various ones open to me and I do not know which would be of more service?

I am Q'uo, and am aware of your query, my sister. First, we would recommend that one determine what it is the other self desires. This may be accomplished by a simple query. It is the explicitly expressed desire for service from another self that is the clearest indication of how that self might be served, regardless of what one might feel would be the greatest service.

To become the other self is a means whereby one might in imagination as closely as possible approximate the other self and its desires if the other self is not present and able to be queried as to how best to serve that other self. The further one moves from the explicitly expressed desire from another self, the more possible it becomes that one's offered service will deviate from an actual service. The desire to serve another which motivates action often goes astray when the other self has not requested a service, however, that desire is the fundamental quality that makes it possible to achieve a redress, shall we say, if the original effort has fallen somewhat short.

Is there another query, my sister?

K: There are times when the explicit request or desire of another entity is something which I do not feel comfortable in being able to fulfill for one reason or another. At those times my assumption is that my responsibility is to exercise my own judgment as to what I feel that I can honestly give, and yet there are times also when I feel that I should be giving what is asked no matter what, because that is what service is, and that I feel that if I don't that I'm not being of service. Can you comment on that sort of dilemma?

I am Q'uo, and am aware of your query, my sister. Indeed, it is a dilemma to be asked to give that which one finds it difficult to give. It is, shall we say, less of a gift if there is the taint of resentment given with the service. It is oftentimes better not to offer the service if it is not possible to offer without the feeling of resentment or guilt or other emotions which would confuse or color the gift in a manner that would disrupt the clear communication, shall we say.

It is, as you have surmised, better to give what can be given with a cheerful heart than to give all of what was asked, but to include the negative emotions as well. It is often helpful in a situation in which one has been asked to give more than one feels one has to offer, to meditate upon that which limits the giving, in order that one might discover a facet of the being which might benefit from attention. There is much that can be learned by studying limitations and facing them in an honest fashion.

There is no shame in recognizing and admitting limitations. These are the boundaries which at one time served one well, and provided a fuller arena of experience, shall we say, but which at the present moment have the opposite effect in reducing that which may be offered as service. The discovery of these limitations increases the knowledge of the self so that there is possible an expanded view of the self that included the limitation and the beginning work upon the balance of the fundamental nature of the limitation.

Therefore, we would agree with your original assumption that it is better, in terms of the purity of service, to give what one can in a cheerful fashion, and when one is unable to give fully, to examine carefully that which limits that which is given.

Is there a further query, my sister?

K: Would the examination of these limitations be with a view to removing the limitation or just to understanding and accepting it?

I am Q'uo, and am aware of your query, my sister. Either may be the case, in our experience, for in many incarnations there are qualities or characteristics which are placed within the character structure that allow certain services to be offered, certain abilities to be expressed, that when seen from another angle, perspective or point of view may be seen as a limitation to yet another kind of expression. In such an instance it is well to accept that quality or characteristic that has been discovered through careful self analysis and meditation to be a fundamental building block of the incarnation, and to accept such freely, openly and with a joyful heart, realizing that service yet grows from this limitation.

In other cases, it is possible that a limitation is a portion of the being that yet remains to be balanced, and when the balancing occurs that there is a greater or wider perspective that allows a larger amount of service, shall we say, for want of a better phrase, to be offered. Only one's careful self-analysis and meditation upon the results of such analysis can determine whether certain characteristics must be accepted or might yet yield further growth.

Is there a further query, my sister?

K: No, that's very helpful, thanks very much.

I am Q'uo, and we thank you, again, my sister. Is there a query at this time with which we may complete this session?

(Pause)

I am Q'uo, and are most grateful to have been able to speak this evening to this group. We take great joy in joining our vibrations with yours, for we find the queries from this group are not only thoughtful and interesting, but come from the deepest concerns of the hearts of those present in the desire to know more of the self in order that the self might be offered to the self and to the Creator in its many other selves as a sincere honestation to that one Creator.

We are those of Q'uo, and we await your calls in your future times as you reckon the movement of time and space. We shall leave this instrument and this group at this time, leaving each, as always, in the love and in the light of the one infinite Creator. We are known to you as those of Q'uo. Adonai, my friends. Adonai. ✤

Sunday Meditation
October 29, 1989

Group question: The question this evening has to do with the great variety that exists in types of beings, those that are incarnate and who go through the incarnational process, those who are incarnate and perhaps do not go through the incarnate process, those that we might call angels that provide guidance and assistance from the inner planes, other types of beings that perhaps do not individualize themselves, maybe the type that we would call the logos or the godhead that comprises the totality of the octave of experience [which we are enjoying,] and provides, actually, that octave for us to go through the evolutionary process. We are wondering about these beings that may not incarnate, those that may not partake as we do in the evolutionary process, and how it is that they exist, how it is they function, and how it is they might progress themselves, if indeed it is necessary for them to progress in any fashion.

(Carla channeling)

I am Q'uo. May I greet each of you upon this beautiful day, within your blessed circle of seeking, quietness and faith. It is indeed a privilege to share this meditation with you, and to offer those few thoughts which are our opinions, and which may be provocative, challenging or inspiring. We hope to give you tools and resources so that you may accelerate your growth upon the spiritual path, your work, and your love of the one infinite Creator. That is the nature of creation, that is the nature of the Creator, and that is the nature of the biggest portion of the self.

Let us begin by saying that one who has moved in consciousness through work in consciousness and the disciplines of the personality, [that] one may gradually become more and more open, able to receive, and able to discriminate that which one receives. Therefore, it is extremely wise to so regulate the in-pouring of consciously channeled energy, that it does not move beyond the boundaries of what is known as physiological capability for work in consciousness. Perhaps the gist of what we have to share is that each entity, no matter what the *(inaudible)*, of angelic beings or *(inaudible)* discarnate entities *(inaudible)*, is responsible for *(inaudible)*, to serve the one infinite Creator in an unique way, for as each soul is different, so is each harmony and conflict special and different, and richer for that.

The question of, so called, discarnate entities, may perhaps be amended to the subject of entities which are not incarnating upon the earth plane at this time. The ones with which you are most familiar are those active and mischievous spirits called poltergeists. It is this kind of phenomenon in which people are most interested, for they are very fond of measuring, *(inaudible)* and *(inaudible)* the, so called, scientific method. This approach, that is, one of the observer who is not taking part in the experience, may yield good results for a time, but it is a false entity who moves continuously along this line.

[Therefore, some things which we have to say are difficult to hear, but we still say them.] For, *(inaudible)*. This entity has spoken much about the process of the *(inaudible)*. There is a reason for that and we would like to go into it and find a pattern. *(Inaudible)*. However, though you are at the mercy *(inaudible)*. The true nature of *(inaudible)* is such that the entire metaphysical portion of the universe, that is, the time/space portion is still with an alternate spiritual velocity. Without the *(inaudible)* which fools entities by appearance, *(inaudible)* is evident no matter what *(inaudible)* no matter how high or how close to the light [the entity has come,] is surrounded by aid and comfort from those entities who *(inaudible)* wish to help and wait for the call to help.

The only way in which one may be decisive and authoritative in the *(inaudible)* process is to become aware of the metaphysical [and imperishable and whole self again.] This entity is whole unto himself. *(Inaudible)* bringing several people together and it may *(inaudible)* pre-incarnatively *(inaudible)* that each entity, whether in a group or alone, has the honor and the duty *(inaudible)* into the trunk of mind becoming able to be in touch with those [painful, carnal, tidal living and desire] *(inaudible)*.

[Why do you not realize this already?] This is an illusion. This is a total [illusion.] All that you see, hear, smell, taste and touch are illusory *(inaudible)* has a personality *(inaudible)* within the incarnation are illusory and ephemeral, and in that persona, it is impossible to realize the true nature of the *(inaudible)* process. Therefore, we strongly suggest that any *(inaudible)* to your studies of how to serve others place one's [first priority] upon the self and the *(inaudible)* that self will have faith in and desire for *(inaudible)*.

These questions are not easy. These questions [are to be the questions] of an entity's life experience. It is upon one's deciding the nature of oneself that one [entered] into service in a way which promotes the gifts [that empathy] and forgives *(inaudible)*. This is true throughout the Creation for metaphysical beings, that you must move from the relative to the absolute, from the pragmatic and practical to the ideal in order to cleanse all *(inaudible)* and make a clear path for the words, the healing or the love of the one infinite Creator.

How does one become a metaphysical being, a magical personality? Perhaps, the first step in this endeavor is the realization that you truly must start from the beginning, that you have the mind of the beginner, that you do not *(inaudible)*. It is wrong to trample any pride or ambition underfoot, for worldly things will keep one upon the surface of life and stifle the thinking and feeling processes which are the very heart of the resources used for spiritual growth within. In meditation each day one might ask, "Who am I? What is my greatest ideal?" Throughout the day, one does many things and at the end of the day one may *(inaudible)* over that day's activities *(inaudible)*. Then you may decide for yourself those things that you wish could have been done differently, that you may experience forgiveness and redemption through your own self to any other *(inaudible)* unhappy and, most of all, to the Creator.

To get one's spiritual feet under one, to be able to stand firmly at spiritual *(inaudible)*, it is necessary to know the self well enough that the self becomes, for the time of the working, an absolute *(inaudible)* with no relativity, no personality but only the impersonal channeling of the infinite love and light of the one Creator. So, before one seeks to receive information, or to attempt healing or any of the other paths of service, it is well to make peace with oneself, peace *(inaudible)* but not worldly [peace]. Indeed, we were speaking of the peace of committing oneself totally to spiritual [thought.] Those who answered this call are no longer sleeping, but are willing and equal partners with the higher self of spirit and the one infinite Creator, weaving a [passage] through [this] life which not only teaches the self but reflects much for others that they may also learn from you, as you learn, complete, whole, perfect [services] to *(inaudible)* any kind of contact.

Now let us move to more transient material. Although it is without bias, neutral *(inaudible)* and information we are happy to share, up to a certain point.

There are two kinds of service *(inaudible)*. One servant-ministry is that of the Confederation of Planets in the Service of the Infinite Creator. This instrument is correct in assuming that we could also be called angels. However, it is our function to indicate mystery, to indicate paradox, to stimulate thinking in seeking, searching for the truth.

We abide by the laws of free will and come only when called. We do not have the rights of those upon the inner planes to move into actual activity upon the Earth plane. To our dismay, we made [several] mistakes in attempting to move into right relationships with incarnate beings in third density by manifesting ourselves among them. The results were egregious and unacceptable to us. We were worshipped. We were over-esteemed. We were thought to be invincible and all-knowing. We still have much to do to uncover that part of light within. Consequently, it was our [detection] that we were living a lie, even as we taught the truth, by our very beingness and therefore the positivity of the work we were sharing was too much upset and offset by the *(inaudible)* involved, and in attempting to receive information without the finally settled notion of who you, as an entity, are. These are the questions of philosophy and religion. We are not capable of acting in the way *(inaudible)* upon the outer planes because we come only when called. We often work with people within their dreaming state or their daydreams. Our touch is subtle and gentle, we hope, and we are limited in what we may do to you, co-creators of the one infinite creation.

Those upon the inner planes who have remained behind after incarnation upon your sphere to work with all others who have not yet created their redemption so that each may become more and more aware that there is a universe within that is vaster, more interesting, more challenging, is more informative than that which may be consciously thought and surmised.

There is a difficulty with those upon the inner planes. An inner-plane decision to remain within the vibrations of third density in a discarnate form is a good expression of martyrdom. For this entity, as long as it desires to be an inner planes teacher, may, itself not progress beyond this density and the study of its lessons. However, these entities have much more capacities to speak personally about specific things than those who, shall we say, are from the outer planes [existence.]

(Pause)

I am Q'uo. We are sorry for the pause but we were asking the instrument to retune. If there could be some chanting at this time, it would be well. I am Q'uo.

(Carla and another sing:)

> We all come from God
> and unto God we shall return.
> We all come from God
> and unto God we shall return,
> like a river flowing into the ocean,
> like a ray of light returning to the sun.

(Carla channeling)

I am Q'uo, and am, again, with this instrument. We appreciate this instrument's fastidiousness with challenging and its desire to retune when it sensed that there was not a satisfactory degree of *(inaudible)*. We shall continue.

The inner planes masters, so called, are often extremely wise. They have graduated to the next density. However, they have turned their back upon their own spiritual evolution that they may aid their brothers and sisters who have come after them. It is a truly sacrificial and, shall we say, theodic ministry of spirit. Yet, many are the spirits who have moved through the incarnational experience as the devoted pupil of some teacher or master. Consequently, one who has had this strong and *(inaudible)* relationship where the teacher basically becomes that which is worshipped, and the Creator worshiped only through that teacher, that you, yourself, begin to accomplish the karmic [mind] of necessity and that is, it is not balanced to receive constantly from the inner planes as much as it is balanced for entities to move on, continue their own seeking and, at the same time, stretch themselves in abundant service to a hungry world.

We do not suggest that the interior monologues and dialogues which you have within yourself—these also being inner-planes thoughts by nature—may indeed be helpful. It is simply that as one is taught, so one will desire to get, and for those entities to whom worship is offered, these entities have the responsibility of steering, most gently, those entities back upon the path of thinking for the self, examining the self, and being aware of one's self-worth [as] an independence of spirit. For you need nothing to make you complete. The Creator, which is love, lives within you in infinite abundance.

Some entities approach the spiritual path as if they were drilling for oil and they do a good deal of harm within their minds, seeking too much too quickly, and unable to assimilate all of it. This constitutes what this instrument would call spiritual constipation. Thus, if you are enjoying a relationship with a discarnate teacher that is of the inner planes and advises one, in addition to speaking of spiritual principles, one is yielding one's free will to that which is the ephemeral personality of the master that speaks within. This will hinder an entity from becoming fully aware of its nature.

All inner planes entities are those who have incarnated, lived and offered much upon your Earth's sphere. Many of them are extremely wise, some of them are mischievous, and some, within the lower astral planes, are most disturbing. However, if one learns from a teacher rather than from one's own heart, one is forever dependent upon that teacher to be without the feet of clay. All entities have the feet of clay, not only in your environment of third density but as one moves on. Of course, that which one does not desire becomes more and more refined in its removal so that where, at first, one took large chunks of the being that did not aid the self and held them upward to the Creator saying, "Take these, these are no longer my personal truths," then one may get on with the business of paying attention to, blessing, nourishing and loving the self. This is the fundamental heart of service to others.

It is impossible to move fully into the heart energy, that is, fully rather than substantially, but to, in whatever manner is comfortable for each seeker, examining the self, discovering and rediscovering the life, gazing at one's choices and asking one self, "Why did I choose? Who am I that I would choose this?" In this context, one looks for spiritual coincidence and for the repetition of the kind of situation which has occurred before and is now occurring once more. This is, if substantial, a part of your inner experience, most probably that which you, yourself, set for yourself to study within this life experience. So we would not particularly suggest that one move beyond one's own angelic *(inaudible)* for the simple reason that is has slowed the development of those teachers who sacrifice the self and in order to balance what this entity calls karma, each entity who works with guru as Creator must, in turn, be Creator to a student. It is a sacred obligation as the choice is constantly made to adore the teacher. This is much more prevalent in the cultures of Asia. However, because of the "global village" effect of mass-communications media, it remains possible to move through one's days in extremely good intentions but unknowing of those things which may be *(inaudible)*. We do not encourage any to seek inner-plane masters unless you, as an entity, wish to spend some time in third-density time/space aiding those who wish to seek from within. If an entity feels comfortable and of service in this regard then we can do no more than encourage the entity to make this sacrifice.

Those who move ahead also have an imbalance of karma because they have left those who still were sick, struggling, miserable, wretched, angry and confused. Consequently, there is, at the appropriate time for each entity, this being also unique, there will be the need for those who have gone on and not stayed in the inner planes to move into the inner planes in thought and offer what inspiration, information and general spiritual guidance we may offer. It is our privilege and pleasure to be of the Children of Sorrow for as we move into your vibration we sense the deep horror, sorrow and anguish each feels over all that there is within this illusion which seems un-beautiful, impossible to restore, broken and hopeless. Yet we of the outer planes and those of the inner planes also, will say over and over and over again: all things are as they should be. An entity who is working within the self, with faith in the self, forgiveness for the self, and strength to the self will realize and recognize, increasingly, those lessons of love which are theirs to learn within this particular life experience. One gazes at one's gifts, whatever they may be, but one does not take these gifts for granted in relation to how one is to use the gifts at hand. It is well to gaze out into the greater community and, in serene and gentle yellow-ray energy, concern oneself with society and culture and all peoples as you are able to meet and know them. Realize that each of you is here at this time either to aid in the harvest as wanderers or to be in the harvest as those of third density reaching graduation for the first time.

We may also remind each who feels his self to be a wanderer that, although, as every entity within Creation, it is whole and perfect, yet if it has ascribed unto itself glory it must balance that within another incarnation. If it has experienced and not balanced any of the deeper feelings it well may be necessary to move back into the life experience and refine, in the fire of third density, the gold from the dross, the light-self from the heavy chemical body.

There are also entities which do not [appear] in any personal form. These social-memory-complexes wander in their own way, for they keep a vigil. They walk the watchtower. They are of the Logos. They are of the principle of unconditional love. And, by realizing the strength of these connections, it becomes more and more possible for an entity which is steeped in its own iniquity and confusion to become more and more able to recognize its needs, its resources, its gifts, and its path of service. If one is of service to one being, one is of service to the planet. If one is of service reluctantly, the energy shared is not pleasant for it is the cheerful giver, the glad giver which acquires no karmic bond by what it offers for it has no desire for any particular outcome, but only the desire to aid other creator-selves. These entities are such as stars …

(Side one of tape ends.)

(Carla channeling)

… and, indeed, the plenum of space.

Perhaps, in order to simplify and express [what is] to us the heart of that which is *(inaudible)* is: there are two kinds of help. There is one help that is of the inner planes in which the entity who has graduated is willing to be the comforter, the redeemer, the savior symbol that the self may reflect self-forgiveness from this mirror. As we said, the drawback is that each of you which does this with a particular teacher incurs karma and must come back to teach that which was learned to balance that dependency with an independence which accepts another's dependency upon it. We suggest, gently, that each think for the self. Each knows that one is not alone, ever. However, the relationship of teacher and pupil is only helpful if the questions asked to the teacher of the inner planes have to do with spiritual principles. This is seldom what is asked of inner-planes entities or, indeed, of any metaphysical entities. Yet, this is what people desire to know. The inner-planes masters are equipped and capable of working with such entities.

We are those who move from another portion of what you would call space/time. We are those future-selves which the decision you make within this density will cause you to become, either positive or negative. Feel the sunshine and know that love unmanifest, unspoken, unuttered and serene is, indeed, that of the Creator. To see yourself more and more clearly, ask oneself the difficult questions more and more deeply. Crystallize the entity within that you know that in which you have faith and that you have committed yourself to that path to an extremely deep extent so that the life experience has become not secular, not laic, but rather a poem, a paean of praise and thanksgiving and prayer to the one infinite Creator. Those who spend time with teachers, either earthly or discarnate, are apt not to value enough the gifts of the spirit within which moves from the outer planes. We suggest that each of you think carefully and at length until you have come to peace with your own definition of yourself, your faith and [your desire.]

Each entity will go through difficult times and prosperous ones, speaking spiritually. We hope that you do not become discouraged at any time because you feel subjectively that you have not created a beautiful, lovely experience. More than us, then, who are not the Creator and do not wish to be worshipped, it is the work within the self in silent meditation that brings the true enlightenment, brings it softly, naturally, quietly, so that one is sure in an instant, whenever that instant may be, that one has found a path for the self that will move one from time into timelessness, from this illusion into that which comes far closer to the reality of All That Is.

Meditate and ask, then listen. The universe is crowded, teeming with populations of various kinds. It is well to be tolerant but, of oneself, we suggest one be somewhat fastidious. Begin to develop the magical personality. Guard one's reaction and create, instead, affirmative and more positive actions than the natural reaction would be. Eventually, you may tap into that deep self within the self, which is the creative self, very quickly, clearing the energy center with rapidity that is not possible for a long period of time but does, indeed, clear the mind for a period of time necessary to begin the channeling process. This is also true in each entity's everyday and mundane existence. There is such a thing as faith and this faith is another word for love.

The faith that you seek is not the faith of the world as you know it. For the world has attempted to place everything in a slot, organizing, rationalizing, thinking and opinionating upon the nature of the creation and the Creator. This is not the job you were sent to do, not the work you came to accomplish. You came to be servants, servants of humankind, helpers in the harvest, those who are truly humble, those who truly wish to serve and do not need the reassurance *(inaudible)*. Set your mind upon that goal and move in the way which seems correct to you but seek always, first, knowledge of yourself, for this is knowledge of the Creator and until you know yourself and have a great and detailed knowledge of how faith and will work in the life, there will not be the peace which passes all understanding. There will only be the difficulties and toil of the spiritual journey. Love, light and merriment come upon those, upon that narrow path, who are able to be merry in their search and pilgrimage for the Father.

May each of you spend time gauging, examining and forgiving the self. In this effort you will have aid, both inner-planes and outer-planes, but as we have said, it is not wise to accept an inner-planes discarnate entity as one's own teacher unless one wishes also, when one graduates from this density, to suspend further learning for what would seem to be very many of your years. It is thought by us that it is preferable to move on and when one has learned more than third-density, then turn back and offer the hand in aid. And this is true of each upon your sphere. It is not well to move within one's human personality in service to others. It is well, rather, to know oneself so well that one may deliberately and consciously move in consciousness to the deeper self and with that deeper self console, comfort and forgive all that there is to be comforted or forgiven.

This instrument is telling us very loudly that we have spoken too long, once more.

The question has ramifications that move beyond what we have said this day but we may say that all questions of a non-transient nature, or that bring forth non-transient information, are those upon which one may expand and expostulate for any amount of time, as you know it.

We are of the principle of the spirit of the one infinite Creator and that one original Thought which created all that there is, that being love. Each of you is whole, perfect and an embodiment of love. May each open the self, knowing who one is and being a citizen of the universe in total democracy with all other spirits, and move and flow and allow that which is offered for one to occur. It is not necessary to push the experience about, for the most part, but simply to observe and become more and more knowledgeable of the dynamics of the mystery of your own self. For, only when you have done this may you chose your contact by the challenging process. In order to challenge a discarnate entity you, as an entity, must see yourself as light. The sparks of the Father within will eventually illuminate the whole of beingness, making it no longer necessary for a heavy chemical body to experience things within. Thus, those of you who are service-to-others oriented, be of service to yourself first. Ask for the comforter, if you wish. Ask for any help that you wish knowing the obligation placed upon you by inner-planes teachers. Move at your own pace and in your own way but be faithful, my friends. Keep seeking persistently, keep hoping, keep loving until you begin to feel as a wonderfully clear aqueduct for the water of blessedness [and aid.]

We would leave this instrument at this time, that the one known as Jim may conclude the working. We are apologetic for our garrulous nature, however, the questions asked us are interesting to us and we find many ramifications therein. We do apologize. We have great difficulty gauging your time as it is not that which is *(inaudible)*.

I am Q'uo, and I leave this instrument in love and light.

(Jim channeling)

I am Q'uo. I greet each in love and light through this instrument. At this time, we would offer ourselves in the attempt to speak to those queries which may yet remain unanswered upon the minds of those present. We hope that we are able to offer ourselves in a manner that does not provide the stumbling block but which, instead, makes clearer and smoother the way that each travels.

Is there a query at this time?

Questioner: I'd just like to know if my daughter's *(inaudible)* last night was a metaphysical event or an event created by *(inaudible)*?

I am Q'uo, and your latter assumption is correct, my sister.

Questioner: Uh-huh.

Is there another query?

Questioner: Yes, Q'uo. Your words are very well taken *(inaudible)*. I take them to heart. I have three brief questions concerning the way that we might pursue the path of our own growth. In posing these questions, I understand that the substance of the answers to these questions must come from within each of us. So, these questions are about form.

Can you give me a form in which any association with an inner master might be politely and gently and appreciatively dissolved? Can you give me a form in which a successful challenge to an entity, a discarnate entity, may be made? Can you give me a form in which a positive, service-to-others discarnate entity of the Confederation might be evoked?

I am Q'uo, and am aware of your queries, my brother. These are thoughtful queries which move to the very heart of the process of seeking, for as one moves within your illusion there is the taking of information from various sources and making it useful within the incarnative pattern. This is an ongoing process that increases with intensity as one becomes more conscious of this process.

It is well, as one continues to seek the nature of the Creation, the nature of the self, and the process by which one moves the self along the evolutionary path, to begin to see the relationships of the self with all that surrounds the self. Thus, there is shone upon this small self, shall we say, light from many directions that reflects to the self its nature in an extending manner. As one becomes more aware of those qualities that are the bedrock, the foundation of the self, one begins to have a firmer ground upon which to build this expanding concept of the self. One begins to have the qualities and ideals being internalized that one has found useful in the, shall we say, outer world. By this construction, one prepares the self for further information from whatever source, or sources.

When there is the establishment of a link between this self and other selves of, shall we say, a discarnate nature, those who have removed themselves to the inner planes of your planetary sphere, the link between these entities and yourself is that which is built upon your desire to know more of what is called the truth in order that one might come closer to this truth, which is ultimately the Creator, and then reflect some portion of this union to those about the self as one attempts to serve those about the self. Thus, it is the desire that one has manifested that creates any link with any other entity whether the entity be incarnate, discarnate or be of one Confederation or another.

Thus, the first step in forming a link, or severing this link, is to first find within the self the desire to do so and, as this desire is discovered, to follow that desire in intensification to the point that the beginning of what you have called a form makes itself apparent as well. In most cases, the form will have been made by the entity of third-density as it repeats its desire and moves in accordance with the intuitive information that is brought forth by this desire. This process, then, becomes repeated as a kind of ritual or mantram in order to either establish a link or to ask that the link be removed. Any entity of the inner planes, or of the Confederation of Planets in Service to the Infinite Creator origin, will respect the request and desire on the part of the third-density entity to either receive or cease to receive information. The entity of third-density, being incarnate within the third-density illusion, has great power over its own destiny, shall we say, in this manner for it is within the illusion and the incarnation and may, through its continued expression of desire, create those opportunities which it wishes to create, more and more successfully as the desire is purified.

If it is desired that entities of the Confederation of Planets in the Service of the Infinite Creator assist a third-density entity, this assistance is most usually offered in a manner which does not include the vocal channeling, as is occurring at this time, for we are well aware that it is necessary for a group to support such an effort for there is the opportunity to share much of that which is light-filled and, therefore, metaphysically potent and desirable upon many different planes. Those entities which would respond in the negative sense would, therefore, have greater success in removing this light were an entity operating singly in the capacity of an instrument, shall we say.

We are most comfortable in sending our love and blessings to entities requesting our assistance and in joining their meditations in order to deepen and enrich these meditations in the manner which the entity has chosen. Thus, my brother, we can suggest that one's desire and the purification of this desire is central in the continuing to seek information, from whatever source, in order that the illumination of the Creation and of the self might occur.

Is there a further query, my brother?

Questioner: No, thank you very much.

I am Q'uo, and we thank you, my brother. Is there another query, at this time?

(No further queries.)

I am Q'uo, and we would take this opportunity to thank each for inviting our presence and for offering us the patience that we find is often necessary as we become somewhat lengthy in our discourses. We do not wish to overtire the mind or the body but we rejoice in the opportunity to offer those thoughts in response to your queries which we found helpful in our journey and which we hope that you will, in some way, find helpful upon your journey as well.

At this time, we shall take our leave of this group, thanking each again for allowing us to walk upon that journey with you in a more manifest fashion. We always walk with those who seek union with the one infinite Creator for we are all portions of that one Creator returning to Itself, rejoicing with each step and blessing each burden.

We are those of Q'uo and we leave each in the love and in the light of the one infinite Creator. Adonai, my friends. Adonai. ✤

L/L Research

L/L Research is a subsidiary of Rock Creek Research & Development Laboratories, Inc.

P.O. Box 5195
Louisville, KY 40255-0195

www.llresearch.org

Rock Creek is a non-profit corporation dedicated to discovering and sharing information which may aid in the spiritual evolution of humankind.

ABOUT THE CONTENTS OF THIS TRANSCRIPT: This telepathic channeling has been taken from transcriptions of the weekly study and meditation meetings of the Rock Creek Research & Development Laboratories and L/L Research. It is offered in the hope that it may be useful to you. As the Confederation entities always make a point of saying, please use your discrimination and judgment in assessing this material. If something rings true to you, fine. If something does not resonate, please leave it behind, for neither we nor those of the Confederation would wish to be a stumbling block for any.

© 2009 L/L Research

Sunday Meditation
November 5, 1989

Group question: The question this evening has to do with joy. What is the function of joy in the evolutionary process in this particular experience and how can we find and utilize joy in our daily round of activities in a way that sustains our growth and service to others?

(Carla channeling)

I am Q'uo. I greet each of you in the love and in the light of the one infinite Creator. How lovely it is to dwell with you at this time in peace and harmony and seeking. We feel most privileged that we are asked to come and share with you our thoughts upon the subject of joy. May we say what a joy it is for us to so share our opinions.

We wish, however, to caution each against looking upon us or any material whatsoever as an infallible authority. We share our opinions. We are not infallible. Thusly, if we speak truth that is the truth of your heart, you shall recognize it. If you do not recognize it as if, though hearing it for the first time, it were a memory, then it is not a personal truth and could well be a stumbling block. We would ask you not to keep those things which do not feel resonant with your own path of seeking but we hope that we are able to share with you some things which may help as you move along the dusty road of pilgrimage.

Firstly, what we would like to say about joy is that, in its primal state, it has no function. It is. For joy is another expression, and indeed a basic manifestation, of unconditional love. Thus, it is of the essence or the beingness of the consciousness of the one infinite Creator, which is love.

To attempt to describe our understanding, limited though it may be, of reality or that which is most real, we may say that we have found the universe at rest to vibrate with the intensity and joy of sexual orgasm in a steady state. This is the energy power, the joy, the, as this instrument would say, élan vital which is its own truth, has its own beingness and needs no reason.

Now, we realize that it was not this ultimate joy, this joy which moves beyond the word, about which you are asking but rather how to find joy in circumstances where an orgasm is out of the question. We hope that you find this analogy helpful because all that manifests is a diffusion, a watering down, a shadowing, a tinting of that one great original Thought which is love and which manifests its energy in the manifested creation of a billion, billion sun bodies and the joyous flames of an infinite number of beings such as yourselves, who have moved into the darkness, into the seed bed of the densities, to root, contemplate and break forth from the earth in due time to bloom.

Each of you is a natural entity. There is a difficulty with experiencing joy, and now we speak in your terms of simple vital energy, love of life and so forth. It seems as though one were disappearing into a dark maze as one encounters the daily routine. Where is the joy, you ask, in taking out garbage and doing chores; in accomplishing well a job for which you have no real fondness? Where is the joy? Somehow it leaks out, it is not with you. It is unfindable and so an entity moves into the desert of indifference or sadness or sorrow or unsatisfied desire.

It is painful there in the desert. One goes through the motions. One does not appreciate the difficulties until a length of your time has passed and, as you gaze back on the mystery of your desert experience, sitting in an oasis that has come upon you, you are able to see the enormously helpful catalytic nature of that which seemed to be no joy but only difficulty, frustration, boredom and distraction, if not even more negative emotions.

When speaking of spiritual work we always move to speaking of a daily practice, one which is faithfully and reliably kept. It is not easy for entities who dwell in your heavy chemical illusion and who have so much to do in order to keep the self going to find the time each day to meditate, to move into silence, to listen and speak not, neither utter a word except, "Here am I."

For as you are aware of your beingness, you are aware of the beingness of all that there is. For the creation is an illusion outside of you. It is actualized within you in that portion of yourself which is of the infinite Creator. It is this portion to which you may turn for joy. In the sense of creating, from the outside in, a way of feeling vital and energetic, we can only say that it is to those who enjoy the athletics of the body or other means of exhausting the self who may find the joy from outside. For the true function of joy is an infinite function and that is growth. Joy may be another word for confident and sure faith.

Now, we have moved away from the state of orgasmic pleasure to a more modest view of joy but we do not wish to give you information that enables you to burn out like a bright comet and become extinguished. We wish to speak of a joy that is peaceful, stable, vital and living. This does not come from the entity within the incarnational experience. Rather, the self which is experiencing the incarnation on the surface level of consciousness must yield to that which is within the self which is infinite.

The practice of this yielding, this tabernacling with the one infinite Creator, the immediacy of this presence, when carried on persistently, patiently and with no dedication to outcome over a period of time begins to set within one a growing awareness of infinity. For as you meditate and listen, you are lost in the present moment. And this present moment is instinct with joy. The present moment is infinity. It is as though one were at the intersection of time and eternity at each present moment. The difficulties people experience are due to living the horizontal life without being aware of the resonances of the vertical life which is moving infinitely within one at all times.

You see, it is so tempting to think of oneself as the physical vehicle which you may see in one of your mirrors. It is so tempting to give oneself characteristics and qualities based upon various parts of one's physical appearance, emotional makeup, and so forth. It is very, very easy to become entwined with many, many intellectual thoughts which always end in mystery and paradox.

It is extremely tempting, in a world which values things and phenomena and fact and proof, to seek some proof of that which is your inward journey to eternity, your journey to the present moment and into the present moment, so that you begin to sense the deep, infinite resonances of your beingness in the one infinite Creator.

You are love. You are the light. But you are not these things within your physical form. Indeed, within this density you are deliberately causing yourself to become stupid in order to be able to partake of the intense catalyst available to one in a heavy, chemical vehicle. You may think of yourself as a distillery or a refinery that begins with the raw material of the harvest of your spirit, your experience, and your meditation and out of which you begin to create that which may be called the magical personality. You begin to know, without knowing what, that there is an immediate presence, an infinite and omnipresent reality lying beneath, above, within, without and in between all that there is. There is a depth and a height to any moment of the life experience.

The point of view may be manipulated by the intellectual mind and this is a tool which is useful in the search for one's own center of vitality, joy, peace and love. One certainly may ask oneself what causes joy within. But the answers are most distorted by the chemical body which is experienced.

And again we move back to the analog of orgasm and joy. To expect one within third density to vibrate orgasmically at each moment would be to ask that which is not possible within the illusion. You are not here to be joyful but rather to make choices. This is that for which you came into this experience: to choose to serve either the self or the one infinite Creator, as seen in the faces of all those whom you meet.

Now, it is difficult to see many entities as the face of the one infinite Creator. For all entities have the clay feet of that which perishes, that which does not know what is hidden within the roots of mind. Thusly, to expect to have the vitality and the joy at all times is to expect to learn nothing, to progress not at all and to make no choices. For with choice there comes change. With change there comes pain.

Each time a truth that has worked in the past ceases to work in the present, much difficult work must be done in consciousness. For your mind must lose or "dump" the program which no longer is effectual for the seeking entity in order to make a place for a new understanding that will inevitably change the seeker in some way. Change is painful. Dumping information is painful. Letting go of old truths is painful. Being uncertain is painful. Being at risk is painful.

You are those who have sought a life of risk. You do not wish to stay in one place mentally, spiritually or emotionally. You wish rather to accelerate the pace of your spiritual evolution. Now, this is sensible. This is in our opinion the very best and most useful attitude to take. But it is not a path which delivers one into the gateway of élan and joy but rather the continuing difficulties of confusion, misunderstanding, realignment of understanding, and ever progressing onward.

There is much more desert in the spiritual life than there is oasis. It is simply a matter of how much you, as a spirit, wish to work in consciousness. The more that you work in consciousness, the more you will change, the more you will be transformed and the more you will be uncomfortable.

Why then, do seekers so stubbornly follow their star? Nothing, my friends, rests in the creation. All things move. And in this activity, in this manifestation, in this movement there is that which, as it is said in your holy works, passeth all understanding. The name for that which passeth all understanding within the holy work of which we speak, is peace. But it is not a peace that is understood among your peoples for it is a peace that is joyful, a peace that is vital, a peace that is merry, that may make light of the serious and may tease and play and feel one's way as a child within the great caverns and grottoes through which one must pass in the spiritual quest, having only one faint light: that of hope. And so you move in darkness, attempting to see. And much of the energy of the incarnation is involved with the simple ability to perceive without distortion.

Now, perception without distortion is a sure yielding of joy. On the other hand, each must distort, through the physical senses, the catalyst which comes to one. The senses you have are those given to all and they are all illusory. To base one's seeking for vital energy on the life experience or anything which it may offer is to put one's trust in that which perishes. The key to joy is the realization that you are an imperishable being. You are a being which is love and is called to love. The Creator created each out of love and placed within each free will and Itself. You are moving through the disciplining of your own free will. And that disciplining must be done freely, the choices your own, in order for that joy which underlies all things to begin to bubble up into the life experience.

We find that a sense of humor, as this instrument would call it, is extraordinarily helpful in the pursuit of a deeper and clearer awareness of the tremendous beauty and resonance of each present moment. As one moves about the illusion doing what one must do to support the needs of the physical vehicle, it is most easy to see life as a horizontal path; a path upon which one literally walks, plods, trudges, ambles or runs, depending upon the mood; a path in which gravity keeps one's feet to the ground, keeps one from rising into the ethereal or sinking into the roots of mind.

One of the choices each spiritual entity makes is whether to move upon that which is consciously known in making life decisions and in living moment to moment or casting all safety to the winds and trusting the self to the risky business of feeling the depths and the heights of each present moment.

It is difficult, when one is working at a job to which one is indifferent, to feel the magnificent resonance of the present moment, to experience the intersection of eternity with that present moment.

Consequently, it is a good exercise, when one is fatigued in the spirit, the emotions and the mind, to move backwards, away from gravity, away from all that has to do with the illusions created by fields of energy.

Moving back, we may see the home planet—fragile, somewhat troubled, and infinitely beautiful. One may imagine the many entities scurrying about on the surface of this celestial globe but one no longer sees the individual selves of the bodies of the third-density beings of the planet, that which will become, in fourth density, a social memory complex.

Thus, when one is peeved, distressed or distraught it is well to move back in the mind, moving away from the surface, flying upwards, gazing down upon, first, yourself and the room, and the dwelling and the town, then larger land masses, then the planet. Then one finally moves back enough to see the infinity of celestial bodies, of centers of the Logos or love which is the great original Thought.

It is well to keep within the mind the resonances of eternity. And if they are not to be found upon the surface of the daily experience, yet still, you are of a certain nature and you may tap into the infinite possibilities of the present moment more and more by persistent faith and hope. Within your illusion all ends in mystery, nothing can be known ultimately.

It is a necessary portion of the illusion of third density that nothing may be objectively proven that would interfere with the free will choices of entities who are deciding upon their path of service. For this reason you came into incarnation, to express and manifest your choice of a path of service.

There are suggestions we may give as to how to compound the joy that is native to you already. If one may draw back from an unpleasant entity enough to affirm that that entity is the one infinite Creator distorting its own illusion in its own way to its own sadness, one is then able to feel an outburst of compassion for an unhappy spirit.

One is similarly able to feel compassion for the one who is happy but without a spiritual vector. Many are those who are asleep and do not wish at this time to awaken. This is acceptable, for there is an eternity in which each has all the time, literally, in creation to move back to the source whence each came before the world as you know it was created.

You are imperishable. You are light. You are moving towards the light. This instrument finds the parable within the holy work which you call the *Holy Bible* of the prodigal son and daughter to be most useful in an awareness of the spiritual journey's constant intersection with the infinite love of the one Creator.

We will now work upon some simple exercises to move into a mental, emotional and spiritual configuration which allows one to follow one's joy.

Firstly, the listening meditation, done persistently and in a daily manner and, if possible, with two or more together, is a basic tool, one which cuts to the heart of a process of spiritual evolution. For those who speak are not listening and those who know all the answers have blocked further questions, further learning, further refinement, further distilling into purity.

You seek to be pure in your service, in your dedication to the one infinite Creator. Yet this seems oftentimes a burdensome and toilsome thing, a yoke you must carry, and a burden that weighs the body, the mind, and the soul down with responsibility. This is where the ability to laugh at the self, to laugh at situations, to laugh at the enormous comedy of paradox and mystery comes in so handy. When all else fails and there is no joy within you and there is much difficulty, one tool you may use is the sense of humor.

Gaze at the entity which is the Creator but is distorting itself in a way which expresses anger or hostility or other negative emotions and remove that entity's clothes. Put this image in the mind so that all the gesticulations, all the pomp, all the mannerisms are those done by an entity in his underwear. It is well, perhaps, to imagine how someone would look with big green spots or a third eye or blue skin. Work at thinking ridiculous thoughts. For the spiritual path is not serious, precisely. The spiritual path is all that there is.

It is possible within the schoolroom to ignore the lessons. But when one is in school, that is the business of the student. One may be an eager student or a lackadaisical one. One may do the homework or not. And we would not judge any, for until the time comes when the demand from within to know infinity and imperishability becomes paramount, it is only flogging and whipping at the self to approximate the state of realization of one's own imperishable nature. Thus, each entity has a rhythm of its own, a time of its own, and a pattern of its own.

There is another tool which one may use to good effect if one is able not to trust the intellect beyond a certain point. That tool is the analytical ability of the mind. When one moves oneself back from a situation which is disturbing one and begins to untie the tangle of distress, one may, through inductive and deductive reasoning processes, come to more and more fundamental realizations as to the true nature of that experience which is difficult for you at this particular time.

You were not of a mind to come here to be happy and content. You were of a mind to come here to graduate into a density that has more light, less heaviness, and no veil between the conscious mind and the roots of mind. Yet you cannot use the light of the one infinite Creator until you have made a profound and persistently chosen choice.

Whom shall you serve, to serve the infinite One? Shall you serve yourself, or shall you, having prepared yourself to serve others in what may seem like service to self, move into the world with the attitude, "How may I help? Send me where there is work for me to do and let me never judge that work or hold it as a goal but only do it for love and let it go." There is a tremendous release of joy in the experience of truly releasing one's good intentions to the caretaking of those who may well not view that joy and wisdom of yours as useful to them but indeed may gibe and carp at the spiritual seeker for his unworldliness, his lack of attention to the important things such as your money, your possessions, your reputations, and your power over other entities.

You see, this third-density experience is biased, in the outer sense, towards service to self. This makes all entities uncomfortable and puts them in the position of choosing. This is the point of this particular density. It is especially the point of the density at this time, as each entity prepares for the walk of light and each entity wishes to move comfortably into the more dense and living light of the one infinite Creator which creates the illusion of fourth density.

A tool which is most helpful in removing negativity from the self that is unwanted is that which this instrument would call prayer. It is not for nothing that a teacher known as Jesus suggested to pray for those who despitefully use you. The concern, the turning to the Creator, the genuine loving and praying for an entity who would never expect such a positive return, is a way of aiding that entity by the love it does receive. It then becomes a mirror to reflect back to you a hundredfold that desire to be of service. It may not come from the entity with which you have the difficulty, as each entity has its own path, but it is inevitable that, as you offer yourself, so you shall receive what others offer.

How to find joy? Know more and more who you are. You are an imperishable being of light. You are doing many ridiculous things within an illusion which is created to be difficult, ridiculous, paradoxical, confusing and destructive of all positive emotions. Yet within you is the one infinite Creator. And the infinity of that imperishable self that is you may always lift the self by prayer, by meditation, by laughter, and simply by the abiding, persistent calling upon the hope and faith that each truly is a portion of the one infinite Creator and of the return of the prodigal.

No matter how long and how difficult the journey, it will occur and the Father will be waiting with a great feast. And in that feast you shall feed each other. For joy comes from others to the self and goes from the self to others. Joy is expansive, generous.

Vitality is a matter of honoring the Creator within each and having the sense of humor to make fun of the illusion that separates each from each. When you touch hands, you touch energy fields. When you love and pray and make a cartoon of an entity to strip him of his negative qualities, you have invoked that which will give joy not only to yourself but to those about you. For one who is centered in eternity while in the present moment is a light unto many, a joy unto many, a source of faith to many. Never consider yourself as unimportant or unworthy. You are the Creator. You simply are learning to deal with the freedom that is the hallmark of the creation of the infinite One. You are free. There is no failure. You choose your own pace.

Before we leave this instrument, we would like to affirm once again that there is not a large number among your people who have the spiritual maturity to experience joy as a steady state. This is not important. What is important is the knowledge within that it exists in a steady state, that it is of love, the Logos, the infinite Creator, and that all is as it should be for your learning.

What sacrifices you made, my friends, coming here. One might well compare this to the basic training in the Army or the Marine Corps. It is difficult. It is taxing. It is wearying. Allow yourself these things and laugh together. Be merry together. Exhort each other, when each is sad, by the silent exhortation of the hug, the smile, the listening ear, and the understanding heart.

If you wish to be joyful, it shall always come to you by reflection. For as you give, so shall you receive.

We would at this time move to the instrument known as Jim so that we may close the meeting through that instrument if he will accept our contact. We thank this instrument very much and we leave it now in love and light. I am Q'uo.

(Jim channeling)

I am Q'uo. I greet each again in love and light through this instrument. We realize that we have spoken for a lengthy portion of your time and that there is fatigue within the circle. But we wish to offer an opportunity for those present to ask the query which may yet remain upon the mind, if indeed such does. Is there a query at this time?

Questioner: I would ask about what, in yogic terminology, is referred to as kriyas[3] which I experience as resistance within the body and mind complex to the free flowing of intelligent energy as it was given from the Creator. I am wondering if this is largely due to mental distortions which have their root in the physical body or are they also maybe preexisting physical distortions? And in what way can I work towards clearing my mind/body complex to allow this freer flowing energy?

I am Q'uo. I am aware of your query, my brother. The distorting effects of which you speak are, for most entities, reflections of mental origin which have as their roots the particular bias that has been desired to be experienced as a portion of a lesson or a service within an incarnation. There is the movement through the deeper portions of the tree of mind that is made as one enters into the meditative state and begins to contact those deeper portions of mind. One experiences this contact as an increase in one's vibratory rate or awareness of this nature of being. One also passes through the area in which the perceptions have been formed and reside, upon a subconscious level, and refracts a portion of this light energy.

These symbolic experiences that, in effect, cause a resistance to the available and increasing energy of intelligence contacted may be seen in their more expansive nature, shall we say, by observing the energy centers affected and the type of expression that occurs within the life pattern in the daily round of activities as a result of this kind of distortion, which is also an opportunity to become more aware of a facet of the being that seeks balance.

Thus, one may observe the daily round of activities in a regularized fashion so that those experiences which register in a polarized form, either toward the positive or the negative, in personal terms, may be noted and used as seed for meditation, so that greater understanding of that facet of the self might be achieved and might be applied to the life experience in a more conscious fashion when similar catalytic circumstances present themselves once again.

This kind of review of the daily experience has the effect of illumination in that the self becomes informed. It has the effect of allowing for balance to occur within the total being as well as the effect of providing the opportunity for forgiveness to be offered to other selves and also the self, which indeed deserves this kind of inner acceptance and requires such in order for the movement from that point to be made.

Is there a further query, my brother?

Questioner: No, thank you very much.

I am Q'uo, and thank you, my brother. Is there another query?

Carla: I don't know, I guess I'm still really aware that no matter how you look at the illusion, if you are having a bad time, you are having a bad time. Is it possible that a constant state of joy is not so much the focus of this incarnation as the constant search for the proper questions about what is truth? I've puzzled over that for many years. It doesn't seem to be part of the human destiny and nature to be unfailingly happy.

---

[3] Kriya is a technique of energy control, or pranayama. It is also a comprehensive spiritual path, which includes additional meditation practices, right living, and a link to the enlightened Masters.

I am Q'uo, and I am aware of your query, my sister. For indeed, this evening we have spoken at length concerning the place which joy holds as that which is ever present and eternal, yet that which is but the oasis upon your long and dusty journeys within the third-density illusion. For if one wishes to progress and to be able to experience a greater unity with all that one sees about one as the one Creator, it is necessary to be in the midst of the catalyst and its effect upon your total being. This requires a forgetting, for the most part, within the incarnation of that unity which indeed binds all that is and of that love which creates and empowers all that is and that light which reveals the true nature of all that is.

This forgetting allows for the self to become affected by the illusion in a manner which will offer the opportunity for the entity to choose more and more to seek, in one fashion or another, to serve the Creator in the self or in others so that an awareness of the Creator might be given to the Creator in a fashion which is unique.

And in providing this perspective and experience, one also expands the ability to accept more and more of the light of the Creator within the being. Thus, you are correct, my sister, in that joy is but a fleeting visitor to those who wish to pursue the work in consciousness that is possible within an illusion that seems so far removed from unity, from love, or from light. This is the sacrifice which you make, my friends, when you enter incarnation.

Yet, there is a pearl, as it has been said, of very great price that may be won by such sacrifice, so that when it is finally won, all sacrifices will seem as nothing in comparison to that great pearl.

Is there a further query, my sister?

Carla: No, thank you.

I am Q'uo, and we thank you, my sister. Is there another query at his time?

(No further queries.)

I am Q'uo, and would take this opportunity to express our great feeling of joy and gratitude at being invited to blend our vibrations with yours this evening and for the journey which each shares with the others at this time. We hope that we have been able to offer a perspective from our experience that will be of service to you. We would, at this time, take our leave of this instrument and this group, leaving each, as always, in the love and in the light of the one infinite Creator. We are known to you as those of Q'uo. Adonai, my friends. Adonai. ☥

L/L Research is a subsidiary of Rock Creek Research & Development Laboratories, Inc.

P.O. Box 5195
Louisville, KY 40255-0195

L/L Research

www.llresearch.org

Rock Creek is a non-profit corporation dedicated to discovering and sharing information which may aid in the spiritual evolution of humankind.

ABOUT THE CONTENTS OF THIS TRANSCRIPT: This telepathic channeling has been taken from transcriptions of the weekly study and meditation meetings of the Rock Creek Research & Development Laboratories and L/L Research. It is offered in the hope that it may be useful to you. As the Confederation entities always make a point of saying, please use your discrimination and judgment in assessing this material. If something rings true to you, fine. If something does not resonate, please leave it behind, for neither we nor those of the Confederation would wish to be a stumbling block for any.

CAVEAT: This transcript is being published by L/L Research in a not yet final form. It has, however, been edited and any obvious errors have been corrected. When it is in a final form, this caveat will be removed.

© 2009 L/L Research

Sunday Meditation
November 12, 1989

Emotions, Part I

Group question: What is the function of emotions in the life of the spiritual seeker, and what value is there to the seeker in attempting to uncover or develop or feel the full range of emotions, especially the caring for those about one, and feeling the vitality of life and being able to express the feelings that move through one?

(Carla channeling)

I am Q'uo. I greet this circle of souls in the love and in the light of the one infinite Creator. It is our privilege to be called to this group of light being, and we bask in the glow of your seeking and your love.

In speaking about emotion, there are semantic difficulties. Emotion has been systematically undervalued among your peoples for a great span of your experience, much to the detriment of the whole and unified self which seeks to manifest through third density illusion the love and the light of the one infinite Creator. What passes for emotion among many are not so much feelings as basic instincts such as reproduction, companionship and practicality. The role of emotions, while idealized within your culture, is in fact a false role, in that emotions do not serve the function which they are capable of serving.

The most usual blockages of energy are two. One is the overactive emotional nature, that nature that wears, as this instrument would say, the heart upon the sleeve, one who reacts with a shallow and instinct feeling to each catalyst that it encounters. The hectic quality of these emotions is a disturbance and a confusion, rather than that which is the true function of emotion, that is, the further knowing of the self and the ennoblement of the expression of life within the consciousness of manifestation. How much we wish we could aid those who are caught in surface emotion, yet always it is the free will choice of each to use its intellect, surface emotion, or to move in consciousness into a more helpful and useful focus of mind and heart, so that one may discover the true, deep and abiding emotions that create a life in faith.

The other common blockage of emotions is also culturally produced. The young ones of your society are not cherished with deep and abiding emotion, quite often and instead there is the rigid rule, the constant request of parent to child for this or that behavior, which, in the course of the young years, causes many souls to become inured and numbed to emotion. The intellect observes the pain of expressing emotion to those who identify deep emotion with misbehavior and unacceptable sentimentality, and so it becomes unproductive, seemingly, and indeed hurtful, to continue

310

experiencing the impact of the full emotional nature of the deep mind.

Almost everyone dwelling upon your sphere at this time, in your culture, tends toward one or the other bias, rather than appreciating emotion in its purified and deeper sense as the profoundest part of one's intelligence. The function of emotion in the spiritual life is the creating of the vitality, the passion and intensity which is not created out of thin air, but discovered from within. In order to make use of these purified emotions which speak of deep intelligence, it is often necessary for an entity to be aided by inspiration, example, and most of all, desire: desire to remove the stumbling blocks which block energy from the heart. With the energy blocked by over-activity or numbness of emotion, the spiritual path is even more muddled, wearisome and confusing than it needs to be. This is because such blockages keep energy from entering the heart in full measure, and it is the heart energy which is lifted up and ennobled by work in consciousness.

Now, what is the definition of purified emotion? We search for vocabulary which is not religious, but rather philosophical, for it is all too easy to say worship, adore, give thanksgiving, offer praise to the one infinite Creator. Instead, we would simply put it in another context. As one is able to experience the self more and more intelligently, consciously and fully, one is able to feel self-forgiven, worthy, hopeful, cheerful, peaceful and oriented toward a lively work on behalf of the one infinite Creator. Humankind is fueled, not by oil or coal so much as by inspiration, passion, sharing and caring. Thus, the more fully one is able to tap into the deep and plangent notes of purified emotion, the greater is one's ability to manifest the light of the infinite One to a darkened world, which rejoices in seeing beacons of light, whether or not they know why the light is there, how the light has come to be there, and what is its function. The emotional nature of a deep and strengthening kind is the basis of intelligence which forms the bedrock of faith. We speak not of faith in this, or faith in that, for the Creator is infinite and mysterious, and any specific belief system neglects much of the whole repertoire of spiritual tools and resources. Therefore, in encouraging one's own deeper intelligence, that is, the deep emotions, one must seek within for that center about which the incarnational experience now [revolves].

It is impossible to create purified emotion by desire alone, for desire will bring you to the border of that emotion, but will make of it a mockery unless the deep self is touched, and felt, unless emotion may inform intellect. Those among your people who are small in years are perfect examples, for the most part, of entities which are in touch with deep emotion. The younger the entity, the closer that entity is to concepts of deep memory concerning the true self and the purpose of the incarnational experience. However, immediately upon entering this illusion the process of enculturation begins, and little by little, young souls react to a lack of understanding, either by moving on a sea of shallow emotions at all times, or by rejecting emotion as painful, unnecessary and undesirable, as it does cause pain to one who does not have a fully energized heart energy center.

Many of your peoples attempt to create within themselves deep emotion, that they may love, and know the joy of deep and spiritual love. This is an exercise in futility. Also to be de-emphasized are those practices of your religions which encourage and even goad participants into an high emotional state which is fed, not by deep emotions in most cases, but by the enjoyable excitement of group joy, that is, when one worships in such a way as artificially to move the hearts of entities from without, so, to the extent that this is so, shall the emotion be that which rings false for deep work in consciousness.

Indeed, the intellect is often the master, even of the most devoted spiritual seeker. Burdened with the rational mind, the seeker often places too little emphasis on the freeing up of deep energies, of keeping open those passageways from spiritual self to mental, emotional and spiritual self. The creation is consciousness, and that consciousness is pure emotion, not the pure intellect. Infinite intelligence expresses itself within incarnation as deep and abiding emotion. Thus, as one feels love pouring through one, one is fulfilling one's fundamental and major mission upon your Earth sphere, and that is to be a radiant being, a light to many, not by action, but by the vital energy, the sweetness of soul, and the expressions of love which move through the seeker who has opened the door to deep emotion.

To remove oneself from the coil of emotion that is shallow, or emotion that is numbed, one may sometimes find it helpful to seek a healer which works with the emotional dynamics and energies of entities. There is, in this type of healer, the energy which may be used, shall we say, as a jump start upon the clearing of emotional blockages. The energy of the teacher in this instance is critical, and those teachers which are not basically moving in joy need to turn within before teaching further, to find the absolute love which is the wisdom of the self for that greater Self which is Love. Love needs must answer love for the creation of each seeker to move into balance.

Perhaps the road to experiencing emotions more clearly and more deeply begins with the contemplation of the astounding, generous and infinite love of the one Creator. The Creator's nature Itself is love infinite. Each of you is likewise imperishable and infinite, but in terms of the experience you now enjoy, you within the body are finite, limited and fooled by the illusion which is to teach you. Therefore, we suggest a daily alignment of affirmation and closeness with the love within one's self which is infinite. Many negative emotions disturb the hearts of those who have not found pure emotion, and, instead of being uplifted by love, they feel judged, inadequate and unloving. This is because the surface healing emotions come from one rather than through one, [and] are easily exhausted or transformed into negative emotions of frustration, anger and guilt.

Thus, one is seeking that which one cannot put into words, that which may fill the being, so that the being is rich and full and vital, and spilling over with love, love infinite. In this atmosphere each entity becomes a healer, each entity becomes a channel, each entity becomes that which one would call Christ to those about one.

Purified emotion, whole and unblemished divine love, is the very axis upon which infinite intelligence built the myriad illusions which lead each imperishable soul along the path of inspiration, closeness to the one Creator, and an infinite capacity for compassion and service to others. Without emotion of a deep nature, the life experience lacks vividness, and it is more difficult for the seeker to make the choice of service to others or service to self with firmness of heart and intensity of passion.

Sometimes it is a long road which the pilgrim must wend upon its way to the experiencing of untutored and unregulated emotional truth. This is as it should be, and we ask each not to be discouraged as one again and again fails to realize the potential within the self, while manifesting this worshipful, sanctified and perfect love. Such deep truths are difficult to find within your illusion. So it was designed that each, by one lesson upon another, by persistence, and by the leap of faith, may become that which one was not before, consciously, that is a very creature of the Creator, a portion of infinite intelligence, an eternal, beautiful and perfect group of energies and expressions.

For, as you well know within your density, all that you see, including your own body, is illusory. That which you are indeed, in truth, is a complex of electromagnetic fields which hold within them the precious and infinite consciousness which, when purified, is one with the infinite Creator. Thus, each emotional blockage which may be found and dispelled, leaves a space, an emptiness, which is absolutely necessary in order that one may move from the emotions of the surface and the involvements of the day to a keener awareness of self as one with the Creator, a bearer of love, a messenger and channel of light to all whom you meet.

There is danger, as in any other pursuit, in working at the discovery of one's emotions. The nature of the deep self is subtle, and is not to be manipulated from without. Rather, it is a matter of seeking faithfully and persistently in meditation and in action, to begin to observe the resonances of deep emotion which lie between the lines of the pages of everyday life. Emotion wells up within, the gift of the nature of the one infinite Creator to its infinite family, its heirs of glory.

We use the word glory most specifically and literally. There is within each seeking entity the dynamic of vitality and numbness, of joy and sorrow, of giving and receiving. It is those which harness the intellect as a dray horse for work upon the surface, and who move into meditation and deeper states of consciousness, which will find the emotions being released from within. A release of blocked emotion is greatly healing, and as one entity is healed and becomes more and more an intense and passionate creature of the light, one becomes less and less addicted to those everyday things which seem so important, and more and more tuned to the spontaneous actions of creative love. The glory of the universe of the infinite One is that each portion of it is full and instinct with profound and whole emotion, that is, the one great original Thought of love, which is the Creator as well as the creation.

There is further aid when one has touched the heart of self and felt the release of blocked energies, and that is that one's abilities to serve others in a compassionate manner are greatly aided, for entities of themselves within the third-density illusion cannot sustain an effort which is ideal. Ideals will always be overtaken by practicalities, adjustments, compromises. Better it is for one to retire from the human arena in a persistently regularized manner, seeking within, listening within, asking to know the deepest portions, the most intelligent portions of the self, which move in emotion and archetype.

The developing of genuine purified emotion is for most a long and toilsome task, where so much of the cultural conditioning is that which, in the case of some, encourages the bubbling of surface emotion, and in others the refusal to express feeling in any way. Such are the ways your culture deadens souls to their true purpose, which is to seek persistently, patiently and prayerfully, to know, and to be with the One.

Once one realizes that within oneself lies holy ground, one knows and trusts far better the path of seeking within, for as we said, emotion that is artificially created is easy emotion, emotion which must be renewed as a library book must be renewed. It is not lasting and it requires constant nurturing and stimulation from without.

Each entity will, because of cultural conditioning, have to more or less extent some measure of blockage within those energy centers which feed the heart energy center. Thus, no one is alone in doubting and asking, yet also no one who seeks to remedy this situation by meditation and contemplation shall be a complete failure, for it is sheer intent, intensity of desire, that moves one beyond the self in surrender to that other self which is the true nature of the ephemeral third-density self.

The instrument informs us that we must cut short our unfortunately prolix dissertation. We are sorry for being unaware of the passage of time, but within your dimension the realization of the time you experience is most difficult for us, and there is much to say upon this subject. We shall simply say to each that the release of negative emotion such as guilt, anger, humiliation and resentment is an incredible healing which is only possible through the infinite love of the one Creator, and through one's identification with that love, and one's dedication to seeking in the deepest and most aesthetically beautiful way possible, to be truth incarnate, to express love divine, to allow oneself to be a channel of compassion and nonjudgmental aid.

We encourage each to seek the holy ground within, to find praise and give thanks for the glory, for beauty, the infinite majesty of the one great original Thought. The heavens sing with His glory, the trees and mountains dance, and all stars and planets sing a song of passionate love for the Creator unmanifest, and for each of you, the Creator made manifest and given complete free will.

We encourage you each to seek the deeper truths within, to allow negative emotions to be balanced and to fall away, as it is natural for them to do in the light of unconditional love. May each of you discover within the inner room the infinity within oneself, the purified emotion which in full strength is the Logos.

What is the function of emotion? It is intelligence which produces profound and fundamental transformation. Only the heart, when released from stricture, may be so. The approach of intellect, the approach from the outside in, the approach of believing this or that, is most frequently fruitless. It is the opening of oneself to free-floating and abstract faith, the faith that all is as it was planned to be, the faith that that which was planned is helpful and full of love, which moves the seeker onward most swiftly upon the path of spiritual evolution.

Rejoice, each soul who finds release from numbness or surface addictions. We rejoice with you as you seek the heart of the self which is the greater Self. Respect deep emotion. Realize that the vital energies are based upon one's ability to have faith and to dwell in an emotional state of unconditional love. Daily meditation, daily contemplation, and what analysis the brain may perform, is suggested for all who seek, for you are seeking to change into the awareness of the self which is imperishable. Forgiveness is an emotion, not a mental process, and it is the key to the advancement of the self in polarization of service to the one infinite Creator. May you respect and encourage intense, loving emotion. May you find it acceptable to release numbness and surface emotion as meditation matures and strengthens the deeper self within.

We thank this instrument, and would like to close the meeting through the one known as Jim. We leave this instrument in love and light. I am Q'uo.

(Jim channeling)

I am Q'uo, and greet each again in love and light through this instrument. We are aware that there is some fatigue in the circle, but are happy to offer ourselves in the attempt to speak to any queries which may prove helpful at this time. Is there a query at this time?

T: I don't really have a question, but I'd like to express my gratitude for the message tonight. It was really what I needed to hear. I thank you very much.

I am Q'uo, and we are most grateful to you, my brother, for posing the query that we were able to offer information upon. It is a great service to have those who bring their heartfelt concerns to our attention that we might have an avenue through which to offer our service.

Is there a query at this time?

K: You mentioned that there is much to say upon this subject. Would it be possible in the future, if we desire more information upon this subject, to ask you to continue from where you left off, or would we need to formulate another similar question in order to continue?

I am Q'uo, and we would be happy to begin at the point which this evening has been our ending at a future meeting, as you measure your time. We would simply request that the query be vibrated again at that time, so that we might again find that focus that has been fine-tuned, shall we say, within this group.

Is there another query?

Carla: No, thank you.

I am Q'uo, and we thank you, my sister. As we have discovered that the evening has grown long in your measurement of time, and that we have, for the nonce, exhausted those queries, we shall take our leave of this group, thanking each again for offering us the opportunity to offer our service at this time, and leaving you in the love and in the light of the one infinite Creator. We are known to you as those of Q'uo. Adonai, my friends. Adonai. ✢

L/L Research

L/L Research is a subsidiary of Rock Creek Research & Development Laboratories, Inc.

P.O. Box 5195
Louisville, KY 40255-0195

www.llresearch.org

Rock Creek is a non-profit corporation dedicated to discovering and sharing information which may aid in the spiritual evolution of humankind.

ABOUT THE CONTENTS OF THIS TRANSCRIPT: This telepathic channeling has been taken from transcriptions of the weekly study and meditation meetings of the Rock Creek Research & Development Laboratories and L/L Research. It is offered in the hope that it may be useful to you. As the Confederation entities always make a point of saying, please use your discrimination and judgment in assessing this material. If something rings true to you, fine. If something does not resonate, please leave it behind, for neither we nor those of the Confederation would wish to be a stumbling block for any.

CAVEAT: This transcript is being published by L/L Research in a not yet final form. It has, however, been edited and any obvious errors have been corrected. When it is in a final form, this caveat will be removed.

© 2009 L/L Research

Sunday Meditation
November 26, 1989

Emotions, Part II

Group question: What is the function of emotions in the life of the spiritual seeker, and what value is there to the seeker in attempting to uncover or develop or feel the full range of emotions, especially the caring for those about one and feeling the vitality of life and being able to express the feelings that move through one?

(Carla channeling)

I am Q'uo. Greetings to you all in the love and in the light of the one infinite Creator, whom we serve in our humble way as do you in yours. We are most grateful to share these few steps of your path of seeking with you, and to explore with you concepts having to do with the nature of consciousness.

Previously, we had established that in truth, although the intellect is highly regarded within your culture, it is, nonetheless, not as intelligent a portion of the mind as the deeper intuitions, what some might call gut instinct, and others call the prompting of the still small voice within, the higher self, guidance, or by whatever name an entity chooses to relate itself to a wider, wiser intelligence. This intelligence is emotion. We established that the surface emotions of life having to do with being caught in traffic, being late, having to wait, feeling negative emotions, feeling quick positive emotions with no depth, is the province of the mundane.

We do not suggest that you follow each whim, each thought, each impulse. We suggest, rather, the trust in the process of seeking within for the truth which will set you free, though it may not set another free. Each of you is unique, and the emotions that are your deeper intelligence are unique to you, their balance is unique to you, and the fruit of that balance in service is unique to you. Thus, we have established a great respect for the intuition and emotion that is the essence of intelligence.

We shall pause as this instrument is concerned.

(Pause while Carla checks with Jim, who has been coughing.)

(Carla channeling)

I am Q'uo, and am again with this instrument, and greet each again in love and light and thanks. We shall continue.

For emotion to be considered the deeper intelligence, a new concept must be created, a word which is not within your working language, to indicate not the emotion of the easy joys and the easy sorrows, but those emotions which move deeply within the roots of mind, moved by the tides of many, many past experiences and many choices made, moved by the guidance of whatever you wish to call that spirit that comforts and supports when all of humankind seems to have failed you. Why would we ask you to dive so deep into yourself when there is a world of manifestation for you to enjoy? There is a reason, and we feel it is a worthy one, and it is from this point that we wish to go forward.

As entities are given physical vehicles at birth and move into the world, their first emotion is anger, their second, love. So begins the dynamic of a lifetime: anger at change, and love at being fed. The anger, that of change, that of moving from the safety and quiet of the womb to the harsh illusion of your world is extremely traumatic, and it creates in the entity, even so small a one, that desire so to use emotion so as to control that which occurs. One cries if one feels hungry, and one is fed. One cries if one is uncomfortable, and one's diapers are changed. This is the beginning of each incarnation, the duality being present from the beginning of hatred of change and love of the ideal.

When we ask you to plunge deeply within yourself—and remember, this is only our opinion—we are asking you to consult the only reliable source of information for yourself. Those such as we may speak words which inspire or aid or otherwise enable entities to know more and more of their true selves. This work is done internally and in the company of intimate friends, mates, children and other family. If one deals with one's own life situation by the use of logic, intellect and cleverness, one shall fall short of one's own desires, for the intellect is intended to be your servant, not your master. In the same way are your deeper feelings to be tools, resources and instruments for your spiritual evolution, not carrying complete authority, but substantially worthwhile to seek out and to hear and to feel.

Now, let us examine the fabric of the universe as we understand it to be. The one great original Thought is not a thought, it is a purified emotion. It is Love. You may call it the Logos, the Creative Word, but it is in essence a pouring through the channel of the self of the infinite love of the one Creator. To attempt to manipulate one's feelings is to attempt the masquerade ball. Yet the ball must end and the masks come off, and the finery, the feathers, the ribbons laid away, and there you sit, all of the masks gone, all of those whom you were to impress having left you alone. And as you sit you ask yourself to take off your mask, and you take that mask off and you find another, and another, and another. The nature of the intellect is such that eventually you will find that the layers enclose a nothingness, for intellect is a cold, logical biocomputer which is designed to make choices. It is not designed to be the vehicle for manifestation. The heart, that which this instrument would call gut feeling, these are those things which enable manifestation among each of those who serve the one infinite Creator in service to others. The primal Logos of all that is, is emotion, the deepest intelligence of all, infinite, without flaw, without distortion, the carrier wave of consciousness.

And so, if you wish to manifest that which you have found to be good, if you wish to manifest your desire to find that which is good, if you seek and hunger for the truth, there is work to be done, for the intellect, the past, the future and all considerations of humankind must needs be put in abeyance on a regular basis for the amount of time it takes to sit in silent waiting until one is able to feel the presence of the infinite One.

We ask each within this group at this time to pause and allow that experience of love poured into your waiting heart to manifest itself to you.

(Pause)

I am Q'uo. I am again with this instrument. Is that love not astounding? Is that love not impossible for humankind to sustain? Yet you are other than human. That of you which is human is that which must do the manifesting, that which creates the inspiration and desire to manifest love of the Creator and love of others, comes from crossing the threshold to the unconscious with the care, persistence and devotion of the lover who is willing to wait and watch and seek from afar, content to sit at the edge of the crowd listening to that faraway voice at the center of the crowd that speaks the truth, for you have many, many voices within you which are manifestations of biases. These biases need to be examined, and in this intellect and logic play a great part. However, as you wish to be of service to the infinite One, and as you wish to love each other, know that the universe is, in essence, an emotion, it is consciousness. Consciousness does not necessarily think. Consciousness allows itself to avail itself of that infinite source of information within.

It is in this way that you are attempting, through meditation and contemplation, through the balancing of the day's extreme emotions, to give to yourself that which cannot be done without some aid. There is, for instance, no possibility of an entity's being able to cogitate, ruminate, ideate and manifest love. Indeed, it is possible for such a person to manifest a universal and very real compassion, but love engages being, love sets on fire the desire to help, love causes soil of the heart to become fallow, that seeds may spring therein which flower out into the tree of manifestation of love with its many blossoms, its beautiful aroma and its faithful use.

Yes, my friends, more than ever as you realize, recognize and respect your own inner wisdom as a portion of the creation, as you continue to meditate faithfully, then you may be undisturbed, insofar as it is possible, by the painfulness of change. For you now seek the beginnings of the fourth density. Within third density the spotlight was on the self, the emerging consciousness, the discovery that that consciousness is one with all and one with the Creator. It is the chief lesson of this particular density, to learn to love, and to learn to accept love, feeling both worthy to love and to be loved.

Much has been written about love. Within your holy works love is described by many phrases, "Love is patient," "Love is long-suffering," and so forth. May we say that love in the sense in which we understand it is in the impatience, is in the misunderstanding, is in every portion and every cell, every iota of creation. You cannot move yourself from the roots of your being. You are rooted in that which you may call the Kingdom of Heaven, and your roots are deep and imperishable, and down, down into the world of illusion do you grow your branches and produce the bloom that promises fruit.

Within your culture, as we have said, the intellect is valued almost to the exclusion of deep, quiet, confident, considered intuition. You are an impatient people, eager, and perhaps running faster with you feet than your heart and your mind can follow. Thus, the first priority may seem very selfish to one, and that is to learn to love the self, unequivocally, with complete self-forgiveness, with full knowledge of the various iniquities of one's own character. You must allow yourself to become aware that the Creator and the creation lies within you, each of you. It is not well to speak as though one were ever and always unworthy to be the vessel for divinity. All of clay and dust, bone and muscle is by definition unworthy to carry imperishable ideals into a world which you experience as that which is not ideal.

Now, you see the interplay of love and faith against the dynamic catalyst of a mundane and sometimes intensive nature. What shall you do in this situation? What shall be your decision in that situation? It is appropriate to use all of the resources at your command. If you have any ignorance of the subject as it is known by humankind, fill the mind with what was written. Use the intellect to discriminate upon the subject in which you are interested, then surrender control of the process, carefully and fastidiously, to the love within, the spark of the Creator within that makes us all one.

Those who have not been able to love themselves are by definition unable to love the Creator, for each is the Creator's prodigal son or daughter, each is an heir of eternity. This is not said to puff you up with pride, but to say that each of you is a cell in the living body of the creation of love. Once you have learned to come into some contact with the Creator on a daily basis, it is then time to gaze at that which lies before you, at the stones in the road, at the stragglers by the wayside, at the thirsty, at the hungry, at the homeless. The manifestation of the Logos that is within you, that of unconditional love, has never been needed more than at this juncture in the passing [of] your planet into fourth density space and time.

It is often said "Thou shalt not judge," not only within your holy works, but also by those whose sense of fairness and ethics makes it mandatory for them to yield to all the same benefit of doubt that one would hope would be yielded to the self in the same circumstances. The density in which you are is a density in which you choose not how to think, but how to love. If you love yourself, you will think in terms of manipulation and control, elitism, perquisites and power on a personal level. If your love is of the Creator and of those in whose eyes you see shining the light of the one infinite Creator, then you are one who may radiate to that person. Often no words are necessary. It is well to move with the deepest instincts, to give a hug, to give a kiss, to give verbal support, to leave alone, to treat as precious each entity, each imperishable light being that is about you.

What is the purpose of emotion? The purpose of emotion within third density is so to engage the mind, the heart, and the soul of the entity which seeks that it becomes more and more aware of the depth and breadth of each present moment and possibilities for loving within each moment. Needless to say, we do not speak of the clinging, dependent love. We do not suggest that the surrender to the higher self be made before the self has been tuned so as to hear the true voice from within. Many are those who would whisper in the ear of one who seeks to be of service. Discrimination remains important always, and this includes those things which we say to you. Let us not be a stumbling block before you.

Now let us look at the way emotion is deepened. Each of you is aware of the system of chakras, or energy centers within the being. It is understood that each needs to be minimally clear and balanced for the full energy of the one infinite Creator, the life force, the prana, if you will, to move upwards within the body to meet that inspiration which comes from the infinite One, from the comforter, from your guidance, from your inner self. Over and over again we suggest to you the daily meditation for the clearing of cobwebs from the mind and the heart, of picking up the old newspapers, the leftover takeout food, the banal junk of a banal society that is intent upon not listening to any voice within which might cause discomfort.

The universe itself is an emotion, it is consciousness, it is love. Each of you will go through many definitions of the word love as you experience various facets of conditional and unconditional love. Your goal, and it is a difficult one within this density, is so to use the deep wisdom of the intuition and choice-making nature of the intellect in harmony to move in the direction that you and the Creator have set for yourself this day. And in that regard we would say that it is not well to create in the mind that which one desires, unless one is absolutely sure that one desires it and will never regret having it, for any desire that is unmet in third density must be met before the entity may move forward to the next level of classes, the next level of illumination, the next level of peace and joy.

How many times, my friends, have you seen a loved one, and found a way to touch that loved one, to strengthen it with your very being? How many times have you been the one to make peace among brothers and sisters? Do you not see the sweet hand of love moving through you in manifestation of the glorious love and light of the one infinite Creator? If you wish to manifest you must feel, deeply, sincerely and honestly. Not all entities can serve in this same way, as not all entities have been given the same gifts, and as we have said before, all services are equal when done for the love of the one infinite Creator.

We would not mislead you. You cannot by any means whatsoever achieve a higher state of consciousness. No mental act, no deliberate series of choices, no action within the illusion shall bring you the paradise of peace that you seek. That which will bring you quietude and serenity is the finding of that deeper self within through meditation, and the surrendering of the minute power of the human intellect to the infinite wisdom, compassion …

(Side one of tape ends.)

(Carla channeling)

I am Q'uo. We shall continue. You are the hands, you are the voice of the Creator, and as you love each other as you love yourself, so you love all that is the Creator. This is the function of purified emotion, to become a channel through which infinite love may flow so that you do not dry up like a shallow well or a desert spring, but remain well watered, well fed, well inspired with food and drink for the soul. In that consciousness you become hollow, and in your purity of love you allow love to speak by surrendering to the Infinite within.

This surrender is not one made without discrimination and care. Surrendering to those who say, "This and this and this you must believe, that and that and that you must do," is an acceptable choice for those who cannot use intellect and feeling, but merely have a generalized need to know what is right and what is wrong to do in life, so that one does not have to think, grow, change, expand and transform the self. For these people, and we do not put them down in insult, this is the way to progress, and progress they will, however slowly. But each of you wishes to move more quickly, to become true channels of light, to feel true peace in the heart, to feel genuine, authentic harmony and serenity, to meet one's companions with joy, trust, sharing and caring. Are these all not words of emotion? Can one reason oneself to this attitude? No, my friends, no.

Why, then, are you in your shell, this thick, impenetrable shell of forgetting? We say to you, you are in this shell of forgetting so that you may make your choice unfettered by the knowledge of the answers to the test. Many are the students who simply write down what the teacher says and parrot it back to the teacher to make a good grade. In spiritual or metaphysical work this line of endeavor is of no virtue, for you are seeking authenticity of self, and only in the authenticity of the self-forgiven self can the Creator move from infinite intelligence through infinite energy into your heart, your spirit, your hands, and your eyes, that you may behold the glory of all that is about you, that you may feel anguish for those many, many things that are awry, and then to affirm that it is possible for this unfortunate condition to cease.

Allow your love to spring forward from within. It is not yours, it is not another's, it is the Creator's. Love one another, my friends, and you shall love the Creator, and this purified emotion of sacrificial love shall move you ever more quickly toward the homeland of peace.

We thank you for allowing us to finish our thoughts on this subject. There is more material in this area, but it would require further questioning.

We would offer to the instrument known as Jim the opportunity to close the session. A simple silence will express this entity's desire not to speak because of the difficulty of speaking at this time. I am Q'uo.

(Pause)

(Carla channeling)

I am Q'uo. I am again with this instrument. We have examined the instrument known as Jim, and find that in order for us to be able to use this instrument's vocal mechanism at this time we would have to induce a trance state. This we are unwilling to do, as without dedication, protection and planning such sacrifice of energy is unacceptable to us as a gift. It is a gift we cannot take unless it is fully offered. We shall therefore open the meeting to any questions which may remain upon the mind of those here. Is there a query at this time?

T: Yes, I have a question. At one point I sort of went away—I missed a small portion of what was channeled, and when I came back you had said something to the effect that "… then you can surrender to the process, to your inner self," something to that effect. My question is, were you at that time talking about the creating process of holding a thought and then creating the desire and then giving up the process to your inner self? Was this what you were speaking of?

I am Q'uo. My brother, we were not speaking of such, but rather were speaking of the work entailed in moving beyond the surface consciousness to the deeper and more trustworthy wisdom that lies deep within the self. We do not ask you to surrender to any outer authority. We ask you only to surrender to that portion of yourself that you have found to be imperishable, worthy, beautiful and able to manifest the fruits of an unconditional love which is your birthright, which moves through you from a deep place of self-acceptance within.

As to the imaging of that which you desire, we exhort you to be extremely careful, as you create what you desire and focus upon it, for you shall receive it. However, there is always, as in many of your myths and fairy tales, the difficulty of attempting to control what occurs. The difficulty is this: for every desire there are unsatisfactory side-effects which will occur when the desire has been met. You are then involved in an unbalanced fashion, and some call this karma, with that which you have created as a life and desired within the life pattern.

Therefore, unless the intuition is most deep, heartfelt and worthy to the self of being held all through the incarnational life experience, we strongly suggest that you are faithful in listening, and when you go forth from your meditation you carry with you the desire to love. One's path is taken one step at a time, one expression of love at a time, one expression of honesty which may lance a boil of misunderstanding and heal. To communicate with the heart and the love of the infinite One is to heal, and by the power of that love the Creator may, if all love, transform and renew the creation of the Father.

This instrument is informing us that we are spending a rather long time, so we would ask if there is a final query at this time. I am Q'uo.

K: I find that there are a number of concepts that I have accepted without perhaps fully understanding them, over the years. One of these is the idea of accepting and loving yourself. Could you offer briefly some suggestions on how to begin to go about the process of accepting and loving yourself in order to move on to loving others?

I am Q'uo. We are most happy to speak to this subject, for within your heavy chemical illusion it is very difficult to have an unbridled love of the divine self within, for one is so taken with the surface iniquities of mundane living, the little disappointments, the little irritations, the hostility, and all the repertoire of negative emotions, that one cannot even believe that one could possibly be worthy, and, indeed, as a human in third density one is not yet worthy of utter self forgiveness except for one thing: the nature of creation is utterly self-forgiven. In finding that basic truth you may claim your worth.

Let us gaze at it in another manner. Upon the surface you are one person, and your sphere is populated with many, many other persons, some of which are very much in sympathy with you, many of which have almost nothing on the surface in common with you. Furthermore, those who wish to be of service are walking a tightrope betwixt service gladly given and the service of the doormat. And when one perceives oneself as a doormat because one is, as this instrument would say, nice, one does not feel that oneself is worthy, but rather than oneself is an hypocrite and a liar, or at least one who tells the fib so as not to offend.

Move within the self at this moment. Consciously allow the awareness to move through the short term memories. Now allow all the pain and joy of this experience of incarnation to be gazed at with eyes of love, for you have learned from each and every challenge. You have not reached the self, you are forgiving the imperfections of the self which an imperfect world was formed on purpose to cause you to feel. If you never felt unworthy your worthiness would have no passion, no strength, and no stamina. It is only when one moves through the awareness of one's human limitations within third density, and accepts each imperfection, each folly, each thoughtlessness as the action of one who simply was not properly tuned, then you may move on to more fertile territory. Not to forgive an imperfect self—and that is the surface self of each—is to deny that there is more, and that that more is a divine mystery which we may only call love.

In claiming the worth of the self it is necessary to gaze at one's relationship with the infinite One. This entity created you before it created the densities, the stars, and the planets which make up your illusion. You are portions of the active consciousness of the one infinite Creator of love and light that is within you. And so you do not honor the small self by feeling worthy, but rather you surrender to the greater Self within, and then you may love all of your idiosyncrasies, all of your faults, because you know, beyond a shadow of a doubt, that as you slip you may forgive yourself, pick yourself up, and walk on. You are imperishable. You are creatures of love.

Once you have made the difficult choice between serving others as a way of serving the Creator and expressing that relationship, and serving the self and so expressing a relationship of total unity with the Creator, then you have made the decision that this density was created to enable you to make.

All upon the outside of the consciousness has a tendency to appear negative, and to evoke negative emotion. Consequently, you, as a spirit of light, are gazing constantly at the darkness of one's own Earthly vessel. This Earthly vessel is made of clay and chemicals and water, and an electrochemical system which enables that which you call consciousness to have a home, and you may be grateful for that imperfect self. You cannot exonerate yourself for the things that you have done amiss. That is not self-forgiveness. When you have done that which you consider amiss, it is well for you immediately to go to the entity whom you feel you have slighted and to create harmony once again betwixt the two, knowing that not only are you an entity of Earth, but also the other is similarly befuddled and confused in a sea of illusion that is the third density.

You must go deeper. You must move from the mind which condemns, judges, evaluates, and so forth to the heart, where resides that infinite spark of imperishability which is the Creator within. It is this portion of the self that is worthy, and because you carry within yourself, within this Earthly vessel, the glorious perfection of the infinite One, so you may move into the point of view of that within you which is the Creator, as the Creator forgives a perishable, various, woeful entity for making the errors of childhood.

Yes, the universe, the Creator has already forgiven all that you may do. Your yourself, however, must forgive the self, be at peace with the self, acknowledge all of the thoughts of the self, and attempt as much as possible to become better. It is well to realize that perfect behavior is not only impossible but meaningless. It is the heart, the love, the emotion that makes you worthy, and as the intensity of your love of the Creator and your love of fellow men and your love of yourself grow, so shall you become a more and more metaphysical light being, moving affirmatively from your strength—that is, the Creator within—rather than running from, avoiding, or being embarrassed about many, many errors that any limited, somewhat ignorant, and often biased child might make.

You in the third density have chosen to be children. You are children of the one infinite Creator. Are you less than worthy? A child may misbehave, but a child is forgiven. You are prodigal, you have squandered your inheritance. All who are Earthly in third density have so done, with extremely few exceptions. Yet, by doing so you strip away for yourself the illusion that this will bring pleasure, that will bring satisfaction, control will give you what you want, and demand will always be heard. A sense of worthiness comes as one becomes aware of oneself as the worthy servant, the least of all, one who is always in error, yet one who carries an imperishable, holy and divine spark of the Creator.

To see oneself as a cell in the body of creation is a most helpful concept, because as you gaze in thought at your own anatomy and physiology you may see that each cell is equally important. The skin, the muscles, the mind, the simple reaching out of the hands that is possible because you are in physical existence, these are causes for rejoicing, these are causes for thanksgiving and praise, for you have the opportunity to act as a channel, a worthy and loving channel for the infinite love and light of the one Creator. Self-acceptance is a good start upon self-forgiveness. To accept one's faults as they are, paradoxically, is to open oneself up to the possibility of change, growth and transformation.

May we answer you further, my sister?

K: No, that's very helpful for now, thank you.

We thank each of you, and would at this time close the meditation, wishing each to respect and seek the heart within, the deep intuition within, not to denigrate the Earthly vessel in which you move, for though it makes many, many errors, yet it has the hands to give, the mouth to speak, the eyes that offer the softness of a loving glance, the breasts that may give the babe nourishment, the loins that shall produce souls whom one may love and by whom one may experience the incredible gift of unconditional love. Love one another, my friends, unconditionally, and if there is a condition, use the intellect for that for which it was made. It is a burro; load it with the information and let it climb the mountain to the answer.

We are no more worthy than you. We are all seekers, all pilgrims, and all imperfect. We could suggest that one may look forward to a time when one is not so, shall we say, imperfect, as seen by the self, but we assure you that these feelings of unworthiness, insecurity and other feelings of this kind are designed completely by yourself before the incarnation to teach you to love, and to love that which is imperfect is to make it worthy.

Examine your soul. All that is, is within you, the bad, as you would call negative emotions and ideas, and the good, as you would call positive emotions and ideas. But the source of your worth is that which makes the universe One, and yourself a citizen as important as any, as worthy as any. You are a part of the infinite Creator; you are worthwhile, necessary and beloved. May you love yourself enough to move the imperfections out of the way of your service, and never ever to hold a grudge against the self, but to forgive the self, to intend a newness which is less imperfect in the ways of doing things.

As always, meditation is the great tool. Prayer, as this instrument understands it, is also a great tool when one is upset with another, for one may pray for that other, and in so doing heal the self of negative emotion as well as being effective in prayer and uplifting of the self in consciousness.

We leave you with that desire to be uplifted, to be transformed, and, indeed, many times, to be uncomfortable. Comfort is for those who are asleep. Comfort is for those for whom someone is willing to tell them exactly what to think about everything. It is a comfortable life. One can attain fourth density light by this means, but it is very difficult, for a feeling of richness and completion of the self is the same problem exactly as the feeling of a great mass of wealth. Clinging to one's possessions is not necessary. When you have made your peace with the imperfections of the self, wait until you feel the presence of the infinite One, of your guidance, of your comforter, and at that point say, "I wish to do the will of my greater Self, I surrender my imperfect human self. What would you have me do?" Be willing; that is the key. Be discriminatory; those discriminations are the lions that guard the truth.

In this truth, love, light, peace and joy of the infinite Creator, we leave you, with blessings and ever flowing love for those who are awake and seeking. We are those known to you as Q'uo. Adonai, my friends. Adonai vasu. ✺

Sunday Meditation
December 3, 1989

Group question: The question this evening has to do with glory and the meaning that glory would have as we say the Lord's Prayer and think about the concepts of "the Kingdom and the power and the glory." What is the glory that belongs to the Father, or to the Creator, and what part in that glory do we play, how do we offer glory, and … that'll do.

(Carla channeling)

I am Q'uo, and greet each in the love and the light of the one infinite Creator. It is a privilege and pleasure to share this meditation with you. May we say, for those sensitive enough to sense the presence of another entity, that the one known as Latwii is with this group this evening, having been called in support but not to speak. Having answered the challenge, the contact prefers to be silent and supportive.

Joy, worship, adoration, praise, honor, glory. Within your illusion you may see glory. It exists instinctually and continuously. Each creation of land and sea and air sharing its rustling leaves, its proud and sturdy branches, its healing magic, its sweet rainfall, sharing all, the glory of a rainbow or of a beautiful scene, is not simply the expression of admiration of geographical territory but a prayer of thanks to its Creator who has made all things well.

This instrument, we find, has asked this question because in this instrument's mind the concept of humility is congruent with the idea of service to others. Thus, the instrument wonders what the place of glory is in the life of the seeker. Within the day-to-day life glory is beheld by many eyes and seen by few hearts in true perception. Most entities sitting in the midst of glorious beauty find that they have a chore to do that must be done, that keeps the eye upon the paper or within the work area, so that one cannot look out and see the easiest, clearest, most eloquent and poignant definition of glory.

Why should the Creator be glorified? The most simplistic answer is, "Look about yourselves, witness the unique character of each dawning, of each dusk, each change of weather that moves the feelings and emotions—quieter when it is pearly, nacreous and rainy; happy and active when the winter sun deigns to shine its glory upon your fair planet. There is an element of "breaking through" to that metaphor, for the glorious light of the one infinite Creator must break through clouds. And in understanding glory itself, you within the self must break through clouds of unworthiness, unhappiness and disquiet.

It is truly said in your holy work named the Bible that in quietness and confidence is your peace. When one becomes still enough to cease the speaking one rapidly becomes aware of the astonishing and miraculous wonder and the beauty of the creation. All of this beauty is within you, all of the Creator is within you, all of the Creation is within you. So, when you give glory to the Creator, you give glory to the deepest part of yourself and affirm your ultimate and far-off nature, affirm that you are a prodigal moving through strange lands, faring variously and aiming at last for the home of the Father.

The Creator does not have a sense of Its own glory. That which you know as glory is that which is recognized by your peoples as an appropriate response to the beauty and blessings, challenges and learned lessons that shape each entity's destiny. One is not always able to focus upon the affirmative, to praise circumstances or to give glory to the source of those circumstances. One often thinks not about one's own incarnation. Had the Creator not felt a glory within thee, would you be? For you are the active principle of the infinite One. You are the crossroads of eternity and time, of reality and illusion. And in any illusion there is the moment when that illusion is shattered and the wonder comes upon one.

The first glory is that which the Creator has invested in you. Thus, it is centrally important to come to an understanding and acceptance and a self-forgiveness within the inner structure of the heart, the mind, and the spirit. As we have mentioned before, it is far more common for the self to be overly judgmental and perfectionistic about the self than for that same self to find many things unacceptable about others. Yet, how can the self be unacceptable to the self? How can the Creator be so distorted that that spark within becomes hidden? You move upon your skis down the white alp, the wind blows by and your face is cold, except for your goggles. Every muscle, every fiber of the being is engaged in this plummeting trip, this sailing upon the Earth, this experience that seems most glorious.

It is exciting. It is that about which one becomes intense. Thus, entities within your culture give glory to many, many things which are not that which is truly glorious. No matter how worthy the entity, the glory of that entity is not the entity, but the Creator within the entity, for one who speaks to another speaks to the Father within that other. And the glory, if there be any, goes solely to the Creator.

Glory is a concept directly at odds with judgment, for in the concept of glory, with the concept that all are one, then all are potentially full of glory, able to generate glory through love and light and service and able to experience glory in the inner room of meditation and contemplation and in the environments which so richly endow each with companionship, laughter, light-heartedness, and a sense of confidence and security that comes from feeling that the self is indeed worthy, that the self at heart is indeed a portion of the glory of the Creator.

It may seem much to you as though we suggest you praise yourselves. By all means, do so. It is known by you to a nicety in this system of illusion that one is not particularly glorious very much of the time. The illusion of difficulty and challenge is heavy; the blockages to self-awareness and self-forgiveness, formidable. To think of oneself as a part of something glorious is very difficult under these circumstances, for one feels humility and somehow it seems that one cannot feel humility and affirming—we correct this instrument—affirmation of glory in the self at the same time. Yet, this paradox is one of the strongest spiritual truths, the dynamics of which a seeker needs to grasp, for the glory lies not within the behavior, not within the surface thinking, but at the level at which each is a portion of the one infinite Creator.

Few there are within third density that are able to manifest perfect glory, for in manifesting perfect glory one no longer has any catalyst to process and one is able to stay in the love and the light of the one infinite Creator, praising and blessing the name of the Creator, speaking hallelujahs for all the blessings of your life. Yet, in the next hour you shall walk away from this beautiful concept, this imperishable ideal, and be unable to live up to that which is truly within you at this time. Yet, the glory is there. It continuously speaks to you, continuously moves within you and, as you become more transparent, more trusting, more accepting of that which occurs, of those conditions in which one finds oneself, one can then allow the glory to flow through the self to all the other portions of that glory.

What do you mean when you say "glory"? In some cases, entities mean heaven; others mean worship; others, praise. Even your flag has the name of "Godhead," undoubtedly named with deliberation. The nature of the Creation is love and the nature of love is glorious. It is much to be awed by, much to be studied. There is much to take into meditation each and every day, and there is the listening ear to develop to the less and less distorted self that lies deeper and deeper within the self, closer and closer to the true self which, in the end, as it was your Source, shall be your Omega.

Now, what is glory to you? Is there glory in serving others in an humble way, in chores, in cooking and cleaning and mothering and fathering and providing and working? The amount of glory you allow into your life is up to you. The glory is there, intrinsic in each moment. Beauty lies all around. Dreams, hopes and ideals abound. And these artifacts of the spirit and the mind and the emotions are wonderful, wondrous and glorious. For, is not love glorious, my friends? Remember that the one known as Jesus removed the commandments of his predecessors, and, instead, asked each to love the Creator and to love each other as the self. This was the new promise that this teacher requested from its followers.

The direct reason that most people do not feel glory, or any intense emotion, is that the culture in which you live is difficult, and in fact, even for it, is going through a difficult period because of the transformation of space and time as your galaxy spins into a new configuration, a new space.

How can one find glory when one has not perceived glory? One may meditate upon glory. But perhaps the best way to approach the understanding of the word glory is to strip [away] all adjectives and gaze at the great noun, "I," the great verb, "AM." To exist is glory. To be conscious is potentially to live in the Kingdom of the Father. Why should a relationship with a father whose love for each is infinite produce anger, confusion and disputation? These things are a portion of your illusion. If you are able to silence your mind, silence your doubts and to open the door to the inner room in private and devout meditation, that silence for you may be a great voyage of discovery, for you will find more and more to like about the self, more and more to see as accomplishments as each entity moves through the life experience and becomes more mature.

Could one do without glory? By no means. To say "glory" is also to say "passion." Glory is the passion of the heart and it has its artifacts in the blue ray of communication of an inspirational nature and the indigo ray of work done upon the self in self-healing, self-forgiveness, self-quieting and, above all, self-acceptance. The beginning of lover—we correct this instrument—the beginning of loving others as one loves the self is to discover the glory within the self, to forgive the self for its behaviors which shall be various due to the workings of free will, so that one may concentrate as much as possible simply on loving and being with the infinite One.

So many things you have seen have been to you glorious and wonderful, awesome and a cause for devotion and worship. Know that this within your spirits is not an artifact of culture, is not a trained portion of an entity, but an instinctive, genuine need. Each entity needs and seeks to find that glory, that joy which somehow, although it may not have been experienced since young childhood, each is aware does exist. One may not become glorious by one's decision to do so. Each has the guidance, the Comforter, within. And this Comforter, with its longer point of view, its wider perspective, may find the glory in moments which seem less than intensely glorious.

Glory is the faculty of the child who finds those things which it likes passionately lovable and glorious objects of love. Were there not an objective referent to glory in the metaphysical sense, there would be no word, for the word "glory" is that which reaches out into eternity for that which it knows not. It knows the glory as a mystery, and, like [buoys] clanging in the fog on a stony coast, it is hidden and it is difficult to navigate through the waters of humanity and ordinary living to create the intensity of consciousness that allows one to glorify and praise and thank the one infinite Creator. Yet, this exercise comes back to you an hundredfold, a thousandfold, a millionfold, for as you recognize the glory of the one infinite Creator, the glory of Creation, the glory of the heart of humankind, one becomes aware of the glory hidden within, that treasure in earthen vessel, that gem within the body. As you become more humble and more aware of how many errors are self-perceived by you, paradoxically you shall become more and more aware of the exploding excitement of the creation in its eternal dance, in its endless beauty, in its infinite love under the powerful strength of pure light.

You shall not always be manifest, you shall not always need to feel glorious, for you shall become glorious as you move back to your source and become a portion of the potentiated Creator that has not yet been potentiated.

It seems odd to use glory as a word which describes the pilgrimage experience. One's shoes are dusty from the road and painful from the stones upon it;

one has hardships, thirsts, hungers and [yet one still] seeks. How can this be glorious? Yet, if you will open the heart and request a sense of praise, thanksgiving, worship and adoration of the one infinite Creator, suddenly glory will be understood by you, the glory of all that there is, the glory of the journey, the glory of its beginning, its ending, and its infinite progression.

You entities call many things glorious. Artifacts of humankind such as music and art and literature receive this adjective frequently and truly, in some cases, the author or the composer has, indeed, touched upon part of the glory of humankind, part of the birthright of the imperishable spirit which you are. You are taught to feel unglorious; you are taught to doubt the self, to esteem the self most lowly and to act defensively. Glory is radiant, quiet, confident, brilliant and radiant. It is an aspect, an attribute of the one infinite Creator that inspires in the seeker purified emotion—the emotion of unconditional love, praise and thanksgiving.

As you move through your life, realize that your life is a divine and glorious gift from the active principle of the one infinite Creator to its source and ending, the unpotentiated Creator. After you have come to this gentle and loving perspective, loving the Creator and loving self as having the Creator within, partially hidden by distortions, one may begin to see the glory of other entities about you.

But always glory is most clearly seen in the second density of Nature, its blooming, its color changing, its infinite variety. Each flower is full of glory, yet it cannot sing praises to the Creator except with its heart. You, too, were given consciousness by the infinite Creator. Is this not a blessing? Glory is not in this case an emotional word but rather a word indicative of a worshipful and adoring attitude toward the mystery of the one infinite Creator. There is no reason to dislike the Creator; there is no reason to be indifferent to the Creator. But to the mind that is lucid there is every reason to see the glory all about one and know that the creation is like the Father.

Before we finish this speech we would like to iterate one important thing. The greatest blockage to an awareness and a feeling of intensity, passion, thankfulness and glory is the focus one has on one's distortions of behavior which does not forgive the faculty of free will for blindsiding you with this variety of feelings and states of mind. You are not intended to be perfect people. You are intended to be pilgrims, but you carry within you great glory. May you always feel that glory and offer that glory back to its source, the Creator, alone.

At this time we would offer a contact to the one known as Jim if this instrument wishes to close this meditation. We leave this instrument in the love and the light and the glory of an inestimably beautiful and truthful and authentic creation. I am Q'uo, and those of Latwii also bid this instrument love, light and farewell. We transfer now if the instrument, Jim, is willing. I am Q'uo.

(Jim channeling)

I am Q'uo, and greet each again in love and light through this instrument. We are pleased that we have been able to make contact.

(Side one of tape ends.)

(Jim channeling)

I am Q'uo, and am again with this instrument. It is our privilege at this time to offer ourselves and to speak to any queries which those present may find value in asking. Is there a query at this time?

Questioner: Yes, I'd like some advice in listening. I'm developing a new and very important relationship, and although speaking helps me it does not help the other person to feel better. Therefore, I feel selfish as I work out my understanding of the nature of that entity whom I love and would like to understand. Could you comment as to how I might circumnavigate, if possible, this somewhat difficult for the other soul's method of becoming aware of the needs of another?

I am Q'uo, and am aware of your query, my sister. You ask us a query which seems upon the surface to be possessed of serious limitations, shall we say, for among your peoples the desire and ability to communicate in a clear and compassionate fashion is one of the greatest tools that entities may utilize in the sharing of the self and the allowing of another to do likewise, for there are few among your people that can be assured that any degree of understanding has been achieved by any other means. Since the telepathic or empathic *(inaudible)* there is little left for an entity who wishes to understand the needs of another if the tool of words is no use. However, one may attempt to reach in feeling, or what you may call *(inaudible)* by utilizing the sense of another entity, shall we say, to make the self available enough to another entity. To accomplish this task is to make of the self a receiver which is sensitive to long variations in the beingness, shall we say, of another entity. It is possible to develop this skill by a system of trial and error whereby one checks the results with another entity. However, one can never be certain that one has been accurate in the sensing.

We apologize *(inaudible)* for this instrument is having difficulty in maintaining the focus necessary for the contact.

(Carla channeling)

I am Q'uo, and greet each again in the love and in the light of the infinite One. May we ask if there are any more queries before we close this evening?

(Pause)

I am Q'uo. We seem to have satisfied your appetite and we are most happy to have done so with our tools, which are fallible and liable to error. Therefore, we ask each to treat that which we say as that which it is—opinions held by those a bit further along the long and dusty path than are those within your density. Still, we do not know all that there is, and we cannot be considered to be truly wise, for still we have identity, and this is not weakness but a resistance to love itself.

How can the Creator love if all It has is Itself? The Creator, in its unpotentiated form, is love. The active principle that moves with free will before each creation to create consciousness and to start a new process is that which …

We are sorry, for this contact is breaking up as this instrument is concerned for the one known as Jim. We simply ask you to open your eyes, to open your hearts, to open your ears to the infinite variety of the glory, the beauty, and the truth of the infinite Creator Who has truly done all things well. We leave this group with obvious reluctance, for, yes indeed, we would chat with you much longer, could we. Yet, we realize that there is only so long that you entities can sit and concentrate. Thus, we urge you to compensate for this day with laughter, merriment and light heartedness. These are also most positive and contribute to a sense of glory. Avoid only those things which rob one of glory: the self-criticism, the criticism of the wisdom of the Creator, the criticism of the wisdom of other selves. When you feel these concerns, honor the glory within and move from concern to clarity and descending light, for so the glorious peace and love of the infinite One may flow through you to engage and kindle another soul, through intensity, passion and the true winds of the glory of the infinite One.

We leave each of you in glory. May you see it everywhere you turn. May you see it in each other and may you love each other. We are those of Q'uo, and are asked by Latwii to thank you for joining with them. We leave you in the love, the light, and the glory of the infinite One. We are known to you as Q'uo. Adonai, my friends. Adonai. ✤

Sunday Meditation
December 10, 1989

Gifts, Part II

Group question: How to discover one's gifts, how to determine what it is that might be the most helpful and beneficial thing for a person to do in the life pattern?

(Carla channeling)

I am Q'uo. Greetings in the love and the light of the one infinite Creator. May we say, as always, what a privilege it is to be called to your group, and may we thank the instrument known as Carla for perceiving a difficulty that was not inwardly visible, but only sensed through the intuition. There was a particularly strong negative entity which was able to stop the contact, but this instrument identified the difficulty with the contact and banished it by calling anathema. We appreciate the instrument's fastidiousness with regard to the challenging of spirits, and especially at this time, since there was no obvious *(inaudible)*, but rather a most clever imitation of our vibration, which is only possible by those of equal ability to use light.

There are very few fifth-density negative entities willing or interested in risking the loss of polarity by working to close down contacts which have promise. This entity has the pathway into this instrument from your times past, but has not been interested in, shall we say, removing the light in the interval since the contact with those of Ra. However, harmony grows within the group, one drop, one understanding, one forgiveness at a time, and, gradually, three independent people become three independent, but harmonious portions of one service, one working, and because this has begun to occur to a small extent in your group, the attention of this entity was caught.

You wished for more information upon how to recognize your gifts, those things which you have to offer in love to the Creator and to those about you. We begin with those things which are most basic, the beingness, and the relatively universal experience of sacrificing oneself in an attempt to rear a young soul to its best advantage rather than your own.

Let us look now a bit further. One who practices the presence of the infinite Creator, and can stop the mouth and open the ears, may rest in a special kind of gift, the gift of presence. This is not the gift of being, for an entity with this gift is one who seeks out the broken and the painful with hands open to heal, and hearts open to listen, for there is a great deal of damage done throughout an entity's lifetime, though only a very small portion of it is damage done to the physical vehicle. Practicing the presence and listening is a universal service. It can never go awry, for as you listen you support and you forgive, and you enable a soul who is troubled to move closer to practicing the presence of its own Creator.

There is a practice which is also most helpful, but difficult to describe in language. It is the state of non-ego, for want of a better term. It is a state of being which has no personality, and therefore no dynamic tension. This utter passivity is not what it seems, for it is the result of giving away all those things which stand between the consciousness of the self and the consciousness of mystery. Well it is that an entity have the gift and the talent of egolessness, but the real entity which has this gift is perhaps the most accurate mirror any spiritual seeker may have.

Now, let us speak of gifts in a different sense, the sense that we believe you meant when you asked this query of us, and that is the gifts or talents which one brings through the incarnational process. Each entity has preferences, each entity has skills and areas of negative skill. Each entity has likes and dislikes, biases too deep to explain. It is not of service to others to express the self if the self has not examined deeply that which is its desire, that which is its joy, that which gives it contentment, pleasure, or the feeling of something well done. This is different for each entity, for each entity comes into the experience of reincarnation with an unique bias, personality, and set of talents or gifts.

The one mistake an entity may make that is a serious error is to offer the gifts of the surface, of the self. Instead, one who wishes to offer gifts to others must needs make the journey within, to seek that seat of joy and peace that is the center of that soul's unique being, for each entity could not be in manifestation were there not a core of perfect wholeness and divine light within.

Thus, one who seeks to offer to others gifts must first move through the process of gazing beneath the surface of things, finding those areas of interest which may translate into help for another, or for giving glory and praise to the one Creator. This instrument, for instance, and the one known as K within this group, have shared a bliss, a joy, and a great service earlier in this diurnal period, as they vibrated and manifested a great hymn to the infinite One, and the principle which you call Christ, that which is forgiven, that which is redeemed.

When you look at your gifts, look not only at those things which you do well, your activities at which you are accomplished, but also look below the surface of things to find the energies within you moving deeply and spontaneously, so that you may spontaneously offer that which is given you only by intuition. Your people are locked in the darkness of manifestation, and so are you, yet within you there is light immeasurable. To be able to find and trust the intuitions which move from the light to the mind is most helpful, for one truly does not ever know when one is serving, one merely attempts such, and leaves the outcome in the hands of the one to whom the gift has been given, for it matters not to the giver if the gift is appreciated or not, but only if the gift is given freely and gladly without the nagging expectation of being paid back.

We speak here of very deep and intuitional gifts, such as the gift of peacemaker, the gift of true humility, the gift of sympathy. These gifts mean a great deal to many, who very much appreciate the sharing of these energies, for not all entities can move to that intuitional place where the hope of peace is true, where the hope of consolation is true.

You will notice that we have spoken mostly of the passive gifts, for they are the most important. In those passive and often nondramatic gifts lie the most free will which entities may give each other. It is respecting and treating each as a colleague, and not as a student to be taught. Thus, no matter what the seeming situation in regard to titles, responsibilities and honors, no matter how many dramatic gifts an entity may have, one may still rate those passive willingness' to listen, and to forgive, to understand, to make peace, to find union where there was none. The gift of humility is especially rare, but it is a resting place for all those who pass by, as they rest in the bosom of one who is no judge, but only sees all as beloved beings whom one wishes to serve.

Now, in order to keep this shorter, as this instrument has requested, we move to the active gifts that undoubtedly were held in mind when the question about sharing gifts was asked. Each entity has a list, short or long, of talents within the illusion. It is difficult to serve fully while staying fully within the illusion. However, that which one has as a gift one has for a reason, for each soul has chosen its manifestations, and fully intends to use each of them.

Thus, as the seeker moves along the path, he notices, without false pride and without false humility, those things at which he is good, and those things at which he is not. The situation often arises where the talent that an entity has is needed. It is neither aggressive nor egotistical to offer wholeheartedly one's talents in the service of the infinite One. And so a great service is simply to offer that which one knows one may do well for the entities about it. The only damage done to this kind of giving of service is a grudging heart.

Thus, each day, it is well for the spirit to ask itself not what its gifts are, but what is blocking it from being a person at peace, a person aware of infinity, a person ready to turn the attention outward to the needs of others. If this is not your attitude with which one awakens, then it is well to look within in consciousness to simplify, clarify and understand the self, and by understanding to have compassion upon the self, so that one does not use one's talents in any negative way. It is the responsibility of the seeker to be firm with the self about the positive use of talents.

The essence of manifested talents is simple, in fact, it is so simplistic that it is difficult to comprehend. When one is in a situation of wishing to be of service, one is already many steps behind the entity which simply is of service, and has responded spontaneously to whatever catalyst is given it. In other words, we wish each soul to follow that which makes it joyful and peaceful and positive and hopeful, and to live in those affirmative vibrations so that when a call comes, it is heard purely, with an unselfish ear and an unblemished heart.

So many, many of your people believe that they serve others, yet because they do not await the balancing and the asking, they become those who are stumbling blocks to others, insistent upon this or that tenet of truth, philosophy or spirituality. There is no truth within your density, except within the heart of your own consciousness, and similarly, within the heart of each consciousness with whom you come in contact. Oftentimes, gifts are learned and then put away like old clothes in a trunk in the attic, and then, one day, deep intuition speaks to the self of a spontaneous need to share a particular gift. We are not specific here, for there are as many gifts as there are entities.

Now, as you gaze at your gifts within the illusion, you may count those artifacts of the human heart and intellect as the writing, the speaking, the poetry, the music, the dance, and all of those creative gifts which pour through one as sweet wine, blessing all upon whom they fall. If the spirit is clear, deep intuition expresses itself in saying, "Use this gift now, and use it for the love of the one infinite Creator." Most puzzling are those entities which have various gifts, talents, which are not used, seemingly. But we say to you that each and every gift of talent subjectively perceived by an entity has a purpose, and the purpose will come forward in due time.

This instrument, for instance, questions why it was given the ability to dance, and then given the disability of arthritis which causes the dance to be clumsy and footsore. Notice that without the gift of dance this particular entity would not be able to move at all. Many, many times, the gift of singing, or of playing a musical instrument, is that gift which creates an atmosphere of love, safety and peace within an abode which may be in need of these things.

There are gifts one does not often think of, the gift, for instance, of gab, as this instrument would call it. One whose joy is in small talk, passing the time of day, sharing in any way what occurs, the life as it is happening, is an entity who will remove loneliness from the consciousness of those about it. Such entities seldom know the wonderful gift they bring to manifested experience, and the catalyst they offer those who are melancholy by nature, and have no small talk, or laughter, of their own. The first laughter may be very rusty, but in time a melancholy soul with faith in the gift of laughter which has been manifested to it will learn to share in that gift, and so give glory to the one infinite Creator, by lightening consciousness upon the planet.

The key to recognizing one's gifts has been already written down in two seemingly paradoxical ways. One is the statement, "Not my will, but thine," spoken by the teacher known to you as Jesus. The other is that willingness to pitch in and do all such good works as appear before one to do. How can one both surrender and volunteer? This is a cause for great study, and worthy of its own time for discussion.

If a gift has been given to you that does not make you happy, it is not a gift that was intended to be used in polarization in service to others, for it is following the gift that makes one happy, evanescent as that concept is, that assures the seeking entity of being at the right place at the right time to be of service in its unique way. "Not my will, but thine."

How can one be of service when one has only the deeper feelings of the heart to inform one as to divine will or the higher self as opposed to the self in manifestation which is blind, deaf and dumb to the actuality of the experience to which you now dance?

It is well for the young soul in your culture to choose that which the entity does in order to create the energy to live on the basis of that which appeals to one, for it is a gift to no one to be wealthy and uncomfortable and unhappy. It is far more a gift in one's poverty to offer in joy that talent which one has.

Gifts and talents come in all shapes and sizes. There are unusual and eccentric gifts which still are able to help others. The gift, for instance, of the gifted mechanic, who can listen to a complicated piece of machinery, and by ear alone detect that which is not correct in the *(inaudible)*. There is the gift of sight, simple physical sight. When it is acute and keen it may be used as a gift as one looks at what gives one joy, and expresses to those who cannot see with loving eyes the energies upon canvas, or the sculpture from clay, wood or stone.

It is a gift given to each and every entity that is self-conscious to express itself, and in expressing itself to learn how to support itself. This may be done in many ways.

(Side one of tape ends. Side two of the tape was not recorded.)

L/L Research

Sunday Meditation
December 17, 1989

Gifts, Part III

Group question: The question this evening is a continuation of the information we were receiving on how to discover the gifts one has that will allow one to be of service to others. Part Three.

(Carla channeling)

I am Hatonn. Greetings to you in the love and in the light of the infinite Creator. It is a privilege and a blessing to be here. We have been given this task by the one known as Q'uo because of the estimation of this instrument's aura. It is not able to function at full power due to illnesses within the body. However, we are a broadband contact, and although we cannot inspire and instruct as well as our teachers, yet we attempt to be of service to you this evening.

As we talk about how to identify your gifts, you have heard this many times and you will hear it again many times: the way to discover your gift is to allow yourself to love. Loving is a risk. It also puts you in the company of people who do many, many, many different things, some of which you may be gifted at; you would never know unless you tried them. If you go through your life trying to be proper and serious you will only become misogynistic, baleful and bitter. When you, in and of yourself—we correct this instrument—in and of the self, the small surface self cannot sustain deep and purified emotions unless they are most, most unusual and do not come from this sphere at all.

So, we would like to close out our speaking upon identifying your gifts by quickly recapitulating what we of the Confederation have said before. We have said that the greatest gift is that of being. The second greatest gift, that of raising children. Everything is a gift to one who feels the presence of the Creator in the inanimate object or the animate object which it is manipulating in order to aid it. How many there are among your people who set up charitable organizations in order to avoid paying taxes. This is not an identification of gifts, but a budgetary decision. What we look for, what we ask for, what we hope for, is people who find that the love of the Creator for them, unblemished, untouched by the human condition lies within them. It is the first step to human-hood; to imperishability.

It is most easy to love some people. Their temperament suits your temperament. They are good listeners, you are good talkers. Or vice-versa. You have many of the same interests, or there is simply the chemistry of working together before that brings people together. But if anything that is attempted is attempted without the free flow of love, infinite love, into the violet-ray chakra from above, upwards from the red-ray chakra, according to the energy blockages of the body, when you sit to meditate, do your best to clear your intelligence of its usual active pattern of contemplation and thought, for those things which can be said to be of an inspiration that is healthy and encourages wellness among the souls of your peoples is not altogether welcome upon your sphere. You must ask for us to be with you.

There are some who are so aware of the love of the infinite One that they naturally radiate love to all whom they see and desire [to be] of service to all whom they meet. This is not the rule among humankind. It is well to consider yourselves as unprivileged in that regard. It is said that to be human is to fail. No truer words were ever spoken. From the moment of your conception, you are dying. You are perishable. You have only a brief time upon this tiny sphere to learn to know yourself and your strong points and your gifts, and to give them with a glad and holy heart.

To some people, the services that they offer is obvious. Housewives who realize the incredible sacrificial service of motherhood in truth, though, however, is not a sacrifice, for love is greater, stronger and more joyful and certainly more confrontive and immediate than other solitary occupations.

This evening we would simply say, "Find your love." What do you love to do? Whatever it is, you may do it in the service of others. Do you love to cook? Try a soup kitchen. Do you love to drive? There are handicapped and helpless people who must be taken here and there. Are you good with your hands? There are programs within your society for rehabilitating the dilapidated house to make it sellable so that people who are poor will have a nicer place to dwell. Is your special forte communications? This entity knows that its best trait, and of course, its worst?, is honest, open communication at all times. Thus, we are able to use this instrument although she is in considerable pain—the heart is single.

In a way, my children, this is what love is. Singleness of heart. One may love this and one may love that. And one may just love banana pudding, and simply adore prime rib. The words are used very sloppily. We do not subscribe to any dogma or dark truth. We are able to inform you inasmuch as we know, and that knowledge is not perfect.

On the foundation and the evolution of spirituality upon your planet, you yourself, however, will come forth from this meeting, this meditation, this circle of joy and sweet peace and move out into a world in which peace seems afar off and life is not sweet always. Thus, as always, we encourage the daily meditation in moderation. That is to say, no more than one half hour at a time, for we can never disclose to you because of your own free will the pace you are particularly able to keep. Each of you is evolving. Some have the capacity to evolve more quickly. The most folly one can assume is to assume that because one seems without love, one is not learning spiritually. You are the one who is not growing spiritually if you do not love the unloved. And we do not talk of empty prayers and dutiful affirmations. We speak of a heart so open that it recognizes the murderer, the rapist, the felon, the abuser, the addict, the street person, one who, in the interest of country, allows ways to be rational for unacceptable means.

The world outside of you is not apparently full of love. Love has an active and a passive form. The most important form for you to become aware of is the immediate presence of the unmoved Logos, that great original Thought which is Love. There's no free will to cause it distortion. And you, my friends, are the active principle of that Creator. Far better it is to attempt to aid and fail than not to attempt because of a fear of failing. No one is keeping score in the heavenly kingdom, except, my friends, you yourselves. You know if you love or if you are merely getting along, being polite, being pleasant and being cheerful. Those are wonderful human traits, but they end, and then you are exhausted and open to the most negative of emotions. It is in the realization that you are [as] portion of the Creator, that your ability to love is there to make itself clear, for it is not your ability at all. Your personality, your circumstances, the island high on which you live, are all illusions. But that which is within your consciousness is no illusion.

Thus, after you have cleared yourself as best you can of the negative thoughts, of the difficulties, of the pocket change of the day, not just in meditation, but moment by moment, you shall be that much closer to your service.

To recapitulate, service is vastly different from the art of pleasing people. When one asks how one can be of service to another, either analysis, intuition or inspiration will inform you. Yes, that person needs help, or I know that person needs to do this on its own. That is compassionate, but it is an enabling process sometimes to allow what is or may be before you to resolve itself that that dear soul which you hold within your arms and heart may grow at its own pace.

Many, many of your organizations began in love, love of mankind, love of beauty. In time, this love became jaundiced and truncated while the necessity of the upkeep of the corporation which houses [its] beautiful objects [replaced it]. So it is with your churches and your schools. One may learn about freedom, but for that, one must pay. Determining your gifts, then, is a matter of observing what it is you love to do the best. Then we suggest you do it; whether it be praying for the peace of the planet, sending healing, it matters not. It matters only that one realizes that one's Lordship dwells within as does the entire universe.

What are your gifts? Only you know. How keen your eyes, how keen your ears, how quick your reflexes, how intelligent your mind, how able your tongue, and how able your body. Only you know whether you are an introvert, an extrovert, a loner, a sociable person. Only you know your own needs. And in serving others, it is not wise to sacrifice too much of that which you enjoy and that which feeds you, for as a channel you are giving, and giving, and giving, and giving without expectations of any return. This is a blessed service for which we thank all of you. But the silence of meditation, the steadiness of day-to-day cheerfulness, the pursuing of work that you love is a great boost forward.

The least important of these, although it would seem that it was the most important because of the time one spends in labor, is in the laboring. Most entities find it reasonable to do something intelligent or unintelligent in order to provide the self with independence by an income. These same people, then, have an obligation that is shared by all, to help with the resources of the planet. It is part of your media, at this blessed time of the year, the Advent of the coming of Emmanuel, [that] many are homeless, many are hungry, many are cold. Some will die. If you cannot bring them food, send them your prayers, for prayers are food for the soul and miracles do occur when prayer is invoked. Sometimes the answers to those prayers are, "No, leave it alone, it is as it should be." And, in that case, one simply holds the one for whom one is praying up and asks the Creator to cradle that entity in His arms.

This, then, is your service to that person—unknown, unappreciated and unexpected. Perhaps the secret of the service to love is to make no fuss or ado about doing what one can to serve. We have a very handy example in this instrument who is having continuous pain flares. This one, however, is aware of the limitations of her service and would have had to have been unconscious not to attempt contact. We look for intensity, passion and dedication in our lives and due to the fact that it is very, very much a secular culture in which you live this feeling of coming home to one's true family is often missing. And people wander the Earth like Noah's beasts in pairs of two, with the lonely ones slipping through the cracks in reality.

My friends, you are asked to love one another as you yourself have been loved. You know the incredible strength of that love. You may lean back against it, and you may open the self to channel words to make peace and harmony and solace available to those who are too tangled in their own details of negative emotion to work out the heart of the problem. Each of you would be in this situation from time to time, thus the offering of love to another by listening, by accepting, by forgiving, and by loving is the gift of which we would speak this evening. Centuries and centuries have gone by with the entities attempting to learn to love. There have been many side trips, many excursions into folly. Many killings, wars and casual death. That is the Creation expressing itself negatively this time.

You may do two things with your love after you have found it. Firstly, you may pray continually without ceasing. This is not a difficult habit to move into, as one knows very small prayers that one has known since childhood, prayers that are to the point and caring. You may also make up your own prayers or simply hold a person with whom you are concerned into the light of the infinite One.

The greatest of active services as opposed to passive services of being is loving in such a way that you are able to hear the words between the lines that plead for spiritual help. We pray you may have the subtlety of wit, the intelligence to take that information which is important to the other, and find a tongue to speak that does not create a stumbling block, while many have been damaged by guilt and excessive judgment in some of your saddled religions.

And now you tread a more difficult road, a road wherein you must believe yourself worthy. Why should you believe yourself worthy? Let us look at this. In the first place, you are worthy because you have been created by the one infinite Creator. You are an active principle which informs the Creator of Itself. This you do by living, not by doing. You are of service to the Creator as you begin to forgive yourself, completely and irrevocably, for the many serious sins of the past, the errors which have caused you humiliation and nausea. It is a difficult thing to wish a living ideal and within your culture it is designed to be impossible.

So, you the pilgrim who seek to be light to the world, will often fall, for stumbling blocks are everywhere. Bruised, tired, dusty, we ask you to pick yourselves up and move along the road that you and the Creator have planned for you. Pray, first of all, that you love yourself. The second portion of the second admission which is found in your holy works is to love your neighbor as yourself. If you do not love yourself, how can you love your neighbor? There is work to be done again until the self is clear enough to hear and appreciate and feel unthreatened by the strength of the feelings, emotions and thoughts of others.

How can one magnify one's ability to share love? Coming to group meditations such as this one is helpful, for as the saying goes in the holy work, your Bible, "When two or three are gathered together, prayers are answered." It is true, too, in the way of information. Three is the minimum number for successful vocal channeling, so that it may be universal. All these things are gestures of love. So, if you do not love yourself or the Creator, stop where you are, do not attempt to strain yourself by opening higher energies without the heart chakra completely open.

It is perfectly appropriate to fail and fail and fail again. We are not speaking of results but of the will to succeed, the persistent desire to run the straight race, as it is written in your holy scripture. Love is emotion that is too soft and too gentle in the way it has become known upon your planet to do that which it was intended to do: act as a balance wheel, giving entities equal opportunities to choose positive or negative paths. The reason for this is that your culture is more positive than negative, consequently, we of the Confederation are aware that there are negative entities also. This is why we charge you with the challenging of all contacts, but if you love the Creator and love yourself, you will then turn to a world that is bright with the light of the Creator's energy.

You do not love energy fields, you do not love that which perishes in entities, although perhaps some of you do. There will come a time when each finds that this is not enough. The experience of loving and being loved involves complete trust, cooperation, sacrifice on all parts, and a yielding up of the little self to a self which is called "us," which has an appointment with destiny. Each of you has gifts and is staring them straight in the face. Some things do not seem like gifts, but if you can love your neighbor as yourself and love yourself as your Creator and love your Creator with all your heart, then those gifts of yours which are needed will be called upon whether or not you express the talent, for the community of those who pray and serve is such that the opportunity is made for those who wish to serve.

We realize that the word "gifts" may have meant to some physiological or mental gifts, such as being athletic, being a good friend, caring greatly about the planet Earth and other subjects like this. This is very good for you to do. But, beneath all the phenomena of a distressed world lies the distress of the one infinite Creator and the planet itself. Practice loving yourself, my friends. The gifts will come to you if they have not already. And when you feel an impulse to do something you have never done before, and you feel you are being led by guidance, do not hesitate, but do that which you feel you are guided to do.

In this atmosphere, each will make many mistakes. That is entirely acceptable. It is the method by which people learn. A mistake is a good thing, for in making the mistake, one can sit, intuit and analyze why that effort to be a light being backfired, and so you learn compassion, sympathy, the single-minded love for humankind, not as humankind but as the Creator would do. This depth of love grinds you upon the rock of spiritual principles.

We are not saying that if you follow your own star or if you follow your own agendas which have welled up within you that people will understand you or give you an easy time. This is not so. This has never been so and will never be so. As long as third-density entities gaze upon the one who is taking a great risk for the good, they shake their heads, they do not understand that death will be preferable to being unable to serve. Sometimes one comes upon a talent later in life. A talent for organization, a talent for money raising, a talent for teaching creative writing, a talent for showing young men how to fix up their cars.

We speak of these talents upon the same level as any other. We do not look down upon your world because [you] yourselves are as sacred to us as your trees and your grass. This is the Creation that you have made and we rejoice and are glad in it. We also see the many pitfalls, the major pitfall being that, in a society that basically thinks [about] the self and accumulating masses of belongings and experiences which are expensive [about one] is not going to be in touch with that part of the self which knows the self and wishes to serve. We therefore ask you, at this time, as the roots of the trees grows deeper and deeper into the Earth, drawing …

(Side one of tape ends.)

(Carla channeling)

… that water from the root system, quite a young thing, there are no leaves on the tree, the trees look dead, they are skeletons waving in the wintry wind, so too are you. This is not aloneness, this is your free will nature. To find your true gift is one thing that is, shall we say, relatively easy, for the ability to give service to others is everywhere. One may volunteer in soup kitchens, hospitals, all sorts of places that need free *(inaudible)*. When you feed a hungry stomach, you know that you have been useful and of service. But never forget the more subtle kinds of service that comes from the heart that loves unconditionally. When you can listen to one who is [in] deep confusion and respond with unrestrained compassion, that is another way of showing love. And, again, it is impossible to do until the self be cleared of all those bits and pieces that don't fit into the living of a life in love and faith. Meditate each day, my friends, and ask for the presence of eternity to be about you, all the day long and all through the night.

We are told by this instrument that we have once again gone overtime. We do apologize for our loquacity. We are most thankful for this instrument, for there was a very large amount of difficulty that this instrument was having and we are very pleased that we are able to use this instrument. We of Hatonn would now close the meeting through the one known as Jim. We leave you in love and light. I am Hatonn.

(Jim channeling)

I am Hatonn, and greet you again in love and light. We are pleased that we have been able to make contact with this instrument, for it has been a measure of your time since we have utilized this instrument as well. We would offer ourselves in the path of seeking to answer queries at this time. If there be any queries which may be upon the minds of those present, we would be happy to attempt our response.

Carla: Is love the same thing as space?

I am Hatonn. My sister, there is, of course, a great ambiguity in the quality of love and of space. However, they are not completely identical. Love is that peaceful, creative energy which accepts all as a portion of its being. When one loves *(inaudible)* one gives of the self, the acceptance of another, the complete embracing of that other of a portion of the self, this acceptance given without condition or expectation that the other shall be any form or manifestation other than that what is.

When one has faith in the other, one begins with an acceptance that is equal to love, and extends that quality of love as a kind of protective field, shall we say, that shields or protects one's sense of purpose or rightness, in order that the sense of rightness within the pattern might firm that pattern or attitude of mind in a way that is likened to the construction of a firm foundation for a building. But when one's heart chakra has been opened enough to allow the movement of this creative energy called love to it, and one has experienced this quality moving from the self to another in a service dependable manner over a period of time, then it is possible to feel the extension of this quality into that quality known as faith.

The faith that [is] all is indeed well, for all is made of love. These are poor words for the great concept of which we speak, and we offer our apologies for our inability to describe in greater clarity the concept.

Is there a further query, my sister?

Carla: Yes, Hatonn. *(Inaudible)*.

I am Hatonn. We look to the general response for application in this regard. We give to this instrument the image of the drill instructor that prepares the troops for battle. The drill instructor motivates and pushes each soldier beyond its limits in order that when it faces that battle, it will be more than prepared to deal with the rigors of the struggle. In a similar fashion does your desire motivate and drive your service in a manner that matches that which you have desired to do. Previous to this incarnation you have prepared yourself with abilities that would be applied within this incarnation. There were also inlaid the various limitations that have purposes for which you are well aware, that of the focusing of the attention in an inward fashion, more than would be possible were the physical vehicle more liable to participate in this mundane world and the many activities.

The great desire to serve then finds its only viable avenue, over a long period of the life pattern, to be that which is concerned with the inward journey and the [companions] of that journey which would also travel with you by inspiration and example. Thus, you have done the equivalent of taking a great engine and, instead of allowing it to move the vehicle broadly across the face of the Earth, you have instead chosen a more [narrow] path for this great power to move upon.

Is there a further query?

Carla: No.

We thank you, my sister. Is there another query?

(Pause)

I am Hatonn. It has been a great privilege for us to be able to address this group this evening. We have for a great portion of your time contented ourselves with observing the activities of this group, and it has brought us great joy to participate even in that fashion. However, due to our previous experience with this group, it has been our heart's desire to once again be able to speak our thoughts and share our opinions with this group, for we feel a great companionship and unity with this group.

We extend our sympathies to the one known as Carla that her distortion of the physical vehicle has been the avenue that allows our experience with your group this evening. We are with you at all times and are pleased to join you in your meditations upon your request that we do so. At this time we shall, in great joy and praise, move from this group in the love and in the light of the one infinite Creator. We are those of Hatonn. Adonai, my friends. Adonai. ❧

L/L Research

Sunday Meditation
December 31, 1989

Group question: The question this evening has to do with the development of the magical personality. How do we go about developing the magical personality, and what, actually, is it that we develop when we develop the magical personality, and of what value is it to us to do so?

(Carla channeling)

We come to you in gratitude and greet you in the love and in the light of the one infinite Creator. I am Q'uo. It is a tantalizing prospect to us, a marvelous avenue of service that you offer us, and we offer to you our humble thanks and our abiding love that you who struggle in the darkness still see and have faith in the light within.

The question offered this evening has to do with the magical personality. But before we speak upon that subject we must speak upon a subject that is fundamental to an understanding of the magical personality. That understanding is the simultaneity of all time, all space, and all action. This present moment is eternal. The past, the future, the feeling of being in the river of time, are part of an illusion which gives you who seek an enormously powerful opportunity, consciously to accelerate the rate of your spiritual growth.

It happens to be the last day of an old year and an old decade among your peoples who count by your calendar. Tomorrow it will be next year. Shall it feel like a different time? Shall it seem transformed? For the most part, no, because you are the same. You have always been, you are, and you will always be.

The choices that you make in this density are predisposed by the biases and polarities that you have picked up in lifetimes long ago and more recent. When biases of love and peace and gentleness and humbleness of heart become your rest and your confidence, then perhaps you may release time and space, allowing it to be a useful and extremely potent offerer of catalyst to those who wish to learn lessons of love.

You see, you are at the beginning of self-consciousness. You have almost finished this year in the school of eternity, this illusory time. However, the choices that you make are made in time/space and speak not to the outer world and its mundane concerns but to the heart and the vital feelings of each.

In this way we may say to you more simply that the magical personality is an artifact of the one who has been able to focus the heart and the mind upon the infinite One. It is, in a way, possible to think of the higher self as being separate from you. But just as you were yesterday and will be tomorrow in a new year and a new decade, so the I AM that is the core of you learns of love, of wisdom, and of loving, wise compassion. When these lessons have been learned to the extent that they are without significant distortion, you turn and, reaching through time, you offer yourself a gift. You offer the biases and decisions and choices that have been made, not up to this point alone in your illusion of time but all the choices that allowed each of you to graduate into fourth density, perfect the lessons of love and learn the lessons of light, to fifth density, when you manifest light and learn the true meaning of wisdom.

In sixth density, there is eventually, in mid-density, a point in which there is no longer any polarity, for if all is one polarity there is no polarity. It is when the spirit has reached this point, full of unity, wisdom and compassion, that the sixth-density self places within the third-density self, in the deep mind, the biases which are to come, the destiny which has been fulfilled, the beauty, the exactitude of service to others.

Therefore, the magical personality, or the higher self, is the last vestige of the self which contains polarity. And as you deal in a world illusion grounded in polarity, this gift can be extremely helpful. Many, many times one is faced with dilemmas and enigmas that cannot be rationally discerned. There is no logical answer. There is only the wisdom of the heart and the compassion of the mind. For this is what the sixth density of unity provides: the realization that compassion is not only of the heart but of the mind, that wisdom is not only of the mind but of the heart.

How many times do your people turn from their heart, refusing to ask, refusing to open the door to that helper or comforter which waits patiently to be asked to aid in decision-making of various kinds?

Our message is very simple. We ask each to love the Creator with adoration and worship as one would normally feel for one's father, for you are truly sons and daughters of the infinite One and within yourself infinite in your own being.

The process of accessing the deep mind, and especially the higher self, may be accomplished best, as we have often said, by repetitious, persistent and daily meditation. Not lasting so long but lasting as long as it feels as though you are in a holy place with the one infinite Creator. Thus, meditation is always the key to the opening of the shuttle from the subconscious or deep mind to the conscious mind. The higher self does not operate by giving instructions, for that would be an infringement of free will and would cause paradoxes within the universe that are not desired. However, the call must go forward within meditation that you may be visited, strengthened and renewed by a longer point [of view], a vaster field of incarnations and of incarnational decisions. For, as each knows, there is no thing upon your planet which is as it seems. You are energy fields, complexes of energy fields, with the energy holding you together, carrying you through life.

It is well to be very kindly toward this physical vehicle for it is the means by which the computer of the mind may gently enter data from the deeper self, the self unperceived even when praying or asking. Perhaps one day one awakens and knows what the proper or appropriate answer to a question may be. Perhaps it comes all of a sudden within meditation. There are as many ways to use the higher self as there are entities.

Now, how does one make use of the higher self, this sixth-density portion of you? The first thing that you must do is give up your physical reality. You are an illusion within an illusion; mystery surrounds you. Consequently, as one asks for guidance from a deeper self, the higher self within, one opens a door that can only be opened by the seeker since the higher self is a far more clear, lucid and defined product of your thinking. Yet, still you will find it most helpful to blend the conscious and rational mind with the deep mind, for they give you feelings and biases that are far more a part of whom—we correct this instrument—of who you are, what your essence is, than you may have by any amount of consideration of these matters within this illusion.

Now, as each sits here, we shall attempt to give the process by which the higher self may be contacted. This is one way; there are many others. This is a way which we feel is simple and therefore easier to grasp.

The first step is the acceptance and the forgiveness of the self within this illusion. It must be clear to each one that one cannot live purely in a world polluted by constant negative thoughts and perceptions, cynicism, and the ugly emotions of fear, terror and the triumph of those who delight in terrorizing others. This is not the personality that you wish to use for that special time during which you are working within consciousness to accelerate the rate of your spiritual growth, to heighten your polarity and to move, may we say, forward. You do not need to gaze at the higher self as part of the self unless you wish. However, it is well to know that the higher self and you are timeless and whole and one.

Now, to attain a magical personality there is much which one can do and, indeed, must do to create the appropriate atmosphere for the gentle lover's touch of the rational mind into the deep mind. This is a slow process for many and infinitely worth it. Once one has been able to contact that part of the self that is sixth-density and which has given the gift back to you within the deep recesses of your mind, you may then have a much wider perspective, a much more clear vantage point from which to view the life experiences which your incarnation brings to you.

We caution each against attempting to live in the higher self mode for any length of time past which one cannot hold the concentration and the clarity which the tuning, the praying and the singing brings about. You cannot plunder your own higher self without doing damage to the quality of information which you receive. Consequently, in putting on the whole armor of light, as this instrument would say, and accepting the self which seems to be in the future, but is indeed yourself, as a good advisor you are moving toward a centered position which will be most advantageous to you in using this deep and lovely resource of the mind. We say lovely because it is considerable effort, a labor of love, for the sixth density to create a thoughtform of all that it has experienced.

It *(the higher self or magical personality)* is placed deep within you. It is not placed without you; it is not placed within your teacher or your student or your colleague. The magical personality is an artifact of the self, the mystery-clad being whose entire experience is recognized to be mystery—we correct this instrument—mysterious.

In preparation for the magical personality's development, the first thing which one needs to accomplish is a full and complete examination of conscience. Not that you as an entity may judge you as an entity—not at all. But rather that you may forgive yourself, for you have forgiven all others, have you not? Yet, still you hold yourself unworthy. This is not a helpful spiritual point of view, for the magical personality is based upon the fact that the spark of the Creator within is the true self of each entity.

Therefore, to begin working with the magical personality one must first go through much searching of the mind, the intellect, the emotional biases that constitute that which you are at this time. This is not for the purpose of judgment but for the purpose of grasping your essence at this time. Perhaps you wish to make changes; perhaps you do not. But to come into contact with yourself as a self is the beginning of the magical personality.

The day-to-day personality wavers. It is happy; it is sad; it is active; it is passive. Life is easy or life is difficult. And all of this is within this illusion. The more attention paid to the difficulties of this illusion, the less likely it is that one will be able to have access to the deeper mind of the magical personality.

So, we suggest to each that the table be cleared, the table of petty prejudice, any unfairness, stinginess, desire to manipulate others, and all of those artifacts whose bias is not helpful in gaining polarity toward service to others in the name of the infinite One. This preparation takes a different amount of time for different entities and at the end of it it is still impossible to live within the higher self at all times. However, it is possible to clear the self for the special and sacred door to the self to be opened.

We suggest that each begin a magical personality meditation with that which has been the call of a white, or positive, magician from time immemorial: "I desire to know in order to serve. I desire to use my subconscious mind to enrich, enliven, enable and engage this third-density mind and heart." It is impossible for most to keep this clarity over an extended period of time, and there is danger in attempting to do so.

Consider yourselves as toddlers, just learning to walk, the spirit so young, so lovely, so strong, and yet so vulnerable. This is how the magical personality sees the outer portion of your behavior and thinking. It is perceived as that of a child who knows not what he does. When one turns one's will and faith to the quest for the philosopher's gold of greater wisdom, then you may begin to see gradually a change within you. But, firstly, you must accept that the magical personality is already your own personality, for all time is simultaneous.

One good way to prepare oneself for meditation upon the magical personality is to visualize each chakra in turn, beginning with the red root chakra, and moving upwards carefully clearing energies, carefully seeing your chakra centers glowing: orange, yellow, green, blue, indigo, violet. When you have reached sufficient humility to be able to listen to advice from the higher self that is not easily understood to be other than the self, then we suggest that you begin with this clearing of the chakras, so that you feel the light streaming from your head, for you have opened all your chakras; you have become vulnerable; you are ready to take a risk.

Firstly, there is a tremendous amount of protection of the body by the body, and we recommend to each that this be observed. For instance, this instrument blends the violet of the crown chakra and the red of the root chakra to cover the self with an energy that is completely personal and denotes that which one is. Upon completing this encapsulization of yourself in the red/violet of body protection, you will then put on a garment of light. That is the Creator's protection, impersonal, loving and infinite.

During the meditations it is helpful for those who call upon guides or angelic presences to do so, for that work which you are doing is work in which you are vulnerable, for you are open to learning and you do not always have truly appropriate vibrations for this energy. This must be seen to carefully. The self must be gotten in order, cleared of the small change of life's miseries, cleared even of the laughter of good times, clear to listen within to what has been called in your holy works "the still small voice." That is your magical personality. It is well to call any whom you wish to call to aid in your protection. This is not an illusion any more than you are an illusion within.

This instrument, for instance, evokes—we correct this instrument—invokes the archangels—Raphael, Gabriel, Michael, Auriel—and with these four pillars standing in the corners of the room there is an overarching golden dome, for these principles of love called the archangels are most powerful and most protective.

When you have prepared yourself for the meditation upon the magical personality it is well to sink into the self with no pressure, no thought, no worry, and no wonder, but rather simply to open the door and invite the wisdom and compassion of the ultimately learned balanced being, which you shall have become, to the self as it is.

It is well, when one wishes to work in consciousness with another by communication, to make these same preparations, for by far the majority of those who channel are channeling their own magical personality, their own higher self, their uniqueness. And it is well, when it is finished, that mentally one acknowledges that one slips off the garment of light and moves back into the illusion of energy fields and the experiences that challenge you to love.

The magical personality is one which is grounded in the deepest humility and in the strongest sense, paradoxical though it may seem, of the worth of the self. Like a string or a ribbon, this unrolling behind you gives you information at each present moment as you request it. Those who wish to maintain a magical personality outside the discipline of meditation may indeed work with the visualizations, to work with visualizations if those visualizations are simply shapes—the square, the circle, the triangle …

(Side one of tape ends.)

(Carla channeling)

I am Q'uo, and we shall continue.

It is well for those who wish to maintain the spiritual magical personality for a longer time than a meditation to work with visualizations. The first visualizations are simply shapes: the square, the circle, the triangle. The discipline it requires to hold this image in consciousness is the same kind of discipline that an artist employs as it studies its technique that it may, in the end, be a better instrument through which music or communication or healing or living may use to allow you to be the shining metaphysical being that you truly are.

It is not advisable, in our opinion, to keep the magical personality any longer than one is able to remain completely clear within. This normally limits that which the magical personality may do to very brief moments within the waking hours and to enspiriting dreams during those hours when the subconscious and the conscious move together in play, in ritual, and in meaning. For, woe betide those who act as if they were acting out of the magical personality when they are less than clear. May we say, this is extremely inadvisable and that the student of the magical personality who does not wish to study the Tree of Life, the Kaballah, and all those things which would inform one of the history of this concept, content the self with knowing that the magical personality lies within you fallow and ready to bloom. When you call upon it may you do so in humility. We hope you may call upon it often, but always protect the self before you open your vulnerable spirit to that which, though it is you, appears within the illusion to be another. For those who do not clear themselves excellently may receive any number of guides which would purport to be the magical personality but which instead are means by which positive polarity is gradually lessened.

We are told by this instrument that once again we have talked too long. We shall cease at this point, though there is perhaps some more upon this subject which would be of interest, for we wish to close the meditation through the instrument known as Jim. We leave you in the love and in the light as we transfer to the one known as Jim. We are Q'uo.

(Jim channeling)

I am Q'uo, and greet each again in love and light. At this time we would ask if there may be queries to which we may speak that have arisen as we have spoken upon the magical personality this evening, or upon any other topic that has interest. Is there a query at this time?

Questioner: Yes, Q'uo. I understand that in the selves of a higher density nature we come together with others, or those that from a third-density point of view seem like others, to form social memory complexes. By the time of sixth density this seems to be a way of life. One's higher self would then seem to be of a social memory complex and therefore would, from the standpoint of third-density experience, be something shared. Is it part of the reason for coming together in groups and joining our seeking together that we share higher selves?

I am Q'uo, and am aware of your query, my brother. This is a most interesting query, for it deals with the nature of the creation itself as it is discovered by conscious, seeking entities, for you are as the explorer that moves into a wilderness area and begins to fashion a means of survival in that wilderness out of what it finds there and as the means of survival are accomplished and shelter is created and food is attained, the explorer begins to discover not that which is foreign to itself but that which is not only familiar but is identical to the self.

As you move through this octave of creation and move into the third density which you now inhabit and refine the definition of individualized consciousness, you then use that defined and individualized consciousness as a means or a trail by which to discover more of that which is unknown, more of that which becomes known, becomes familiar, and is recognized as the self. The country through which you travel, the brothers and sisters with whom you travel, reveal themselves to you and give of themselves in a fashion which forms a unified conscious seeking so that what is available to one is available to all and is utilized in furthering the journey of discovery. So, as you come together, utilizing the pooled resources, you add information, experience, response and discovery, and all of these things and concepts become further definitions, or refinements, or broadening of the small self that has become a group self that is, indeed, transforming to a greater self that continues this spiraling process, so that that which you seek, that which is your goal, eventually is seen to be a portion of the self in an expanded quality.

Thus, at some point in your experience, you will no longer seek the light but shall become the light; you shall no longer seek the love but shall become love; you shall no longer seek the one Creator but shall become the one Creator. Thus, the pattern of your seeking reproduces the nature of the creation, which is unity.

Is there a further query, my brother?

Questioner: Yes, from the point of view of the seeking, the distance *(inaudible)*, as we gaze toward the unity which we *(inaudible)*, it seems to us something not yet. And yet the further we get in the exploration and in the unfoldment toward that unity, the more it seems that what is discovered is discovered as something already. We already have a higher self, already in sixth density there seems an already preparedness of all of the stages in life's way. Have we had to go stage by stage downward to the furthest point removed from the one infinite Creator, then to begin the journey back? I'm not sure I understand the why of that.

I am Q'uo, and am aware of your query, my brother. It depends upon one's point of view as to whether one has gone in a downward fashion in order to move upward, or has moved from an upward fashion to that which seems to be down. To be more precise, when the one Creator harvests the experience of all Its portions through an octave of creation It then utilizes that harvest, which is the refinement of each of Its portions of experience of unity, and enters again into the great cycle of creation and spins forth another universe, beginning in the chaotic movement of first density that is in your measurement without time, without order. And from this seeming chaos, then moves into that which has the spiraling cycles of increased conscious awareness, that the harvest of the previous creation might become the foundation for that which shall further refine the experience and knowledge of the Creator.

Each of you, as individualized portions of the one Creator, partake in this process by particularizing what is simultaneous, taking a small portion of what you would call the river of time from the ocean of eternity, and viewing that river of time as if under the microscope, looking at what seems to come before that which follows, creating the past, the present, and the future, in order that that which is and that is unity in many portions might be experienced in a more intense, varied and purified fashion. That small sliver, then, of experience that is chosen for each incarnation has working upon it your free will choice, so that that which is eternal becomes magnified and particularized enough that it may be examined carefully within an incarnation, be worked upon by free will, be refined in this process and be purified as an expression of Beingness, of the identity of the one Creator within yourself.

Thus, you enter into this entire process in order that you might pick a portion of that which is yourself and, by working upon it intensively, cause it to become as vivid as possible that it might become an adornment, an honestation for the one Creator. Thus, you refine as one who takes the raw ore from the mountainside and removes from it by this process of particularization that which is gold so that the product of this process, then, is bright, brilliant and shining and is purified in its nature in a manner which would not have been possible were not you to have chosen to expend your consciousness and your effort upon it.

Is there a further query, my brother?

Questioner: Yes, just one more. As we move into a greater realization of our goal as selves, we find that self is in God and yet we need now to learn to develop the magical personality, which for us means to develop that self which is in the sixth density, not yet God. Is there a reason that we do not invoke directly our Godness? Is it a matter of taking one step at a time?

I am Q'uo, and am aware of your query, my brother. If we understand correctly that which you have asked, we would say that this Godness, the quality of the Creator, residing whole and full within, is not immediately available in its complete sense to each entity in any portion of the evolutionary journey in order that that journey might have, what we might call, a greater span of experience possible. For, if any portion of the one Creator shall come into the full realization of its nature as the one Creator, then the journey is complete. The opportunity for further refinement through the application of free will to catalyst then has no further purpose, the goal having been achieved.

Thus, the octave of creation through which each portion of the one Creator moves provides each portion and the one Creator within each portion an opportunity that is more varied because of the lack of full knowledge of the nature of the self. Thus, one may say that ignorance provides opportunity. The veils that are placed within the consciousness of each entity provide the mystery which draws the seeker onward. If all veils were removed and the nature of the self were seen, it would be as if there were no more debts, no more gains, shall we say.

Is there a further query, my brother?

Questioner: Thank you very much.

I am Q'uo, and we thank you. Indeed, we thank you very much as well, my brother. Is there another query at this time?

Carla: I would like to know if I was, in fact, experiencing psychic greeting before this meditation, and, if so, why. And I will certainly appreciate the problem if you cannot answer because of the Law of Confusion.

I am Q'uo, and am aware of your query, my sister. The nexus of this experience is likened to the crossing of paths or of opportunities that have been noted by those entities who have been your companions for some time upon this journey, of that which you call the negative polarity. The cycle of the adept is such that within your own experience there was noted a particular sensitivity, as has been noted on previous occasions by these entities and one in particular. Added to this cyclical sensitivity were the chemical medications that further enhanced your receptivity, or susceptibility, to impressions, shall we say. The state or nature of the mind complex when under the influence of these various medications provided an opportunity which then took advantage of the dysfunction of the otic portions of your physical vehicle that were damaged from youth, so that it was possible to render a certain degree of what you would call dizziness that would have the potential of rendering you unconscious for a brief portion of time. This effort was offered more as an attempt to enter fear into your experience than to enter true difficulty or danger.

Is there a further query, my sister?

Carla: No, Q'uo. I appreciate it. Thank you.

I am Q'uo, and we thank you, my sister. Is there another query at this time?

Carla: Could you comment on how aware cats in our household are of these contacts, if they are able to participate in any way?

I am Q'uo, and am aware of your query, my sister. The entities that you refer to as the cats are quite sensitive to not only our presence and others of the Confederation of Planets in the Service to the One Creator, but are also sensitive to the negatively oriented that would offer their service in their own way. The feline entities have, throughout the history of your peoples, been seen by those of a metaphysical sensitivity as being able to perceive much which is unseen to your physical eye. The cat has been utilized as the guardian of many temples in the past of the Egyptian race of your peoples. For this reason and because of the sensitivity of the cat entities, the negatively oriented entities find some difficulty in offering the full impact of their services when the feline entities are present, for there is a natural kind of guarding or protection that is offered by the cat entities. They are not always aware of each entity as an individualized portion or person as they are aware of you in that nature, but are often aware of a feeling tone or attitude or ambiance that has changed or has a certain quality.

Thus, it is sometimes as if these creatures sense a presence as you would hear a certain sound that would alert you to activity. The cat entity, however, is also able to ascertain the nature of the presence, whether it is beneficial or deleterious, and will respond differently to each of these qualities.

Is there a further query, my sister?

Carla: Are they, then, beginning to develop their own biases toward the positive or the negative path at this point?

I am Q'uo, and am aware of your query, my sister. In some cases this is so, especially those cases in which a cat entity is invested in the position as a pet, as we find in this domicile there are six such entities. In other cases, it is possible for the cat entity to become aware of the presence of unseen entities and simply be aware that a presence is there, much as they are aware you are in their presence when you are indeed in their presence. Their beginning bias toward one polarity or the other, then, is a function of the quality of investment, shall we say, that has been given to them.

Is there a further query, my sister?

Carla: Is there a *(inaudible)* that in our participation *(inaudible)* that would aid them in the investment process? And also I am assuming that our contributions toward investment is a service that we perform?

I am Q'uo, and am aware of your query, my sister. The participation of the cat entities in these meditations enhances this investment quality in that they share their experience with you and with us. The nature of investment is that the quality of beingness of a greater energy source, shall we say, is manifested in a direct fashion that is the proximity of one presence to another with the motivation being to share freely of the self or to radiate a certain vibration or information that then will find a resonance with the essence or basic quality of the entities with whom the vibration or information is shared. Thus, though the cat entities are not able to perceive in a mental or spiritual nature in the same manner as are you that which is shared in these meditations, they are aware of and receptive to the basic frequency of vibration that is radiated in a resonate fashion with their own essence.

Is there a further query, my sister?

Carla: No, thank you.

Is there any other query at this time?

(Pause)

I am Q'uo, and we wish to take this opportunity to thank each present for asking with an whole heart that of which is the greatest concern, for we cannot be of service without the asking and we treasure each opportunity to respond to your queries with that which we have found helpful in our own journeys of seeking and of asking the same questions that you ask with your hearts, with your minds and with your being. We walk with you upon this journey and rejoice with each step. We thank each for every particle of experience that is brought into these meditations that we may share with you that which is your experience and which is your desire. The bridge that is fashioned by your invitation is that rainbow bridge which connects heart to heart.

At this time we shall take leave of this group, thanking each for the joy and the love that is given to us, and leaving each in that joy and that love and in the light of the one infinite Creator. We are known to you as those of Q'uo. Adonai, my friends. Adonai.

Year 1990

January 7, 1990 to March 13, 1990

Sunday Meditation
January 7, 1990

Group question: The question this evening has to do, to start with, how does one maintain the attitude, and the manifestation of the attitude, of joy, and of praise and of thanksgiving, sincerely and heartfelt, when one is undergoing assaults of pain and limitation, nausea, discomfort, general run of the mill bad news? Then we will follow with other questions, concerning, perhaps, was Christ the only Son of God, what does it mean to be a Son of God?

(Carla channeling)

I am Q'uo, and am with this group, thanking each in the circle for calling for the kind of information that we are able to offer an opinion upon, for it is a great service to us to teach, as the teach/learner learns always more than the student.

You ask this evening firstly about the prickly business of mood balancing during difficult conditions. We are aware that it is this instrument's question, as this instrument is going into two hospitalizations and wishes with all its heart to create within those experiences a poem of praise and thanksgiving for the Creator, and not the nattering of complaint and whining.

Firstly, we would remind all that they are in the third density. The amount of will which it takes to balance pain and the counting of blessings is enormous, and if it is not balanced, but merely suppressed, it does much more harm than good. It is well to ventilate any negative emotion while it is small, that it does not escalate into a crisis in the spiritual walk of a pilgrim. Breathe in; breathe out. This is the first blessing. You are alive. You are in this illusion, and you are learning. You earned this position, this incarnation. Carefully did you select that which shall come to you. Carefully did you estimate your limits and move catalyst to the very limits, for you wish once and for all to learn the lesson of unconditional self-forgiveness that opens the door to compassionate love. Therefore, the first thing that we should suggest is dwelling whenever possible upon the all-compassionate love and the immediate presence of the one infinite Creator.

We realize it is difficult for the mind to work well when the physical vehicle demands a great deal of energy in pain control. But the words to give praise and thanksgiving are simple. Merely thank the Creator for your creation, for the safety in which you have lived to this day, experiencing and learning, for opportunities of the moment and the moments to come. You have been created, and you are sustained, and all that is given you is given you by your Higher Self, in sure knowledge that with that which this instrument would call grace, that which we would call the principle of unconditional love, can be made to be the natural and essential being of each, no matter what the condition.

You, as humankind, must face the fact that you are mortal and given to weakness of the flesh. There are few who have not the aches, the pains and the irritabilities. The basic secret of protecting the self from the self's own self-judgment is the practice of self-forgiveness, for Christ, Christ consciousness, the Higher Self, whatever you wish to call this principle of unconditional love, stands waiting for you to ask for help. May your heart be as soft as the earth in the springtime, that it may be amenable to plowing, and that seeds of love are planted in the ashes of pain, and fertilized with meditation and caring to do better in a persistent way.

When you wish to count your blessings, and you are not in a position to think clearly, you are still in a position to count the blessings of personalities close to you. You may give thanks that the Creator loves you personally, that you are as important to the mystery as the mystery is to your mystery-clad being; not your variousness, not your free will, but that of you which is in the Creator, and that of the Creator which is in you. Kindness to the self is helpful.

We find also that for some the using of breath is very helpful, for when one uses one's breath one is using one's vital energy. Thus, the reading to the self of material designed to increase one's awareness of thanksgiving is recommended. Even repetitious reading of inspiring words is helpful, for sometimes those of humankind are resistant to feeling better about themselves, to accepting their limitations, and to continuing to offer the praise and the thanksgiving that is rightfully the one infinite Creator's, Who offered each of you and each of us a magnificent opportunity, the opportunity to grow, to be, to perceive and to act. Always have you control of some degree over the behavior which you must express.

This instrument is telling us that we should be short, as there is more than one question. We believe that an instrument, such as this one who is in pain, may, through the help of medication which is causing mere sleep, slide into thanksgiving for all those souls that care about the entity, for the Creator's love of the entity, for the gift of faith to bear that which cannot be born, and to endure the unendurable.

We credit each pilgrim with persistence. Persistence, more than any one trait, though it lacks somewhat in a sense of humor, is the key to spiritual growth. You cannot pick up items on the spiritual shelf and gaze at them, and try them, and put them back, unless you have learned from them, and applied those learnings in the life. Therefore, we suggest the very simple giving of thanks, thanks for creation, for preservation, and for all those people and things that are blessings to you. In any circumstance there are many blessings, not the least of which is the fact that many environments which an entity knows not that it touches, moves into prayer as it cares and shares that caring with the metaphysical instrument of unconditional love, and the request that the will of the One Creator be perceived, and the entity given the strength to act upon what is perceived.

You must see yourselves as heroes. You are mythical characters. You are not mundane. That is the illusion. The pain that you feel is within the illusion. Far worse is it to feel the spiritual pain of rejection, low self-worth, frustration and anger. These things cannot be avoided, for you are of humankind, but in the controlled situation of recovery from serious illness, it is good to attempt to pray without ceasing, giving thanks for all that you can think of—for those who love you, for the Creator which nurtures you, for the skill of those healers which work with you. Repetition is a good and useful tool for the learning of a habit, and that is what a positive attitude is—it is a habit. You may complain, or you may count your blessings. It is difficult to do both in the same breath.

To increase the energy which is available for praise and thanksgiving—that is to increase the vital energy—the use of the breath is recommended, either through chanting, singing, praying out loud, or reading from inspirational works to the self. Again, repetition is no bad thing. If something is important to you as you read, savor it, and bless it with your recognition of its personal truth for you.

We are told we must stop at this point, that we may answer other questions that you may have. And so we open this meeting to questions.

Jim: What does it mean to be a Son of God, and how do we manifest that? Is it possible to in our lives? Was Jesus the only Son of God?

I am Q'uo. The phenomenon known to you as Jesus is a principle of the Logos, or Love, that has moved through the densities as any other entity, but was created slightly differently than those of you who swim beneath the sea of illusion. This entity also wished to live a life that was a poem to the Creator, and again, and again, on planet after planet, this entity comes into incarnation with the special character of partial remembrance. In other words, this entity contains more of the Logos, or Love, than free will, whereas each of you contain the bonding of Love and free will, against which you must challenge yourself to find a unity of being.

This entity was a good teacher of the message of the Law of One. Again and again the message is misunderstood. Again and again the Creator sends forth that special part of Itself which retains the consciousness of unconditional love rather than having it disappear beneath the veil. This entity has helped many, many civilizations.

Each of you is equally son or daughter, heir or heiress, Christ, of God, but each of you are deeply enmeshed in a negatively oriented mundane world. You do not have the ability which this special entity had to perceive and do the Creator's will in joy, no matter what the circumstances, no matter what the cost. However, each of you is brother or sister to the Christ principle. The Christ principle resides within each of you. You are Christ. But you are separated from the knowledge of that portion of yourself, that you may feel iniquitous, guilty, angry, frustrated and disharmonious, and thereby offer to yourselves the catalyst which is needed for growth and polarization in the choices that you make to serve others or to serve the self.

Shall you one day be a Christ? There is only one Christ that is part of the Creator or the Logos that has been given the dispensation not to forget in third density. This does not mean that you are lesser. It means you struggle against more difficult circumstances, for you struggle in a life full of faith instead of knowledge. To the one known as Jesus there was little mystery in the Creator, in itself, and in humankind. To the rest of creation there remain grave questions to be answered, a truth for which to be sought, although the truth shall not be forthcoming within this density. There is the instinctive hunger to move closer and closer to that principle of consciousness which is freely given, unconditionally given, love. You labor against an immense handicap. Do not be discouraged. In the words of this particular entity, when mistakes are made, they are not counted. It is merely an opportunity to realign the life pattern so that the lesson may once again come before the entity.

There is no judgment save the judgment of the self by the self. Consequently, we suggest that each spend time forgiving the self and praying for those who are not seemingly helpful to you, for so would the Christ consciousness do. So is the I AM of love. Each of you has an I AM deeply buried in the resources and contents of the deep mind. It is overlaid with stratum after stratum of bias, experience and reaction. As always, we recommend the faithful daily meditation, or some form of prayer, that one may spend time aware that one is on holy ground. There is no ground that is not holy. But when one is moving very quickly through the mundane routine of the day, one is prone to forget one's relationship with the Infinite One. Call yourselves prodigal sons or daughters, for you have squandered your inheritance. As a planet, damage has been done that rests upon the head of each. May each be aware of each and pray that the situation be ameliorated, and if possible, may each entity volunteer to make things better for those who have nothing.

Yes, my friends, there is only one Christ, but it is a consciousness, a principle, that can incarnate, and incarnate again, and incarnate again. When it incarnates, its only difference is that it does not forget that which all those upon your sphere do forget: the glory, the wonder, the beauty, the peace, the laughter, the love and the light of the one infinite Creator. It is not impossible for you to move along the path that the Christ consciousness has shown you, for you too are the sons and daughters of the Infinite One. And as you meditate and slowly become more and more conversant with the deep self which is worthy, limitless and eternal, you may find yourself humbly pleased that you are able to be a servant of the principle of Love.

May we ask if there is another query at this time?

Jim: Who are you as Q'uo as you speak to us?

I am Q'uo. I am two social memory complexes, the one you know of as Ra, and the one you know of as Latwii. We have combined because this instrument constantly asks for the highest and best contact it may stably carry. The energies of the one known as Ra, which is a social memory complex of sixth density, is an energy band narrow enough that it requires the locking in, and therefore the unconscious state, of the mind of the channel. The entities of Ra were appalled to see the toll it took upon this instrument to bring forth that which it did channel. It was not expected that there would be so much interest from what this instrument calls the loyal opposition.

When our energies are stepped down to those of Latwii, an energy this instrument feels most comfortable with, we are able to offer concepts that are to some degree more precise, and may we say, perhaps more interesting to the advanced student of metaphysics, than that which is called Latwii would be by the self, for Latwii is of the fifth density, the density of wisdom, and as you can feel, our vibrations are the vibrations not only of unconditional wisdom, but compassion as well.

Thus, we are composite, and as this instrument has often suspected, our name is a pun, a quibble; not a joke, but merely an identification which was clear. We are the I AM, and you too are the I AM, and all that is in creation is the I AM. We chose a language this instrument knew, and used the word meaning "who," or "which." It was designed to make the instrument ponder this very point, and we are delighted (in the) results so far, for we of Latwii have been able, with the help of our teachers, those of Ra, to offer information in a way which is clearer and more compassionate, perhaps, than we of Latwii, in and of our own social memory complex, could accomplish. We find that our senses of humor are not at all the same, and so we have attempted to give up our sense of humor, that the higher sense of humor or wisdom informed by compassion may do its subtle work in these meditations.

May we answer you further, my brother?

Jim: Not at this time. Thank you.

We thank you, my brother. Is there another query at this time?

K: Can you talk about what it means to accept your limitations?

I am Q'uo. The acceptance of limitations is both simple and excruciatingly difficult. To accept a limitation is to fight not against it, and it is humankind's nature to fight, to see any limitation, or lack of freedom, as a fault, and to move body, and soul, and mind, and spirit, in will and faith that the condition experienced—which may be difficult at the present moment—by the activities of good attitude, proper care of the body, and proper discipline of the mind and personality, may become more and more able to be themselves.

When one is doing that which one does out of a sense of duty, one is not accepting one's limitations, for the limitations of which we would speak are not only those physical limitations which may occur, but also mental, emotional and spiritual limitations, which are just as valid, though unseen. To accept the self as it is is to accept the limitation.

Now, this instrument, for instance, is a good example of those who are unable to accept limitation. This is a human characteristic, and is designed in direct opposition to the spiritual principle of surrender of the self. However, this determination and will was given to each seeking entity to use in complete free will. And so if the limitations are not respected and are pushed against, this is no mistake, nor is it an error. It simply increases the distractions and discomforts of the limitations against which one is fighting. If one were to accept all of one's limitations, one would never change.

What we truly mean by accepting limitations is accepting whatever condition one finds oneself in. Certainly it is well to help the self, insofar as the self may be helped …

(Side one of tape ends.)

(Carla channeling)

I am Q'uo. I shall continue. The acceptance of limitations is a very personal, metaphysical question. If one accepts limitations that are unacceptable to the personality, one is not accepting limitations, but rather becoming dutiful, and duty is a negative emotion. So we suggest to each that one do what one can to improve one's condition, with joy, and to meet that which one cannot meet with joy with a sense of peace and acceptance.

Each entity was born without this or that gift, and with other gifts. Each entity is unique. Each entity has unique limitations. Therefore, we suggest to the one who wishes to accept one's limitations that in any circumstance one offer praise and thanksgiving for one's being, one's preservation, and one's son- or daughtership in relation to the one infinite Creator.

May we answer you further, my sister?

K: Not at this time, thank you.

I am Q'uo. Pardon us for taking the time, as you would say, to luxuriate in what seems to us a warm and frothy waterfall of each entity's love of the Creator and of each other. We are aware that within this group there is not the strength of the group which Ra was able to use. This identity, Q'uo, is able to use the level of this group in a stable and safe manner. We rest here with you, in quietness and peace and comfort and immunity, for you are light to us, beautiful, dramatic, and at the very heart of the adventure of consciousness. Now is the time for choice—to serve the Creator by serving others, or to serve the self and so serve the Creator within.

We ask each to be persistent with the daily routine of morning offering. We realize that anywhere two or three, as it is said in your holy works, are gathered together, unconditional love is within the group as a member, an actual principle or being of consciousness. Thus, the group meditation, the group focus upon the truth and love and peace, creates a very strengthening resource for each as it moves from the group into other environments which are not controlled, which are not safe, which are puzzling and risky. May you pray for such risks, and such chances to utilize that which you have learned, to move closer and closer to the polarity of the unconditional love that is the core of your imperishable being.

We would leave you at this time in the love and in the light of the one infinite Creator. We are most pleased that you asked who we were. We would have called ourselves "Ego," except that it would have been misunderstood by each of you, for though it means I AM, the same difficulty would have caused conflict that has caused conflict ever since the entity with consciousness of Jesus said "I AM the Way, I AM the Truth, I AM the Life." We speak to those within a Christian culture, and we find that this is one of the most misunderstood passages ever offered by the teacher known as Jesus. His I AM was the principle of unconditional love, the nature of the Creator. The great I AM is love, unmanifest and manifest.

You are the dancers now which dance the dance of your destiny in third density. May you choose well to learn from each mistake, to forgive the self for all, to move forward in newness of spirit and renewal of commitment each and every day. You are lifted up into the light of the Infinite One. Feel that blessing as we call it to your group. It is intense, is it not? We ask you to find your own center of being, your own essence, your own passion, commitment and center, for then you shall be able to express more and more of the I AM principle within.

We leave this group in love and light. I am known to you as Q'uo. We wish each to take that which we have said not as infallible, but as our opinion, as we leave each in thanks and blessing of being allowed to share those opinions with you. Adonai, my friends. Adonai vasu borragus. ✼

Sunday Meditation
January 21, 1990

Group question: The question this evening has to do with the means by which those who are in mated relationships might use the mated relationship to further, not only the relationship, but also the metaphysical or spiritual growth that each wishes to accomplish within the incarnation.

(Carla channeling)

I am Q'uo. Greetings to each of you. *(Inaudible)* of the one infinite Creator. *(Inaudible)* bask in the beauty of each unique *(inaudible)* unique spirit within this dwelling place. The beauty and the *(inaudible)* within this heavy [illusion] is very moving to us.

We would like to remind each that we are but those brothers and sisters on the path that you are following. Our *(inaudible)* are perhaps a bit dustier, our experience is perhaps richer and fuller, but we are not infallible, we are not authorities, we speak our opinions and some of our opinions may not be those truths which may personally pertain to you in the conditioning that your *(inaudible)* at this time. Therefore we ask you to beware of relying upon our authority, or any authority. But rather, when you hear truth that is your personal truth, you will feel as though you are remembering it rather than learning it for the first time. And you will resonate as an instrument does, a harp when touched by the wind, and you shall be inspirited and in your inspiration lies the removal of the fate of this planet. So listen in faith, but accept only those things that seem so to you as being helpful and allow the rest to pass away from your memory as not being part of your personal truth at this time. For there are many, many levels of learning upon this path of seeking and each entity moves at a different pace and in a different creation. In a creation as unique as that person is. Which brings us to the subject which was requested this evening.

Each entity of the mated relationship is a unique being. There will always be an "I" and a "thou." One may gaze at this as a centrifugal force, a dynamic which swings each within the union away from the center of that union into those specialized environments which are made for the path of service that each has chosen. No two entities have the same path of service. No two entities can do everything together and if they were to do everything together they would be far more poorer than their relationship because of their slavishness to behavior. A mated relationship is not strengthened at the level of behavior, but, rather, is nourished by deeper and more dynamic forces from within.

Thus, the first thing that will aid the mated relationship is the constant respect of the free will of the other self. That other self may do things which are not understandable to the self. It is not necessary that each understand the other. For yours are not the lessons of reason, yours are the lessons of love. And so you attempt, in freeing each other, to move outwards from the center of the relationship, to encourage that self to be that self, to nourish and enrich that self, knowing that the self is accepted unconditionally as it is, with no desire for any change or variation. In this way, the mirror one holds up to the other becomes clear and still and accurate.

Because each is unique, there is sometimes a frightening realization that honest disagreements of a fairly deep nature exist. In the atmosphere of honest disagreement, there needs to be a realization of that which is beyond the surface, intellectual and emotional thinking. That awareness is a centripetal force that brings the couple back to the center to become "one." This becoming one does not diminish either self, but is rather a different entity which you may call "us." [Each us] is an unique blend of perspectives, biases and viewpoints, just as each are unique in self. This us-self is the beginning of what has been called a social memory complex. Total acceptance of another, without the need to understand, creates an atmosphere in which understanding becomes possible. Intellectually, one can only be hagridden[4] by attempts to understand and rationalize the behavior of another.

To attempt to live as a couple, moving from the mind and not from the heart, is to imprison both in the very narrow room of logic *(pause)* and sacred or cherished belief systems. We urge each in a mated relationship to remember that the most precious thing they possess is invisible and is an entity that is created by both selves, working together in service to the one Creator.

Thus, there is the self, the other self, and the Creator. That is the "us," for which you may strive with all good health and faith.

The degree of purity and honesty between two entities is the key to clarity within mated relationships. To allow one misunderstanding is to set the plumb line and lay the first brick in a wall that can never be broken down completely. When the occasion occurs wherein the mated pair feels that there is an antagonistic relationship, both entities need to step back and gaze at that stumbling block. Are two mated entities adversaries if they pull the same cart, carry the same hopes, and strain with every fiber of their being toward the passion of mystery? Certainly not! So when there is antagonism, objectify, acknowledge and accept this momentary antagonism. Discuss it, dissolve it, forgive it, and move on. Do not allow the first brick to be laid in a wall of separation.

This is an enormous challenge. We put you to it, for you have asked us how you may best use the mated relationship. It is hard work. We may mention also that the "us" of each in the relationship is enhanced greatly by that great enhancer of the unique individual. That is, meditation on a daily basis.

Meditation together is possible. Quiet times, reading times, inspiration times. It could be only five minutes long, it could be only ten minutes. If it be just a few seconds with the meeting of the eyes, in the understanding that each is on the other side, that each is in there pitching for the other and is never over against the other, then have you won through to a level of trust that will enable each to mirror to the other that which the self is actually manifesting in an objective sense. For subjectively it is entirely probable that the self shall be the own—we correct this instrument—shall be its own best stumbling block, fooling itself with rationalizations about the self.

In a mated relationship, each is the teacher to the other. In the complete and utter equality of children of the one infinite Creator, each is equally equipped to serve as a mirror to the other self. Each is perfectly equipped by that within, that we may call the Creator-self, for each of you is a mixture of the Creator and free will. When two entities come together, they come together willfully, their wills are variant, and the road is bumpy indeed, nor does it ever smooth out entirely, for there is no end to the lessons one may learn, no end to the refinement of those lessons.

Thus, do not fool yourselves if you feel you are smarter, more intuitive, an older soul, or in anyway elite or other than completely equal as a metaphysical being to the mate. This mutual respect and recognition offers to each the potential for great works in faith.

Before we close we would wish to address the subject of the paths of service that each has. Each has certain environments, peculiar to that person alone and not shared by the other. These environments begin quite

---

[4] hagridden: to be afflicted by worries.

subjectively within the mind and the heart of the individual. Two entities may stay in the same room gazing at the same scenery through an entire incarnation and learn completely different lessons. But more than that, each entity shall move out into the world, hoping to aid it, to serve it, to be one with that which makes things better, more unified, more peaceful, more beautiful, more of a gift to the infinite Creator. The path of service that is most often overlooked is the path of service called parenthood. There is no more difficult path of service. It is an extremely sacrificial, daily and devotional path of service.

Those who realize that they are dealing with imperishable spirits, that they are nourishing metaphysical entities in small physical bodies, may aid those entities as they grow by paying attention to those questions that are asked and answering them in all seriousness when the question is a serious one. It is a path of service that shall either separate a mated couple or bring it forcefully together, joyfully together, so that each [offers] the other consolation as they gaze in constant bewilderment at the chaos which is inherent in the process of rapid growth, the rapid growth of each child. You may best be of service to that entity by being a steady influence. For instance, if there is no formal worship within the family group, no sense of wonder or mystery explored, no time set aside for the beauty and the love and the peace of the infinite One, then the guidance that each intends to give to the young ones who have been given into your care is greatly [diminished]. Allow and expect your little ones to participate in some ritualistic recognition of the great mystery of the one infinite Creator. Talk about faith and abiding, talk of peace and consolation and forgiveness. Talk of those principles and ideas which are worn so shabbily and made so ragged by consensus reality, which is indeed an extremely skewed and distorted perception of that which truly is.

Do not abandon your little ones in your path of service. If they are entrusted to you, it is up to you to allow them to know the joy and the healing peace of worship of the infinite. Nothing is known, nothing can be known, we offer to you no doctrine, no dogma, but simply posit a theory which we have found so far to be correct in practice and that is that each is a child of the one infinite Creator. Each is a being of love. Each has choices to make about how to use that love. For each is a powerful person, able to give and to receive.

Share with your little ones the awe and the wonder of summer nights, the smell of burning wood, and the sweet smiles on otherwise sour faces when your Christmas tides are opening up. Share in a little piece of each day and spend some ritualistic time in respective silence or in vocal praise, in whatever way the mated pair feels comfortable with the little ones, that as they grow they may know that they have been created, that they have been loved not only by the parents but by the universe itself. Then they are at home in the universe, for the universe loves them. This is the most precious gift that this particular path of service offers. The creation of the biases within the incarnational experience of the small ones, that they are accepted, forgiven and loved unconditionally by that great mystery which is love itself, the great moving force of creation, and indeed the Creator Itself.

We suggest to each that a very strong lesson in the armament of fighting through to togetherness and comfort together is the sense of humor. It is not well to take things too seriously. For situations constantly change and that which yesterday was a mountain, today is the mole hill. Attempt to remain within the present moment.

Let us make an analogy. Each of you is a aware of how animated cartoons are made. Each slide is drawn slightly differently, that a movement may seem to take place when those slides are run past the eye in rapid sequence. In reality, all of the incarnational experience is those slides of the present moment resting upon one another in one pile of presence. There is only the present moment. You are heaping up the present moment. The path is a dream within a dream. The future? The same. Your link with eternity? Truth, reality and love is the realization that now is a resonant and sanctified moment. We ask you to become intense in your appreciation of this present moment, of the beauty within you and all about you.

We are being told by this instrument that we must be short, so we shall at this time end this most pleasant conversation with you, hoping that we have said some few things that may be of help to each. For truly, two learn better together than one by themselves. For does one have a mirror to gaze into? No. The only true mirror you shall ever have is the mirror of your friends and especially that of your mate, who knows all your secrets and has seen all your imperfections, and who has forgiven them, accepted them, and now simply reflects that which is given. This is the heart of accelerating spiritual grown by using the mated relationship. Follow your paths of service as they diverge. Fling yourselves into your environments with joy. They will be different and you shall learn different lessons and so shall you teach each other. But above all treasure the "us" which is created in the mated bond and which includes, as a third partner, the Creator Itself, the great original Thought, which is love, love impersonal and impassable.

May you share laughter and tears, And may you remember that such relationships and such learning are the work not of a week, nor a year or a decade, but of a lifetime. You may feel you are making no progress. But look back ten years and see the value of shared experience. Above all, refuse to become adversaries. Always attempt to put the self in the place of the other self. And to give that other self every consideration, as their freedom, every ounce of love within your being. Release and surrender your mate to the love of the one infinite Creator. And allow your mate to release you. For each of you is strong, independent and able. Your differences are the dynamics which make your "us"-ness strong. So do not fear disagreement. Simply recognize that there will be honest disagreement and that this is acceptable. May you live in faith, faith that that which is happening is that which is supposed to be happening. Faith that there is love in the moment, if one looks hard enough for it. Faith in the difficulties, that the difficulties is a challenge which shall bear fruit. And faith that recognizes and rejoices in those times which are easy and warm and loving. Remember always to give thanks and praise for such moments. For if you may give sufficient praise and include the Creator in these special moments, then you need not so much suffer disagreements. For you are doing your work of becoming more and more a strong union. While in good humor, the more you may do in a conscious work. While in a good humor, the less need you will have for the challenge and the learning inherent in trauma. Yet trauma there shall be, for as you meditate, as you learn together each shall change, not once but many times. And there is a continuous need for acceptance, forgiveness and for encouragement, one to the other.

We leave you in each other's hands. May you cherish each other as if each were the Creator, for in truth that is what you are. You are just a very young creator with much to learn, as are we.

I am Q'uo, and we thank this instrument for its effort at this time with the one known as Jim McCarty. We would at this time leave this instrument in love and light and transfer to the one known as Jim.

(Jim channeling)

I am Q'uo, and greet each in love and light through this instrument at this time. *(Inaudible)* to offer ourselves in the attempt to speak to any further queries *(inaudible)* may find value in the asking. Is there a query at this time?

(Long pause.)

I am Q'uo, and as it appears that we have, for the nonce, spoken to those concerns which each has for this evening, we would again extend our great gratitude to this circle of seeking for offering itself in service this evening by asking for our presence and enabling us to speak to your concerns. We rejoice at each opportunity to blend our vibrations with yours and would remind each that we are with you in your meditations upon your simple request that we join you there in order that we may aid your meditation by deepening your concentration. We do not speak at these times, nor vocalize in any manner, but simply lend our vibrations to yours, that your desire to know more of that which you call the truth might be enhanced.

At this time we shall take our leave of this group, leaving each, as always, in the love and in the light of the one infinite Creator. We are known to you as those of Q'uo. Adonai, my friends. Adonai. ✸

Sunday Meditation
February 4, 1990

Group question: The question this evening has to do with how the various light groups around the [world], in different countries, different cultures and different religions, who are all working towards the realization of some sort of love, light or unity within their group, can blend their efforts and help to bring forth this light and unity for the entire planet.

(Carla channeling)

I am Q'uo. Greetings to each of you, my friends, in the love and in the light of the one infinite Creator, in whose service we humbly are. We thank each of you for calling for our information and for accepting our love and blessing, for we do indeed feel loved and blessed in return a thousandfold, and learn a great deal from the bravery and charity which each of you manifests within the world of illusion in a purified manner. We think of you as gallant heroines and heroes, and though we know that often you are tired, yet shall you always begin again, for you are hungry in a way that cannot be fed by the bread of humanity or wisdom, but only by the mystery of the infinite One, and in this dance, in this journey, we are one with you.

Your question this evening is difficult to answer in a simple manner, for first we must undo what, in our opinion, is somewhat false consideration before we may go on to that answer which we would offer. The falsity within the illusion is complete. That one group or another may contact, move together, combine energies, and so forth, is subjectively and to the entities involved a most joyful and helpful experience, and many are the times that your groups have communicated with each other in the name of the infinite One, creating a palpable and metaphysical web of love, light and service which spans your sphere and which causes the spiritual gravity of your peoples to approach the point of harvest.

It is a great comfort for one who is on the road to have companions, and we do not deny you that comfort, nor suggest in any way that it is not helpful to you. Indeed, we encourage all such gatherings and communications betwixt those pilgrims who are upon the same path, for as you love each other so you empower each other, and engage each other's passion in love and service to others. But this, my friends, is a bare beginning, the preparation for that service which you came to give. No matter how beautiful the vibrations of many entities together worshipping the infinite One, yet still the emphasis is towards the center, towards the self-growth and the mountaintop experience of sharing in wholeheartedness the infinite love of the one Creator with each other.

This does indeed have its place, and may be considered spiritual food for you, just as this group feeds as it will upon the humble grass of our thoughts, opinions and ideas. However, each of you that is already one who has chosen the path of service to others has now a deeper, honorable commitment, and that is to turn outside, to face away from the center of love and joy, that your light may pierce the darkness about you, that that which comes through you may shine from you, not into the eyes of another who is already radiant, but into the eyes of those who know not light.

Thus, the preparatory step of working with lightening the consciousness of the planet begins with a long-term journey of understanding of the self, of seeing the self as not elite and always equal to each and every other complex of consciousness which may pass before you. When this lesson is learned, the desire to meet only with those who meet your subjective standards of spiritual ability can be released more easily, for one is able to see that within each pilgrim lies the consciousness of love that, when purified, is a channel for love and light not only from the infinite Creator, but from all those co-creators who serve at the harvest, such as yourselves.

When we speak of social memory complexes, we are not speaking of a group consciousness which focuses upon each other, but a group of consciousnesses whose goals and balances are so well known to the self and to the other selves that each has finally become independent and able to stride forth into the abyss of unknowing, ready to risk that which may be risked, to be of service and to respond to the calls for aid that are all about you at this time.

We realize that it is difficult when one has spent many, many years pondering thoughtfully upon metaphysical data to conceive of the sleeping, the indifferent and the ignorant among your peoples as being your true equals. This is, however, a most important point, for we would have you see yourselves as servants, not masters, as the most low, not the most high. We ask you to bend the knee and wash the feet, metaphorically speaking, using your biblical reference, of those who shall never understand you, those who may not ever hear the clarion call to service, those who shall remain blissfully inattentive to the trumpet call, to the destiny, of harvest.

(Pause)

I am Q'uo. We apologize for the pause, but we found that this instrument's vocal mechanism was becoming quite dry and unable to enunciate our thoughts, and so we paused while this entity recovered a level of consciousness able to perform the duty of replenishing the supply of water.

Now we may look at the one known as Christ, a teacher and prophet in his own time and place. He had those who were his students, but he did not encourage them to love and serve him, but to love and serve those who sought him. So we encourage each of you to consider yourselves sources through which the light of the Creator may flow. Yes, indeed, you are holding hands and forming the first harbingers of fourth-density social memory complex. You have the making together of so many entities in love, communication and service. But remember always that when strength has been given to the group by the group, it is then time to turn away from that great center of love and light, and to be that channel through which light flows into a world darkened by the heavy illusion of despair, loneliness, sickness and distress.

Have you never been lonely, sick, mournful or distressed? You see, you too, each of you, have all of humanity within you, and you can be of the greatest help to those about you by remaining humble, attentive and listening rather than determining to teach, to effect change and to transfigure others' mental and emotional patterns of thinking and manifestation.

Let us gaze at the community of the faithful upon your sphere. You know intellectually that time is an illusion. This means that all of you are together now, linked, whole and entire. All your prayers, your meditations and your thoughts, mingle in glorious harmony and ring in euphony to the honor and the glory of the one Creator. As there is no time, there is no space. So all of you are linked far more closely than you may ever realize. As each of you approaches more and more purity of service, so you approach more and more closely the unity of those who serve.

Thus, the first service is always that of consciousness. Sometimes it takes a considerable amount of work to begin to remember the original self, the self that is beneath all of the masks, the protections and the armor which each sensitive soul has placed about it in order that it may endure this harsh third-density illusion. For those who wish to teach, fear is most inappropriate. The desire to belong, to be special, or to be aloof is most unfortunate, and will result always in a gradual lessening of the polarity that you have come so far to accomplish. We ask that you see yourself as a minister of some kind, not as the world calls minister, but as we call one who ministers to another, a caretaker, one who loves, one who gives.

Upon one's knees, metaphorically speaking, one bows the head and says, "I am ready to serve. My free will is open to the impression of divine guidance. May this day bring to me that which I should do, and may I do that which there is for me to do with single-mindedness of love and light."

Once a seeking entity who wishes to enable those of the [Earth] sphere to become more conscious of the light has realized that they are indeed all one, that they are indeed interwoven and cannot be otherwise, then one need never feel alone or solitary again, for in one's seeking, in one's doubting, in one's searching and in one's suffering, the spiritual journey is played out again, and again, and again with those who are as you, heirs of the everlasting.

Now, as you turn outwards to the world before you, gaze upon its city streets, its country fields, its great expanses of water, and the beautiful harmonies and colors of the second-density illusion, gaze upon the grief, the sadness, and the woe that is contained in the heart of each. Gaze further and see the merriment, the joy, the childlike quality that lies sometimes buried very deeply within each entity, and know that you are one among many. You simply have remembered that which you came to do. The greatest aid that one pilgrim may be to another is to share the insights of the practical spiritual journey, to share the pebbles in the shoes of spiritual experience caught in the mundane world.

You are not in this mundane world to seek a way out of it. You have chosen to be in this mundane world not to help each other, but to reach out to those who call to you, that is, to the Creator, the I AM within you, that you may serve, humbly, and without wisdom, but only compassion. We ask that none of you attempt to be wise, for wisdom within the density which you now enjoy is a snare, a trap set for the unwary by those who wish to put out the great light of compassion and love. In compassion there is often not understanding; there is always the accepting.

Paradoxically, the more one wishes to aid, the more one seeks and is desirous of being of service, the less spontaneous, flowing and effective will that service be. See yourself as in a flow of service already. See that the infinite One has prepared for you that work which you have to do from day to day. To the metaphysical mind and heart there is no difference between the task of being a parent, the task of working with one's hands, the task of using one's communication, or the task of working in consciousness, for all work is blessed. And for those who do nothing, who resist efforts to be awakened to that illusion of life and that mystery that lies beyond it, we say this is acceptable. This is not something about which you, as an harvester, need be concerned. There shall be other springs, there shall be seeds that find good ground in other seasons. There shall be an infinite number of blooming summers and the reaping of a harvest in autumn.

Release yourself from the limitations of the physical and mental energy complexes, and feel the attunement which you have with entities you do not know all over this sphere. Feel at this moment the intensity of love that is radiating through so, so many of you at this time, and know that the connections are already made. They are made below the level of consciousness within that nascent group mind which shall be the nucleus of fourth-density social memory complex.

We know that you desire to help, to serve, to love and to give. Love and serve that which is nearest to you. Cherish that which is given unto you, and release with gladness that which moves from you, for you shall pass in and out of many lives, and in your interactions those things will occur which you know not of, nor shall you know until you enter a larger life in which the veil is lifted and you are able to see clearly that which you have been able to do in service during the incarnational period that you now enjoy.

To turn inwards and link up with each other is to be comfortable, to be joyful, to experience the mountaintop, the glory, the positive infinite energy of divine love. This, my friends, is a luxury, a heavy, intoxicating and sometimes addictive drink. it is not well to overdo that nourishment, but rather it is well, as if that nourishment were food from a table, to rise from that table and go forth into the mean and beggarly streets of the grimy, garbage strewn surface of your Earth sphere, sending your clear love and your best light to those who lie in the gutter, to those who hunger but have no money for food, to those who know not what they wish.

You are there for them. You are there in service as a sacrifice. You are within this density in concentrated and purified sorrow and compassion, and when you realize that you can fix nothing, that you can recreate no perfection, but only stand as lights piercing the darkness, the peace of the one infinite Creator begins to steal over you as the dawn steals over the horizon, blinking out the hopeful stars of night, and taking on the rosy radiance of the manifestation of daylight. Sing your songs, my friends. Rejoice in heart and go forth to serve. You are linked in an inward way. May you enlarge, by example and by service the company of those who have joined in the web of life.

At this time we shall leave this instrument and transfer to the one known as Jim. We thank this instrument for allowing us to use it, as it was experiencing much difficulty physically. However, its channel remained determinedly open, and we thank this instrument for its faithfulness. At this time we would transfer contact. I am known to you as Q'uo.

(Jim channeling)

I am Q'uo, and greet each again in love and light. It is our privilege at this time to offer ourselves in the attempt to speak to those queries which may yet remain upon the minds of those present. We remind each again that we offer that which is but our opinion. We do not wish to be seen as those who are infallible. At this time we would ask if there is a query to which we may speak?

T: I have a query. As Simon Peter once said to the ascended Christ, "Quo vadis domine," and in my ministry to others, "Quo vadis domine?"

I am Q'uo, and we would ask that for the benefit of this instrument that the Latin be translated.

T: "Whither do you want me to do? Where am I most needed?"

I am Q'uo, and we thank you for your indulgence, and for your query, which is asked with great sincerity. We appreciate the great desire to be of service to the Creator that you have expressed. This is a query which is asked to that being that is the Christ of all, the Christ within, that small and still voice, which, when petitioned with an whole heart, makes clear the way for the feet of clay and the heart of compassion. This clearly may be asked of any entity by any entity, and wise and careful counsel may be given by many. And yet, the response which is truly sought is that response which will fill the heart and inspire the spirit within, for each portion of the Creator exemplified by each entity within the creation is guided, most lovingly and precisely, by the voice of the Creator that speaks from that deep and still point within the heart.

(Side one of tape ends.)

(Jim channeling)

I am Q'uo, and am again with this instrument. Is there another query at this time?

Carla: I'd sort of like to follow up on the preceding query and just make sure I have the principle straight, because I think it's a really important one. Basically, what you're saying is the harder that you try to figure out what your service is and where you should go and so forth, the harder it will be for you to find out, whereas the more intensely you ask these questions and then surrender them to the infinite One, the more easily and quickly the path that is yours will be shown to you. Is this the principle that you are explicating?

I am Q'uo, and we would suggest that this is a close approximation. We shall attempt to refine this statement by suggesting that the process involves not so much the analytical mind figuring the pros and cons, as you say, of one possibility over another, as it is the willingness to be of service and the great desire to serve being generated from within, and then allowing the self to surrender its small will and idea or ideas of what is proper, that a greater will might utilize the instrument as is most appropriate for that instrument at a particular time within its process of evolution.

Is there a further query, my sister?

Carla: In a related way, I have seen a lot of people who feel that they have missed the boat spiritually, who feel that they had a chance to do something, and that that moment passed and that they failed to grasp it, and so they feel that there is not another path of service for them but that they have simply lost their direction and are forever, therefore, unable to be of the kind of help that they would need to be. I have always personally questioned this point of view, feeling that there is always a new hope and a new life and a new way of serving. Is it true that there is one service designed for each person and that that person must find it, or is it true that there are many paths of service for each person, and the person is perfectly free to choose that one which offers to that person the greatest degree of service that that person may bear stably?

I am Q'uo. Again, the small will in its ability to analyze and decide oftentimes becomes a stumbling block in its own activity when it takes over full responsibility for the service and actions of the entity. This is to say that where an entity is, and what an entity does are those ingredients which for that moment and that entity are the most appropriate in that entity's journey. If the entity then begins to feel that it has missed its opportunity, it then begins to ignore the opportunity which is before it, and the prophecy is, as you would say, self-fulfilling.

However, if it is recognized by the entity that its opportunity to serve and to learn are with it always, and that any future opportunities that shall be added unto it are additional to that which is, then the life pattern can be seen as that of abundance, for that indeed is true for each. There is but one Creator in many faces. Each face one encounters is the same Creator. All faces need service. All may instruct. All may receive. Thus, there is nothing but opportunity to learn and to serve. The attitude of the entity in its breadth or in its narrowness determines the abundance of opportunity for that entity.

Is there a further query, my sister?

Carla: I find that when I gather in group worship of any kind, or when I am with people who are spiritually involved and dedicated, that my heart really does soar, and I feel strengthened, and I rather got the feeling that you were suggesting that this, in its importance, be somewhat downplayed. However, I have always found it to be an integral part of my being able to be of service to others. Perhaps you addressed this and I simply missed it because I was busy with the mechanics of channeling, but I wonder if you could clarify this point?

I am Q'uo, and it is our intention to reaffirm the value of group worship for each within any such group which offers itself in the joyful praise and thanksgiving that is a natural part of the Creator as It speaks to Itself through Its many portions. Each entity that engages in such a service of worship lends a certain vibratory reaffirmation, shall we say, to that vibratory level of being which is sought as the ideal, the goal, the grail, and makes more steady and sturdy the rainbow bridge that is girded from the mundane to the metaphysical in order that that which is of the spirit may inspire the mundane and ennoble it in a fashion which calls for the spirit from within the center of all created things. Thus, the joyful noise, shall we say, that is made unto the world is that which causes the creation to sing within the heart, and the heart to sing within the creation.

Is there a further query, my sister?

Carla: I would like to ask a personal query, and I realize that you will be severely handicapped in answering me, which I accept. I had an experience in this contact which I have never had before, and that was that my mouth grew so completely dry, and it's still like that, that I was completely unable to free my tongue from the roof of my mouth or my lips from each other, and was forced to stop long enough to get water. I also had to adjust the chair to my back because, although I am not normally conscious of being uncomfortable, at this time I was severely conscious of being uncomfortable. There were several adjustments that I seemed to have to make that I don't usually make. Is this a form of greeting, and in general, what may one do beyond the challenging and the protection that I am already doing to avoid these inconveniences and to be a clearer and more useful channel?

I am Q'uo, and am aware of your query, my sister. The energies of which you speak are more various than described. Your increasing desire to speak in a clear and positive fashion, along with your predilection for the dry mouth syndrome have been accentuated so that these minor inconveniences would perhaps disturb the centering process and provide some small degree of difficulty. However, as one is able to meet each challenge successfully with an happy heart, shall we say, the ability to serve as an instrument is enhanced. One must expect that there will be some difficulties, for there are those entities of what we find you have called the loyal opposition which would exercise their desire that a portion of the light which is formed in groups such as this one might belong to them. We encourage the steadfastness to principle and the perseverance in the practical sense of achieving that degree of comfort which allows one to serve in the manner desired.

Is there a further query, my sister?

Carla: No, thank you, Q'uo.

I am Q'uo, and we thank you once again, my sister. Is there another query at this time?

(Pause)

I am Q'uo, and as it appears that we have, for the nonce, exhausted those queries, we would take this opportunity to thank each for allowing us to join your circle of seeking for this evening. We again have greatly enjoyed this opportunity and look, as you say, forward to these gatherings, for in such gatherings we have our being within your illusion, and may for this brief moment take part in that great dance of seeking the One within the illusion of many.

The illusion in which you find yourselves at this time is one which presents the greatest of challenges, in our humble estimation, for the nature of your illusion is that of the mantling over of the many jewels of the one Creator in a fashion which seems to suggest that each entity is truly separate one from another and that the strength of one must pit itself against the might of the many for any portion of peace or pleasure. This is the illusion which presents itself to your senses each day, and it is a brave and courageous act indeed to place oneself in the heart of such illusion and to hold steady to the ideals of unity of light, of the ability of each entity to fashion a pathway to that light and to that unity, both within and without the self. We salute each in each effort that is made, for each effort builds upon each previous effort and redoubles the strength of the seeking. You seek, you seek, you seek, and slowly you find, and that which you find becomes strong and firm within your being as you continue seeking, and seeking, and seeking. That light which you create is not easily seen within your illusion, but, my friends, we may say that it shines about you as brightly as those stars and suns that populate the universe about you.

At this time we shall take our leave of this instrument and this group, thanking each again for inviting our presence. We are those of Q'uo. We leave each in the love and in the light of the one infinite Creator. Adonai, my friends. Adonai.

Sunday Meditation
February 11, 1990

Group question: The question this evening has to do with the general topic of dreams. From previous information we understand that Q'uo is one who works with people in the dream state. We would like to know first of all how Q'uo works with people in the dream state, and does Q'uo work with everyone, or what are the preconditions necessary in order to have Q'uo work with you in dreams, and how can we further this process of having either Q'uo, or our own personal guides, or Higher Self, or any other helpful entity work with us in dreams? What is the benefit that we can get from this type of dream work?

(Carla channeling)

I am Q'uo. Greetings to you in the love and in the light of the one infinite Creator. This circle of seeking this evening is most harmonious and beautiful to us, and it is with great pleasure and gratitude that we share in your meditation. We thank you for calling us to you for our opinions upon the matters that you have chosen to consider. We wish you well, we are one with you, and we would wish you to know that we are not infallible, and that all that we have to say is the product of our experiences and our biases at this time, as you would call it. Our vision sees perhaps farther than yours, yet infinity still beckons, and recedes always before us. We still are finite, and therefore prone to error. Therefore we ask, as always, that you listen with discrimination, taking those ideas which may help, give you pleasure, or assist you in your seeking, and allowing to drop from you those things which do not feel resonant with your own inner seeking, for the rudder is yours, not anyone else's, not anything else's. You are all that is. We are part of you. You are the creation.

We speak in this wise, for you have asked this evening about dreams. Dreams take place in an unified state of creation, in an unified, timeless, spaceless nexus where all things are simultaneous, where the universe is truly malleable, for it is all within you. As you are awake at this time, you are aware of shape and figure, the shape of your bodies, the weight pressing down upon the cushions upon which you sit, the sounds, the smells, the sensations of time and space. It is indeed a complete and excellent illusion, but within you lies that which is beyond illusion, and though you cannot ever plumb the depths, and know what is called the truth, yet the truth may be known in you, and you may be the truth, so that each is truth to another, but never to the self. The self is always unknown, the creation is always unknown.

This instrument has requested that we speak for one of your recording devices tape's measure of time. We shall have the utmost difficulty even beginning to speak of this large subject in so short a time, yet we shall attempt to speak most generally, and if further searching is required, we are happy to continue at a later period within your illusion.

You are the dreamer, and you are the dream. The unity of yourself and all that is must be seen as the fundamental property of the dreaming state. Freed from the bonds of illusion, freed from the responsibility of the knowledge which you contain, you are able to work upon the disciplining and examining of the creation that lies within at whatever level, and with whatever bias you choose. The mind is as unfettered as you wish it to be by conscious preference, or unconscious determination. If there is no conscious determination, there is seldom a clear experiencing of the dreaming in an individual soul's incarnational pattern. Therefore, the first project undertaken to awaken one's ability to recall and to structure the dreaming state is the conscious determination to do so.

You may not peer through the veil that keeps you from the knowledge that lies within. Such sight would be a killing blow while within all illusions of which you are aware. This is a difficult concept to grasp, but what we are trying to express is that we know that there is a noble unknowing. We have become convinced that we know that which we do not know, that which we can never say, that which when known shall be unknown because it shall be the Creator unmanifest at last, and your journey as a seeking soul shall be at its end, the course having been reached, the prodigal greeted, and the breath of creation inhaled again.

We realize that you are curious as to how entities such as we may aid you in the dreaming. Within the dreaming state, with illusion unnecessary, for sleep is protection, we are one with you, we are you, and you are we. As to who shall work with you, each entity may call whatever energy it wishes in whatever way it understands, and it shall be done. We suggest that you wish for that which you truly desire, that you suggest help that you truly desire, for you shall receive it, and as you study and form opinions in your conscious mind, you shall be responsible for living so, and expressing in manifestation that which has come through the veil into conscious knowledge.

Thus, some prefer to ask for personal individualities. Many who do so are hampered by their own opinionated desires for a certain source. Each entity has an unique vibratory complex and is most ably helped in an unique way. If all ask for Q'uo, many shall receive information that is relatively opaque and meaningless, for those of a certain energy vibration such as we who speak through this particular channel are those who are of the nature to blend well with this particular entity.

Thusly, we would suggest not that you call for Q'uo, or for any individuality, but for that which would be most helpful, most consoling, most comforting and most informative to you. That which you receive shall make itself known to you in its own way. Some have visions, some simply come to conclusions knowing not why. Some are most expressive, and have dreams full of clarity and richness of detail. Others may have the need for a path that is stepped down in power, so that some energy blockage that has reached into the subconscious mind may not be disturbed while learning is taking place. Further, many of you have responsibilities of which you do not know, and you yourselves aid others while the complex of energies which create the illusion of your body rest and recuperate from the tensions and stresses of the illusion.

It is well to remember that no matter how simple or how complex the dream landscape may be, no matter how deeply you seek or how far you travel, there is, in the end, an unity, an ultimate oneness of dreamer and dream. The meaning of all of creation is held within the unity of your true self.

Now, there are many created methods of studying the structure of that which you call the subconscious mind, the most helpful perhaps being those studies which you call archetypical, for though each is unique, yet are all one beneath those biases which are necessary for you, beyond the illusion and into the noumenal. This archetypical mind is still an unique mind for each, but has characteristics far more in common with all others than the conscious seeking mind. There are geometries within the subconscious which are dependable. That which is a question is the method of studying those geometries without being harmed by an excess of understanding or emotion, joy or terror. You deal with infinite power when you deal with the unconscious self. Gaze in your mind at the creation. Imagine the farthest view your scientists have created the instrumentation to make of your universe. There is no end to this universe. It is within your illusion, even to the most careful eye, infinite. This power, this character, is yours, and this is the kingdom wherein you dwell in dreaming.

Thus, it is well to move thoughtfully and carefully, and most of all, seriously, in your examination of, and remembering of, dreams. Do not attempt to over-program the self, but attempt to move naturally with the tides of event and circumstance that focus your attention upon various phases of the illusion, remembering always that your lessons are those of love, your density is that which seeks a greater grasp of the nature, meaning and power of love.

Thus, in your waking life, gaze at all that occurs with a view towards what aspect of love may be presenting itself to you for examination. Then flow naturally with this desire to know as you move into the dreaming state, being patient, for you shall dream, and dream, and dream again, about the same thing, gazing at it always in a slightly different way, as the dream attempts to speak to finity that which is infinite.

It is the patient entity, the persistent and daily entity, whose dreams begin to make a kind of sense, and become more and more of a tool and a resource for learning. Those who expect dreams to explain themselves to the conscious mind shall be disappointed for the most part. There are, of course, among your peoples, those who have the gift of clear vision, because of the character that they possess within the illusion and the work that has been done before this particular incarnational experience. However, the vast majority of seeking souls do not receive the crystal clear explanations of love, but nuances, clues, stage settings and masks.

Thus, the study of the archetypical mind in the conscious state is helpful in that it creates a vocabulary for examining the structure of dreams, for you are who you are, and all things are in relation to you as you are in relation to yourself. You are who you are, and you are who you become, and each of these is the same statement.

The depths of this truth may begin to be plumbed in the conscious mind best by working in some way with the archetypical mind. Some favor the system of the tarot, others the glyphs of the tree of life, and as these are the two most helpful we shall express our opinion as to the difference between the two. Those personalities who are focused upon the dynamics of positive and negative, yin and yang, passive and active, will find most rewarding the study of the major Arcana of the tarot. Those who see in a less personal sense, or who need in a less vital sense the necessity for choosing betwixt the positive and the negative shall find the study of the tree of life, though more complex in some ways, more rewarding in that rather than the self being summed up in relation to the choice between positive and negative, positive and negative are two pillars betwixt which are placed the middle pillar Malkuth, Yesod, Tifareth, Kether, Ain Soph Aur, Ain Soph, Ain.

We feel that this is an introduction which suffices for this moment, and will at this time thank this instrument for its willingness to be used. We would now transfer this contact to the one known as Jim. We are those of Q'uo, and in love and light we leave this instrument.

(Jim channeling)

I am Q'uo, and greet each again in love and light. At this time it is our privilege to offer ourselves in the attempt to speak to any further queries if there are further queries. May we begin now with the first query?

S: Yes, Q'uo, you mentioned that we have natural protection when we sleep. We are, in that case, in a state of unity which involves having passed through the veil. In some sense as we study consciously the systems of the deep mind, we attempt in a partial way to do the same thing, but one quickly learns of the necessity for protection in doing so. If one were to take the first step on the path, for example, of the study of the Kabbala, one passes through the dark night of the soul, the Malkuth, through Yesod, I wonder if that involves passing through the veil, entering what is sometimes called the light body, and if so, if there is a danger in doing so, what is one's best protection in doing so?

I am Q'uo, and am aware of your query, my brother. As one undertakes any study of the nature of your evolutionary process, whether it be that path followed by those who study the tree of life, the path of the tarot, or any other path that leads eventually to the realization of unity, it is well to surround oneself with the desire to seek this unity within that quality that you may call love. Love, being the energizing and creative force of all that is, then, can speak to itself within all other beings and forces that may be encountered, calling from each its creative and sustaining nature. To so configure the conscious and subconscious mind with the quality of love is to provide to the self the greatest protection that is possible, for where there is love there cannot be fear, and fear is the only avenue available to any entity that would wish to enter fear and manipulation into one's pattern of life experience.

Thus, it is well to begin any serious study and application of any particular avenue of ritualistic discipline of the personality with this quality. As one progresses along whatever path is chosen and begins to bear the fruit of that path in service to others it is especially important to fashion the armor of love and light about oneself in order that the endeavor to seek unity in order to be of service to others might be protected.

Is there a further query, my brother?

S: Yes. One does find instances where there are correspondences made between the tarot and Kabbala. For example, I have read recently a correspondence between the major Arcana twenty-one, the Great Way of Spirit, and the first path working upon which the aspirant adept may step in the Kabbala *(inaudible)*. I wonder if you could tell me if these correspondences are useful, if they have a truth to them, and how they might be used?

I am Q'uo, and am aware of your query, my brother. Indeed, my brother, in an universe of unity there are correspondences all about one. The usefulness of any correspondence is much like the beauty of any work of art. It is in the eye of the beholder or the efforts of the practitioner that the usefulness is to be determined. For each entity, no matter what portion of the study is undertaken, will be moving from a place in his or her understanding that is unique, and whatever correspondence is available or noticeable to that entity will be useful insofar as the entity has prepared itself to utilize that which lies before it.

This is to say that the preparation in understanding and practice will call to the seeker those succeeding steps and the perception of those steps that is appropriate in order safely to place the foot upon new understanding and new metaphysical ground. Thus, as the quality of the ...

(Side one of tape ends.)

(Jim channeling)

I am Q'uo, and am again with this instrument. Is there a further query, my brother?

S: There's just one. It occurs to me now that the greatest protection we may need is from ourselves, and as you have said, the surest protection is provided by the loving and open heart. You have mentioned on other occasions that the heart may be used as a springboard to the higher energy centers. A question I have had is, does that springboard effect work directly, say from the heart center to the throat center, and then again directly from the heart center to the indigo center, or does it simply rise up through the channels, going first through the throat center, then through the indigo center? Is there a way to draw directly on the energies of the heart?

I am Q'uo, and am aware of your query, my brother. The nature of the heart center is for the adept as the foundation is for the carpenter. This is the foundation upon which the structure of any effort shall be placed. It is necessary in order to be able to move beyond the blue-ray energy center that there be a considerable amount of work accomplished, not only at that center, but also within the indigo-ray center, for the opening of the green-ray or heart center is an opening which allows a movement from that center to the next center for the beginning of work within the throat or blue-ray center.

It is necessary to master to a minimal degree the study of each center beyond the green-ray center for the opening of any center beyond the green ray to occur upon a regular and dependable basis. Thus, when such work has been accomplished within the blue and indigo rays, it is possible for the adept to choose whether energy shall be moved through the green-, the blue- or the indigo-ray center for work of either the healing nature within green ray, the freely given communication within blue ray, or the work of that which you may call the white magical nature within the indigo-ray center.

Is there a further query, my brother?

S: No, thank you very much, Q'uo.

I am Q'uo, and we thank you, my brother. Is there another query at this time?

Carla: I'd like to follow up on a couple of questions, and then just a thank you. To follow up on S's question, would not, once the green-ray center was established as fully opened, the energy be drawn naturally to one's chosen path of service, that path of service which was chosen before the incarnation? Is it not something that happens naturally and doesn't have to be chosen, or is the conscious choice necessary?

I am Q'uo, and am aware of your query, my sister. This statement we find, if we understand it correctly, to be much as one of your sayings which states that it is putting the cart before the horse. In this regard we mean to say that the opening of the green-ray center is most often accomplished by those who have begun, and well begun, the following of what you have called the life's work, or chosen service, and the pursuing of this service has been refined to such a degree that the opening and energizing of the green-ray energy center then becomes possible, and when accomplished, acts much as your magnifying glass does to enlarge that service which has been chosen.

Is there a further query, my sister?

Carla: Yes, I see from that answer that it is desirable to continue always to wish to seek higher and higher in the indigo ray. I understand now. But I did have a feeling from the whole message that you were inferring a simplicity beneath the various ways of studying dreams, in other words, that you said the dreamer is the dream and the dream is the dreamer; that if you were studying the archetypical mind the first of the major Arcana would contain the whole of the Arcana, and the first station, or I guess it would be the last in the *(inaudible)* [Tree Of Life], Malkuth, would contain the whole of the tree of life. Is this inference correct?

I am Q'uo, and am aware of your query, my sister. Not only is this inference correct, but it may be applied to any of the stations, any of the Arcana, and any portion of one's life experience, for all may be seen to be individualized and particularized facets of the one Creator, viewpoints from which the one Creator may be experienced, may be observed and may be glorified. Each station, Arcana and experience, then, is as a facet upon a jewel, the jewel being the one Creator, the facet being a window through which a portion of the one Creator may be viewed, and when viewed with a perception free of distortion, all facets of the one Creator are then made available through the one facet that is observed, much as your holographic picture will yield the entirety of the picture from any portion.

Is there a further query, my sister?

Carla: No, Q'uo, but I'd just like to thank you for the blessing of the most incredible light that I've ever seen—actually I didn't see it, I felt it, and the only word I can use to describe it is splendor. I thank you very much for this experience.

I am Q'uo, and we thank you as well, my sister, for the service which you and each within this group provide us. It is a light to us as well, of great beauty. Is there another query at this time?

M: Yes, Q'uo, I have a question. I *(inaudible)* that could be used in understanding archetypes, the Tree of Life and the tarot. I understood that perhaps astrology would also be useful *(inaudible)*.

I am Q'uo, and am aware of your query, my sister. It is true that astrology is also quite useful in the study of the nature of the archetypical mind and the evolutionary process as an whole. However, we did not mention astrology in our original statements because there is much that has been attributed to this study which is confusing to those who have not engaged in intensive and long-term study of the origins of this particular field of inquiry. This is a study which differs significantly from that of the tarot and that of the Tree of Life in that much of the work of the study utilizing astrology must be accomplished within the meditative state where certain tones or resonances, harmonics between concepts and energies, are felt and intuited. This type of study is one which is highly informative to those who are quite sincerely dedicated to penetrating beyond the surface appearance of what is usually given in books and treatises upon the study of astrology. The necessity of penetrating the outer appearance of this study is so great as to cause us to, shall we say, give the caveat that it is a most difficult study to master without great dedication and perseverance.

Is there a further query, my sister?

M: No, thank you Q'uo.

I am Q'uo, and we thank you, my sister. Is there another query at this time?

K: You spoke this evening of the protection inherent in the consciousness of love. It seems to me that there may be different types of protection available, but maybe not, maybe they all stem from that one source. Earlier you spoke about the protection that is offered by the cat entity, and I'm wondering if you can talk a little bit about how they offer that protection and if that's related to that same love consciousness?

I am Q'uo, and am aware of your query, my sister. The entities known as your cats have a history within the archetypical experiences of your third density that dates back, shall we say, using your reference of time, to many, many thousands of years ago, moving especially through that culture that you know as the Egyptian culture, moving back even farther to the roots of this experience into that culture known to you as Atlantean.

Within that culture there were those who sought sincerely and successfully the Law of One, and in this study used as a portion of their ritualized worship and seeking of the One the companionship of the entities that you call the cat. These entities have a correspondence by their nature to that quality within the human being that may be seen as the feminine, the subconscious mind, the High Priestess as given by the tarot, which inspires, nourishes, protects and potentiates experience within that portion of the mind exemplified by the male, the conscious, the third-density entity which exists upon the level of the illusion.

Thus, the cat has for great eons of your planet's metaphysical experience become associated within the mass mind of your planetary sphere with that which is protective, nourishing, loving and inspirational. Thus, the connection between this creature and that quality known as love is one which is steeped in metaphysical experience and within the roots of your subconscious mind.

Is there a further query, my sister?

K: Has there been any decision on the part of the feline species to offer themselves in service to us in that way?

I am Q'uo, and am aware of your query, my sister. The decision, as you call it, is not that which you would understand as a decision made in a conscious fashion, but one which is rather as is the given in their nature, a gift or quality which by its very nature offers itself in this service without either being consciously made or even being conscious.

Is there a further query, my sister?

K: No, thank you very much.

I am Q'uo, and we thank you, my sister. Is there another query at this time?

(Pause)

I am Q'uo, and we would like to take this opportunity to thank each entity present this evening for inviting us once again into your circle of seeking. It has been a great honor to join you here and to walk with you in that light and love of the one infinite Creator in which we leave you at this time, rejoicing at each step, praising the light and sharing the love. We are known to you as those of Q'uo. Adonai, my friends. Adonai. ✤

L/L Research

Sunday Meditation
February 25, 1990

Group question: The process of evolution can be seen as the process of learning to discipline the personality, or to focus our expenditures of energy in a precise manner, one that moves us closer to our metaphysical goals. What is the nature of discipline? Does it have to be difficult and tedious? What qualities enable the strengthening of discipline? What qualities detract from the strengthening of the discipline?

(Carla channeling)

I am Q'uo. I am Q'uo. We have most happily been able to contact this instrument, and we greet you in the love and in the light of the one infinite Creator, in Whose service we move and have our being. It was a good example of your query upon discipline in the process which this instrument has spent the previous approximate hour of your time as we find this instrument is aware of time. In the attempt to banish the genuine exhaustion of the physical self due to pain and exertion, this instrument's red-ray energy center was most dim, and therefore the instrument, in preparing to offer words of inspiration, neglected to be enough aware of the need for the focus upon the reenergizing of the will to live joyfully that is the mark of the open red ray.

Thus, to this instrument's surprise, we asked the instrument to move backwards in the tuning process to repeat several times prayers of supplication for the uplifting of joy in life. The instrument is now in satisfactory balance, however we would have done this instrument some harm by calling upon vital energies had we not requested repeatedly that the instrument work within its own faith, its own path, its own ways of recalling and reviving the joy of living. This takes patience, and when there is additional work to be done after an hour of prayer it is, shall we say, indeed an effort.

We find you have the term "no pain, no gain." This is a shallow statement, yet in most cases accurate enough in terms of learning the discipline of any activity of third density, for each entity is unknown to itself, and there must be put forward the effort to know the self in deeper and more profound ways. This illusion which you now enjoy is upon the level of molecular structure, magnetic relationships, and the geometry of what you call matter, placed in order. However, the divine Thought within, which is love, that which is the true self, is covered over, as is the molten center of your planet, with honeycombs of many, many kinds of material, and finally the shallow waters and land masses of the topography of the surface of your sphere.

This planet is an analogy to that which is the consciousness of love within. That is how deeply it is buried. Your passion seems far from you. The discipline of your personality to know the self seems nowhere upon land or sea, in the air or underneath the waters of the earth. There is no conscious way to break into or to tunnel into the heart of your true nature, which is not personality, but which is desired by your free will at this time.

Much effort has already been expended by each of you. Each of you has made choice after choice after choice. When weary, you have sat by the road of seeking; when energetic once again you take up the burden of humanity and walk the path of the seeker, seeking in the air, the earth, the water, and the fire of energy that which is completely unable to be found by the conscious mind. There is, however, that oneness between the molten center of your being, the passion of the divine love within you, and the one great original Thought that is the Creator. And you are within this illusion to learn the nature of yourself and to choose how you wish to shape that nature, how you wish to make choices within the life to serve, to be inspired, to rest, to seek, to be patient, to be despairing, to be thoughtless. All these are equally permissible. There is no judgment, only free will. That is the law of your density, and free will brooks no discipline. You are free. Thus, as in any classroom, when you who do not know decide to know, effort must take place.

Now, there are two answers to your question about the pain of discipline. Firstly, in the deepest sense, all discipline is painful, for it denies free will, the full action of chaos, and chaos is the natural atmosphere into which you, as mind and body and spirit, are birthed in this illusion. You have complete freedom. On the other hand, the first choice is perhaps the most difficult, the most humbling, the most painful, for it is a final, deep and complete awareness that chaos is not desirable, that chaos is but the wind upon the water, the waves upon the shore. Without observation of order, without faith in any order within the self, without faith in any work to the self, beyond this little shadow of a life that flickers briefly and moves from dust to dust, it is the choice to have faith, that is the painful, hard-won, difficult and almost impossible to remember cornerstone of all spiritual work.

Once this choice has been not only consciously made—that is, the choice to seek in faith the true orderly nature of the self, ignoring the obvious chaos about one that one may begin to seek out tools for learning and decide when, how and how intensively to apply them to the life experience—once this cornerstone decision has been made, the difficulty level of increasing the discipline of the personality will vary widely with the random actions of free will upon catalyst. Sometimes the desire is very strong within and the work that needs to be done in meditation, contemplation, study, analysis and service seems to be joyful, easy and most pleasant. Sometimes the self is so far removed from any knowledge of its own true heart that there is almost no possibility of spiritual work, and it takes the greatest effort to bring oneself back to that original cornerstone decision to live a life of faith that you are more than a shadow that will fall into dust.

Each of you has this faith. Each of you is therefore through the most painful and difficult portion of the spiritual search. For once you have put your foot upon the path of the seeker of the true self, the energy of that decision comes as a gadfly to nag and move you again and again no matter how far you stray, aiding you to mindfulness.

This is the tool we would give you this evening: mindfulness. How heedless you are. You are heedless of beauty, you are heedless of pain, you are heedless of much that goes on about you as are all entities. There is too much catalyst to process for any entity to process completely, and so a series of choices is constantly being made as to what in the environment of the self shall be heeded as to where the mind shall be placed, the attention drawn. We encourage meditation with the regularity that must seem endless to those who hear our words, but meditation is the key that unlocks the door to that shuttle into that molten passion of love within, awareness of which inspires and enlivens each portion of the experience of your illusion. This entity, for instance, has been heedless of the needs of its physical vehicle, focusing upon outer works and not focusing upon that for which it has dedicated its life. If it is not joyful in living all else must cease, and joy must again be found, for without that foundation, without that energy, all other energy centers are depleted, flaccid, weak and unable to bear the energy of inspiration.

It is not in any way unspiritual to evaluate the self each day, beginning with the fundamental energy of love of life. To be of good cheer, to care for experience and welcome catalyst is the first priority of the most spiritual of beings. It is not to the one who denies the need for care of the self that glory is given, but to the one who keeps that energy open, that joy alive. This is true for each energy center in an ascending pattern. So mindfulness begins with a mindfulness of the need for the instrument of incarnation, which is your physical vehicle. Mindfulness then continues to evaluate energies, to ask the self if there is joy in knowing the self and in knowing others, then in knowing and appreciating the group in which one experiences incarnation, the job, the friendships, the society of your nation state, the quality of that sphere which you call your home at this time. Others who have not enjoyed the clear yellow-ray environment of freedom and the passion for it—and at this time there is much movement upon your planet, passionately to seek it for all people—yet you who already have won your freedom and are the children of freedom and the grandchildren of freedom, how do you value it? How to you use it? How do you support it? How do you care for it? Where is your balance of joy in freedom?

All this is discipline that must be attended to before you may work with the heart to open the heart, to have compassion on the self, on others, on your planet. First you must do your work with your own self, finding your joy, finding your passion. You have chosen faith, you have chosen to believe that there is a reality beyond this illusion. You have done the hardest work. The rest is learning. The rest is the discipline of the personality that began in the chaos of unlearning into which you were born. As we have spoken, each of you has examined the energies, has opened the heart, has begun to feel each other's presence as seekers, the unity of this group with all who seek, with those such as we who seek to help, and are ourselves seeking further to refine evermore the discipline of the personality. All this must be done before you can begin to discipline your personality. You must first find joy. You must first allow your faith to show forth in a love of life and living. Sometimes you do most, most beautifully at this, at other times there is a woeful lack of work because the self does not feel worthy of such fundamental work, wishing only to serve others. Nay, my friends, prepare the self first for service.

Now we speak of mindfulness itself, a mindfulness of your choice, a mindfulness of your faith that there is indeed within you the passion that created the universe and all that is in it. In meditation roads are built that create a pathway to an immediate experience of this love. This is work done in discipline. When the energy of living within you is good, and the desire to learn is strong, there is only joy in this work. It can also be the most difficult work you can imagine. A great deal depends upon the preparation of your self to be a person of joy and lover of life. Be mindful of who you are. You are love, you are a co-creator with the original Thought of your own experience and your own creation. There is not one creation, there are as many creations as there are perceptors of creation. Each personal truth is absolute. One cannot give to another faith, but only the desire to find that faith and the realization that such a thing is possible.

We come to speak to you as those who have learned mindfulness. We find in this instrument's mind the phrase "to pray without ceasing." This is a good phrase to express that which we mean by being mindful. In meditation you tabernacle with the infinite One, you listen to the silence that speaks deeply, without words, and gives the information that will give you the energy, the joy, and the faith to move ahead. Without the meditation it is very difficult to remain in a state of unity with your greater self, with the Creator within. This is the heart of the discipline of personality.

Each of you has read many, many texts which attempt to aid in the process of accelerating the evolution of mind, body and spirit. The catalyst for the discipline of personality is joyful remembering of who you are. As you remember who you are, more and more of that which you may willfully seem to be, but which you are not, is no longer needed and falls away. The effort is not in pushing away the things of this world, as this instrument would say. The effort is in creating within the self a joyful remembrance of love as the nature of the true self, which creates an atmosphere in which gradually, and in a rhythmic, appropriate time, one after another, those things which are hindrances to joy fall away. Anger is not overcome, it is simply no longer needed to express the passion of the self. Distress, despair, all negative emotion is distorted love. It is passion turned and bent and unrecognizable. But as love is all there is, so with your free will you may create ponderous illusion upon illusion, finding perverse comfort in negative emotion, for it is familiar, and that which is familiar is safe, and that which is unfamiliar is not. When one is mindful one finds oneself slowly able to release the fear that has caused the distortion that has created for the self an armor against that which is perceived as a threat. To one continuously aware of the self as love there are no threats, there is only remembrance of the truth of love.

We are mindful of this entity's weariness, and would therefore transfer this contact, with many thanks to the instrument for its remembrance of its great desire to love, to the one known as Jim. We hail each through the mouth of this humble one in love and light. I am Q'uo.

(Jim channeling)

I am Q'uo, and greet each again in love and light. At this time we would offer ourselves …

(Side one of tape ends.)

(Jim channeling)

I am Q'uo, and am again with this instrument. We find some difficulty with this instrument. We shall pause.

(Carla channeling)

I am Q'uo, and am again with this instrument. We find that as we have spoken to this instrument it has moved in sympathy with our words and glows with its usual brightness despite its tiredness. This instrument was simply forgetful, mired in the cares of physical difficulty and mental confusion. There is no need for such. There is no need to give oneself the great drama of difficulty. But it is important, as one relaxes into the rhythms of life, and accepts what sisters and brothers come to one, be they pain, or wellbeing, confusion or simplicity, joyful surroundings and happy friends, or difficult relationships and difficult feelings. These are the surfaces, these are the wind that blows where it will. These are those things to which you give up your will instead of remembering. In meditation, remember; in action, remember; in all things, remember how thankful you are, how blessed you are to have consciousness, life and the opportunity for the accelerated advancement of this great choice-making density.

Yes, my friends, to you who are not of this density it is a foreign land. The language is difficult, the people barbaric sometimes, the feelings too intense, too painful. Suffering seems inevitable, and so you forget the joy of being. Be mindful, be faithful to yourself, to the love within you, to the consciousness that abides eternally, infinitely within you. You are the creation. Create well, my friends.

We shall go no further this particular evening, for indeed this instrument has overspent its energy upon the physical plane. But we wish to leave you with gentle words and merry thoughts. There is one within this room which has experienced great joy in recent past, the joy of that yellow-ray activity of great vitality and companionship. This is a wonderful and inspirational memory. Of itself it is only useful ephemerally; as a memory; as a knowledge of how things can be, its use is inestimable. Others within this group are battle weary and worn. Reach within that weariness for the tenderness, love and the cherishing that has moved within each in service to each as difficulties have been recognized, accepted and perhaps allowed to take center stage instead of mindfulness. There is no discipline in despair, but only the chaos of distortion. Be mindful of this lesson. Be mindful to look for the blessings, for the beauties, for the peace and serenities that lie around you in the creation of the Father, and in the hearts of those whom you meet. And most of all, remember your choice, rejoice in your decision to have faith in your beingness. Accept yourself as eternal, and be mindful of joy everlasting.

We leave you in the love that you are, and the light that can come through you as surface beings from that passion, that love which is your Creator, your beingness, and that Omega towards which you travel as you unravel the mysteries of the disciplines of the personality. We are those of Q'uo, and shed our love, and let light shine through us to you, in the name of the one infinite, glorious and everlasting Creator. Adonai, my friends. Adonai. Adonai. Adonai. ☙

L/L Research

Sunday Meditation
March 4, 1990

Group question: The question this evening has to do with the type of event or movement that has been happening around our planet, perhaps in the mass consciousness of the planet, with the concepts of freedom and democracy and self-determination seeming to win ascendancy in various places where they have not been in place for some time—in Eastern Europe, in the Soviet Union, South Africa, Nicaragua and elsewhere. We would like to know the principles behind this type of shifting consciousness, what has perhaps brought it about, what the potential outcome might be, and what it would mean for our planet and each of the inhabitants upon the planet.

(Carla channeling)

I am Hatonn. I greet you in the love and in the light of the infinite Creator. We come to you this evening in response to your call for information, and in very deep gratitude for our rare opportunity to speak through this instrument. The one known as Carla is most wise to request only that channel which may stably be held, for this instrument is in considerable physical deficit, and our contact is far less demanding of the vital energy than others with which this instrument is wont to have contact. We hope we may in our own way share our opinions with you. We are most distorted in our own thinking upon the question of freedom, as we have only progressed one density beyond your own, yet those thoughts which we may share, we shall, as we safeguard this instrument and this group.

We would ask each to be aware of the need for sending light in clockwise fashion about the circle of one that you create, that this contact be strengthened, steadied and even, as this instrument is less able than usual to be at the full power of its usual tuning. This instrument has absolutely no idea what we shall [say]. This is a good beginning for any contact.

When we speak to you of the spiritual principles of freedom, we must, as you know, speak generally, but we may address ourselves in general to the ebb and flow of that which is known to you as freedom, and to describe some of the dynamics which cause its apparent rise and fall amongst the many cultures which your sphere has begotten and then lost. Time and time again, empires have arisen, either because of ideals or because of strength. Time and time again ideals and strength have in the end equally failed to engage the caring and the attention of those who give power to authority.

We shall speak first of that which has been noted as the worldwide hunger for freedom. When entities have, for countless centuries past, been accustomed to serving, it is that service which is assumed to be inevitable. It is the rare visionary, the heretic, the madman or the fool which decries, in the face of that which seems to have been and always will be, another and impossibly idealistic way of associating with others of humankind. So it is in many cases that freedom has meant the freedom to live, to continue the race, to keep the belly fed and to find shelter for the body. These basic needs are seen by those who think not upon ideals or impossible things to be the culmination of that which is possible to achieve in the name of liberty. Gradually, through the centuries, the truly free entities of what you would call primitive societies have been infected by that concept which you may call power or dominion over others.

Gaze at the savage. This is an entity truly free, for this entity does what it wishes to do at all times. The demands of survival are parameters accepted as given, and there is no ambition for any but the comforts of eating and sleeping, mating, and communicating in some way with that great spirit which is known by all primitive peoples as the giver of all blessings, the lover of all entities, the source and the ending of each consciousness before birth and after death. This peace, this true freedom, takes its purity from the purity of the spirits of those who do not have greed, ambition or thought. They are indeed very close to second-density consciousness, and are aware of the sanctity of all things, of the utter and unquestionable reality of magical and divine power, and within these lives is a rhythm of obedience to what civilized entities would call the myths and the shamanistic practices inherent in primitive cultures.

Yet the third density was not intended to be one which remained at the level of unquestioning faith. Rather, it was specifically designed to encourage each entity to seek, to think, to acquire, and to learn the vices, as you would call them, of humankind. Thus, the divine plan moved entities into groups which had awareness not only of themselves, but of other and differing groups, of other and differing gifts, of other and differing territories, arts and personalities. And so the learning process began many, many thousands of your years in the past. That which drove the spirit forward was an inner quest for freedom which we have often called the Law of Confusion, or free will. The concept of freedom is a paradox, for as one thinks of freedom one is bound by one's thought of freedom. One distorts the concept even as it is used in a reasoning and intellectual manner. Thus, freedom became infected with that trait of humankind which is absolutely necessary to set the stage for the making of choices, and that is the chaos of complete free will.

In very few cases, once the concept of freedom was born, was an entity content with that which it already had, but, rather, there was the wish to improve the circumstances of one's incarnation. This touched each and every facet of the life experience. Gradually entities began to choose to perpetuate the species with mates which they preferred, in a way which is inexplicable and has only to do with the vagaries of the spirit of humankind. Inevitably there arose each and every excess of which the human mind is capable of creating. Enough food to fill the belly became less than enough, and gluttony was born. The desire to enlarge one's territory at the expense of those who peacefully lived in that territory created the greed and the destruction of hostile action.

The pure and simple realization of the love all about one began to be questioned, for within the third density mind and spirit nothing is obvious, nothing is known, and there are only hints that there is a reason for existence beyond the viewing of the seasons, the participation in the rhythms of life, the opening of the eyes at birth and the closing of them at death. As you are aware, there was, again and again, prophecy, vision and the perfect ideal communicated through those gifted in mysticism and communion with love itself. In each case, this original message of love, love given, love shared, love enjoyed, was distorted by the need to convince others of this love, of this way of understanding, of this method of enlarging the scope of the experience of humankind.

Gradually, many, many of the societies which you would call pagan or savage became aware that they craved a structure which was created not simply by instinct, but also by the use of the intellect, of the minds of humankind. And so each mind that found itself in the position of power began to use that power to express the distortion of freedom and love which it considered to be correct. Since the beginning of your experience upon this third density planet, the stage has been set again and again for entities to make the choice as to what they consider their relationship to the Creator to be, for it is in that relationship that the concept of freedom rests. It is the birthright of that relationship that gives a seemingly limited entity the birthright to infinitely worthwhile and ideal principles.

Those who call upon their own powers, and not upon the powers of any but themselves, have found always that their empires do not last long. Those, upon the other hand, who have been biased towards idealistic rationalizations for the use of power have been able to engage the spirit, the confidence and the energy of the cultures which they lead, thus guaranteeing a longer and more productive society in terms of the society's ability to offer to the individual a number of options or choices to be made in relative freedom from swift and merciless action if there is disagreement.

Now, let us look at those concepts which moved through those who wished to follow the steps of one which desired only to serve others, and which refused worldly power. This entity, known to you as the master Jesus, was able to engage the ideals of many differing cultures, and thus the effect that this incarnation and its implications had upon various cultures was never the same in any two cultures. However, there were those which were able to choose to seek without ambition, to offer themselves in faith and hope without a desire for a reward. In every culture, in every generation, there have been those radiant beings which have been, as was the one known as Jesus, Christed entities, those through whom true freedom flowed, those who were able to engage the imaginations and the hearts of those with whom they came in contact.

A large concentration of this system of thought, by chance, was spread throughout much of the world which was ruled at one time by that civilization which you know of as Roman, for by happenstance, and by the folly of one superstitious entity, a vow was made that if a battle was won all of the empire would embrace the teachings of this humble master, who had no interest in this Earth and its kingdoms, but who looked always beyond to eternity. Because entities were ordered to worship this entity instead of another, there came to be a more and more unified concept of love, of creation and of freedom. This may be traced through that which was called the empire of the Romans, through all of the decadence of a falling empire. Yet, the word of a gazing beyond was spread, and entities of the Celtic races, those nation-states of that which you call Europe, were enkindled to a passionate love for love itself. Again and again the teachings of this entity were used in a distorted and incorrect manner. Yet, again and again the vitality of the original message came forward, and moved finally to the continent which you call North America, in this broad and pleasant land.

The birth of the nation was wrought by ideals, yet tainted from the beginning by warfare, separation and those choices to which humankind may often fall prey that involve using pragmatic means towards an idealistic end. Thus, as the culture which you now enjoy has matured, the concept has more and more been sullied by those which have not had to fight for it, which have not had firsthand experience of tyranny, and of the blessing of a deep and passionate faith in the ideals of infinite love.

So it is that at this time, in spite of the great influx of those within your culture which are attempting to lighten the consciousness of this once greatly blessed people, more and more the negative service to self pragmatism of greed and the desire for more and more control over others has begun to manifest itself. Thus, the nation state which you now enjoy is in the throes of its greatest difficulty since its inception. This is because of the growing distortions having to do with the true identity of the ideal of love. There is no bargaining to love, there is no taking to love, there is no possessiveness, there is no discord. There is only the desire to work together in more and more harmony, allowing for more and more tolerance of differences, more and more of that which is true freedom, which includes each entity's birthright to choose its manner of living and of dying.

This culture has become obsessed with its own safety. It has become fearful, and with each fear, with each law enacted to protect those who are afraid, true freedom bows its head and becomes less apparent as the ideal bows to pragmatism in the very name of freedom.

Meanwhile, in those places upon your sphere which have had far less of the advantages of choice, through the globalization of information, entities have begun to awaken to the possibility of a freedom beyond that of survival. This ideal inflames, excites and engages every sense, every iota of the beings which have come upon the incredible possibility of true freedom, to be oneself.

And so those tyrannies which depended upon control and a pragmatic approach to the control of the nation-states which were their responsibility have begun to yield to that new generation of those to whom freedom is alive, new, pure and exciting. There has not yet been time enough in these cultures for the portions of the nature of humankind which move towards possessiveness, greed and pragmatism to take hold, and so as you see within your own culture more and more of a threat to true freedom, you may see at the same time the dawning of the realization of freedom in those cultures which are only now beginning to become able to make choices for the ideal that transcends all pragmatism.

Each upon this sphere has, as its birthright, freedom. This freedom lies within, and when it is looked at as an outward right given by [the] dispensation of nation-states, distortions occur almost immediately. Examine the motivations of those who began the culture of your own nation-state. They were not greedy for land, or riches, or anything that this incarnation could offer. They were greedy for the freedom to worship the infinite Creator in the way that had meaning for them. And now that pure and undefiled desire to worship, to adore, to praise and to give thanksgiving has been sullied by the very entities which designed a government based not only on ideals but upon a pragmatic look at the nature of humankind. It accepted the basic venality of the species, and attempted, by a complex system of placing power against power in many, many balances, a government which had the most chance of saving the central ideal.

Yet, in so doing it sowed the seeds of its own destruction. And so inevitably, one day this culture which you now enjoy shall be made new, altered and begun again by those in whom the vision is clear, the ideal unsullied by pragmatic concerns. This will not occur within this density. Within this density the strife and the struggle of positive against negative has been the whole point, has been the source of learning for all. Critical mass, shall we say, of a hope and a belief and a faith in the birthright of infinite life and freedom to worship that infinity is more and more globally understood, and it is on this account that so much of the rest of your globe in its various nation-states now cries for freedom.

Freedom does not and can never bring happiness. Therein lay the seed of the destruction of that liberty which began the experiment of your nation state. Yet the pursuit of this intangible happiness has created many, many choices betwixt vice and virtue, betwixt pragmatism and idealism, betwixt compromise and absolute value. Each of you may choose in your own freedom within a series of compromises or a series of that which may seem to be foolish: the choice for purity of action, speech and ideals. As each chooses in the face of a most pragmatic and confused society the purity of love given freely, so each approaches a true understanding of the nature of freedom; that is, the freedom to be the best of oneself, to rest in hope, and peace, and joy and in faith, no matter what the outer circumstances may appear to be.

We realize we have spoken too long, and we apologize, but this instrument had reserved this amount of energy expecting a much more narrow-band contact, and so in our less demanding way we have been able to speak in a more lengthy term through this instrument. The concept of freedom is one of which we have barely scratched the surface, yet we shall content ourselves with these thoughts, hoping that they may provoke thoughts within each, self-examination and rededication to the ideal.

We would close this session through the instrument known as Jim. It is in gratitude that we leave this instrument and transfer. We are known to you as Hatonn.

(Jim channeling)

I am Hatonn, and I greet each in love and light through this instrument at this time. Before we close this session we would ask if there may be a question or two that we may speak to. Is there a question at this time?

Carla: I do have a question, but I don't really know how to put it into words. I wonder why it took so long for so much of the rest of the world, which really did have wealth, to come to any sort of realization of the pure concept of freedom?

I am Hatonn. We thank you for your query, my sister. The qualities of spirit which are necessary to be translated, as you may say, into the mundane world, and into the personalities, both of individuals and of societies, necessarily begin within a few entities within each culture. We say necessarily begin, because there are always those students who learn more quickly than do others the solutions to riddles, problems and puzzles, whether they are of the nature of the life pattern or of the curricula within your educational institutions.

It is therefore these seedlings that find the first glimmers of the expanded view of the self and its ability to move and express itself in an unrestricted manner, for within most cultures within your third-density experience the individual entity had existence only insofar as it was a part of the larger culture, and enacted its part in a certain and expected manner. The definition of the individual was small, and the boundaries which surrounded its expression were large. Thus, the most likely venue for the expansion of the definition of the individual, and for the ability to crack the formidable boundaries surrounding the individual, was a, shall we say, change of venue which would allow for the formation of a new idea for the culture or the state, as you call it.

Thus, the creation of your own nation-state provided the circumstances necessary for this redefinition of the individual, the state or culture, and the relationship between the two. As this process began, the first entities that were to populate the new nation were those who were for the most part cast out of the old nations and cultures because there was the determination that they did not fit existing definitions. Thus, the beginning with the outcasts, the criminals, and the misfits of one kind and another was a beginning which would seem at first glance to be inauspicious, but upon closer examination was a beginning which could be depended upon to provide a radical departure in the determining of new definitions.

Thus, the birthing of your nation was one in which the concept of the freedom of expression was the foundation stone, for those first entities settling within your boundaries were responding to an enhanced need for the ability to express themselves in one manner or another that was greater than was possible within the old setting or venue. Thus, though there was much wealth of a monetary nature of learning, of the expression of the arts, and wealth of all kinds, there was still not the opportunity for each entity within any existing nation-state to express itself in a manner that exceeded the limits that had been known for generation upon generation. Only the new setting of a new nation with seemingly endless boundaries could provide the opportunity for the concept of the freedom of expression for the individual to be sown, and for the garden of humanity to flourish.

Is there another query, my sister?

Carla: No, Hatonn, I would just request the speediest possible termination of the contact because *(inaudible)*. Thank you very much.

I am Hatonn, and we wish to extend our great gratitude to you, my sister, not only for your query, but mostly for your willingness to serve as an instrument this evening, knowing that your service would be given under very, very difficult circumstances. We are honored and humbled at your service to us and to others. We thank you. At this time we shall bring this gathering to a close, thanking each for allowing our presence. We are those of Hatonn. We leave you now in love and light, my friends. Adonai vasu borragus. ✣

L/L Research

L/L Research is a subsidiary of Rock Creek Research & Development Laboratories, Inc.

P.O. Box 5195
Louisville, KY 40255-0195

www.llresearch.org

Rock Creek is a non-profit corporation dedicated to discovering and sharing information which may aid in the spiritual evolution of humankind.

ABOUT THE CONTENTS OF THIS TRANSCRIPT: This telepathic channeling has been taken from transcriptions of the weekly study and meditation meetings of the Rock Creek Research & Development Laboratories and L/L Research. It is offered in the hope that it may be useful to you. As the Confederation entities always make a point of saying, please use your discrimination and judgment in assessing this material. If something rings true to you, fine. If something does not resonate, please leave it behind, for neither we nor those of the Confederation would wish to be a stumbling block for any.

© 2009 L/L Research

Sunday Meditation
March 11, 1990

Group question: The question this evening has to do with what is perceived by many as the end or apocalyptic times that we live in, where there seems to be a great deal of activity both upon the physical and the metaphysical planes occurring on our planet. We see a great deal of difficulty around the world, a lot of turmoil, a lot of suffering, war, pain, misery. There is also the appearance of the Virgin Mary in various places, and other signs and symbols given to people that are interpreted in one way or another to help them deal with their own personal life and perhaps larger life as well. How can we find a meaning in, say, the appearance of the Virgin Mary in various locations around the world, and the message that she has to offer us in these times?

(Carla channeling)

I am Q'uo, and I greet you in the love and in the light of the one infinite Creator, in whose name we come to serve as you have called us. We are most grateful to share in your concerns at this time, and in the beauty of your vibrations and the unity of your seeking and meditation. We ask each to continue tuning throughout this session, as that which we offer to this instrument, though within the bounds of free will, has the opportunity, through weakness of contact, of moving far too close to those areas of information best left to the study of each individual seeker.

This evening you have asked us about the appearances in these latter days of the Virgin Mother of God made flesh. This is to your people the construction placed upon these occurrences, nor would we deny the truth to each person of that personal truth, for the nature of the evolution of the individual in spirit is utterly personal and subjective, and that which is true for the entity is quite simply true, but true only for that entity, and not of that universal nature which may be passed as common things are passed from person to person, the news of the town, the food at the end of the day. No, indeed. Such things as the concept of latter days and the concept of the appearance of that which is known as the Virgin Mary have an universal meaning which may fruitfully be explored. We must pause.

(Pause)

I am Q'uo, and we shall continue. Each of you moves in a way which enables each to live and move and serve and conduct within the tortured confines of an illusion that does not fit people, but rather asks people to fit it, a life of balance, of beauty, of poetry and of truth which are manifestly denied by the vision of the waking eye.

Within your experience, within your own lifetimes, and within the lifetimes of the generations preceding you, the nature of time which is not the time of clocks, but the subjective time of those who sense the imminence of transformation, has begun a speeding up process, first, many hundreds of years ago upon your inner planes, and then, as a result of this, moving downward gradually into the waking conscious awareness of entities who do not seek for information such as you ask, but who must deal with it nevertheless, as they find themselves faced with the instincts of the ideal and the environment of the completely pragmatic.

This speeding up process has been occurring for several thousand of your years, and is especially noticeable within your culture at this time, as those of one generation experience an entirely different illusion than the experience of the parents. One of your poets has said, "The center does not hold," and, indeed, the center has not held, the bird no longer obeys the master, the hawk flies free, and the hunter is left with only its instincts, its faith and its intuition.

Yet, in that faith there is begotten aid that is of meaning to each entity separately. See each of yourselves as hunters in this analogy, and you will see more clearly that while those eyes which saw clearer than yours detected you, while all was in harmony with you, there was a protection against that which you call evil which has flown from you in the face of planet-wide transformation. This transformation has already begun.

What is it to be alive? What is it to be conscious? What is it to attempt to find meaning of that instinctual hunt which each of you engage in? Are not each of you searching for the center that did not hold, that did not stay, that in and of itself, because of humankind's uncleverness, removed the easiness with which faith and simplicity were achieved? Without the feeling of being protected, without the feeling of a living faith, vital and alive, one feels prey, not to the positive, but to the negative, for we may note that within the biases of your minds it is far easier to conceive of negativity as having power than of positivity as having power, for that is the way the illusion seems to work, and this cannot be gainsaid by the most idealistic of entities.

The nature of the illusion is to challenge your ideals to the very bedrock of your existence. The nature of this illusion is to attempt to deaden the living spirit within, to give that spirit a solid picture of the creation which is not as you would choose it to be, so that you discover the possibility of choice. And as the time grows further and further into that which has so often been called the New Age, the newer vibrations, though subtle, disturb those without a living and vital faith.

(Pause)

We are sorry that we must pause so often, but we find that this instrument is being greeted continually, and were we not able to pause while this instrument consumed liquid, it would soon not be able to speak. We thank you for abiding through these short silences, for we of Q'uo can only maintain contact as powerful as the energy of the group.

To continue with that which we were discussing, the end times are not drawing near, the end times have well begun, and they shall continue for many of your years to come. It is impossible to tell you, even if we could, when the transition will be complete. We can tell you that it shall be non-dramatic, that those who are harvested shall be harvested as their natural lifetimes of incarnational lessons draw to a close. But there shall come a time when those both incarnate and discarnate shall need to walk a path walked only by those who are alive in faith and love, adoration and worship of the one infinite Creator, and so, able to receive and use and praise the more intense light, the more dense vibratory patterns of being, which characterize that illusion which is at the end of this gradual graduation process.

Always have there been signs and wonders, but never have these signs and wonders been more exciting to those whose faith is shaken than now, for such phenomena which are public, witnessable and undeniable, are to people who are not able to believe, in faith, evidence of a sort of that love which is alive. And because many of those entities upon your sphere call the one known as Jesus "Lord of all," it is natural and appropriate that images connected with this entity be given to those of simple enough faith and childlike enough hearts to receive without doubt that which is alive, not in the illusion, but in the spirit, which exists in imperishable reality.

Thus, many signs and wonders connected with the various religions, philosophies and spiritual practices used by many incarnate entities to further their progress have come to life, have stood before the least learned, the least sophisticated, the most open, the most willing to believe, and through the energy of that faith have been able to manifest not only to these people, but through that faith to others who doubt, and yearn not to doubt, but know not how to stop.

Now, let us turn specifically to the energies of that entity known as the Virgin Mary. Let us look at the story of this entity's relationship with the one infinite Creator. This entity was barely fifteen years old when the historical event—the visitation by a messenger of the Living Creator—came to this entity. This young woman had been reared in an extremely restrictive environment, one which would be called in your own terms, a man's world. The very idea of the Creator was couched in puissance and every masculine attribute. The gentleness, the nurturing, the tender quality of the love of the one infinite Creator in this particular society was not valued greatly, nor were those who represented that side of the Creator—that is, women—regarded as anything but property, those who were totally subservient, those who spoke not unless spoken to, those who watched carefully all that they did, those who would not dream, nor even imagine, breaking a vow of marriage, once promised. Such an entity was this pure virgin, too young to know precisely that which was ahead, but old enough to know that she was marrying an older, responsible and very fatherly man, not at her wish, but as an arrangement, for such was the custom.

In this context a vision appeared to this young girl, at an age that is now thought of [as] being completely irresponsible, untried, and unworthy of being given the credit of adulthood. Yet the one known as Mary listened to an angel—as she perceived this energy—say that she would be with child because of the will of the infinite and unnamable Creator, that she would bear a son before she knew her husband intimately.

The normal reaction of such a well brought up, carefully reared woman as the one known as Mary, should without faith most certainly have [been to] run in horror from such a vision. Who could believe her? Who could feel that she had not somehow broken her vows and known another intimately, and borne a son who would be a shame to the responsible and greatly revered man to whom she was promised? It would have seemed, in fact, a sentence of doom, swift and certain, if it could be countenanced at all, which in itself would be somewhat unlikely.

Yet this entity, though young and pure and naive, was a woman of timeless and ageless faith, and her reaction was the reaction of those who have the ultimate bravery of acting idealistically in the face of the impossibility of the ideal. She accepted at once the authority of this vision, and rather than pulling away from the situation in which she would be a shame to her future husband, she threw all caution to the winds, and glorified the one infinite Creator that she might be part of this beautiful story, part of the great promise that had been made to her people, the promise of "him who comes in the name of the Lord."

How could she believe? How could she find a living faith in such an unusual and bizarre occurrence as this visitation? Such was the power of her faith that she accepted the Creator first and all else after. And so she leapt into a situation which seemed doomed, glorifying the Creator and speaking most eloquently of all those things which seem to be plenteousness, but are in fact rewarded with little, and examining those things which seem to be full of poverty and lack, and exclaiming upon their riches.

Such was the entity, Mary, and so luminous was she with her faith, so alive with her vision, that the one to whom she was vowed could not disavow her, but claimed her and the babe she carried as his own. It is a dramatic and telling tale of a living faith in the midst of a world in which faith seems impossible.

When Jesus the Christ moved back to the Source, to the Creator, this entity left a feminine and nurturing spirit available to all each day, everywhere and always. This entity is often called the Holy Spirit, and within other belief systems which are more comfortable to those of this generation they are now known as guides and masters. This is acceptable, as long as it is realized that these entities are part of a living faith in a living Creator. However, the one known as Jesus could not return in person, in visions to simple folk, for this entity released the Christ of itself into the Holy Spirit, into that Comforter which is different for each and every one, and which is invisible and only to be discovered and trusted through a process of living faith.

However, the one known as Mary retained a most blessed part in the story of redemption that has seized the imaginations, the hearts, the minds, the souls and the loyalties of so many, through so many generations. This entity is a living feminine principle. The one known as Jesus the Christ was dealing from a position in which women are not even allowed in the same place to worship as the men, where women were not regarded as the gift that they are, for are not all men and women gifts one to another?

Thus, Mary remained most, most important to those who sought the nurturing side of what had been heretofore a masculine, harsh and judgmental concept of the one infinite Creator. It is of course true that love may sometimes be harsh, that its lessons may seem capricious. However, it is also true that the one infinite Creator is infinitely nurturing, infinitely a female energy also, and this energy, within the culture in which you now enjoy existence, has been personified by many as the one known as Mary.

It is to the nurturer that men and women alike turn, because they do not wish to face the stern face of the Creator, of judgment, which has come through centuries of misconception, without regard to the change in societal and cultural biases. Stubbornly, entities cling to a masculine side of the Creator, the generative and destructive side of the infinite One, at the expense of the realization of the everlasting tenderness, gentleness and caringness of this same Creator.

Thus, Mary is recognized by the one known as Jesus in the deeply moving story of his death, while of all of his family, his brothers, his sisters, his relatives, his disciples, his friends, he picked one person to be sure was cared for, and that was Mary. He gave his own precious mother, not just to a disciple, but to the world. It is important to see the universality of this act, just as it is important to see the feminine side of the Creator, forgiving upon the cross one who had sinned admittedly, and was told simply, "This day you shall be with me in paradise." Both of these elements of this great and archetypical story are meant to indicate the infinite and nurturing nature of the Living Creator.

And so from time to time when there is a window of opportunity, when there is a special group of simple, pure and believing people, usually children, Mary appears and speaks. She is as she always was, a mother, brought up as a Jew, one who wished above all things to take care of her children, to be there for them, to care for them, to worry about them, and to pray for them. And many who are jaded and lost in doubt have come across the undeniable evidence of these occurrences, occurrences which continue and will continue throughout the transition period into fourth density, in order to give the weary soul rest at last when it needs, in a thirsty dry land of intellectual belief and thought, the sweet, warm love of a living Creator.

This Mary personifies, as do all women. May each woman be aware of the vast potential within for nurture, for safety, for the being of a harbor and a haven to those who come near. It is in the weakness and the smallness of the woman's heart that the greatest personal compassion resides. The Holy Grail that each seeker seeks is a feminine symbol, a nurturing, caring, protective symbol. You do not see the dagger, you do not see the sword. You bow your head before the love of the infinite One.

You may take that which we have said on any level you choose. We have no interest in the level at which your belief or faith works within your incarnational experience to accelerate the pace of your spiritual development. We wish only for you to see the balance of the Creator. The Creator does not just create and destroy, but is a personal, caring nurturer of every moment of every day of every spark of consciousness in the creation. In passion were you all created, and in passion are you nurtured.

The symbols that you choose to be important to you are your own choice, but we ask that you gaze steadily and carefully at the concept of compassion, that it may come to heal you, to mend that which is broken, to cure sorrow, to turn the wrangling reality as it seems for a quiet and pleasant place for the soul to rest and to love. Your world may seem unsafe, but within you is a world of complete safety, beauty and sanctuary. May you meet the Creator there in that holy place within, realizing the love of the one infinite Creator at every moment. Give yourself up to this love in meditation. Give yourself up to this using of the ideal and allow all that seems chaotic about you to recede into the love and light of eternity, for therein do you truly dwell, and from that viewpoint you may open your eyes and be a beacon of light to those about you, as within you compassion is felt.

We thank you very much, as always, for asking us to be with you. We have attempted to be brief, and we are sorry that we have difficulty with the time. Please forgive the length of this message. At this time we would like to end this working by transferring this contact to the one known as Jim. We are those of Q'uo.

(Jim channeling)

I am Q'uo, and greet each again in love and light through this instrument. It is our privilege at this time to offer ourselves in the attempt to speak to queries which may yet remain upon the minds of those present. We remind each that we share that which we have to share with a full and joyous heart, but wish each to realize that we are not infallible in our opinion, and we wish each to utilize the inner discrimination that will allow those words which are helpful to be discerned from those which are not. Is there a query at this time?

S: Yes, Q'uo. Your words I take very much to heart, and I too feel the need to soften the edges, and feel the attraction to the feminine side of the Creator as a safe haven. Yet still the severe energies surge within. As one attempts to cope with these, is there a strategy other than negating the severity? Is it somehow transmuted in the experience of compassion?

I am Q'uo, and am aware of your query, my brother. As one observes the nature of one's own manifestation of beingness within your illusion, it is well to allow the experience to run a full course, shall we say, without the forceful attempt to negate and replace that which is not as one would have it be. By allowing the more wisdom-oriented nature to express itself within your thoughts and actions, you may then use this tone of experience as the focus for further meditation where you may experiment, shall we say, with alternate possibilities, examining how you'd feel if a more compassionate response would have expressed itself in the particular situation in which you feel there was given the wisdom instead of the compassion.

Look at the necessary frame of mind or perceptions that would engender the more compassionate response. Look within your being for those qualities which already exist of the compassionate nature. Find the connection between them and the expression of greater compassion in the situation that is the focus for your meditation. Examine the connections carefully. Concentrate upon those qualities which now exist which you wish to enhance in order that the garden of your being might be prepared for the producing of a new way of perceiving. Repeat this process as often as is necessary, for it shall be as the watering and fertilizing of this new plant. Thus, you shall assist in the alteration or transmutation of that quality of wisdom which you describe as being somewhat severe rather than compassionate.

Is there a further query, my brother?

S: No, thank you very much.

I am Q'uo, and we thank you, my brother. Is there another query?

Carla: How may we become more alive to the nurturing quality of the Holy Spirit which was the feminine principle of the Christ which Jesus left to comfort us?

I am Q'uo, and am aware of your query, my sister. To become more aware of that which you have called the Holy Spirit is to widen the doors of perception, shall we say, and to invite this spirit within one's inner dwelling. We find again that the meditative state is that state most conducive to opening these doors, and to begin to perceive that the Holy Spirit does indeed move through these doors upon your invitation and dwells with you within your inner room. Practice this feeling of the presence of complete nurturing and inspiriting in a regular fashion, so that your inner feelings begin to permeate your consciousness to such a degree that the daily round of activities is then touched, colored, transformed in some degree by that feeling of wholeness within the heart that is the product of this presence as it is practiced in a regular fashion.

Is there a further query, my sister?

Carla: *(Inaudible)* of which I would like *(inaudible)*. It seems to me that biological women as well as biological men are brought up in this society to be rather vigorously male, in the use of the intellect, in the use of logic, in competitiveness having to do with the daily world, the job, the getting done of things, *(inaudible)* to neglect that nurturing portion of themselves which *(inaudible)*.

I am Q'uo, and we would basically agree with your observation, my sister, for the illusion which you inhabit is one constructed for the exercise of the conscious mind that has been, shall we say, insulated from the nurturing and informing qualities of the subconscious mind, in order that the choices made by the conscious mind might carry more weight in the process of polarization within the totality of one's being than would be possible if there were completely open and free access by the conscious mind to the subconscious mind.

The ease of such an interaction would not provide the difficulty necessary to provide the pearl of great price, shall we say. To any seeking entity, treasures long sought are far more valued than that which is easily won, and your illusion, my sister, is one in which each choice made is one step farther along the great journey of evolution which each of us finds ourselves moving upon.

Is there another query at this time?

Carla: Not from me, thank you Q'uo.

K: You mentioned that Jesus had left behind the Christed portion of himself, or a portion thereof, as the feminine principle of the Holy Spirit. I'm a little confused about what you said about the entity known as Mary. You mentioned that a principle does remain, which from time to time appears to entities here and now. Did the third-density entity, Mary, choose to remain behind through the time of harvest for this purpose, or did that entity continue on with its evolution, leaving behind a similar principle?

I am Q'uo, and am aware of your query, my sister. The entity known as Mary, after the completion of its incarnation, moved again into those realms from which it had come to be of service, and offered itself from those realms in manifestation at the appropriate time and place for the observation of those who revered this entity, in order that the light body which was seen by these entities would inspire the further seeking and perception of inspiriting—we search for the correct term—that the process of seeking for these entities might then become more enabled due to the appearance of this entity in accordance with the belief structure which had been accepted as a significant portion of the path of seeking for these entities.

Thus, the one known as Mary works from the, as you would call them, inner planes of this particular planetary sphere, and communicates via what is called the light body at appropriate times for this inspiriting and enabling of the seeking process for many.

Is there a further query, my sister?

K: Has this entity then chosen to put its own path of evolution on hold for the time being in order that it may be of service at this time in that manner?

I am Q'uo, and am aware of your query, my sister. To serve is to learn, thus there is no waiting or putting off of one's own progress when one chooses to serve, but rather there is the enhancing and the acceleration of that growth.

Is there a further query, my sister?

K: No, not from me. Thank you.

I am Q'uo, and we thank you, my sister. Is there another query at this time?

Carla: I have just one last confusion. It was my understanding that those entities who stay within the inner planes of third density, instead of going on to higher densities, were indeed making a great sacrifice, as even though they learned and could serve, they were not learning in the same way as they would, had they gone on: that they were making the sacrifice to the people of third density as long as this particular third density experience lasted. Am I incorrect in this understanding?

I am Q'uo, and am aware of your query, my sister. It is not that this perception is incorrect, simply that it is incomplete. There is the opportunity to progress wherever there is the opportunity to serve. Indeed, it may be so that an entity, removing itself from one opportunity, would increase the chances of growth by so doing, and in many cases this is so for those who remain within your inner planes. However, it is not true that the growth is, as was stated, put on hold. It is accelerated in comparison to what would be possible if no service were attempted.

Is there a further query, my sister?

Carla: No, that clears that up, thank you.

I am Q'uo, and we thank you once again, my sister. Is there another query at this time?

(Pause)

I am Q'uo, and we seem to have exhausted the queries for this evening. We hope that our lengthy discourse is not too much of the reason for the exhaustion. We do thank each present for inviting us to join your circle of seeking this evening. It is a great honor to join this group. We would at this time take our leave of this instrument and this group, leaving each, as always, in the love and in the light of the one infinite Creator. We are known to you as those of Q'uo. Adonai, my friends. Adonai.

Intensive Meditation
March 12, 1990

Group question: We would like some information this evening about beginning the channeling process for this group of S1, M and S2, that is going to begin working as a group with the intention of developing S2 as a channel, and of being able to share information with other people through the channeling process. We would like to know the most important information for S2 and the support group to concentrate on at this time as they begin this journey.

(Carla channeling)

I am Laitos, and I greet you in the love and in the light of the infinite Creator. This instrument challenged us several times because she felt we were too merry, but we are very, very happy to be speaking through this instrument, through whom we have not been able to speak for some time, as there has not been a calling for that which is our own particular kind of information. We come to you in joy, and bid you all be merry, and ask that you allow yourselves a moment to rest in joy that we do not understand, but can feel, for the universe, and the air about you, and every cell in your body is dancing, whirling, joyous with life and love. Let your minds be still for a moment and feel the joy of being. We shall now pause.

(Pause)

I am Laitos, and am again with this instrument. We thank each of you for allowing us to enjoy and feel the beauty of living with you. You call for information about that which is known as channeling. It is a large subject, but we should begin with one simple concept which is at the basis of all channeling, and that is that each channels at all times, at every moment. None can avoid being a channel, for in truth you are consciousness, and those energies that you choose out of that consciousness build upon themselves because of your choices, and thus you channel emotion, attitude, feeling, desire and manifestation.

Very, very few entities have the awareness that they are, in fact, not entities acting unto themselves, but instead are part of one infinite Creator, undifferentiated from that Creator except by the choosing in free will to express in an independent and co-creative way. Consequently, most take no care in that which they manifest in the life experience, but rather assume that they are to react to that which occurs outside of themselves, one thing following another in the pattern of your society in the environments of work and home and play.

You make choices you know not of. How little credit you give to your own creative power. There is, in truth, no reality in third density but your consciousness. You dwell within an illusion which is densely opaque, through which one cannot see, in order that you may, more and more, learn to choose in a consistent fashion those biases which move the consciousness into a less distorted form of the manifestation of the love of the co-creator and of the Creator. So each of you channels yourself, each of you cannot help being a channel. It is no effort, it is simply not recognized that this effortless process is not the process of expressing the self, but a series of choices about what the self is being in the process of becoming a being, for you are both being and becoming.

This is an obvious paradox, and when you meet paradox within your studies, rejoice, for then you know that you have moved into the realm of that which is spiritually helpful. A spiritual path is a series of paradoxes. How easy it is not to heed these words. How easy it is to yield responsibility for the choices one makes to the press of circumstance. The illusion, a series of vibratory complexes and patterns of energy, designed to manifest themselves to your senses as opaque reality, is, in fact, malleable and plastic and most willing to bend to the instrument who is aware of the process that is taking place.

Thus, as this group begins what this instrument would call a ministry that takes a great deal of dedication and patience and work in consciousness, it is well to come to terms with your own inestimable power. It is in no case necessary for anyone to react to circumstance. It is always, even in the most extreme circumstance, true that there are choices to be made, and the more consciously they are made the more rapid shall be the acceleration of each entity's spiritual evolution. The work of realizing the self that lies hidden as a gem of infinite worth within the clay of manifestation cannot be seen by the self or by another until it is realized and valued by the self.

You are each imperishable beings of light, heirs of grace and glory, an infinitely important and necessary portion of the one great Thought which created all there is, that being divine love. That is the crystal that is within you—love. Not love as humans would understand it to be, not the weak and watered love of kindness and courtesy, not even the love of personal passion and romance, but the love of such immense power that it generated the infinite creation in balance and in perfection.

This seems to be without you: the perfection, the balance, the divine love. You are projecting into an illusion that has been created with your own cooperation so that you may move forward one step at a time, one small step at a time. You began as unmanifest love. You were joined with free will and flung outward to become prodigal sons and daughters of love itself. You are information givers, for all that you experience is that which the Creator experiences and knows of Itself. You cannot make any errors, for in each action the Creator learns of Itself. You can, however, make choices about that which you wish to learn.

Since your density is a density which is attempting to learn lessons of love, you may depend upon your incarnational patterns being planned to allow you to meet those ways of loving which you felt needed further refinement. We do not send understanding or wisdom, for these lessons are not of this density. All too often, the heart has been lost in those who seek the truth that lies within the illusion of third density. But wisdom is not the answer, and the questions one asks cannot be answered wisely, but only compassionately, for compassion is in the heart of the choices each of you make day by day.

Thus, as we speak to this group which wishes to be of service to others, we ask it, first of all and always, to be conscious of the nature of the lessons to be learned by the self and in harmony with other selves. These are lessons of love and compassion. Not love partially given, not compassion partially withheld, but unstinted, foolish, quixotic love, love that fears no hurt, that can ignore and smile at pain, knowing that new things are painfully learned, knowing that opening up the heart to love is dying to those things which block the heart from opening like the flower that it is. It is as if you were infected by a disease called doubt: self-doubt, doubt of others, doubt of the worth of that which you are doing, doubt of the nature of the infinite One. There is no need and no room, for the seeker who wishes to work towards finding the treasure of love within.

It has been said that love casts out fear, but it is not explained how one may love. We shall explain. You are love. You need to find out more and more clearly how to express your true being. Those about you who are not seeking as you constantly offer the catalyst of the unexamined life, of the measured love, of the stinted compassion, of the carelessness and fine scorn for the fragile treasure of this brief dance of an incarnation. You shall not exist long in this body, in this illusion. Use the time that you have, for time itself is part of that illusion, and as you become aware more and more of the love within each moment, as you choose to ask yourself, in the face of difficult catalyst, where is the love in this moment, more and more shall you drop away those things which are not love from the being which you are becoming. More and more shall you be able to shine and be the love that you seek. You are simply uncovering that which you truly are.

Now we move to that part, that all important part of a support group which creates for the channel the nature of that channel. The channel itself does not create its own nature, it is the group harmony, the group love, that is hard won through the fierce loyalty to truth with each other and with the self. We could say simply, "Be merry together," and that would be the heart of the harmony of which we speak. But, in truth, each of you has stumbling blocks to teach each other with, each of you presents challenges and catalyst which each other may learn to love without let, without hindrance, unsparingly, unstintingly. It is the job of the support group—and this includes the channel—to love at all times, most especially when the manifestation of one of the group seems to be less than lovable, when the behavior seems to be unacceptable, when a thinking seems to be unforgivably erroneous. Love accepts the unacceptable, forgives the unforgivable, loves the unlovable, and by that environment creates a catalyst by which that self may choose a new path.

In a support group you are not bound by what you think of each other, but by the love that you know is each other's true self. You set each other free, and each of you teaches each. Let no one feel shame at lacking courage, making errors, or falling by the wayside in some self-perceived manner. It shall happen to you again, and again, and again. The support group, when it sees that one of its members is in need, forgets all need of its own, and reaches out in love to pull the needy one out of the mire of confusion and self-doubt.

This is a most intimate relationship. It is the beginning of what you call the social memory complex, and each group's balance of harmony is unique to that group, and will thus form the basis for the information which comes through the channel of that group. So be aware of that great truth, and seek to love, not to be loved. Seek to understand, not to be understood. Rest in your mighty power and give the gifts that you have freely and gloriously, rejoicing in the infinite Creator. See yourselves as those who pull the wagon, pulling together, working with such joy that labor becomes play. Love each other, and allow with all generosity the burgeoning and blooming self that is you, as daily you change, to be melded anew into the ever-changing, subtle patterns of group energy.

We are suggesting that which will cause you great discomfort for as long as you work together, for this sort of effort causes one to change, and as the mind perceives itself changing, and realizes that its old programs no longer work—or as you say, in your technical society, compute—then you must dump that program, and this is most painful, and feels much like loss, and feels, indeed, like a grievous loss. The energy which could be taken to be lost could be used up in grieving, may instead be turned by faith to the building of programs which are fully representative of that which you have learned, that love which you have uncovered within yourself.

More than this, there is a basic program within the subconscious, and this too is heavily veiled in distortion. This is where the work with dreaming, with keeping a journal, with taking oneself seriously, becomes centrally important, for it is, shall we say, a metaprogram[5], in which you accept the socially unacceptable dictum of a chosen path of service.

Within your society it is not considered healthy to feel that one is on a mission of a spiritual nature. Nevertheless, this is, in actuality, the truth. You have come here, intent upon expressing and manifesting in poetic beauty the mission in service to others which you chose preincarnatively. Yes, you chose much personal work, but you chose more. You chose your paths of service, and in each path of service to others much must be yielded and given up. Thus, we encourage you to encourage each other, to love each other, to allow no disharmony to rule for one moment longer that it takes to recognize that there is something which must be discussed, which must be forgiven, which must be balanced, so that love and harmony again may be the environment in which you follow your path of service.

---

[5] meta: as a prefix means "higher" or "transcending." A metaprogram, then, would be a program that is higher than and takes precedence over the other programs being used.

During sessions of working, the support group needs continually to realize and send for the power of love, that the instrument may not have to depend upon its own strength and will alone, but may rest against the cushion and support of an environment of love. Tuning, then, is done continuously throughout a session, not as a heavy burden, not as a heavy duty to perform, but as that which becomes second nature, as that which becomes a simple and constant visualization of living, revolving light, which raises itself round about the whole group in spirals and reaches unto the one infinite light of the Creator in its first manifestation.

We shall end by speaking of channeling itself. There are many, many kinds of channelings. As we have said, the life itself is a channeled experience. This instrument and we who are called to this instrument are those who teach, as we learn, about spiritual principles, about tools and resources that may aid in the acceleration of spiritual evolution. This particular teacher, and we, as those who speak through this instrument and have been called by this group, are not concerned, nor can we be, with those details of mundane existence which open with the first breath and close with the last, for we see the incarnation in its illusory form only as a learning opportunity. We cannot tarry there long.

Yes, at each turn it is important to be able to orient the self within one's environment, to be able to see the nature of the changes of the illusion as they affect the day-to-day workings of the incarnate, self-willed, little self. There are many, many teachers who are most pleased to speak through channels and guide one through each day, each experience, each choice. It is our nature to give that responsibility to the self of your self.

The material that we offer, therefore, will not be material that is sweet and easily taken, the candy of the spirit. We move rather towards the more substantial meat and drink of spiritual lore, working to enlarge the viewpoint in order that those questions which one might have about the day, the hour, the experience, this or that, become questions that are small, become questions which beg for a larger question, and that is, "Where does this concern fit into the life that I know lies within me?"

Many will seek of any channel specific information, especially during these generations of change, when time itself is speeded up and finally swallowed by the density to come. Those who work with this instrument and with us will find themselves often unable satisfactorily to answer specific questions, for to do so would be to lose the purity of the contact. And so, if being of apparent help in reading the, shall we say, tea leaves of the day, the dream, the occurrence, the concern, which are things which can be taught by other teachers, but not by us, if this is any part of the ambition of the channel, let it be faced now, that we may not, in our teaching, be a disappointment, be a stumbling block before you.

We are a comparatively impersonal contact. We look at questions and value the question more than the answer, for in the question lies the quality of the life experience that is being sought by the questioner. In an illusion where there are no true answers, it is the questions that are important. You will again and again as a channel find yourself pointing and ending to and in mystery, speaking in riddles and paradoxes, seeking out of the maelstrom of dizzying, excited questions and observations the still and quiet waters of silent truth that lie stably and eternally within each consciousness.

The mechanics of channeling are those easily taught but difficult to learn, because it is always thought that if something is worthwhile it must be difficult to achieve. We cannot teach you to be faithful in your practice. Teaching an entity to channel is much akin to teaching a beginning violinist how to finger the scale, how to play the simplest of tunes. The teacher does not teach greatness, but only a simple mechanism which must be practiced, and practiced, and practiced, in infinite patience and dogged determination and persistence, for it is practice alone which creates that level of trust which allows the surrender of all expectation.

Many are the times we have demonstrated through this instrument the nature of that trust. We do so at this time. Six, six, five, three, seven, one, four, three, six, six. That is what we gave this instrument—nonsense. That is what you will feel you are receiving—nonsense. That is acceptable, being able to accept that you do not know what you will say is important to one who wishes to be a faithful channel. It is not up to the channel to judge the channeling, but only to prepare itself, first by attempting to become the best self it knows how to be, and secondly, by opening itself completely in surrender to a greater will, a higher self, a larger point of view.

We believe we have given you things to think about, enough for one session. We are still very excited at being able to be with this group again, and thank the one known as S2, the one known as M, and the one known as S1, for giving us an opportunity which is all too rare, to share that which we have learned, that which is our specialty within the Confederation of Planets in the Service of the Infinite Creator, for those who truly wish to follow a path of service [that] exists before the little life began, and shall exist long after the last breath has quieted, and the physical vehicle crumbled to dust. Imperishable ones, we greet and bless each of you, and would close this working through the one known as Jim. We leave this instrument in thanks, in love and in light. I am Laitos.

(Jim channeling)

I am Laitos, and greet each again in love and light through this instrument. We would now offer ourselves for any queries which this group would have for us. Is there a query at this time?

S2: Yes. May we know how we would *(inaudible)* start in safety, and what we would do well to know to preserve that safety by tuning and challenging our contact?

I am Laitos, and we are aware of your query, my brother. It is well, most especially for the one serving as the instrument, to have knowledge of the self in regards what the core belief is that the instrument would live and die for. This information is well presented in the handbook that has been compiled by the one known as Carla, for in this essence of the self one may offer a challenge to any unseen spirit that will ensure that that spirit comes in a manner which is acceptable to you as you offer yourself as instrument through which it may speak. This is centrally important, and it is well that this be considered in depth by each within the group, most especially the instrument, between this time and the time during which you shall again sit in session with this group.

At that time it shall be our honor to begin the initial contact with your instrument in order that you shall become acquainted with the feelings and perceptions that begin this contact process, as it is used by this group. The group tuning, by listening to music that is meaningful to each within the group, the visualizing of light, the joining in voice in the repeated mantram, are also other techniques in preparing the group for the contact and in tuning the individual entities into one seeking entity that acts as the receiving mechanism for the desired contact.

Thus, we would suggest, in the intervening time, that you not only consider that core quality that enlivens your entire being, and which will become that concept through which you will offer your challenge, but that the group sit in silent meditation upon a regular basis in order that the energies of the group might become harmoniously blended. This will greatly enable this process of harmonization to occur.

Is there a further query, my brother?

S2: No, thank you very much.

I am Laitos, and we thank you. Is there another query?

Carla: I just have one. I was planning, on my own, to have a session during the day tomorrow before these people leave. I don't want to rush them, I understand the principle of the baby steps, but I was planning to start the instruction immediately *(inaudible)*.

I am Laitos, and we are aware of your query, my sister. This is acceptable as long as it is understood by each within this newly forming group that the first attempts at a contact are those which shall be contemplated in the intervening time until the new group again sits in circle with this group, and that there shall be no verbal contact attempted until there have been a number of successful contacts achieved within the group that now sits in seeking circle.

Is there a further query, my sister?

Carla: No, thank you.

I am Laitos, and we thank you, my sister. Is there another query at this time?

S1: I have two questions. One is, do you suggest a mantra for a group, and secondly, in our existences on all levels, what is the best way to surrender all expectations?

I am Laitos, and am aware of your queries, my sister. We suggest only those means of tuning, whether by mantram, singing, group visualizing or whatever other means is available that have meaning to the group. This is decided by your own free will choice, for you are by now aware of those means by which you are most inspired, and we would suggest that you follow those yearnings and preferences which are already in place within each of you, and that as a group you make this choice.

As for the means by which one may give up the expectations, again, this is that process which has most effect when it is decided by each individual. It is in our humble opinion that which is most easily accomplished by a simple decision that serves as the foundation stone upon which any service to others is offered, and that is that one seeks with all the heart, the mind, and the soul to serve in whatever way is most appropriate, and that all other cares for the duration of the session of working are released.

One may see them as put aside, as one would discard cares and worries at the foot of a series of stairs, leaving them behind, or putting them in the pockets of a coat and hanging the coat in a closet, or by whatever means carries weight within your way of thinking, so that one becomes as an hollow vessel during the session of working, with no concern for any particular outcome, but concern only that one offers oneself wholly and completely in order that one may serve the one Creator in whatever manifestation [that] presents itself to one.

Is there a further query, my sister?

S1: No, thank you.

I am Laitos. We thank you for your concerns. Is there another query at this time?

Carla: Not from me, thank you very much.

I am Laitos, and we also thank each within this circle for allowing us to offer ourselves in service, for it is our great joy to do so, and we rejoice with you at this new opportunity to serve that is presented to each, not only within this circle and the newly forming circle, but to each portion of the Creator that resides upon your planetary sphere and will in some fashion be touched by each effort of service, for are not all one being, joined in seeking, joined in serving? And as each portion becomes awakened unto that desire living within the heart of the self, then does each other portion resonate in harmony with that same single desire. Again we thank you, my friends. We cannot thank you enough. We shall take our leave of this group at this time. We are those of Laitos. Adonai, my friends. Adonai.

Intensive Meditation
March 13, 1990

(Carla channeling)

I am Laitos, and I greet you in the love and in the light of the infinite Creator. We are most grateful for your call to us, for your request of our humble opinions which, as always, we must warn, are quite fallible. We are not those of final authority, but like you, seekers upon the path of truth, beauty and the nature of the Creator.

We have spoken much about the preparation for channeling. It is now time to move forward into a more active mode, the mechanical learning of that which is called channeling. It is akin to teaching a child to play a simple tune upon the piano. This instrument would call such a tune, "Chopsticks." This we can teach. We cannot teach persistence, or a love of harmony, an assiduousness of practice. We must pause.

(Telephone interruption.)

I am Laitos, and am again with this instrument. We shall continue. The mechanics, the way of production, of channeled material, is so simple that it is normally resisted by those who wish to make it harder and more complex, who are learning to be little children who simply repeat what they hear or feel inside. This is the condition of the instrument as it begins the contact. It has prayed in whatever manner it deems most deeply worthwhile, to reach as high a tuning as the instrument may achieve in a stable and continual manner. This requires a crushing and absolute honesty, a knowing of the self and of the limitations of the self, for one does not go into the ministry of channeling to remove oneself from the world about him and dwell upon an higher plane.

One chooses to channel inspirational, spiritual and metaphysical principles because the Christ consciousness which permeates your Earth plane has, in the majority of cases, no chance at speaking in conventional ways, that is, through church attendance, involvement in the community of the Creator. There is no way for many to experience community. Thusly, to those whose distortions cause them to be unable to find the inspiration, the renewal, and the strength which they need day by day, to realize by grace that which is asked of them and to do that with a cheerful heart, there must be an alternative place of genuine worship.

We are not those who disregard or denigrate compassion, for especially within your own density the deepest truths lie in purified emotion. The job of a channel, therefore, is to provide catalyst, to evoke that purified emotion which is the daily food and bread for which you pray each day in the Lord's Prayer. Think you then that you are asking for bread to eat and wine to drink? This was not the intent of a teacher who spoke always in parables. The daily bread which you seek and which you seek to share is that manna that contains the healing, the peace and the love of the consciousness of Christ; by whatever name you know the Christed entity, this is so.

This, then, is your goal, to become more and more able to perceive the ramifications of each point made in discussions about queries that have been asked by a group. Be humble before this gift. You are not reciting scripture, you are not offering infallibility. You are offering that food which otherwise would not be there and would cause starvation of the soul to many. Vocal channeling is only one of the myriad of services. It happens to be a more conspicuous one. This in no way means that the vocal channel is any different or better than the mother who nurtures a child, or any other entity whose path of service lies not in blue-ray communication, but in green-ray healing, whether it be of physical things, the rebuilding of old neighborhoods, feeding the hungry, working with the here and now of souls that need to be fed, not manna first, but food for the body, all across the spectrum to those who have put those things to rest by circumstance, work and luck, and are therefore able to take the leisure to move into contemplation, to seek out purity, to fall in love with love in the Creator, in yourself and in others.

No one within this density, as far as we are aware, has ever been able to keep this consciousness constant as a steady state throughout the incarnation or period of service. What is important is that you are able to clear the mind, to empty it as you would the contents of your pockets, before resting for the nighttime watches, until you become so much a part of the silence, so focused within, that thoughts begin coming to you. Now, you have continued to tune during the entire process of protection of the self, protection of the group, and protection of the working. When the time comes to channel it is time to cast away every inhibition, every care, every distraction, and put on the clarity of the white light of the infinite One.

The nature of the channeling which we prefer doing, because it is much easier upon the physical complex of the instrument, is conscious channeling. We are of the fourth density, the density of love and understanding. We are not as wise as many of our colleagues, and so our specialty is working compassionately with those who wish to build compassion for themselves, for others and for the Creator within themselves. We are humbled and grateful that the one known as S has made a serious commitment to learn this discipline of the personality and lend his unique voice to the explication of that very simple message that is repeated time and time again in various ways, in order that various kinds of people may find spiritual enlightenment available.

To begin familiarizing the group with the energy which we use, and we are a broadband energy, which means it is easier to experience us, we would like at this time to dwell with each within the mind in silence for a few moments. Allow anything that happens, or does not happen, to be acceptable. Simply, as we pause, experience being touched by this energy. We would now pause. We are those of Laitos.

(Pause)

Those energies which you feel shall not always be overwhelming. It is extremely common to the new student to find a great disorientation when beginning the work of channeling, for you upon your sphere of existence have the concept of solidity, of objective reference. We simply offer thoughts to your subconscious in the form of concept rather than language. It is the portion of the channel to hear the clarion call of those thoughts, to waste no time considering whether it is you channeling yourself, or yourself channeling an outer source. This process moves on despite all doubt, all questioning, and all fear, as long as the entity who wishes to channel continues to feel that this service is a path of service chosen.

Since much has been said already about preparing for contact, we shall await questions in order to clear up any confusing points you might have, but at this time we wish to speak directly to the teaching process of channeling. Channeling is a process much likened unto the catching and the throwing of a baseball, in a rapid fashion, which requires that the mind be kept single-mindedly upon the succession of balls, and the hand be nimble to empty itself of the ball it has just caught, that it again may be empty to receive the new ball. In this analogy we equate these balls with intuitionally validated thoughts and inspirations which are yours alone as you move along the path of life.

Now, we will tell you that which is not told those of the students who come to this instrument who do not wish to channel, and that is that the way to begin is to cast aside all powers of analysis, all resistance, all fears of saying or doing the wrong thing. This is often a difficult thing to give up, for entities truly wish to be of great service, and they wish to move forward as quickly as possible, but we ask you to take our instructions verbatim, and then think about them in as many different ways as you wish, ways in which you may come into adjustment with the seeming loss of the self. You certainly are not losing yourself, but gaining a deeper and more impersonal portion of yourself, for yourself is the Creator.

When we transfer a contact to a channel, the channel waits until a thought comes into its mind. It is distressing to many channels, and the first words that they get are the words with which we always open and close each meditation, greeting you and bidding you farewell alike in the love and the light of the infinite Creator. It is a great temptation to feel that there is a tremendous conspiracy of those who pretend to channel, but are, indeed, less than honest, less than rigorous, less than prepared, so that their material remains inferior and uninspiring. Channeling is a series of concepts that are caught and spoken without thought, without judgment.

After the experience is over, you may examine, analyze, probe, discuss and attempt to measure that which you have experienced, but during the process itself, a complete surrender to the Creator of all things, in certain knowledge of His plan for your existence within this incarnation, is in place, and that all is as it should be. This relaxed and peaceful state is aided only in some cases by the ingestion of caffeine in order that, although calm, quiet and listening, one also has the energy which such substances give to the physical vehicle and to the mind complex.

As we work with the one known as S, and gaze at the dynamics of the support group, we see that the one known as S's greatest difficulty will be in releasing himself from an attempt to be objective and to make sense in a mundane way of that which transcends day-to-day living and moves the mind and the heart into the vast eternity of imperishability. The energies that are carried are strong. This is the reason we have put much emphasis upon the work upon the self, not so much to be a better person, but to be able to discipline the personality enough to clear the self at the time of self, and therefore be an ideal and magical entity.

The process is as simple as repeating what you are thinking. New instruments, as we have said, feel again and again that they are making up those things that are being said. This is because we start upon familiar territory, common to all seekers, and common especially to those who have studied the work of this particular group. It takes a certain very powerful courage to have faith that the thoughts that are springing into mind from the subconscious will in the end have created a document that is as full of inspiration and information as you are able stably to convey.

You channel—and we speak quite seriously here—your own thought processes. You choose your behaviors, your reactions or lack of them, and all the attitudes of life. When one decides to become a vocal channel, one is drawn into a powerful energy nexus of which it is one point in the planetary light. Whether or not the channeler turns out to be proficient, if there is great sincerity in the attempt, that alone will lighten the consciousness of your beloved planet that is so sadly in need of light. We repeat again, do not analyze, do not allow the mind to judge the contact. It is of the greatest normalcy that an entity will begin channeling with perhaps only fifty percent of channeled material of an outer kind, and the other half the wisdom of the deeper self, so that in fact the channel in the beginning is very much aided by its unseen spirit, or guides, or [moods].

We would at this time request that the one known as S relax, take several deep breaths, and allow apprehension and fear to leave the aura of the physical vehicle, for in this first session we wish no more than to establish the experience of a momentary contact. When we transfer to the one known as S, we shall simply be sending the information of who we are and what we stand for. The simple perception of that name, which you require within yourself if spoken aloud, begins the brave and foolhardy Don Quixote upon his path towards the windmills of doubt, temptation and distraction. Thus, we would at this time attempt to make our presence known just as an energy, and when the instrument hears a greeting beginning, simply repeats that which it hears, judging not whether that thought is coming from the expectation of entity after entity greeting in the same way those who call. Once this is accomplished, the work is well begun, but the first step is to be able to open the mouth and speak that which spontaneously rises into the consciousness with no analysis and a complete faith in the service provided.

We would at this time like to announce ourselves in such a way to the one known as S, that he is able to vocalize thoughts that come from his subconscious spontaneously. It is impossible to tell in terms of the experience of the bodily senses whether such contacts are real or unreal. It is simply your job as channel to speak the words that we give you. You are, as an instrument, a person of great power, for you may choose the manner of the channeling, the focus of a life in faith and the joy of each individual lay ministry. Relax, rest back, and simply repeat that which is given without question and without thought. We will at this time move to the one known as S, that it may experience us and be able to vocalize at least one sentence of spontaneous thought. We would at this time transfer this contact to the one known as S. I am Laitos.

(S channeling)

I am Laitos. I greet each in the love and the light of the one infinite Creator. It has come about that …

(Side one of tape ends.)

(S channeling)

I am Laitos, and am again with this instrument. We rejoice that this instrument finds within itself the heart to speak that which it does not know. The instrument is telling me that it is reaching the limits of its ability *(inaudible)*. We rejoice *(inaudible)* and the experience of the deepened commitment. We understand the great difficulty *(inaudible)*. We leave this instrument now in the love and in the light of the one infinite Creator, wishing each well, in the paths of your chosen, thankful, *(inaudible)*. We wish at this time to transfer the contact back to the one known as Carla.

(Carla channeling)

I am Laitos, and am again with this instrument. First of all, we would wish to say to the one known as S that this entity is a joy to work with, cooperative, straightforward and single-minded to move into the heart and into heartfelt communication in service to others. We rejoice in the support group as well, for each is equally important, and we thank each for that dedication.

We are aware that controlling, handling and experiencing our energy for the length of time which it took to speak the sentences which the instrument spoke was great, and we commend this instrument for trusting in a teacher who is surely fallible, but who may have something to share. The key is trust. We hope you may come to know us and others of the Confederation, that you will begin to discriminate between one another of those entities to find that entity which best meshes with your own vibratory patterns, my brother, but how wonderful it is that such a beginning has occurred, that the soul was ready to open and bloom as a beautiful rose, or the unfurling leaves of spring which you may see in your countryside at this time.

We find that there is some adjustment necessary for the new instrument's maximum comfort in the contact. Because of the fact that we cannot directly experience those discomforts that need adjusting, we would ask that the instrument aid us by mentally asking for adjustments of any offshoot of strong energy which may prove distracting or troublesome. This is not our wish, we do not wish to deplete anyone, but merely to add to the information available to those who seek, and seek in such a way that this little room is church, as this instrument would call it, and the channel opening itself to contact is patterned after Christ consciousness, willing to give up all to do the work of the Father with a glad spirit and a steady heart.

Each time this entity practices the channeling it needs to be very clear with us mentally as to how we may serve it by entering into its energy fields in the most comfortable way possible. We especially congratulate one whose pride is in logical thought, but whose desire to serve has been so purified, the egoistic demands of the small self so well put aside, that much has already been done.

You may well question that which you may do between times of meeting with this group until the instrument itself feels it is strong, stable and full of discernment that it may channel within its own support group without the more experienced channel to aid it. As the process of meditation begins, or as it ends, we would suggest the discipline of tuning. The mantram of this particular teacher is the Lord's Prayer. There is an outer mantram and an inner mantram. The outer mantram brings the energy of the group into a circle that flows through the channel, strengthening and stabilizing the contact. That which is inner is of faith, the will to serve and the power of concentration.

Thus, we ask that the most difficult part of preparing oneself to channel, indeed, the most difficult part of the channeling process, be practiced, until one feels the vibration of whatever member of the Confederation you have called. Since those of Laitos have long been specializing in working with new channels, their's is likely, though it would be most efficacious for the instrument to request our presence, but it is the tuning process that must be practiced until it falls so deeply into the grain of the mind that it becomes impossible to consider channeling without doing the appropriate preparation.

Preparation is different for each entity. We will express to you this instrument's preparation in detail, not as an instruction, but as an example of how one moves from one state of consciousness to another, clearing the mundane pockets of the litter of life within your physical beings, and creating the hollowness within that asks and seeks and is ready to serve, and say, "Here am I, use me, send me, let me do the work you have prepared for me this day." Under no circumstances would we suggest that the entity, without the aid of the support group and the more experienced channel, at this time do any experimenting with channeling by the self alone.

Now we shall describe this instrument's own idiosyncratic way of preparation. Since the one known as S knows the idiosyncrasies of the one known of Carla, it may extrapolate the principles involved into equivalent values of equivalent intensity and meaning within its own life.

When the instrument known as Carla prepares to channel, the instrument does a symbolic act. Were this instrument more able to do things without aid it is possible that this instrument would prefer actually to shower and cleanse the whole body. Instead this instrument cleanses its hands, empties its bladder, brushes the teeth. As one empties the body of those waste materials it can no longer use and gives praise and thanksgiving to the Creator for having been able to use the food that the creation has provided, as one washes one's hands, prayer may turn towards the cleanliness of the self, asking and seeking always to be centered, consciously aware of the presence of the one infinite Creator, and systematically cleansed for the moment of the tedium and hubbub of civilization. As one brushes one's teeth, prayers are offered up on behalf of the purity of the words which come from that instrument's mouth.

There are as many different ways of praying, as many different symbolic ways of changing personalities and personas, of becoming that entity which is capable of taking its place in the world of spirit, as there are entities. The goal, however, is to feel at one, peaceful, stable, safe and fearless, and whatever ritual best creates within the self those feelings is acceptable to us, as long as the prayers involved concern service to others, for though there are teachers of service to self, we are not they, we have made our choices, and we believe each has made its own choice in this group also. Relax, be merry, take things lightly, and yet ponder them deeply. Allow the consciousness you experience in channeling, and meditation to a lesser extent, to begin to color your existence, and always, daily if possible, practice the tuning process.

To move back to this instrument's process of tuning, there is, as you know, the reproduction of the exact question asked, if there is a question which has been asked, while the instrument is in a slightly altered state of consciousness. In this state of consciousness the words are heard differently than if the words were heard before the cleansing process and the fervent, passionate prayer has been done.

Then the tuning of the group begins. Some prefer to "om," so that all entities within the circle are expelling the breath of life at the same time. Some enjoy the singing, and others enjoy the inspirational music. Indeed, there need not be a seriousness about such tuning devices. For instance, an extremely good tuning song is an old nursery rhyme, "Row, row, row your boat, gently down the stream, life is but a dream." This places you squarely in the consciousness of time and space, and it is from time/space that you are receiving information.

Then, there is the breath given together in the mantram of your choice. This instrument chooses the Lord's Prayer. There are many other invocations that have resonance for some people which the Lord's Prayer does not. As long as the import of this mantram is love of the Creator and love of each other, it is of the Christ consciousness and is acceptable to us.

When one has come this far, one then sees to the protection of the self and of the group. This instrument does so by visualizing each chakra in turn, asking it to receive, for this working, the unblocking of all difficulties, that full energy may rise to the heart chakra, and therefrom to the blue-ray energy center, which the vocal channel uses. In order to use the green healing ray, or the blue communication ray, it is vitally necessary to pay constant and close attention to the indigo ray which lies betwixt the brows in the center of the forehead. These lobes of the brain are those lobes in which eternity resides, now safely and securely, and hardly ever touched by human thought or imagination. When one feels that the protection of the working and of the self is complete, you may go on.

This instrument's method is to move each chakra into its normal balanced brilliance and spinning and life-giving energy, so that there are no blockages for that time, then surrounding the bodily energy in mind with the mixture of the violet ray of identity, and the red ray of life itself. These two colors create a mixture of lavender and red, the kind of color this instrument might call burgundy, and one visualizes it covering and coating the body as if the body were a capsule, and the covering that which held the great medicine of that capsule within it so that it may be useful upon its taking, and not be scattered, so that one is taking small bits and pieces into meditation, but has found a way to be whole.

After that, this instrument visualizes the white light, the full armor of light, placed upon its form, missing no spot, of undifferentiated love manifesting as pure white light. Once that feeling has been achieved—and it is often so that there is a lightness, either physical or mental, experienced during this portion of tuning—one then visualizes, as does each of the support group, this same white light that is first simply a small ball of enormous beauty and luminosity in the middle of the group, by bowing before its wisdom, by accepting its protection, you each allow it to expand, until all of you are bathed in unconditional love and light, the greatest protection available within the personal reference frame.

This instrument then asks the archangels, with whom it has a long history of acquaintance and love, to stand guard over the meeting, to warn of any intruders, and to act as champions of the light which the channel and its group are attempting to produce. The four archangels are Raphael, Gabriel, Michael and Ariel. If you wish to use the same technique as this instrument, you would see the one known as Raphael dressed in raiment so white that it glistened yellow and crimson. It is a silent witness, not a jovial personality. Then, behind the self, one asks for the presence of Gabriel, that great nurturer, who is normally visualized wearing a blue robe, standing in water, which is running and fresh, and offering up a holy cup to the thirsty. To the right there is Michael, the only [one] of the archangels which bears what you would call a weapon. It is the archetypal dragon slayer, it is the protector. It is always alert, and as one becomes adept at these visualizations one may see from the expression on these entities' faces what the atmosphere is truly like, not seen or felt from the outside, but from the inside, for Michael, more than any of the others, changes posture, changes the angle of its sword, changes its degree of alertness. Lastly, moving from the crimson robes of Michael, we ask that our left side be guarded by the archangel Ariel, which is the personification of Earth cycles. As it moves its multicolored cloak, a wind blows, and leaves, fallen from the trees and dry, rustle across its path. It is a mystery-clad entity, just as death and transformation are unknown until after the fact.

Asking for these archangels, one may begin, upon practice, to feel the great golden dome of metaphysical protection which has been begun by the energy of the group moving in a spiraling, clockwise fashion. This dome is impervious to damaging psychic greeting. It is possible, with this protection, for entities to take advantage of the instrument which falls prey to temptation, or in other ways has some chink in the armor of light, some Achilles' heel. But if the preparation has been complete and wholehearted, protection reigns within the place of working, and as you repeat over and over this process, it will cease taking so very, very long to do.

The protection having been done, the instrument known as Carla, and again we use this as an example, turns to the prayer of St. Francis, for that is the prayer that is its personal mantram, and we shall recite it in full.

Oh Lord, make me an instrument of Thy peace. Where there is hatred, let me sow love; where there is injury, pardon; where there is discord, unity; where there is doubt, faith; where there is despair, hope; where there is darkness, light; where there is sadness, joy. Lord, let me seek not to be loved, but to love; not to be understood, but to understand. For it is in consoling that we are consoled. It is in pardoning that we are pardoned. It is in giving that we receive. And it is dying that we rise to eternal life with Thee.

At the end of this private prayer, this continuing inner tuning, the instrument then declares itself as a metaphysical spirit. Let no mistake be made by one who feels unworthy, the universe is a complete democracy, no matter what density, no matter what differences of wisdom or compassion, each is made of the same stuff, that being love itself. The one known as Jesus said, "I am the vine, you are the branches." Settle yourself with your roots in the ground, and in divine consciousness. When you have declared who you are, with no doubt, no holding back, and no reservation, you have become a being of light in the great democracy of all spirits. No discarnate spirit is ever confused about its identity. Its very existence depends on its knowing who it is, and if an instrument wishes to work with spirits, and have control over that spirit to which it connects, the instrument, too, must know who he is. Then there is a prayer said that the energy not be more than can stably be accepted.

With all of this done, the entity opens itself to contact, declaring precisely who it is, and what challenge any spirit who wishes to speak with it must meet. This instrument challenges in the name of Jesus Christ. It is most important to challenge as each knows, but the challenging depends upon the utter, naked and sometimes hard line honesty of the instrument. You cannot behave as a spiritual being in the presence of discarnate entities. You must be, and consciously be aware of being, an undying and eternal source of light, part of the Creator, and part of the great democracy of all spirits.

The challenge should take place once one hears an identification, "I am Laitos," or, "I am Oxal," or, "I am Q'uo." There are many within the Confederation who teach, and you will find that contact which is most helpful to you and most productive of good, inspirational and information material. This is a matter of practice and of time. To go further in your acceptance of the contact is not only folly, it can lead to madness. We ask that the instrument never move beyond the signature, the identification, but simply ask the identified contact to be with the instrument in its meditation, for we of the Confederation have a strong and general carrier wave which aids in deepening and making more useful the meditative experience.

We apologize for taking such a great length of time to give this information, but we are aware that the instrument shall be many weeks upon its own. However, we feel we have given tools and resources not only for the instrument, but for the very concept of the support group, for the support group, too, may do this same work, not because it wishes to channel, but because it wishes to be the self it truly is, and thus be a stronger and more powerful battery.

We thank you very much for your patience with us. The information you have called for exceeds greatly that information which is normally called for by new students, and we are most happy and most grateful to respond. We find there are unasked questions upon the minds of those present. It is a free will choice whether or not each wishes to ask them, but we would prefer not to use this instrument in this capacity at this time, and would therefore transfer the contact to the one known as Jim. I am Laitos.

(Jim channeling)

I am Laitos, and greet each again in love and light through this instrument. We would offer ourselves at this time in attempting to respond to any query which may yet remain upon the minds of those present. Is there a query at this time?

S: Yes, Laitos. Could you expand just a little bit on the meaning of caution you gave having to do with the greeting of the disincarnate entity, that we go no further than the greeting—is that what you said?—lest we meet with madness.

I am Laitos, and am aware of your query, my brother. It is our recommendation that the greeting of any discarnate entity be all that you receive before offering your own challenge to that entity as to whether it comes in the name of whatever quality or essence is at the core of who you are. The one known as Carla challenges in the name of Jesus the Christ. The one known as Jim challenges in the name of the Christ consciousness and the service-to-others polarity. It is up to you as instrument to determine that quality which is most central in your life pattern and by which quality you will offer your own challenge after hearing the greeting from any entity which wishes to utilize your instrument and to speak through you.

Is there a further query, my brother?

S: Yes. So the danger is in allowing some greeting to take place before one gets a chance to register the challenge, is that right?

I am Laitos, and this is correct, my brother. Is there another query?

S: No, thank you very much.

I am Laitos. If we have, then, exhausted the queries, we shall again thank each most humbly and gratefully for allowing us to work with this group and the new instrument. It has been a great joy and we feel that much has been accomplished this day. We commend each for the dedication and perseverance necessary to begin and continue this form of service through the vocal channeling. We, as you would say, look forward to those times in which we shall again be able to serve in refining this process which is well begun.

At this time we shall take our leave of this group, leaving each, as always, in the love and in the light of the one infinite Creator. We are known to you as those of Laitos. Adonai, my friends. Adonai. ❧

www.ingramcontent.com/pod-product-compliance
Lightning Source LLC
Chambersburg PA
CBHW080420230426

43662CB00015B/2154